YEARS

SIMON & SCHUSTER

OPUS

The Cult of
DARK
MONEY,

HUMAN
TRAFFICKING,

and

RIGHT-WING
CONSPIRACY

inside the
CATHOLIC
CHURCH

GARETH GORE

SIMON & SCHUSTER

New York   London   Toronto   Sydney   New Delhi

1230 Avenue of the Americas
New York, NY 10020

First Simon & Schuster hardcover edition October 2024

SIMON & SCHUSTER and colophon are registered trademarks of Simon & Schuster, LLC

Simon & Schuster: Celebrating 100 Years of Publishing in 2024

For information about special discounts for bulk purchases,
please contact Simon & Schuster Special Sales
at 1-866-506-1949 or business@simonandschuster.com.

The Simon & Schuster Speakers Bureau can bring authors to your live event.
For more information or to book an event, contact the Simon & Schuster Speakers Bureau
at 1-866-248-3049 or visit our website at www.simonspeakers.com.

Interior design by Ruth Lee-Mui

Manufactured in the United States of America

1   3   5   7   9   10   8   6   4   2

Library of Congress Cataloging-in-Publication Data has been applied for.

ISBN 978-1-6680-1614-5
ISBN 978-1-6680-1616-9 (ebook)

In memory of my parents,

Dorothy and Jimmy

Contents

INTRODUCTION

WHEN BANCO POPULAR SUDDENLY COLLAPSED IN THE EARLY HOURS OF June 7, 2017, attention naturally turned to those caught up in what turned out to be one of the largest bank failures ever seen in Europe. Spanish television broadcast scenes of angry customers outside shuttered branches all over the country, brandishing placards, demanding answers—and prison for those responsible. Reporters interviewed tearful pensioners who had lost everything in the collapse: elderly men and women who had entrusted their life savings to a bank once hailed as one of the strongest and most profitable in the world. The financial press pursued another angle, focusing on supposedly savvy bond investors like Pimco and Anchorage Capital, who had lost hundreds of millions of dollars overnight. Around the world, everyone was asking the same question: How could a well-known Spanish lender, an institution with a proud ninety-year history, which owned another bank in the United States and had offices as far afield as Shanghai, Dubai, and Rio de Janeiro, just disappear overnight?

But, amid all the coverage, no mention was made of the biggest casualty of all. For more than sixty years, a shadowy group of men sworn to a life of celibacy and self-flagellation had secretly controlled the bank and taken advantage of their positions there to siphon off billions of dollars. This is the previously untold story of how these men hijacked Banco Popular and transformed it into a cash machine for Opus Dei, the controversial religious sect they belonged to—transforming this tiny, secretive religious movement into one of the most powerful forces in the Catholic Church, bankrolling the creation of a vast recruitment network targeting children and vulnerable teenagers, and creating a beachhead in the world of U.S. politics that would make Opus Dei a secret but critical force behind the recent erosion of reproductive rights and other civil liberties. In a world obsessed with conspiracy theories—of QAnon and Bilderberg—this is a real-life story of abuse, manipulation, and greed cloaked in the mantle of holiness.

I was one of the journalists who covered the collapse of Banco Popular and who—like everyone else, it now seems—missed the most important part of the story. I had spent much of the previous decade reporting on the rolling banking crises that had ripped through Europe in the years after the 2008 global financial collapse. My work had taken me to France, Germany, Greece, Italy, Portugal, Russia, Spain, Sweden, and Turkey to write about the various crises, interviewing the people who ran the banks and building out the story through conversations with regulators, central bankers, lawyers, investors, and ordinary folk. I initially covered the Popular story in much the same way. At first, the collapse seemed all too familiar: the usual tale of unbridled ambition, poor decision-making, a hubristic belief that risks were being controlled, and an unwillingness to recognize mistakes until it was too late. But the deeper I dug into the story, the less sense it all seemed to make. Many aspects of Banco Popular's rise and fall simply defied any logical explanation, even for a seasoned financial reporter. Gradually, it became clear that huge pieces of the puzzle were missing.

I moved to Madrid to investigate further. I had lived there as a correspondent for Bloomberg a decade earlier, reporting on the country's spectacular boom and bust. Ten years on, the city looked just as I had left it—but with one notable difference. The Banco Popular name, once a fixture in every neighborhood, was now gone. The bank had once boasted more than two thousand branches across the country—including three hundred in Madrid alone—making it almost impossible to walk through any of the

Spanish capital's many *barrios* without seeing its purple logo, instantly recognizable to millions of Spaniards. But, while Popular had vanished from the streets, its name lived on in the newspapers. The bank's collapse had become a legal quagmire, spawning more than a hundred lawsuits—most involving the 300,000 shareholders who had seen their investments turn to dust. Other lawsuits had been brought by the bank's creditors, who were owed billions. One by one, I met with the disaffected groups. Keen for any coverage of their fight—especially in the international press—everyone seemed eager to talk.

Or almost everyone. Absent from these conversations was the most affected party of all: the bank's biggest shareholder. Enigmatically named The Syndicate, the group traced its roots back to a gentlemen's agreement in the 1940s and controlled almost 10 percent of the bank when it collapsed, a stake worth more than $2 billion at its peak. But, within weeks of the collapse, the main company at the heart of The Syndicate had quietly given notice to the authorities that it was to be dissolved. While the bank's other shareholders were mounting a public battle to recoup their money, this shadowy group that had once controlled the bank seemed to be intent on exiting the scene. My curiosity piqued, I began to investigate further and soon discovered that there was much more to The Syndicate than met the eye. At the heart of the consortium was a company obliquely called the European Union of Investors, which turned out to be a nest of Russian dolls stacked in such a way as to hide the real beneficiary of this giant holding. Each of the dolls had innocent-enough-sounding names—the Fund for Social Action, the Institute for Education and Investigation, the Foundation for International Development and Cooperation, the Fund for Social Cooperation. But, as the dolls were unstacked and laid out beside each other, curious similarities began to emerge. Many of them shared the same shareholders. They were run by the same group of seemingly interchangeable men. As much as $100 million a year passed from the bank down through this network. I started to realize why The Syndicate had been so keen to remain silent, why the company behind it had applied for dissolution while others so publicly fought for justice: it had a secret to hide.

My reporting took me to the tiny Swiss municipality of Crans-Montana, a luxury resort in the Alps famous for its skiing and ultra-wealthy residents.

I was there to interview Javier Valls-Taberner, who had spent more than forty years at the bank—including fifteen as chairman alongside his older brother Luis. If anyone could help me get to the bottom of the Banco Popular mystery, I figured, it was him. Javier greeted me at the door of his Alpine lodge with a beaming smile and a warm handshake. We had met briefly in Madrid a few months earlier, and he seemed genuinely grateful for my having come all this way to see him. He had agreed to spend the next three days being interviewed about his time at the bank.

It was clear from the start that he worshiped Luis, who had died some years earlier. He regaled me with stories of their youth—of how they had dressed as peasants to escape war-torn Barcelona, of their exile in Italy, and of the death of their father, a well-respected politician. At eighty-nine, his voice was weak, his health clearly in decline after the recent diagnosis of a rare blood disease. But his eyes glistened as he recalled how he and his brother had transformed Popular—a sleepy regional bank with just a handful of offices—into a global player. The two brothers were very different: while Luis was a devout member of Opus Dei, a conservative Catholic sect, sworn to a life of chastity, poverty, and obedience, Javier was well known in Madrid's staid banking circles as a *bon vivant* who enjoyed travel, good food, good wine—and a good party. "They had nicknames for the two of us," Javier told me, chuckling. "They called us Opus Dei and Opus Night."

We reconvened early the next morning and got down to business. Top on my list was understanding what The Syndicate really was. I asked him straight out.

"Well, it was all fake," Javier told me. "Previously, there had been a *real* syndicate—but we stripped it of any legal status. Later on, it was basically made up of anyone with shares who wanted in—the only condition being that you had to vote in favor of whatever the board proposed. There were loads of us. But it was one big ruse because they double-counted those of us in The Syndicate. All of the big shareholders were involved . . . it meant they got counted as individual investors *and* as members of The Syndicate."

What Javier was telling me amounted to fraud on a massive scale. Here was a set of investors who had systematically clubbed together to swing important votes at the bank—in order to head off any real accountability about the way Banco Popular was being managed. But why? Now an old man, with his health in serious decline, Javier clearly had few qualms about admitting to this clear abuse of power. He also had an axe to grind. Back in 2006, just days after the death of his older brother, Javier had been unceremoniously ousted from the bank. After four decades at the helm of Popular, Opus Night had evidently outlived his usefulness to the real power brokers behind the bank.

His ouster coincided with the sudden emergence of the European Union of Investors, the enigmatic company that had first caught my eye back in Madrid.

"The Syndicate began to fall apart when they started to behave badly towards me and towards Luis, and a lot of people decided to pull out," he told me. "So, they put together a company called the European Union of Investors."

"Just a minute—who are *they*?" I asked.

"It was Opus Dei *one hundred percent*. It ended up taking the place of The Syndicate—which wasn't really a syndicate."

Javier then told me about his brother's dying days.

"When Luis became really sick and was admitted to hospital, they tried to stop me seeing him," he recalled, his eyes glazing over. "They tried to keep me away while he was still alive because—I think—there was already some kind of plan within Opus Dei stipulating that, as soon as Luis was dead, the other brother would be out."

"But why didn't they want you to visit him?"

"Because Opus Dei was controlling him. They didn't want me telling him things—or him telling me things. Already, over the previous two years . . . I noticed . . . it was already decided . . . Opus Dei had a plan. They were controlling everything, more or less. I think they had decided that, as soon as he was gone, they would have it all for themselves."

"Do you think Luis realized what was going on?"

"I don't know whether he realized—or whether he knew but couldn't say anything."

The memory of his brother's dying days—and of his dismissal from the bank—clearly pained Javier. He told me about how, at the time, he couldn't help but think of Roberto Calvi, the Italian banker who had been murdered in the early 1980s—at the hands of people close to Opus Dei, according to legend. Fearing for his family's safety, he decided to leave Spain, where the organization's tentacles ran deep, and move to Switzerland. From his home in the Alps, he had watched with a mixture of sorrow and Schadenfreude as the bank he and his brother had propelled to prominence collapsed—taking down with it the web of Opus Dei interests that knifed him in the back years earlier.

While my father had been raised as a Roman Catholic—his grandparents were from Ireland and he spent much of his childhood being looked after by nuns in a convalescent home for sick children—he gradually became disillusioned with the Church's unrelenting fixation on guilt, and he resolved to raise his own children free to make their own moral judgments about the world. As a result, I knew next to nothing about the Church or about Opus Dei when I first set out investigating the collapse of Banco Popular—but I soon made it a priority to get up to speed. I read voraciously and spoke with current and former members to try to understand the organization. My first interactions threw me somewhat—after what Javier had told me about them, the members of Opus Dei who had worked and lived with Luis Valls-Taberner, the ones he had accused of manipulating his brother's illness and death to wrest control of the bank, turned out to be amiable, forthcoming, and delighted that a journalist from England was taking an interest in the late banker, whom they clearly revered.

But one thing struck me as odd. Almost every conversation would begin the same way: with the member of Opus Dei explaining how everyone within the organization acted with complete freedom and that anything that any of them did—whether that be in business, politics, or more generally—was of their own initiative and nothing to do with Opus Dei. After the fourth or fifth rendition of this spiel, I began to wonder whether the men—and they were all men—had been told what to say. The weird thing was that they would each offer up this statement unprompted, before we had even begun to discuss *what* Luis Valls-Taberner had actually done. Why would they feel the need to preface our discussion with this disclaimer—before I had even asked anything? Little did I know, this disclaimer would become an almost constant refrain in my conversations with Opus Dei members over the next few years.

Newly alert for anything to do with Opus Dei, my attention was caught by an article from the Associated Press about a group of forty-two women in Argentina who alleged they had been recruited by Opus Dei as young girls and forced to work effectively as slaves—cooking, cleaning, and scrubbing the toilets for years without pay. They had filed a complaint at the Vatican for alleged labor exploitation, abuse of power—and abuse of conscience. They were demanding financial compensation, an acknowledgment of their suffering, disciplinary measures for those responsible, and a formal apology from Opus Dei. While I obviously felt sorry for the women, the story seemed unrelated to my own investigation. But all that changed on a subsequent visit to the Banco Popular archives, which had since fallen into the hands of a rival bank, which had bought up Popular's assets following its collapse. This was my third visit to the archive, located in a business park off a coastal highway in northern Spain, since securing access the previous year. While sifting through towers of boxes, I happened upon an "unofficial" archive that had been kept quite separate from the main Popular collection, which had been discovered in a mansion up in the mountains outside Madrid that was once owned by the bank and where Luis Valls-Taberner had once lived. I learned about how one of the archivists had been sent to the mansion to recover this "stray" collection and to arrange for its transportation—only to discover that someone had been there before him to purge this mysterious cache. But it had been a rushed job and, buried in the stacks and stacks of seemingly unorganized piles of paper, he said there might be documents of interest to me.

For three days, I sifted through the piles. On my last day at the archive— that evening I was due to fly back home to London—I discovered a thick document with the words "Balance Sheet of International Cooperation" on the front. The report linked the bank to more than sixty seemingly innocuous companies around the world—including one connected to the alleged enslavement of the forty-two women in Argentina. During the late eighties and early nineties, tens of millions of dollars had been sent all over the world, with records of the transactions kept separate from the official Banco Popular archives—and seemingly missed by those sent to purge the hidden cache. As I checked off the list of recipients—in countries including Australia, Cameroon, Ireland, Nigeria, and the Philippines—I found that many of these companies ran "vocational schools" similar to the ones implicated in the scandal in Argentina. These schools actively recruited young girls living in some of the world's poorest countries into a life of servitude. I had stumbled on a vast operation to entrap these young girls and then traffic them to work in the service of Opus Dei all around the world—and all of it financed by Banco Popular. On subsequent visits, I found other pieces of the puzzle—records of millions of dollars channeled through one of the bank's subsidiaries in Switzerland to accounts in Panama, Liechtenstein, and Curacao, offshore havens for secrecy and money laundering, which were directly controlled by leading figures in Opus Dei in the United States, Mexico, and elsewhere. I soon began to realize that the story was about much more than a Spanish bank. Here was a network of hidden largesse that had been used to catapult Opus Dei onto the global stage. The strands would eventually stretch deep into the Vatican, into the world of American politics—and to the sudden disappearance of a man fifty years earlier.

On the morning of May 20, 2023, Father Charles Trullols proudly led the congregation of the Catholic Information Center through the streets of Washington, D.C., on the first of what he anticipated would be an annual tradition of a eucharistic procession in the heart of the nation's capital. Elegantly dressed in the elaborately adorned vestments normally reserved for feast days, the Spanish priest gazed intensely up at the golden monstrance he carried before him as he made his way along K Street, over petals that had been scattered on the sidewalk, flanked by priests and altar boys who held a white canopy high above him. Trullols had envisioned the procession as an expression of faith and a reminder of the presence of God—even in this most ungodly town. "I have absolute faith in the many graces God will bestow onto our country when Christ's real presence is carried through the streets of D.C.," he said. "The procession will express our belief that Jesus is passing by and bestowing his love and help on all of us."

Many of the regulars at the Catholic Information Center's daily noontime Mass—the politicians, lawyers, and lobbyists who came to take communion during their lunchbreaks—had taken Father Charles's words to heart. Almost five hundred people had taken time out of their weekend for this special event. As they made their way along the mile-long route, down

Seventeenth Street, onto Connecticut Avenue and in front of the White House, the crowd trailed behind in reverent silence, stopping to kneel and pray at two altar stops along the route. Father Charles led their prayers, asking God to come to the aid of America.

This was the friendly, public, acceptable face of Opus Dei that Father Charles, as chaplain of the Catholic Information Center, had been tasked with projecting onto the politicians, the lawyers, and the lobbyists who came through its doors every day. Situated in the heart of the city—a virtue celebrated by the blue plaque outside boasting how it was the closest tabernacle to the White House—the unassuming chapel and bookstore was a shopwindow for Opus Dei in the most powerful city on earth. For forty years, the Catholic Information Center had pushed the organization's same uncontroversial message that had drawn countless Washingtonians into its bosom. This message—that Catholics best serve God by striving for holiness in everything they do, by offering up their everyday work and aiming for excellence in their professional lives—had struck a chord among the city's believers, many of whom had long struggled with the question of how to live out their faith in this deeply transactional, amoral town. Members of Congress, Supreme Court Justices, and prominent figures from the worlds of finance, law, and journalism had been drawn to this simple message over the years. Its success had transformed the wider Washington metropolitan area into the largest Opus Dei community in the United States—made up of eight hundred members and countless sympathizers.

From Colombia to Japan, Nigeria to Sri Lanka, this is the face that Opus Dei projects to the world: of an agglomeration of ordinary Catholics, the vast majority of which are married with children, who are doctors and lawyers and teachers inspired to live out their faith in everyday life. Drawing on the legitimacy conferred upon it by the Church—Opus Dei was elevated to the unique status of personal prelature by Pope John Paul II in the eighties and its founder, the Spanish priest Josemaría Escrivá, was canonized and proclaimed the "saint of ordinary life" two decades later—the organization presents itself as nothing more than a spiritual guide for members of the faith searching for a way of serving God in their daily lives. Across the websites maintained by Opus Dei in the sixty-six countries in which it operates, and in the literature handed out at the Catholic Information Center and in hundreds of similar centers around the world, the testimonies of members underscore this message: of how the organization, and the teachings of Escrivá, have inspired them to live out their faith. "The Work, as the faithful of Opus Dei call it, is part of the Church, and the Church is a family and Mother," relates one high-ranking Brazilian member. "Saint Josemaría spoke of the great family of the Work. I like to think of the Work as a family of families." The organization talks about how almost ninety thousand people—from many different backgrounds, cultures, and languages—have been inspired to follow in the ways of Opus Dei, ways which were supposedly communicated to the founder directly from God during a retreat in Madrid in October 1928. Some share their testimonies of how, from heaven, Saint Josemaría has interceded in their daily lives to resolve problems, cure illness, and inspire them to become better Catholics.

But, beneath this veneer of deep faith and inspiration, there is an underbelly to the organization that few—even among the most longstanding members—know anything about. While 90 percent of its members live respectable Christian lives, at home with their families, striving to live out their faith more deeply, at the heart of the organization lies an elite corps who live highly controlled existences. Having taken vows of chastity, poverty, and obedience, this elite group live according to a dystopian set of rules and regulations—an Orwellian blueprint for society laid down by the founder and kept hidden from authorities at the Vatican. Normal members are prohibited from reading these documents, which are kept under lock and key at the residences where the celibate members live together, to be consulted only by their superiors, who often abuse their authority to control the lives of those in their charge. Nine thousand members live this tightly controlled existence of prayer and indoctrination, where almost every move is meticulously prescribed and watched over, where contact with friends and family is restricted and monitored, and where their personal and professional lives are subject to the whims and needs of the wider movement.

Living in closed, segregated communities, they operate as clandestine cells in almost every major city in the world, following a detailed playbook of surreptitious recruitment drawn up by the founder and geared toward a single aim: extending the movement's influence among the rich and the powerful. Constantly pressured by their superiors to generate more and more "vocations," these elite members are encouraged to follow a playbook common to many religious cults to generate more followers and expand Opus Dei's power and reach. Potential recruits are targeted while they are still children and are enticed into friendships with current members through "love bombing," who then collect and exchange information on the targets in order to whip them into a "vocational crisis" designed to push them into joining. Once inside, recruits are cut off from their families, and their lives are intricately controlled until they become pliable and submissive—at which point they are turned to recruiting more members.

This elite corps is aided in its task by a clandestine network of foundations and companies, which once counted Banco Popular at its core, that funnel millions of dollars around the world to initiatives aimed at recruitment and at expanding the influence of Opus Dei deeper into society. Opus Dei denies that it controls any of this network, but this is a legal fiction designed to protect the organization from any scandal or blowback—and to absolve it of any responsibility toward the thousands of individuals whose lives it controls and abuses. This hidden network of money, much of which can be traced back to the organization's cozy relationship with the Spanish dictator Francisco Franco, has enabled Opus Dei to buy power and influence across six continents—from Santiago to Stockholm, Los Angeles to Lagos, and Mexico City to Manila. Publicly, it is officially affiliated with nineteen universities, twelve business schools, 275 elementary and high schools, 160 technical and hospitality schools, 228 university residences and countless youth clubs and summer camps. Covertly, its tentacles run much deeper—into the very fabric of our supposedly secular, civil society.

Opus Dei boasts special privileges enjoyed by no other organization within the Catholic Church that for years have allowed it to effectively function outside the usual hierarchy, giving it unprecedented freedom to operate wherever it likes—answerable to nobody but the pope. These special powers were granted in the early 1980s, at a time when the Vatican was mired in deep financial trouble and amid swirling rumors about Opus Dei's role in a huge financial bailout for the Holy See. These privileges catapulted the group into the upper echelons of the Catholic Church, legitimizing it among the faithful, turbocharging its recruitment efforts, and facilitating the canonization of its founder.

Since the 1990s, Opus Dei has exploited this legitimacy to ally itself with conservative forces within the Church—especially in the United States. This has opened the door to billionaires and dark money, which in recent years—and especially following the collapse of Banco Popular in 2017—have become a critical means for Opus Dei to sustain this hidden network. For all its talk about allegiance to the Vatican, the Church, and the teachings of Jesus Christ, Opus Dei seems unconcerned that many of the conservative forces it now embraces in the United States are openly hostile to the pope— even going so far as to undermine his authority and plot against him. For the veneer presented to the vast majority of its members—of upholding Church doctrine and offering spiritual guidance for Catholics to live out their faith— is a false one. The principal things that drive Opus Dei are the cult-like worship of its founder and its own expansion. Its methods and practices have corrupted the outlook of even its own leadership, which has time and time again proven unwilling and unable to reform, even in the face of incontrovertible evidence of abuse and coercion in its ranks. Opus Dei is a danger to itself, its membership, the Church—and the world.

For decades, the organization has operated with effective impunity, but there are signs that the walls are beginning to close in. In July 2022, Pope Francis made his first tentative attempt to rein in the organization— through a *motu propio*, effectively a personal decree, which downgraded the institution within the hierarchy of the Church and tasked it with "updating" its statutes. Few realized it at the time, but this was a delicate way of telling Opus Dei to put its house in order. When the organization failed to take heed, Francis issued a second *motu propio*—this time severing the authority of the organization over its members and laying the ground for direct intervention by the Vatican if it fails to reform. A vicious fight looms between Opus Dei and the progressive forces of the Catholic Church.

Opus traces the origins of this secretive religious sect, challenging its official history and directly linking its ascent to the hijacking of Banco Popular. At the heart of this story is Luis Valls-Taberner, a prominent Spanish financier still widely regarded as one of the greatest bankers of his generation. As the man who ran Popular for almost fifty years, before his death in 2006, he is credited with transforming the bank from a small player with just a handful of branches into a global powerhouse that commanded the respect of its peers. But he was also a man with a double life. By day, he carefully cultivated his image as a tycoon, holding court in his opulent penthouse office where he received politicians and titans of industry. By night, he retired to his sparse room at the Opus Dei lodge just outside Madrid, where he changed out of his business suit into casual clothes and attached a cilice—a small, spiked chain—to his thigh to remind him of the suffering of Christ. There, he plotted how to defraud his own bank and the shareholders he supposedly served, running a network of companies that funneled billions from Spain to offshore accounts and onto Opus Dei operations around the world.

This book offers a window into the movement, its predatory recruitment techniques, the psychological abuse borne down on members, and the control over their daily lives. It explores the medieval practices of corporal mortification that members are instructed to perform, as well as the daily rites and rituals—from cold showers to sleeping on wooden planks—that they still observe today. It also casts a new light on the rushed canonization of the founder, despite huge resistance from many within the Church.

But this isn't just a story about the past. The book also explores the vast empire that Opus Dei controls today. In New York, Murray Hill Place rises seventeen stories from the corner of Lexington Avenue and Thirty-fourth Street. There is no signage on the redbrick and limestone building, just a single discreet entrance onto each of the two adjoining streets—one for men and one for women, who are prohibited from mixing inside. Behind the walls of this nondescript building, a well-oiled brainwashing machine is at work: shut off from their families and the world outside, dozens of young recruits are subjected to a grueling timetable of prayer, introspection, and corporal mortification. Those with university degrees are encouraged to seek well-paid jobs in law or finance, and to hand over all their earnings to the order. Men without a university degree are usually not admitted—although the organization actively recruits lesser educated women—some only teenagers—who are pushed into a life of servitude, of punishing fifteen-hour days cleaning and cooking, their nights spent sleeping on wooden planks. It's a scene repeated across the globe—in London, Nairobi, Sydney, Tokyo, and numerous other cities. These residential centers are fed by a network of schools and universities, where teenagers are educated using only those books approved by Opus Dei priests and where newspapers and magazines regularly have "inappropriate" content cut out. Television and the internet are censored. Meanwhile, in Rome, the leaders of the movement live a life of opulence at the palatial Villa Tevere, where the life of Saint Josemaría is commemorated in a solemn ceremony every day at noon.

Lastly, the book raises important questions about the forces that shape our society, shedding light on some of the hidden actors that lurk beneath the surface. As the organization approaches its centenary, it presents an opportunity to reassess Opus Dei, showing the cult to be the centerpiece of a real-life conspiracy.

1

THE SYNDICATE

Madrid, Spain—June 2004

ON THE MORNING OF JUNE 24, 2004, A SKULK OF GRAY-FACED BUSINESSMEN gathered in the basement of the Banco Popular headquarters in central Madrid to formally sign off on the previous year's accounts. The annual shareholder meeting was a tedious but immutable affair in the business calendar, a legal requirement that was supposed to give the tens of thousands of investors who owned shares in the bank an opportunity to ask questions, to raise concerns—and generally to hold the men who ran Popular to account. For years, it had paid only lip service to such requirements, electing instead to hold the meeting effectively behind closed doors in the boardroom on the seventh floor, where the men in charge signed off on the accounts without debate. For years, regulators had turned a blind eye—but had recently begun to ask questions and enforce the rules more strictly. The clampdown mirrored a wider revolution sweeping through Spanish society triggered by events three months earlier, when—in a cynical attempt to stay in power—the ruling conservatives had lied to the country about a series of train bombings that had killed 193 people only days before a general election, blaming the atrocity on Basque terrorists rather than Islamists protesting the country's role in the Iraq War. The gambit had backfired spectacularly, losing them an election they had been poised to win and unleashing widespread ire against the crooked elite. With the youthful new Socialist prime minister promising a new society based on transparency, the men assembled were apprehensive about what the coming revolution might mean for them—and the secret at the heart of Banco Popular that had been kept hidden for more than fifty years.

The shift in landscape could not have come at a worse time. Luis Valls-Taberner, the chairman and figurehead of Popular since the late fifties, hadn't been seen in public for months. Don Luis, as he was respectfully known to everyone within the bank, had turned seventy-eight a few weeks earlier. Though he wasn't one for birthdays—he preferred to congratulate people on their saint's day rather than the anniversary of their birth—the last few had been ominous markers for the gradual decline in his health. The chairman had spent his seventy-sixth birthday recovering from emergency surgery on his stomach; his seventy-seventh had been spent preparing for another procedure to remove a growth above his left eye. The years were beginning to take their toll: more recently, his movement had become increasingly slow and awkward, and he had begun to suffer from dizzy spells and blurred vision—symptoms of advanced Parkinson's disease. But, rather than step down or name a successor, Don Luis had elected to stay on and cover up his failing health. While he still came to the office religiously—arriving at nine each morning, often with a layer of fresh stubble (he preferred to shave at the office so he could spend more time at home reading the Bible)—Don Luis remained conspicuous by his absence. In years gone by, the chairman would frequently be seen around the building, stopping for chats with the rank-and-file, addressing employees by their first names, taking care to remember small details about a child's communion, a sick relative, or the travails of their favorite football team—all the while gathering information about the bank, which departments were working hard, what needed attention, who was slacking. But those walks had all but ceased.

This charade went on for months. But more recently, things had begun to occur that threatened to transform the relatively benign problem of the chairman's hermitic existence into a major crisis. The first sign that something was wrong came at the end of 2003 when, just a week before Christmas, eleven members of the board were suddenly dismissed en masse. The bank tried to spin the departures as being part of a long-planned reduction in the number of people on the board—a line swallowed hook, line, and sinker by the press. But then, a few weeks later, one of the bank's biggest shareholders unexpectedly announced that it was selling its entire $400 million stake. The news came as a huge surprise, not least because the investor had only recently bought the stake—and had done so amid great fanfare, heralding the purchase as the beginning of a new alliance that promised an exciting future for both parties. Understandably, such an abrupt reversal set off intense speculation. Had the investor decided to sell after seeing what was *really* going on behind closed doors? Had he concluded that Don Luis was unfit to run the bank? The liquidation also cast a different light on the mass dismissal of more than a third of the board a few months earlier. There was now talk of a failed coup against the chairman, who refused to retire, who refused to listen to reason. Was a confused old man in charge of one of Spain's largest banks? Why was he being allowed to stay on? Why hadn't the rest of the board done something to remedy the situation?

Through the spring, speculation about Don Luis's fitness to remain in his post had wiped more than a billion dollars off the value of Popular. In banking, a business built on instilling confidence in customers and convincing them their money is safe, uncertainty can be a very dangerous thing. For one, the bank's depressed share price could make it an easy target, opening it up to a hostile takeover from a larger rival—or a vulture fund. Given the need to keep a lid on the bank's secret beneficiary, such a scenario was clearly unacceptable. But more worryingly, if confidence among investors continued to evaporate and spread to the bank's five million customers, Popular could very quickly have a major crisis on its hands—in that situation, a run on the bank couldn't be ruled out.

The tightknit team around the chairman devised a plan to quash the rumors, to project an image of business as usual—and of solid support among the board members for Don Luis. Given the new requirements to hold an actual gathering of shareholders, rather than the closed meeting of board members up on the seventh floor, executives at the bank decided to kill two birds with one stone: by having the chairman give a speech to the annual gathering, which could be recorded and distributed to the media. The meeting was already on the calendar, so there was no need to invent a pretext for the sudden appearance of the chairman after so many months. In fact, it nicely reinforced the message they were trying to push—of business as usual. Given what was at stake, the team also decided to take a few precautions. They kept Don Luis's speech as short as possible and printed it for him in an oversized font—double spaced—to help with his blurred vision.

That morning, they had held a rehearsal in the auditorium, just to be sure. Smartly dressed in a dark woolen suit, white shirt, and a patterned blue tie, Don Luis had delivered the speech without a hitch—to the great relief of everyone present. The guest list had also been kept to an absolute minimum. While the meeting had been moved from the boardroom to the auditorium, located in the basement, the cast of characters in attendance was much the same as always. In a clear breach of all the rules, the smaller shareholders— the ones who might cause a scene or ask difficult questions—had been kept away. The room was less than a quarter full—just twenty out of the more than seventy thousand shareholders were in attendance. The auditorium was a sea of friendly faces, of men personally appointed to the board by Don Luis over the years precisely because of their discretion and their willingness to turn a blind eye to the bank's big secret.

But all those precautions were in vain—the meeting was a disaster from the start. On his way up onto the stage, Don Luis tripped and fell on the stairs. He seemed slightly shaken—embarrassed perhaps—but fine. The chairman was helped to his seat. For a while, there was silence—both on stage and in the audience. Nobody knew quite what to say.

The first to break the silence was Ángel Ron, seated immediately to the right of Don Luis. A portly Galician with thick bushy eyebrows, a cleft chin, and a roguish smile, Ron was chief executive of the bank, the man in charge of the day-to-day. Despite the difference in age, the two men had an excellent relationship. Ron was one of the few people at the bank who still saw Don Luis regularly—the two had lunch a couple of times a week. Ron had a soft spot for his boss, who had picked him out for greater things at a young age and, over the years, trusted him with some of the bank's most difficult and delicate business matters—as a test of his competence and his discretion. Ron had passed with flying colors, and two years earlier had been named chief executive at the age of just thirty-nine.

"You need to start . . . look, we have it here in the script," said Ron, attentively, pointing at the oversized words in the text laid out for Don Luis. "You start by welcoming everyone."

"That's right, you start by welcoming everyone," chirped in a friendly voice from the other side. It was Francisco Aparicio, known to everyone as Paco. Aparicio had joined the bank's board at the end of the previous year. A slight man with a prominent nose and small, piercing eyes, Paco was a lawyer by trade—although his area of expertise was something of a mystery. On the court circuit, he wasn't well known. Instead, he seemed to spend most of his time working for enigmatic charitable foundations. He had no experience running a bank, but for some reason Don Luis had decided to name him not only secretary to the board but also secretary to the executive committee, both critical roles in the day-to-day running of the bank. Perhaps sensing surprise among those around him, Don Luis had asked people to treat Paco as one of their own. It wasn't hard: helped by his disarmingly friendly demeanor and infectious smile, Paco had quickly become a popular figure.

But a certain mystery hung over the new board secretary. It was an open secret that Luis and Paco lived together. Neither man spoke openly about their life outside the bank, but it was known that both were members of Opus Dei, a secretive, ultra-conservative branch of the Catholic Church—and that they lived in an all-male lodge run by the movement, located just north of the capital. There, they led a hidden existence bound by vows of celibacy, poverty, and obedience, and were expected to follow a strict timetable of Mass, rituals, and silences. The appointment of Paco as board secretary had been a risky move: for decades, Banco Popular had been branded by some in Madrid as the "Bank of Opus Dei," owing to the religious allegiance of its chairman. Don Luis often laughed off such accusations, pointing to the many thousands of bank employees who had nothing to do with the religious movement. Keen to counter the rumors, he had even banned the few Opus Dei members who did work there from greeting each other in the traditional way—in Latin, with one person saying "*Pax*" (peace) and the other responding "*In ætérnum*" (for all eternity). Still, the reputation was hard to shake off and to some extent had become internalized. The canteen staff had stopped serving meat on Fridays during Lent—not because anyone had told them to but because they thought it might upset Opus Dei. If the staff were unsure about who was in charge, it was little wonder that the Madrid rumor mill was full of speculation about the links between Popular and the religious movement. The appointment of Paco risked fueling such talk. But given the urgency of a seamless transfer in power, such optics were no longer so important.

Luis picked up the script laid out before him, raised his left hand to adjust his glasses, and in his head, began to read through the first few lines of his speech. He signaled for Ron to turn on the microphone: he was ready to begin.

"A very good afternoon," he began. Not a great start—it was still morning. Luckily, most of the audience hadn't heard anything because Don Luis had grabbed the microphone right as he had begun speaking, provoking a deafening eruption of interference that filled the room. The assembled men raised their hands to their ears.

Clearly on edge, both Paco and Ron then grabbed the microphone and together dragged it closer to the chairman, placing it over some of the papers laid out in front of him. The moving of the equipment reverberated in a series of pops that rang out around the room.

"Can you all hear?" said Don Luis.

"And now?" A short pause.

"Welcome to the AGM," Luis said at last. He smiled, paused, and slowly looked around the room, before returning his gaze to the script. He had been told to follow the script. "For many years, we have gathered in the final week of June. . . ."

The chairman was quite clearly slurring his words.

The men gathered in the auditorium glanced around nervously at each other.

"We meet not just to . . . not just to obey the law but also to keep wider society informed . . . as we have been doing throughout the year . . . so that they can . . . can approve, censure—*or stay silent*—about the management of the bank."

His words were slow, almost pained, and every few seconds he made a strange sideways movement with his jaw. Paco, seated to his left and clearly uncomfortable at what was happening, nervously took off his glasses and looked at Don Luis, ready to intervene. He knew the fragility of the chairman's health. Back at the lodge, various modifications had been made to address his difficulties: an elevator had been installed and, following some recent falls, the exposed bricks on the staircase had been covered with thick padding for his safety.

"Given the fact that last year's results were presented back in January," continued Luis, "and have been analyzed and discussed for five months, right now in June—with our homework done"—he looked up from his glasses—"there is little to . . ."—a long pause—". . . to discuss."

Luis seemed to sense the unease in the room.

He leafed through the script nervously.

"Because these are short paragraphs, I'm pausing to help distinguish one section from another," he offered as an odd explanation for his difficulty in finishing the previous sentence.

Among the men gathered in the auditorium, the embarrassment was palpable. While none of them were under any illusions that any part of the annual general meeting was actually about holding management to account, if word got out, their complicity in this entire charade could be damaging. They were scions of industry, top lawyers, the crème de la crème of the Spanish economic elite, who had their own reputations to think about. But they were also part of what Don Luis used to call his *núcleo duro*, a hard core of steadfast, unswerving allies who could be counted on to protect the interests of the bank—and the real power behind it.

While the chairman allowed—encouraged, some believed—Popular to be described in the media as the Valls-Taberner brothers' bank, in truth he and his brother Javier owned only a few shares. The bank also liked to talk up a 9 percent stake owned by the German insurance giant Allianz, which had bought into the bank in the 1980s. But nobody really mentioned the real power behind Popular. Its biggest shareholder was actually a mysterious alliance of unidentified investors collectively known as The Syndicate. Various layers of companies—all registered at the same address as the bank, and all run by the same roster of faceless, enigmatic men—made it difficult to trace who exactly was the ultimate owner, the ultimate beneficiary of this huge stake. Over the past few years, the stake had generated hundreds of millions of dollars in dividends alone. Tracing the flow of money through the various layers of companies, it seemed the beneficiaries were charitable foundations with one thing in common—links to Opus Dei.

But after fifty years, this arrangement was under threat. Within Popular, a bitter struggle for power was now taking place that threatened to expose—and possibly close off—the steady flow of funds from the bank to Opus Dei. The slow decline of Don Luis's health had awakened the long-dormant ambitions of some of the most senior executives at the bank. In the past couple of years alone, he had witnessed separate coup attempts from two of his closest lieutenants. With Don Luis aging, isolated in his office and cut off from the politics of the bank, they had made their move. Board members were beginning to think of succession, of who—and what—might come next, and fissures were beginning to appear in the fabric of the board. Those fissures risked eroding the power of The Syndicate and interrupting the flow of money to Opus Dei.

As Don Luis continued his speech, he turned to the delicate issue of succession, which hung menacingly over the room.

"We have to ensure that the essential unity of the bank doesn't come under threat," he said. "In business . . ."

Electrical feedback once again filled the room. Don Luis had hit his microphone while turning the page in his speech. After a few seconds it died down. The room waited for him to resume his speech. And waited. And waited. Up on stage, the chairman turned to the previous page of his speech and then leafed back. He looked lost. From either side of him, Ron and Paco turned toward the chairman, anxious looks on their faces.

"In business . . ."

He tried to resume, but again he lost his place. He looked blankly down at the script before him and moved his jaw nervously in a sideways motion. Paco leaned over and pointed out where he was. After a few seconds of awkward silence, the chairman resumed, before losing his place again. He was clearly struggling. Every word seemed a real effort. What was meant to be an assertion of power, a demonstration of unity, was rapidly descending into farce. His authority was ebbing away. It was clear that Don Luis was fast becoming a liability—to the men present, to the bank—and to Opus Dei.

Don Luis headed home early that afternoon, having excused himself from the long lunch for board members that traditionally followed the annual general meeting. From the Popular headquarters in central Madrid, it was a twenty-minute drive back to Mirasierra, an upscale neighborhood on the northern fringes of the city, where he shared a residence with about a dozen other men who, like him, lived as numerary members of Opus Dei. Tucked away on the corner where two quiet streets meet, the modern, red-brick, residential complex looked ordinary, unassuming. Perhaps its only distinguishing feature was its size: the house was the largest in the neighborhood. To the left, behind a fence, was a sixty-foot-long pool, a tennis court, and a separate padel court where the men living at the residence could blow off steam.

Numerary members were the elite corps of Opus Dei. While the vast majority of members—the supernumeraries—had ostensibly ordinary existences, living in an everyday family home with their spouse and children, a select group of members like Don Luis had decided to devote their entire lives to Opus Dei, and had taken vows of poverty, chastity, and obedience to the movement. The residence itself was split into two parts: the main building where the male numeraries lived, and a smaller building where the numerary assistants—the women who cooked and cleaned for the men—had their quarters, with its separate entrance around the corner next to the garbage. The two buildings were connected through a double set of internal doors, each fitted with a different lock. The director of the men's residence had a key to unlock one door, while the directress in charge of the numerary assistants had the key for the other. It was a foolproof system designed to create a hermetic seal between the two residences. Mixing of genders was strictly prohibited—although they effectively lived in the same building, the founder had left specific instructions that they were to live as though they were miles apart. The doors were opened at fixed times for the women to serve dinner or clean, and then were locked all night long. During the daily cleaning of the male residence, the men were expected to vacate not just their own rooms but the entire floor of the house in order to avoid accidental encounters. Even the director and directress weren't allowed to come into physical contact. Any conversations to coordinate mealtimes or cleaning had to be done over an internal telephone system. Even then they weren't allowed to use each other's name. For more complicated matters, it was permitted to pass a note under the door—although it had to be typed and unsigned as a safety measure to prevent any personal bonds from forming—from seeing the other person's name or handwriting, for example.

The car pulled up at the residence, and Luis took the elevator up from the garage to the second floor. Once there, he walked along a short corridor and turned left. He opened the door to his room, which was sparsely furnished—containing a bed, a simple bedside table, a desk and chair, and an armchair. Over the bed was an image of the Virgin Mary, a mandatory decoration, which numeraries were required to greet—a simple movement of the eyes was enough—whenever they entered or left. After greeting the Virgin, Luis closed the door behind him and began to change out of his work clothes into something more comfortable. Before putting his trousers back on, he attached a cilice—a small, spiked chain—to his thigh. Numeraries were expected to wear the device for two hours each day, as a pious custom of chastisement designed to keep the body in a state of servitude and remind it of Christ's suffering. The cilice often left small prick holes in the flesh, which could be embarrassing when swimming in public, and which made having a private pool all the more justifiable. Mortification was a central tenet of Opus Dei and regular acts—however small—were encouraged throughout the day, whether they be taking a cold shower or drinking coffee without milk. Once a week, the men were expected to sleep on a wooden board—women did this every night because they were considered more sensual and so needed to make an extra effort to ward off temptation. On Saturday, further mortification came in the form of the discipline, a cordlike whip that members struck over their shoulders against their back while chanting a prayer to the Virgin Mary, "Hail, holy Queen." The practice occasionally left specks of blood on the wall.

After changing, Luis went down to the chapel. Thirty minutes of prayer in the afternoon were a fixed part of the "plan of life" that members were expected to follow, and Luis—even as the busy chairman of a large bank—was no exception. The norms, as they were known internally, had been laid down by the founder and were a critical part of life within Opus Dei. Members were instructed to follow them meticulously, and to honor and defend them as the irrefutable course of the path that God had laid down for them. The norms regulated the lives of every numerary from morning until night. Each of them was expected to wake at dawn and offer up to God the first minute of the day, which was done by kneeling, kissing the floor, and uttering *Serviam*—Latin for "I serve"—under their breath. Then there was a half hour of prayer in the morning, followed by Mass in Latin and communion. Even at work, the norms continued. Numeraries were expected to recite the Angelus Prayer at noon, take some time for personal introspection, and to pray the rosary. Ideally, they were expected to refrain from speaking for three hours after lunch—although that wasn't always possible at the office. After work, there was another half hour of prayer, usually followed by religious study—a text specially chosen by the spiritual director, as well as something from the Bible. Then before sleep, members were expected to kneel beside their bed, arms stretched out, before saying three Hail Marys and then sprinkling holy water over their bed. Each of them was expected to then observe a strict silence until the next morning. So precise and demanding was the schedule that special cards were printed for members to tick off their compliance over the course of a month—which the director could check at any time. Every minute of the day seemed to be accounted for. Any spare moment was supposed to be dedicated to recruiting new members, progress on which was regularly checked by the director. Numeraries had barely a moment to think for themselves.

Evenings at the residence were quiet. On the few days like this when he arrived early back from work, Luis liked to stretch his legs a little, and would sometimes squeeze in a short walk between his "family" obligations. He was also an avid reader, a passion he tried to share with the other men he lived with. While it was prohibited for numerary members to give presents to each other, even small items, he had a habit of buying books for the residence and laying them out in the living room for other members. His benevolence was sometimes a source of frustration for the director, the nominal head of the residence and the one in charge of upholding the rules governing every aspect of everyday life.

Many of the director's duties revolved simply around maintaining the apparatus of control over the residents—he was expected to go through the newspapers each morning to censor any sensitive material and also keep precise records about goings-on at the residence, which were shared with the regional Opus Dei headquarters in Madrid. Other duties had more to do with particular obsessions and paranoias of the founder, which—despite being dead for almost thirty years—still determined daily life in all Opus Dei residences around the world. The director was required to turn off the gas supply at the mains every night, to keep internal rulebooks under lock and key in his office lest they get into the wrong hands, and to compile regular reports for regional headquarters detailing how much was spent on food. There was an elaborate system for sending such reports. Regular mail deliveries were not to be trusted, meaning any communications with regional headquarters had to be delivered by hand. For residences in Madrid, that wasn't such a big issue. But those farther afield had to send numeraries as couriers. As a nod to the founder's paranoia over secure communications—and to ensure that nothing compromising ever got out—the guidelines had even been updated to specify that neither email nor telephone was to be used to communicate with the regional headquarters.

The books that Luis brought home frequently put the director in a difficult position. What numeraries could and couldn't read was strictly controlled, with all books assigned a rating of between 1 and 6—1 designating that a book could be read by anyone, rising to 6 for a book prohibited unless special permission had been granted by the head of Opus Dei. Gustav Flaubert, James Joyce, Jack Kerouac, Stephen King, Doris Lessing, Karl Marx, Toni Morrison, Harold Pinter, Philip Roth, Bertrand Russell, Gore Vidal, and Tennessee Williams were among hundreds of 6s. A special department in Rome was in charge of issuing the ratings, which were recorded on a huge database and distributed by CD-ROM to all Opus Dei residences around the world. Unfortunately for the director, so new were the titles that Luis picked up at the bookstore that Rome hadn't yet classified many of them—which left him in a quandary. Occasionally, the director had to "disappear" some of the books that Luis brought home so that other members wouldn't be morally sullied. But it wasn't Luis's only act of subversion. Officially, numeraries were normally only allowed to watch one movie a month—and even then, it had to be something approved by Rome. But Luis regularly watched movies on the projector in his office. It was an open secret, and something which normally wouldn't have been tolerated among the other residents, who were encouraged to inform on each other even for the most minor of infractions— as a loving act of "fraternal correction."

But Luis was given a long leash. Other numeraries had been specifically told by their superiors to leave him be. There was a good reason for not antagonizing him. Years earlier, the oppression of daily life at the residence had become too much, prompting him to spend most of his week living alone in the mountains. Such an arrangement wasn't usually permitted, but the regional commission had concluded that, given the importance of Luis to the financial operations of Opus Dei, it was wiser to turn a blind eye than to risk angering him and driving him out. But Luis had been forced to abandon his independence seven years earlier, after police raised the alarm about a suspected plot by Euskadi Ta Askatasuna, the Basque terrorist group known as ETA, to kidnap him from the mountain retreat. Since then, he'd reluctantly moved back into the residence.

On the second floor hung a painting of Saint Nicholas of Bari. Born into a wealthy Greek family in the third century, Nicholas was said to have performed many miracles—calming a storm at sea, saving soldiers from wrongful execution, and destroying a tree possessed by a demon. But he was perhaps best known for saving the virtue of three sisters, whose once-devout father had frittered away their dowry money after succumbing to the temptations of the devil, and who as a result faced a life of almost certain prostitution. Saint Nicholas, having heard of their situation, threw a bag of gold coins through the family's window one evening—which the father used as a dowry to marry off his eldest daughter. Nicholas then repeated this generous act for her two sisters. He was caught by their father on the third attempt but had sworn the man to secrecy. Over the years, the story had grown into folklore, with Saint Nicholas eventually becoming better known as Santa Claus. Within Opus Dei, he had become a revered figure, too. Early on, the Opus Dei founder Escrivá had prayed to Nicholas for his intercession in the financial needs of the movement and had clearly stipulated that every residence hang a portrait of the saint. But Nicholas had a particular significance in the Mirasierra residence. Don Luis, who just like Saint Nicholas had been born into wealth, had made a pledge as a young man that he would make it his life's mission to liberate the founder from any worries about money. So successful had he become in that endeavor that Escrivá would sometimes jokingly refer to Luis as "my Saint Nicholas." The Opus Dei founder clearly didn't see the irony that the bags of gold coins being generated by this modern-day Saint Nicholas were being used to entrap young women in lives of servitude rather than liberate them. Luis himself liked to bask in this moniker by spending his few weeks off in the summer visiting various shrines around Spain that were devoted to Saint Nicholas.

At nine or so in the evening, the men would congregate in the dining room for a simple dinner that had been laid out by the women who lived next door. As they ate, the men would share small tidbits from their day—although Luis barely spoke about his work at the bank. Certain topics were strictly off limits—under no circumstances was the governance of Opus Dei ever to be openly discussed among the numerary members themselves. This rule was another way of ensuring discipline among the ranks—of precluding open discussions about the meticulous regulations that governed every aspect of their common existence and of preventing any collective dissent from forming among the residents. The director was supposed to be the only person who knew about how the Opus Dei governance machine really worked. But things were different at the Mirasierra residence. Given his importance within the movement, Luis often knew more than the director. He traveled to Rome frequently to meet with members of the general council there.

Much of the conversation at dinner—and afterwards, in the sitting room—revolved around the recruitment of new members. All numeraries were expected to be constantly grooming new recruits to join the ranks. Each of them was expected to have about fifteen candidates they were actively working on, and every night around the dinner table they would update each other on how close each of these young men and boys were to "whistling"—the internal parlance for asking to join Opus Dei. Unlike the wider Catholic Church, which was open to anyone, Opus Dei was picky about its membership. It was important that prospective members projected the right image—not necessarily of piety or devotion, but of worldly success. Numeraries were specifically instructed to steer clear of anyone of a nervous disposition, including—curiously—anyone with a history of sleepwalking. They were also warned to exercise caution around anyone who might physically find it difficult to live as part of a "family." This was code for avoiding anyone with an obvious disability, and it echoed comments made by the leader of Opus Dei a few years earlier at a gathering in Italy, during which he had said that 90 percent of disabled children were born to parents who had failed to keep their bodies "clean" before marriage. Medical check-ups were preferable before anyone was formally admitted—that way Opus Dei could be sure that nobody would become a financial burden. They were also advised against targeting anyone with bad grades—or anyone who was illegitimate.

Numeraries were told that children could become "aspirant" members from as young as fourteen and a half, and reminded of the fact that it wasn't compulsory to consult with their parents beforehand—such matters were to be referred to the regional commission for advice. Luis, for his part, liked to visit a nearby university residence, where he would often give the young men there a lecture on etiquette while he peeled an orange using a spoon. It is unclear how many new recruits he won this way, although given the impact that his work at the bank had on Opus Dei recruitment efforts around the world, he was under little pressure for results.

After dinner and the get-together in the sitting room, it was time for the final communal ritual of the day—the recitation of the *Preces*, a set of prayers written in Latin that had been devised by the founder and which were specific to Opus Dei. Once more, the men made their way downstairs to the chapel, took their positions in the pews, and knelt in unison.

"*Ad Sanctum Iosephmaríam conditórem nostrum*," chanted the priest.

To Saint Josemaría, our founder.

"*Intercéde pro fíliis tuis ut, fidéles spirítui Óperis Dei, labórem sanctificémus et ánimas Christo lucrifácere quærámus*," chanted the kneeling numeraries in unison.

Intercede for your children so that, being faithful to the spirit of Opus Dei, we may sanctify our work and seek to win souls for Christ.

After prayers for the pope and the local bishop, the numeraries sang a prayer whose purpose was clearly to underline the importance of unity—and obedience—within the ranks.

"Every kingdom divided against itself will be laid waste," sang the priest.

"And no city or house divided against itself will stand," the men chanted back.

"Let us pray for our benefactors," sang the priest.

"Grant everlasting life, O Lord, to all those who do good to us on account of your name," the kneeling numeraries sang in response. "Amen."

The prayer, with its call for the everlasting life of Opus Dei benefactors, was particularly poignant for the Banco Popular chairman. Financially speaking, Luis was the greatest benefactor in the movement's history—he had been the source of its financial stability for the best part of five decades. His claim to everlasting life was strong. But whether the system he had created, the hidden web of companies that generated millions every year for Opus Dei, would outlast his time on earth was far from certain. As he knelt there on that balmy June evening, Luis must have known that his time—at least at the bank, and possibly in this world—was coming to an end.

"*Pax*," sang the priest at the front.

"*In ætérnum*," they chanted back.

Four thousand miles away in Washington, D.C., another prominent Opus Dei figure had also mysteriously vanished from public view. Charles John McCloskey III was a fifty-year-old priest who had grown up in Falls Church, Virginia, a small town on the outskirts of D.C. Fresh-faced, with piercing blue eyes, thick black eyebrows, and prematurely silver hair combed neatly to the side, Father C. John—as everyone knew him—was a popular figure among the city's Catholic elite. As a priest without a parish, he lived in an Opus Dei residence for numerary men in Kalorama Heights, an affluent neighborhood favored by diplomats and power brokers. Wyoming House was a four-story mansion built in the 1920s, with twelve bedrooms and ten bathrooms, and it boasted the Thai and Yemeni embassies as neighbors. The property had been purchased a couple of years earlier using a donation of several million dollars from an undisclosed source.

His living arrangements weren't the only unconventional aspect of Father McCloskey's priestly existence. He'd started out on Wall Street, where he'd worked for Merrill Lynch as a trader during the stock market boom and bust of the late 1970s. He'd spent his days cold-calling potential clients, fine-tuning the high-pressure sales tactics that would later transform him into one of Opus Dei's most effective recruiters.

Deeply religious, McCloskey had joined Opus Dei as a young man and had initially sought—like the majority of its members—to serve God as a layman with a normal job, in his case on Wall Street. But he suddenly quit his job in the summer of 1978, after receiving a letter from Álvaro del Portillo—who had been appointed as the general president of Opus Dei following the death of the founder some three years earlier—proclaiming that the movement needed him to become a priest. Such pronouncements from Rome weren't unusual for numerary members like McCloskey, who frequently found themselves required to suddenly change city or leave their careers in order to fulfill the movement's latest needs. Such was a life of obedience.

He first went to Rome, where he arrived in a city still mourning the sudden death of John Paul I, who had died just thirty-three days into his papacy. His funeral followed a couple of days after the American's arrival. He then moved to the Spanish city of Pamplona, home to an Opus Dei university financed by Luis Valls-Taberner and Banco Popular, and the primary training ground for priests affiliated with the movement. He sought to rationalize the abandonment of his career in pseudo-economic terms. "I was not fleeing the evil world of Wall Street . . . but rather, changing professional occupations to serve in another way," he explained. "I suppose you could also say that I was dedicating myself in the priesthood to selling a better product, on which the returns are infinite."

Three years later, McCloskey was ordained at a ceremony at Torreciudad, a vast Opus Dei shrine in the Pyrenees, which was attended by his parents, and an aunt and an uncle, who had made the journey from Falls Church. Afterwards, the five of them drove the six hours to Madrid, where they visited the Spanish headquarters of Opus Dei, just a few blocks north of Banco Popular. After returning to the United States, McCloskey moved into a numerary residence on New York's Upper West Side, before relocating to Princeton in 1985 to serve as a university chaplain. There, he soon developed a reputation as an "in-your-face" champion of traditional Catholic values—a conservative, by-the-book priest who spouted controversial views on contraception, abortion, and homosexuality with his hallmark Wall Street swagger.

"A liberal Catholic is oxymoronic," he would explain to students, while advising them on which classes to take and which to avoid, based on his own assessment of the theological outlook of the teacher giving the course, as well as of how closely their views aligned with his own and those of Opus Dei. He acknowledged the uphill battle he faced on an Ivy League campus, where the students were more interested in listening to Madonna or AC/DC than to the word of God. He jokingly referred to his own chaplaincy as "the most exotic pagan mission territory" when talking to other priests who had been posted to Africa or Asia.

He wasn't always so flippant about his difficulties connecting with the students, whom he resentfully described as a "rarefied group of people" raised by "small families marked by contraceptive selfishness." At times his view of the Princeton population took on a dark edge. "The values of the secular elite university are so radically anti-Christian," he warned. "They are the harbingers of the culture of death. They create the culture of death. This is where the seeds are planted. You can see what is coming down the line by just looking at the atmosphere there now: hedonistic, naturalistic, secularistic." Unsurprisingly, his aggressive views and manner upset many on campus. A group of students began to meet regularly to lobby for his dismissal. For five controversial years, McCloskey held on. The straw that broke the camel's back was a public spat with a comedian over her routine that touched on safe sex and feminism. In 1990, McCloskey was finally kicked out. But he didn't go far, moving into a numerary residence that was a ten-minute walk from Princeton's main campus on Mercer Street and that had just been bought by Opus Dei after its previous owner—an elderly woman—was found murdered in the basement. From there, he continued his unofficial chaplaincy.

But then, in 1998, McCloskey received a phone call from his Opus Dei superiors that would herald his big break. The prelature had recently been entrusted with a small, poorly attended bookshop and adjoining chapel in downtown Washington, D.C. But the priest who had been sent to run it had been taken ill, and they needed a replacement. Despite—or perhaps owing to—his firebrand reputation, McCloskey had been picked for the role. Early the following year, at the age of forty-four, he moved to D.C. to become director of the Catholic Information Center, determined to transform it from a sleepy, largely irrelevant operation into a vibrant spiritual, intellectual, and political hub.

He quickly made his mark, converting a number of high-profile Washington figures to Catholicism—and specifically to the ultra-conservative Opus Dei interpretation of it. During his first few years in the capital, McCloskey was personally responsible for the conversion of Speaker of the House Newt Gingrich, Supreme Court nominee Robert Bork, several congressmen, and high-profile political pundits such as Robert Novak and Larry Kudlow. Soon, worshipers were flooding to midday Mass at the CIC, which was rapidly developing into a Who's Who of the Washington Catholic elite. At the center of it all was McCloskey, who celebrated Mass, heard confession, and provided spiritual direction for his flock, who were encouraged to follow his "Catholic Lifetime Reading Plan." The hundred or so books on the list—including those by Dante, Tolkien, and the Opus Dei founder—were all stocked in the Catholic Information Center bookshop.

Worshipers weren't the only thing streaming in during those years; soon, money began to flood in, too. As well as political heavy hitters, McCloskey converted several big business names—including conservative publishing executive Alfred Regnery, financier and former New York mayoral candidate Lewis Lehrman, and Tyco International general counsel Mark Belnick. Flush with cash, McCloskey moved the Catholic Information Center to larger premises on Fifteenth Street.

Soon, the CIC outgrew even those premises, and in April 2002, it moved to a larger location on K Street, placing it at the heart of the vast lobbying industry that sought to influence senators and congresspeople. The move coincided with an enormous scandal in the Catholic Church. It began with a series of articles in the *Boston Globe* exposing sexual abuse of children dating back decades and involving five priests in the city. The news provoked outrage—and the prosecution of the five men implicated. But the scandal didn't stop there: over coming months, more victims came forward. The *Globe*'s Spotlight team continued their investigation, uncovering a vast cover-up operation that could be traced right to the top of the archdiocese—the cardinal himself was implicated and resigned. Eventually, more than five hundred victims filed suit against one hundred and fifty priests.

Never one to shy from controversy, McCloskey spotted an opportunity and soon established himself as the go-to cleric for journalists striving to inject some "balance" into the debate—for those looking for someone to defend the Church. He rapidly became a regular fixture in television coverage of the Boston sexual abuse scandal, appearing on NBC's *Nightly News*, on CNN, MSNBC, and shows such as *Crossfire*, *Dateline*, and *Meet the Press*. It was a risky strategy and one that could have easily backfired. But his defense of the Church in the face of the growing public backlash only seemed to elevate him within the Catholic conservative clique. Many saw his brash, combative approach as something that was long overdue in the battle against liberalism taking place in society at large and within the Church—with Opus Dei on the far right of that fight. To his supporters, McCloskey personified a reawakening of the Church's original evangelizing mission that would win millions of new converts and return Catholicism to its traditionalist roots. "It's delightful, delicious, the irony," McCloskey would say of liberal Catholics who supported abortion rights or who countenanced gay civil unions. "Those types of people, those nominal Catholics, will not be there in twenty or thirty years."

So, it was a huge shock when, at the height of his fame, McCloskey suddenly disappeared without warning from Washington in late 2003. He no longer celebrated Mass or heard confession, and he no longer came to the Catholic Information Center, the vibrant spiritual and intellectual hub that he had almost singlehandedly transformed. At first, many put his absence down to potential health issues: McCloskey had a difficult relationship with alcohol dating back to his Princeton days. But then people started to suspect that something else was afoot. Perhaps Opus Dei, known for its secrecy and discretion, had finally had enough of his brash, in-your-face ways? Perhaps the headquarters in Rome had sensed the way the wind was blowing on the Boston sexual abuse scandal and had concluded that McCloskey's defense of the accused priests was a liability?

These theories were wide of the mark. McCloskey had, in fact, quietly fled the country following allegations against him for sexual assault. A female parishioner had first made the complaint over a year earlier. The victim, a forty-year-old woman and member of Opus Dei, had approached Father C. John for help with her marital problems. He offered her counseling in his office at the CIC. But on several occasions during and after these sessions, he sexually assaulted her—putting his hands on her hips, pressing himself against her, kissing her hair and caressing her. "He absolutely radiated holiness and kindness and caring and charisma," she said. "He persuaded me that I needed to be hugged, which of course I did, but I needed to be hugged by my husband, not by him." He also asked her detailed questions about her sex life with her husband, and at times she smelled alcohol on his breath.

She recalled thinking, *Am I crazy? This can't be happening. He knew what buttons to push and then just let me go and glided serenely in his cassock to his desk and asked, "When would you like to make the next appointment?"* After one assault, she expressed shame and guilt about what had happened during a subsequent confession with him. McCloskey absolved her of sin without acknowledging his own. During this time, he continued to give interviews defending priests accused of sexual assault and appealing for their privacy to be respected. Finally, the victim went to another Opus Dei priest, who told her not to tell anyone "so he could fix it."

For more than a year after the woman first reported the assaults to the Opus Dei priest in Virginia, nothing much seemed to happen. McCloskey continued his work at the Catholic Information Center. "I love Opus Dei," said the woman he abused, "but I was caught up in this cover-up—I went to confession, thinking I did something to tempt this holy man to cross boundaries." But when she was encouraged by another priest to seek legal action against McCloskey, Opus Dei was suddenly jolted into action. Fearing the worst—for Father C. John and for itself—McCloskey was bundled off to London, where arrangements were made to shield him at an Opus Dei residence in the leafy suburbs of Hampstead. McCloskey had a cover story for anyone who asked, telling them that he was on sabbatical and had come to Europe to write a new book on evangelization—although this was never communicated back to his flock in Washington.

In truth, Opus Dei was keen to keep any news about McCloskey's disappearance as quiet as possible. The allegations against its most high-profile priest could not have been at a worse time. The initial complaint had come just weeks after the canonization of its founder. It was a coming-of-age moment for Opus Dei, a seal of approval from the Vatican, a legitimization of the sanctity of the movement and its founder, who henceforth would become known as Saint Josemaría. The canonization promised to give Opus Dei, which already boasted around ninety thousand members worldwide, real momentum—especially in the United States, a country long coveted by the newly consecrated founder. After five decades of trying—and failing—to win influence in the United States, Opus Dei—through Father McCloskey—had finally broken into the corridors of power. Just before the allegations had surfaced, he'd boasted to the *New York Times* about the growing stature of the movement in the United States: "It's increasingly seen as more mainstream and more normal," he said. "There is a certain gift that Opus Dei has in terms of dealing with people of influence."

Its advances in the country weren't confined to Washington. In New York, Opus Dei had just opened a new national headquarters, a seventeen-story brick and limestone building that rose from the corner of Lexington Avenue and Thirty-fourth Street, which—at a cost of $70 million—symbolized its ambitions for the United States. Across the country, around a hundred non-profit organizations had been set up, with hundreds of millions of dollars in assets—regional launchpads for the movement to recruit more souls to its mission, and soldiers in the fight to shape the public debate around abortion, same-sex marriage, and prayer in schools.

The accusations against McCloskey put all this in jeopardy. At precisely the moment when Opus Dei had reached the peak of its power—politically, financially, and ecclesiastically—it had been hit by twin crises in Washington and Madrid that threatened the foundations on which that influence had been built. In Madrid, the movement had a fight on its hands to secure the financial web that had driven its global growth for fifty years and which had been used to secure influence on the political stage and at the Vatican. In Washington, it faced a fight to retain its presence in the corridors of power, its influence in shaping legislation, and its position in the coming battle against the liberal elite. Then another bombshell dropped: in France, a magistrate ordered a raid on the French headquarters of Opus Dei in Paris, linked to an ongoing investigation into the possible enslavement of young women who had been recruited to cook and clean for numerary members in lodges run by the movement.

The legacy of Saint Josemaría hung by a thread.

2

THE FAMILY BUSINESS

Madrid, Spain—April 1927

THE YOUNG PRIEST CLIMBED DOWN FROM THE TRAIN ONTO THE PLATFORM
and anxiously made his way through the crowd. José María Escrivá was already two weeks late for his new job at Saint Michael's. The rector there had
written a month earlier requesting that, with Holy Week fast approaching,
he should report for duty as soon as possible. With his paperwork in order
and a letter of recommendation from the archbishop, the twenty-five-year-
old had been ready to leave Saragossa for his new job in the capital—only to
have his plans scuppered at the last minute by a letter from the local chan-
cery office, informing him that he was to spend Easter filling in for another
priest in a small village six hours away. He suspected the whole thing was a
ruse cooked up by someone in the archdiocese just to annoy him. "They sent
me there to screw with me," he complained.

While he was quick to play the victim card, his superiors had every right
to be frustrated with him. He'd been offered an idyllic posting shortly after
being ordained—a tiny village just outside of Saragossa, where his main tasks
would be hearing confession from the local farmers and village folk, anoint-
ing the sick, and presiding over weddings, baptisms, and communions. But
he lasted only six weeks before requesting a transfer back to the city. His

frustration at his latest posting was the second time in as many years that he had turned his nose up at the menial parochial work that most priests his age would have jumped at. Despite his youth, Escrivá already harbored airs of grandeur.

As he dashed through the station, he was unsure how his new boss would react to the two-week delay. It wasn't the best start: not only had he failed to get to Madrid early, as requested, but he'd also missed Holy Week entirely. Plump-faced, with slicked-back hair and round, wire-framed glasses, Escrivá looked much younger than his years—more the teenage seminarian than a fully ordained man of the cloth. But what he lacked in experience he more than made up for in style. He took particular care about his appearance—a habit that had attracted great ridicule at the seminary, where he'd struggled to make friends and occasionally got into fights with the other trainees, who mockingly called him "the little gentleman." Vanity was a trait he inherited from his father, who spent his Sundays promenading along the river, wearing a bowler hat and carrying a cane. Such public demonstrations of grandeur were a nod to a lost era for the Escrivá family: his father had fallen into bankruptcy when José María was twelve, forcing the family not only to sell their home and give up their four servants but also to leave their hometown of Barbastro in search for work. This fall from grace capped a tragic four years for José María during which three of his younger sisters died in quick succession. The events deeply affected the boy and prompted him to question why God would inflict such suffering on good, devout people while other, less pious families lived free of such hardships. "I realized that God in some way has to reward them on earth, since he won't be able to reward them in eternity," he concluded. "They also feed the ox that will go to the slaughterhouse." His reasoning betrayed a gnawing sense of entitlement, righteousness—and a certain darkness in his personality.

From the station, he headed straight for Saint Michael's, although his haste to get there was driven perhaps more by guilt than by enthusiasm for his new job. For Father José María had a confession to make: his reasons for moving to the capital were not altogether devout. He'd actually applied for the job at Saint Michael's as a pretext to secure the relevant permissions to move from one diocese to another so he could pursue his real passion—a doctorate in law. The job, which involved giving the early-morning Mass in exchange for a daily stipend of five and a half pesetas—about $20 a day today—fitted perfectly with his plans to study and would even leave him with spare time to teach law to undergraduates and earn a little extra cash. Escrivá was unsure about the priesthood. Like many boys growing up in the provinces, he had joined the seminary, not out of a strong desire to go into the Church, but as a pathway to a better life and for opportunities beyond his hometown. "I had never thought of becoming a priest, or of dedicating myself to God," he confessed. Although he took care to project the image of the devout clergyman, always immaculately turned out in his black cassock, his outward appearance hid a burning ambition to make something of himself—and a deep uncertainty about his future in the Church.

After presenting himself to the rector, he checked into a hotel a short walk away and, over the next few days, he gradually got himself installed in the capital and enrolled in the relevant courses at the Universidad Central. He soon found cheaper accommodation—a boarding house for priests that was owned by a group of aristocratic women who had been inspired to help the poor after going on a pilgrimage to Lourdes. José María wasted no time in ingratiating himself with these rich women. The Apostolic Ladies of the Sacred Heart of Jesus, as they called themselves, had just been given permission to open their own chapel, and they were so taken with Escrivá that they soon offered him the chaplaincy of their new church. Ambition trumped any loyalty or obligation to the rector at Saint Michael's, who had patiently waited for his delayed arrival from Saragossa. In July, he handed in his notice. He had been there only two months.

Moving to the Apostolic Ladies brought Escrivá into contact with real poverty for the first time. Although he liked to bemoan his family's financial situation, their poverty was relative only to the good life they had once enjoyed. Even after their fall, the Escrivás still had a lifestyle that was far detached from the appalling conditions in Madrid's slums, where many thousands of people faced a daily struggle of existence and where homelessness, malnutrition, and disease were rife. The Apostolic Ladies had set up a string of schools and soup kitchens, and part of the young chaplain's duties involved going out to the city's slums to anoint the sick or give catechism classes. The women also enlisted him in one of their pet projects—a campaign against what they saw as blatant anti-Catholic propaganda being pushed by the left.

The work involved countering talk of workers' rights and social justice with readings from the Bible and defending the Church against claims that it was a defender of the brutally unjust political order. Escrivá threw himself wholeheartedly into these "apostolic missions." It was an early indication of his willingness to defend the Church at all costs, even if that meant turning a blind eye to the suffering around him.

Escrivá didn't allow his work in the slums to take up all his time. During his first year in Madrid, he completed two courses toward his doctorate—one on the history of international law and the other on the philosophy of law. He also took on another job teaching at a private academy in the afternoons and he had enough time left over to give private classes to undergraduate law students at home. Soon, his economic situation had improved markedly— he was able to afford an apartment in Chamberí, a well-to-do neighborhood with large open spaces. By the end of 1927, his mother Dolores, older sister Carmen, and eight-year-old brother Santiago moved to Madrid to live with him.

But the pressure of juggling three jobs and a doctorate soon started to take its toll and, before long, his studies—the thing that had brought him to the capital—were slipping. The grades in his first year were only average and in his second he started to fall behind. The feeling of his academic career stalling weighed heavily: since his father's death five years earlier, he had been the family's main breadwinner, and the Escrivá family's prospects lay squarely on his shoulders. His mother also heaped pressure on him. When he was a toddler, he had suddenly taken ill and a doctor had warned that the young boy might not make it through the night. His mother had prayed to the Virgin Mary, promising her that if she saved her son, then she would take the boy to a shrine fourteen miles away at Torreciudad. The next day José María staged a miraculous recovery. "It must be for something great that our Lady left you in this world, because you were more dead than alive," she often reminded him. It was little wonder, then, that he felt pressure to make something of his life.

In September 1928, he took time out at a retreat. He planned to use his time there to think about his future, and he took with him a bundle of papers—jottings he had made over the years about life and faith. He arrived on a Sunday night and, freed from work and his studies, began to embrace the daily rhythm of the retreat—waking at five, going to bed at nine, with a program of talks in between. On the third day, he went back to his room after morning Mass to read through some of his papers. What happened next would change his life. For years, the notes had seemed a sprawling mass of disparate ideas with no clear link. He had prayed to God for clarity—but to no avail. Suddenly, that morning it all became clear: Escrivá saw the outlines of a new way to serve God.

Over the next few days, while still on retreat, he started to formulate the rough outlines of what would eventually become Opus Dei—the Work of God. At its core was the idea of a universal call to holiness. He envisioned a lay brotherhood of men—"never—no way—will there be women in Opus Dei"—who would serve God by striving for perfection even in the most everyday tasks. "The extraordinary for us is the ordinary: the ordinary done with perfection," he wrote. "Always with a smile, ignoring—in a nice way—the things that bother us, that annoy us; being generous beyond measure. In a word, making our ordinary life a continuous prayer." At its birth, Escrivá's vision for Opus Dei was a deeply Christian one, embracing notions like compassion, forgiveness, and charity. But over the years that vision would become warped by his need to grow and control the movement.

From the outset, he maintained that God had sent him the idea directly—but in reality, his vision borrowed heavily from more earthly foundations. The idea for a lay brotherhood was nothing new—the Jesuits already had various sodalities that sought to extend the order's spirituality beyond its clergy. The timing of the vision was also convenient. It was a clear response to a debate raging about the intransigence and outright complicity of the Church in the country's social problems. Escrivá would have been well aware of the potential appeal of a new back-to-basics Catholicism among those who were questioning the actions of the Church and who were seeking a way to return to the core teachings of their faith. Still, he maintained his vision was from God—and God alone. "It would take the imagination of a novelist who is a raving lunatic, or who has a fever of 105, to come up with on one's own the idea of a Work like this," he wrote in his journal. "If it was not of God, it would have to be a plan concocted by someone drunk with pride."

Despite being convinced that the Lord had spoken to him directly, for the next four years Escrivá did surprisingly little to realize God's will. Instead, he drifted between his three jobs and his law studies. Occasionally, he spoke about his idea for Opus Dei with those around him. Sometimes, after class, he took his students to a local bar, but his evangelical efforts bore little fruit. In 1929, the year after his vision, just two people tentatively expressed interest in joining Opus Dei—although one of those was his own deputy at the church, who might have felt awkward about saying no to his boss.

Perhaps frustrated with his failure to recruit anyone in the sixteen months since receiving the vision, in February 1930, Escrivá had an epiphany during a Mass being held at the home of one of the aristocratic women he knew—and he decided to ditch his previous opposition to women joining Opus Dei. A contradiction was already emerging within the foundations of the movement. On the one hand, he insisted that the vision he had received in October 1928 had come directly from God—and had been fully formed. "I received an illumination about the entire Work while I was reading those papers," he explained. But on the other hand, he showed a readiness to make changes to that divine vision for practical, recruitment purposes. Evidently, the word of God was malleable.

But even that volte-face failed to generate recruits. At one stage, Escrivá became so despairing of his own failure that he asked one dying woman to intercede for him when she reached the next life. During this period, his frame of mind seemed to swing from one extreme to the other. At times, he felt inspired, and he looked back on that October morning as the moment that changed his life. "Yesterday evening, while walking down the street," he wrote, "it occurred to me that Madrid has been my Damascus, because it was here that the scales fell from the eyes of my soul . . . and it was here that I received my mission." Other days, he thought about leaving the priesthood entirely. At one stage, Escrivá decided to forget about the Work of God and instead apply for a job as a civil servant. Even direct intervention from God seemed insufficient to quiet the competing demands of his faith, his worldly ambition, and his family.

Money—or the lack of it—soon became an obsession. While his life was comfortable, it was a far cry from the affluence the family had once enjoyed—a contrast much remarked upon by his mother. With a generous salary of

2,500 pesetas a year, the civil service job would have been a big step in the right direction. But his application was unsuccessful. Having failed to find a decent job in the civilian world, he began looking around for ecclesiastical openings. His decision to switch jobs probably wasn't only based on money; it also coincided with a dramatic shift in the political landscape. Over a few days in April 1931, the brutally unjust political order was swept away. The left won municipal elections by a landslide and called for King Alfonso XIII, who had presided over years of incompetence and corruption, to abdicate. Within two days he was gone. A republic was proclaimed, headed by a new government dedicated to improving the lives of millions of Spaniards. With the working classes newly empowered against their former oppressors, the city's slums would be an even more dangerous place for a young priest. Escrivá, like the king, could sense the way the wind was blowing. It was prudent to look for another, less frontline position.

Despite having seen the conditions in the slums himself, Escrivá was horrified at the priorities of the new regime. "May the Immaculate Virgin defend this poor Spain!," he wrote. "God confound the enemies of our Mother the Church! Madrid, for twenty-four hours, was one huge brothel. . . . Things seem to have calmed down. But the Freemasons are not sleeping." He became obsessed with right-wing conspiracy theories that claimed the declaration of the republic was a secret plot concocted by a shadowy group of Jews, Masons, and Communists who wanted to overthrow Christian Europe.

With tensions rising, a misunderstanding over the alleged killing of a taxi driver by a group of monarchists finally led to outright violence in the city on May 10. Initially, it was mainly directed at pro-monarchy symbols— including the newspaper ABC. But the next day, the crowd turned against other symbols of oppression. A Jesuit church in the middle of the city was burned to the ground. On its scorched walls, the words "justice for the people against the thieves" were chalked in bold letters. Over the next three days, violence against the Church exploded across the country: more than a hundred buildings—churches, monasteries, convents, and religious schools—were torched. "The persecution has begun," he wrote in his journal.

A month after the church burnings, his job hunt finally paid off. Escrivá was offered a chaplaincy at the Santa Isabel convent, on the eastern edge of the city. It was far from ideal—the position was temporary and offered no pay, meaning a hit to the family's finances—but it would keep him out of the slums. His departure led to a falling out with the women at the Apostolic Ladies, which may have been rooted in what they saw as the abandonment of his duties. His life at Santa Isabel certainly was more comfortable: over the coming months, he had more time to develop his ideas about Opus Dei. Stirred by the events around him, what had been a relatively benign vision of core Christian beliefs began to evolve into something darker, more political, and almost militia-like. Escrivá initially described his vision of Opus Dei as being an example to others, an inspiration for how everyone—no matter their station in life—could dedicate their everyday actions up to God. By the spring of 1931, amid growing discontent with the ruling elite, that vision had evolved slightly to underline the importance of prayer, of standing firm against temptation, of remaining faithful. But a year later, following the spate of church burnings and violence against members of the clergy, his outline for Opus Dei was transformed. In his writings in the spring of 1932, Escrivá stated that being a member of Opus Dei meant offering your life up to God—it meant complete loyalty to the movement, unquestioning obedience, and the renouncement of any individual rights. Clues outlining this calling had been clearly outlined in the Gospel, he explained—but the true meaning of this message had been misunderstood by Church scholars for close to two millennia. But *he* now understood it. "You don't come to the Work in search of something," he wrote. "You come to serve yourself up, to renounce—for the love of God—any personal ambition." The evolution in his thinking was a clear reaction to current events, and to his obsession with the conspiracy theories swirling around him. While he still had no followers, he was outlining a battle plan for an "army" of the faithful, a call to arms against the Freemasons, the Jews, and the Communists.

After his lack of success recruiting followers through his daily pastoral work, Escrivá decided to change direction—taking inspiration from the Jesuits, who had recently opened an academy where law students from the university could study and worship safely, away from the violence on campus. Escrivá decided he would do the same. At the end of 1932, he borrowed some money and moved his family to a new, larger apartment where he could hold regular classes and study circles. Within a few weeks he had two new recruits.

Invigorated, he began to formulate plans for a full-scale academy and he actively began to recruit potential tutors. The plans gave him fresh motivation after four years with little to show for his efforts. He went on retreat in June 1933 and, on a sheet titled "immediate action," he resolved to dedicate himself completely to Opus Dei. "I need to give up everything—even things that are truly apostolic—that isn't directly connected with fulfilling the will of God, which means the Work. Plan: Every week, I have been hearing confessions in seven different places. I will give up hearing those confessions, except for those two little groups of university girls." Once again, his own ambitions took precedence over his priestly duties.

His resolve coincided with a sudden change in the family's fortunes. His uncle, also a priest, suddenly passed away and left two properties to his mother. Shortly after this windfall, Escrivá rented another apartment a short walk from the family home in what was to be the new location of the academy. Over the next few weeks, work began on decorating and decking out the new premises. At Christmas, Escrivá unveiled the name: the academy would simply be called DYA, to stand for *Dios y Audacia*—"God and Audacity"—although he asked for the name to remain a secret to anyone beyond his immediate circle of recruits. Instead, they were to say that the three letters stood for *Derecho y Arquitectura*—"law and architecture"—the two main subjects that would be taught there. Right from the start, Escrivá was choosing to conceal what was really going on behind closed doors. The very first Opus Dei center, the hub that he planned to use to recruit unsuspecting university students to his movement, was presented to the world as nothing more than a secular academy.

DYA opened its doors on January 15, 1934. Even though months had already passed since the start of the academic year, it had no trouble attracting students. Like the Jesuits, Escrivá was tapping into huge demand for private tuition among the city's law and architecture students, which was unsurprising, perhaps given the huge education reforms being pushed through by the government, which had led to a shortage of qualified staff. During the first three months, around a hundred students passed through its doors to attend classes. Thirty of them also signed up for the extracurricular spiritual formation classes given by Escrivá. Afterwards, he often met students one-on-one and explained how they could improve their lives through Opus Dei. In those first three months, seven more students asked to join, swelling membership to the double figures. Escrivá held a special weekly meeting for the small group and asked them to begin calling him *Padre*—Father—instead of the Don José María used by other students at the academy. He also told them to look out for each other. A new, semi-covert inner circle was developing.

Father soon had bigger plans for the group. Drawing on his observations of the students who came through the doors of the academy each day—and taking note of which methods worked and which ones failed—he began to compile a detailed set of what he called "instructions" for his small but growing membership. It was the first of what eventually would become dozens of "instructions" totaling hundreds of pages, all written by the founder, which would dictate every aspect of life within Opus Dei, controlling the daily activities of its members and restricting their contact with the outside world. The first of these documents, titled *Instruction Concerning the Supernatural Spirit of the Work of God*, was the first time Escrivá had set down in writing for others what it meant to be in Opus Dei. He referred to the "tempestuous times" they were living through, which demanded men and women who were "strong willed, with supernatural resolve, ready to enter into battle against the enemies of Christ." Right from the beginning, then, it was clear that Opus Dei was deeply political at its core; it was a reactionary stand against the progressive forces that were transforming society. To his list of prayer and atonement the founder now added an additional duty required of his followers—action. He wrote that the movement was part of "a rising militia" of "apostles carrying out the orders of Christ." His words were a rallying cry to young conservatives keen to defend the Church and roll back some of the progressive reforms of the last few years. "The disease is extraordinary— and the medicine is just as extraordinary," wrote Escrivá. "We are an intravenous injection, inserted into the circulatory torrent of society . . . to immunize the corruption of mankind and to illuminate all minds with the light of Christ."

A few weeks later, Escrivá put together his second "instructions" document, which set out a detailed guide his followers could use to entice more souls into Opus Dei. The document, called *Instruction Concerning How to Proselytize*, would become a blueprint for Opus Dei members in the decades ahead— a secret manual for recruitment that would be hidden from the outside world, including Vatican authorities. Escrivá ordered his followers to focus their efforts on young people and avoid anyone over the age of twenty-five, explaining that older people had a tendency to be set in their ways—although perhaps it was simply that they were less susceptible to being recruited into what was increasingly looking like a religious cult. He warned them to be wary of people that asked too many questions. Members were told to operate covertly, and to begin by planting seeds in the mind of the person being targeted. Drawing on his own methods, Escrivá even suggested that his followers might arrange charitable visits or cultural talks as a pretext for getting people together—but he warned against trying to recruit lots of people at once. "Never—ever!—try to capture a group," he advised. "Vocations need to come one by one, unpicking—in this case—the group with snakelike calculation." He advised members to tell anyone showing interest in joining Opus Dei to keep it to themselves. "Instruct the new ones to *shut up*," he wrote, "because their calling is like a little candle that has just been lit . . . and it would only take one small breath to extinguish it completely in their heart." Recruits were also to be encouraged to distance themselves from their families. Anyone having any doubts was to be directed to an Opus Dei priest; Escrivá was the only priest within the movement at this stage, but even in 1934 he had plans to roll out his movement much more widely. If they were reluctant to meet a priest, he encouraged his followers to invent a pretext for the meeting, to present the priest as an expert in law or history or literature who might be able to help them professionally or with their studies. They were to target men at the top of their field—although such were Escrivá's ambitions for Opus Dei that he added that it would also be necessary to recruit mediocre men as the movement grew, as they would be needed to fill internal roles within the organization. He also encouraged recruiters to use any resource at their disposal, including public funds and government buildings. With membership barely in the double figures, Escrivá had created a system that would underpin its expansion for the next ninety years—a system based on secrecy and deception.

Escrivá soon decided that the time had come to bring his followers under one roof. He resolved to open a student residence before the start of the next academic year and convinced his mother to sell the two properties she had just inherited to invest in his new venture. The residence would make it easier for members to follow the grueling daily schedule—a program of spiritual life, as Escrivá liked to call it—that he had begun to formulate. Every day, there was a half hour of prayer in the morning, followed by Mass and communion, the praying of the Angelus and the rosary, spiritual readings, and another half hour of prayer in the evening, a visit to the Eucharist, supplications, examinations of conscience, and other prayers throughout the day. This intensive program filled up a large chunk of members' days, leaving them little time to actually go out and serve God through their everyday jobs—as they had been told they would. Instead, their lives became ever more insular—and ever more dependent on Opus Dei and its founder.

Then there was the mortification. His failure to get Opus Dei off the ground had taken its toll on Escrivá in the years since first getting the call, and at times he had turned to corporal mortification as atonement. Those close to him had become alarmed at his incessant use of the discipline—a cord-like whip, to which he added bits of metal and pieces of razor blade to enhance his suffering—during his lowest points. While the discipline had been used over the centuries by various orders, including the Cistercians and Capuchins, by the 1930s it had fallen completely out of use by everyday priests like Escrivá—and certainly among lay Catholics. He used the discipline three times a week, with an additional lashing once every two weeks and also on feast days. He also used the cilice, a small, spiked chain worn around the thigh, multiple times a day—twice before lunch and then in the afternoon. On Tuesdays, he used a cilice that wrapped around his waist. On Saturdays, he fasted—although he would often find any excuse to deny himself food or water. Some of the mortification—the fasting, the cilice around the waist—was linked to a growing obsession with his weight, which had begun to increase. "It is precisely against gluttony that I need to fight hardest," he explained. At one point, his confessor became concerned about his health and had to ban him from fasting.

The bloody sessions with the discipline had also begun to alarm those closest to him. At his mother's house, he would turn on the faucets to muffle the cracks of the whip and carefully clean up afterwards. But she would still find specks of blood on the floor and the walls. When she agreed to give him the money for the academy, she voiced her concerns. "Don't beat yourself or put on a long face," she begged him. But the daily acts of mortification continued. He asked that his followers do the same: they were expected to wear the cilice every day, sleep on the floor three times a week, and observe a total fast—no bread or water—once a week.

He quickly realized that money from his mother wouldn't be enough to pay for the new Opus Dei residence, and he ordered members to go back to their families—the families they had been encouraged to turn away from—and ask them for money. This selective distancing—of cutting oneself off from one's family, apart from when money was needed—would become a recurring theme for Opus Dei members. "A student residence is essential," he wrote. "We are doing what we can, but we have not yet come up with the money we need. Help us: do some asking yourselves and get others to ask, too. We must make our Father-God dizzy with our pleading." Soon, Escrivá was in a position to rent three apartments on Calle Ferraz, a short walk from the university. Over the next few weeks, two of the apartments were converted into sleeping quarters for twenty-five students; the other was converted into classrooms, a new location for the academy. By the end of October, it was all ready. "Classes have started at DYA," wrote Escrivá, "and I expect much supernatural fruit, fruit of Catholic formation and culture, from this house."

Things did not go as planned. Tensions had once again been rising across the country following the victory of a Catholic-led coalition at the end of 1933. Sporadic protests from those on the left broke out across the country—spurred on by counter-protests on the right. José María Gil Robles, the leader of the Catholic coalition, called a rally at the royal palace in El Escorial, just outside the capital. A group of twenty thousand men turned up to the meeting, which resembled a Nazi rally, and swore allegiance to Gil Robles with chants of *Jefe! Jefe! Jefe!* The army brutally quelled a popular uprising in Catalonia and a miners' strike in Asturias. With political unrest breaking out everywhere, the government thought it prudent to delay the start of the university year—just as Escrivá was launching his new student residence. The decision was devastating for DYA: not a single student signed up to live at the residence, and advertisements in various newspapers went unanswered. With no income coming in, Escrivá struggled to pay the four members of the staff who had been hired ahead of the opening of the residence—two housekeepers, a cook, and a porter.

By Christmas, Escrivá was in serious financial trouble. He prayed to Saint Nicholas of Bari, pleading for him to intercede in the financial problems of the DYA residence, even going so far as to name him as the patron saint of Opus Dei's business affairs. But Opus's fortunes did not improve. During this period, Escrivá's use of the discipline increased. With his finances in dire straits, he made the difficult decision to hand back the keys for one of the three apartments—the one that had been earmarked for the academy—leaving him with only the residence.

Once the universities reopened, their money troubles abated a little. By March, the worst had passed, and Escrivá turned his attention to making improvements. His new obsession was having his own chapel on the premises, and he wrote to the local diocese to ask for permission. Before he even had a reply, he bought an altar and altarpiece. A few days later, he secured a tabernacle, altar cloths, candlesticks, and various other items. Unable to contain his excitement, he decided to baptize the new chapel with an initiation ceremony for his small group of followers, which would mark their official incorporation into Opus Dei. Standing before a plain wooden cross in the yet-to-be-sanctified chapel, the Father asked them, one by one, to declare their allegiance. His impatience in bringing forward the ceremony before approval had been granted—and the pledge that members were expected to make—indicated a growing disregard for the rules of the Church. "If the Lord calls me home before the Work gets all the canonical approvals it needs for stability, will you keep working to carry forward Opus Dei, even if it costs you your property, your reputation, and your career?" he asked each one of them. "Will you, in other words, put your whole life at the service of God in his Work?" Afterwards, he gave each of them a ring engraved inside with the date and the word *Serviam*—"I will serve." Ominously, Escrivá named the ceremony "The Enslavement."

By the end of the academic year, business was booming at the academy. DYA had one hundred and fifty students on its books by the spring—half of whom also attended Escrivá's spiritual formation classes. But the large numbers of students who passed through the doors of the residence and the academy weren't yet converting into the stream of Opus Dei recruits he had hoped for. He started to refine his recruitment methods, asking residents and visitors to fill out questionnaires. Using that information, he kept report cards on all the students and carefully honed his recruitment methods for each. It was a method that would eventually become standard practice within Opus Dei. One architecture student who had put down painting as a hobby turned up at the academy a few days later, only to be presented with a large canvas and asked to paint something for the dining room. Escrivá would sit with him while he painted and talk to him about Opus Dei. Meanwhile, two other architecture students who were already members were encouraged to push him into joining. Such aggressive recruitment techniques paid off: seven more students asked to be admitted to Opus Dei before the academic year was out.

In September, his followers wrote to high schools outside the capital and placed advertisements in national newspapers in an effort to boost enrollment at the residence, making no mention of its affiliations with this new religious movement. The residence was getting so crowded that Escrivá had to rent an apartment in the building next door to handle the overflow. The DYA residence and academy was rapidly becoming a booming line of business. While it hadn't yet generated the army of followers he yearned for, the sheer number of people passing through its doors had the potential to turn it into a hotbed for recruits that was far more effective than anything Escrivá had tried before.

Following months of infighting and a series of scandals, the conservative government collapsed in early 1936 and the left returned to power, sparking renewed clashes on the streets. One of the DYA residents was arrested for his involvement in the botched assassination of a left-wing politician and was sent to prison. Following the incident, Escrivá introduced a new rule—any talk of politics was banned inside the residence. The move wasn't an attempt to condemn the attempted murder—indeed, he asked some of the residents to visit the assassin in prison—but instead a clear attempt to protect Opus Dei from any political fallout. He took other precautions, too, setting up a new company called the Foundation for Higher Studies that would handle the business affairs of the residence and the academy behind an entity that was financially and legally separate from Opus Dei and the Escrivá family. It was a method that Opus Dei would eventually use for all its business and apostolic interests around the world.

Escrivá started making plans for expansion beyond Madrid. He also started looking for a larger property in the Spanish capital, and in June 1936 the Foundation for Higher Studies signed off on the purchase of an entire building near the DYA residence. The new building looked out over parkland and the imposing Montaña military barracks, home to several hundred soldiers. It's unclear where the money came from, although it's likely the company took out a loan based on the profits being made at the academy and residence. Clearly, Escrivá had hit on an efficient and lucrative business model. At this point, only twenty-one men and five women had taken the enslavement ceremony, but Escrivá had big ambitions. "Madrid? Valencia? Paris? The world!" he wrote.

In May 1936, he authored another set of "instructions" addressed to the men who would be tasked with running Opus Dei residences in these cities. The document, entitled *Instruction for Directors*, covered 103 different topics, from the level of anger deemed appropriate for a director to show to the levels of tidiness expected. During the early expansion of Opus Dei, Escrivá had himself been able to groom each of the young men who had asked to join the movement, and this document laid bare his unease about losing direct control over the formation of new members. He stipulated that the local directors were required to write everything down—including details about spiritual matters, everyday incidents within the residence, the personal details about residents' family and professional lives, as well as observations about their particular talents, skills, and interests. These report cards would eventually evolve into the internal "reports of conscience" that local directors would prepare for the regional headquarters, using information gleaned from members during the supposedly confidential spiritual guidance sessions—a mainstay of Opus Dei's control over its members' lives that would remain for decades to come. Directors were also encouraged to open and read the personal correspondence of anyone living at the residence. They were also told to exercise caution interacting with any clergy from the local diocese and to remain silent about any "contradictions"—presumably between Opus Dei's precepts and Church teachings. "People who don't belong to the Work don't have the spirit of Opus Dei," explained the founder. "Nor do they have the grace of God." He wrote that the directors would, for the time being, have to also take charge of domestic tasks—but added that he was working on detailed plans for his daughters in the women's section, who would eventually do all those jobs "without being seen and without being heard, an apostolate that will go unnoticed." He was clear that this would free up men's time to recruit.

On July 13, a Monday, Escrivá and his followers moved into the larger new residence in Madrid, just hours after the brutal murder of a conservative politician at the hands of a police squad, who were avenging the killing of one of their own—probably by a right-wing hit squad. As Escrivá and his small band of followers unpacked, frantic meetings were taking place across the capital to try to figure out what to do next. Socialist politicians said now was the time to begin distributing weapons to workers. Hundreds of miles away, in the Canary Islands, General Francisco Franco took the murder as a green light for the military to take over and restore order. A coup, which had long been talked about among senior army officers, was planned for Friday, July 17. By Saturday morning, July 18, garrisons in the Canary Islands, Spanish Morocco, and the enclaves of Ceuta and Melilla on the North African coast had all risen up and taken over. By Sunday, military uprisings were taking place on the mainland—although the picture was confused and, in Madrid, the main radio station was broadcasting the message that "no one, absolutely no one on the Spanish mainland, has taken part in this absurd plot."

That report was inaccurate. A senior general had arrived at the Montaña barracks opposite the Opus Dei residence that morning dressed in civilian clothing, tasked with taking over the city. Inside, several hundred troops were told to wait for backup. On Sunday afternoon, Escrivá began to notice unusual activity on the street below; groups of people—loyalist troops, police officers, people's militias and ordinary workers—were marching with weapons, flags, and raised fists toward the barracks, determined to prevent the army from taking over the city. The gates were blocked—nobody could get in or out. The standoff continued for hours.

During the night, an occasional gunshot rang out, as a reminder of the tension in the street below, but the stalemate continued. The calm was shattered first thing Monday morning, when the forces outside launched their attack. Five hours of fighting followed, with the government loyalists showering the barracks with bullets, amid cries of "Death to Fascism" and "All to the aid of the Republic." Reinforcement came from the air and from two pieces of artillery that had been drawn through the capital's streets by a beer truck. As Escrivá and his followers cowered inside, stray bullets ricocheted off the walls and splintered the balcony. They took refuge in the basement. By mid-morning, several hundred people were dead. The loyalists had won, and they rapidly took control of what remained of the barracks—and the cache of weapons inside. Across the city, dozens of churches were set on fire. The workers were taking control. In Madrid, at least, the coup had failed.

Fearing for his life, once the battle at the Montaña barracks had abated, Escrivá changed out of his cassock and into a set of blue overalls that had been left over from the recent refurbishment of the residence. At one o'clock, he made the sign of the cross and exited through the back door. He was the first to leave. He headed for his mother's apartment and called the residence to check on his followers. Everyone was safe. Escrivá spent the rest of the afternoon and evening listening to conflicting radio reports and praying the rosary. That night, the heat and the tension made it difficult to sleep. Occasionally, he heard militias creeping around on the roof of the building.

In the coming days, while Escrivá remained in hiding, he asked his followers to run errands for him, sending them to collect his keys, a briefcase, and his identity card and to check at the post office for mail. His sister went out multiple times to buy food. Escrivá remained in the relative safety of the apartment and whiled away the time by playing cards with his mother or listening to the radio. It gradually became clear that the military uprising had only partially succeeded: while the coup had been successful across much of rural Spain, it had failed in the main cities, where workers were making a stand against the reactionary forces. From radio reports and telephone conversations, Escrivá began to piece together the reality of a country that was now divided in two. Santa Isabel, the church attached to the monastery where he was still officially a priest, had been burned to the ground. He also began to hear talk of priests being rounded up.

Over the next couple of weeks, as rumors of house-to-house searches intensified, he took further precautions to hide the fact that he was a priest, wearing his father's wedding ring, growing out his tonsure, and also growing a moustache to throw off anyone who might have recognized him. Early one morning, the building's doorman told them that there was to be a search.

Escrivá left immediately and spent the next few hours walking the streets of the capital aimlessly, in constant fear of being stopped and thrown into prison, or worse. That evening, unsure of the situation at his mother's apartment, he went to the home of a young professor who frequented the DYA academy, and there he was reunited with two of his followers. During the first three months of the war, Escrivá stayed in eight different homes belonging to friends and relatives of Opus Dei members, taking care to not stay in any one place too long. He had good reason to be scared: in the first few months of the war, around a third of the two thousand priests in Madrid were killed.

Meanwhile, the search continued for a more secure hiding place. Arrangements were made for Escrivá to be admitted to a mental asylum on the northeastern edge of the city. On October 7, the Opus Dei founder was picked up from the apartment where he was staying by a car sent by the hospital. The "patient" was put in the back, while one of his followers got into the front of the car with the driver. "I told the driver that the person in the back seat was mentally ill, not dangerous but beset with delusions of grandeur, and that I was taking him to the sanatorium for treatment," he later recalled. Escrivá spent five months in the asylum. An atmosphere of suspicion and fear hung in the air. It was unclear which patients were genuinely ill and which were feigning their illness. The doctor in charge seemed happy to turn a blind eye to anyone masquerading as a patient so long as they paid their bill. At one point, Escrivá's mother concluded that her youngest son Santiago—fast approaching eighteen and at risk of being conscripted into fighting—would be safer alongside his older brother José María and so she sent him to live at the asylum as well.

In March 1937, another of his followers who had taken refuge at the Honduran consulate secured permission for Escrivá and his brother to join him there. Across the city, more than ten thousand people—predominantly, though not exclusively, people from the right—were holed up in the embassies and consulates of foreign governments. At the consulate, he was reunited with four other members of Opus Dei. Escrivá and Santiago were also reunited with their mother and sister, who were allowed to visit briefly. The first few weeks were happy ones: various embassies had been holding negotiations with government forces about a mass evacuation, and the priest and his brother had moved from the asylum on the assumption they would be part of that. They had even paid for their passage and been assigned numbers 23 and 92, respectively. Again, it's unclear where the money came from.

Week after week, Escrivá thought his escape was imminent. But it never came. Conditions inside the consulate were difficult. During the day they were pushed into the corridors, and at night they arranged their mattresses side by side under the dining table; blankets, suitcases, books, and toiletries were strewn everywhere. In May, the priest, his brother, and the three Opus Dei members were given a room of their own—an old storeroom that wasn't even big enough to lay out their mattresses. Then news arrived of a raid at the Peruvian embassy, where three hundred Spaniards and thirty Peruvians had been rounded up. Escrivá did his best to keep his spirits up. Outside, on the streets of Madrid and across the country, tens of thousands of people—possibly hundreds of thousands—had died; the country had been torn apart and living conditions for millions were atrocious. In the relative safety of the consulate, the thoughts of Escrivá and his followers were focused on Opus Dei. They wrote to members, usually in code, and sought as much as possible to follow the daily schedule of prayers and introspection drawn up by the founder. Against the backdrop of horror and death, Escrivá decided to file a claim for compensation against the government for damage to the DYA academy and residence. He claimed one million pesetas in damages.

Trapped inside the consulate, unable to go outside, after a few months Escrivá's mental health started to deteriorate. As had happened during the previous financial crisis at the academy a few years earlier, he became ever more obsessed with violent acts of mortification as he began to slide into depression. Occasionally, he would ask the others to leave the room; other times, he would wait for them to go to the dining room. Once, when one of his followers was in bed with a fever and could not leave, he asked him to cover his face with a blanket, before proceeding to whip himself with his discipline a thousand times. The floor was spattered with blood.

Things improved in the summer, when Escrivá persuaded the consulate to issue him a false document naming him as an employee—as chief supply officer. The document gave him the confidence to begin roaming the streets of Madrid once again. He began to regularly visit his mother, and his mood improved. Soon, his resolve returned, too. He concluded that the only way to secure the future of Opus Dei would be to leave Madrid. Word got back to the Opus Dei men at the consulate about a possible escape route, through Barcelona and the Pyrenees into France, that a handful of priests had already used. Escrivá decided that he, too, would give it a try and he began the process of obtaining the paperwork that would allow him to make the journey to Barcelona, the first stage of his escape. He also started raising money to pay the people smugglers.

The founder would leave behind his mother, sister, brother, and six of his followers, including three men who had been holed up with him at the Honduran consulate. But at the same time, he contacted some of his followers outside the city to invite them along. Another five Opus Dei members and the brother of one member would eventually join the expedition. Miguel Fisac, one of those who was contacted, suspected that Escrivá had picked him for not altogether altruistic reasons. "I supposed they tried to find me when they found out how expensive the guides, who would help them escape over the Pyrenees, were going to be, as it meant a great deal of money," he later said. "They supposed my father would supply it, which he did."

The journey across the Pyrenees was long and perilous. On October 8, Escrivá set off—first to Valencia by car and then to Barcelona by train. There, the eight fugitives waited for a signal from the traffickers. And waited. And waited. On November 19, they finally got the signal. Over the next five nights, the six men walked more than fifty miles over mountainous terrain. They slept at safe houses pre-arranged by the smugglers and they breakfasted on hearty meals of bread, wine, and sausages. Finally, on the morning of December 2, they crossed the border into Andorra—to shouts of *"Deo gratias! Deo gratias!"* from the Opus Dei founder.

From there, they crossed into France and headed north to the border at Hendaye, back into Spain and Franco-held territory. They made the crossing on December 10, 1937. Life was noticeably different in the Franco-held zone, where people—at least those who hadn't been rounded up and shot for being leftist sympathizers—were able to worship freely. Once across the border, the young men who had accompanied Escrivá on the dangerous crossing over the last few weeks almost immediately signed up to fight for General Franco. By contrast, the Opus Dei founder, who was just a couple of weeks from his thirty-sixth birthday, decided to go to Pamplona, invited by the bishop, to rest. There, he read and renewed his determination to rebuild Opus Dei. On January 8, the day before his birthday, he relocated to Burgos, which Franco was using as a temporary capital and where he would sit out the remainder of the war.

The war had dealt a bitter blow to Opus Dei at precisely the moment when it was beginning to build real momentum. On the eve of the conflict, Escrivá had twenty-one followers in the Work. But they were now scattered across the country—some in Franco-held territory, others still in the government-held zone; some fighting on the front lines, others in hiding. Now settled at a boarding house in Burgos, Escrivá turned his full attention to maintaining contact with the group. He began once again to keep detailed records on each of his followers and was resolved to contact all of them. Over the next six weeks, he sent eighteen letters to Opus Dei members in Madrid but received only seven responses. Escrivá couldn't tell whether the lack of response was due to severed communications between the two zones, down to personal doubts about their membership in Opus Dei, or because they were dead.

Returning to Madrid soon became his focus. As the war continued, Escrivá opted to spend his time not by helping out at a military hospital or even by helping the Francoist war effort, but by attending a women's sewing bee that made decorations for Opus Dei residences for use after the war and by giving them spiritual formation classes. He also became obsessed with finding the money to fund the re-establishment of the Work. He wrote to his followers in Madrid and implored them to push the claim for compensation he had filed while at the Honduran consulate. He wrote to those on the frontline, men facing death daily, and asked them to send him money. To the Bishop of Vitoria, he wrote "I need a wee million, along with fifty men who love Jesus Christ above all things." He also returned to writing, adding to the notes that he had taken to the retreat when he had received his vision. He set a new target for himself, that of expanding these notes to 999 maxims—words of wisdom, anecdotes, and spiritual advice—that would guide his followers.

On March 28, 1939, the government finally surrendered, and victorious Francoist troops entered the capital. Escrivá followed the next day. His own entrance into the city was just as triumphant as that of the troops. He rode in on a military truck, defiantly wearing his cassock and holding out his crucifix to the city's disheveled and malnourished inhabitants. For many, he was the first priest they had seen wearing a cassock since the conflict had begun. The country had been torn apart during the previous two and a half years: three hundred thousand people lay dead; another quarter of a million were held in concentration camps; half a million more had fled Spain altogether. Madrid lay in ruins, and its people were struggling to survive—food supplies were close to running out, there was no heating, hot water, medicine, or surgical dressings.

Escrivá focused on what he called "the family business." Before the war, the DYA academy and residence had been the engine behind Opus Dei; in its small chapel, Escrivá had presided over the enslavement ceremonies of its two dozen or so members. The war had severely depleted their numbers, though—two had been killed and another seven had left the movement. Just fourteen men and two women remained. Escrivá headed immediately for Calle Ferraz to get the academy and residence back up and running. But it wasn't to be. He arrived to find it bombed out, burned, and ransacked. His work—the Work of God—lay in ruins. But thanks to his "instructions," he now had a detailed blueprint to resurrect the movement. Armed with his tried-and-tested methods for targeting and controlling prospective recruits, Opus Dei would quickly regain its lost ground.

3

AN AUTOGRAPH FROM THE POPE

Barcelona, Spain—October 1944

AFTER MASS ON SUNDAYS, CONCERNED CHURCHGOERS HANDED OUT pamphlets warning about the goings-on at the apartment on Carrer de Balmes. The whole of Barcelona seemed to be ablaze with stories of the unspeakable acts that supposedly went on inside the Opus Dei residence two blocks north of the university. Some said there was a priest who used lights to hypnotize the innocent young men who had been tricked into going inside and make them believe that he was actually levitating. Others talked of Opus Dei members being nailed to a huge wooden cross. Caught up in the frenzy, the Jesuits had even begun to station priests on the other side of the street to observe those who went inside. Afterwards, they paid visits to the families of regular attendees to report that their sons had been drawn in by a devil priest and to warn that the young men risked being refused confession if they persisted in attending. The stories struck a nerve with the locals, whose own sense of reality had been numbed by a diet of conspiracy theories constantly fed to them by the Franco regime—of Jews and Masons and Bolsheviks intent on destroying their way of life. The overflowing prisons and forced labor camps, summary executions, and stories of women who had been raped and had their children stolen were a constant reminder of the dangers of standing out from the crowd. Five years after the end of the war, an atmosphere of fear and repression still hung over the country.

Eighteen and devout, Luis Valls-Taberner was a prime target for the Opus Dei members who roamed the campus looking for fresh recruits. Mindful of this growing menace at the university—and perhaps also of her son's susceptibility to it—his mother had warned him to stay away from the apartment on Carrer de Balmes. "If you want to take up orders, you can join the Franciscans or Capuchins," she told him. "But not Opus Dei!" Her survival instincts were well honed: as a wealthy, politically conservative, and deeply religious family, the Valls-Taberners had come perilously close to losing everything in the early days of the war. The military uprising had taken over vast swathes of the country but had failed in Barcelona, put down by gangs of workers, policemen, and anarchists who soon took over the city and eyed families like the Valls-Taberners with suspicion.

After hiding out for a few weeks at their summer house outside the city, their father—a politician and prominent figure on the right—discovered his name was on a hit list. Fearing for their lives, the family decided to make a run for it, returning to the city dressed as peasants and buying their way onto an Italian ship bound for Genoa, arriving the next day with nothing but the clothes on their backs. The experience left an indelible mark on Luis, who was only ten at the time. After a few months in Italy, the Valls-Taberners returned to Spain—at least to the rebel-held zone, where their father reinvented himself as a Franco loyalist, going on speaking tours of Nazi Germany and Latin America to sing the Caudillo's praises. By the time he passed away in 1942, the Valls-Taberners were once again part of Barcelona's elite. But, as Luis's mother knew, the Caudillo was unpredictable, and a scandal involving Opus Dei might easily bring about a swift reversal of their fortunes.

Luis decided to ignore his mother's advice. The young law student was befriended by another student not long after joining the faculty. As a quiet, introspective young man still reeling from the sudden death of his beloved father two years earlier, attention from someone who knew his way around campus was welcome. Jorge Maciá Masbagá—known to everyone as Jordi— was a few years older and stood out because he had his own motorcycle. He was also a member of Opus Dei who had been encouraged to make friends on campus with potential recruits, and his dogged pursuit of the shy freshman was a masterclass in how to apply the Opus Dei recruitment playbook. Just as the founder had instructed, Jordi made an effort to separate Luis from his peers, picking him up most days after class on his bike to play hockey or polo. Over the coming months, he groomed Luis, dropping comments about study sessions and prayer meetings at the apartment on Carrer de Balmes, which was known as El Palau—The Palace—to those who went there. He explained that the founder of Opus Dei, a priest called Escrivá who visited occasionally from Madrid, had baptized it with that name as a joke, because of its shabbiness. The founder sounded unlike the priests Luis knew.

Luis went along to see for himself. He quickly saw that Jordi's comments about El Palau's shabbiness were true. The apartment was dark, dilapidated, and sparsely furnished. The common room, which doubled as a library, was tiny, with only two small tables, some mismatched chairs, and a bookcase. Another room had been converted into a small chapel, with a makeshift altar made from a chest of drawers. A few men lived there, although dozens more frequented the apartment every week to study, worship, and attend spiritual formation classes. Over the following weeks, Luis gradually learned more about life within Opus Dei. The seriousness of the men—toward their work, their studies, and their apostolate—was a stark contrast to the world outside, where everything from government ministries to export licenses and military promotions were doled out, not according to merit but, rather, based on loyalty to Franco's regime. The rituals of prayer and the discussion of faith brought a new focus to his life—something he had struggled to find in his studies. He was following in his father's footsteps by studying law, but the concepts and principles he debated in class seemed pointless when justice was meted out by military generals who mounted sham trials where they chose the judge, the prosecutor, and the defense lawyer. Before his freshman year was up, he had decided to join Opus Dei.

On university campuses across Spain, hundreds of students like Luis were having similar epiphanies. Opus Dei had been almost completely destroyed by the war—a third of its members had left or died, and those that remained were scattered across the country. The DYA academy, its main recruitment center in Madrid, had been left in ruins. But Franco's victory soon created the perfect conditions for Escrivá to make the "family business" thrive. Keen to bolster his image as the Catholic savior of Spain, while simultaneously quelling any potential subversion, Franco made religious studies compulsory for all students and encouraged religious orders to set up halls, where students could be watched and reported on by trusted members of the clergy. The measures played into the hands of Opus Dei and its prewar years of experience running a student residence. Just three months after the end of the war, it rented an apartment in Madrid as a new residence. Expansion soon followed. In September 1939, it rented another in Valencia. By the summer of 1940, it had expanded to Valladolid and Barcelona.

With the new rules in force, Escrivá's old business model thrived. Given the shortage of student accommodation that met the regime's strict new requirements and with half the city reduced to rubble, his residences quickly filled up. Just as he had before the war, the founder took full advantage of his packed dorms to recruit for Opus Dei, reviving his system of report cards, which he consulted continuously to tailor and hone his recruitment methods. He encouraged those who were already members to make weekend trips to other Spanish cities to target students there. Armed with Escrivá's detailed—and effective—manual for recruitment, and convinced they were doing the Work of God, his followers were highly successful. Their targets were clear: they concentrated their efforts on the top students, often hiding their affiliation to Opus Dei. Once someone was identified as close to joining, they were invited to special study weeks held by Escrivá at his empty residence when the rest of the students had gone home for Easter or for the summer; there, they would be pushed into making the final leap. His methods proved highly effective: seventy people joined the Work during the first academic year after the war—almost three times the number of people he had recruited during the previous decade. "I think we will end up having to bless the war," he wrote.

By the time Luis began frequenting El Palau in 1945, Opus Dei had grown to almost two hundred and fifty members, spread among twelve residences across six Spanish cities. New "vocations," as fresh recruits were known internally, kept on coming. The Barcelona apartment became so overcrowded at one stage that Luis twice wrote to Escrivá about the urgent need to find another property in the city. While there was an almost monkish seriousness to their spiritual lives and to the norms of prayer and mortification set by the founder, there was a spirit of camaraderie among the young men. The architecture students among them would organize sketching trips to interesting sites, while the law students passed the time on the beach with amateur boxing matches. Those who lived at the Opus Dei residence were expected to pay bed and board, while the older men with jobs were expected to hand over their entire salaries. But behind the camaraderie, there was a darker element to life at the residence that remained hidden from vocations like Luis. As the movement grew in the early 1940s, Escrivá added a new set of "instructions" detailing how young recruit like Luis were supposed to live their lives. The document, kept under lock and key at each of the residences, was designed to reinforce the effectiveness of the methods of control set out in the separate "instructions" for directors, which regular members were likewise unaware of. Escrivá made clear to the directors the importance of keeping detailed report cards about each of the men in their charge—including about spiritual and deeply personal matters—which were to be shared with regional headquarters whenever it was deemed "opportune." To facilitate that intelligence gathering, in his "instructions" to the rank and file, Escrivá emphasized the importance of "opening up your heart" during the weekly "chat" they were supposed to have with their director—without mentioning how their intimate thoughts would be recorded and shared. He also made it clear that members were expected to comply with any advice they were given by the local director during these sessions. "During the chat, the Lord shines a light to show us—so we might learn—what must be done to conduct yourselves properly, with Christian perfection, in each situation," he wrote.

Beneath this veil of religious formation, Escrivá was creating a mechanism to control not just members' spiritual outlook but their actions, too. This carefully crafted duality—split between the friendly, benign vision that Escrivá wanted to project to the outside world, and an apparatus of control and manipulation hidden from all but the movement's most senior members—also extended into the public sphere. Escrivá soon became a minor celebrity on university campuses, where a book of pithy maxims he'd written was beginning to accumulate a sizable following. He'd written *The Way* during the war. It was a collection of 999 points touching on a wide range of subjects, including how crucifixes ought to be made from iron rather than plaster, on how prayer should be manly and not effeminate, and how women shouldn't aspire to being learned—only to be discreet—that all members of Opus Dei were encouraged to read and reread. Many of the maxims were utterly banal. "Don't leave your work for tomorrow" stated one. "Get used to saying no" was another.

Through *The Way*, many students began to see Opus Dei as a modern, innovative, and avant-garde offshoot of the Church. Escrivá soon received requests to give retreats and formation classes all around the country, which elevated both his profile and Opus Dei's even further. His rising star had even caught the attention of the Franco regime, which at one stage considered nominating Escrivá to be ordained as a bishop. A report was sent up to the Caudillo's desk, assuring the dictator that Escrivá's politics were "absolutely" aligned with those of the regime. General Franco seemed impressed: "very loyal," he jotted down next to Escrivá's name. While he wasn't nominated for a bishopric in the end, perhaps because of his youth, Franco invited Escrivá to give a private, six-day retreat for himself and his wife at the El Pardo palace, where they lived.

Given his rising celebrity, the aristocratic airs that had attracted such ridicule at the seminary could now be lived out. Soon, he began traveling by air, a method of transport that no ordinary Spaniard—let alone a priest—could dream of at the time. He moved into a three-story mansion in the well-to-do Salamanca neighborhood of Madrid, and he declared it the new headquarters of Opus Dei. He moved his mother, sister Carmen, and brother Santiago in, too, which raised eyebrows among some, who asked why they were living there when they weren't even members. "That's their business," responded Escrivá, who said that the Escrivá family revered God in their own way. In a sign of his growing self-importance, the founder also applied to change his surname from plain old Escrivá to the much grander Escrivá de Balaguer.

He also began to draw up plans for expanding Opus Dei well beyond its core of numerary members—the growing ranks of men and women who had sworn an oath of fidelity to the movement and who lived lives of chastity, poverty, and obedience in the dozen or so residences dotted across the country. Escrivá began to draw up "instructions" for a new class of membership: married men and women, who might live at home with their families and hold normal jobs, but who nonetheless would be critical members of the "mobilization of souls" who would take back control of the "paganized world" and reinvigorate it with "the spirit of Christianity, which will permeate absolutely everything in the world." Evidently, for Escrivá, Franco's victory and the subsequent elimination—through murder and imprisonment—of any remaining traces of progressivism were insufficient. Escrivá envisioned a complete re-Christianization of the entire world. He saw this new class of membership—the supernumeraries—as a hidden guerrilla army, told not disclose their membership of Opus Dei to anyone else without express permission, tasked with infiltrating every element of society, and gathering intelligence about "the plans of the enemies of Christ." In an echo of the subversive recruitment methods he had drawn up before the war, he suggested that the new supernumeraries might try to influence—or even take charge of—cultural, social, and government institutions as part of their mission.

Given that such members wouldn't have to take vows of chastity, they would also have an additional task: to "foment the multiplication of numerary vocations"—that is, breeding the next generation of recruits. In this new set of "instructions," he outlined a vision of how this new class of membership would fan out across the world—"to America, to Africa, to Australia"—and how Opus Dei retreat centers would be set up with hotels attached to them, where entire families could stay. But the movement wasn't quite ready: this new breed of supernumeraries would require its own, separate system of manipulation and control to ensure it worked that would eventually be enforced by a sprawling army of numeraries tasked with overseeing the "spiritual formation" of the supernumeraries in their charge. Unfortunately for Escrivá, the number of numeraries wasn't yet large enough to make that practicable. The supernumerary vision would have to wait.

Although the Work of God had been initially envisioned as a *universal* call to holiness, university students had become a major focus during the years after the war. Escrivá understood the potential in recruiting from the next generation of government officials and businessmen—the men who would shape Spain's future. Recruiting them was his chance to influence that future. "To reach everyone, we first target the intellectuals, knowing that any attempt to influence society must go through them," he wrote. On university campuses across the country, gatherings like those at El Palau were taking place every day—for many, it was an act of rebellion against Franco and against the Church. *The Way* was a motivational handbook for a new generation.

But the targeting of students made some in the regime uneasy—especially among the Falange, the fascist paramilitary group with almost a million members that Franco relied on to stay in power. In 1941, Opus Dei had been reported to the Special Tribunal for the Repression of Masonry, a court set up to root out an imaginary network of Masonic lodges that the Caudillo was convinced was out to get him, on charges of clandestine activity and the corruption of young people. The accusations had the paranoid hallmarks of the Falange, but they were not wholly unjustified. Numeraries, after all, had been told to keep their membership of Opus Dei secret during their initial recruitment of potential targets.

Faced with this new, existential threat to the family business, and with rival factions within the Church continuing to put out pamphlets and spreading rumors about what went on inside its residences, Escrivá concluded that the time had come to seek ecclesiastical cover. He began to cultivate a relationship with the Bishop of Madrid, and he asked him to consider officially approving Opus Dei as a "pious union," a designation that could be easily handed out at diocese level without having to consult anyone in Rome. Escrivá sent him documents outlining what Opus Dei was—while omitting the detailed "instructions" that dictated precisely what went on inside the movement. It was the beginning of a strategy to hide its real workings from the wider Catholic Church, a practice that continues to this day. The strategy seemed to work: Opus Dei was designated as a "pious union," and the special tribunal threw out the charges against it. "I have never known a chaste Mason yet," the judge explained in his decision.

But ecclesiastical approval brought other problems for Escrivá. Much to his annoyance, the Bishop of Madrid began to meddle in the internal affairs of the Work. Once, when Escrivá was away, the bishop took advantage of his absence to visit some Opus Dei members, telling them that they—as good Christians—should sign up to fight for the Nazis as part of a Spanish volunteer force known as the Blue Division, which was going to support the Germans on the Eastern Front. Escrivá, on his return, was horrified—but not on moral grounds. He had seen the Work decimated by war before and he was loathe to see it happen again. He told his followers that, since they were but a few, it would be irresponsible take such risks.

The incident highlighted what was fast becoming a problem for the rapidly expanding movement: how to control its members' interactions with other parts of the Church. Confession was a particular concern. Growth of the Work had made it impossible for Escrivá to hear the sins of all its members. Years earlier, knowing that he himself couldn't offer regular confession to every member, Escrivá had allowed them to take confession with other priests although he had drawn the line at their continuous spiritual formation, which he stipulated must be done only within Opus Dei. Now, he realized that regular contact with priests outside the movement threatened his authority over and control of the membership. The only solution was to have priests of his own. He began preparing some of his most loyal members for ordination. The irony that they had joined Opus Dei precisely to live out their faith as ordinary Catholics with normal jobs seemed quite lost on him. But he had two problems: first, priests couldn't be members of a pious union such as Opus Dei; and second, all clergy had to be affiliated with a preexisting order or diocese. Escrivá had to draw on his legal studies to come up with a solution: a separate body called the Priestly Society of the Holy Cross.

Needing approval from the Vatican for a new priestly society, he sent Álvaro del Portillo, one of the earliest members of Opus Dei, to lobby the Holy See in person. A timid young man with a wispy moustache and sad, hound-dog eyes framed by horn-rimmed glasses, Del Portillo was the third of eight children in a devout Catholic family, who had joined Opus Dei before the war, during his time as an engineering student at the university in Madrid. He spent part of the war holed up with Escrivá in the Honduran embassy—although he had been left behind when the founder staged his escape over the Pyrenees. Nonetheless, this didn't dent Del Portillo's devotion to the priest twelve years his senior—a devotion he would carry throughout his life. Now that Del Portillo was a twenty-nine-year-old engineer, Escrivá told him he had a vocation to become one of Opus Dei's first priests, and he asked him to go to Rome on his behalf to meet with the pope. It is unclear why Escrivá didn't make this important journey himself, or why he sent Del Portillo on this delicate mission. It was a dangerous journey, perhaps too risky for the increasingly important Escrivá. Italy, after all, was at war. On his flight over,

Del Portillo's plane was almost shot down by the British. But Escrivá's confidence in Del Portillo was proven right; eventually, the Priestly Society of the Holy Cross was officially approved. The following June, the young engineer was one of three priests ordained into the Priestly Society in Madrid. Opus Dei now had its first priests—although Escrivá made it clear that they were not to use the title "Father," which was to be reserved exclusively for him. Instead, all priests were to use "Don," a generic term of respect.

While the ecclesiastical attacks abated, the political attacks did not. The Falange compiled its own report on Opus Dei, concluding that it was set on "the conquest of power through cultural institutions." It was an astute observation and an aim that Escrivá had clearly stated in his "instructions" for the membership. The Falange had no access to these secret internal documents, but Opus Dei's growing presence on university campuses across the country had evidently raised suspicions about its true aims. Young members like Luis were fed the line that Opus Dei was the embodiment of a vision clearly laid out in the Bible. The founder told them they were the foot soldiers, serving a much greater mission to transform the world into something altogether more wholesome and devout. "You and I are effectively following the orders of a King—Jesus Christ—trying to find the soldiers who will enlist in the army of our Lord," Escrivá explained. But the only king was Escrivá himself. A cult of personality was being built around him, cultivated and encouraged by the man himself. Directors told the members in their charge that they were expected to write regularly to the founder and share with him their devotion to doing the Work of God. He barely ever wrote back. But on trips around the country to visit his sons, the founder often picked out individuals—often the ones with money—and showered them with attention. For these members, receiving such personal attention from a man they considered to be a living saint often pushed them to go even further in showing their dedication to fulfilling the Work of God. Luis persuaded his mother to make a large contribution to Opus Dei to help furnish a new residence. Evidently, with the movement gathering in popularity, she had dropped her objections.

In June 1946, with recruitment gathering momentum, Escrivá made his first visit to Rome to seek Vatican approval for the expansion of Opus Dei to new territories. While the Work had been officially recognized as a "pious union," that authorization was valid only in Madrid. Residences had of course been established in other Spanish cities, but each one required delicate lobbying of the local bishop, and not everyone was quite so accommodating as the Bishop of Madrid. What Escrivá wanted was approval from the Vatican. By gaining pontifical approval, Opus Dei would automatically have the green light to expand to anywhere it wished. It would be a real game changer, effectively allowing the movement to operate outside the Church's traditional hierarchy. Don Álvaro had been sent ahead to lobby for the change a few months earlier, but the results had been mixed. He had written to Escrivá in Madrid, pleading for him to come. Only the founder could break the deadlock.

After an overnight boat journey from Barcelona to Genoa, and a drive of several hours, Escrivá reached Rome at around nine in the evening. The city appeared majestically on the horizon, with the splendor of Saint Peter's illuminated by the setting sun. He became emotional and began to chant in Latin. It was his first sight of the Eternal City. They drove through to the Piazza della Città Leonina, a small square by the Vatican where Del Portillo had rented an apartment ahead of the Father's arrival. Its rooftop balcony boasted one of the most sought-after views in the city, looking out over Saint Peter's. Clearly, the apartment didn't come cheap. After the others went to bed, Escrivá, unable to sleep, sat outside and drank in the air of the midsummer evening. He prayed. How life had changed for the son of the bankrupt merchant from Barbastro. He thought of his early difficulties, his escape over the mountains, his "children" back in Spain, and the huge steps already taken. Occasionally, he looked up at the lit window of the pope's private library and dreamed of the great future ahead.

Over the next few days, he held meetings with various Vatican officials—often using a signed photograph of the pope intended for him that Del Portillo had managed to procure as a way to get people to see him. The signed photo projected papal support even if that was far from the truth. "I have a handwritten blessing from the Holy Father for 'the Founder of the Priestly Society of the Holy Cross and of Opus Dei,'" he wrote back to his followers in Spain. "What a thrill! I've kissed it a thousand times." He also asked them to start fundraising for a new house he intended to buy in Rome. As he waited for an audience with the pope, and inspired by his new surroundings, the expansion of Opus Dei to Rome became his new obsession. He wrote to Madrid to request that the women there begin work immediately to make altar linens—for not one but *two* houses in Rome. He also requested that three numeraries and five "numerary servants" be sent out by the end of the summer.

Numerary servants were a new development in Opus Dei. Escrivá had sworn in the first ones at a ceremony just outside of Madrid only a year earlier, creating a new class of members that stood apart from the numerary men and numerary women, who tended to be well-educated and from wealthy families. By contrast, the numerary servants were uneducated women from poor backgrounds, who had been employed as domestic staff at the various Opus Dei residences and were gradually recruited to join by the superior numerary members. Escrivá saw this new underclass as vital to creating a more rarefied atmosphere within the residences, making the numerary members feel even more special.

The numerary servants were given spiritual formation classes and were taught how to cook, clean, and serve properly. They were also encouraged to abide by the strict timetable of prayer and mortification that their superior numerary members followed. The new numerary servants category was also a shrewd business move; like other numeraries, the numerary servants were expected to hand over their pay to Opus Dei, meaning the movement effectively now had teams of women who cooked, cleaned, and served at its residences for free. One female numerary who helped recruit and train several numerary servants herself later confessed that the system allowed Opus to keep up the standards of a luxury hotel for its members through cheap or even semi-slave labor. Escrivá reveled in the brilliance of the idea. "The numerary servants—I really mean this—seem to me the greatest miracle our Lord has done for his Work," he wrote at the time of the first admissions. "Before she 'only' peeled potatoes, but now she attains holiness by peeling potatoes."

In July, Escrivá secured an audience with the pope. Pius XII was a native of Rome, with a hooked nose and dark, piercing eyes, who had been accused of turning a blind eye during the Second World War, as millions of Jews, communists, and homosexuals were murdered. Escrivá had his own strong views on the Holocaust, telling one confidant some years later that Hitler had been unjustly accused and that it was "impossible" for the Nazis to have killed as many as six million Jews. The pope and Escrivá got along well, and Escrivá left the meeting optimistic about his prospects. He began work on a formal application for pontifical approval under a new constitution being drawn up by the pope, which would for the first time sanctify "secular institutes"—bands of pious Catholics who lived normal lives but who strived toward ideals of charity and evangelization. Opus Dei hoped to be the first secular institute to be recognized under the new constitution. Over the coming weeks and months, there was a constant back and forth among Escrivá, Del Portillo, and various Vatican offices. Escrivá soon became frustrated with the process, criticizing those around the pope for being controlling, inflexible, and derogatory. Clearly, his own sense of importance blinded him to the necessary due process. But it didn't take him long to hone his political skills to help expedite the process. He began to pitch Opus Dei as a critical organ in the Vatican's own fight against Marxism. "In Rome, I lost my innocence," he later said. Many suspected that Escrivá viewed the political chicanery he saw in Rome as a sanctification of the kind of scheming that he would later use to justify his own controversial actions.

The approval finally came in February 1947. Escrivá was ecstatic. It had been less than eight years since the end of the Spanish Civil War. In that time, he had rebuilt the family business almost from scratch. Opus Dei now boasted around three hundred members in several cities across Spain—and a new house in the Portuguese city of Coimbra. The Work had successfully defeated repeated attempts by fierce rivals both within and outside the Church. And most important of all, what had once been no more than the personal project of an unknown priest had now been formally recognized by the Vatican. With approval as a secular institute, Opus Dei now effectively had a green light to expand to anywhere in the world. In Rome, the founder celebrated by buying a former palace that he had seen just a few days before. He renamed it Villa Tevere, after the river that flowed through the city.

In September 1947, Escrivá gathered a select group of his followers at a ranch in the mountains to the north of Madrid. The property had been bought a year earlier as a place to hold retreats and formation classes, and had been baptized Molinoviejo by the founder, after an old windmill on the grounds. He had summoned them there to outline the next phase in Opus Dei's rapid expansion. Escrivá told the men that he had chosen sixty numerary men to ascend to a new tier within the movement. They would henceforth become *inscribed* members of the Work, would receive additional formation, and would be expected to participate in the government of Opus Dei. He asked each of them to make a pledge before God to obey three strict conditions: to watch over each other like brothers and remedy any improper conduct whenever necessary; to never aspire to lead Opus Dei; and to consult the founder or his counselors for all important matters. The three pledges marked a step change in Escrivá's efforts to control his followers, formalizing not just their loyalty but also a system for "brotherly correction" to root out any dissent. The move was rational, given the planned expansion of Opus Dei around the world and Escrivá's own decision, after being so enamored with the Eternal City after his first trip, to relocate to the recently acquired palace in Rome. The inscribed membership would form an elite corps at the heart of the movement, an ultra-loyal band of men who watched each other suspiciously and who pledged never to usurp their leader.

For members like Luis Valls-Taberner, the news of meetings with the pope and plans for a new headquarters in Rome were confirmation that God was indeed behind Opus Dei. Just two years after requesting admittance, Luis was a changed man. Now twenty-one, and in his final year at the university, he was no longer the quiet, sensitive boy who had cowered aboard a ship on the family's escape to Italy. He was now a self-assured young man with grit and determination who stood apart from the crowd, just as *The Way* had taught him. He had shown his loyalty by trying to recruit his brothers and sisters and persuading one of his relatives to donate a house they owned. Always on the lookout for money, such overtures from a young member rumored to have a large inheritance soon caught the eye of Escrivá, who began to cultivate a closer relationship with Luis, singling him out for special treatment. The founder invited Luis to accompany him on a visit to an abbey in the mountains near Barcelona. The two were shown around the grounds by the abbot and two monks. Escrivá looked every inch the VIP in his flowing black cassock, dark sunglasses, and shiny black shoes adorned with a large gold buckle, which contrasted sharply with the simple black leather shoes worn by the abbot and his monks. Luis followed close behind in a suit and striped tie, smoking a pipe, a camera slung over his shoulder.

After completing his degree and military service, in 1949 Luis moved to Madrid to begin a doctorate in law. There, he settled into a student residence run by Opus Dei on Avenida de la Moncloa, a short walk from the main university campus. The property was a former hotel that the movement had bought in 1943 and heavily remodeled to create a residence for about a hundred students. By 1948, it had become the biggest—and most lucrative—asset in the family business. It also served another purpose. The Moncloa residence was treated as a shopwindow for Opus Dei. Great pains were taken to foster a welcoming atmosphere and project an image of vitality and youth. Residents were encouraged to bring their friends back to participate in the extracurricular activities there, which revolved around sports, academic talks, and spiritual formation. Although the majority of the students weren't part of Opus Dei, all the senior staff were and Luis quickly fell in with a small group of members like him, who together followed the daily rituals of prayer and mortification prescribed by the founder and who sought to live their lives according to *The Way*.

Soon, one of his fellow members in Madrid got him a new job as head of publications at the Spanish National Research Council. To his family and his fellow doctoral students, this appointment must have seemed an odd one. Luis had no experience whatsoever in publishing. Why would this prestigious institution even give him a job, let alone task him with running an entire department? And Luis had barely begun his doctoral studies. As a top student, he had been determined to do well—to honor the memory of his father, who had been a respected academic, as well as a politician. Surely, taking on a full-time job would dramatically impact his ability to do that? It wasn't like he needed the money. Unlike some of the other students on campus, Luis didn't have to earn extra cash to pay his way through school.

But anyone familiar with the Research Council would have understood quickly exactly what was going on. The institution had been created by Franco in the first months after the war, tasked with imposing on the world of culture "the essential ideas that have inspired our Glorious Movement." The Research Council was given a huge budget; between 1945 and 1950, it received almost 260 million pesetas in funding, which was more than triple what was spent on rebuilding the hundreds of war-damaged schools across the country. José María Albareda, one of the first members of Opus Dei who had made friends with the future education minister while hiding out at the Chilean embassy during the war, had been put in charge. Almost immediately, he abused his position by directing the state funds at his disposal to his friends in Opus Dei. During his first few years, one of every sixteen of the lucrative academic research grants handed out by the Research Council went to Opus Dei members—even though the movement had only a tiny number of qualified academics. Some of them used the money to study abroad and took advantage of their overseas stays to put down roots for Opus Dei in those countries. Those that remained in Spain were expected to hand over any income to Opus Dei. By the time of Luis's appointment, the Research Council had effectively been captured by Opus Dei, which bled the institution dry of state funds at a time of acute need to rebuild the country.

One of Luis's fellow members had taken Opus Dei's pilfering of state funds to a whole new level. Miguel Fisac, who had joined before the war and whose father provided the funds to pay for Escrivá's escape over the Pyrenees, had fully qualified as an architect in 1941. One of his projects caught the eye of the Minister of Education, and soon Fisac became one of its principal contractors. Given the government's tight finances, contractors were encouraged to work at a discount. But Fisac was instructed by his Opus Dei superiors to mark up his contracts and pass on the difference. This continued for five or six years and, by 1948, Fisac had become a major source of funds. "It really ate at my conscience," he later admitted.

By 1949, when Luis started his job at the Research Council, the institution was overrun with members of Opus Dei, all paid salaries using public money that—in full or in part—ended up in the movement's coffers in Madrid and in Rome. Despite his clear lack of experience, Luis was awarded a generous salary of ten thousand pesetas a year, which he was expected to hand over in full. Securing a job for him was a way of extracting extra cash for Opus Dei, and for filling his time and monopolizing his thoughts. Bombarded with tasks and the Work's messaging, numeraries such as Luis had little time to think for themselves. By the end of his first year, under pressure to earn money for Opus Dei with his day job at the Research Council, to recruit new members at the university, and to comply with the norms of prayer and mortification set by Escrivá, Luis had begun to fall behind in his studies.

The pressure to squeeze the membership—and the public purse—for money came directly from Rome, where Escrivá's demands increased with each passing day. In February 1949, following a standoff with the previous tenants, Escrivá moved into Villa Tevere. The property, which was entered through enormous gates that led into a garden of pine, eucalyptus, and fig trees, was made up of two buildings: the main house, a three-story mansion constructed in Florentine style, and a separate caretaker's house to its left. Escrivá worked on plans to transform the entire property into something more suitable for the Work of God. The refurbishment would take eleven years to complete and come in more than ten times over budget, costing well over a billion lira—equivalent to about $20 million today. Some of that money went toward the construction of accommodations and office space for the growing movement, but vast sums were also spent on deluxe accommodation for Escrivá. The original palace, where Escrivá lived apart from the other members, had two new floors added, which placed such a stress on the structure that additional support had to be added. After the death of his sister, Escrivá also had a crypt installed—which would eventually house his own remains.

The finances of Opus Dei were already stretched enough with the purchase and expansion of Villa Tevere, but Escrivá's ambitions knew no bounds. He decided he would also need a separate building to house the regional headquarters—he had already divided the world into seven separate regions. He also required another to house the headquarters of the women's branch, a training college for numerary members, and two study centers, a conference center next to the papal summer residence at Castel Gandolfo, and four residences across Italy. Added to that, Opus Dei was rapidly expanding in Spain: it had just bought the mansion on Calle Diego de León, where the founder's brother and sister lived, for six million pesetas, as well as two ranches for retreats. As a further financial drain, Escrivá had sent two of his disciples on a six-month tour of the Americas, visiting the United States, Canada, Mexico, Peru, Chile, and Argentina, with a view to expanding there.

With such enormous expenses, it soon became apparent that profits from the student residences and the numeraries' wages wouldn't be enough to support the movement. Escrivá had already taken a huge step toward diversifying his revenue sources by finally signing off on the admission of supernumeraries at the beginning of 1948. After more than a decade of prevaricating about when would be the right time to admit married people, evidently the purchase of Villa Tevere a few months earlier and the prospect of raising funds for the coming expansion of the palace forced his hand. Critically, these new members would be expected to give Opus Dei a tenth or so of their household income. Within the first couple of years, almost seven hundred people became supernumerary members.

But even with the additional revenue from the supernumeraries, Opus Dei still had a huge hole in its finances. The founder saddled Del Portillo with the responsibility of finding the cash to pay the builders, who demanded up to three million lira every couple of weeks. At times, the stress of finding enough money left him unable to sleep. Regular prayers to Saint Nicholas proved insufficient, leaving Del Portillo with little choice but to turn to the Franco dictatorship for help. He shamelessly asked the government in Madrid to make a sizable contribution to the project, requesting eight million pesetas of public funds—the equivalent of almost $4 million today. The funds were earmarked for Escrivá's latest pet project, which he had grandly named the Roman College of the Holy Cross. Essentially, it was a refresher center for numerary men, a place where the most dedicated members of Opus Dei would be sent for periodic "formation" to ensure they remained on message.

The request to the Franco regime made no mention of this. Instead, Del Portillo described the college as an "international center of research and culture," where Catholics from all over the world could come and unite in battle against the "unorthodox tendencies of thought that so seriously threaten the Church and the values of Western civilization." The Franco regime eventually donated one and a half million pesetas.

By the summer of 1950, the Roman College of the Holy Cross was up and running. In June, Luis was sent to Rome to attend one of the new spiritual formation courses there. It was his first trip outside the country since the family's wartime escape—and his first ever on his own. He stayed in Italy for two weeks, sleeping at Villa Tevere, where once again he spent time with the founder. Luis was clearly impacted by his trip to Rome. Seeing Del Portillo struggling to raise money left such a mark on the young man that he resolved to make it his personal mission to liberate the founder from the burden of ever having to worry about the finances of Opus Dei.

Luis returned to his full-time job and his doctoral studies in Madrid at the end of June. Then, the following month, he was sent on another Opus Dei course at the Molinoviejo ranch just outside the capital. His formation was taking on a new intensity. In September, he was granted a visa to enter Andorra, a strong indication that—after his summer of formation and private conversations with the founder—the twenty-four-year-old was now being entrusted with secret missions to smuggle money over the border. At the time, the Franco regime had strict currency controls in place, making it illegal to transport large sums out of the country. This produced a big headache for Opus Dei, which needed to get money from Spain, where the family business generated substantial amounts of cash, to Italy. A system was established whereby members would cross borders into Andorra, France, or Portugal with large sums in cash hidden under their clothes or in their luggage—sometimes without their even knowing what they were carrying, having been handed packages by their spiritual directors. Such smuggling was at great personal risk to the individuals themselves. They could easily have been thrown in prison. Luis traveled a great deal for a man of his age during the first half of the 1950s: to Italy five times—usually via France; to Portugal three times; and twice to Switzerland, where banks asked few questions.

By 1952, Luis had moved into the Opus Dei headquarters in Madrid, the mansion on Calle Diego de León where Escrivá had once lived with his mother and siblings. There, his life—already busy because of his job at the institute and his doctoral studies—took on a new intensity. Constant pressure came from the founder in Rome, who sent an endless stream of letters demanding more money and berating members for failing to raise enough new funds. Construction at Villa Tevere were now into their third year and trouble was brewing with some of the builders, who had threatened to stop working if their wages were delayed any longer. "We are financially drained—and must finish those buildings," Escrivá demanded.

As the plans for Villa Tevere began to grow ever more grandiose, a few members began to see them for what they were—vulgar and ostentatious. Miguel Fisac even confronted Escrivá directly about it and before long had decided to quit the movement. But Escrivá stood firm, defending Villa Tevere's twelve dining rooms and fourteen chapels. "It shows that we pray more than we eat" was his strange logic.

Back in Madrid, the drain on the movement's finances was keenly felt. There was no money available to repair the broken heating system or even to buy coal, and numeraries like Luis seemed to survive on a diet of potatoes. But their souls were nourished with news of fresh signs of divine intervention at Villa Tevere, where the founder had supposedly collapsed at the dinner table, the color draining from his face. He was unable to see for several hours. But with the return of his sight, the diabetes that had plagued his health throughout his life was suddenly, miraculously cured. Nobody could explain it, but the timing was certainly helpful in lifting the spirits of followers back in Madrid, who were constantly being pressured to find new recruits and to visit family members who might make donations. Rumors were widespread of report cards being kept on individual members' recruitment and fundraising efforts. Father Escrivá had a vision and everyone was expected to play their part. "I don't know if you fully realize what it will mean, *for the whole Work*, to accomplish what we're attempting in Rome. . . . Villa Tevere means advancing or holding back the work of our institute by half a century," the founder wrote. His vision was often the sugar coating in increasingly aggressive letters, which drove home the message that the founder's demands had to be met—by whatever means. Although there were never any explicit instructions, members were encouraged to push harder wherever they could.

Such shamelessness was evident in Opus Dei's dealings with the Franco regime. In July 1952, Del Portillo returned to Spain to request an audience with the Caudillo. In previous conversations, Franco had expressed his "sincere wish" to help out Opus Dei—"if only they could find the right arrangement." The regime had already shown itself to be extremely accommodating with Opus Dei, through its financial help and the granting of various privileges, including the use of a castle on the Valencian coast. Del Portillo had a proposal for the Caudillo that could be mutually beneficial. After its success among the intelligentsia, Opus Dei had plans to extend its reach to the lower classes—to workers in the factories and in the countryside—but it needed money. "There is so much work that can be done in the service of God— and of the Fatherland," Del Portillo wrote. "And it's so urgent if we are to ensure that the efforts of the state, under your supreme leadership, toward the complete restoration of a just and Christian social order toward which we must strive so diligently—and at whatever cost—aren't thwarted by the influence of shadowy sects and subversive doctrines." He closed his proposal with a direct appeal to Franco to intercede in Opus Dei's application for a fifty-five million peseta loan from the state and asked the Caudillo to bear in mind the solid financial situation of Opus Dei. "Things in Spain would have to go very badly indeed to leave us unable to pay it back," he concluded. In public, Escrivá was at pains to distance himself from the regime back home and to insist on Opus Dei as an apolitical institution. But in private, he was more than happy to sweet-talk the regime and take the dictator's money. The Caudillo turned down their request—there were more pressing needs for public money—which provoked great distress within Opus Dei. Luis, who had helped put together the loan request to the Spanish central bank, wrote to Escrivá and pledged to come up with "a definitive solution" for the movement's financial needs.

Thirteen years after the end of the war, Escrivá had successfully rebuilt his movement, which had been almost completely destroyed by the conflict. Opus Dei now counted about three thousand members. The vast majority of those members were numeraries—men and women who had pledged their lives to the Work; who had taken oaths of poverty, chastity, and obedience; who lived in single-sex residences under the watchful eye of the local director, waited on by a small but growing army of numerary servants recruited from the lower classes. The supernumeraries, Escrivá's guerrilla network which would fight to re-Christianize the world, was also expanding fast, having grown to almost seven hundred people in just a few years. Opus Dei had also made its first tentative steps abroad; by 1952, small cells of numeraries were operating in Portugal, Italy, Great Britain, France, Ireland, Mexico, the United States, Chile, Argentina, Colombia, Venezuela, and Germany. Escrivá had approval from the Vatican to extend Opus Dei to every corner of the globe. The only constraining factor was money—as the experience with Villa Tevere had proven. While Opus Dei coffers swelled with each passing year as the membership—and their financial contributions—grew, the increase in revenues was insufficient to keep pace with Escrivá's ambitions and his capacity to spend money he simply didn't have. Fortunately for the Work, Luis was about to find "the definitive solution" he'd promised.

4

NOT A THING OF THIS WORLD

Madrid, Spain—April 1954

THERE WERE TWO UNFAMILIAR FACES IN THE CROWD THAT AFTERNOON AS investors gathered at the Banco Popular headquarters for the annual general meeting. None of the other hundred or so shareholders in attendance paid either man much attention—seemingly unaware that their presence there that day would change this small Spanish bank forever, transforming it into a secret weapon that would reshape the Catholic Church and impact the lives of thousands of people across the globe. Both men were supernumeraries—ground troops in Escrivá's hidden army tasked with infiltrating every element of society—and both men had been sent there that day on a secret mission. Word had reached Opus Dei of a huge scandal involving the chairman of Popular—a large man with thick bushy eyebrows and thinning hair by the name of Félix Millet—who had signed a secret business deal in Paris that risked landing the bank in big trouble with the Franco regime. A tip-off had come from an executive at the bank—a devout Catholic who received spiritual direction from Opus Dei and who had shared his qualms about the chairman's recklessness with his numerary handler. Betraying the executive's confidence, the numerary had in turn shared the information with his Opus Dei colleagues and together they had come up with a cunning plan to profit from the situation—and somehow turn it to the religious movement's advantage.

As Millet began speaking, the first man launched the first phase of the plan, hurling abuse at the Popular chairman that was infused with subtle hints of the dodgy deal in Paris. The intervention was designed to send a message to Millet without alerting the rest of the assembled shareholders— that there were people out there who knew about his secret. The first man was hushed and booed, and eventually retook his seat, allowing a shaken Millet to continue his speech. Once he had finished, the second man—a government bureaucrat by the name of Mariano Navarro Rubio—initiated phase two of the plan, congratulating Millet on his excellent speech, before launching into a series of incisive remarks about how the bank might best position itself to take advantage of the current environment. His intervention would raise his profile with other shareholders ahead of the coup that the small Opus Dei group was planning. Within months, Navarro Rubio would be placed in charge of the bank's day-to-day operations. Three years later, the group would have complete control of the bank.

While the carefully planned hijacking of Banco Popular was perhaps the most audacious, the takeover of the bank was just one piece of a much larger plan hatched by a close-knit group of numerary and supernumerary men to infiltrate the Spanish business world. The ranks of utopian students who had been drawn to Opus Dei on university campuses a decade earlier were coming of age and were—just as the founder had envisioned—settling into respectable careers in business and commerce, creating opportunities for the Work to generate new streams of revenue to finance Escrivá's grand plans for expansion. Opus Dei members with their own businesses or with a share in a family venture were pressured to syphon off money and donate it to the cause. Others were encouraged to do their bit, too. Anyone with a job was pressed to use his or her position to benefit the movement in some way. A small band of entrepreneurial members had taken things a step further, spotting an opportunity to set up a series of new companies that members could use to take advantage of their solid contacts within the corrupt regime to win contracts and privileges, with the profits going back to Opus Dei. Escrivá had raised the possibility of members running what he called *support companies* in his "instructions" for supernumeraries written in the early

1940s. The founder had himself dabbled in the business world, setting up a holding company to buy the DYA student academy, although that company had eventually gone bankrupt. But these were different times: with a bit of start-up capital, hard work, and the right connections in the regime, such ventures could be very lucrative indeed.

By the early 1950s, several companies had been set up to tap into a wide range of business opportunities. There were newspapers and magazines, publishing companies, a publicity firm, film distributors, and even a news service. These "support companies" were officially owned by Opus Dei members in a personal capacity, distancing the movement from this new line of economic activity and also limiting its liability—financially, legally, and politically—should anything go wrong. But the guiding hand of Opus Dei was never far away. The movement even set up its own business department to oversee this growing network, which in turn appointed men of confidence to the boards of the individual companies who would report to and take orders from regional headquarters. Opus Dei even established its own rules for how these "support companies" were to be run. Many of the firms were eventually owned through a single holding company called Sociedad Española Anónima de Estudios Financieros—also known as Esfina, which was headed by two numeraries, both of whom were rising stars within Opus Dei: Alberto Ullastres was named chairman, and Luis Valls-Taberner was deputy chairman. Its board read like a Who's Who of the Opus Dei elite. The family business was quickly turning into a vast conglomerate, with tentacles extended to every part of society.

Business ventures were not limited to Spain, either. Luis and his associates soon established contact with a hotshot New York lawyer, who exchanged regular correspondence with them across the Atlantic, discussing potential opportunities. Sol Rosenblatt was a Hispanophile and a lawyer to the stars; he was featured in *Life* magazine after being shot at three times on the streets of Manhattan. The attempted murder had come in the middle of a bitterly fought court battle over the estate of one of J. P. Morgan's granddaughters, who had decided to leave her entire fortune to Rosenblatt. Her family had accused the lawyer of using "undue influence" over her—a ruthlessness which perhaps made him attractive to his Opus Dei clients in Madrid. Rosenblatt had been critical to establishing the Work in the United

States, helping secure a mortgage for the movement—against all the odds—on a property in Boston, close to the Harvard campus. He wrote to Luis and his associates about possible opportunities in the insurance business. He stated clearly that Opus Dei would be the ultimate beneficiary of any such deal, although—perhaps conscious of Franco's censors in Madrid—he was keen to present any arrangement as more widely beneficial to the whole country. The sums on offer were clearly large, with Rosenblatt making it obvious that he was willing to cross the Atlantic with his glamorous wife whenever his Opus Dei clients needed him.

While such business opportunities were not to be sniffed at, what the Work wanted most was a bank of its own. Luis had been working closely with Navarro Rubio on the idea for a couple of years before the opportunity to take over Banco Popular had arisen. The two had come close to buying a small savings bank a year before, but had eventually backed out after concluding that the price tag was too high. Despite the collapsed deal, getting into the banking industry remained a top priority for Luis. Taking control of a bank's balance sheet—made up of the savings of hundreds of thousands of Spaniards—would give the group ready access to billions of pesetas that could be loaned to other parts of the sprawling Opus Dei business empire. It would be a complete game-changer. So, when news filtered back to the group about the kompromat they had on the chairman of a national bank, they were ecstatic.

There was only one problem: Félix Millet, the target of the planned attack, was a first cousin of Luis's mother. Capturing the bank would mean betraying his own family. But the young numerary embraced the plan; indeed, he took charge of it. While one group threatened to expose the Banco Popular chairman with the kompromat they held, Luis played the role of savior, offering to buy Millet's stake and provide him with a way of bowing out of the bank with his reputation intact.

Within weeks of the intervention at the shareholder meeting, the wheels of Opus Dei's takeover of Popular were in motion. Millet had arranged for a Belgian consultancy firm to advise the bank on how to turn around its lackluster performance. In June 1954, they reported their findings, identifying a series of grave issues concerning the way the bank was run. Working in tandem with the Opus Dei group, Millet used the report as a pretext to fire his chief executive—the man in charge of running the bank—and proposed installing Navarro Rubio in his place. As word of all this maneuvering—and of Luis's role in it—reached Rome, Escrivá rewarded him by promoting the twenty-eight-year-old to "elector," granting him a seat on the governing council tasked with voting on any major changes to the Work and determining who would succeed Escrivá when the time came.

At the start of 1955, the Banco Popular board gathered to appoint Navarro Rubio as chief executive. Opus Dei now had day-to-day control of Popular. But Rubio's tenure in the job was to be short-lived. In April, just a few weeks after his appointment, Navarro Rubio was offered a job in government as the new Undersecretary of Public Works. He sought to demur, protesting that he had only just taken on the Popular job, but the Caudillo was not a man to be turned down. A compromise was offered, with Navarro Rubio given a special dispensation to hold both jobs. That did little to solve the problem; given the inevitable demands on his time at the ministry, there was no way he could possibly keep tabs on everything going on at the bank. Opus Dei's control of Popular risked slipping away even before it had properly begun.

This development created a new urgency to complete the purchase of Millet's stake and to solidify control over Popular. Using their access to the bank's confidential records, the group identified other large shareholders who might also be coerced into selling. The aim was to acquire more than half the bank's shares, which would give Opus Dei complete control. They identified one board member with a string of hydroelectric plants, who had taken out a series of loans and had fallen into difficulties with repayments because of an unexpected drought. Millet wrote to him about a deal, telling him that *someone* was willing to buy his shares. Within days, the deal was done. The purchase, totaling five million pesetas, was made by a company called Eolo, one of two vehicles set up by some Opus Dei members a few years earlier to spearhead the movement's plans to move into construction and transport. Three months later, the same company paid ten million pesetas to buy shares from another big shareholder.

Two Opus Dei members were appointed to new positions in the bank, giving them oversight of critical parts in its lending operations. More friendly faces were also elected to the board. Just a few months later, the bank signed off on a fifteen million peseta loan for Eolo, which was imme-diately used to fund the purchase of yet another huge slug of shares. It was a highly unorthodox move. The bank was effectively stumping up the cash to finance a hostile takeover of itself—and by a group that hadn't even declared its intentions to the board. It showed the lengths—and the brazenness—that Opus Dei was willing to go to secure its prize.

By January 1957, the group had enough shares in their possession to give them complete control of the bank. Millet resigned from the board, and a new chairman—a man called Fernando Camacho, a trusted ally of Opus Dei who had run one of their "support companies," was named as his replacement. He duly appointed a young, relatively unknown figure to be his right-hand man as deputy chairman: Luis Valls-Taberner. In the space of a year, control seemed to have passed from an experienced group of well-known men with long, storied histories in the banking world to a group of unknowns. The changes began to worry some long-time Popular executives. One board member voiced his consternation that Luis was being handed so many powers. But the new owners of the bank paid little attention to such resistance. News a few weeks later that three fellow Opus Dei members had been appointed to senior positions in the Franco regime must have embold-ened them even further. Among their ranks was none other than the super-numerary Navarro Rubio, who was named as the new Minister of Finance. Alberto Ullastres, the numerary who had been Luis's boss at one of the "sup-port companies," was named as Minister of Commerce, while Laureano López Rodó—a numerary at the same residence as Luis—was named special advisor to the Prime Minister. At least in Spain, Opus Dei's ascendancy now seemed complete. But it was just the beginning. Armed with a nationwide bank that commanded billions of pesetas in resources, the ambitious plans of the founder could now be unleashed. He wrote glowingly to Luis from Rome: "It's good, your constant attention to the work of Saint Nicholas."

On a cold Sunday morning in November 1960, a long motorcade carrying the Caudillo cautiously snaked its way through the mountain passes just north of Madrid, headed for the Valley of the Fallen. An army of twenty thousand political prisoners had worked on the site, often in inhuman conditions, hollowing out a mountain for the vast underground basilica and hauling a gargantuan cross onto its craggy summit. Many had died during construction. Officially, the monument was a symbol of national reconciliation—but not even Franco's staunchest supporters believed that. It towered over the city below, a constant reminder of the enduring power of the victors, who had supposedly saved Spain from a coalition of Jews, Masons, and Communists bent on overthrowing the country's Christian traditions and heritage. In an adjoining abbey, twenty Benedictine monks held a constant vigil, a reminder of the Church's complicity with Franco's regime. Each day, they conducted Mass in the basilica, giving thanks to God and asking Him to take away their sins, all while standing over the tomb of José Antonio Primo de Rivera, a thug and a bully who had founded the Falange movement and modeled it on the Nazis.

That morning was the anniversary of Primo de Rivera's death and Franco had made the journey up into the mountains to pay homage to this fallen hero. The two men had never been close, and while their paths had crossed several times over the years, neither had really warmed to the other. But during and after the war, the Falange and its one million members had provided critical support to Franco, so his attendance at the ceremony that morning was his way of cementing that relationship. On arrival, the Caudillo was led under a processional canopy carried by the monks—from the parade ground and into the basilica, where hundreds of Falange members were gathered. At the most poignant moment in the ceremony—with the lights turned down and the congregation knelt in silent prayer—a shout rose out from the back of the nave: "Franco, you traitor!" A commotion broke out and a uniformed member of the Falange youth wing was frogmarched out of the basilica and taken away for questioning. After a grueling interrogation, the police made a startling discovery: the lone agitator said his entire regiment had planned on shouting in unison but had lost their nerve at the last minute. The source of their ire: Opus Dei and its growing power.

Franco's decision to appoint three Opus Dei ministers to his Cabinet in 1957 had suddenly shone an intense spotlight on a group that had until then been relatively unknown beyond a few university campuses. The rapid rise of the three ministers had only intensified public attention. In less than four years, their package of landmark economic reforms had almost certainly saved the regime from bankruptcy, triggering a series of articles in the *New*

York Times, Le Monde, and *The Economist* that extolled Opus Dei's political ascent. Franco himself was ecstatic with the results and gradually began to cede more and more autonomy to the three so-called technocrats, freeing up more time for him to spend on his favorite hobbies—hunting, watching Westerns, and playing the football pools. Escrivá wrote to Franco to express his personal joy over the Catholic vision that the dictator had for the country. "I ask the Lord Our God to bestow good fortune on Your Excellency and to provide you with an abundance of grace in the execution of the lofty mission entrusted to you," he fawned.

But the Falange, which had seen one of its most prominent members demoted in the 1957 reshuffle, and much of its influence diluted in the years since, eyed the shift in power with increasing alarm. The situation wasn't helped by Escrivá, who couldn't resist his own impulses to bask in his movement's growing influence. At a meeting of his top lieutenants in the Swiss mountains in 1956, he had introduced a requirement to kneel in his presence. Following the government appointments, he ordered that all Opus Dei ministers were to come personally to receive him whenever he came back to Spain. The requirement was inconvenient enough when the founder flew into Barajas airport, just north of the capital. But he occasionally traveled back to Spain though France by car, forcing three of the busiest and most powerful men in the country to drop everything and drive five hours north to the border at Irún. To the Falange, the ministerial receptions at the border were confirmation that the Opus Dei men in government answered not to the Caudillo but to another authority entirely.

Matters were made worse when a gleeful Escrivá returned in October 1960 for a triumphant homecoming tour. His first stop was Madrid, where Opus Dei had just been granted custody of its first church—none other than Saint Michael's, where the founder had worked for a few months in 1927. Before hundreds of Opus Dei members, who were worshiping as a large group for the first time ever in public, Escrivá gave an emotional address. "The Lord brought me here with hints of our Work," he told them. "I never dreamed that I would see this church full of souls that so love Jesus Christ. I am truly moved." From there, he left for Saragossa to collect an honorary doctorate, and met with crowds who pushed and jostled to get close. Then it was on to Pamplona, where Escrivá was to attend a ceremony at a law school set up by Opus Dei that had just been granted the status of pontifical university by the Vatican—the new University of Navarre. The city was filled with a festival atmosphere: colorful flags adorned the old town and Opus Dei members roamed the streets singing songs and chanting "Long live Father Escrivá!" The founder sat on a velvet-padded throne during the ceremony. Directly behind him sat Luis Valls-Taberner, literally the power behind the throne. The thirty-four-year-old businessman, sporting slicked-back hair and a pencil moustache, stood out among the older men seated around Escrivá not just because of his youth but also because he was the only one in the front rows who wasn't wearing an academic robe or a cassock.

By 1960, after less than four years at the bank, Luis had so successfully rewired Popular to benefit the Work that the founder had begun to refer to him affectionately as *mi banquero*—"my banker." But his transition to his new role at the bank hadn't been easy. Indeed, Luis's first few years there had been decidedly mixed. Although he outranked everyone apart from the chairman, Luis learned to stay quiet at the monthly board meetings so as not to embarrass himself, deferring to his much older colleagues—many of them twice his age—who had long, illustrious careers in banking and who, unlike him, could offer wise opinions on the bank's liquidity coefficient and other abstruse subjects. The silences might have been taken as a sign of reflection and concentration, were it not for his occasional attempts to get involved with the daily business of the bank with strange pseudo-philosophical musings. These were on topics such as brotherhood, equality, and responsibility, and were published in the company magazine to inspire Popular employees, but they struck the bank tellers, security guards, and secretaries as strange. In one missive, he warned his colleagues against using their reason to understand the world around them. "In our interactions, and in social, professional, and family life, we must turn to a more transcendental and at the same time more simplified idea—that of faith," he wrote. While blind faith may have been a cornerstone of Opus Dei, it was an odd principle to extend to the world of banking, where billions of pesetas were at stake every day.

Luis had an ulterior motive for discouraging his colleagues from using their powers of reason. By 1960, Banco Popular had become the central cog in a sprawling financial engine of Opus Dei businesses that reached deep into the Spanish economy. On the face of it, the bank continued to operate as it always had, taking in savings and lending money out again in mortgages and business loans. But its new owners had made subtle changes to the way Popular operated that directly benefited the Work. Some of the changes were almost imperceptible, such as Luis using his position to invite important clients and other members on the board to special V.I.P. retreats hosted by Opus Dei. Other moves were more overt. Many of the "support companies" that had been set up in the 1950s to generate cash for the renovation of Villa Tevere in Rome had been onboarded as clients and given loans on extremely favorable terms. Popular's overseas operations had been overhauled completely. After years of doing business in neighboring Morocco, the bank suddenly pulled out; evidently, its predominantly Muslim population offered few prospects for Opus Dei. In its place, Popular's new owners created a much more ambitious overseas network spanning Switzerland, Germany, the UK, and several Latin American countries—coincidentally, these were places where the movement had put down roots and was keen to expand. Numerary members were put in charge of the overseas push. The appointments created a double windfall for Opus Dei, which not only got every peseta of their generous salaries but also gave Opus a critical say in all new business in those countries.

The role of Banco Popular in fueling Opus Dei's rise was not lost on the Falange, which soon began a campaign to expose this hidden financing network. On the streets of Madrid, pamphlets began to appear detailing how Escrivá's followers had built a sprawling web of business interests. "Did you know that Opus Dei is absolutely bound up and embedded in Spanish daily life?" it asked. It detailed eight newspapers and magazines, a newswire, a publishing company, fifty bookshops, a film distributor, and a movie rental chain that were all linked to the group. The pamphlet also revealed Opus Dei's ownership of a majority stake in Banco Popular—and another bank in Andorra, which it said was involved in transferring vast sums overseas. Over the next two years, the Falange's attacks against the bank intensified. In the early hours of June 8, 1962, two bombs exploded at the Popular headquarters in central Madrid. Nobody was hurt in the explosions, but the message was clear. While the authorities blamed the attack on communists, the facts all pointed in the same direction. Luis and the bank were now targets in a bitter fight being waged by the Falange to thwart Opus Dei.

The attacks did little to break the growing ambitions of Escrivá, who continued to heap pressure on his foot soldiers back in Madrid to keep the cash flowing. Given the cult of personality that had built up around the founder, care was taken to distance him from any grubby decisions involving money. But it was all a smokescreen: in fact, the founder demanded to be kept regularly updated on his rapidly expanding family business, and detailed reports were sent frequently to Rome for his attention. The founder flew into frequent fits of rage whenever he felt that his recruits weren't sending enough money, and he barked out orders that were sent back to Spain using a secret code of numbers and letters kept inside a copy of a book about Saint Jerome, the wise old sage of Christian morality. Back in Madrid, the orders were cascaded down to members, who were encouraged do whatever was necessary to further the Work of God—even if it involved abusing their positions at work, betraying their friends and family, or acting against their own conscience. Members were asked to come up with lists of people who could be swindled, which were sent up to superiors to ensure there was no duplication. Even the three government ministers were not immune from such demands. Alberto Ullastres, the Minister of Commerce, was initially reluctant when asked to name a fellow numerary to his ministry to help waive through export deals that directly benefited the Work, but eventually he gave in after pressure from his Opus Dei superiors.

Luis soon became a critical bridge between Madrid and Rome, flying out to see the founder whenever he was summoned and often spending eight or ten days there, even during intensely busy periods at the bank, despite the fact that Popular—at least officially—had no business in Italy. Escrivá soon began to consider the young banker as his eyes and ears in Madrid. Back at the numerary residence in the evening, he and Laureano López Rodó—the de facto deputy prime minister—held court, receiving their fellow members and doling out orders and advice on how to game the system. Such late-night politicking awakened Luis's long-held ambitions to follow his father and his grandfather into politics. Like many numeraries, he had been encouraged to set aside his own dreams and aspirations in favor of the professional path that his superiors deemed most beneficial to Opus Dei. Leaving the bank wasn't an option, but he nonetheless allowed himself to dream of a world in which he would be completely free to decide his own destiny. He started to look across the Atlantic to another young Catholic from a political dynasty. As a womanizer who enjoyed the good life, President John F. Kennedy was an unusual role model for a man who had taken vows of chastity, poverty, and obedience. But Luis lapped up every article he could get his hands on that mentioned Kennedy and even jokingly began to refer to his assistant as his Mac Bundy, in reference to the president's right-hand man, McGeorge Bundy.

But his political abilities often fell far short of those demonstrated by the young American president. Frequently, Luis found himself unable to smooth over the day-to-day problems, disputes, and contradictions that resulted from the stream of demands that came from the founder. His inexperience, having been parachuted into the top echelons of Popular, also led to grave mistakes. By 1962, five years after the takeover, a festering crisis was beginning to emerge at the bank that threatened its role as the financial engine behind the religious movement. Luis had allowed Opus Dei to bleed Popular dry, saddling the bank with huge amounts of debt and then using the money to fund its various projects. Some of the more experienced bankers on the board from outside the takeover group had warned against such a reckless expansion, but the needs of Rome had trumped those of the bank. It all soon came to a head. Under intense pressure from regulators to strengthen its finances, Popular finally relented and asked its shareholders to inject seventy million pesetas to forestall a possible crisis. Luis was tasked with coming up with Opus Dei's own contribution to ensure that its power at the bank wasn't diluted. For a while, he borrowed money from the bank. But that could only ever be a temporary fix; if the regulators found out, the bank could be in deep trouble. Unable to find the money, a clearly distressed Luis was left with no option but to turn to his wealthy family for help. His mother and younger brother Javier came to the rescue, bailing out Opus Dei with a huge cash injection. The Valls-Taberners weren't awarded any shares—they were simply buying Luis out of a hole. The young numerary suffered a breakdown shortly afterwards and disappeared for weeks, bundled off to Pamplona, where he was cared for by Opus Dei's own trusted set of doctors. Given the pressure being heaped on numerary members, such "medical retreats"—and the widespread use of prescription drugs to dull any mental and physical damage—became increasingly common. This was combined with feigned concern and affection that had been absent in the years running up to these increasingly common health crises. "You and I, who have both been endowed with huge hearts by the Lord Our God, have to keep smiling—we both know how to do it—and not build mountains out of molehills," Escrivá wrote to Luis after his own breakdown. "Agreed?"

For all his inspirational words to Luis, the pressure from Escrivá to keep the money flowing was unrelenting. By the early sixties, Opus Dei had reached as far as Kenya, Japan, and Australia and its membership had climbed to about six thousand people across six continents. Such rapid geographical expansion had never been seen before in almost two thousand years of Christendom—perhaps because nobody else had access to such large amounts of cash or the convenience of the airplane.

Escrivá's self-importance burgeoned along with the Work. He began to change the way he signed his name, merging the compound José María—a very common boy's name at the time in Spanish-speaking countries—to the one-word Josemaría. He told his followers that he did it as a sign of his devotion to both Joseph and Mary. But the founder perhaps also had an eye on his legacy; rather than be yet another Saint Joseph, of which there were already several, he might be the first Saint Josemaría. He told his followers to begin collecting artifacts connected to his life, explaining that God would—one day—demand an account of their time with him. But at the same time as he was planning for his sainthood, in private conversations with his followers Escrivá acknowledged the underhanded methods that Opus Dei had used to fuel its expansion. In one meeting, Escrivá made it clear to Luis and others present that they were to distance themselves from what they were doing to help Opus Dei. "Don't use the term *we*, use only the term *I*," he ordered. Such personal culpability would become a mainstay of Opus Dei for years to come, giving it a cover of deniability whenever something went wrong. "Defend the Work," was the new mantra.

By the mid-'60s, some 138 "support companies" had been set up to generate funds to finance Escrivá's ambitions. About a quarter of those were in Spain, where the group's deep penetration of the Franco regime was generating large sums, while the rest had been set up in other parts of the world—in the United States, Mexico, and across Latin America—as financial spring-boards into those countries. Opus Dei had already established a complex sys-tem of bank accounts—both within Spain and abroad—held in the names of trusted numerary members to avoid the country's strict capital-control rules. But that system wasn't infallible, and sometimes the group had to re-sort to the basics to get money out of Spain. Ahead of a trip abroad, mem-bers were sometimes suddenly presented with a money belt to wear—often containing many thousands of dollars—and were effectively encouraged to break money-trafficking rules, to risk arrest and even prison. Numerary businessmen with a good excuse for traveling abroad were prime candidates. Gregorio Ortega Pardo, Banco Popular's man in Lisbon, was particularly ac-tive. Through the 1950s, he had established himself as Opus Dei's money smuggler in chief. Members often visited Madrid carrying large wads of cash, taking advantage of the lax controls on the Spain-Portugal border, to give to Ortega, who would then arrange for the money to be sent on. Luis himself made several trips to Portugal during that time.

But this route for Opus Dei money out of Spain would soon come under threat. On October 16, 1965, Ortega flew to Caracas and checked himself into a suite at the Hotel Tamanaco, a luxury resort on the eastern fringes of the Venezuelan capital that was frequented by the rich and famous. Despite being a numerary who had taken vows of poverty, chastity, and obedience, Ortega had a taste for the good life. Elegant and debonair, the forty-three-year-old businessman was a familiar face around Lisbon's trendiest and most elegant nightspots—although hardly any of the city's elite knew much about the Spaniard. There were many stories about him, including the one where he announced he was the Archduke of Austria at the chic Montes Claros restaurant and paid the orchestra a thousand escudos to dedicate a waltz to him. Such eccentricities, which clearly flouted not just the letter but also the spirit of Opus Dei rules, had gradually seeped into the lifestyles of some of the elite numerary businessmen in Madrid and beyond, who en-joyed certain liberties and immunity from reprimand because of their status within the movement. In part, such privileges reflected a shift within Opus Dei—from an organization primarily concerned with the spiritual realm, to one more interested in money and expansion, with a willingness to be more flexible toward those members who contributed most to achieving its goals.

Such liberties were vital not only to keep up appearances—Ortega was linked to a long list of companies that touched on everything from automobiles to construction, and even cinema—but also to serve as a pressure valve for elite members who lived under constant stress and who often put themselves in harm's way to meet the founder's demands. Like Luis, Ortega had begun to feel the pressure of late. He had begun to skip meals and for a time subsisted on a diet of whisky and coffee. A year before his trip to Venezuela, it had all become so much that he needed to take some time away and returned to Spain for a period of "medical retreat"—first in Pamplona and then in the mountains outside Madrid. By the time of his journey to Venezuela, he seemed much better to the people around him. He bumped into the Spanish ambassador on the day of his departure at the airport, who remarked that he had seemed recovered and completely normal.

Ortega spent his first full day in the Venezuelan capital by relaxing at the hotel. The next day, he took a cab downtown to the Banco de Caracas, where he presented a suitcase full of banknotes to the manager, who immediately became suspicious and reported him to the authorities. The police, assuming Ortega might be part of a communist cell linked to a clandestine arms factory that had been discovered a few days earlier, decided not to bring him in for questioning straight away, but instead to follow him around the city. For two weeks they kept him under surveillance, logging his meetings with a mysterious woman. They also followed him to the office of a lawyer long suspected of working with communists, which only confirmed their suspicions. On November 5, they arrested him in his hotel suite, where they found almost a quarter of a million dollars—as well as several pieces of antique jewelry. Under questioning, Ortega panicked and lied; he told the police he was a university professor who had brought the money into the country to buy some property. He made no mention of his affiliation to Opus Dei, or of the coincidence of his visit with the group's plans to open a new school for boys in Caracas, for which a briefcase full of dollars would be extremely helpful. Happy that he wasn't a communist—and having established that the money had been withdrawn legally from accounts controlled by Ortega back in Lisbon—the businessman was released without charge and told he was free to leave the country.

Back at the bank in Madrid, the arrest of one of its most senior executives with a suitcase full of unexplained cash created panic. While the scandal had been hushed up in the press, news of the incident had reached the Caudillo, and the situation—if not properly handled—risked exposing the huge flows of dollars from Banco Popular to Opus Dei operations across the world. Luis took the news particularly badly and shut himself in his office for several days, refusing to see anyone. After almost twenty years inside Opus Dei, his ability to rationalize the situation was seriously compromised. He had known Ortega for many years and it was Luis who had entrusted his old friend with the delicate operations in Lisbon. Not only had he failed the founder but he had failed God, too. Worse still, every part of his life—from the moment he woke and kissed the floor at the residence, to his day at the bank overseeing the sprawling web of Opus Dei companies, to his evenings of politicking with the minister and doling out orders and favors to his fellow members—was tied up with the movement. He depended on Opus Dei. At any moment, with one word from the founder in Rome, everything—his job at the bank, his status among his peers, his life in Madrid—could be taken away. Shut away in his office, his mind clearly still not recovered from his breakdown two years earlier, he began to grow paranoid. Had one of his fellow numeraries, jealous of his status within the movement, engineered all this? One of his colleagues finally managed to get in to see him and was shocked at what he found. "How do we know you're not a sleeping communist, that you haven't been working normally all these years, just waiting for this moment?" Luis barked at him. He finally emerged after a week and announced that he was moving out of his large office and relocating to a room barely big enough to fit a desk. This act of penance might have been interpreted as the natural Catholic response, were it not for what was to happen next—which exposed the lengths that supposedly devout members of Opus Dei would go to protect the interests of the movement.

The Work soon moved to cover up the incident. The numerary residence where Ortega had lived in Lisbon was particularly active, selectively leaking information to the friendly Spanish ambassador, implying that the businessman had suddenly severed ties with Opus Dei shortly before his departure. They produced a series of letters in which Ortega had suddenly resigned from several companies linked to the movement, which wasn't true. Luis and his colleagues were more than conscious of this, given the enormous work they were putting into extricating Ortega from the web of companies he still headed, and as the Venezuelan police had themselves established. Such fabricated letters were a well-known threat that hung over any numerary who traveled abroad, as they were expected to sign several blank sheets of paper before leaving on any trip. Opus Dei members also pushed the line that Ortega had suddenly gone crazy and might cause further public embarrassment for the Caudillo and his regime. As a result, after landing in Madrid on November 13, Ortega was bundled off to a mental asylum to be assessed. The doctors there found nothing wrong with the patient and discharged him. The Caudillo was informed a few days later that Ortega was being cared for by a group of people "with good sense and authentic love for their neighbor" who had "put him under a medical regimen appropriate to his condition."

Ortega was in fact being held at a ranch in the countryside while Luis conspired with the Opus Dei men in government on what do to about their embarrassing little secret. The scandal refused to die down; reports began to emerge abroad that Ortega may have helped to smuggle as much as two million dollars abroad, prompting a pair of Vatican journalists to travel to Lisbon to investigate further. Conversations at the bank took on a dark turn; Luis and one of his trusted lieutenants talked about the option of a possible "incapacitation or subjecting him to medical treatment proportionate to the danger he poses." That same day, Luis paid a courtesy call to Franco's security chief to thank him for his assistance in the matter.

Such duplicity and moral perversion was by no means unique to Luis. Across Spain, many members were going to extreme lengths to protect the movement. Opus Dei doctors were encouraged to medicate fellow numeraries who were having doubts about their membership. For his part, there were some indications that Luis was uncomfortable about his role. He never went to see his old friend Ortega in person, but instead usually sent his brother Pedro or one of his Opus Dei colleagues from the bank. By the end of March, after almost four months of being held against his will, Ortega finally capitulated. "He can't cope with staying in the asylum any longer because he isn't crazy," Pedro reported back to Luis after spending eight hours with Ortega. "He understands and accepts whatever solution. If things drag on, he will go to the police himself." Two weeks later, the deal was done. After signing various documents, including a confession and some legal documents, Pedro met with him once again—this time in a house owned by the Valls-Taberner family—to discuss a new life that had been arranged for him in Argentina. Shortly after, the name Gregorio Ortega Pardo seemed to disappear forever.

Luis was deeply scarred by his role in betraying his close friend and colleague. Perhaps sensing the growing unease of a man who was now playing an increasingly critical role in the expansion of Opus Dei, the founder took him aside following one Mass and spoke to Luis directly about the Ortega Pardo affair. "Don't get upset about any of it," he told his banker. "Everything can be fixed—apart from death. Everything. Sometimes we only see one part of the whole." "Never judge things by appearances," he continued. "Many people, who we quite clearly witness doing bad things, we will see once again in Heaven." Numeraries like Luis were not to view their actions through a prism of earthly morality. "Opus Dei is not a thing of this world," he explained. Rather than sate Escrivá's ambition, the huge sums generated by Luis and by Banco Popular had only reinforced the founder's self-importance, fueling his ambition further and leading him to justify whatever means were necessary to fulfill what he had convinced himself and those around him was the Work of God. As the Ortega Pardo incident illustrated, things had now spiraled out of control. The founder's insatiable ambition would soon bring him into direct conflict with the Church itself.

5

BECAUSE I SAY SO

Rome, Italy—October 1965

THERE WAS NOBODY WAITING FOR HER AT FIUMICINO AIRPORT, SO MARÍA del Carmen Tapia decided to head straight into Rome, where she found two friendly faces waiting for her at the bus terminal. The women were overjoyed to see her. The three of them had worked together years earlier, before Tapia had been sent to Venezuela. Both asked about the reason for Tapia's visit, but she had no explanation to give them. All she knew was that her colleagues in Caracas had received a note from Villa Tevere a few days earlier, instructing María del Carmen to return to Rome as soon as possible. For days, she had racked her brain trying to try to figure why. One of the priests she knew suggested that the founder, conscious of the passing years, was probably just keen to see a few old faces. Tapia had been sent to Rome in the early 1950s, not long after being recruited as a numerary by her boss at the Research Council in Madrid, who happened to be a priest and—like almost everyone else in the building, she later discovered—a member of Opus Dei. After a few years at various residences across Spain, she had been invited to live at Villa Tevere, where she spent four years working alongside the founder before being sent off to Venezuela.

Returning to Rome all these years later, she was taken aback at some of the changes—and not just those to do with the extensive remodeling of Villa Tevere. The room she was given had a thick mattress placed on top of the wooden planks that female numeraries usually slept on. She soon learned that such comfort, which the male numeraries had enjoyed right from the beginnings of the movement, had recently been extended to women—but only those over forty. The older women were also now allowed to take hot showers. The changes had come into force after an outbreak of health issues, including rheumatism, bad backs, and gynecological problems linked to the harsh conditions the women endured.

Before she had finished unpacking, a message came over the intercom that she was to report immediately to the dining room in Villa Vecchia, the original palace at the heart of the Villa Tevere complex, around which a labyrinthine city of newer buildings, chapels, and offices had been constructed over the years. Villa Vecchia was completely hidden from the street and retained much of its former elegance and charm. Escrivá had chosen the palace as his personal living quarters, where his suite of rooms included an office, a chapel for the sole use of the founder—and a private dining room. There she found him having dinner with Del Portillo, the head of the women's section and the prefect of servants. As was customary, she approached Escrivá, knelt before him, and kissed his hand.

"How was the journey?" he responded, without getting up.

"Good, thank you Father," she replied.

"How were they when you left?" he enquired, referring to the women who shared the numerary residence with Tapia back in Caracas.

"Good, Father—although I am really worried about Begoña, given her bad news."

Begoña lived at the residence and had just been diagnosed with cancer.

"*Bad news* you call it, knowing that she will soon be with God?" Escrivá retorted. "What a blessing! She should count herself lucky, knowing that she will die soon. Anyway, who is this Begoña—and how long has she been ill?"

Tapia was surprised that Escrivá seemed to know nothing about the news. Begoña had established the women's section in Venezuela and she held important positions in Opus Dei's regional government there. As instructed, Tapia and her colleagues in Caracas had sent regular reports back to Rome about the evolution of her condition. She assumed it had simply slipped his mind.

"And you—how is your health?" he asked.

"Good, Father," she replied.

"Has the doctor seen you?"

"Yes, Father. Every year we have a thorough check-up."

"Never mind! You"—he turned to the prefect of servants—"take a look at her. Make sure she eats. It's important that she sleeps and that she rests, because we are going to give her lots of things to do. We will speak in due course. But, for now—rest, eat, and sleep."

With that, he left the room.

The exchange left Tapia feeling confused; she was still no wiser about the reason she had been forced to trek five thousand miles. While the founder had been courteous, she sensed that something wasn't quite right—there was a certain annoyance in his voice. She tried to put her instincts aside. After all, these were testing times for any devout Catholic—and the founder, as a loyal servant of the pope, was probably riven with anxiety about the Second Vatican Council, which was expected to conclude within weeks. The gathering was the first ecumenical council in almost a hundred years, and it had been convened by Pope John XXIII to modernize the Church so that it might better address the challenges of an increasingly secular society. But such good intentions had soon collapsed into acrimony and division, exposing huge fault lines running through the Catholic faith. Over the previous four autumns, hundreds of cardinals, bishops, and Church leaders had convened in Rome for weeks of debate and to vote on a long list of proposed reforms. Escrivá wasn't invited to participate in the general congregations where such debate and voting took place—attendance there was reserved for cardinals, bishops, and the heads of the main religious orders. As the mere head of a secular institute, Escrivá did not qualify, although two Opus Dei bishops from Peru and another from Portugal did participate. After lobbying from the movement, the pope's personal secretary offered a compromise: Escrivá could attend as a consultor to the various commissions that had been set up to work on documents for the general congregations, alongside Del Portillo and two other Opus Dei priests who had also been invited to participate. But Escrivá turned down the offer. Evidently, being relegated below three of his own bishops was unsatisfactory. Instead, the founder was forced to follow the proceedings from afar.

Escrivá's relationship with the Vatican had already been floundering even before the Council. The Opus Dei founder had taken umbrage at a sudden spate of approvals of other secular institutes, which—in his eyes—diminished the status of Opus Dei within the Church. Suddenly, the Work of God was relegated to the same ecclesiastical bucket as the Institute of the Maids of the Poor and the Company of Saint Ursula. Clearly offended, he even wrote to the membership to state unilaterally that Opus Dei was no longer a secular institute because the meaning of that label had become distorted over the years—even though only the Vatican had the authority to confer or withdraw that status.

His relations with the papacy had also begun to sour. Escrivá had never warmed to Pope John XXIII, who had been elected after the death of Pius XII in 1958 and quickly became known as the "good pope" for his efforts to liberalize the Church. On the pope's death in 1963, Escrivá had hoped that his successor would show more respect to Opus Dei, and possibly confer on it a new status more befitting such an important movement within the Church. But the selection of Pope Paul VI—the former Archbishop of Milan, who had already had several run-ins with Opus Dei in the city—dealt a blow to any such hopes. On hearing the news, Escrivá flew into a rage, accusing the new pope of being a Mason and predicting that all of those who had elected him would go to hell. "God in his infinite wisdom should take this man away," he told one member. Other influential figures at the Vatican also looked down on Escrivá. One respected Swiss theologian, who would later become an advisor to two popes, dismissed *The Way*, the founder's seminal work, as nothing more than a "handbook for senior scouts" and openly criticized Opus Dei for "purchasing" spirituality through its various business interests. "Purchased spirit is a contradiction in itself," he surmised.

The day after her conversation with the founder, Tapia went to visit Saint Peter's, but rushed back in case Escrivá wanted to speak with her again. She heard nothing. For the next three days, she was stuck in her room with nothing to do. On the fourth day, she asked to be assigned a task and was told to catalogue all the books in the library—first alphabetically and then by subject. She realized that the work would take her months. Handing out such menial and Sisyphean tasks was a common tactic used by Escrivá to test the commitment of his followers—and to assert his control over them. Another numerary, who had already been instructed by his director in London to give up his very successful academic career to focus his time on recruiting schoolboys, was sent to Rome around the same time as Tapia in order to retrain as a priest—even though he had no interest in doing so. "Whatever the director told me to do was God's will," he recalled. "Opus Dei and God gradually merged into one. I had been instructed that criticism was a sign of pride." On arrival, he was given the task of cleaning the central-heating boiler—hot, dirty, and arduous work. Only after passing this "test" was he given a better job. "I was told that in bullfights the bull had to be weakened, reduced to his knees, if it was to be controlled and mastered before being slain," he recalled. "Inside Opus Dei, the paramount virtues were whole-hearted, uncritical obedience and annihilation of personal feeling and tastes—all for the benefit of the institution."

During the obligatory spiritual guidance conversations, and even during confession, Tapia began to sense that something was wrong. The director and the priest made some insinuations that she had done something terrible back in Venezuela—that she had done something that went against the founder and the spirit of the Work. She pleaded with the head of the women's section to tell her more, to no avail. It was only after a month that she was finally summoned to see Escrivá again. He received her in the offices of the women's section and was seated in a high-back chair upholstered in red velvet.

His demeanor was completely changed from their first encounter.

"I have called you here to tell you I want you in Rome," he announced. "You will *not* be returning to Venezuela. We brought you here under false pretenses"—he was smiling, almost amused—"because, with that temper of yours, who knows how you might have reacted. We had no option but to do it that way. So now you know—you aren't going back."

"But Father, I want to live—and die—in Venezuela," begged Tapia.

Her defiant tone took everyone in the room by surprise.

The founder rose to his feet, visibly angry.

"No and no!" he screamed. "Didn't you hear? You aren't going back because *I* say so and I am the one with the authority to order him . . . and her . . . and you." His finger stabbed its way around the room. "Such arrogance! You. Are. Not. Going. Back."

That evening, she was summoned before the founder again to receive a formal admonition—for her reaction to his order that afternoon.

"These people have told me," he said, gesturing around at some of the other female numeraries in the room, "that you have received the news that you aren't going back to Venezuela with hysteria and tears." He suddenly raised his voice. "Very bad spirit!" he screamed at her. "You are not going back to Venezuela—nor will you ever go back—because your work has been all about you and bad. And you have been saying things about my documents!"

He raised his fist up against her face.

"This is serious—serious, SERIOUS!" he screamed. "I hereby give you a canonical admonition. Let it be recorded! Next time, you are on the street!"

Over the coming days, it became clear to Tapia that the reason she had been summoned to Rome—and the reason for the founder's anger toward her—was that she had dared to question Escrivá's rules and regulations. Back in Venezuela, she had suggested to one of her colleagues that members be allowed to make confession with priests from outside Opus Dei—something that was allowed on paper, but which was deemed "bad spirit" for anyone to actually do. She'd also failed to follow the founder's guidelines that numeraries were to make a monthly visit to the countryside. Given that Venezuela had little "countryside" in the European sense, she had taken the women in her charge to the beach. To cap her insubordination, she had dared to suggest that a Spanish magazine set up by Opus Dei that Escrivá had tasked all numeraries with finding subscribers for might not be of interest to anyone in Venezuela. She also learned of the punishment for her transgressions. She would be banned from communicating with anyone back in Venezuela—and if anyone were to come looking for her at Villa Tevere, they would be told she was sick. Her colleagues back in Venezuela were to be told of her bad spirit—although she was banned from talking about "her lamentable situation" with anyone in Rome. She was told that only through prayer and blind obedience could she save her soul.

For the next four months, she was a prisoner inside Villa Tevere. She was prohibited from leaving the villa, making or receiving phone calls, and writing or receiving letters. She shared her despair with a friendly numerary from Venezuela called Gladys, taking care to speak to her only in certain rooms of Villa Tevere because Tapia knew about the microphones the founder had installed in many parts of the complex, which were connected to his private quarters and which allowed him to listen in on members' private conversations. By the sixties, Escrivá had so successfully groomed a circle of sycophants around himself in Rome that nobody seemed to question such blatant breaches of members' personal rights. "Surrounded by a bubble of affection, I was utterly uncritical," recalled one numerary who helped install the listening devices. "It seemed perfectly normal to install a microphone behind a picture in an interview room so that every word uttered there could be taped for posterity and a record kept of who said what." Gladys felt sorry for Tapia and thought she was being treated harshly. She agreed to set up a post office box for her, opening up a way for Tapia to correspond with Ana María Gibert, a colleague she was close to back home—with Gladys dropping off and picking up any correspondence. The restrictions finally began to ease at the end of March—although Tapia was usually accompanied by another numerary whenever she left the complex. Things continued like that for several weeks—until one day she was unexpectedly summoned to see Escrivá.

"This has to stop," he said. "You won't keep making fools of us."

He picked up a sheet of paper and adjusted his spectacles.

"They tell me you have been corresponding with Ana María Gibert—that wicked woman," he continued. "And you have a post office box here in Rome."

He put his spectacles down and began to shout.

"What is this? You enormous hypocrite—you deceiver, you wicked woman!"

"Yes, Father. I have written to Ana María Gibert. But she isn't a wicked woman."

"And that procurer, Gladys!" he shouted. "The swine! Bring her here!"

Gladys was brought in and shouted at by Escrivá. He ordered her out.

"See to her afterwards," he told the representatives of the women's section who were present. "Pull up her skirt, pull down her pants, and smack her on the ass until she talks. Make her talk!"

He then turned to Tapia.

"I herewith give you your second admonition, you hypocrite," he snarled. "Tell them everything—everything!—you piece of work. I'm waiting for some affidavits to arrive from Venezuela . . . then you'll see. You are a wicked, ruined piece of trash. That's what you are! Now—go! I don't want to see you."

Her superiors interrogated her about the details of the post office box—for hours on end, repeating the same question over and over. After each interrogation, Tapia would return to her room to find they had been through her things in search of any incriminating evidence. Before the end of the month, she was asked to leave—and told what to write in her letter of resignation, explicitly stating that she had been happy in the Work but had been unable to fulfil her obligations and as a result wanted to be dispensed from them.

Before she was released, Escrivá gave a piece of advice.

"Don't you dare talk about the Work—or about Rome—with anyone," he screamed. "Don't make us upset with your parents, because if I find out that you have been saying anything negative about the Work, I—José María Escrivá de Balaguer, who have the world's press in my hands—I will publicly disgrace you. Your name will be on the front pages of all the papers, because I will personally make sure of it—bringing you disgrace before men and before your own family!"

Escrivá's own growing sense of self-importance was fueled—at least in part—by the rapid growth of Opus Dei. By 1965, the movement had expanded to thirty-one countries—and extended well beyond its footholds in Europe and the Americas to countries that included Kenya, Nigeria, Japan, the Philippines, and Australia. Much of this expansion was fed by the Work's burgeoning business empire. During the first half of the sixties, Escrivá officially spent almost three million dollars on expansion overseas, equivalent to more than $30 million today—although in reality the figures were likely much higher. The United States was a particular focus. Such were the flows of cash into the United States that, by the mid-sixties, they were beginning to provoke unease among the Catholic establishment there.

In 1964, the Archbishop of Boston wrote a letter to Opus Dei's top man in the city, seeking answers about some big real estate purchases. Richard Cushing was a popular, no-nonsense priest born to Irish immigrants, with slicked-back silver hair and a prominent hooked nose. He had become a poster child for Pope John XXIII's modern, more compassionate Catholic Church. Cushing had initially wanted to be a politician before going into the priesthood and he prided himself on knowing the way to his parishioners' hearts—and to their wallets. On one occasion, he marched a visiting delegation of police officers into a tavern—mitre and all—and ordered a round of beer; on another, he visited a local orphanage to announce his gift of vast quantities of ice cream to Boston kids, jokingly telling one girl, "If you ever marry a millionaire, introduce him to me." His fundraising had borne fruit across the archdiocese and helped swell church attendance to record numbers. Officials boasted that Cushing was responsible for at least $250 million worth of construction, including 120 schools, 86 new churches, and 4 hospitals across the Boston area. He was also close to the Kennedys—he had presided over the marriage of Jack and Jackie and had baptized Bobby's son Chris. Millions of Americans had watched him deliver a prayer at the 1961 presidential inauguration; less than three years later, he led the nation in grief as the priest chosen to oversee the funeral of the murdered young president.

The cardinal didn't take well to any attempts to muscle in on his turf. So, when Opus Dei bought a one-acre lot four blocks from Harvard Yard for $200,000 in cash and announced to the *Boston Globe* that it had been given permission to build a residence for two hundred students there—big enough to accommodate one in ten Harvard students—Cushing was taken aback. "I don't know anything about your work in Boston and the only time I ever hear from your Community is when the male or the female branch of this Society wants to expand," he wrote. "In my opinion, there is too much tax-exempt property in Boston and in adjacent areas." Cushing certainly had a point. The purchase of the plot close to Harvard Yard was just the latest in a string of large property purchases made by the group in just a few years. Opus Dei owned two six-story redbrick houses in the wealthy Back Bay area of the city, which it ran as student residences and where several men were said to live like monks, as well as a large clapboard house on Follen Street in Cambridge that it had paid for in cash a couple of years earlier. It also ran a separate residence for women close to the university and owned a ski chalet in Vermont, where it hosted weekend retreats for young men and boys.

How a tight-knit group of Spanish priests and students had built up this empire so fast was a mystery to the archbishop, who declared himself "mighty upset." Cushing clearly suspected Opus Dei of hiding information and its true intentions from the archdiocese. He demanded the group immediately halt any plans for expansion and instead submit a report detailing all the properties it owned and any money it had raised.

The Work's property holdings in Boston were just the tip of Opus Dei's rapidly growing property empire in the United States. It was an iceberg that stretched deep into the Midwest and beyond, owned through a series of companies set up in places like Maryland, where rules on corporate transparency were notoriously lax. The numeraries leading the push seemed to have access to an almost endless stream of cash. Careful observers would spot a number of red flags. For instance, Manolo Barturen, who ran a numerary residence in New York, often crossed the Atlantic by air. What was he bringing back from Spain in his suitcase? The Federal Bureau of Investigation had also been tipped off about possible links between Opus Dei and corrupt export deals involving salad oil from Europe. Anthony "Tino" De Angelis, a former New Jersey butcher who had become one of the biggest players in global commodities trading, had been arrested the previous year for his role in the so-called salad oil scandal, in which he tricked banks into lending him millions of dollars by filling storage tanks, supposedly containing soya oil earmarked for export to Europe, with water instead. Tino blamed the whole thing on Opus Dei, which he said had worked with his enemies to steal his multi-million-dollar salad oil contracts in Spain and had even sent one of its members to his hotel room in Madrid to threaten him to back off.

This world of unexplained property purchases and scandal was a million miles from how Opus Dei had started out in the United States, and reflected the slow erosion of the movement's morality and purpose as it grew in size. José Luis Múzquiz and Salvador Ferigle had been sent there by the founder in February 1949, a priest and a graduate student who shared just a few dollars and a burning desire to spread the Work of God to new pastures. After landing in New York, they took a train to Chicago to join up with another Opus Dei member who was working in a laboratory, where Múzquiz—or Father Joseph, as he preferred to introduce himself to the locals—established the Work's first American outpost. By June, he had purchased a fifteen-room house at 5544 South Woodlawn Avenue, a few blocks from the university. The property was registered to a company called Work of God, Inc., which Father Joseph had set up. His spiel about Escrivá's divine vision and the good work that Opus Dei was already doing in Spain resonated with the locals. Some ladies in the neighborhood started fundraising for the new venture, while others donated furniture to the residence.

By the end of their first academic year in Chicago, the Opus Dei pioneers had their first American recruit—Dick Rieman, a naval artillery officer in World War II who was studying for a degree in sociology. His cousin Pat also joined not long after. By Christmas, another five men asked to be admitted— one was a resident at the Opus Dei house who was pursuing a music doctorate, the other a freshman at the university, and the remaining three were high school students who had worked with Rieman during the summer. It didn't take long for letters to arrive from Escrivá asking Father Joseph to send money. "We are making progress on furniture and decorations, but I've had little success in raising cash," Muzquiz wrote back. "I have a few leads. I've been following a number of them for several months without much result, but *in verbo autem tuo laxabo rete*"—at your word I will lower the net.

By 1953, Opus Dei had expanded to Boston, where it once again tapped into the generosity of the local Catholic population. With the help of Louise Day Hicks, the daughter of a wealthy judge who would later go on to make a name for herself in politics as a staunch opponent of racial desegregation, the Work of God, Inc., closed on another property—a former boarding-house on Marlborough Street that it would convert into a student residence for young men attending Harvard and MIT. Escrivá sent another priest to oversee spiritual formation at the new residence—Guillermo Porras, the American-born son of Mexican immigrants who was one of the first native English speakers in Opus Dei, and who preferred to go by the name Father Bill. His arrival freed up more time for Father Joseph, who was working on a translation of *The Way* into English. While overseeing the renovation of the new residence, Porras began to cultivate a relationship with the local archbishop. Cushing took a liking to Porras and asked whether he might be interested in taking over the Harvard Catholic Club. Its previous chaplain had been excommunicated from the Church after making a speech about the incompatibility of Catholicism with American culture, and for inciting the club's members to leave their studies. Cushing, who had been invited to Spain by Opus Dei some years earlier and had seen first-hand its great work there, viewed Porras as a safe pair of hands for the Harvard Catholic Club after all the scandal of the so-called Boston Heresy Case.

By the early sixties, the platform given it at Harvard—as well as the hard work of members who had set up student residences in Madison,

Washington, St. Louis, Milwaukee, and elsewhere—had begun to bear fruit. After a dozen years in the States, Opus Dei had recruited about four hundred Americans. The United States had become one of its biggest strongholds outside Spain. But its relationship with the Catholic Church there had begun to sour—especially in Boston, where complaints were streaming into the archbishop's residence on Commonwealth Avenue. Cushing had already had a run-in with Porras over the admission of women into the Harvard Catholic Club after the university's decision to let women study the same degrees as men. Porras was against it. "It is my experience that in a mixed group, even though the women might be fewer in number, they seem to be able to do more work than the men and they eventually take over," he explained, failing to mention Opus Dei's strict separation of the sexes. Porras quit before the merger was pushed though.

But the conflict between Opus Dei and the archbishop was just beginning. Soon, the new chaplain at the Harvard Catholic Club had to ask another two Opus Dei priests, who had been brought onto the books by Porras, to leave. "I possess several documents and have many facts which I can substantiate that indicate to me and to many others that the tactics and methods of Opus Dei are questionable, equivocal, and at times underhanded and deceitful," he warned the archbishop. But Cushing's demand that Opus Dei halt all activities fell on deaf ears. If anything, its activity picked up in the years that followed. Amid its frosty relations with the Vatican, Escrivá was increasingly becoming a law unto himself, willing to ignore direct orders of the Church in his quest for self-aggrandizement. The archbishop had given the group a platform to recruit from the top echelons of American students—and nothing was going to stop them taking full advantage of that position. Just weeks later, Opus Dei bought a private school sitting on more than eighty acres of land in Pembroke, Massachusetts, about forty-five minutes south of Boston, intending to transform it into a boarding school for rich girls.

Opus Dei also pushed ahead with its expansion in Boston. In December 1964, it made its biggest purchase yet—a five-story Tiffany mansion on Commonwealth Avenue, replete with tall fireplaces, vaulted ceilings, and a spiral staircase under a glittering arch of mosaic tiles. The property, together with two adjacent houses, set Opus Dei back $400,000. The complex would soon be renamed as the Bayridge Residence, where female numeraries would live alongside paying students. The acquisition was just one in a string of lavish property purchases around the world that year. Opus Dei also bought a seventeenth-century château outside Paris, a manor in the East Sussex countryside near London, a huge estate in Ireland, and a French Renaissance-style mansion on the banks of the St. Lawrence River outside Montreal, in Canada. The movement was also in the middle of setting up a sixth-form college in Kenya and a university in Peru.

Escrivá sought to use the rapid expansion of Opus Dei as a way to convince the Vatican to take him—and his movement—more seriously, and to persuade them that the time had come to finally give this secular institute a more befitting canonical status. Such overtures fell on deaf ears, though. Less than a month after the conclusion of the Second Vatican Council, and with Tapia still imprisoned at Villa Tevere, Escrivá had an audience with Pope Paul VI, where he pled his case for granting Opus Dei some higher status within the Church. That plea was rebuffed. Escrivá had another audience with the pope the following year, with the same disappointing result. It would be his last meeting with the pope for six years. Desperate for recognition, at times his lobbying became frantic. During the late sixties, Escrivá begged ten times for an audience with the pope—but was turned down every time.

It dawned on Escrivá that Rome might be unwilling to show him the respect and import he felt he deserved, and he began to ponder drastic measures: a complete rupture with the Catholic Church. In 1967, he sent Del Portillo to Greece to see whether he might bring the movement into the Orthodox Church. The trip was ultimately unsuccessful, but Del Portillo's willingness to even countenance such a move shows that the movement had reached a point of no return—maintaining a cult of personality around Escrivá was now the defining motive of Opus Dei, even if that meant betraying the interests of the Catholic Church.

The gradual betrayal of the movement's professed ideals soon led to a number of senior departures—especially among the earliest of Escrivá's disciples who had joined Opus Dei as a symbol of change, of Christian renewal and virtue. Antonio Pérez-Tenessa, a priest who had held the positions of secretary general and head of the Spanish region, was the most senior departure. He had wanted to leave for years—something his superiors knew all too well, but they had made it almost impossible for him to go. He disappeared from his residence in the middle of the night, prompting Escrivá—who was perhaps worried about the compromising information that Pérez-Tenessa had about Opus Dei finances—to launch a manhunt to track him down. The "traitor" was finally located in Mexico, where the Opus Dei members who found him passed on an order from the founder that he keep quiet about his time in the movement. As he did with Tapia, Escrivá probably threatened to use his influence within the Franco regime and the Spanish business world to make his life a misery if he disobeyed. Other heavy hitters soon followed. Raimundo Panikkar, a priest who had recruited hundreds of young men at the Moncloa student residence, also quit. Those who left were often harassed—when Miguel Fisac, one of Escrivá's first disciples, lost his six-year-old daughter after a botched polio vaccine, he was visited by two Opus Dei priests who told him that her death was God's punishment for leaving the Work.

Such instances betrayed a mood of discontentment in Opus Dei residences across Spain, where a mass exodus was kept in check only by assurances from local directors about the purity of Escrivá's message—and the occasional use of prescription drugs to pacify dissenters. Many were unable to contemplate escape because of how dependent they were professionally and emotionally on the movement. The reality of Opus Dei was a world apart from the principles Escrivá espoused in public. The founder's incessant demands, and his obsession with money and expansion, had transformed what was once a devout group of people unified by prayer and mortification into a Wild West of lawlessness, where members actively competed for resources and fought against each other in order to meet his capricious demands. As news of the spiritual crisis within Opus Dei began to seep through to the mainstream, a frustrated Escrivá decided the time had come to reset the narrative. He granted a series of interviews to some big, international publications, including the *New York Times*, *Le Figaro*, and *Time* magazine. The "interviews" were in fact entirely stage-managed; Escrivá refused to be interviewed in person. Instead, Opus Dei members drafted answers to written questions, and sent those answers to him for approval. Another reason for stage-managing the interviews was Escrivá's declining health: the founder was once again being treated for his diabetes, which had supposedly been miraculously cured years earlier.

The timing of the interviews was not coincidental. By the late 1960s, recruitment was starting to peter out—especially on university campuses, where student protest movements were mobilizing against traditional attitudes about gender, race, capitalism, government, and religion. Even in the stuffy confines of dictatorial Spain, senior members within Opus Dei openly talked about a growing crisis. In his interview with the *New York Times*, Escrivá pointed to initiatives his movement had begun to attract among a new generation—those targeting children and teenagers. The founder pointed to a new school called The Heights in Washington, D.C., as well as a new sports and cultural club in Chicago's Near West Side. These initiatives were part of a huge school-building program in Spain and Latin America that had begun a few years earlier and was now being rolled out in the United States and beyond. With recruitment becoming more difficult among adults, this was the start of a new strategy to recruit children.

But any efforts to clean up Opus Dei's image would soon be shattered by an enormous scandal in Spain. In July 1969, a businessman close to Opus Dei was detained at the airport in Barcelona. Juan Vila Reyes owned a textile company called Matesa that held the patent for a supposedly groundbreaking loom, and he had secured huge sums of public money to finance the production of machines for export—aided in part by his Opus Dei friends in government. Luis Valls-Taberner, perhaps knowing something that others didn't, had kept his distance from the affair. While other Spanish banks piled on to finance Matesa, Popular had held back. It all suddenly came to a head that summer, when a consignment of looms, supposedly destined for New York, was found abandoned at the docks in Barcelona. The Ministry of Finance soon opened an investigation and uncovered that $200 million of public money—about $1.5 billion today—had been embezzled in an immense fraud involving fake invoices and shell companies spread across the world—in Switzerland, the United States, and Latin America. The loans were purportedly to finance the manufacture of hundreds of looms to meet orders that had flooded in from around the globe, but the money had instead made its way to various Opus Dei initiatives including the University of Navarre, its business school in Barcelona—and countless other projects, including Richard Nixon's election campaign.

The Falange, sensing an opportunity to land its great rival, leaked the news to the press, a move which backfired badly. The Caudillo was furious that this scandal at the heart of the regime was being splashed across the front pages—in Spain and abroad. "What have you got against Opus Dei?" fumed Franco when the Falangists complained about the behavior of their colleagues in government who were members of the movement. "Because while they work you just fuck about." According to the Caudillo's warped moral compass, a little graft here and there was immaterial. But the red line that absolutely could not be crossed was bringing the regime into disrepute. The Falangist leaks to the press had broken that vital rule. Unbeknownst to the Falangists, Opus Dei had also been lobbying the Caudillo, who was being heavily medicated at the time for his worsening Parkinson's disease, and putting their own spin on the scandal. They sought to portray the Falangist leaks to the press as a scandalous politicization of a private matter that was made possible only because of changes in the press law that had been pushed by the Falangist propaganda minister Manuel Fraga.

The ailing Caudillo sided with Opus Dei. He announced that he would be dismissing the Falangists from their posts immediately. The size of the Opus Dei victory that night became apparent only when the evening news broadcast was interrupted for a special announcement from the El Pardo palace. The Caudillo had formed a new government: of the nineteen ministers announced to the nation that evening, ten were allied with Opus Dei. Franco would later admit that he had been taken advantage of. It was a crucial moment for the movement to snatch the reins of power. Just days later, one of the founders of the Falange walked into the Santa Barbara church in the center of Madrid. He took confession and then calmly walked back out to the street, took out his gun, and shot himself in the head. A note was found on his body that condemned Opus Dei. The Work's political rise was complete.

By 1969, the movement's position in Spain was secure, but it was under increasing threat at the Vatican, where a special commission was being set up to investigate a raft of criticism against Opus Dei. Accusations had been swirling around the Vatican for some time that the movement had begun to openly challenge the pope's authority. The new commission would bring Opus Dei back into line by settling the question of its status within the Church hierarchy once and for all, and by unilaterally rewriting the movement's constitution. To his horror, Escrivá discovered that three of the five of the cardinals being proposed to oversee the commission were openly hostile to the movement.

Scrambling to head off the challenge, Escrivá pulled a shrewd political move, asking the Holy See for permission to convene an extraordinary general congress of members—as per its constitution as a secular institute—during which they would revise its rules and practices in accordance with the Second Vatican Council. On the face of it, the move was a public demonstration of fidelity to the pope, a recognition that Opus Dei needed to be reformed and that the movement was willing to push through those reforms itself. But in private, it was a different story. Among his followers, he shared his despair at the changes ushered in by Pope Paul VI, which had updated the liturgy, given a larger role to the laity, and allowed priests to perform worship in languages other than Latin for the first time. Escrivá banned Opus Dei priests from implementing many of the changes, a significant riposte to pontifical authority. When the extraordinary general congress convened in September 1969, Escrivá made it clear the numeraries and priests assembled were there not to update Opus Dei for the modern age but to reaffirm its original spirit—by rewriting the parts of its constitution that it had been forced to compromise on in order to win its approval as a secular institute. The congress concluded by tasking its members to come up with amendments at another congress a year later—a move which would buy it more time.

His ego swelled by the multitude of members who had come to Rome for the meeting, Escrivá was unable to contain his indignation when he wrote to the pope to update him on the meeting's outcome. In it, he openly criticized the idea of a special commission looking into Opus Dei—branding it as secretive, accusing its members of being partisan and of actively seeking to undermine the internal process of reform that was now underway. The Vatican's Secretary of State wrote back, admonishing Escrivá for the tone he had dared to use with the pope and forcing the founder into a groveling apology.

The pope accepted the founder's act of contrition. Within a few weeks of the apology, Villa Tevere received news that the special commission had been dropped. But Opus Dei would find itself in trouble with the Church again in 1971, amid accusations that one senior member had been using his position at the Vatican to spy on the Holy See and communicate his observations back to his superiors at Villa Tevere. Escrivá was asked to give "explicit assurance" that its members were not expected to reveal anything learned in their service to the Church or the Holy See in general. Despite knowing that Opus Dei's own internal rules explicitly required members to share everything about their personal and professional lives—and for that information to be methodically recorded and passed up the chain—the founder wrote back stating that members would never be asked to betray "professional secrets."

A few months later, in June 1973, Escrivá was granted his first audience with the pope in almost six years. The meeting was brief and tense.

"Why don't you come to see me more often?" asked Pope Paul VI, provokingly.

An uncomfortable silence ensued. Escrivá broke it by describing how Opus Dei had used the past few years to expand its presence to five continents.

The Pontiff interrupted: "Oh, you are a saint," he said.

"No, no, your Holiness doesn't know me well—I am just a poor sinner."

"No, no," responded the pope. "You are a saint."

The pope's cold shoulder contrasted sharply with the feverish adulation that met Escrivá elsewhere—thanks in part to a series of highly choreographed "apostolic trips" that Villa Tevere arranged for the founder across Latin America. Footage of his public appearances—usually heavily edited—would later be played over and over again at the hundreds of numerary residences around the world, as a way of enhancing the cult of personality that already surrounded him. This was Escrivá for posterity: friendly, charismatic, and loyal to the Church. Occasionally during the trip, a former member or worried relative of a current member would openly challenge him—but such altercations would be edited out. The same was true of any instances where Escrivá would let slip his public, benevolent mask. During one appearance in Chile, Escrivá launched into a diatribe about the sexual obsessions of young people. "There are others, who in their youth, seem to do nothing but have sex—what wretches!" he told one audience. "If a rooster or a bull were capable of thinking, it would think like they do. How noble, correct?! Then they form a disgusting family, and the rotten children come—poor creatures, who are victims of the incontinence of their parents." In private, he also sent out missives to the membership bemoaning the state of the Church—fueled by his anger and frustration over the pope's refusal to grant him the recognition that he craved.

His ego was appeased somewhat by the construction of an enormous shrine in the Pyrenean foothills—supposedly dedicated to the Virgin who had saved his life when he was a toddler, but really a monument to Escrivá himself and the movement he had built. Plans for the site were ambitious: a whole mountain had been leveled to house the planned complex of buildings, which would include an immense basilica, four smaller chapels, two conference halls, a research center, museum, soaring bell tower, and vast courtyard. Escrivá stipulated that there should be forty confessional boxes—as many as Lourdes—for the vast numbers of pilgrims he predicted would visit the site each year. In May 1975, he visited the site by helicopter. "It is marvelous," he declared. "What sighs the old ladies will let out here! And the young people! What sighs! Good! Only we Opus Dei crazies can do this, and we are very happy to be crazy."

Escrivá would never see the completion of the shrine at Torreciudad. Just before midnight on June 26, 1975, the founder collapsed in his rooms at Villa Tevere. Unwilling to believe that he had died, his followers tried for ninety minutes to resuscitate him, giving him oxygen and various injections, and trying to restart his heart. Del Portillo knelt by his side praying repeatedly for the absolution of his soul. A call was put through ordering that the numerary servants in the adjoining building be woken up and sent straight to the chapel, where they were to pray for an urgent intervention from heaven. Their prayers went unanswered.

As if the founder's death weren't enough, another calamity awaited Opus Dei. The movement was about to lose its benefactor—General Franco. On October 1, the Caudillo appeared before a huge crowd at the Palacio de Oriente in Central Madrid—against the advice of his doctors. Hunched over on the balcony, he spoke in a weak, croaking voice, and he wept as he waved and turned to go inside. It was his last public appearance. Exposure to the stabbing autumn winds set off a series of medical crises over the coming weeks: first a runny nose, then other flu symptoms. News of a Moroccan attack on the Spanish-held Western Sahara prompted a heart attack, followed two days later by another attack. Three days after that, he was diagnosed with internal bleeding, and he died soon after. In less than five months, Opus Dei had lost the two figures who had made possible its phenomenal spread across the world. Cast adrift, with the Vatican openly hostile to the movement, it faced an uncertain future.

6

HABEMUS PAPAM

Rome, Italy—August 1978

ON A STIFLING SUMMER EVENING, A SILVER-HAIRED PRIEST WITH BROAD shoulders and a slight hunch walked up to the unmarked door on Viale Bruno Buozzi and disappeared inside. Karol Józef Wojtyła had been in Rome for a couple of days, having been summoned by the Vatican to attend the funeral of Pope Paul VI—and to participate in the conclave to elect his successor. That evening, in a welcome break from the seemingly endless "congregations" to discuss the merits of potential candidates, the Archbishop of Krakow had been invited to a quiet dinner with an old friend. Wojtyła had known Álvaro del Portillo since the days of the Second Vatican Council and had immediately warmed to a fellow conservative who shared his own anxiety over the slow, progressive drift of the Church. The two soon developed a friendly and mutually beneficial relationship, with Wojtyła speaking at conferences hosted by Opus Dei, which repaid him by publishing his speeches as books and circulating them among the Vatican hierarchy. That night, the two priests exchanged views on the challenges facing the Church—and those facing Del Portillo as the new leader of Opus Dei. Afterwards, they went down into the crypt to visit the tomb of the founder, marked with a simple stone engraved with the words "THE FATHER." Escrivá had actually asked for a different inscription—he had wanted his tomb to be marked with the word "Sinner" alongside an entreaty for visitors to "pray for him," but a decision had been made that such a description would be unbefitting for the beloved founder of Opus Dei. That evening, Wojtyła and Del Portillo knelt in silence before his tomb and prayed for his soul—and for the Church.

Given the divisions within the Church, the conclave to elect the successor to Paul VI was surprisingly straightforward. Such a strong consensus had already formed around the candidacy of Cardinal Albino Luciani of Venice, a popular bishop known for his simple tastes and dislike of the Venetian elite, before the election that the 111-member conclave reached the threshold of two-thirds plus one vote on the first day. Vatican officials rushed to release white smoke from the chimney of the Sistine Chapel for the waiting crowds outside. They tried. And tried again. And again. And again. Four different signals, each of indeterminate color, appeared over the course of just half an hour, spreading confusion to the thousands of faithful assembled in Saint Peter's Square. Finally, they announced the news over loudspeaker. The omens were not good—and soon got very much worse. On the morning of September 29, just thirty-three days into his papacy, John Paul I was found dead in his bed.

Once again, Wojtyła trekked back to Rome—this time to a Church deep in crisis. The conclave was a world apart from the one just a few weeks earlier, as the cardinals struggled to understand what God was trying to tell them—first with the mixed smoke signals and then the pope's sudden demise. Seven ballots were held, but the conclave remained in deadlock. Unable to choose between the two leading candidates, the cardinals eventually settled on Wojtyła as a compromise. The Archbishop of Krakow had barely attracted any votes at the conclave just seven weeks earlier—and was considered such an outsider in the run-up to this one that the Vatican hadn't even included his name in a list of thirty-six possible successors put out to the press. While the politics of the new pope remained a mystery to many— Wojtyła's speeches had over the years been hailed by progressives and conservatives in equal measure—this robust priest from behind the Iron Curtain who enjoyed skiing and wrote poetry seemed like the perfect antidote after the deaths of two elderly popes in as many months.

This fortuitous turn of events was also the perfect antidote for Del

Portillo, who had been cultivating his relationship with Wojtyła for years through an Opus Dei organization known as the Centro Romano di Incontri Sacerdotali—the Roman Center for Priestly Encounters. Like other anodyne-sounding Opus Dei initiatives, the association had more sinister motives. "I was asked on to the team setting up CRIS, one of Opus Dei's most successful projects—ever," recalled Vladimir Felzmann, a numerary priest. "Overtly, it was there to support students and lost souls in Rome: a spiritual and emotional anchor in a city swirling with *La Dolce Vita*. In fact, it was a honey trap: a platform to attract 'the great and the good' when they were in Rome, so they could get to know Opus Dei. It worked very effectively with Archbishop—then Cardinal—Karol Józef Wojtyła." The timing of Wojtyła's election as pope was a godsend to Del Portillo, whose tenure as general president of Opus Dei was already beginning to stall just three years into the job. While Franco was now dead, the movement had found it difficult to shake off its reputation for scandal and fascist sympathies. During his first few months in charge, news broke that Opus Dei had worked alongside a paramilitary group in Chile to overthrow the country's democratically elected government—using money from conservative foundations based in the United States. A scandal had also broken out in Spain, where an Opus Dei priest had publicly confessed to conspiring to defame a former numerary who had written an embarrassing exposé about his time in the movement. Quiet, erudite, and intellectual, the election of this sixty-one-year-old priest as the group's new figurehead in November 1975, just months after the passing of "Our Father in Heaven," as Escrivá was now called, marked a dramatic shift in tone. Gone were the founder's bombastic, tyrannical, ego-fueled outbursts, which cowed the membership into submission. By contrast, Del Portillo sought to lead through careful consideration and consensus among the movement's elders. In a mark of this change in style—and in a bid, perhaps, to roll back Escrivá's excesses—Del Portillo ordered the removal of the sprawling network of listening devices that had been installed around Villa Tevere, which had allowed Escrivá to secretly monitor his followers' private conversations. His death was an opportunity for the movement to return to its founding philosophy—supposedly handed down from God—of sanctifying every act in life.

But Del Portillo was torn. While the new general president had personally witnessed many of the founder's failings, having lived alongside him since 1946 and been his personal confessor for almost thirty years, his reverence for the man had remained steadfast. He owed so much to Escrivá—*he* had been the one who had helped him see his religious calling before the war, *he* had selected the young engineer to become one of the first Opus Dei priests in the 1940s, *he* had asked him to come and live in Rome, *he* had been the one who had specifically named Del Portillo as his successor. As general president of Opus Dei, it was his duty to protect the spirit of the movement—precisely as it had been written down by the founder, who himself had been given inspiration directly from God. "We have been bequeathed a gift, which is the spirit of the Work," he declared to the male numeraries who elected him, in his first speech as head of the movement. "We have to pass on that gift intact to those that come after us, without distorting it, without changing it, without diminishing it, without adding to it—precisely as it is!" Given the hundreds of pages of meticulously detailed "instructions" penned by the founder, this early pledge would place Del Portillo in a bind. While his instincts told him that Escrivá's controlling tendencies had spiraled out of control—as demonstrated by his decision to remove the listening devices from Villa Tevere—challenging the written word of the founder risked undermining his commitment to preserving the gift bequeathed to them "precisely as it is." Ultimately, his natural meekness would leave him unable to address this contradiction at the heart of the movement.

As part of this pledge to preserve the "gift" of Opus Dei for future generations, Del Portillo dedicated himself to fulfilling Escrivá's dying wish: that the movement he founded be accorded a more befitting status within the Church. In March 1976, four months into his new job, Del Portillo secured an audience with Pope Paul VI. During the meeting, he reiterated Escrivá's argument that the classification of Opus Dei as a secular institute was no longer appropriate—words that the pope had heard countless times before. Diplomatically but vaguely, Paul VI acknowledged that—twenty years into the movement's lobbying efforts—"the matter continues to be open." It was more than two years until Del Portillo's next papal audience. This time, he was told to prepare the proper documentation—a response Opus Dei sought to present as clear progress, but which could just as easily be seen as an attempt to delay the matter indefinitely. As it happened, nobody would ever know what the pope's real intentions were, because he would die of a massive heart attack a few weeks later. Del Portillo spoke with John Paul I during his short reign, who agreed to consider the matter—before his own passing. But the election of John Paul II changed everything. Less than two weeks after being elected, Wojtyła welcomed Del Portillo to the pontifical palace. "This isn't an audience, it's a family meeting," he warmly told his old friend. A few days later, he wrote a letter of congratulations to Opus Dei on its fiftieth anniversary. The Cardinal Secretary of State, handing it over, made it clear that the new pope wished to quickly resolve the question of Opus Dei's status.

Del Portillo wasn't the only one looking to curtail some of the movement's abuses and excesses. By the late seventies, Luis Valls-Taberner had effectively moved out of the numerary residence and had begun to build a new life for himself in the mountains outside Madrid. He spent most of his week at a country house owned by Banco Popular in San Rafael, about an hour's drive north of the capital, which in years past had been used by the bank's employees as a vacation spot—with a swimming pool, soccer field, and walking routes. Luis had closed down the facility on cost grounds and commandeered use of the house for himself. He grew to love the autonomy it afforded him: after thirty years of life in the confines of the residence, his newfound freedom was like a breath of fresh air. It wasn't the only extravagance he afforded himself. After being promoted to the chairmanship of the bank, he commissioned an opulent new headquarters. The Beatriz Building, as it was known, was a modernist concrete hulk that occupied an entire block in the heart of the city. Luis had named it after Beatriz Galindo, a Renaissance writer who shared his love of books—and of God. Beatriz had been a nun before giving up her vows to marry a handsome captain but was renowned for her unusual custom of donning her old nun's habit for walks around the city. Luis also led a weird double existence: while the Opus Dei numerary—at least on paper—remained committed to his vows of poverty, celibacy, and obedience, the construction of the Beatriz Building had allowed him to indulge a few of his vices. The entire top floor had been converted into a luxury penthouse for his sole use, complete with a rooftop tennis court and swimming pool.

While he now spent most of his time away from the residence, Luis remained committed to the ideals of Opus Dei. Having transformed the movement's prospects over the previous twenty years, he now turned to the challenge of maintaining the power and influence that a core group of members had accumulated during the dictatorship. With Franco now dead, and the country transitioning to democracy, the old system of reward and patronage that Opus Dei had turned to its own advantage was slowly unraveling. Adolfo Suárez—a former television executive and supernumerary member of Opus Dei—was elected prime minister. But Spain's future remained an open question. In years past, Luis had relished his position in the shadows. "The press has always been very kind to me, especially with its silences," he said. But he soon shifted his view, concluding that, with the country transitioning to a different political structure, his best chance of maintaining power was by *projecting* power. He began to write articles for various national newspapers—about government, the monarchy, and economic policy. He also gave television interviews clearly aimed at carefully crafting a reputation for himself as the *éminence grise* of the emerging political elite. "I've never had the power to *name* ministers," he playfully explained in one interview for national television, before cryptically adding: "It's been at least a year since anyone has asked me for a minister." As news reached him about the election of a new pope, Luis was engaged in plans to host Spain's political elite at a grand Council of Europe summit at the bank's headquarters.

When he was away from the cameras, there were other changes, too. By the late seventies, serious work was underway to legitimize the huge flows of money between the bank and Opus Dei. With the forces of democracy slowly being unleashed, the movement could no longer depend on its contacts within the regime to cover up its scandals, as had happened with Matesa. The Banco Popular chairman had already begun cleaning up these flows in the last days of the Franco regime by establishing a nonprofit organization called the Hispanic Foundation that received 5 percent of the bank's profits every year. By the late 1970s, the Hispanic Foundation boasted more than two billion pesetas, equivalent to $150 million today. The bank's employees and shareholders were vaguely told that these sums were going to "good causes"—although most of the money went toward Opus Dei's expansion. Millions of dollars were spent on a huge school-building program all across Spain, as well as funding a holiday camp for children run by Opus Dei priests and numeraries. Flows from the Hispanic Foundation reflected a growing shift in the movement's recruitment strategy—away from targeting university students, and toward targeting teenagers and children instead.

The Opus Dei network would eventually stretch to three hundred schools around the globe. Like every other aspect of life within Opus Dei, Escrivá was keen to maintain complete control over what went on inside the schools, which sometimes made for unusual arrangements. Numeraries—rather than qualified teachers—were chosen to instruct the children. In Spain alone, by the late seventies, there were eight hundred numeraries teaching children in Opus Dei schools. In the United States, where the movement opened its first school in 1969, in the Friendship Heights neighborhood of Washington, D.C., it even tried to make a virtue out of this highly unconventional arrangement. The Heights, as it was known, billed itself as "unique" and "experimental" because classes were taught by "experts" rather than normal teachers—glossing over the fact that they were numerary members of Opus Dei. By 1978, the movement's secondary-education scheme was expanding, with schools in Chicago and Boston. Such was its success in Washington that it bought larger premises in Potomac, Maryland, and began drawing up plans to almost double the size of The Heights. The movement had evidently hit on an effective model for generating new recruits and profits.

The shift to schools and away from university residences was also a reaction to the growing resistance that Opus Dei was beginning to experience with young adults, who increasingly questioned the recruitment methods being used on them—and the control that the movement exerted over their lives. In Australia, where Opus Dei had opened its largest student residence yet—a dorm for two hundred affiliated with the University of New South Wales, in Sydney—the slow failure of the once-reliable model underpinning the family business had become all too apparent. Warrane College had been controversial from the moment it opened its doors in 1970, not least because of its arcane rules that prohibited its male residents from taking women to their rooms, even to do college work. The residence struggled to fill its dorm from day one, with only three-quarters of rooms rented out. Within the first year of operation, the reputation of Warrane took one hit after another. Word got out that the master of the college, a member of Opus Dei, roamed the halls and burst into the rooms of students, who were forbidden from locking their doors, to wake them up because they had overslept. One student social was canceled when Opus Dei discovered that adult men and women might dance together. Residents also raised concerns that intimate details shared in confidence in pastoral discussions were being methodically recorded by the college and then used to emotionally blackmail residents. "Opus Dei is a very deadly form of cancer and it is the duty of every thinking Christian student in the college to eradicate it by any means possible," one resident warned in an open letter.

When six thousand copies of the student newspaper *Tharunka*, whose cover story was a piece about sexual freedom, were stolen from the presses, attention naturally turned to Opus Dei. Over the next few weeks, amid a constant stream of new accusations against the movement, two thousand students called on university authorities to throw Opus Dei off campus. Six hundred students marched on the college, only to be pelted with objects, rubbish, and water bombs from people hidden inside. Several protesters managed to get in, prompting the police to be called. The "Siege of Warrane College," as it became known, made national news, and it dealt a severe blow to Opus Dei's reputation in Australia. While the college offered token concessions, the tensions persisted. Three years later, protests broke out again. Students mounted a mock Passion Play, during which a black coffin inscribed with the words "Opus Dei R.I.P.," and borne by four hooded pall bearers, was led in a procession to the college, where 1,500 students "exorcised" what they called the "Holy Mafia" with cries of "OPUS OUT NOW!"

To prevent residents from bringing women to their rooms, the Opus Dei members that ran the residence took drastic action, locking all the fire escapes of the eight-story, two-hundred-bed building. They explained that it was better for all the residents to burn in this life and be saved rather than for a few to burn in hell. Several days later, this glaring risk to student welfare was reported to university authorities, which said such actions were unacceptable and ordered that the fire escapes be unlocked. Opus Dei complied, but when the attention died down, the fire escapes were locked once again.

Naturally, all this negative publicity had a serious impact on recruitment. With bills needing to be paid, the numeraries that ran the residence were encouraged by their superiors to falsify the college's accounts to give the impression that everything was in order—both to their superiors back in Rome and also to the local banks, which continued to offer the college and other Opus Dei initiatives access to credit based on the college's sound profits. When one numerary shared with his spiritual director how the pressure to cook the books was preventing him from sleeping, he was encouraged to take sedatives prescribed by an Opus Dei doctor.

The movement had a similar experience in New York. Its first attempt to open a residence in the city in the early fifties drew few boarders and had to be closed down not long after opening. But in 1966, Opus Dei bought a large property located a block from Columbia University, intended to be its flagship student residence in the city. Schuyler Hall, as it was named, had wood-paneled rooms hung with Spanish paintings and two grand pianos. It took out ads in the *Columbia Daily Spectator*, describing itself as "a private residence hall for men who want something special" and boasting the "nearest thing to home-cooked meals in Morningside Heights." No mention was made of its affiliation to Opus Dei. Things did not go well for the venture. Soon, the campus was filled with stories of residents being pressured to follow Opus Dei practices, of their movements in and out of the building being logged—and even a ban on residents seeing their families for more than four consecutive days at a time. Then came reports about residents who had been beaten up for speaking to the press. At one stage, the residents of Schuyler Hall tried to stage a mutiny, even going so far as to set up their own, alternative governing body. University authorities removed information on Schuyler Hall from their packets for freshmen. After a collapse in numbers, Opus Dei eventually gave up and sold the building.

While Luis had legitimized some of the financial flows between Banco Popular and Opus Dei, parts of the network had yet to be cleaned up. Over the years, Luis had established a web of offshore companies registered in places like Panama and Liechtenstein to facilitate the transfer of large sums to Opus Dei to wherever in the world they might be needed. Transfers to these offshore companies were routed through a private bank in Switzerland called Banque d'Investissements Mobiliers et de Financement—also known as Imefbank—that Popular had bought into during the sixties. The acquisition had been dodgy right from the start. Officially, Popular had only bought a 40 percent stake in Imefbank—but had been allowed to transfer double the asking price, supposedly as a "guarantee" to the seller. The extra money was actually used to buy a secret additional 35 percent stake on behalf of a Panamanian company run by one of Opus Dei's top men in Switzerland. The whole operation, which was signed off by Mariano Navarro Rubio, governor of Spain's central bank and a supernumerary member of Opus Dei, was a scam designed to get large sums of money out of the country—in clear breach of Spain's strict currency controls—and park them offshore, where they could be controlled by the movement. Popular never mentioned this side deal to the Spanish government—or even to its own shareholders.

Imefbank soon became firmly established as a conduit that covertly moved money out of Spain, through Switzerland, into shell companies in Panama and Liechtenstein, and finally to Opus Dei numeraries stationed around the world. Tens of millions of dollars—equivalent to more than a hundred million dollars today—passed through this system. Some of the money, having been washed abroad, even made it back to Spain—including millions of dollars that coincided with the construction of the shrine at Torreciudad. Other shell companies that received money were run by senior members of Opus Dei in the United States and Mexico. When some numeraries in New York struggled to pay back the $6 million that had been lent to them, Imefbank was plunged into crisis. With the authorities starting to ask difficult questions about the Swiss bank's finances, Luis had to ask for outside help. He turned to José María Ruiz-Mateos, a Spanish entrepreneur and supernumerary, who agreed to wire millions of dollars to save the Swiss bank from collapse.

The bailout would mark a critical turning point in the relationship between the two men—and a shift in the way Opus Dei would use its numerary base to target wealthy Catholics for donations. While Luis had known Ruiz-Mateos since the late fifties, the two men had never been close. They had different personalities. Luis came across as cold and obtuse, whereas Ruiz-Mateos was warm and outgoing, with a big grin and an endearing Andalusian lisp. The businessman had risen from humble beginnings, transforming the family's small sherry business into a vast conglomerate that included banks, hotels, vineyards, a department store, the Loewe luxury brand, a dairy, and four insurance companies. By the late seventies, he was one of the wealthiest men in Europe—with plans for expansion into the

States, where he was in negotiations to buy the Sears chain of department stores. He was a workaholic who had few interests outside the office, other than his thirteen children and the Church. He went to Mass twice a day and was a devoted member of Opus Dei, which he credited with helping him get started in business, through the contacts he had made within the movement in the early sixties. He showed his gratitude with large regular donations. But he always felt looked down on by the Opus Dei elite and became obsessed with breaking into what he saw as the inner sanctum of the movement. Luis tapped into that insecurity. He began inviting the billionaire to his mountain retreat. Stoking Ruiz-Mateos's desire to be part of Opus Dei's inner sanctum, Luis played music during their meetings, telling his guest that it was to prevent anyone from listening in.

These cordial exchanges disguised a disdain that Luis secretly held toward the Andalusian. He still held a grudge about a business deal involving a German brewery that Ruiz-Mateos had reneged on in the sixties, leaving the bank with a huge headache. The Banco Popular chairman viewed the entrepreneur as uneducated and vulgar—an attitude shared by much of the top brass within Opus Dei. Animosity toward Ruiz-Mateos extended right to the top of the organization. On one trip to Madrid, Del Portillo expressed irritation at seeing bees—the symbol of Ruiz-Mateos's vast business empire—all over the city. "I see too many bees," he complained. "Seriously, why do we have to see this little bee everywhere?" But both Luis and Del Portillo were happy to take the businessman's money. The lunches in the mountains were all part of a lobbying effort being overseen by Luis—and various other numerary men also considered part of the "inner sanctum"—to convince Ruiz-Mateos to bankroll a new foundation called the Institute for Education and Investigation, which was being set up to finance various Opus Dei educational initiatives around the world. During their lunches, Luis encouraged the billionaire to make a contribution to this new initiative. Ruiz-Mateos made a donation of one and a half billion pesetas—equivalent to about $100 million today. But the conversations weren't entirely one-sided. Ruiz-Mateos had gotten into deep trouble with the authorities after failing to pay billions of pesetas in tax and the government was threatening to come after him. Luis indicated to Ruiz-Mateos that he might be able to help. As the country transitioned toward greater transparency and accountability, the

Opus Dei network was itself evolving—into a hidden back channel for political favors, where well-connected numeraries and supernumeraries were willing to help their fellow members in exchange for their support of the movement's initiatives. It was a blueprint for a new age, and one that Opus Dei could export to dozens of other countries.

In February 1979, just three months after the surprise election of Wojtyła, Opus Dei formally submitted its application to change its status. What that status might be was an open question. As an organization of priests and lay people, Opus Dei was something of an anomaly within the Church. But by the end of the seventies, a consensus had begun to form around the construct of "personal prelature" as the least bad option. The structure had been created by the Vatican in the sixties primarily as means for ordaining priests outside of the local diocese structure, freeing them of their geographical bonds to the local bishop or archbishop so that clergy could be easily distributed from one diocese with a surplus of priests to another where they were sorely needed. As just one of hundreds of changes approved at the Second Vatican Council, the wording had been rushed and clumsy—opening the door to an ambiguity that Opus Dei could work to its own advantage. Although thirteen years had passed since the proposals had come into force through a papal decree, the sheer number of reforms passed at the Council had created something of a legal backlog, meaning that the relevant canon law governing these personal prelatures hadn't yet been written. The structure held great appeal for Opus Dei, critically bestowing it with the authority to ordain priests into the movement. While the proposals were clearly written for priests, they also mentioned lay people—who could "dedicate themselves with their professional skill" to projects linked to the personal prelature. Even more important, given that the law concerning personal prelatures was yet to be established, Opus Dei had a chance to write—or at least influence—its own rulebook.

A few weeks later, the pope wrote to the Congregation for Bishops, which had jurisdiction over the matter, stating that he expected them to study the application closely. It wasn't the last time that Wojtyła would intervene in the process to ensure that Opus Dei got what it wanted. The Congregation for Bishops did not view the application favorably, however. At the end of

June, it held a meeting, at which the cardinals and bishops present almost unanimously threw out the application, stating that there were no grounds for transforming Opus Dei into a personal prelature. The application would eventually be approved, thanks to the personal intervention of the pope, who overruled widespread objections across the entire Church. His reasons for doing so extended much further than simply doing a favor for his old friends. Opus Dei convinced Wojtyła that an elevation in status would create a new mobile battalion of priests and laymen at his personal disposal. For Wojtyła, a man just months into the job and still figuring out the Vatican's power dynamics, having his own, independent mobile corps of likeminded conservatives was an appealing prospect. Opus Dei was also keen to emphasize its ability to influence public opinion. Contradicting its own official line about the autonomy that members enjoyed in their professional lives, in private correspondence with the Vatican it boasted about its infiltration of higher education and the media, detailing that it had operatives working at almost seven hundred newspapers and magazines, five hundred educational facilities, fifty radio stations, and a dozen film distributors. Opus Dei appeared to be so keen to secure its new status that it massively overstated its membership, telling the Vatican that it had more than seventy-two thousand members in eighty-seven different countries, when the actual membership was much smaller according to the movement's own records—probably fewer than sixty thousand.

With the backing of the pope, Villa Tevere launched a huge lobbying effort to convince influential bishops and cardinals to change their minds, sending ambassadors around the world to privately press Opus Dei's case. Wojtyła intervened again, instructing the Congregation of Bishops to set up a "technical commission" tasked with overcoming any obstacles to the erection of Opus Dei as a personal prelature. It was an extraordinary move, designed to silence growing discontent within the Church about the proposed changes—even among some of the pope's most conservative allies. Many argued that elevating Opus Dei would allow it to bypass the Church hierarchy, which was based on more than two thousand local dioceses taking responsibility for the spiritual and pastoral needs of Catholics living within their boundaries. Pamphlets began to appear warning that approval would create a separate branch of the Church with complete autonomy. For the pope, such concessions were justified as part of the battle of ideas that was playing out within the Church, with some parts of the clergy openly questioning his pronouncements on birth control, priestly celibacy, the barring of women from the priesthood, and clerical involvement in politics—and by extension undermining the principle of papal infallibility, a relatively new notion within the Church but one which the pope clung to dearly. He had already reined in arguably the most powerful force within the Church—the Jesuits—by suspending its constitution and replacing its superior general with someone of his own choosing. Having a staunch ally like Opus Dei that could operate anywhere in the world outside the normal Church hierarchy would tilt the power balance further in his favor.

Having experienced the abuses of life within the organization, former members saw the danger of granting Opus Dei even greater autonomy. They feared that the proposed changes would enable further psychological abuse, granting the movement impunity in its control over the lives of its members. John Roche, an Irish numerary who had secretly photocopied internal documents and put together a report outlining widespread systematic abuse within Opus Dei, decided that the time had come to release his findings. He sent his report to the Church and shared the main points with two journalists from *The Times*, who published an exposé on the darker side of Opus Dei—the indoctrination, manipulation, and control of its members. The Archbishop of Westminster was appalled and decided to conduct his own investigation. After receiving evidence from around the world, he imposed a series of measures designed to prevent potential abuse: ordering Opus Dei to stop recruiting minors, to respect the freedom of members to receive outside spiritual direction, to allow people to leave freely without undue pressure, and to be transparent about its recruitment activity.

Even some of the pope's staunchest allies balked at his willingness to rip up centuries of tradition. Cardinal Joseph Ratzinger, who would eventually succeed John Paul II as pope, was one such voice. He warned that approving the changes as proposed by Opus Dei would effectively create a church within a church, where Opus Dei had the power to admit or turn away members who would otherwise be welcomed by any normal diocese. "It would be a Church of the elect and we cannot have that!" he said. Such warnings had little impact. In April 1982—after a year of deliberations—the technical commission tasked with overcoming the hurdles to establishing Opus Dei as a personal prelature delivered its six-hundred-page report to the pope for approval. A month later, an assassination attempt on the pope by a Turkish gunman nearly derailed the whole process. Wojtyła approved the movement's new status from his hospital bed. As news was disseminated to cardinals and bishops around the world, opposition flooded into the Vatican, with more than sixty cardinals voicing opposition. The Spanish Catholic Church, which knew Opus Dei better than anyone else, was particularly opposed. Ignoring calls for a pause in the process, the pope pushed on. By 1982, Opus Dei's new status was in striking distance.

The discovery of a male corpse would soon cast a shadow over Wojtyła's motives and raise questions about Opus Dei's involvement in the circumstances surrounding the man's death. On the morning of June 17, 1982, the body of an Italian banker was found hanging from scaffolding under Blackfriars Bridge in London, his pockets stuffed with thousands of dollars in foreign banknotes, and he was weighed down with bricks from a nearby building site. Roberto Calvi had, until the day before, been the chairman of Banco Ambrosiano, an institution with a rich history founded in 1896 by a priest in Milan with a vision for providing credit to the local community in a way that was in keeping with Catholic teachings. It was also a bank mired in scandal, after the discovery that Calvi had authorized hundreds of millions of dollars to be secreted out of the company to a network of shell companies registered in Panama and Liechtenstein. Most shocking of all, investigators had discovered that these companies were owned by the Vatican itself.

Calvi had stood trial for his role in the affair two years earlier. Despite his having been found guilty of breaching Italian currency laws, and having been handed a four-year suspended sentence, the Ambrosiano board had voted to keep him on. Its continued stewardship by a convicted felon and lingering questions about the credibility of the bank were a lethal combination. In the months following his trial, vital credit lines had disappeared one by one as creditors sought to distance themselves from Ambrosiano's dealings. In the weeks before his sudden death, investigators had unearthed new information on $1.4 billion in assets secreted out the country to the Vatican-owned companies. With creditors circling and options fast running out, Calvi had suddenly vanished, prompting the board at Ambrosiano to fire him. His trusted secretary, a woman in her fifties, climbed out the window of her office upon hearing of the news of his dismissal and threw herself to her death.

Given the circumstances, the police and the coroner in London were quick to conclude that Calvi's death had been a suicide. But evidence soon emerged that heaped doubt on those initial findings. Two days before his death, Calvi had given a rare interview to La Stampa, a leading Italian newspaper, detailing threats he had received and describing his situation as precarious. "Survival in an environment that is fast becoming one of religious warfare is not easy," he warned. "In this environment, any barbarism is possible." Soon, new information emerged about a meeting in which John Paul II had entrusted Calvi with finding a solution for the hundreds of millions of dollars in losses that the Vatican was facing as a result of the scandal. With the authorities in London coming under increasing pressure to reopen the case into Calvi's death, his son went public with startling revelations in the Wall Street Journal about how Calvi had been negotiating with Opus Dei to bail out the Vatican just before his death. The accusations were repeated by the dead banker's wife a few weeks later. "The answer lies in the final act of Roberto, which had taken him to London, and which had to do with Opus Dei's assumption of the debts of the Vatican Bank," she said. "It was a risky business—politically as well as economically. In exchange for its help, Opus Dei asked for precise powers in the Vatican that included determining the strategy toward communist and Third World countries. . . . How can we exclude the possibility that Roberto was assassinated to prevent him from completing a conservative project like the one of Opus Dei?" Soon, the case was reopened. A jury later ruled the cause of his death to be inconclusive at a second inquest.

Calvi's death would cast a shadow over Opus Dei for years—and eventually drag it into an Italian parliamentary investigation into the influence of secret societies there. Neither the police nor the parliamentary investigation would ever prove whether the movement had anything to do with the events that led up to the Italian banker's death. Whether or not it was involved is perhaps beside the point, however. That Opus Dei was dragged into this scandal at all shows the deep unease that many within the Church felt about the new pope's sudden elevation of this controversial group. For many, the discovery of Calvi's body, and his ominous statements just before his death, offered a ready explanation for why the pope would make such an unprecedented move.

In spite of the rumors, on August 23, 1982, the pope issued a decree establishing Opus Dei as the first personal prelature in the Church. It was an extraordinary move, given that the Pontifical Commission for the Interpretation of Canon Law was still in the process of establishing a set of rules for this new juridical structure. The pope, in his haste to grant his friends the status they so coveted, had approved the new constitution of the personal prelature without knowing what the rules governing it would be. When the rules were eventually published some months later, there would be glaring contradictions between what the pope had approved and what canon law actually said. The papal decree would give Opus Dei carte blanche to ignore canon law for the next forty years. Del Portillo, as an experienced canonist, would eventually take full advantage. But events in Spain would soon offer a reminder of the movement's murky past and stall its efforts to take advantage of its new canonical status to rapidly expand its membership before they had even properly begun.

In February 1983, Spain's new socialist government, which had been elected four months earlier on a promise to flush out the lingering corruption of the Franco years, decided that it was time to take action against José María Ruiz-Mateos and the billions of pesetas he owed in unpaid taxes. As police surrounded the headquarters of his sprawling business empire in central Madrid, a statement was read on the evening news announcing that the prime minister had signed an emergency decree expropriating the entire conglomerate. Fearing arrest, and unsure of what to do, the disgraced billionaire turned to the one man he thought might be able to help him: Luis Valls-Taberner. The Banco Popular chairman had supposedly been working behind the scenes for months to help his fellow member of Opus Dei. Acting on advice from Luis, the businessman had even arranged for a billion pesetas in cash to be left in a safe deposit box, which was to be used to bribe government officials. But unknown to Ruiz-Mateos, instead of trying to help the desperate businessman, Luis Valls-Taberner had actually been working *against* him. A month earlier, having heard about the government's plans, a memo was sent around Banco Popular ordering staff to halt all outstanding operations with any of Ruiz-Mateos' businesses. Around the same time, Opus Dei had also sent two emissaries to question the billionaire about who else knew about his financial connections with the movement. Having secured his donation for the education foundation, Opus Dei was moving to protect itself—just as it had with Ortega Pardo and the Venezuela scandal two decades earlier.

When the call came through from a desperate Ruiz-Mateos, Luis advised him to flee the country. Heeding his advice, the disgraced businessman staged a dramatic escape. Evading the police who had been sent to surveil him, he fled the city in the trunk of a Mercedes with diplomatic plates, and he made his way over the mountains into Andorra and then—using a counterfeit passport—into France, where he boarded a plane for London. There, he was met by a numerary sent to collect him, told to await further instructions, and ordered to conceal his membership in Opus Dei. Back in Spain, government investigators soon discovered huge holes in the accounts of his business empire—including almost $50 million that had been secreted out of the country to companies in Panama, as well as the billion pesetas that had been withdrawn in cash. The Spanish authorities, still owed billions in taxes, demanded the money be paid back. As they went deeper into the accounts, they made more shocking discoveries. A Swiss lawyer named Alfred Wiederkehr, a controversial figure who had made a small fortune profiting from Jews wishing to escape the Nazis and who had helped set up the first Opus Dei foundation in Switzerland, was identified as a central figure in some of the transfers. On the demands of the Spanish government, he helped recoup some of the money—including one payment which mysteriously was made from an Opus Dei foundation in The Netherlands.

After a few weeks in London, Ruiz-Mateos began asking about what had happened to the billion pesetas that had been earmarked for bribing government officials and realized that Luis might have played him. He shared his suspicions with one of his advisors and asked him to go to Luis and challenge him directly about it. "I want you mention the theory to him and look straight into his eyes," he explained. "Let's see what he says and what kind of a face he makes."

Luis immediately wrote Ruiz-Mateos a letter apologizing for what had happened and feigning innocence with regard to the missing billion pesetas. But the Rumasa chairman remained unconvinced. Relations between the two men quickly deteriorated, and the row went public, with an angry Ruiz-Mateos leaking stories to the press about Luis's corruption. "I never met Calvi, but some people say I will end up like Calvi," he told the *Financial Times*. In a bid to prevent the allegations from spiraling into another public scandal, Luis flew to London to calm the situation during the final week of June.

Ruiz-Mateos invited the banker over for lunch at his house in Chelsea. He was tense and agitated but tried his best to put on a brave face and be cordial to his fellow Opus Dei member. They were joined by Ruiz-Mateos's wife, Teresa. The businessman served some wine, and the three of them made a toast.

Ruiz-Mateos accused Luis directly of not following through on his promises, and Luis remained silent.

After a while, the businessman left for a meeting with his lawyers, and it fell to his wife to press Luis on what exactly had happened.

"The number of times you two saw each other . . ." she pleaded with the banker. "You simply have to give him some kind of explanation."

"I tried to help him," Luis explained. "Yes, we used to eat together—he used to come and ask me for advice with things. But this isn't my fault."

"But you've seen how he is," she replied. "You have to say something to him . . ."

Just then, the children arrived. Luis made his excuses and left.

Seeking to rationalize what had happened to him, Ruiz-Mateos concluded that there were two sides to Opus Dei. On one side was the spiritual philosophy underpinning the movement, as revealed to the founder by God Himself. That was the real Opus Dei. But there was also another side, Ruiz-Mateos thought, which he called "Opus Homini"—made up of corrupt, power-hungry men like Luis Valls-Taberner. He wrote a forty-five-page letter to Álvaro del Portillo asking him to root out the evil that had infected the religious movement. "Everything has been taken from me," he wrote. "I have been dishonored, discredited in my work, and thrown out of Spain. I have been persecuted and slandered. . . . I beg of you, Father, to put yourself in my situation and try to understand me. I'm sure you will feel compassion."

Shortly after, he received a visit from someone at Opus Dei's headquarters in Rome. The visitor asked him "How is your soul? Have you been following the norms?" When Ruiz-Mateos asked whether Del Portillo had a response for him, the emissary replied, "What letter? Do you know that you could die tonight? Have a heart attack? Or die of cancer?"

Del Portillo had more pressing business to attend to. A solemn ceremony to mark the official creation of the Prelature of the Holy Cross and Opus Dei, as the movement was now officially known, had been held at the Basilica di Sant'Eugenio in Rome on March 19—always a special day for members because it was the feast day of Saint Joseph, the founder's namesake. For three generations, the movement's reputation had been tarnished by its close ties to the Franco regime and its complicity in the corruption and brutality meted out by the dictatorship. But now, having secured Escrivá's dream of a new status, Opus Dei eyed the third millennium of Christendom with optimism, fresh legitimacy—and ample funds. But its advance had come at great personal cost for two of its most loyal soldiers. In February 1984, the Spanish authorities issued an arrest warrant for Ruiz-Mateos. Following a decision by the British government not to renew his visa, the disgraced businessman fled to the United States—then to the Caribbean and on to Germany, where he was finally intercepted on an Interpol arrest warrant. He would respond by going public with his accusations about Luis and the missing billion pesetas. The two men would see a bitter court fight that would go on for years. While Ruiz-Mateos and Luis Valls-Taberner battled to save their reputations, Opus Dei turned its attention to reaping the fruits of plants seeded by its two biggest benefactors. With the cause for the beatification of the founder racing through the Vatican, the years ahead promised untold power and influence.

7

BLESSED DAY

Los Angeles, California—February 1988

WITH HIS HEAD BOWED AND HIS HANDS CLASPED BEFORE HIM IN PRAYER, Álvaro del Portillo knelt before the gilded altar of the Church of Our Lady Queen in downtown Los Angeles and pleaded to God for help. The church, which traced its roots back to 1784, was the oldest in the city, built to support the work of a mission of Spanish priests sent to evangelize the local population. Two centuries later, Del Portillo had come to California with that same spirit of evangelization—backed up by an army of numeraries rather than a battalion of Spanish troops. Having fulfilled the founder's dream of securing a new canonical status, the new "prelate"—as members now called Del Portillo—set his sights on achieving another of Escrivá's big ambitions. The founder had spoken of Opus Dei's building a shrine in North America dedicated to Mary, as a counterweight to Hollywood's corrosive cultural dominance. The shrine would remain a pipe dream for decades. But, as Del Portillo knelt in prayer, he asked the Lord for assistance. "We want Christ's reign here on Earth to become a reality," he said. "To help us accomplish this re-evangelization of the world, we ask you give the work of Opus Dei here in California a special blessing."

Los Angeles was the sixth stop on a grueling two-month tour of North

America that had already taken Del Portillo to New York, Puerto Rico, Florida, Texas—and briefly across the border to Mexico. The trip showed the rising importance that he and Opus Dei were placing on the region—and on the United States in particular. The visit was also opportunistic, coming at a time of deep division within the American Church. A groundswell of moral outrage had risen up among ordinary Catholics against U.S. policies in Central America, where the Reagan administration was sponsoring military attacks that targeted left-leaning priests. Many American bishops had felt compelled to speak out, openly criticizing the administration—a move that put them in direct conflict with an increasingly authoritarian Vatican, which turned a blind eye to the deaths of left-leaning priests in Central America as part of the conservative renaissance being led by the pope. Wojtyła had responded with disciplinary measures against the bishops—a tactic which only made things worse, prompting some wealthy American dioceses to withhold their contributions to Rome in protest. The divisions almost derailed a papal visit to the United States in 1987 and gave birth to a new, vocal breed of conservative Catholics who felt increasingly alienated by what they saw as the leftward drift of the American Church—and who pumped money into new publications and foundations that exposed liberal bishops.

The schism created a twofold opportunity for Opus Dei: opening the door for it to position itself as a refuge of orthodoxy for conservative American Catholics; and to demonstrate its unwavering loyalty to the pope. As Del Portillo traveled around the country, he made it clear that Opus Dei stood with the pope on the most divisive issues. "Love your children—do not block the sources of life," he told a gathering in San Francisco. "I ask you to go forth and spread the true doctrine of the Church: that it is not lawful to block the sources of life, to use contraceptives, and that God makes your heart bigger the more children you have."

The tour, which would also take him to Chicago, Milwaukee, St. Louis, Washington, and Boston, was designed to project an image of a movement on the march, gaining popularity among the nation's Catholics. But the heavily choreographed public gatherings masked Del Portillo's growing frustration with the pace of expansion in the United States—and disappointment with the amount of money the movement had raised in the country. Back in Rome, the prelate had shared his irritation with two American numeraries who were training to become priests, explaining that Escrivá had once dreamed of being able to draw from the financial resources of the United States in order to fund the growth of Opus Dei in other parts of the world. Regrettably, that dream had not come to pass—so precarious were the movement's finances in the United States at one stage during the eighties that it was forced to borrow money from one wealthy supernumerary family to pay its bills there.

The movement's finances in America had since improved owing to the hard work of a handful of numeraries in New York. John Haley, who had joined Opus Dei while studying at the University of Notre Dame, was the brains behind that transformation. Haley had moved to New York in 1978. After a spell in charge of the movement's recruitment efforts with teenagers, he was asked to take on the role of regional administrator—which effectively put him in charge of managing Opus Dei's finances at a national level. The accounts were in a dire state: as money flowing out of Spain slowed to a trickle, many of the opulent properties owned by the movement in the United States had been mortgaged to the hilt. Various initiatives—such as the student residence near Columbia University—had failed and saddled it with even more debt.

Haley ripped up the old system of managing the movement's property portfolio centrally and set up each individual residence and retreat center as a religious nonprofit. The switch in status had huge tax advantages. He also set up a new nonprofit called the Woodlawn Foundation, where numeraries were told to send their paychecks after they had paid their local center for living expenses. The system allowed Opus Dei to avoid falling foul of the Internal Revenue Service, which had strict rules about passing off living expenses as charitable donations and which had already investigated dozens of numeraries because of suspicious activity. It also had another advantage—creating a firewall between Opus Dei as an organization and the operations of its numerary members on the ground. It was a legal fiction; in the United States and elsewhere, entities like the Woodlawn Foundation were set up and closely controlled by a small group of trusted numeraries specially selected by Rome to run the affairs in each country. The group would appoint more junior members to officially run these supposedly independent entities—although in practice they had absolutely no autonomy and were effectively told what to do. On occasion, these junior members who on paper ran these nonprofits would be asked by the numeraries who were really in charge to sign fictitious minutes of meetings that had never taken place. Over the next two decades, this web of supposedly independent foundations would rise to well over a hundred in the U.S. alone.

Haley also sought to professionalize the process of extracting donations from supernumeraries and the wider Catholic population. He brought in Marts & Lundy, the leading consultancy firm in the philanthropy industry, which advised Opus Dei to compile a list of potential wealthy donors—basically anyone who might be able to contribute at least $10,000, which was equivalent to about half of what the average American earned annually—and write to each one with a clear, one-page pitch. It was here where the detailed report cards mandated by Escrivá in his "instructions" for directors came in useful. Haley asked the directors of Opus Dei residences across the country to put together lists of names. They were able to draw on their report cards of local supernumeraries and sympathetic Catholics, which included detailed information on their personal, professional, and spiritual lives. Letters were sent out and about fifty people responded positively. Haley had been hoping to raise a million dollars. But indications for $3 million came in. Opus Dei now had a way of using the information gathered about members and Catholics at the local level to generate cash.

Having discovered this rich seam of money, the numeraries who ran Opus Dei in the United States began to get ahead of themselves. They hired a full-time fundraiser, who was put in charge of raising the money for another project that regional headquarters saw as a priority—a $3 million refurbishment of a retreat center outside Boston. The campaign was a failure, generating commitments that were barely enough to cover the fundraiser's wages. Marts & Lundy were brought in again to advise on what had gone wrong. The consultants told them it had been a mistake to frame the fundraiser as a refurbishment of an existing property. "Everybody needs a new kitchen," explained one of the firm's experts. Opus Dei was told to ditch the campaign and instead recast it as something completely different—something the membership could engage with.

Word had got back to Haley that one wealthy supernumerary—a Wall Street lawyer named Edward Lisk Wyckoff—might be willing to donate as much as $1 million for the right project. The regional council heard that

Wyckoff had a particular obsession with female lawyers who prioritized their careers over having children. He was convinced that they must be deeply unhappy and had spoken about the need to intervene early with these women—ideally at university—and instill in them good Catholic values. Opus Dei spotted an opportunity. Instead of talking about the expensive refurbishment of a country house that was used for retreats, the fundraiser was rebranded as the "Second Generation Campaign." A narrative was constructed about how a generation of Spanish priests had risen up to bring the message of Opus Dei to the United States—and how a new, second generation was now expected to rise up and fund an expansion of this important work. The $3 million refurbishment of the retreat center would of course remain the priority, but Opus Dei emphasized other plans: expanding its network of residences to university towns, where it would disseminate Catholic values to a new generation of young professionals. Wyckoff bought in. It was the first $1 million donation for Opus Dei in the United States. Its relationship with its wealthy base there would be changed forever.

Opus Dei also established strong relationships with other wealthy heirs. Dorothy Bunting Duffy was one of them. After the First World War, her grandfather began selling skin cream that he branded as "Dr Bunting's Sunburn Remedy," but soon renamed the recipe as Noxzema—"no-eczema"—as a way to open up a wider market. The product was a runaway success, and by the late fifties the company had branched out into shaving cream, suntan lotion, and its CoverGirl line of cosmetics. The family business made the Buntings extremely wealthy. In 1957, she married Joe Duffy, a naval officer who went on to work at the U.S. Naval Academy in Annapolis, and the two began a new life in the Virginia suburbs of Washington, D.C.—first in Falls Church and then in McLean. There, they fell in with Opus Dei and became supernumeraries. As a wealthy couple, they gave generously to the movement. When approached to help fund the renovation of the retreat center in Boston, Dorothy initially pushed back. But after it was rebranded to the "Second Generation Campaign"—and after she heard of the $1 million contribution from Wyckoff—she decided to match his donation.

The Duffy family fortune exploded in 1989, when the company was sold to consumer products giant Procter & Gamble for $1.3 billion. The sale coincided with another huge fundraising push by Opus Dei. John Haley branded his next initiative "The Campaign for the Twenty First Century," which chimed with a similar campaign being pushed by the Vatican ahead of the 2000th anniversary of Christ's birth. The Duffys became increasingly important donors. Over the next three decades, Duffy and her daughter would donate tens of millions of dollars to Opus Dei.

The strides made by Haley and the other senior numeraries in opening the purse strings of the supernumerary base supercharged Del Portillo's ambitions for the United States. He outlined his plans during a visit to Boston toward the end of his two-month trip. Speaking to a meeting near Harvard and MIT, he reflected on what Opus Dei members could do to thwart liberalism at such prestigious institutions. He wanted to build an Opus Dei university in the United States—as the movement had already done in Spain, Peru, Mexico, and Colombia. Del Portillo had other priorities, too. Before his visit, the prelate had decided to install the first native-born American to head Opus Dei in the country. The change at the top would help underscore the "Second Generation Campaign" narrative. Jim Kelly had grown up in Massachusetts and joined Opus Dei as a numerary while studying at Harvard. After a stint in New York, he moved to Rome to study as a priest, and there he'd caught Del Portillo's eye. The prelate had taken him aside at Villa Tevere and explained his priorities. Kelly was told to get better at asking for money from the rich seam of supernumerary wealth the movement had identified. He also had another instruction, telling Kelly that the region was henceforth to target its recruitment efforts at teenagers.

Del Portillo had spent much of his time since securing the movement's new status updating its recruitment playbook, penning a detailed *Vademecum on the Apostolate of Public Opinion*. The document detailed how every member had to disseminate the "divine truth" that Escrivá had received from God—and told them precisely how to do it. Priests were encouraged to write for newspapers and magazines, and to infiltrate ecclesiastical gatherings to discuss the Church's policies and initiatives at national level. Lay members were encouraged to write letters that might be published and read by the general public. The most detailed guidelines were reserved for Opus Dei members who worked in the media. They were encouraged to talk about the founder and his teachings in their professional work whenever the opportunity arose, although any articles examining Opus Dei in depth were to first be run by the regional commission. The guidelines stipulated that Opus Dei spiritual directors were to provide them with material and check that they were fulfilling the movement's expectations. Members were encouraged to strike up friendships with others that worked in the media and offer their "help" in reading over articles before publication to check for "inaccuracies." The level of detail concerning what members should and shouldn't do, and the clear stipulation that spiritual directors should involve themselves in the professional and private lives of members in order to shape the public image of Opus Dei, contradicted the prelature's public position: that members were free to do and say whatever they wanted.

Del Portillo also used the process of updating Opus Dei's secret internal documents to cover up his own failings as successor. The erection of Opus Dei as a personal prelature had been rushed through by Pope John Paul II in the final weeks of 1982, through a papal decree that unilaterally approved its application before the relevant canon laws governing personal prelatures had been finalized. It was a desperate move designed to ensure that Opus Dei won its coveted new status—but a risky one, given the uncertainty about what being a personal prelature would actually entail under canon law. That had become apparent two months later, when the laws were finalized. To Del Portillo's horror, the bishops had refused to back down in their assertion that personal prelatures—in accordance with the original thinking behind their creation at the Second Vatican Council—were to be made up only of priests. This created a huge problem for Opus Dei, which in its haste to win its elevated status had effectively lost its ecclesiastical authority over the vast majority of its members, who were lay people and not members of the clergy. Unable to backtrack because of the adulation that followed the granting of Opus Dei's new status, which now turned out to be a dud, Del Portillo chose to cover up his mistakes by lying to the membership. They were told that, having taken vows, they were ecclesiastically bound to Opus Dei and could leave the movement only by obtaining a personal dispensation from the prelate himself. This misleading interpretation of canon law would place a hold on the membership, forcing many to remain in Opus Dei because obtaining a dispensation from the prelate often proved lengthy or difficult. Effectively, it was a form of spiritual abuse. To reinforce its grip on the membership, Del

Portillo made it clear that leaving without *his* permission would be considered a serious sin. In an acknowledgment, perhaps, that these internal rules contradicted canon law, he ordered that they were to be kept under lock and key and never removed from Opus Dei premises.

Opus Dei also routinely violated canon law regarding minors. The Church specifically prohibited the recruitment of anyone younger than eighteen. Publicly, the movement acknowledged this in its official statutes that had been presented to the Vatican. But in its secret guidelines for members, Del Portillo effectively encouraged numeraries to target children as young as fourteen. He explained that there was nothing to prevent children from becoming what he called "aspirants"—a new category invented to get around Church restrictions. Such "aspirants" were not members as such, but were to receive regular spiritual guidance from a numerary adult and attend retreats and summer camps where the only adults present were usually numeraries. With the adults who ran such recruitment activities under acute pressure from their superiors to generate new "vocations," the well-being of the children in their care was often an afterthought. Spiritual—and sexual—abuse of minors festered in such an environment. In New York, one numerary ran catechism classes for young boys in the basement of one large and influential Catholic family. During these meetings, he would sometimes encourage the boys—some of whom were only thirteen—to masturbate in front of him, according to one participant. He took them away on trips to Opus Dei houses and told the young boys that they had a calling—while also subjecting them to horrific sexual abuse. "You were a special recruit—I was told they felt the calling in me," said one person who was repeatedly sexually abused by one numerary when he was between the ages of twelve and sixteen. He was convinced others knew about it. "It was an offense that could be overlooked if you were bringing in money or recruits," he added. The numerary was later selected by the Opus Dei headquarters to become a priest, and was then sent back to the United States, where he ran youth activities in New York.

Elsewhere, similar abuses also occurred at other Opus Dei activities targeted at children. In England, Johnny Daukes was encouraged by his mother, who was a supernumerary, to attend a youth club in nearby Oxford that some members had just set up. "These clubs had much to recommend them," he recalled. "Activities including sports, filmmaking, camping, car mechanics, and lots of other things appealing to teenage male youths. They did, however, have a key component—disguised by the attractions of tents, balls, and grease—of praying. Boys' Club was a Trojan horse to ensnare unsuspecting youth in the religious activities of Opus Dei." There, one of the men who ran the club was appointed as spiritual advisor to the young boy and instructed him to share *everything* so that he might be forgiven by God. The older man abused his privilege as spiritual advisor to groom Daukes into submission for regular acts of sexual abuse, which took place at Grandpont House, the numerary residence in Oxford—and also at Wickenden Manor, an Opus Dei retreat center out in the English countryside. "Whilst my abuse was the actions of one man, it frequently took place on Opus Dei premises," said Daukes. "The degree of contact I had with him was very obvious to everyone at Grandpont House and it is, at the very least, surprising that no one chose to question the propriety of that relationship and its unhealthy proximity." The serial abuser later took a senior position running Opus Dei schools. Daukes said the man sexually abused at least one other boy during that time. When new allegations surfaced many years later, the new victim was sent to an Opus Dei priest and supernumerary psychiatrist. The abuse was never reported to the authorities.

This surreptitious targeting of children—in clear breach of canon law—did not go unnoticed. In New York, a group of Catholic parents who felt they had lost their children to the movement published a book called *Parent's Guide to Opus Dei*, in which they detailed the group's recruiting techniques. The parents illustrated how Opus Dei was a modern cult according to the criteria set out by the Vatican three years earlier, in a report about the "Characteristics of Destructive New Religious Movements." Accusing Opus Dei of brainwashing and mind control, of cultivating group pressure and instilling guilt and fear, they called on the Vatican to take action. Opus Dei hit back with a letter from the main author's daughter, asserting that she had joined the organization of her own free will. It denied that a recruitment handbook even existed—glossing over the *instructions* and *vademecums* locked away inside Opus Dei centers.

At the same time it was issuing these rebuttals, a group of numerary women in Boston were running a summer school for high school girls from abroad. The school had been purportedly set up to teach them English and about the American way of life, but it was really a front to lure minors.

Tammy DiNicola was one of the numeraries tasked with this mission. She herself had been recruited three years earlier, while in her junior year at Boston College, and was taught the techniques that numeraries were expected to use to generate new vocations. Such methods were openly talked about at the Bayridge residence where she lived. The numeraries were even encouraged to sing an Opus Dei song celebrating their surreptitious recruitment techniques that compared them to "underwater fishing." They sang about how they should never wait for the fish—a euphemism for the children they were targeting—to bite, but instead position themselves, lie in wait, and shoot at their target with a harpoon. "Then you grab it—and that's the end of that," she would sing at the residence, as the director beat the rhythm with a tambourine. The girls at the summer camp had no idea why they were really there. One week into the camp, DiNicola and the other numeraries were called to a meeting. One of them had a sheet with the names of the girls attending. Then a tailored plan for how to recruit each specific girl would be devised, and a numerary would be chosen to carry it out. Her sudden realization that the girls had been brought to Boston on false pretenses made her deeply uneasy, but she felt unable to resist because doing so would be deemed "bad spirit." "They were vulnerable, unsuspecting youth unable to handle the intensity which was thrust upon them," she later reflected. "There was one girl in particular who was upset all the time, and who I believe experienced a minor breakdown near the end of the program." DiNicola left Opus Dei soon afterwards. Among numeraries around the world having qualms about what they were being asked to do, not everyone found it so easy to just leave. One numerary from Venezuela was told by her superiors that she was being tempted by the devil when she asked to leave, telling her that she would never be happy or be able to live in the grace of God ever again if she were to act on her impulses. She said they forbade her from speaking to her parents, hid the keys to the residence to stop her leaving—and even gave her Rohypnol, explaining that it would help her get some rest. By the late eighties, the prescription of antidepressants and amphetamines was widespread among many numeraries. In Barcelona, one supernumerary doctor seemed to work in cahoots with the local Opus Dei bosses and was notorious for prescribing such medication to numeraries—and sharing the confidential discussions he had with such patients with the numeraries' superiors.

While Opus Dei set detailed guidelines on how to recruit minors, its attention to the welfare of the children placed in its care was an afterthought. "Opus Dei aimed to spread the Kingdom of God using deceit," recalled Vladimir Felzmann, an Opus Dei priest who spent twenty-three years inside the movement. "Members were encouraged to become pretend friends with the aristocracy of brains, blood, and wealth. Nowadays that is called grooming. Activities had a covert as well as an overt agenda. Camps, educational events were officially there to help young people. In fact, they were there to attract possible vocations." Felzmann recalled that male numeraries were encouraged to smoke to show they were macho—and told that offering a cigarette was a great way to break the ice. Female numeraries were told to target girls who were attractive—as they would in turn be more successful in recruiting more members to the cause. But when it came to doling out advice about the spiritual or physical welfare of such recruits, there was no real guidance or supervision. In the same year as it held the Boston course for girls from abroad, Opus Dei hosted a summer camp for young boys in Buenos Aires. One of the numeraries asked an eleven-year-old boy to sleep in his bed. In the middle of the night, the boy awoke to find the numerary fondling his genitals. The following year, the same numerary abused another boy. When the case was reported years later, Opus Dei sought to wash its hands of the incident, telling the victim that it couldn't look into it because the summer camp hadn't actually been run by the prelature but, rather, by a separate foundation that happened to be run by numeraries.

Luis Valls-Taberner and the money from Banco Popular were critical to these recruitment efforts. By the late 1980s, the Spanish banker had created a new system of legitimate international funding for Opus Dei to replace the nefarious route that had slowly been dismantled in the years since Franco's death. Officially, the bank had spun off a large portfolio of businesses in the late 1960s to comply with new banking regulations. The portfolio included various real estate companies, including one that owned the Banco Popular headquarters. Unknown to anyone but a tightknit group around him, Luis had used a bunch of dormant subsidiaries to buy up these assets with the bank's own money. One of the subsidiaries was run by Santiago Escrivá, the founder's younger brother. Discreetly, Luis had transferred ownership of these assets to the newly created Foundation for Social Action. By 1989, this system was up and running. Over the next few years, almost six billion pesetas—equivalent to about $100 million today—would flow from Spain to projects all around the world.

Projects aimed at minors and young people were the biggest recipients. Using assets syphoned off from Banco Popular—and topped up with a portion of the bank's profits earmarked for "good causes"—the Foundation for Social Action pumped millions of dollars into the expansion of Opus Dei in thirty-seven countries, including Argentina, Australia, France, Italy, the Ivory Coast, Kenya, the Philippines, Sweden, and the UK. Two new high schools were built on the outskirts of Sydney, youth clubs were created in the Paris suburbs, university residences were constructed in the newly liberated Poland, and cultural centers were established in Kinshasa, in what was then Zaire. While huge sums went into expanding the public face of Opus Dei—the schools, youth clubs, and student residences designed to entice future numeraries into the movement—an equally sizable amount was pumped into supporting the hidden underbelly of the prelature: recruiting underprivileged girls as numerary assistants, who were needed to cook and clean facilities in the sprawling network of new residences being planned by the prelate.

Freed from having to justify its actions to the local diocese because of its status as a personal prelature, and liberated from the oversight and accountability that might have come from regular donors—professionally run charitable organizations or local congregations—Opus Dei operatives allowed abuse to fester in plain sight. Such dynamics were evident in France, where hundreds of thousands of dollars generated by Banco Popular were sent to support the École Hôtelière Dosnon, a recruitment center for numerary assistants set up under the guise of a school for young girls interested in working in the country's burgeoning hospitality sector. Based in Couvrelles, a small village a couple of hours northeast of Paris, the school was attached to a seventeenth-century château that had been converted into a center for Opus Dei retreats. The château had been acquired in the early 1960s, as part of a rush of property acquisitions by Opus Dei that included historic castles and mansions. By the early 1990s, the château had become the preeminent center for Opus Dei retreats in the whole of France. Hidden from view for most retreatants was an adjoining building housing the hospitality school, connected by an underground tunnel, where twenty teenage girls were pressured to join Opus Dei as numerary assistants—and to provide cheap labor for the retreats being held next door. The château had no employees; all the cleaning and cooking was done by the teenage girls, who had little time for study. Each morning they rose at dawn and often worked through until ten at night, seven days a week.

Catherine Tissier had been fourteen when her parents signed her up for the three-year hospitality course at the École Hôtelière Dosnon. She would later become the first public whistleblower of the systematic abuse of numerary assistants. During a visit to the school, the family had been impressed by the staff's friendliness and professionalism, and had come away convinced that Dosnon was the perfect place for a girl like Catherine, who had struggled academically. None of the staff mentioned the school's affiliation with Opus Dei. Only after her parents left did the religious rituals that defined life for the girls become apparent. At first, there was little pressure to attend daily Mass—or the catechism classes, sermons, and meditations given by an Opus Dei priest. But all that changed in the second year, when the pressure to attend the religious activities was ratcheted up—spearheaded by Catherine's tutor, whose job should have been to prepare her for a life in the hospitality industry, but who instead quizzed her about that day's sermon and pushed her to follow the strict timetable of prayers and meditation followed by Opus Dei members. Under acute pressure, she finally relented. When she was sixteen, at the beginning of her third year, her tutor dictated a letter for her to write to Álvaro del Portillo asking for admission into Opus Dei as a numerary assistant, pledging to offer up her work and her prayers for the founder. Her tutor instructed her not to tell her parents. A year later, she took the oblation, which signified her official incorporation into Opus Dei. She was still only seventeen. She was asked to write a will ceding all her earthly possessions to Opus Dei, which was immediately sent to the regional office to be put on file. She was rewarded with the gift of a Bible and a crucifix. She was sent to work at an Opus Dei student residence in London. Her parents were told it was so that she could learn English. But all she did there was work—ten hours a day, seven days a week. It was only after her return to France that the reason for the transfer became obvious. She was by then eighteen. "Your daughter is now an adult," her parents were told. "Her family is no longer you—it's us."

Tissier's account of life as a numerary assistant was bleak. Many girls were moved from one residence to another on short notice to meet the movement's needs—as was the case with Catherine, who was assigned to a residence in Paris, where she was taught to lower her gaze to avoid eye contact with any of the men and where she was only allowed out if accompanied by another member so they could watch over each other. She worked ten-hour days. A bank account was opened in her name, and her wages were deposited in it. But she had no access to it; all the statements were sent to her employer, and she was regularly asked to sign blank checks, which she later found out were used to make payments to support an Opus Dei publishing house. She was allowed to visit her parents only once a year. Between visits, any contact with them was controlled—her letters were opened, and her telephone calls were monitored. This went on for eight years. Years later, suffering from depression, she was sent to see an Opus Dei doctor, who prescribed for her antipsychotics and tranquilizers. Shortly after that, she was sent as au pair for a supernumerary family, but ended up being hospitalized, after which she was sent back to the École Hôtelière Dosnon. It was only after a visit to her parents that the alarm was raised. She weighed less than ninety pounds and had stopped eating. They took her to see a doctor, who advised that she stop work immediately—and be taken off the cocktail of drugs that the Opus Dei doctor had prescribed. After deciding to sue, the Tissiers soon found out that other parents had made similar allegations against the school.

Living his isolated existence in the mountains around Madrid, Luis Valls-Taberner continued to sign his own blank checks. Encouraged by internal reports that these hospitality schools were helping young girls, the Banco Popular chairman funded similar initiatives all around the world: in Argentina, money from the bank paid for several "maid schools" that were later linked to abuse; facilities were also set up in other countries including Belgium, Sweden, and the Philippines. The system would ultimately claim hundreds—if not thousands—of victims. Most of the women would remain for years, locked in the system or silent about the abuse they suffered. Catherine Tissier was the first to publicly seek justice. She sought to sue Opus Dei for the exploitation she had suffered as a numerary assistant. Rather than take responsibility, Opus Dei chose to hide behind the web of companies that had been set up in the country—as a tax-efficient way of running its finances, and as a way of protecting the movement from any potential legal problems. During deliberations with the judge, Opus Dei successfully argued that it had only been responsible for the spiritual formation of the young numerary assistant—and not for any breaches of labor law or alleged enslavement. It was the first of many times over the next three decades that such a tactic would prove successful.

But activity back at Villa Tevere in Rome told a different story. There, one of the most senior members of government in the women's section was tasked with keeping Del Portillo updated on the global push to recruit more numerary assistants. Her work took her all over the world—including to many of the "hospitality schools" financed by Banco Popular. While Opus Dei publicly distanced itself from any legal responsibility for the girls and young women, she ran a department for numerary assistants in Rome which was charged with coordinating this global operation. Part of the department's work was seeking accreditation for the schools' training programs. The accreditation efforts were part of a process of securing visas for the numerary assistants so they could be moved from the developing countries where they were increasingly being recruited to developed countries where few young girls had any interest in the lifestyle that Opus Dei offered. While in court it washed its hands of any responsibility, in Rome an entire team was working to intricately coordinate which girls would be sent where. Given that many of them were unpaid, and that many had been duped or pressured into their vocations, the department was essentially engaged in human trafficking. Occasionally, when the immigration authorities asked too many questions, the department would ask supernumerary families to sponsor the girls' visa applications. When they arrived in their destination country, they didn't live with their sponsor family—but instead went straight to work in a numerary residence. Beneath the façade of these girls "discovering" their vocations to serve God through domestic work lay a system of abuse and deception whose only purpose was to generate a cheap—and at times entirely free—system of labor for Opus Dei residences around the world.

The United Nations has defined human trafficking as the recruitment, transportation, or receipt of people by means of threats, force, or coercion for the purpose of exploitation—even if the victim in question has given their consent. The system of recruiting, grooming, and moving around the young girls and young women who were brought into Opus Dei as numerary assistants certainly appears to fit that definition. According to dozens of interviews with numerary assistants who worked in several different countries—as well as published reports—many of the young women were coerced into joining, usually by Opus Dei elders. They would tell the girls in their charge, many of whom were still teenagers, that the girls' families would be condemned to hell if the girls refused to join. The young women were pushed into lives of servitude and expected to work long days, often without pay and with no time off. They were also transferred and transported around the world to wherever they were needed by the organization. While such transfers were presented as a choice and the consent of the women was sought, many of them felt they had no option but to accede to such moves and were told that it was "bad spirit" to question the decision of their superiors to move them to another city—or even to the other side of the world. They were often denied contact with their families.

At the center of this was the numerary assistant department in Rome, which coordinated operations around the world, offering guidance on how the women recruited as numerary assistants were to be treated and managing logistics that determined where the girls would be sent. Opus Dei has always maintained that the women joined the organization freely, that their consent to move was always sought, and that they were always free to leave—although this glosses over the psychological hold that the organization often had over these impressionable young girls and women. Many remained trapped in the organization for years—even decades—and some became clinically depressed and at times suicidal because of the exploitation and hardship they were subjected to. As the United Nations definition of human trafficking states, the consent of a victim is irrelevant when it has been coerced. While Opus Dei has never been charged with human trafficking, the testimonies of the young girls and women recruited into this system of exploitation indicate that the practice was widespread.

In May 1992, Opus Dei members from around the globe converged on Rome to take part in what promised to be a watershed moment in its history: the beatification of the movement's founder and father in heaven, Josemaría Escrivá. In the days building up to the ceremony, planeloads of pilgrims landed at Fiumicino Airport on more than a hundred flights that the prelature had chartered. For those unable to secure a seat, a fleet of buses had been put on to transport the faithful from every corner of Europe. In anticipation of the crowds, the coffin containing the mortal remains of the founder had been moved from the crypt of Villa Tevere and transferred half a mile down the road to the Basilica of Saint Eugene, a modern church close to the banks of the Tiber, so that more people could pay their respects. The delicate operation had been closely overseen by the city's police department, following a tip-off that terrorists from the Basque separatist group ETA were planning to kidnap his remains. While the threat never materialized, the information was a reminder of Opus Dei's dark past—of its complicity with the Franco regime and of lingering questions about the vast wealth it had amassed during the dictatorship. But for the pilgrims who had come to Rome, such thoughts were far from their minds. They filed past the coffin that had been placed in front of the altar, decorated with a red mantle and freshly cut roses.

On the day of the ceremony, two hundred thousand people flocked to Saint Peter's Square for an open-air Mass with Pope John Paul II. Many had nothing to do with the prelature. As well as the hoards of tourists who regularly packed Saint Peter's Square, Opus Dei had tempted thousands of students from its universities who had no interest in the founder's beatification to Rome by offering to heavily subsidize their trips.

Luis Valls-Taberner watched the ceremony from his seat on the steps of Saint Peter's, among the other invited dignitaries given a front-row view almost within touching distance of the pope. Although something of a social outcast in Madrid's political circles owing to the allegations of corruption that still hung over him, his prominence in the audience that day left no doubt of the Banco Popular chairman's status within Opus Dei. Close to him sat Santiago Escrivá, the only surviving sibling of the Opus Dei founder, as well as Giulio Andreotti, the senator for life and seven-time prime minister of Italy, who had slipped out of a parliamentary vote on the country's next president to attend the ceremony. Dozens of countries where Opus Dei had a strong presence had sent delegations. Also in attendance was Mother Teresa, whose own popularity was the envy of the conservative wing that now so dominated the Vatican. "Why does the press speak so favorably of Mother

Teresa but it doesn't do the same when it speaks about Opus Dei or about me?" the pope had remarked in a private audience with Del Portillo.

The furor that had been whipped up in the press concerning the beatification of Escrivá was proof in point. The decision had been highly controversial, both inside and outside the Vatican. Opus Dei had begun the process well before the statutory five-year waiting period, hiring a team to put together the paperwork and compile a list of potential miracles. The process had then been pushed through at unprecedented speed: less than seventeen years elapsed between the death of Escrivá and his beatification, a third of the time it normally took. There was even controversy surrounding his supposed miracle: a Carmelite nun, who had recovered after being on the verge of death just a year after the death of Escrivá, turned out to be the cousin of Mariano Navarro Rubio, one of the most prominent members of Opus Dei and a minister under Franco. The doctor charged with confirming there was no medical explanation for the miracle was also a member. Opus Dei also made a series of pre-emptive strikes to discredit the testimonies of people it assumed would speak out against the beatification—including Antonio Pérez-Tenessa. He was the former priest and head of the Spanish region who had run off in the middle of the night and subsequently been hunted down in Mexico. Some former members who had tried to give evidence to the Vatican opposing the beatification soon came forward to reveal that they had been refused a hearing. Father Vladimir Felzmann, a former Opus Dei priest who spent years working alongside Escrivá in Rome during the sixties, gave an interview to *Newsweek* in which he alleged that Escrivá feared human sexuality, believed everything he wrote came from God, possessed a filthy temper, and—most damning of all—defended Adolf Hitler. "He told me that Hitler had been unjustly accused of killing six million Jews," he told the magazine. "In fact, he had killed only four million. That stuck in my mind."

Within the Vatican, there was much unease over the damage that the fast-tracked beatification of such a controversial figure might inflict on the Church. For many, the speed of the approval—based on selective evidence and a silencing of critics—was proof the beatification had been bought. In a sign of just how uncomfortable some in the Church were, two of the nine members of the Vatican council tasked with considering the application had voted against it, requesting more time to investigate Escrivá's alleged failings—including his repeated clashes with the Jesuits, his alleged lack of humility, and even questions about the miracles supposedly associated with him. One senior Spanish cleric had been particularly scathing: "We cannot portray as a model of Christian living someone who has served the power of the state and who used that power to launch his Opus, which he ran with obscure criteria, like a Mafia shrouded in white," he said. "Beatifying the Father means sanctifying the Father's Opus, including all its negative aspects: its tactics, dogmas, recruiting methods, and manner of placing Christ in the midst of the political and economic arenas." Despite such fierce opposition, the application had been approved.

For John Paul II, the crowds packed into Saint Peter's Square that morning confirmed that elevating Escrivá had been the right decision and that his counterreformation against the Church's leftward drift was gaining traction among the faithful. Since his election in 1978, he had made it his mission to rein in those elements of the Church that had interpreted the Second Vatican Council as a green light for liberalization. But rather than stamp out dissent, his vindictive pursuit of enemies effectively opened up more wounds. At times, some thought he had gone too far. One German theologian who had been banned from carrying out his priestly duties by the Nazis was traumatized at the way he was treated after being summoned to Rome to account for his views on sexual conduct. He compared the hearings at the Vatican to the Third Reich show trials he had endured as a young man. "The Hitler trials were certainly more dangerous," he wrote in an angry letter to the hearings afterwards, "but they were not an offense to my honor, while those of the Holy Office were a grave offense." During a trip to Nicaragua, the pope refused to let one cardinal kiss his ring because he had disobeyed a papal order. Millions watched on television as he admonished the priest, reducing him to tears. During the same trip, an outraged pope had shouted *"Silencio!"* during an open-air Mass after some in the crowd dared to express their desire for peace.

Through all this, Opus Dei had proved itself a loyal ally. The pope had even chosen a prominent numerary as his press secretary and close advisor. Joaquín Navarro-Valls was a former apprentice bullfighter who left the ring to train as a doctor—before later abandoning that career to retrain as a journalist. By the early 1990s, he had become one of the most powerful men in the Vatican, controlling access to the pope—and one of the most ruthless. In a trick he may well have learned during his time in Opus Dei, he was not averse to putting out fabricated stories about the pope in order to maintain John Paul II's image as the virile, athletic picture of health—even when many in the Vatican knew he was ill. At times, he also abused his position to benefit Opus Dei. On one occasion, he invited the Vatican press corps to his house under the pretext of giving them a big story about the pope. When they arrived, he showed them a recruitment video for Opus Dei. As the pope's health deteriorated, some within the Vatican even began to fear that Navarro-Valls might start to unduly influence decision-making. Still, in the battle to assert his own authority over what he considered to be wayward factions in the Church, John Paul II regarded Opus Dei as a trusted ally. The relationship was mutually beneficial: Opus Dei could pitch itself to potential recruits as a leading force in the pope's counterreformation, while the Vatican had a loyal ally on the ground to counter any dissident rival clergy. As a reward for his loyalty, Del Portillo had been named a bishop—one of ten Opus Dei priests elevated to bishophood since his election as pope. John Paul II would eventually appoint twenty-one Opus Dei priests as bishops—compared with three under Paul VI.

Emboldened by his elevation and Opus Dei's higher status within the Church hierarchy, Del Portillo renewed his resolve to build the movement's power in the world's most powerful country.

8

A NEW DEMOGRAPHIC

Washington, D.C.—October 1994

DEAL HUDSON PACKED THE CONTENTS OF HIS WESTCHESTER HOME INTO THE
back of a car and drove south to Washington, where he was set to start a
new life as a staff member on an obscure Catholic magazine called *Crisis*. It
was an odd career move: up until the summer break, the forty-four-year-
old Texan had been a popular philosophy professor at Fordham University in
New York. He was considered a rising star. He'd edited two volumes—one on
the teachings of Thomas Aquinas and another about Sigrid Undset, a Nor-
wegian author and Catholic convert—that had been well received. Hudson
seemed to thrive on academia. Raised a Protestant, he had joined the Baptists
while at college and even trained as a minister, but then left the movement
after finding it lacked intellectual rigor. "Something seemed wrong about
a Christian outlook that excluded all the world's greatest writers and artists from the conversation about truth," he explained—a cultural depth he
later found in Catholicism. Hudson's admiration of the great thinkers perhaps made him an unlikely recruit for Opus Dei, whose main philosophical
text *The Way* had been dismissed as nothing more than a "handbook for senior scouts" by one of the Catholic Church's most respected scholars. Yet the
movement still went after him at Fordham. Opus Dei had helped him forge

useful contacts: his second book was published by the Wethersfield Institute, one of the foundations set up by the supernumerary and banking heir Chauncey Stillman.

When he arrived in Washington, Daryl Glick, a numerary from the Midwest, came over to help him move in. Hudson soon found that the movement looked very different in the nation's capital. Unlike New York, where its "apostolate" with young people was restricted to extracurricular clubs and study groups, in Washington the prelature had two schools of its own: The Heights, for boys in Potomac, Maryland, and Oakcrest, for girls close to D.C.'s American University. Both schools had initially struggled to gain much of a following within the city's sizable Catholic community. At one stage, enrollment was so low at The Heights that the school was forced to sell off a large chunk of its grounds, just to stave off bankruptcy. But Opus Dei's positioning of itself as a bastion of conservativism within the divided American Church during the eighties had improved its fortunes—so much so that The Heights now regretted selling off that land because it restricted its options for expansion to accommodate the steadily rising number of applications coming in.

The schools had helped draw hundreds of families closer to Opus Dei. By the early nineties, the movement boasted a growing community in D.C., with the schools' two popular chaplains at its heart. Malcolm Kennedy had been a fixture at The Heights since it started out as an after-school club for bright children in the sixties. Tall, gaunt, and silver-haired, Father Malcolm liked to describe himself as both a liberal *and* a traditionalist, explaining that the one true path to liberation was through the traditions of the Church. But his outspoken views on the plight of modern America undermined that argument. He criticized feminism for being against the spirit of the Virgin Mary and railed against the sexual revolution for having contributed to a decline in purity and innocence in American culture. His counterpart at Oakcrest was Ron Gillis, an affable Bostonian who had been sent to Rome in the sixties to train as a priest. This was right at the height of Beatlemania. "I remember thinking this music is the most fantastic. But it's immoral for them to wear their hair that long," he recalled, while also lamenting the revolution that had ripped through society in the years since then. For many, these two priests fulfilled a collective yearning for the days before the sexual revolution—and symbolized a return to a devout outlook on life and family that was now bestowed on the next generation at The Heights and Oakcrest.

While its two schools were the public face of Opus Dei in the capital, it also operated three numerary residences there. The Tenley Study Center for men and Stonecrest, a residence for women, were both located in the Tenleytown neighborhood, close to American University. A third residence, mainly inhabited by priests and members of Opus Dei's national government, occupied an old mansion in the wealthy Kalorama neighborhood. At these three locations, a small army of numeraries were tasked with generating fresh recruits from the unsuspecting souls cast into their orbit—through the schools or other initiatives, like the highly regarded S.A.T. program that some of the male numeraries ran. Their main task was to identify individuals who might be recruitment material, "with the aim of creating the conditions for them to respond with generosity should the Lord call them," as one of the Work's internal documents put it. The numeraries were also tasked with providing spiritual guidance to the ranks of supernumerary parents whose numbers were beginning to grow around The Heights and Oakcrest. On paper, that meant giving the weekly "chat" that supplemented confession and which involved supernumeraries sharing their innermost thoughts and concerns. Another task involved hosting a regular meeting of about six of the supernumeraries in their charge—the "circle"—a study group that delved deeper into topics that usually related to Escrivá's teachings.

This guidance often veered beyond the purely spiritual, with the "chats" touching on personal, professional, and even political matters. The numeraries were instructed to use these sessions to extract more money from the supernumerary base, to give them "apostolic tasks" deemed helpful to Opus Dei, and to offer "clear guidance" on any political matters considered "immoral or contrary to the common good." They were instructed to dole out professional advice, too. "It may be that, in some cases, they are simply not aware of their capabilities, and so it might be necessary for them to discover their possibilities so that—freely and in their own personal capacity—they might take on tasks of greater importance," said another internal document. The "circles" often doubled as networking events, during which the numeraries running them were encouraged to connect supernumeraries with other members who might be deemed useful allies in the "doctrinal and moral battles" ahead. Leading academics and journalists such as Hudson were sometimes invited along, too. "The importance of engaging with leading intellectuals—whether older, established ones who already wield considerable prestige, or younger ones who are starting out—in order to re-Christianize society is obvious," the movement's documents declared. "It is key to work to ensure that scientific truth and progress serve as a means to imbue men and culture with the knowledge of God. The local councils will be able to encourage and direct those with the necessary qualities to enter scientific or humanities bodies, or so-called think tanks, so that they can write, publish, and create a following."

In many ways, spiritual guidance was a front for building a network of like-minded Catholic political activists—the guerrilla army that Escrivá had long envisioned. In a political town like Washington, such social engineering could have an outsized impact in the battle to re-Christianize society. But it would take Opus Dei many years to realize that potential. In the early nineties, this Washington network was still very much in its infancy—and very much based around the families who sent their children to the movement's two schools. There was, however, one other Opus Dei outpost in the city. Two years before Hudson's arrival in Washington, the movement had taken charge of a small bookshop and chapel on Fifteenth Street. The Catholic Information Center, as it was called, had been run by the Redemptorists since the 1950s. But money generated from book sales and the collection at midday Mass weren't enough to cover the rent and, in 1991, the Redemptorists informed the archdiocese that they would no longer be able to keep up with rent payments. A numerary called Bob Best used to visit the chapel regularly with one of the supernumeraries in his charge. This was an executive at the World Bank named Damian von Stauffenberg, a relative of the Nazi general who tried to assassinate Adolf Hitler. Upon hearing about the Redemptorists' handing in their notice, Best had an epiphany: Opus Dei should take over the chapel and bookstore. He outlined to von Stauffenberg how the Catholic Information Center could be an ideal shopwindow for Opus Dei in the heart of the most powerful city on the planet. "The vision was to lure people in through books," von Stauffenberg recalled. "While people would think twice about entering a rectory, to walk into a bookstore you don't have to overcome very many hurdles."

Bob Best had impetuously joined the Work during high school without really knowing what it was. The decision came after he'd had a particularly aggressive scuffle with another player on the football field, only for his opponent to die the following day. A teammate called him a "killer" in the locker room, prompting Best to desperately turn to God. He went to a talk at an Opus Dei house in Boston and decided it must be a sign. He asked what he needed to do to join and was told to write a letter to the Father. Best assumed they meant the pope and addressed his letter to the Holy Father. "As I drove back, I was pretty worried about having jumped into something I knew little about—but since the pope seemed to be in charge of things, I thought it must be OK," he later recalled.

After college, Best moved to Washington in 1959 to join the U.S. Treasury Department. From there, he moved to the Senate Finance Committee, eventually becoming its chief economist. He helped negotiate international trade agreements, and his work took him all over the world. On one trip to Paris in 1971, he bumped into two other Opus Dei members who were heading up the Spanish delegation. The three men greeted each other with the traditional "*Pax.*" He met the founder several times. On one occasion, Best shared his dread about the way America was headed, describing the country as a body without a soul.

"No, my son—America has a great soul," Escrivá responded. "If it were not for the United States, we would all be reds," he explained.

On another occasion, Best gifted the founder with a pen that President Nixon had used to sign a piece of legislation. Escrivá smiled and handed it to some Spanish bankers, who used it to sign a check to pay for a new Opus Dei project. "I always thought that was Nixon's finest hour, but he never knew it," recalled Best. After leaving the Senate Finance Committee in the late seventies, he became a lobbyist—a job that allowed him to indulge in his one great passion apart from God: golf. He worked to further the interests of his clients, which included a raft of defense and aerospace manufacturers—as well as a Hawaiian hotel and a grower of Christmas trees.

His suggestion that Opus Dei take over the Catholic Information Center was unlike anything the movement had ever done before. Escrivá had envisioned the Work as a hidden army of Christian soldiers, so putting that army on display in a major city seemed to contradict everything the founder had taught them. His superiors rejected the idea and told Best to go back to his regular apostolate. There was good reason: by 1992, the fifty-five-year-old numerary had become a critical source of funds for various Opus Dei projects around the world. After a spell in lobbying, in 1992 Best set up a nonprofit called the Private Sector Initiatives Foundation, which sought to tap into growing discontent with how public money was being wasted on aid programs in the developing world; instead, it would raise money in the private sector and direct it toward worthwhile causes. Naturally, much of the money went to Opus Dei projects. Best sought to tap the contacts he had built up during his time at the Treasury, in Congress, and as a lobbyist to generate millions for such projects.

Best's plan to turn the Catholic Information Center into a shopwindow for Opus Dei was thus put on the back burner. But then, at a meeting between Álvaro del Portillo and the Archbishop of Washington in Rome, the subject came up unexpectedly. Cardinal James Hickey began complaining about a problem he had—a bookshop and chapel in the center of the city that had been entrusted to the Redemptorists, but who had asked to give up that commitment. With the lease still open, the archdiocese looked set to foot a huge bill. The cardinal asked Del Portillo whether he could help. Suddenly, the plan to take over the Catholic Information Center was resurrected; helping out a fellow conservative in the world's most powerful city evidently trumped any reluctance Opus Dei had had about contradicting the original spirit laid down by the founder. Within weeks, Opus Dei had selected a priest to take over. Father Michael Curtin had been born in Ohio but grew up in California and had joined Opus Dei while studying to be an engineer at Harvard. After a few years as a priest at Opus Dei student residences in Chicago, Milwaukee, and Delray Beach, Florida, he had been sent to Washington to work at The Heights. By the time Deal Hudson arrived in Washington in 1994, Curtin had been running the Catholic Information Center for more than two years—although it still seemed a relatively sleepy outpost. It would take the magic touch of another priest to realize the bookshop's real potential in the crusade to re-Christianize American society.

Away from Fifteenth Street—through its work at The Heights and Oakcrest—Opus Dei was beginning to build an impressive network of members and sympathizers that it would eventually plug into its operations at the Catholic Information Center. This network was soon revealed to Hudson, who—within months of starting his new job at *Crisis*—received an unexpected promotion. His boss Michael Novak had launched the magazine in 1982 as a response to what he saw as the leftward drift of the American Church. In a reflection of that angst, he had initially called the magazine *Catholicism in Crisis* before settling on its shorter, more forthright name. While the magazine had established a cult following among conservative Catholics—drawn by its pieces extolling the morality of nuclear deterrence, supporting Reagan's controversial foreign policy in Central America, and defending capitalism against its critics—Novak was no businessman and "emergency dinners" to stave off bankruptcy were common. The magazine had come close to ruin several times. In March 1995, just five months into his new life in Washington, Hudson was asked by Novak whether he might like to take over. The former academic soon demonstrated an untapped entrepreneurial streak, boosting the magazine's circulation through a targeted direct-mail initiative and raising its profile by hosting radio and television programs. Over the next decade, Hudson would revolutionize *Crisis*, quadrupling its readership and its budget. That revolution would soon extend into the world of politics, catapulting the interests of a small group of conservative Catholics onto the national stage—and creating a platform for Opus Dei to transform American society.

Having already established contact with Hudson when he first moved to Washington, Opus Dei intensified its courting of the Texan almost as soon as he was promoted to editor. Hudson was invited along to one of the V.I.P. retreats that the movement held for select members and supporters at Belmont Manor House, a former slave plantation in northern Virginia. Supreme Court Justice Antonin Scalia was one of those in attendance. A devout Catholic, he'd been familiar with Opus Dei since the late fifties, when Bob Connor—one of his childhood friends—suddenly dropped out of medical school to go and live with the founder in Rome. Horrified, Connor's parents asked Scalia to talk him out of it. Instead, he ended up getting drawn in by his friend's enthusiasm. During his honeymoon, Scalia took his wife Maureen to visit Villa Tevere, and the two newlyweds went out for dinner with Antonin's old schoolfriend, who had since been ordained as an Opus

Dei priest. From there, their paths diverged. But Scalia's nomination to the Supreme Court soon put him back in Opus Dei's sights. Connor, now installed in a numerary residence in New Jersey, contacted Scalia and put him in touch with the local Opus Dei center in Washington, D.C. Before long, the Supreme Court Justice was a regular at the V.I.P. retreats hosted by Opus Dei. Drawn in by the movement, he even asked for a list of colleges where Opus Dei had a presence—for his son Paul, who would later become a priest. A numerary sent him a list of thirty-six colleges. Scalia became close to Father Malcolm Kennedy and regularly had him over to the family home for dinner.

Hudson was gradually introduced to other attendees to the V.I.P. Opus Dei retreats—the lawyer and baseball commissioner Bowie Kuhn, the economist and political operative Larry Kudlow, a young congressman from Pennsylvania named Rick Santorum, and Domino's Pizza founder Tom Monaghan. These men helped Hudson raise the cash for the magazine. Monaghan was particularly supportive, signing up for a thousand subscriptions—equivalent to almost a fifth of its entire readership at that stage. They also put him in touch with the right-leaning Bradley and Scaife foundations, which made six-figure contributions. Monaghan—together with the Bradley and Scaife foundations—would later fund various projects linked to the prelature. Together, Opus Dei and Hudson were forming a new alliance that would eventually transform a small and obscure group of conservative Catholics into the most consequential force in American politics.

In September 1997, the New York City Department of Buildings received an application to redevelop six properties at the intersection of Lexington Avenue and Thirty-fourth Street. Such a request wasn't unusual: with New York City now booming after years of crime and decline, investors regularly bought up old lots with the intention of redeveloping them into prime real estate. Unusually, the investor—a nonprofit based in the quiet commuter town of New Rochelle, known as the National Center Foundation Inc.—had bought the properties four years earlier for $5 million, but had done nothing to develop the site. Most of the money for the purchase had actually been transferred from another nonprofit with an equally vague name: the Association for Cultural Interchange Inc. Residents of Murray Hill had grown so used to the vacant lots at Lexington and Thirty-fourth Street that these days they barely paid attention to them. They had no idea they were about to have a front-row seat for the next act in the Opus Dei story. The movement—now flush with cash and renewed ambition following the beatification of its founder—made its boldest move since the acquisition of Villa Tevere in the 1950s.

Its plans for the site reflected its hopes and aspirations for this new era. From this spot a new national headquarters for Opus Dei would rise, soaring seventeen stories high. Made from red brick and limestone, the new headquarters would include a hundred bedrooms, six dining rooms, various libraries, living rooms, meeting rooms, and offices—as well as four outdoor terraces and three chapels, ornamented with millwork and marble. For any other Catholic organization, such grandiose plans for the new headquarters—and the $70 million cost of making them a reality—might have been difficult to justify, especially given the fact that the movement had just three thousand members across the entire United States. But for Opus Dei, the project expressed its ambitions for expansion in the most powerful nation on earth.

Thanks to its growing influence in Rome, where the pope had appointed several bishops and priests from Opus Dei to important roles within the Vatican administration, and its successful efforts to cozy up to conservative elements within the American Catholic Church, the movement had by the early nineties already made some important ecclesiastical inroads in the States. Several friendly bishops, seeing the movement as a vital ally in the fight against liberalism, appointed Opus Dei priests to districts under their mandate—although the appointments weren't always welcomed by local parishioners. The movement also became adroit at using its vast financial resources to persuade bishops who weren't aligned with its views to give it a foothold in their diocese. Such tactics were evident in Chicago, where Opus Dei persuaded Cardinal Joseph Bernardin, a staunch defender of the modernization of the Church, to effectively hand over one city parish after the prelature offered to raise the cash to save a church from demolition. The move provoked an outcry from clergy and parishioners alike. Undeterred, around the time of the Murray Hill purchases, Opus Dei was also in negotiations to buy a former seminary for $9 million in Chicago, which it intended to turn into a school. The purchase would later be voted down at committee level after a number of priests voiced concern about the organization's aggressive, dogmatic approach, which they believed was counterproductive to the real work of the Church.

Given the success of its Second Generation Campaign and the latest Campaign for the Twenty-First Century—the two initiatives would eventually raise more than $70 million—Opus Dei had the firepower it needed to launch a major new offensive to make inroads into Catholic America. But plans for the new headquarters were punctuated by two important events: the death of the prelate and a sudden, unexpected windfall within its ranks. Del Portillo passed away in March 1994, following a major heart attack hours after returning from a trip to the Holy Land, where he had set another hugely expensive project in motion. That would be a retreat center of its own in the Holy Land, a place where members could pray, kneel, and kiss the ground trodden by Christ Himself. This longstanding dream of Escrivá's would eventually become the Saxum Visitor Center, a $60 million development on the outskirts of Jerusalem and named after the founder's pet name for Del Portillo (which means "rock" in Latin).

Del Portillo's body was put on display in the nave of the main chapel at Villa Tevere. Several Masses were held for an endless stream of mourners. At one point, the pope visited Villa Tevere to pay his own respects. It was an extraordinary gesture—the pope never attended funeral Masses, even when a cardinal died in Rome—and was illustrative of the deep friendship between the two men.

Despite the adulation that attended his passing, Del Portillo's tenure as prelate was, by many measures, a failure. Having targeted 120,000 new recruits for the movement over an eight-year period, the membership actually grew by less than a tenth of that target. He left behind an institution even more corrupt than the one he'd inherited. During his reign, he had further tightened the screws on the membership through his intricately detailed *vademecums*—and outright lied about the authority that Opus Dei held over them. The poisoned chalice would now pass to the next prelate.

Four weeks later, 138 "electors" convened in Rome to choose a successor. Given the failures of the past decade, the meeting might have been an opportunity for Opus Dei to take stock and somehow return the movement to what was supposed to be its guiding principle—the sanctification of everyday life—rather than the artificial, controlled existences many of its members lived. But that didn't happen. Instead, the men present opted once again for continuity. Javier Echevarría, another of Escrivá's proteges, was duly elected as the new prelate. Sixty-one, with piercing eyes and silver hair, he had joined Opus Dei in 1948, and had spent his adult life working alongside the founder and Del Portillo. In his first message to the membership, he set three objectives: family, the recruitment of the young—and an "evangelization" of the cultural sphere. "These people are the moderators of civic society," he explained, "the ones who are in a position to profoundly influence the ways of thinking and of living for future generations."

The second important event that punctuated the plans to redevelop the property in Murray Hill would double the funds available to Opus Dei in the United States and effectively remove many of the material limits on expansion there. In January 1996, the head of a wealthy pharmaceutical family in Pittsburgh died at the age of seventy-three. Ben Venue Laboratories had been established by R. Templeton Smith, a Cornell University graduate and serial entrepreneur, during the Depression. The company's fortunes had been transformed by the Second World War, when it won a lucrative government contract to manufacture human blood plasma from donations collected by the Red Cross. The company ventured into insulin production after the war. The Smiths, who were Presbyterians, used their wealth to champion a number of civic causes—advocating for women's rights and fighting against government corruption. One campaign bankrolled by them led to an investigation that landed Pittsburgh Mayor Charles H. Kline in jail on forty-eight counts of malfeasance. Both Smiths would have probably turned in their graves had they discovered what the family money would later go on to finance. After his death, control of Ben Venue passed to their youngest son Kennedy, who would run the company for the next twenty years. Kennedy Smith and his wife had met in the U.S. Navy during the war and had initially lived in Boston, but they moved to Pittsburgh to join the family company and start a family. They would have six children. It was there that the Smiths met Opus Dei. While Kennedy would hold out as a Presbyterian until shortly before his death, when he was converted to Catholicism by a Byzantine priest, his wife and some of their children joined the Work. The two youngest sons—Frederick and Mark—even became numeraries. Frederick Smith, known to everyone as Sandy, trained as a pathologist, going on to practice in Chicago, where he lived at a numerary residence. Mark Smith continued to run the Ben Venue company alongside his older brother Edward, commuting from an Opus Dei residence in Pittsburgh.

When their father died in 1996, both Sandy and Mark became extremely wealthy, although almost all that wealth was on paper, tied up in the family business. But that changed when Ben Venue became the subject of a takeover bid by a German company the year after their father's passing. The family decided to sell. Sandy and Mark would receive $80 million from the deal. Opus Dei moved to cement its claim on the good fortune of these two numeraries almost immediately. Two nonprofits were set up to manage the enormous windfalls. Sandy's money was moved into an entity called the Sauganash Foundation, after the residence where he lived, while Mark's money was shifted into an entity called the Rockside Foundation. Both were registered in New Rochelle, New York, with John Haley named as president and another numerary from the regional council named chief financial officer. Sandy and Mark were named secretaries of their respective foundations, but they could easily be outvoted by the other two numeraries. Curiously, both foundations had a clause inserted in their founding documents blocking either of the brothers from taking back control of their inherited family wealth. The clause stipulated that both brothers were allowed to nominate additional people to the board, but that the Woodlawn Foundation—the entity set up by Haley in the late seventies to manage the paychecks of its numerary members—was to have that same right. "The number of Woodlawn Trustees shall at all times be greater than the number of Donor Trustees by at least one," it stipulated. The clause guaranteed that Opus Dei would always have control of the money—no matter what happened. Over the next sixteen years, Opus Dei would whittle their inheritance down to almost nothing.

Opus Dei's caution in regard to the Smith windfall was perhaps not coincidental, given a recent incident in Argentina which had caused huge embarrassment for the prelature. Opus Dei had begun construction of a new university on the outskirts of Buenos Aires only a few years earlier. It had been made possible by a donation of around $100 million from one of the country's wealthiest businessmen—Gregorio "Goyo" Pérez Companc, who had built a vast conglomerate with tentacles stretching into oil and gas, banking, agriculture, and paper. Plans for the university envisioned a sprawling academic city on the edge of the Argentinian capital, with its own hospital and with more than a dozen large faculty buildings. But construction had been halted less than halfway through, amid rumors that the billionaire donor had pulled funding after discovering false invoices revealing that money had gone missing. By 1996, just two of the three planned wings of the hospital had been built, while many of the planned faculty buildings had been canceled.

This wasn't the only instance of Opus Dei members in Argentina falsifying invoices at the time. One of the senior numeraries there was asked by her superiors to overstate what she was earning by 600 percent so that one donor wouldn't discover his money was being detoured to side projects he hadn't approved originally. While Opus Dei protected itself against the blowback from such underhandedness through the network of supposedly independent foundations it had created, it showed a glaring disregard for its members, who say they were being encouraged to break the law and commit fraud. By legally distancing itself from the criminal activity carried out in its name—but simultaneously perfecting methods that systematically controlled its members and pushed them to take risks for the Work—Opus Dei allowed this Wild West atmosphere to permeate the entire organization. The loss of the Pérez Companc money was doubly humiliating for Opus Dei because Austral University was one of its "corporate works"—that is, one of the initiatives given the official stamp of approval, rather than those informally attached to the movement. The half-built campus was an embarrassing reminder of its failure to make good on its grand plans.

By asking the Smith brothers to effectively sign away their money, with no strings attached, Opus Dei avoided opening itself up to the vulnerabilities it had faced in Argentina. Much of the brothers' money would go toward funding the construction of Murray Hill Place. Opus Dei never explained the true origins of the cash—even to its own members. Internally, it promoted the narrative that a wealthy Catholic couple from Pittsburgh had made this generous donation. Members were encouraged to call these two benefactors "Mamoo" and "Papoo," copying the names the Smith children affectionately used for their parents. But the truth was very different. Two of its numeraries had received a huge inheritance, and Opus Dei had moved quickly to take control of their good fortune and ensure they could never claw it back. In the years ahead, it would use this largess to fund its schools in Washington, D.C., and Chicago; to start a failed university in New York; to cover up for excessive spending at the Woodlawn Foundation; and as seed money for the next part of its plan to influence U.S. society. Having positioned itself to take advantage of the deep schism in the American Catholic Church, by having learned how to extract money from its base and by having consolidated its presence in the country through the addition of more residences and parishes, Opus Dei would now set its sights on influencing the political world.

In June 1998, Father Michael Curtin was forced to step down from his position as chaplain at the Catholic Information Center, after being diagnosed with a serious heart problem. His replacement was Father C. John McCloskey, a former stockbroker and a numerary who had quit his life on Wall Street to become an Opus Dei priest. McCloskey had grown up across the Potomac River in Falls Church, Virginia, and so he knew the city well—although his appointment as the new chaplain at the Catholic Information Center was more than just a homecoming for the forty-four-year-old clergyman. After being fired as the chaplain at Princeton University after a series of run-ins over his aggressively conservative preaching style, McCloskey had been forced to continue his recruitment efforts clandestinely from the numerary residence on Mercer Street, after being banned from campus by university authorities. While the prohibition had hardly dented his ability to generate new recruits for the movement—including several high-profile businessmen and politicians—having to operate under the radar was not something that came naturally. The transfer to Washington, D.C., meant that McCloskey would be able to preach openly again. During a visit to the capital a year earlier, for the baptism of a recent convert—the political columnist and television pundit Bob Novak—his eyes had widened at the potential that the city held for Opus Dei. "I was looking out from where I was standing and it looked like a Who's Who of political and journalistic Washington," he recalled.

He wasted little time in reaping the fruits of his labors, carving out a special niche for himself as Washington's most preeminent proselytizer and becoming known as the "convert maker"—especially within Republican circles. McCloskey split his time between the Catholic Information Center, where he presided over Mass and heard the confessions of the political elite, and the refined splendor of The University Club a block away, on Sixteenth Street. It was a popular spot for Republican Party grandees—Richard Nixon used to play poker there, while Supreme Court Chief Justice Earl Warren favored its grand surroundings for social gatherings. McCloskey soon installed himself there among the political set. He played squash with the powerful and the influential. Afterwards, he was often seen in the bar, deepening his friendships and expanding his network. Though he looked incongruous in his black cassock while among the business suits, he was in his element.

While McCloskey's conservativism had impeded his apostolic efforts at Princeton, the University Club set embraced his views. He held forth on everything from abortion to tax policy, soothing the consciences and stroking the egos of his interlocutors with his doctrinal endorsements of their rightwing stances. One by one, he converted several prominent conservatives to the Catholic Church, including Senator Sam Brownback, Supreme Court nominee Robert Bork, publishing heir Alfred Regnery, and Lew Lehrman, a former banker and candidate for governor of New York. While he was never so tactless as to tell them how to vote, he did offer clear guidance on any issues that were—in his opinion—matters of "natural law" or of "divine revelation." One recurrent idea that McCloskey pushed to those in his network was the rise of theologically inspired politics in the United States—and the role that people like themselves should play in the upcoming battle for the nation's soul. For McCloskey, priests were warriors for Jesus Christ—they were Navy Seals, Army Rangers, the Green Berets of the Catholic Church. Politicians also had their role to play. "Do I think it's possible for someone who believes in the sanctity of marriage, the sanctity of life, the sanctity of family, over a period of time to choose to survive with people who think it's OK to kill women and children or for—quote—homosexual couples to exist and be recognized?" he asked. "No, I don't think that's possible. I don't know how it's going to work itself out, but I know it's not possible, and my hope and prayer is that it does not end in violence. But, unfortunately, in the past, these types of things have tended to end this way. If American Catholics feel that's troubling, let them. I don't feel it's troubling at all."

His apostolate was particularly fruitful among men experiencing some form of crisis. McCloskey had developed his own theory about a particular malaise that seemed to affect American men of a certain age—a condition he called Friendship Deficit Syndrome—and developed techniques to cure them through what he called "apostolic friendship." He took inspiration from Sir Thomas More, the sixteenth-century martyr and patron saint of lawyers, politicians, and statesmen who had befriended the leading figures of the Tudor court. McCloskey sought to become a modern-day Saint Thomas, offering apostolic friendship to men in power who had found themselves adrift and unable to seek help because of their status, celebrity, or inhibitions. It was essentially a turbocharged version of the love-bombing technique Opus Dei had carefully honed over the years—but one specially fine-tuned for the Washington elite. He was often dogged in his pursuit. "Once Father John gets his claws into you, he never lets go," remembered Larry Kudlow, an influential economist on the right and a senior figure in the first Reagan administration who was befriended by McCloskey while struggling with an addiction to alcohol and cocaine—and who later converted to Catholicism under his tutelage.

Just before his return to Washington, McCloskey had been working on a high-flying lawyer from New York who had emailed the Opus Dei priest by mistake—but whom the "convert maker" had sunk his teeth into regardless. Mark Belnick was a former synagogue president who had begun to flirt with Christianity during a serious mid-life crisis that some of his friends feared might even push him to suicide. McCloskey invited the lawyer to Opus Dei retreats in Massachusetts and Maryland and the two became good friends, emailing almost daily and seeing each other every few weeks. "I thank God every day for the gift of mistaken e-mail addresses," Belnick wrote in one exchange. McCloskey introduced him to several of his Opus Dei friends—men like Bowie Kuhn, Lew Lehrman, and Bob Best, who reinforced the priest's own efforts to recruit the New York lawyer. Soon, the stupor that had so worried his friends was gone. Belnick started a new job as the top in-house lawyer at Tyco International, a vast conglomerate. "I'm on fire with the faith," he wrote to McCloskey, whom he liked to call his "human guardian angel." When McCloskey moved to Washington, Belnick wrote to say how much he missed him. "Jesus is a great companion, having Him is having everything (but I still miss you . . .)."

McCloskey's explosion onto the Washington political scene in the fall of 1998 coincided with another twist of fate that would transform how Republican strategists thought about the Catholic demographic. The architect of this change was Deal Hudson, the publisher of *Crisis* magazine, who—by 1998—had like many other conservatives become despondent about the inability of the Republican Party to capitalize on the moral transgressions of President Bill Clinton. Attempts to derail Clinton's reelection prospects in 1996 by drudging up an old real estate scandal from almost twenty years earlier had spectacularly backfired. Not only had Clinton won a second term, but he had done it with a much larger share of the vote. But then the Monica Lewinsky scandal exploded, whipping up the moral outrage of conservative Catholics like Hudson. The irony of his outrage seemed to be lost on him; unknown to all of his new friends in Washington, the *Crisis* editor had been forced to leave his tenured position at Fordham University after a complaint from an eighteen-year-old student following a drunken sexual encounter between them. Hudson didn't let his own transgressions dilute his ire toward Clinton. "After we have stripped away all idealism from offices that bind our culture together—president, father, husband—what will be left for us to aspire to?" he asked. "Who will want to sacrifice personal desires for public responsibilities?"

Determined to do *something*, Hudson earmarked $75,000 of the magazine's budget for the first major poll into the political attitudes of American Catholics. He hoped the survey might force the political elite to finally take this constituency seriously. He published the findings in *Crisis* in November 1998. "Stripping away inactive Catholics who retain the label as a cultural identification, the real swing voters are *active* Catholics," he concluded. The findings caught the eye of Karl Rove, who saw an opportunity to tap into a new demographic—just as Ronald Reagan had done with Evangelicals in the eighties. He invited Hudson down to Texas to meet George W. Bush, the state's governor, who was considering a run for the presidency. They asked Hudson to become an advisor to the campaign, which he did. It didn't take long for the news to spread among Hudson's fellow conservative Catholics in Washington. This small and hitherto relatively unimportant group of faithful men actively courted by Opus Dei through its V.I.P. retreats in Virginia had suddenly been catapulted onto the political stage.

Meanwhile, McCloskey's evangelization efforts with Belnick soon began to generate sizable donations to Opus Dei. By 1999, the former synagogue president had—through his new job as general counsel for Tyco International—become one of the country's highest-paid attorneys. In September, on his one-year anniversary of joining the company, Belnick received the first of several huge bonuses—$3.4 million from the sale of restricted shares. He emailed McCloskey six days later to announce that he wanted to make a donation for a new chapel dedicated to Josemaría Escrivá at the Catholic Information Center. "I'm sending you my check for $2M toward my pledge to the new Sanctuary/Altar," he declared. Over the next three years, the Tyco International general counsel would receive more than $50 million from his employer. His good fortune soon caught the eye of McCloskey, who encouraged him to donate to other "good" causes—including a new initiative that had recently been set up by Bob Best. The Culture of Life Foundation, as it was called, was a lobby group imbued with Christian values which sought to promote a "more humane society" respecting the dignity of all its members—"especially the poor, the elderly, and those who have no voice." The initiative had been personally endorsed by the pope and counted a number of high-profile supporters. But it was basically a one-man band run by Bob Best, out of the old offices he had once used for the Private Sector Initiatives Foundation. As the initiative grew, the boundary between the Culture of Life Foundation and the Catholic Information Center became increasingly blurred. Best and McCloskey lived at the same numerary residence in the Kalorama neighborhood. They fundraised together for the foundation, tapping into McCloskey's growing coterie of converts. At one stage, Best even transferred the registered address from his old Private Sector Initiatives Foundation offices to 815 15th Street—where the Catholic Information Center was located. The bookstore and chapel was slowly being transformed into a fundraising center for dozens of new initiatives, many of them launched or run by Opus Dei members and co-operators, to tap into the growing political influence of conservative Catholics—all thanks to Hudson's survey.

In April 2000, Belnick was baptized at a small ceremony held at Saint Thomas More Church, on the Upper East Side of New York. The ceremony had been supposed to happen two months earlier, but Belnick hadn't told his wife—who was Jewish and who had been married to him for twenty-six years—until a few days before and she hadn't taken the news well. Evidently, the founder's "instructions" to Opus Dei members that they encourage potential recruits to keep their vocation secret from their families was still alive and well. At the postponed baptism, most of those present were members of the prelature. There was McCloskey, of course—but also Bob Best and Bowie Kuhn, an Opus Dei supernumerary who had inspired Best to get the Culture of Life Foundation off the ground. A few weeks later, Belnick showed his gratitude. In July, the Securities and Exchange Commission wrapped up an investigation it had been conducting into suspicious accounting practices at Tyco. Belnick, as general counsel, had undermined the probe by failing to produce documents and even misleading government investigators. When Tyco received the all-clear, Belnick emailed the company's top human-resources executive, seeking payment of a $12 million bonus he had been promised. He asked for $2 million in cash to be wired immediately. The same day, he sent an email to McCloskey. "Justice triumphs—and the Founder comes through again!" he wrote. When he received the $2 million, he immediately made a six-figure donation to the Culture of Life Foundation. The bequest would transform the lobby group's work—and propel Bob Best to political prominence.

In September, a commemorative mass was held at the Catholic Information Center to celebrate the completion of another project Belnick had helped to pay for—a new chapel dedicated to Josemaría Escrivá, the first in the United States honoring the Opus Dei founder. Javier Echevarría and other members of the Opus Dei leadership had flown in from Rome for this symbolically important event. The guest of honor was Cardinal Hickey, who had gone to the prelature for help in running the bookstore and chapel eight years earlier—and who had seen the venue transformed in the years since. Hickey had led the city's Catholic elite for more twenty years—and had become a man revered across the political spectrum because of his ability to straddle both sides of the deep fissure running through the U.S. congregation, both as an outspoken defender of the poor and a fierce critic of the powerful gun lobby but also as a man who proudly defended controversial Vatican policies on contraception and homosexuality. On the cusp of retirement, this was one of his final acts. The ceremony was like a passing of the torch from an inclusive church of the masses to one unified by a conservative reading of the Gospel and propelled by power and money. Welcoming the cardinal, McCloskey lauded the new premises as "another effort in the new evangelization" that had been called for by the pope. Behind him, to the right of the altar, a bronze statue of the Opus Dei founder looked down on the assembled dignitaries.

With numbers on the increase and its political influence rising, across town Opus Dei was laying the stones for further expansion. Evidently, more numeraries were needed to work this growing influence. A few weeks earlier, the Fairfax County Planning Commission, across the river in Virginia, had approved plans for a $9 million development that was to be called the Reston Study Center—a new residence for numerary men that would offer events, study sessions for high school children, and father-son workshops for the burgeoning, and now politically important, Catholic community in Washington's sprawling suburbs. The money man behind the new project was a little-known financial consultant and supernumerary called Neil Corkery, who would play a critical role in the coming battle to reshape—and re-Christianize—American society.

9

CLOAK AND DAGGER

Vienna, Virginia—February 2001

BONNIE HANSSEN NERVOUSLY GLANCED AT THE CLOCK FOR THE UMPTEENTH time that afternoon and wondered where on earth her husband had got to. Bob had left the house several hours earlier, after offering to drive an old pal, who had been staying with them for the Presidents' Day weekend, out to Dulles Airport—and had promised his wife he'd be back in time for Sunday dinner with the family. An F.B.I. officer with more than twenty-five years of service, Bob was an upstanding member of the community who doted on his children, and regularly went to dawn Mass at Saint Catherine of Siena Catholic Church on his way into the office. Going missing like this was totally out of character. Bonnie, for her part, was a part-time theology teacher at nearby Oakcrest School. The couple were both supernumerary members of Opus Dei and had dutifully sent all six children to its two schools in D.C. Bonnie had known the Work all her life—back in Chicago, her mother had been a childhood friend of Robert Bucciarelli, one of the movement's most senior men in the States, while her father had helped set up its first school in the city, back in the seventies. All her brothers had gone there, and one—John, the youngest—was now an Opus Dei priest in Rome. While Bob had been brought up a Lutheran, he had converted to Catholicism shortly after marrying his college sweetheart Bonnie and had grown to embrace his membership in Opus Dei. He had a reputation for being holier-than-thou at work—some knew him as rabidly homophobic and cartoonishly anti-communist, and it was not uncommon for him to aggressively foist his Catholic faith onto his colleagues. Since moving to the D.C. area twenty years earlier, the couple had become esteemed members of the local Opus Dei community. Bob carpooled with Joe Duffy, husband of the wealthy Noxema heir who was a big donor to the movement, to attend the regular "circle," and the Hanssens went to Sunday Mass at the same church as Bob's boss, F.B.I. director Louis Freeh, who was widely rumored to be a member, too.

With no news of her husband, by early evening Bonnie decided to get into her car and drive out to Dulles Airport herself. She was surrounded by F.B.I. agents in the parking lot, who escorted her back to the family home in Vienna, Virginia. She was told to pack some clothes and toiletries for herself and her children—her husband had been arrested, and the agents had a warrant to search their house. Earlier that afternoon, after dropping his friend at the airport, Bob had driven to Foxstone Park, less than a mile from the family home on Talisman Drive, to leave a stack of classified documents for the Russians. He'd been intercepted by an elaborate sting operation conducted by F.B.I. agents and their colleagues at the Central Intelligence Agency. They had known for years they had a double agent in their midst but had failed to track down the mole until a former Russian agent had provided them with letters, an old recording, and a plastic bag used to make a dead-drop that had Hanssen's fingerprints on it.

The agents had created a fictitious new division within the Bureau and promoted Bob to run it, as a ploy to reel him in. They wired his office with video and audio recording equipment, bought a house on Talisman Drive to monitor his movements, and even orchestrated a shooting contest within F.B.I. headquarters to pry Hanssen away from his desk so that an agent could swipe his beloved PalmPilot. The ploy, three days earlier, had revealed information about a dead-drop planned for that Sunday. The agents had caught Hanssen in the act. They had been lucky; among the bundle of secret documents was a letter from the supernumerary saying he planned to lay low for several months after picking up on some suspicious activity which might mean he was being monitored.

The agents at the Hanssen house were somewhat surprised at how calm Bonnie was, given the misfortune that had just befallen her family. At one point, she indicated she wanted to talk—so she and an agent went up to the bedroom and sat on the bed. There, she revealed that Bob might have been spying for the Russians as early as 1979. The agent was stunned; the team knew only about spying that Hanssen had been doing since 1985. Bonnie recounted a story about how, years earlier, she had discovered him in their basement in New York, reviewing what turned out to be a communication with the G.R.U., Russia's foreign military intelligence. Hanssen had told her everything. Panicked, Bonnie took him to Father Robert Bucciarelli to confess and seek guidance. The Opus Dei priest advised Hanssen to do the right thing and to turn himself in to the authorities. The couple went away and prepared themselves for what was to come. But the next day, Bucciarelli called to say that he had changed his mind. He advised Hanssen that, instead of turning himself in, he should give away to charity any money the Russians had paid him and move on with his life. It is unclear why Bucciarelli suddenly changed his mind—or who else he discussed the case with at the New Rochelle national headquarters where he lived. But, as the most prominent Opus Dei figure in the United States, he must have known that a scandal involving one of the movement's most prominent families would reflect badly on the Work. This was 1980, in the middle of Opus Dei's battle to dispel widespread opposition within the Church about its application to become a personal prelature. As a result of Bucciarelli's advice, Hanssen remained at large. Over the next twenty years, he would become the most notorious double agent in U.S. history. Hanssen gave up valuable military and counterintelligence secrets that placed countless lives in danger, and he provided information that would lead to the execution of at least three Russian double-agents whom the Americans had recruited.

Within days of Hanssen's arrest in February 2001, Opus Dei moved to protect itself from any blowback—just as it had twenty years earlier. Tom Bohlin, a numerary from New Jersey who had taught history to Bonnie Hanssen's brothers at the Opus Dei school in Chicago before being sent to Rome to train as a priest, was the man tasked with creating distance between the prelature and the actions of its supernumerary superspy. Bohlin requested an urgent meeting with the chargé d'affaires to the Holy See at the American Embassy. At the meeting, he told the U.S. official that Opus Dei had conducted an audit of "all financial contributions" made by Hanssen and had concluded that he had only contributed $4,000 during the previous thirty years as a member—and not a single penny after 1992. Bohlin did not go into detail, but it is highly unlikely that this supposedly thorough financial audit told the whole story. It was unthinkable that an Opus Dei member close to the top of the F.B.I. pay scale would have chosen to forgo their monthly donations to the prelature—given that such payments were widely viewed as one of the supernumerary's essential duties. Bohlin's calculations also likely ignored the thousands of dollars Hanssen spent on tuition for his children at the Opus Dei schools, much of which went to pay the many numerary teachers there. Once again, the network of arms-length foundations created by John Haley probably came in very useful, making it possible for Bohlin to argue that Opus Dei itself hadn't received a penny from Hanssen for almost a decade, when that money might have been sent to the Woodlawn Foundation or one of the many other nonprofits the prelature indirectly controlled. Bonnie probably also provided it with a loophole; maybe she was the one to mail the check to Opus Dei each month? What had happened to his ill-gotten money? Hanssen reaped more than $600,000 from the Russians in exchange for the information he supplied. The chargé d'affaires seemed unconvinced. "Request for urgent meeting struck post as unusual," he reported in a cable to the State Department following the meeting. "This is the first time Opus Dei has officially asked for a meeting. It appears that Opus Dei is attempting to preempt any charges that it profited financially from alleged activities of Hanssen."

Villa Tevere had good reason to be careful about how it handled the Hanssen spy scandal. By 2001, as Opus Dei approached the ten-year anniversary of the founder's beatification, the membership figures were finally starting to show some improvement, thanks to the prelature's embrace of the pope's conservative agenda and the inroads made in dozens of cities through the roughly three hundred schools it now operated. At the turn of the millennium, Opus Dei boasted more than eighty thousand members worldwide and had a physical presence in sixty countries across six continents. In the United States—the center of the Hanssen scandal—it had much more at stake. A month before the arrest of the double-agent, the pope had named

José Horacio Gómez, an Opus Dei priest born in Mexico but naturalized as an American citizen, as auxiliary bishop to the Archdiocese of Denver. The appointment caused some controversy, forcing Gómez to go on the defensive. "We are not a sect," he said in response to allegations about the movement's secret practices. "We are part of the church. Opus Dei is so simple, but so difficult to explain."

The appointment had huge significance for the movement. Gómez was the first Opus Dei bishop appointed in the United States, and he marked the prelature's successful courting not just of the pope but also of the ecclesiastical ranks of the American Church itself. In Washington, the Opus Dei community continued to amass money and influence. Around the time of the Hanssen arrest, the founder of the power company AES Corporation, Dennis Bakke, donated more than $10 million earmarked for the purchase and renovation of an 844-acre property near the Shenandoah Mountains, southwest of the capital. Once completed, the property—named as the Longlea Conference Center—would host silent retreats and become a primary tool in Opus Dei's effort to win over the D.C. elite. Work was also nearing completion on its new national headquarters in New York City. A handful of numeraries had begun moving into Murray Hill Place the previous fall and a grand opening was planned for the middle of May—with Cardinal Edward Egan, the Archbishop of New York, slated to bless the new headquarters. But Opus Dei suddenly canceled the event because of what it said was unfinished construction. It later transpired that the event would have coincided with news of the indictment of Hanssen on twenty-one counts of espionage.

A few weeks later, news finally broke about Opus Dei's complicity in the affair. The *New York Times* carried the exclusive as the lead story on its front page, with the headline "Wife Says Suspect Told a Priest 20 Years Ago of Aiding Soviets." When reporters got through to Father Bucciarelli, he initially confirmed that he had known the Hanssens in 1980—but followed up with a written statement saying that he would not discuss whether he had ever met with the double-agent in the context of spiritual guidance. The news kicked off frenzied speculation about which other members of the country's political and economic elite might be part of this mysterious religious movement that had so undermined the U.S. national interest. In Washington, the revelations sparked a brief witch hunt about which other members of the

D.C. establishment might also be involved with the group, with F.B.I. Director Louis Freeh and Supreme Court Justice Antonin Scalia both named as possible sympathizers. Against this backdrop, Opus Dei's new $70 million headquarters in New York opened with little fanfare. The prelature's grand ambitions for the United States were now seriously compromised.

In July 2001, Bob Best appeared on *Washington Journal*, a popular call-in show on the cable network C-SPAN, for a special segment on stem cell research. The issue had been thrust into the national spotlight within weeks of George W. Bush's entering the White House. The new president announced a review of federal government guidelines established by the Clinton administration only a few months earlier, related to the use of aborted embryos for ground-breaking scientific research. The review made good on a pledge the Bush campaign had made to Catholic voters. They had rallied behind the Texan to help him narrowly beat Al Gore to the presidency—albeit only after the Supreme Court invalidated thousands of votes for his Democrat opponent. In the months since announcing the review, a fierce debate had broken out within the administration. It divided the pragmatists, on one hand, who saw the potential medical breakthroughs promised by such research, and the political strategists such as Karl Rove, who understood how important the Catholic base was to Bush's hopes for reelection. With public debate still raging about how Bush should balance the religious beliefs of a minority against the clear scientific benefits of such research, Bob Best—president of the Culture of Life Foundation—had been invited onto the show to field questions from viewers about this issue. While the foundation had been created with the broad mandate of promoting a "more humane society" respecting the dignity of all its members—"especially the poor, the elderly and those who have no voice"—it had more recently focused all its efforts on opposing any stem cell research using human embryos.

Anchor Connie Doebele cut right to the chase.

"Once people have made a decision to discard the leftover embryo—after they have made their family planning decisions—the question, the ethical question, then is why not go ahead and use it for research?" she asked.

Bob Best spoke slowly and with a hint of a Southern drawl as he made his rebuttal.

José María Escrivá entered the seminary at sixteen, where his vanity soon attracted ridicule from the other students. He struggled to make friends and occasionally got into fights with the other seminarians, who mockingly called him "the little gentleman." *Album/Alamy*

Once ordained, Escrivá (center) opened an academy offering classes to law and architecture students in 1934, which was a front to lure young, impressionable students into Opus Dei. He honed and refined his techniques, eventually drawing up a manual that he instructed his followers to use in order to isolate potential recruits and slowly draw them into the movement. *Album/Alamy*

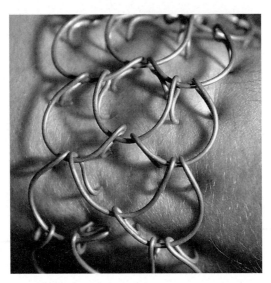

Recruits were instructed to follow a "plan of life" that included wearing a cilice—a small spiked chain worn under the clothing around the thigh—every afternoon. The practice, alongside other sacrifices such as not drinking water for long periods, was supposed to remind them of the suffering of Christ. *Orjan Ellingvag / Corbis / Getty Images*

Corporal mortification was an essential part of membership. Recruits were expected to whip themselves with a "discipline" like this one once a week. Escrivá liked to add bits of metal and pieces of razor blade to enhance his suffering, which sometimes left the room spattered with blood. *Wayne Perry / Alamy*

Escrivá (center) moved to Rome in 1946, where he successfully lobbied Vatican authorities to officially recognize Opus Dei as a "secular institute." The status gave the organization legitimacy among ordinary Catholics and helped make its recruitment efforts increasingly effective. *Franco Origlia / Opus Dei Archive / Getty Images*

In Rome, he moved into a former palace and transformed it into a vast complex that included twelve dining rooms and fourteen chapels. Escrivá ordered his recruits back in Spain to do whatever was necessary to find the money to pay for it. Many defrauded the government and their families. *Antonello Nusca / Gamma-Rapho / Getty Images*

Opus Dei flourished under Francisco Franco (left), the brutal Spanish dictator who conspired with Adolf Hitler to aid the Nazi war effort. Escrivá fostered his relationship with Franco and devised various schemes to help the dictator, who considered the Opus Dei founder as "very loyal." *OFF / AFP / Getty Images*

The Franco regime forced twenty thousand political prisoners to hollow out a mountain and erect a cross on its summit. Many died in the inhumane conditions. At the same time, Opus Dei offered to work closely with Franco "towards the complete restoration of a just and Christian social order." *Philippe Desmazes / AFP / Getty Images*

By 1969, ties between the Franco regime and Opus Dei were so close that more than half of the seats in the cabinet belonged to men who were members of the organization. *Album/Alamy*

Opus Dei's relations with the Vatican were more strained—particularly under Pope Paul VI (left). At one point, the Holy See launched an investigation into claims that the movement was openly challenging the pope's authority. Escrivá toyed with the idea of moving Opus Dei into the Greek Orthodox Church.

Opus Dei Rome / Getty Images

Escrivá developed an acute sense of self-importance. He changed his first name—rather than be yet another Saint Joseph, he wanted to be the first Saint Josemaría. He also told his followers to collect artifacts connected to his life, which might be revered as relics after his canonization. *Opus Dei Rome / Getty Images*

He also ordered the construction of a vast shrine in the Pyrenean foothills. Escrivá stipulated that there should be forty confessional boxes, as many as at Lourdes, for the vast numbers of pilgrims he predicted would visit the site each year. It remains unclear where the money to construct it came from. *Mauritius Images / Alamy*

Opus Dei's methods of recruiting university students began to falter in the 1970s, triggering a series of protests against the organization in Sydney, New York, and elsewhere. Instead, it turned its attention to recruiting children through an ambitious school-building program. *Martin James Brannan / Fairfax Media / Getty Images*

Escrivá died in 1975 and was buried in the crypt underneath the Opus Dei headquarters in Rome, in a tomb bearing the words "The Father." He was succeeded by Álvaro del Portillo, whom Escrivá had groomed since his student days, and who pledged not to change anything about the organization. *Eric Vandeville / Gamma-Rapho / Getty Images*

Luis Valls-Taberner was part of a group of Opus Dei members who ruthlessly took control of Banco Popular in the 1950s and transformed the Spanish bank into a cash machine for the movement, siphoning off hundreds of millions of dollars over the next sixty years. *Paco Junquera / Cover / Getty Images*

Banco Popular helped to finance a global network of so-called vocational schools that targeted young women, many of them still children, from poor backgrounds and coerced them into a life of servitude for Opus Dei. Many were trafficked around the world to meet the needs of the movement. *Robert Wilkinson / Alamy*

Pope John Paul II (at right, in white) was close to Opus Dei and frequently met with Álvaro del Portillo, its leader. He saw the organization as a critical conservative bastion of support within a divided Church and elevated it to a special new status—that of "personal prelature"—that gave it unprecedented power. *Edoardo Fornaciari / Getty Images*

The elevation in status coincided with the death of the Italian banker Roberto Calvi. His family later said that Calvi had been negotiating with Opus Dei to bail out the Vatican just before his death, following a huge scandal involving money laundering that implicated senior Catholic figures. *Archivio APG / Mondadori Portfolio / Getty Images*

Pope John Paul II rushed through the canonization of Escrivá. Today, he is revered as Saint Josemaría within the Catholic Church. Opus Dei strived to discredit serious allegations made by former members during the process, and the testimonies of many of them were never heard. *Gabriel Bouys / AFP / Getty Images*

The remains of Escrivá were subsequently transferred from the crypt to be displayed below the altar in the main chapel at the Opus Dei headquarters in Rome. A solemn ceremony is now held every day at noon to commemorate the founder of the movement, which today counts more than ninety thousand members worldwide. *Eric Vandeville / Gamma-Rapho / Getty Images*

Opus Dei has sought to capitalize on Escrivá's canonization by expanding its reach—especially in the United States, where it has carved out support among the conservative Catholic elite. In the late nineties, it built this $70-million national headquarters in the heart of New York City. *Mike Albans / New York* Daily News *Archive / Getty Images*

The organization's treatment of its lowest class of members—the so-called numerary assistants—has continued to dog its reputation. Catherine Tissier, a French former numerary assistant, has sued Opus Dei for exploiting her while she was a numerary assistant. *Lionel Bonaventure / AFP / Getty Images*

After Álvaro del Portillo's death in 1994, the leadership of Opus Dei passed to Javier Echevarría, who would remain in charge for the next twenty-two years. Under his leadership, the organization would make new inroads into the United States—especially among the wealthy conservative elite. *Eric Vandeville / Gamma-Rapho / Getty Images*

Robert Hanssen, a supernumerary member, gave valuable military and counterintelligence secrets to the Russians that placed countless lives in danger and led to the execution of at least three double-agents. His Opus Dei priest was made aware of his treachery twenty years before Hanssen's arrest and told him to keep it to himself. *Pictorial Press / Alamy*

Father Tom Bohlin, who was recruited into Opus Dei during his time at the University of Notre Dame, ran the organization in the United States during the 2000s and 2010s. He sought to counter the unflattering depiction of Opus Dei in *The Da Vinci Code* with several television appearances, including this one on *Meet the Press*. *Alex Wong / Getty Images*

Pope Benedict XVI had objected to the unprecedented powers granted to Opus Dei by his predecessor. Such was the organization's influence by the time Benedict became pope—a statue of Escrivá was literally built into the walls of the Vatican, pictured here—that he felt unable to reverse the changes. *Vincenzo Pinto / AFP / Getty Images*

C. John McCloskey (left), an Opus Dei priest at the Catholic Information Center in Washington, D.C., converted some of the city's most powerful figures. He fled the country in 2003, shortly after being accused of sexually assaulting one member of his congregation. The allegations were later settled for $1 million. *Alex Wong / Getty Images*

The academic Robert P. George helped create a "beachhead" at Princeton University for the conservative Catholicism pushed by Opus Dei, using money provided by the organization. That blueprint has since been extended to more than a dozen other universities across the United States, including Harvard, Yale, and Stanford. *Chris Goodney / Bloomberg / Getty Images*

Powerful conservative activist Leonard Leo (right) supports Opus Dei through his network of nonprofits and through his role as a director at the Catholic Information Center in Washington, D.C., which the movement runs. *Aurora Rose / Patrick McMullan / Getty Images*

Leo has been a critical figure in reshaping the U.S. Supreme Court. He was involved in the nomination of the five conservative justices who joined the court in the 2000s and is a longtime friend of the sixth conservative justice, Clarence Thomas. *Jabin Botsford / Washington Post / Getty Images*

In 2021, forty-two former numerary assistants in Argentina filed a complaint with the Vatican detailing Opus Dei's systematic abuse of women. The document named Opus Dei's leader, Fernando Ocáriz, and his deputy Mariano Fazio, pictured here with Pope Francis, as being complicit in the abuse. Since then, the pope has made a series of moves to rein in the organization—including issuing two papal decrees that downgrade the institution and that strip it of its authority over members. Opus Dei has sought to shrug off the moves, setting up a major fight between it and the Catholic Church. *Independent Photo Agency / Alamy*

"Well, the key point in this whole debate is that a human embryo is a human person and has all the biology, all the D.N.A., all the chromosomes that a human person has," he responded. "The sex is decided even at the single cell. As a human person and as a human being, it deserves respect, and to use them for experiments—to deliberately and directly kill a human embryo for whatever reason—it's immoral, it's illegal, it's against every principle of Western civilization, and it's totally unnecessary."

In the four years since launching the Culture of Life Foundation, the one-man political lobby group had grown dramatically. Thanks to a six-figure donation from the Tyco general counsel Mark Belnick, whom Best had met through Father McCloskey, the foundation had hired more staff and established itself as a major political force on the issue. Best drew on Opus Dei's growing network to recruit several high-profile pro-life figures to the foundation as advisors. Robert George, a Princeton academic who had become good friends with the director of an Opus Dei numerary residence there, and who had been introduced to Best through McCloskey, joined the board. George would soon become a critical figure in another under-the-radar Opus Dei project. William Hogan, an obstetrician who had known the Work since the late seventies after being aggressively hounded by Father Bob Connor (the childhood friend of Supreme Court Justice Antonin Scalia) at his house and outside of his office, became a medical advisor. McCloskey was named ecclesiastical advisor—alongside Charles Chaput, the Archbishop of Denver who had consecrated José Horacio Gómez as the first Opus Dei bishop in the United States. From the Culture of Life Foundation offices adjoining the Catholic Information Center, Best sought to capitalize on the sudden rise in interest in the stem cell with a stream of press releases. The announcements oscillated between presenting the foundation as a serious, scholarly institute backed by prominent medical, legal, and ecclesiastical advisors; and a sensationalist publicity machine that put its own spin on unsubstantiated news pieces about how people were now selling their organs in England or a new pro-life song from a Grammy-nominated artist.

C-SPAN anchor Connie Doebele seemed confused by this oddly mixed messaging.

"So, what *is* the Culture of Life Foundation?" she asked.

"The Culture of Life Foundation collects and communicates the medical, scientific, philosophical, psychological, ontological, and even theological truths that confirm the dignity of each human person and the sacredness of human life."

"And who funds it?"

"It's funded by donors—you're looking at one," Best responded, smirking. "But it's not a big organization. We're very small. We're almost like a little embryo, operating with four people in a Washington office. We have a nice board of directors and a board of advisors."

"Are you religious based?" asked the anchor, probingly.

"Not really," the numerary answered. "We have people from different religions. If you looked at our website, which is—can I put a plug in for that . . . ?"

Best wasn't giving much away. He made no mention of the donation from Mark Belnick, which had helped double the foundation's budget from two years earlier, or its links to Father McCloskey and the Catholic Information Center. He made no mention of his own affiliation with Opus Dei, or the fact that he was a numerary member. Such opacity, which purposefully covered up any links back to the prelature, would become a blueprint over the coming years for the myriad political action groups born of the Catholic Information Center and the city's growing Opus Dei community.

"Sure," said Doebele.

"It is www.culture-of-life.org—got to get the dashes in," he added in a folksy drawl.

"What will people see there?"

"People will see sections that deal with medical and biological truths, they will see philosophy, they will see psychology—and they'll see religious truths. And among those religious truths are truths from the Roman Catholic, from Orthodox, from mainline Protestant groups, from Jewish groups, and also from the Moslems."

"Let's take some phone calls for you," she interrupted. "Jacksonville, Illinois—*for* stem cell research. Good morning."

A breathy caller came on the line.

"In the battle between science—which establishes fact—and belief, it appears to me down through the years that science always wins," said the voice. "You can't stop good science. Thank goodness. And I believe this is good science—and religious belief won't stop it."

"Well, I disagree with that premise," interjected Best. "I don't believe there's any conflict at all between good science and the truths of faith. Truth is indivisible, and so to make the point that science always wins over faith is absurd—in my opinion."

His argument echoed the internal Opus Dei documents used to guide numeraries like him about how to "ensure that scientific truth and progress serve as a means to imbue men and culture with the knowledge of God." Best had certainly done his work in that sense. The Culture of Life website pumped out reams of disinformation and pseudo-science on its website— such as about how oral contraceptives could be deadly and about how new medication to abort pregnancies had been developed in Nazi death camps. Best added to this disinformation drive with articles warning of his dark vision for modern-day America—a dystopia unnervingly similar to that of McCloskey, his Opus Dei comrade. "We see teenagers killing their own baby at a prom, then going on to dance the night away. We have enshrined the killing of innocent human beings under the bogus Constitutional phrase, *a woman's right to choose*," he wrote. "It is not difficult to imagine an electorate or a court 10 or 50 years from now who would favor getting rid of useless old people, the homeless, retarded children, anti-social blacks, illegal Hispanics, gypsies, Jews, gays, lesbians . . . the list goes on and on." He outlined his vision to replace this culture of death with one of life, starting on Capitol Hill. "Our government will indeed be *by the people, for the people and of the people*, losing its tendency to be oppressive and intrusive," he declared. "Our leaders will see power as an opportunity to serve, not as a podium for personal glory."

In the run-up to the 2000 presidential election, Best had also used the foundation's website to mount calculated slurs against Al Gore, with sensationalist articles about the Democratic candidate's "tolerance" of homosexuals, which echoed other homophobic material on the site—including a piece urging readers to write to DC Comics and any companies that advertised with them to complain about plans for two openly gay superheroes.

"You also have had some personal communication with the president on this issue," said the anchor Connie Doebele, referring to stem cell research.

Best had brought along a letter from Bush addressed to him, as president of the Culture of Life Foundation, outlining his opposition to federal funding for research based stem cells extracted from aborted embryos—and effectively pledging to restrict funding to research on tissues extracted from adults. With no policy announced yet, the letter was a coup for the Culture of Life Foundation. Best had been given advance information on a policy that would be announced in a televised address to the nation the following month.

In January 2002, more than a thousand dignitaries gathered at the Palazzo dell'Apollinare, in central Rome. Dating back to the thirteenth century, the palace had once been a seat for cardinals, who used it to scheme and plot far from the watchful eye of the Vatican, across the Tiber. These days, the palace was home to the Pontifical University of the Holy Cross, which Álvaro del Portillo had founded shortly after the erection of Opus Dei as a personal prelature in the early eighties—and later given pontifical status by his old friend, the pope. The university had racked up huge losses every year since, with millions of dollars diverted from Opus Dei's sprawling global network of foundations at the start of each academic year to cover the vast expense of renting such a palatial location and hiring the two hundred people required to run it. That year alone, a foundation run out of an office in Princeton, which acted as a conduit for money diverted from other Opus Dei foundations, would wire more than $2 million to the university. Other foundations in Chile, Germany, Italy, and Spain performed similar roles. While Villa Tevere sought to frame this huge drain on its financial resources as a selfless sacrifice—a realization of the founder's dream to have an ecclesiastical institution in Rome "at the service of the whole Church"—the money spent on the university bought the prelature power and influence around the world. The vast majority of students enrolled there were priests in training from hard-up dioceses in Europe, Latin America, and Africa. Opus Dei covered much of their tuition and living costs. Such generosity created goodwill with local bishops, who otherwise would struggle to send their priests to Rome for their studies.

The university also allowed Opus Dei to position itself as an authority in canon law and Church communications—two critical keys to power at the Vatican. The numeraries who taught there were frequently called upon by the Holy See to offer their advice and expertise. The university's longstanding dean of canon law would eventually become secretary of the Pontifical

Council for Legislative Texts—also known as the Vatican's Supreme Court— a body already presided over by Julián Herranz, an Opus Dei bishop close to the pope. The school of canon law had been particularly successful in "cornering the market"—as senior figures within Opus Dei liked to joke— on any debate concerning personal prelatures and publishing dozens of papers that explained away the contradictions in canon law.

But over five chilly days that January, the university had a very different role—as the host of a major conference to celebrate the centenary of the founder's birth. Haughtily titled "The Grandeur of Ordinary Life," the event portrayed the prelature as a powerful influence at the Vatican and around the world, with important conservative allies such as the Italian Cardinal Camillo Ruini and the Archbishop of Sydney George Pell due to deliver speeches. The event was the start of a year of celebration centered on the life of the founder, which would include conferences in Belgium, Hong Kong, Kenya, Spain, and the United States, and where eight separate events were planned in Washington, Chicago, New York, Saint Louis, San Francisco, Boston, and Minneapolis. Such huge expenditure was a build-up to the canonization of the founder, expected later that year. The five-day extravaganza in Rome would include the premiere of a new documentary film about the founder and the launch of a new set of stamps in Italy commemorating his life—and would culminate in an audience with the pope on the final day for the Opus Dei faithful who had journeyed to Rome from around the world.

Among those invited to speak at the conference was a future U.S. presidential candidate. Rick Santorum, a senator from Pennsylvania and the third most senior Republican, had been introduced to Opus Dei through his wife's devout Catholic parents and regularly attended its V.I.P. retreats in rural Virginia. While already a fervent supporter of the movement, Opus Dei had further enticed the senator to fly to Rome for the event by paying him a speaking fee—covered by the foundation in Princeton which sent millions to the Pontifical University of the Holy Cross. Nonetheless, Santorum claimed on his congressional declaration that he was attending the event in an official capacity as a U.S. senator. Such blurring of private faith and public function was a recurring theme of the talks given at the conference. Speaker after speaker reiterated the need of Opus Dei members—and Catholics more generally—to use their positions in society to shape public policy, citing one famous phrase attributed to the founder. "Have you ever bothered to think how absurd it is to leave one's Catholicism aside on entering a university, or a professional association, or a scholarly meeting, or a congress—as if you were checking your hat at the door?" he had supposedly asked. Santorum echoed that sentiment, telling the conference that—in his public fight at the U.S. Senate to uphold absolute truths—"blessed Josemaría guides my way." He also used his appearance to question a speech given by John F. Kennedy before the 1960 election, in which he stated clearly that he would not take orders from the Catholic Church if elected president. Santorum declared that such views had caused "much harm in America." "All of us have heard people say, 'I privately am against abortion, homosexual marriage, stem cell research, cloning . . . but who am I to decide that it's not right for somebody else?' It sounds good," he added. "But it is the corruption of freedom of conscience." His words were lapped up by McCloskey, the man who had invited him there, whose efforts to capture people who could have an influence were beginning to pay dividends.

McCloskey stayed on after the conference to celebrate Mass with the pope in his private chapel at the Vatican. After the private Mass, Wojtyła presented McCloskey with a rosary. He explained that the gift was a reminder that, whenever Christ—or anyone else—found themselves "on the cross," the Virgin Mary would always be by their side. The example set by the eighty-one-year-old—Pope John Paul the Great, as McCloskey called him—in standing up to the criticism that had beset his papacy would inspire the Opus Dei priest, who soon found himself "on the cross" defending the Church against allegations it had systematically covered up the abuse of minors in the United States.

That news had broken just two days before "The Grandeur of Ordinary Life" event, following the publication of the first in a series of devastating exposés by a group of journalists at the *Boston Globe*, detailing systematic efforts within the Archdiocese of Boston to cover up sexual abuse dating back decades. Over coming months, as hundreds more victims came forward, similar stories emerged across the country, revealing an endemic culture of concealment and suppression across the Catholic Church that protected sexual predators in its ranks. As the U.S. Conference of Catholic Bishops scrambled to take action in response to a rising groundswell of anger from ordinary Catholics around the country, McCloskey adopted a contrarian attitude, seeking not only to downplay the grievous criminal acts committed by his colleagues within the Church but also to twist the narrative around this widespread problem as part of a liberal plot threatening the Church and wider society. "This is a problem of active homosexuals within the clergy—not a problem of pedophilia," he said at the height of the scandal. "The American press does not want to recognize this. On the contrary, many media have been advocating that the Boy Scouts admit homosexuals among their monitors. The press and 'dissident' Catholics have used the conduct of a small proportion of the clergy to relentlessly attack the priesthood and the Church hierarchy, to advocate the abrogation of priestly celibacy and the ordination of women."

McCloskey's comments mirrored the Holy See's own response to the scandal, which was being handled by the pope's press secretary, Joaquín Navarro-Valls, the most prominent member of Opus Dei within the Vatican. He had been the one who had persuaded Cardinal Bernard Law, the Archbishop of Boston and a man directly implicated in the cover-up of sexual abuse, to resist calls for him to resign—imploring him to hang on and warning that stepping down risked creating a "domino effect" that could rip through the Church. Navarro-Valls sought to frame the allegations against the Church as a homosexual rather than a pedophilia problem, claiming that most of the cases involved teenage boys rather than children. "People with these inclinations just cannot be ordained," he said in response to the mounting scandal, referring specifically to the role that homosexuality had played in the scandal.

McCloskey seemed to revel in his newfound stardom as the last line of defense for a Church besieged by liberal elements. At the Catholic Information Center, which moved to larger premises on K Street at the height of the scandal in April 2002, a television screen placed in the reception area of the bookstore and chapel played his recent appearance on *Meet the Press* on a continual loop. In the interview, he made it clear there should be no room for debate among Catholics about the moral issues of the day—that the views of the aging, now heavily medicated pope were not to be questioned. "The church is not run by opinion polls," he explained. "It's not a Chinese menu which you can choose things. You have to assent . . . to all the truths the

Catholic Church teaches. That's what the essence of Catholicism is." Mc-Closkey's delight in his growing celebrity angered some among the Catholic Information Center's flock. It wasn't the only element of his behavior that had begun to ring alarm bells in Washington. Deal Hudson, the publisher of *Crisis* magazine, had a very public falling out with McCloskey after he discovered proof that the Opus Dei priest had broken the seal of confession by sharing personal information with someone else. Hudson had unintentionally hit on a widespread technique used by some in Opus Dei who sometimes shared information gathered in the confessional with local directors to guide them in controlling members and sympathizers in their charge.

By 2002, Opus Dei was experiencing phenomenal growth in the city. The Longlea Conference Center, which had just opened its doors, was the latest big development. Within its first year alone, the venue would host five hundred people to its weekend retreats. Back in the capital, a similar number of people were attending its monthly evenings of recollection. All of them were drawn in by Opus Dei's public message—that they could best serve God through the sanctification of the everyday, whether at work, at home, or in their friendships. Few saw the hidden side of the movement: the violation of the confessional, the systematic targeting of children, the numerary assistants being trafficked from other parts of the world.

With Escrivá's canonization fast approaching, in 2001 and 2002 the organization updated its internal documents to strengthen the system of control that had been devised by the founder and carefully enhanced by his successors. Following the *instructions* of the founder and the *vademecums* of Del Portillo, Javier Echevarría called his own set of edicts "experiences." The name sought to give the impression that the documents were mere tips and observations accumulated by thousands of numeraries and priests over the years, although their contents were no less authoritarian than those of his predecessors. The first document, issued in March 2000, was titled "Experiences of How to Carry out Fraternal Chats" in reference to the regular "chat," also known as the "confidence," that all Opus Dei members were expected to have with their spiritual director. The practice was an extension of confession under which members were expected not only to divulge their sins but also to provide intimate details of their professional, personal, and sex lives. In centuries past, such "manifestations of conscience" had been an important element of life within religious orders. But the practice was so open to abuse that the Vatican had effectively banned it in 1890. Revisions of canon law in 1917 and 1983 reinforced the ban on forced manifestations, emphasizing the freedom of all Catholics to choose if, when, and how often they took part.

But the "chat" had become such an essential tool of control over the membership that Opus Dei chose to ignore canon law. In the movement's secret internal documents, the founder's successors enforced the practice in direct contravention of canon law. "The confidence—that sincere chat, full of supernatural meaning—is the highest means of sanctification, apart from the sacraments, that we have in Opus Dei," Echevarría stipulated. His instructions deliberately blurred the boundaries between God and the intricately designed system of abuse and control that underpinned Opus Dei. "The directors are instruments of God who are gifted with the necessary graces to help you," he wrote. "Therefore, we always come with a disposition of complete sincerity, with the desire that they might attain a knowledge of our ascetic struggle that is ever clearer, fuller, more intimate—wishing to facilitate, to those who have the mission of forming us, the knowledge of all our personal circumstances . . . it brings us joy to make our souls so transparent."

Reinforcing the controlling element of the "confidence," Echevarría stated that any advice received was not optional. "Advice will normally take the form of guidance or suggestions," he added, "but whoever receives them must accept them as if they had come from Jesus Christ, Our Lord himself." In direct contravention of canon law, he made it clear to the membership that such manifestations of conscience were not to be a free choice but, rather, a mandatory element of membership.

That October, the Opus Dei membership converged on Rome to witness Escrivá's canonization. On the face of it, the event was an even more impressive demonstration than the beatification some ten years earlier. This time, the crowd stretched all the way down to the Tiber—an estimated three hundred thousand people were in attendance, although yet again many students unaffiliated with the prelature had been enticed with heavily subsidized tickets. In a weak, trembling voice that betrayed the extent of his Parkinson's, which the Vatican was struggling to keep secret, Pope John Paul II proclaimed the founder of Opus Dei as a modern-day saint following the confirmation of another miracle—a Spanish doctor supposedly cured of his cancer. After the ceremony, a hundred priests standing beneath white umbrellas fanned out into the crowd to give communion to the assembled masses. Afterwards, the pope invited Echevarría into his vehicle to tour the crowd, stopping occasionally so that John Paul II could kiss a baby passed up from the crowd.

In that moment, with the elevation of its founder to the Catalogue of Saints, it seemed Opus Dei's ascent was complete. But its position remained precarious. Its two biggest benefactors were gravely ill. Within months of the ceremony, the Vatican would at long last admit what had been obvious for many years—the pope was seriously unwell. Luis Valls-Taberner was suffering from the same disease. Opus Dei faced the prospect of a future without the two men who had so developed the Work. Unknown to its leadership, new challenges were also emerging on both sides of the Atlantic that threatened to deal a huge blow to the movement at precisely the time it should have been looking forward to a promising new future. The first would become apparent just a few weeks after the canonization ceremony, when Opus Dei was informed of sexual misconduct allegations against its star priest in Washington, D.C. The second would come from an unexpected quarter.

10

THE ALBINO ASSASSIN

Murray Hill Place, New York—January 2003

BRIAN FINNERTY WAS STILL RIDING HIGH FROM THE POSITIVE COVERAGE HE and his fellow numeraries in the Opus Dei press office had whipped up about Escrivá's canonization three months earlier, when he came across an article in *Publishers Weekly* that stopped him in his tracks. Hard working and meticulous, Finnerty liked to monitor the trade magazine for the latest nonfiction releases, so that he might get a heads-up about anything that could cause trouble for the Work. Such prudence had already proven valuable. Over the previous fourteen months, no fewer than five books had been published about the Hanssen spying scandal, each with more salacious details than the last—and Finnerty's diligence had allowed the prelature to prepare for trouble ahead of time. Curiously, it was an article in the fiction section that caught Finnerty's eye that day. It was about a new novel by Dan Brown, a former schoolteacher from New Hampshire, whose previous three books had sold modestly but whose latest offering had set the publishing world ablaze with excitement. *The Da Vinci Code* was a well-paced thriller about the murder of a museum curator in Paris who leaves behind a set of mysterious clues pointing to a dark truth long buried by the Church.

Finnerty inwardly sighed at this latest attempt to profit from sacrilegious nonsense. But a throwaway line in the second paragraph grabbed his attention. "What keeps this baroque conceit from collapsing is the way Brown grounds it in historical facts about Da Vinci's life, along with two actual secret societies: the Priory of Sion, a pagan brotherhood to which Da Vinci belonged, and a contemporary, Vatican-sanctioned Christian sect called Opus Dei." An *actual* secret society? His heart sank. With the publishing frenzy about the Hanssen scandal finally dying down, he had been hoping to dedicate the coming year to promoting the cause for beatification of Del Portillo, a clear priority for his bosses at Villa Tevere. Only recently, he had even dared to think that, following the glowing coverage of Escrivá's canonization, Opus Dei might finally have turned a corner in its relationship with the press. Now, it was clear he had another potential public relations crisis on his hands.

Finnerty knew he had to move quickly. A former computer programmer who had quit his job at IBM after discovering that his true vocation was in public relations, the numerary had been an early champion of the web within Opus Dei, and he often boasted about how he had saved the prelature from malicious content being posted in its name, having had the foresight to secure the opusdei.org domain in the web's early days. Faced with this unexpected crisis, he again turned to the web as a potential savior. He stumbled across a set of bound galleys of the book for sale online. Bound galleys were advance copies that the publisher sent out to reviewers, booksellers, and salespeople to drum up interest ahead of the official launch; some of them had somehow found their way onto eBay. Finnerty bought one and read it from cover to cover.

Despite clearly identifying itself as a work of fiction—the words "A Novel" were emblazoned on the cover—the book began with a special "fact" section. "The Vatican prelature known as Opus Dei is a deeply devout Catholic sect that has been the topic of recent controversy due to reports of brainwashing, coercion and a dangerous practice known as 'corporal mortification,'" it read. Worse was to come. Dan Brown had dredged up a series of allegations which had been thrown at the prelature over the years. As well as the Hanssen spy scandal, there were mentions of Opus Dei's bailout of the Vatican Bank, charges about its thirst for power, and allegations of its "medieval" views on women. The book's main villain was an escaped convict turned numerary, an assassin tasked by the prelate with murdering the members of a rival sect—a man who would stop at nothing to safeguard the Work's interests.

Given his role as communications director, Finnerty enjoyed certain privileges denied to other numeraries, who were subject to draconian rules controlling the information they consumed—which books they read, what news they heard, and which movies they could watch. The practice traced its roots back to medieval times, when the Church first began to issue lists of books deemed heretical or immoral, lists which were later published as the *Index Librorum Prohibitorum*. The Vatican had scrapped the index in the sixties, concluding that Catholics should be free to make their own decisions about what they read. Escrivá had mutinied against the Holy See by putting together his own list, which had been fine-tuned over the years as yet another method of control. By the early 2000s, even as billions of people around the world were enjoying an information revolution that put knowledge instantly at their fingertips, most numeraries remained locked in the Dark Ages, limited to reading books that had been approved by an Opus Dei priest in Rome. Flaubert, Joyce, Kerouac, Pinter, Roth, and Tennessee Williams were all off limits. Special dispensations were occasionally granted—but only when absolutely necessary. Access to the news was equally controlled. While most residences received deliveries of safe, conservative-leaning newspapers, local directors would pore over them first for any inappropriate material. It wasn't unusual for numeraries to pick up the morning paper to find photos or articles cut out. As a result, most numeraries lived in ignorance of anything remotely negative about Opus Dei—other than what they were told by superiors, who framed these false accusations as acts of religious persecution.

As one of only a handful of numeraries allowed to read anything remotely critical, Finnerty was well aware that *The Da Vinci Code* presented a major problem for the prelature. He raised his concerns with Tom Bohlin, who had only just arrived in New York to take up his new assignment as Opus Dei's most senior man in the States. Originally from New Jersey, Bohlin joined Opus Dei as a numerary while studying history at the University of Notre Dame in the seventies, and he was instantly drawn in by the philosophy that ordinary Catholics like himself could best serve God not by becoming priests, but by living out their faith in the world as lawyers or doctors or politicians. But it wasn't long before the practical needs of the Work took precedent over the fiction that had been sold to him. With Bohlin set to attend law school after his graduation from Notre Dame, he was unexpectedly asked to remain in Chicago to help out at a school that Opus Dei had just opened there. He agreed—refusing the request would have been deemed "bad spirit"—and deferred his entry to law school by a year. The next year, he deferred again. After three years of teaching, he began to like the job—but was soon transferred to another role, this time as an administrator for the various clubs aimed at teenage boys that Opus Dei ran across the Midwest. Bohlin embraced this opportunity to bring Escrivá's teachings into young people's lives. Keen to cultivate this loyal lieutenant, Bohlin's superiors decided to send him to Rome for World Youth Day. Opus Dei arranged for him to appear on stage in front of three hundred thousand young Catholics who had journeyed to Rome to celebrate their faith; he would talk about his work in the Midwest. The pope embraced him and gave him a rosary.

Quiet and withdrawn, Bohlin had never been keen on becoming a priest. But one day in 1993, he received a memo from Villa Tevere informing him that the prelate had specially selected him to move to Rome and study at the Pontifical University of the Holy Cross, in preparation for ordination. Such memos were not unusual within Opus Dei: while many numeraries may have harbored a burning desire to enter the priesthood, and may even have requested permission from the prelate to do so, becoming a priest of Opus Dei was not a decision numeraries were allowed to make themselves. Candidates were monitored and selected—whether they had expressed a strong desire to enter the priesthood or not—and informed of their new posting when the needs of the Work required it. Bohlin was duly sent off to Rome to study, finally becoming ordained at the age of forty-three. While there, he caught the eye of Javier Echevarría, who singled him out for greater things. Bohlin was invited to work alongside the prelate as part of his personal staff. He soon realized he was being groomed for another, more important role. Once again, Opus Dei used its status with the Vatican to woo this rising star. During the canonization, Bohlin was seated next to the altar and was invited to receive communion from the pope. A few weeks later, Echevarría called him to ask whether he would be willing to return to the United States as regional vicar. He told him to pray on it and come back with his answer. A couple of hours later, Bohlin went back to accept. Within a few years, he had gone from running clubs for teenage boys in the Midwest to being the most senior Opus Dei man in the United States.

Bohlin's appointment was part of a wider refresh of the organization's most senior cadres. While on the face of it, the prelate had notched up a long list of successes—expanding to seven new countries, mining the rich seam of wealth that cut through its membership, infiltrating the D.C. conservative Catholic elite, and the canonization itself—beneath the surface the worrying trends were evident. Echevarría was particularly upset about the unsatisfactory number of new vocations. Under Del Portillo's ill-fated recruitment drive in the eighties and nineties, the organization had attracted twenty thousand new members over an eight-year period. If those figures were disappointing, then Echevarría's efforts were truly galling. Over roughly the same period—and with a much larger pool of numeraries operating over a far bigger number of countries—just five thousand new members had joined. The consequences of the prelate's frustration were borne out by the ordinary numeraries, who lived under inordinate pressure from their local directors to meet unrealistic targets set by the regional headquarters. Rather than ask deep questions about why Opus Dei had failed to gain more traction with young people, Villa Tevere focused its efforts on oiling the internal propaganda machine to produce an image of rapid expansion and to reinforce the cult of personality surrounding the founder. Millions of dollars were spent on two supposedly serious academic institutes—one at the Opus Dei university in Rome and the other in Spain—that did little serious scholarship, but pumped out paper after paper extolling the virtues of Saint Josemaría. Opus Dei's internal magazine *Romana* was filled with accounts sent in by ordinary members, who told of the many souls being drawn to the Work. Such accounts were occasionally so heavily embellished that the original authors barely recognized the events they had supposedly experienced. Having lived in this alternative reality ever since his university days, Bohlin was blinded to the potential threat posed by *The Da Vinci Code* and he responded to Finnerty's concerns by dismissing the book as a zany piece of fiction that was unlikely to have much impact. "Brian, don't worry, the novel sounds so silly that nobody will ever buy it," he said.

It didn't take long for Finnerty's instincts to be proved right. When his boss visited from Rome a few weeks later, the two men visited a Barnes & Noble store in New York, only to find to their horror that the entire front window display had been decked out with promotional material for the book. The display was an indication of the huge resources that the book's publisher, Doubleday, had put into the promotional campaign. Roughly ten thousand advance copies had been mailed out to whet the appetites of booksellers, while Dan Brown had been sent on a promotional tour to meet executives from all the big chains to convince them to feature the book prominently. As the launch approached, the campaign cranked into high gear, with newspaper advertisements, an innovative online "Crack the Code" contest, and a six-city author tour. The reviews were glowing, with the *New York Times* describing the book with a single word—"Wow." "In this gleefully erudite suspense novel, Mr. Brown takes the format he has been developing through three earlier novels and fine-tunes it to blockbuster perfection," it enthused. *The Da Vinci Code* surged to the top of the bestseller list during its first week on sale, leading many to hail its relatively unknown author as the savior of the struggling publishing industry. Opus Dei's decision to ignore the book and hope that any interest would quickly wane had proved to be a serious miscalculation. With copies flying off the shelves, it wasn't long before the press would start to look for stories about the *real* Opus Dei. Organizations representing former members pounced on the opportunity to draw attention to the movement's abusive and predatory practices. Finnerty and his colleagues were soon fielding calls from journalists asking tough questions about the organization.

For six months, Opus Dei held off putting out a public statement. Internally, a frantic operation was underway to coach numeraries on what to say about the book if they were asked about it by supernumeraries or co-operators. They were told to insist that it was all lies and that Opus Dei couldn't sue because the book had a disclaimer saying it was fiction. In September, under the weight of all those inquiries, Opus Dei finally broke its public silence and condemned Brown's depiction. "Notwithstanding the book's marketing promotion and its pretension to authentic scholarship, the truth is that the novel distorts the historical record about Christianity and the Catholic Church and gives a wholly unrealistic portrayal of the members of Opus Dei and how they live," it stated. "The numerous inaccuracies range from simple factual errors to outrageous and false depictions of criminal or pathological behavior. . . . All of this is absurd nonsense." The prelature also included links to several reviews critical of the book, in a futile attempt to create a narrative of failure around its release. But rather than put out the fire, the statement only fanned the flames. Over the coming months, a feeding frenzy ensued, with pieces in the *Chicago Tribune* and *Newsday*, and on National Public Radio giving voice to former members willing to talk about its abusive practices. CNN aired a segment on Opus Dei as part of a series it was doing on secret societies, with host Anderson Cooper hearing from a former numerary assistant who talked about the "cult-like" practices of life within the prelature. To make matters worse, Sony Pictures acquired the rights to turn the book into a film. Bohlin wrote an angry letter, demanding a meeting with the studio's head of motion pictures and requesting that the name of Opus Dei not be used. The request fell on deaf ears.

As work began on the screen adaptation, Finnerty and his colleagues were left to take stock. In just a few months, all the hard work regarding the canonization had been undone by a single book. In the cultural psyche, the prelature had suffered its own great Fall—from the high altars of the Church to an object of public ridicule and derision. Confirmation of that came in the form of a call to the press office from the producers of *The Sopranos* to ask about the burial rites for members. When Finnerty became suspicious, the producers called again, pretending to be a funeral parlor. The offending episode aired a few months later, and only confirmed Opus Dei's new status as the bogeyman of American culture. After finding his father in his casket holding a rosary with a strange medal attached, Little Carmine decides to confront fellow mobster Johnny Sack. "You think I don't know what that is? It's for Opus Dei," he barks. "What the fuck is that about?" He then accuses Johnny Sack, whose wife is a supernumerary, of placing the medal there against his late father's wishes—arguing that he would never have believed any of "that New Jersey housewife fundamentalist shit." The scene was aired during primetime on HBO. If even a group of ruthless mobsters were too ashamed to be associated with Opus Dei, what would it mean for the prelature's relationships with the wealthy American Catholics it had spent the previous decade cultivating?

Against this backdrop, the last thing Opus Dei needed was another scandal. Sexual abuse allegations had first surfaced against Father McCloskey, the prelature's star priest in Washington, in November 2002. A supernumerary woman who had gone to him for help with her depression and marital problems had reported to another Opus Dei priest how McCloskey had sexually assaulted her multiple times. On several occasions both during and after counseling sessions, he put his hands on her hips and pressed himself against her, kissed her hair, and caressed her. Racked with guilt, she challenged McCloskey about his behavior—only for him to absolve her of her sins. She eventually turned to another Opus Dei priest for help, who told her not to tell anyone—including any other priests—"so he could fix it." Bohlin, who had only just arrived back in the States and who had no real on-the-ground experience as a priest, let alone in handling a serious sexual assault, sent someone to investigate the matter. The investigation was a farce, failing to even ascertain the charges against McCloskey—although the woman was given assurances that Father McCloskey would be dealt with. He wasn't. Instead, the matter was swept under the carpet. There was no real attempt to get to the bottom of the allegations, and McCloskey was let off with a reminder that spiritual direction should take place in the confessional, not in his private office.

Months later, the woman realized that her accusations had not been taken seriously. She was shocked to find that, rather than being reined in, McCloskey was still giving interviews to the press and—to her dismay—publicly reveling in his reputation as the chief converter of the rich and powerful. "I'm a salesman for the church," he told one reporter. "I'm into helping transform people into serious Christians. The only way we're going to transform society and the culture is to have believing, prayerful, scripture reading, sacramental Catholics who with their own drive and energy will have an enormous impact on entertainment, the arts, music, culture and politics." Astonished, angry, and feeling betrayed by the organization that took so much interest in every other aspect of her life, she resolved to seek justice through the courts.

The threat of a lawsuit against one of its star priests came at the worst possible time for the prelature—coinciding not just with the media frenzy around *The Da Vinci Code* but also as its apostolate in Washington was beginning to bear real fruit. By mid-2003, Opus Dei's infiltration of the upper echelons of power in the United States was reaching new heights. Its influence wasn't limited to the political sphere, either. In May, Supreme Court Justice Antonin Scalia was the main speaker at a fundraiser event for the new numerary residence that Opus Dei was building in Reston, Virginia. Despite being the ground zero of the Hanssen spy scandal, the D.C. area had become the nation's largest community of Opus Dei members, with several hundred based in the Virginia and Maryland suburbs. News reports of the arrest had initially shone an uncomfortable spotlight on Opus Dei's role in covering up the affair—and sparked a brief witch hunt for other members of the D.C. establishment who might also be involved with the group. But the media frenzy had died down quickly. Within weeks of the Hanssen arrest being made public, and the prelature's own role in the twenty-year cover-up exposed, Opus Dei was welcoming the great and the good of the Washington elite to its new $10 million retreat venue in the Shenandoah Mountains, a two-hour drive outside the city.

Conservative Catholic circles in the capital were particularly excited about a new initiative to imitate the National Prayer Breakfast, an annual event dating back to Eisenhower's presidency that brought politicians and business leaders together through their shared faith. Over the years, the event had become a staple on the Washington calendar, attracting legislators, the president, and several other heads of state—as well as high-wattage guests like Mother Teresa and Bono. At this point, the Catholic initiative was an attempt to reassert the interests of its conservative elite ahead of the next presidential election, following a slight chill in relations with the Bush administration. After early optimism about the president's willingness to push their agenda, Bob Best and other prominent Opus Dei figures had been disappointed about the White House's willingness to seek compromise on complex issues, conceding ground to scientific advancement over Catholic doctrine. Best had been particularly incensed by the president's willingness to green-light federal funding for research on previously discarded human embryos, even though a ban would be enforced on funding research that involved newly discarded embryos.

While rushing to appear on television to criticize the decision, Best fell on some marble steps and broke both kneecaps. The fall would end the numerary's active lobbying career. He passed the mantle at the Culture of Life Foundation to a vocal young supernumerary called Austin Ruse, who became heavily involved in the creation of the National Catholic Prayer Breakfast. So close were the two organizations that the Culture of Life Foundation provided seed funding and office space for the National Catholic Prayer Breakfast. Various influential Catholics were invited onto its board—including a young Leonard Leo, not yet forty, the vice president of the Federalist Society and an advisor to the White House. The move linked Opus Dei and Leo politically for the first time in what would prove to be an extremely fruitful relationship for both parties.

McCloskey should have played a starring role in the new initiative. As the most prominent defender of their shared values, the numerary priest should have been center stage. But he was thousands of miles away. Bohlin had quietly ordered the accused priest to get on a plane to London and check into a numerary residence in the leafy suburb of Hampstead. Moving McCloskey out of the country made it more difficult for the priest to be asked hard questions or to be served with legal papers. Within Opus Dei, a narrative took hold that McCloskey had been sent abroad for specialist psychological help—apparently his colleagues had spotted some cognitive issues that made it difficult for the priest to write. With him safely in England, those cognitive issues seemed to disappear. There, rather than face justice or disciplinary proceedings, he played an active role in the Catholic community—meeting with Members of Parliament, writing regularly, and even leading retreats. Back in Washington, his gaping absence was particularly noted at the first National Catholic Prayer Breakfast in April 2004, which turned out to be an enormous success—with almost five hundred people at the Mass beforehand and a thousand in attendance for the breakfast itself.

Within days of the breakfast, McCloskey broke his silence and attempted to explain his absence. "In the middle of the journey of my life unexpectedly I was able to take several months of sabbatical from my normal pastoral work in Washington, D.C., in order to write a book on conversions and evangelization," he wrote in a misleading article. His words offered little in the way of contrition. Instead, here was a man above the law, shielded by an institution that had no interest in holding its star priest accountable for his sins. Before long, McCloskey was rebuilding his profile, appearing on CNN to talk about the faith of U.S. presidential candidate John Kerry, while Opus Dei lobbied the local archbishop in London to let him exercise his ministry there, where he might win more converts and donations for the prelature.

Opus Dei's failure to properly address the McCloskey abuse scandal reflected a much deeper problem within the organization that had made it taboo to challenge anything regarding the way it operated. At the root of this taboo was the foundational myth that Escrivá had established the Work according to a vision sent to him *directly* from God. This myth created an aura of infallibility around everything to do with that vision. If Opus Dei had been born as a human initiative—as other Catholic movements such as the Benedictines, the Franciscans, or the Dominicans—then it would have been perfectly appropriate to scrutinize and debate its errors and imperfections. But Escrivá had been a mere instrument of God, and to question anything about Opus Dei was to cast doubt on God Himself. This way of thinking had permeated the organization for decades, creating an expectation of blind obedience and quashing the smallest element of dissent about the rituals, customs, and structure that underpinned life within the organization. Even after the passing of Escrivá, this unquestioning philosophy had been encouraged by his successors, who perhaps also saw advantages to keeping the faithful in line following the death of the charismatic leader. Del Portillo had come to power pledging to continue the Work "without distorting it, without changing it, without diminishing it, without adding to it—precisely as it is!"—an approach endorsed by his own successor, Echevarría. Such thinking had become even more entrenched by the early 2000s. The canonization of Escrivá was widely depicted by many within the organization as the Church's official confirmation of Opus Dei's infallibility. Protecting that vision—precisely as it was, against any form of attack or criticism—was every member's solemn duty.

While it was useful to internally promote this aura of divine inspiration for the Work in order to maintain discipline among its numerary members and to thwart any dissent about the way their lives were controlled, Villa Tevere was all too aware of the fallibility of the vision handed down by the founder—and had even taken measures to protect itself from any potential fallout. Legally and financially, the central government of Opus Dei distanced itself from the work being carried out in its name in the sixty-two countries where it operated. While its activities in each of those countries were run according to the detailed "instructions" laid down by Villa Tevere, officially Opus Dei had nothing to do with anything its members did—other than providing them with vague "spiritual direction." Legally speaking, other than the headquarters and two other properties in Rome, Opus Dei had no legal or financial connection to any of the hundreds of numerary residences, youth centers, schools, and universities that had been set up in its name around the world—other than the occasional "voluntary" donations that these operations made to the central government each year. On paper at least, these initiatives had been set up by local members, who owned and managed them—often through vaguely named foundations. The system helped foster an image of local communities inspired by Escrivá's teachings, that had spontaneously come together to spread his divinely inspired vision for the Work.

But this was a mirage. According to numerous testimonies from around the world, most new initiatives were set up by trusted numeraries acting on instructions from their superiors, having been ordered to leave behind their jobs and communities. These numeraries arrived with seed funding provided by the prelature, money transferred from other supposedly independent initiatives, or occasionally from tax havens overseas. The initiatives were set up in their names, but their control was only nominal, with all major decisions first vetted by Opus Dei's regional or central government. As an added protection, these numeraries were asked to sign documents relinquishing ownership to other foundations or companies in the Opus Dei network—copies of which were kept under lock and key at the regional government to be used in the event that the appointed numerary failed to follow orders or left the Work. Critically, the system also acted as a circuit breaker between Opus Dei and anything being carried out in its name. It saddled individual numeraries with all the liability, while guaranteeing legal immunity for the prelature. Most important, it protected the narrative of infallibility concerning Opus Dei: if it didn't own or control anything, then it couldn't do anything wrong. Of course, this was a sham, as the McCloskey incident had demonstrated. For all the organization's attempts to push back on its portrayal in *The Da*

Vinci Code, the novel captured the prelature's innate reflex to protect Opus Dei at whatever cost.

This network of foundations and companies would soon unite in the defense of the most important and lucrative asset in the prelature's hidden portfolio: Banco Popular. Five decades had passed since a loyal band of numeraries had hijacked Popular, and the Spanish bank remained the jewel in the crown of the personal prelature. By 2004, following a steady rise in the share price of Banco Popular, Opus Dei's stake in the bank was worth more than a billion dollars. Of course, the prelature's name never appeared on any documentation—that would raise too many questions. Escrivá had told Luis Valls-Taberner to always avoid any connections to Opus Dei, even when specifically carrying out deeds in its name. "Don't use 'we,' conjugate using only 'I,'" he had said. Instead, the stake was held through a series of shell companies and foundations that worked like a set of Russian dolls to hide their real beneficiary. Officially, each of these companies operated independently of the others—they had their own boards, their own shareholders, their own projects they financed—and they *just so happened* to all own a stake in the same bank. But, as the dolls were unstacked and laid out beside each other, strange similarities began to emerge. Many of these companies and foundations shared the same shareholders; they were run by the same tightknit group of numeraries; and they all seemed to donate huge sums to Opus Dei projects. Close to $100 million passed through this network every year—with the money moving from the bank to recruitment initiatives all over the globe. About half of that money came directly from the shares these companies and foundations owned in the bank, which were generating close to $50 million a year in dividends. This was topped off with additional contributions from the bank itself—thanks to the cunning of Luis, who had taken advantage of the lack of oversight at board meetings to ensure that almost every cent the bank made in charitable donations went straight to a single foundation linked to the prelature. An additional $50 million was generated along this route, passing first to the recipient foundation in Madrid, and from there to others in the Opus Dei network. As a young man, the Banco Popular chairman had made it his personal mission to "liberate" the founder and the Opus Dei elite from any financial worries. He had spent his lifetime building this system. Now on the cusp of retirement, he seemed to have firmly established a mechanism to finance the Work for many years to come.

But in the early 2000s, a confluence of forces would threaten a collapse of this system. The declining health of the bank's aging chairman was the root cause—awakening the ambitions of a generation of executives just below him, many of whom critically had no interest in maintaining the bank's delicate links with Opus Dei. In 2002, when the first real signs of the chairman's ill health became apparent, the bank's chief executive—a tenacious manager nicknamed "The Terminator," who had been tasked by Luis with taking on the powerful unions—was caught plotting a coup with one of the bank's largest shareholders to oust him as chairman in a move that would have almost certainly cut off the huge flows of money to Opus Dei. The coup was averted at the last minute thanks to Ángel Ron, a young protégé of Luis. Ron alerted the chairman to what was happening, who dismissed the rebel chief executive. He installed Ron to replace him, in gratitude for his loyalty. Allianz, the large shareholder that had sided with the rebellion, was seething: one of the world's biggest investors had been outmaneuvered by a sickly seventy-five-year-old who made a mockery of corporate governance by pushing through the appointment without consultation. "We would have expected that a measure of such magnitude would have first been agreed with partners and large shareholders, but that isn't how it was," an Allianz board member wrote. "According to some, the role of Allianz in your bank is nothing more than a 'scarecrow' designed to scare off any undesirable aggressors."

The failed coup left Luis shaken. Forced to hide in his office because of his declining health, the chairman had seemingly lost control of the delicate balance of power that for years had protected Popular's independence—and by extension the financial interests of Opus Dei. Frail, tired, and increasingly unable to play the critical role he once did, the Banco Popular chairman should have been thinking about retirement. But instead, with Allianz now having showed its hand and the allegiance of other outside investors far from assured, he had no option but to remain in place until he had secured control of the bank for the prelature. Over the coming months, he made a series of moves to bolster Opus Dei's position. Francisco Aparicio, a fellow numerary at the residence where the Banco Popular chairman lived and a trusted ally who had helped design the web of foundations and shell companies that funneled money back to the prelature, was appointed to the board. Warm, friendly, and twenty years younger than Luis, Paco—as he preferred to be known—was a safe pair of hands, a man who had sworn allegiance to Opus Dei. He could be an additional set of eyes and ears, gathering valuable information that could be fed back to the chairman. Meanwhile, tentative signals were put out to other potential investors seen as friendly to Opus Dei. Luis's younger brother Javier was sent off to court Américo Amorim, a Portuguese cork billionaire and long-time Opus Dei sympathizer. A deal was soon struck for Banco Popular to buy his bank. Critically, the billionaire would be paid in Popular shares, overnight turning him into one of the Spanish bank's largest investors—and a crucial source of support at a critical juncture for the interests of Opus Dei.

The defenses held for a few months, but toward the end of 2003 there came another betrayal—and this time from within the ranks of Opus Dei itself. For years, Jesús Platero had been a trusted confidant of the Banco Popular chairman. Both men had trained as lawyers in Madrid, and both had become numeraries at a young age. While Platero later abandoned his vows, opting to downgrade his membership to supernumerary so that he might marry and start a family, his fidelity to the Work was never in doubt. During the 1970s and 1980s, he represented The Syndicate on the bank's board. Indeed, when the Ruiz-Mateos scandal broke, Luis rushed to his house with a pile of sensitive documents for supposed "safe keeping." By 2003, Platero had racked up twenty-five years on the Popular board and was seen as unwaveringly loyal. But ambition eventually got the better of him. After convincing himself that Opus Dei would back him as a successor to Luis, Platero launched a takeover bid of his own, allying with a Spanish insurance company that began buying up shares in Popular. Luis was distraught when he found out. Unable to gather the strength to sack Platero himself—or perhaps too worried about revealing the extent of his Parkinson's disease—he sent Ron to do his dirty work, who dismissed the traitor with immediate effect. Perhaps realizing what he had done, Platero was so overcome that he needed to be taken to the hospital. Over the coming weeks, during the long hours he spent alone in his office on the seventh floor and often under the influence of heavy medication, Luis set about rooting out any remaining threats.

Weeks after the Platero betrayal, he oversaw a "night of the long knives" at the bank, sacking eleven board members and installing his fellow numerary Paco as general secretary of the bank. Popular tried to bill the move as an efficiency measure, a long-planned slimming back of the board. One large investor sold an entire $400 million stake in the bank, only weeks after boasting about it as a "safe" and "very profitable" investment.

In June 2004, Luis made his disastrous appearance at the annual shareholder meeting, where the urgency of finding a successor became obvious to all. With investors jittery following the drama of the previous few months, and Luis's bumbling performance at the shareholder gathering, he knew that naming his fellow numerary Paco—a lawyer with no real banking experience—to the top job might destabilize the stock price further, leaving the bank open to predators. He soon settled on a compromise. Ángel Ron, the young chief executive who had proven his loyalty during the attempted coup two years earlier, would be elevated to the chairmanship alongside Luis's trusted younger brother Javier. While neither man was Opus Dei, both were familiar with the bank's unique relationship with the prelature. By dividing the power within the bank between loyal members of Opus Dei, on the one hand, and his chosen successors Ángel Ron and Javier—neither of whom had any affiliation with the prelature—on the other, Luis was safeguarding this prized asset for generations to come. He was also protecting it against the dangerous tendency of numeraries to blindly follow orders from Rome.

His resignation was announced at a board meeting at the end of October. Over the coming months, Luis's visits to the bank became less and less frequent—so much so that by the summer of 2005, and barely a year into his retirement, the seventy-nine-year-old was largely housebound, shut away from the world and behind the walls of the numerary residence. Cut off from his former life and from colleagues at the bank, and increasingly unable to venture outside his room unaided—let alone leave the residence—his existence became ever more dependent on the other numeraries there. His loss of independence was more than just physical. Unlike Luis, who for years had been exempted from the strict rules and regulations that governed every aspect of a numerary's life because of his special status within the prelature, the other men at the residence were expected to follow to the letter the norms laid down by Escrivá, which meant that everything—every personal phone call, every letter, every visitor—was subject to the watchful eye of the local director. After years of freedom, Luis had come full circle. The men he lived with were now his gatekeepers to the outside world; the system of control and manipulation that they lived under was now effectively extended to him. Outwardly, this shift in the power dynamic between himself and Opus Dei wasn't always apparent. Friends and former colleagues—at least the ones approved by the local director—were allowed to visit, and many did so to pay their respects.

But there were other signs that indicated all might not be as it seemed. Javier in particular began to sense that he was being prevented from seeing his brother. Whenever he called to arrange a visit, he was told that Luis was asleep, or too sick to receive visitors, or that a doctor had advised him to rest. Javier began to suspect that information was being fed to Luis to turn him against him, a man he had known all his life, a trusted confidant whom he had brought in as his right-hand man during one of the most difficult periods at the bank—and a man he had trusted with Banco Popular's most intimate secrets. Why were they preventing the two men from seeing each other? Javier suspected that the other numeraries were acting on instructions from Rome to safeguard the assets still in his brother's name and prevent him from rewriting his will during his final weeks.

Before long, other signs began to emerge that led Javier to suspect something even bigger might be afoot. He began to receive messages supposedly from his older brother—although it was unclear whether that was true, since the notes were typed and had no signature. "Your brother has asked me to pass on a request, which won't come as a surprise to you," read one. "The request is that we terminate the transition, that is to say that you leave the co-chairmanship now, in a natural way; and the proposal is that you pass to being honorary chairman." It was an odd request to be receiving from a man who had resigned from the bank more than a year earlier, who officially had no shareholding in the bank and no vote on its board—but it was a reminder, as if any were needed, of the hidden forces that really controlled Popular. "The offer is the best solution for the bank and for you, because a friendly and natural exit is the most honorable, would allow you to stay on as honorary chairman, would be the culmination of a career—and it would also avoid any unnecessary tensions."

Behind the walls of the residence, a plan was unfolding to rip up the carefully thought-out succession plan designed by Luis to divide power between people allied to the prelature and people with no affiliation, so as to protect this vital flow of funds from being plundered by Rome.

The suggestion that Javier opt for "a friendly and natural exit" and "avoid any unnecessary tensions" was the opening salvo of a much bigger battle to consolidate Opus Dei's interests in the bank and avoid a potential takeover by another bank. The concern about Popular's being bought up reflected how deeply the connections still extended between the bank and the prelature. If its interest in the bank had been restricted simply to the shares bequeathed to the various foundations linked to the prelature, then a possible takeover could have been great news for Opus Dei. An approach would send Popular's share prices soaring and allow the prelature to cash out with a hefty premium.

But a takeover would cut off the "charitable donations" which, though scaled back by Ron, still amounted to tens of millions of dollars every year. Other arrangements between the bank and Opus Dei risked being exposed, too. Popular paid millions in rent to the Opus Dei foundation that owned its headquarters. It also allowed the Banco de Depósitos—a bank within the bank that was owned by another Opus Dei–linked foundation—to use its vast branch network across the country. Many members received loans from this bank that they would have been very unlikely to get from any other bank, and their resulting debts would be another tie binding them to the Work.

Opus Dei still had one frail but powerful weapon in its arsenal: Luis Valls-Taberner. Bedridden and increasingly disoriented because of his illness and the cocktail of drugs Opus Dei doctors had prescribed for him, the seventy-nine-year-old acquiesced to a change in strategy. Some of the once-loyal supernumeraries who sat on the board were summoned to see Luis. Struggling to speak, and occasionally drifting in and out of consciousness, he implored them to swap their shares in the bank for shares in a company that would consolidate all the interests in the bank allied to Opus Dei. When asked why they should agree to swap their Banco Popular shares, which could easily be sold on the open market, for shares in the Opus Dei vehicle, which could not, Luis shot back: "Because you are loyal." Grouping the supernumerary families together would bind them in a pact and help defend the bank against attack. Over the coming weeks, plans were put together to merge their various holdings under a single umbrella: a shell company called European Union of Investments, a real estate vehicle set up by the bank in the eighties that had since been repurposed as a front for the various foundations and their stakes in the bank. That would be the first stage in the plan. The second would see another $380 million spent on buying additional Banco Popular shares. The lion's share of the money would come from the foundations and would confirm the huge sums at their disposal. It would also confirm their priorities—namely in protecting Opus Dei's interests, rather than spending the money on the social programs they supposedly existed to support. Eventually, the move would help create a solid bloc of Opus Dei–allied shareholders holding 20 percent of the bank that could easily defend itself against any takeover attempt.

As this plan was coming together, Luis's health took a sudden turn for the worse. He died on February 25, 2006, three months short of his eightieth birthday. His body was moved to the chapel of an Opus Dei male student residence a short walk away, financed by the former Banco Popular chairman in the late seventies. The students were encouraged to file past the corpse of this great man, draped in a simple white sheet, and kiss him on the forehead. Many knew this man only from the stories handed down to them by alumni.

A few days later, the men charged with consolidating Opus Dei power in the bank made their move against Javier. Amid rumors of his attempts to sell off the bank and fears that a formal approach might be imminent, two of the supernumeraries who had heeded Luis's plea to swap their bank shares for foundation shares confronted him. They asked about an unscheduled trip he'd made to Barcelona, where two of the banks interested in buying Popular were based. During his absence, much had been made of this sudden trip—and of Javier's supposed attempts to keep it secret by not asking for one of the bank's drivers to pick him up from the airport there. He denied everything.

Whatever the truth was, the cards were stacked against him. In his absence, a consensus had formed among the other members of the board that it was time for him to move on. Their decision was relayed to him, but Javier refused to back down. With the younger Valls-Taberner digging in his heels, his opponents decided to fight dirty, moving his office out of the headquarters in the middle of the night and disabling his security clearances to enter the building. The showdown culminated in a shouting match in the lobby of the building, which also drew in Javier's wife and daughter. Exiled to a new office on the other side of the city, he was told that the board would vote on whether to retain him—a vote he would surely lose.

Javier conceded defeat. He felt bitter and betrayed—he was ousted from the bank where he had worked for more than forty years, including seventeen as chairman alongside his older brother. When his bodyguards and driver were suddenly removed, he started to think he might lose more than his job. The image of Roberto Calvi, the banker found hanging under Blackfriars Bridge, began to haunt him. He flew to London to speak with the Spanish ambassador there, a man known to be high up in Opus Dei, and asked him to inform Villa Tevere that he had incriminating documents in a safe in Switzerland, which would be released if anything were to happen to him or his family. He resolved to sell his shares in the bank and live in the Alps, a long way from the Opus Dei cabal that had ousted him.

Back in Rome, attention was turning to how to manage the imminent release of the movie adaptation of *The Da Vinci Code*—a blockbuster starring Tom Hanks and Audrey Tautou that threatened to deal another blow to the prelature's image. Having failed despite numerous attempts to elicit any kind of reassurance from Sony Pictures about how Opus Dei would be depicted in the film, the prelature had decided to take matters into its own hands. A few months earlier, Opus Dei had flown its communications teams based in New York, Montreal, London, Paris, Madrid, Cologne, and Lagos to Rome for a crisis workshop to figure out how to handle the upcoming release. The meeting had been triggered by comments from the movie's director, Ron Howard, who had confirmed to *Newsweek* that the screen adaptation would be faithful to the novel. "That's news to me—I'll have to get back to you," the U.S. spokesperson Brian Finnerty had responded, when the magazine had approached him for comment. Over the next few days, Finnerty and his colleagues put together a plan of action, codenamed "Operation Lemonade," after their attempts to make something palatable out of the lemons they had been dealt. A central part of the plan was depicting the film as being an affront—not just to Opus Dei but also to all Christians. It was a clever tactic to shift the media's focus away from some of the very real criticisms of Opus Dei—around brainwashing, coercion, and misogynistic behavior, all of which could be corroborated—and to refocus attention on Brown's sensational claims about Jesus Christ's relationship with Mary Magdalen. The team also recognized that they needed to be proactive with the media, strategically feeding them packaged stories with clever hooks and a cast of readily available interviewees who would show the "real" Opus Dei.

In the weeks leading up to the movie's premiere, the plan kicked into action. In an attempt at a light-hearted take on the assault it was facing, Finnerty and his colleagues discovered one of its members was actually called Silas, just like the murderous monk in Brown's novel, and pushed the story out. The "real-life Silas" was covered by the *New York Times*, *Time* magazine, CNN, CBS, and ABC. Meanwhile, the team put on tours of Murray Hill Place for the media, and even put up a small box outside the entrance, containing literature about the prelature, enticing passersby to take a pamphlet with the inscription: "For fans of *The Da Vinci Code*: If you are interested in the 'real' Opus Dei, take one." Even the prelate joined in with the charm offensive. "Ignorance is always a great evil and information a good," Echevarría told *Le Figaro* when asked to comment on Opus Dei's apparent new openness with the media. "Communication is not a game and it does not suffer from amateurism."

In May 2006, the night before the movie went on global release, the MSNBC show *Hardball with Chris Matthews* was invited to Murray Hill Place. Bohlin was the man put up to be the friendly face of Opus Dei.

"To millions and millions of readers of *The Da Vinci Code*, this building at Thirty-fourth and Lexington in New York City is a den of horrors," began the host. "You've got thugs wandering around here dressed like monks, hitmen to be sent off to various parts of the world to kill people to defend the faith. What do you make of that?"

"We thought it was just kind of a joke at first, because, you know, who was going to believe this kind of thing?" responded the Opus Dei priest. "Because we're real people, we are a real organization—we have bishops around the world, cardinals in Opus Dei, fifteen universities affiliated with Opus Dei around the world. And along comes Dan Brown saying that Opus Dei is an organization with mad monks, albinos, and there are no monks in Opus Dei—albino or otherwise."

"Let's talk about the pieces of it that they have used to make the book sell, the pieces of reality," continued Matthews. "In Opus Dei, there is corporal mortification. There is this form of whipping. The cilice, the wearing of the cilice."

Bohlin began to laugh.

"You're laughing, but—but tell me what the facts are," continued Matthews.

"OK," replied the priest. "There's nothing in Opus Dei like the grotesque portrayals in *The Da Vinci Code* movie—or the book. That's all a gross exaggeration. We promote a spirit of sacrifice—in little things every day. Smiling when you're tired, holding your tongue when you feel like you could say something cutting, persevering at your work when you feel tired."

Bohlin made no mention of the other sacrifices—such as the $1 million settlement that had just been agreed with the victim of McCloskey's sexual misconduct, or the nondisclosure agreement attached to it designed to silence her from ever revealing anything about its star priest. He never mentioned the sacrifice of the numeraries and numerary assistants whose lives were intricately controlled and who were systematically abused according to the "instructions" distributed by Villa Tevere.

"I could use all that," Matthews responded with a smile. "But what about the whipping, the self-whipping? Is that part of Opus Dei, the self-flagellation?"

"Within the Catholic Church, there has always been a long tradition of more serious sacrifice—fasting, and also this practice . . . that has been used in religious orders for centuries, in great religious families, by celibate people. And these are part of the Catholic Church. They're not part of—Opus Dei adopts them for some members who freely undertake some of these things, but it's not a majority of members, and it's nothing like what's in the movie."

"Why are people willing to believe the worst about their own Church and about Opus Dei?" continued Matthews.

"I'm not sure that it's necessarily Catholics who want to believe the worst," answered Bohlin. "I think people read this on different levels. There are people out there who just see a nice thriller. Other people think they are learning a lot of things that they have never heard before, because the way the facts—the so-called facts—are presented in the book as facts, that everyone knows who has studied something. And there is a third level of people, who want to kick the

Church while it's down, who want to take advantage of anything that attacks the Church, traditional morality, the teachings of Jesus Christ."

"Let me ask you about your strategy," said the host. "It's wonderful of you to let us in here. I know that from our past experience dealing with Opus Dei, this hasn't always been your practice—to let people into this headquarters here at Thirty-fourth and Lexington in New York. Why did you change your position?"

"We're here in order to be known," said Bohlin. "We work in a very private way—one-to-one—in helping people live their faith and passing on from one person to another. But this movie gives us a great opportunity to get our message out, and we want to seize it. You know, if they are giving us lemons, we want to make lemonade out of it."

Its experience with *The Da Vinci Code* had taught Villa Tevere an important lesson: that control of the message was just as important outside the organization as it was within. Controversy was nothing new to Opus Dei. Since its founding, the organization had faced an almost unending series of allegations—about its abusive practices, about the vast network of hidden assets at its disposal, about its corruption and willingness to work with even the most morally repugnant of regimes. For years, such accusations had been localized and relatively easily brushed off as the work of embittered former members seeking revenge. *The Da Vinci Code* had threatened to expose the organization for what it was, inspiring victims to break their silence and prompting the media to scrutinize the movement more carefully. Coinciding with the McCloskey scandal, *The Da Vinci Code* had threatened to undermine Opus Dei's success in the United States. Thanks to its shrewd communications strategy—and a $1 million payout to silence one victim—Opus Dei had indeed turned lemons into lemonade. "God's mercy is much greater than our sexual sins," McCloskey explained in an interview for a documentary aimed at helping Catholics become "marriage material" that was filmed shortly after his return to the United States. "It's just like getting a wound or getting cut on your arm or your leg. There can be a big scar, but over the course of time—we've all experienced this—perhaps that scar gradually, almost disappears; you never know it even happened. That can also be the case with sexual sins." By presenting itself as a bulwark of Catholic tradition and any attacks against it as an onslaught against the Church and religion in general, Opus Dei hoped to make its own scars disappear.

11

A MARRIAGE OF CONVENIENCE

The United States Senate—June 2006

ON A BALMY DAY IN LATE SPRING, THE SENATOR FROM KANSAS TOOK TO THE floor of the U.S. Senate. Raised on a farm in the Midwest, Sam Brownback had something of the Midas touch among voters in America's rural interior. He was also a champion of the religious right—a staunch pro-life activist and the co-sponsor of an amendment, along with Rick Santorum, to force schools to stop teaching evolutionary theory as a fact. With these two important bases covered, the forty-nine-year-old was widely seen as a rising star within the Republican Party, and a leading candidate for the presidential nomination two years hence. Wearing a crisply pressed suit and burgundy tie, he stood up to make his opening speech. This was the first of what were expected to be several days of debate on a constitutional amendment proposed by Republicans to outlaw same-sex marriage. The proposal was a political stunt by party grandees that had no real chance of passing. Its real aim was re-energizing the conservative base, which had grown frustrated with the botched Iraq War and high gas prices, ahead of the mid-term elections later in the year. Brownback himself needed no re-energizing when it came to matters of faith. Since his conversion by Father McCloskey a few years earlier, his politics had become increasingly defined by his conservative interpretation of Catholicism. The Opus Dei priest had actively encouraged Brownback and other powerful politicians in his orbit to reconsider how they thought about democracy. "How many constituents do you have?" Mc-Closkey challenged one group of senators. Four million, nine million, twelve million came the answers from around the room. "May I suggest," the priest replied, "that you have only one constituent?" That moment had changed Brownback's life. Shortly after, in a ceremony at the Opus Dei chapel on K Street presided over by McCloskey, he converted. Ever since, he had devoted his time in the Senate to serving that one constituent—God.

"There hardly could be a more important issue than the foundational structure of how we build society and how societies have been built for thousands of years," Brownback told the chamber. "They have been built around the institution of marriage—of a man and a woman bonded together for life. Out of that, families develop and grow and prosper. Children are raised, and that is the next generation. The next generation after that is brought forth and the generation preceding them is cared for or nurtured."

The passion in his oratory came not just from his conservative Catholic beliefs but also from a growing alarm with a trend sweeping the country. Massachusetts had recently become the first U.S. state to legalize marriage between same-sex couples following a landmark ruling by its state supreme court. The decision had energized campaigners across the country, leading to pressure on other states to do the same. It had also stirred opponents, who were now organizing to prevent other states from falling.

"The problem we have in front of us is the institution of marriage has been weakened," continued Brownback. "The effort to redefine it in this vast social experiment that we have going on . . . the early data that we see from other places, harms the institution of the family, the raising of the next generation. And it is harmful to the future of the Republic. I think we can hardly have a more foundational debate regarding things of importance than the marriage amendment."

The amendment, if passed, included a provision that would enshrine into the U.S. Constitution a clause preventing individual states from defining marriage in any way other than between a man and a woman. According to Brownback, the clause was a way of taking power back from the cabal of lawyers who had conspired to impose their liberal vision on American society through the courts—and to hand that power back to the people, through an amendment passed by their democratically elected representatives. His argument was ironic, given the tactics that Opus Dei and its allies on the conservative right would use in coming years to force their dystopian views on the American people through the courts—against the clear democratic will of hundreds of millions of voters.

To back up his argument, Brownback wielded a study that had just been published at Princeton University, arguing why the defense of marriage was in the public interest. The study, called *Ten Principles on Marriage and the Public Good*, had been put together by a group of scholars from the fields of history, economics, psychiatry, law, sociology, and philosophy. It claimed that, with divorce rates rising and an increasing number of children born out of wedlock, those who suffered most from the nation's retreat from marriage were minorities and the poor. Defending these vulnerable communities was the moral obligation of Congress, it claimed. The Princeton scholars maintained that marriage had enormous benefits to society, arguing that higher rates of marriage—specifically between a man and a woman—had an enormous impact on the well-being of children, on the creation of wealth, on lessening inequity, on encouraging political liberty, and on fostering limited government. The study linked almost every advancement in Western society to marriage between a man and a woman. Its conclusion was a specious case of correlation misconstrued as causation.

But the report had seemingly strong academic credentials.

"This is a Princeton group of scholars," affirmed Brownback.

The senator made no mention of the study's origins, or of its links to Opus Dei. The publication of *Ten Principles on Marriage and the Public Good* had grown out of a conference held at Princeton, in December 2004, on "Why Marriage Is in the Public Interest," which had been attended by a series of right-wing academics and activists like Robert George, Hadley Arkes, and Maggie Gallagher. The conference was the first major project of the Witherspoon Institute, the brainchild of a numerary from Mexico who had been tasked with creating a beachhead for Opus Dei at American universities across the United States. The Princeton report was just a harbinger of the influence that Opus Dei would soon wield on college campuses nationwide.

Luis Tellez grew up in a little town on the Mexican side of the Sonoran Desert and was one of three brothers in a family of eight who joined Opus Dei as numeraries. Trained as an engineer, Tellez found work at a chemical company in Saint Louis, where he was also made director of the numerary residence there. In 1981, he was assigned to New York, where he was asked to help out with an endowment being set up by a wealthy Mexican couple—the wife was a supernumerary and the husband received spiritual direction from an Opus Dei priest—who wanted to leave their fortune to good causes. The priest introduced Tellez to the couple and they agreed to put him in charge of the endowment, which they initially called the Mass Foundation but which was later renamed as the Clover Foundation. It would eventually swell in size to almost $130 million and be absorbed into the sprawling web of supposedly independent Opus Dei foundations in the United States, becoming a vital source of funds for its initiatives not just there but also all around the world. Following Del Portillo's two-month tour of the States in 1988, Tellez was also put in charge of youth programs—specifically a team charged with infiltrating the university sector. Del Portillo and many of those close to the prelate were obsessed with exporting what they called "the Spanish model"—building an Opus Dei university and a network of feeder schools— to the United States. The system had been exported to other countries, including Argentina, Chile, Colombia, Mexico, Peru, and the Philippines, and that had helped generate thousands of new numeraries for the movement.

To help him achieve his goal, Father McCloskey invited Tellez to Princeton, and the Mexican numerary immediately became enamored with the town. It was small, teeming with intellectual stimulus, and full of potential for recruiting the right kind of people: bright, wealthy kids destined for successful careers. Tellez decided to move his operation to a small office on Mercer Street, which would give him an excuse to spend more time in the town and also would provide a venue to host "circles" for students. These circles were small catechism classes designed to introduce students to the philosophy of Opus Dei, but which were often also used to slowly lure people into the organization. It was a difficult time for the prelature in the town following the McCloskey furor, and Tellez's quiet, understated approach was welcomed by those students who were still interested in Escrivá's message.

For the new numerary in town, it was also a chance to learn how

American universities really worked—and to build relationships with potentially useful figures. It was at Princeton that Luis Tellez met Robert George, a legal scholar and champion of "natural law." This was a theoretical framework that had begun to gather momentum among a small group of conservative, religiously minded lawyers, and it argued that certain moral "truths"—usually ones that dovetailed with Catholic teachings—were inherent to human consciousness. Using this framework as a guide, George had advocated for leaving state laws prohibiting adultery, fornication, and sodomy on the books in order to assert these moral standards. Just before meeting Tellez, he had published a book advocating the legal enforcement of morals, which had secured him tenure and also established him as a rising force among an increasingly activist band of conservative Catholics. As a respected Princeton scholar, George would eventually become the public, acceptable face for dozens of Tellez's initiatives to infiltrate the American university system. Their relationship would eventually transform their reactionary agenda and thrust Opus Dei into the center of the battle to tear down hard-won progressive rights.

But it was another, more unlikely academic figure who would give Tellez his first big break into the Ivy League. The Mexican numerary often played tennis with the distinguished Dante scholar Robert Hollander, who as a humanist and an atheist was perhaps an unlikely bedfellow, but whom Tellez revered because of his stimulating conversation. Around 1995, Tellez heard on the grapevine that the humanities school at Princeton was keen to expand, but lacked the money to do so. He approached Hollander about possibly funding a postdoctorate chair using money from the Clover Foundation. He pitched it as a way of fostering new talent in a world increasingly dominated by aging academics. Hollander set up meetings with the university, and Tellez's offer was accepted. The numerary didn't even convene the Clover Foundation board to get the donation approved; in the end, he convinced the foundation's benefactors to authorize the payment in lieu of paying him a salary. Of course, he could have taken a salary and paid for the fellowship himself, but the foundation offered cover and distanced the initiative from Opus Dei. The recipient of the first Clover Fellowship in the Humanities, the philosophy lecturer Michael Sugrue, wasn't exactly new talent; he was an academic already at Princeton whom the school wanted to retain. But everyone was happy. Sugrue got a raise, Princeton got to keep a gifted lecturer, and Opus Dei had a foot in the door of the American higher education system. "I wanted to learn how the university worked. I wanted to make friends. And I did both," Tellez explained. "It was probably the most important investment I ever made. It changed the course of my thinking."

Buoyed by his experience, Tellez became more brazen in his approach. When he began to hear rumors that the distinguished history professor William Jordan might be leaving, he approached his friend Robert George to discuss how they might tempt him to stay. The two devised a plan to use money raised by Tellez to fund a new initiative, which they called the James Madison Program, after the founding father who had helped draft the U.S. Constitution and Bill of Rights. Ironically, the program would later play a critical role in dismantling the rights of women, the LGBTQ+ community, and minority groups. "He says 'this will give me the opportunity to create something independent of the department, that I will run' and which will do many of the things that, presumably, I was interested in," recalled Tellez of the meeting. "It was establishing a footprint—a beachhead—controlled by Robby." Tellez sounded out Fernando Ocáriz, the number two in Opus Dei who would eventually succeed Echevarría as prelate, about what he was doing and was told to continue his good work. He was given permission to relocate full time to Princeton.

The James Madison Program was launched in 2000. In its first two years, the program raised $8 million, with large amounts coming from Tellez and his network—including the Clover Foundation and some Opus Dei donors—and won plaudits from across the right. While the program purported to be a model of academic rigor and debate, underneath it functioned as a vehicle for conservative interests—supporting gatherings of activists and fellowships for conservative professors and students. "Princeton's Madison Program is a model for solving the political-correctness problem in the academy as a whole," wrote conservative commentator Stanley Kurtz. "We may not be able to do much about tenured humanities and social science faculties at elite colleges that are liberal by margins of more than 90 percent. But setting up small enclaves of professors with more conservative views is a real possibility."

Three years later, around the time that Father Bohlin was facing the twin crises posed by McCloskey and *The Da Vinci Code*, Tellez was launching his third big initiative at Princeton in eight years. Through the James Madison Program, the numerary had established contact with a number of major conservative donors. One of them was Steve Forbes, the billionaire and heir to the *Forbes* publishing empire who had twice run for president. Forbes had withdrawn his donations to Princeton in a furor over its controversial decision to hire the Australian philosopher Peter Singer, a secular, utilitarian moralist who argued in favor of vegetarianism and of donations to help the global poor. His ideas would later give birth to the Effective Altruism movement. Singer's support for abortion rights and euthanasia outraged Forbes and conservative moralists like Robby George. Forbes pulled his donations to the university and directed his money to George's new institute instead. The Smith family, heirs to the Ben Venue pharmaceutical fortune, also contributed. With such strong backers—and additional recourse to Opus Dei money—Tellez concluded the time had come to expand. He decided against plowing more money into the James Madison Program, which sat within George's department, because of the control that Princeton would have over it. Setting up a new institute would give Tellez and George complete control—and allow them to expand way beyond Princeton to other Ivy League universities and later around the world.

The Witherspoon Institute was founded in 2003 on a promise to support the study of constitutional law and political thought. But it soon became a locus for intellectuals opposed to abortion and same-sex marriage, and its only discussion of the Constitution seemed to revolve solely around the question of religion's role in society. It was supported by hundreds of thousands of dollars from Opus Dei. During the nineties, after Del Portillo's suggestion about an Opus Dei university in the States, the prelature had created a new non-profit—using some of the money from the Smith family—called the Higher Education Initiatives Foundation. Run out of the same office as the Clover Foundation, on Nassau Street in Princeton, with Tellez on the board alongside a bunch of numeraries and supernumeraries, the foundation was effectively a conduit for money to Opus Dei initiatives in the higher education sector. One recipient was a school called the Institute for Media & Entertainment that the prelature was setting up in New York City as a way to infiltrate the industries. It eventually turned out to be a complete failure. But the biggest recipient was the Witherspoon Institute, which received almost $500,000 in donations from the Opus Dei foundation during its first three years. The James Madison Program received an additional $187,000. "We did create a committee—with which I was involved . . . this is in the nineties—to fund several projects to experiment, basically give people money . . . to see what they could do," recalled Tellez about the Higher Education Initiatives Foundation. He initially denied that Witherspoon ever received any money, but later said he forgot when presented with information contradicting that. George also did his best to distance the James Madison Program and the Witherspoon Institute from Opus Dei. "I can tell you categorically we have never taken a dime from Opus Dei," he told one reporter from *The Nation*. The ties weren't only financial, though. The executive director of the Witherspoon Institute was the supernumerary Ana Samuel, who had encountered Opus Dei while studying at Princeton, where she had dreams of becoming a photojournalist for *National Geographic*—until a numerary challenged her about how compatible that would be with her role as a future mother. She would later go on to write a book called *No Differences? How Children in Same-Sex Households Fare*, which laid bare the "truth" about the damage of growing up with same-sex parents.

Despite suspicions about Opus Dei's involvement with these two initiatives, the prelature successfully painted itself as nothing more than a benign group of devout Catholics who largely kept to themselves. But this was a façade. Tom Bohlin, the organization's most senior man in the States, took particular pride in the Witherspoon Institute as a vindication of his policy of removing internal bureaucracy and actively encouraging numeraries and supernumararies to launch such "apostolic" initiatives. "Unless you're an active leaven, you're not going to raise the dough," he explained. "It doesn't take a lot of leaven to raise the dough and make a little bigger—but you gotta mix in well, you gotta be active. Our job is not to do one thing—like run hospitals, or run schools, or run parishes; it's to set people on fire and then throw them wherever they belong, and set fire to wherever they are and take initiative where they are." The leadership occasionally helped stoke those fires with practical help—or money. At one stage, Opus Dei even offered to advance Tellez the money for the multi-million dollar purchase of a new office for the Witherspoon Institute on Stockton Street. But at the same time, Tellez was at pains to publicly distance his private, religious existence from the role he played on campus at the James Madison Program and the Witherspoon Institute. "Nothing I do is a recruiting tool," he told the *Daily Princetonian*. "None of that happens on my watch. I'm interested in people joining Opus Dei, but I know that the only way that's going to happen is if God wants it and if they want it. So there's no pressure. The process starts with the person. People make up their minds on their own. I'm simply a facilitator."

Tellez's subtle approach could not have been more different from that of John McCloskey, whose presence on campus had shone an uncomfortable light on Opus Dei little more than a decade earlier. His careful projection of what he called "the nice kind" of conservatism—respectful of divergent views, committed to serious scholarship, employing dialogue rather than invective—quelled suspicions about Opus Dei among the fresh crop of students on campus, who were oblivious to the scandals that had marred its presence there in the eighties and nineties. By the mid-2000s, the prayer sessions and Friday dinners at Mercer House, the Opus Dei residence in town, were again teeming with students and potential vocations. The success of Tellez's apostolate was not lost on the men in charge back at Murray Hill Place, in New York. "It's a matter of having the right people in the right places—and seeing what they can do," Father Tom Bohlin reflected.

Robby George occasionally made it down to Washington, where he had taken over from Deal Hudson, following the *Crisis* publisher's fall from grace because of a sexual encounter with a freshman during his time at Fordham. He would now be one of the chief advisors to the Bush administration regarding their outreach to Catholics. He occasionally stopped by the Catholic Information Center, which—following the departure of Father McCloskey—was struggling to revive its former status in the capital. Father Bill Stetson, who had joined Opus Dei in the 1950s while studying law at Harvard and moved to Rome shortly afterwards to study under the founder, was his first replacement. Quiet, soft-spoken, and possessing an almost ethereal air that contrasted with the earthy charm of his predecessor, Stetson had served out much of his priesthood filling internal positions within Opus Dei, and he evidently found it difficult to work the Washington social and political scenes that had generated so many converts for his predecessor. Attendance at the daily Mass began to suffer. Donations dramatically tailed off, too. It wasn't long before the Catholic Information Center fell into financial difficulties. At one stage, the situation was so bad that it was unable to pay its rent and it had to be bailed out by the Opus Dei headquarters in New York. At a time when Washington Catholics were in the ascendancy—demonstrated by the growing numbers coming to the National Catholic Prayer Breakfast, which George W. Bush attended every year—Opus Dei seemed unable to capitalize on this great Catholic renaissance that it had helped create.

Its struggle to take full advantage of its foothold in D.C. was reflective of a much broader struggle to exploit the inroads it had made into the Catholic Church. The reign of John Paul II had been a high-water mark for Opus Dei, an important period that had not only seen elevation as a personal prelature but also its founder canonized, dozens of priests promoted to the bishop-hood, and two made into cardinals. As the pope's health began to deteriorate in early 2005, one of those two—Cardinal Julián Herranz—became well-known for convening meetings of carefully selected cardinals at an Opus Dei villa on the outskirts of Rome. German Cardinal Joseph Ratzinger, who had befriended the movement as a conservative bastion within the Church, quickly emerged as the favorite to succeed Wojtyła among those on the right. As the pope lay dying, Herranz began an active campaign to lobby the cardinals—most of whom had been chosen by Wojtyła—on behalf of Ratzinger. "Opus Dei is the only group well organized enough working within the power structure of the Roman Curia that can make a difference," one Vatican expert commented at the time. As soon as Ratzinger won the election, the Opus Dei kingmaker Herranz wrote to him on behalf of what he called the "pre-conclave" about what the priorities of his papacy ought to be.

But power at the Vatican didn't equate to popularity among the more than one billion Catholics around the world who were turning their backs on the message of Saint Josemaría. The failure to generate enough vocations was a flashing red light on the dashboard at Villa Tevere, where the prelate Javier Echevarría had tried—but failed—to boost recruitment by installing a new generation of regional vicars, including Tom Bohlin, and setting them ambitious targets. Membership numbers remained stubbornly low despite all the movement's efforts.

At the Catholic Information Center in Washington, the prelature opted for a change in tack. Stetson's initial three-year term was not renewed, and in September 2007 he was replaced by Father Arne Panula. Blue-eyed and silver-haired, Father Arne was a big figure within Opus Dei. For a period in the nineties, he was the prelature's most senior man in the United States—and the choice of such a heavy hitter indicated the importance of the Catholic Information Center to its superiors in New York and Rome. A native of Minnesota, Father Arne had grown up in a small town on the shores of Lake Superior and had joined the Work while at Harvard. He moved to Rome after graduating, where he lived alongside Escrivá and trained to become a priest. After ordination, he moved back to the States to take on the role of chaplain at The Heights school in Washington, which was still in its infancy. During his forty years in Opus Dei, he had also spent some time in California, and had become a close friend of Peter Thiel, the billionaire entrepreneur who helped found PayPal and who had been an early investor in Facebook. On long hikes in the Marin headlands, just north of San Francisco, the two men bonded over their shared disdain for government—and the dangers of liberal attempts to correct the ills of society through policies like affirmative action. Father Arne liked to blame almost all of society's ills on this slow liberal drift. He believed that Catholic priests had lost their way and sexually abused children because of efforts to liberalize Mass by the Vatican in the sixties, which had led to "confusion" for men of the cloth. Opus Dei's own "discipline" was the reason none of its priests had been caught up in the scandal, he explained. When Thiel talked about technological growth stalling out around 1973, Father Arne attributed it to *Roe v. Wade*. "Obviously, if a platform is open to eliminating future citizens, including without any care for their potential contributions, that's inimical to society's flourishing," he said. "Think about it: How many—sixty, seventy million children who have never seen the light of day? Might there not have been some changes on account of that? Couldn't one of those unborn citizens have gotten a handle on the cure for cancer?"

To take Father Arne out of Silicon Valley, where he had made important connections among some of the world's most influential tech entrepreneurs, was a clear indication of Opus Dei's priorities. Warm and outgoing, he was much better suited to working McCloskey's old network than was Stetson, although—perhaps through no fault of his own, given the global financial crisis that was raging at the time—during his first few years he failed to reinvigorate the pipeline of donations that Father C. John had been so successful at. He did, however, make some important contacts—he became spiritual director to Arthur C. Brooks, president of the American Enterprise Institute, an influential conservative thinktank that held huge sway over the Republican Party, and which was devoted to cutting taxes and reining in government. He asked Brooks to meditate on a homily Escrivá had given about serving God through work—a message that Brooks described as "the most powerful direction I have ever received." Father Arne also made friends in the judiciary, and fondly became known within Opus Dei circles as a "friend and confidant to billionaires and Supreme Court Justices."

He also became close to another Catholic luminary who might have described himself in the same way. Leonard Leo had been born on Long Island in the mid-sixties and, while only a toddler, lost his father—a pastry chef—to cancer. At the age of five, his mother remarried, and the Leos moved to New Jersey, where he attended Monroe Township High School. Leo was chosen as the "Most Likely to Succeed" in the yearbook—a distinction he shared with classmate Sally Schroeder, his future wife. In the yearbook, the two were shown sitting next to each other, holding wads of cash and with dollar signs painted on their glasses. He was so effective at raising money for his senior prom that his classmates nicknamed him the "Moneybags Kid." His grandfather, who emigrated to the United States from Italy as a teenager, started out as an apprentice tailor, and went on to become a vice-president of Brooks Brothers. Throughout his life, he remained steeped in the deep Catholicism of his native land; he and his wife attended Mass daily, and encouraged the young Leonard to follow their lead. After high school, Leo went to Cornell University, studying under a group of conservative academics in the university's department of government and with the wider national backdrop of iconoclastic scholars led by Yale University's Robert Bork and the University of Chicago's Antonin Scalia, who were building the case for a novel legal doctrine known as originalism. He got a series of internships in Washington, D.C., during the final years of the Reagan administration, then returned to Cornell to join the law school, where in 1989 he founded the local chapter of a student organization called the Federalist Society. That group had been set up by three conservative-leaning students from Yale, Harvard, and Chicago seven years earlier as a way of challenging what they saw as the dominance of liberal ideology at the country's law schools.

After graduating, Leo married his childhood sweetheart Sally Schroeder, who had been raised as a Protestant but who used to go to Catholic Mass five times every weekend because she played the organ. She decided to convert not long before her marriage. The couple moved back to Washington, where Leo clerked for a judge on the court of appeals and became close with another appellate judge who had recently been appointed to the D.C. circuit—a man from Georgia called Clarence Thomas, who had toyed with becoming a Catholic priest. Despite being ten years older and from much more humble origins, Thomas shared Leo's conservative outlook, and the two soon developed a deep friendship that would endure for many years. During this period, Leo was asked by the Federalist Society to become its first employee—although he delayed his start date so that he could help his good friend Thomas through his contentious confirmation process for the Supreme Court. Despite accusations of sexual harassment hanging over him, Thomas won Senate confirmation by a slim margin. It would be the first in a series of fights in which Leo would have to put aside the teachings of his Christian faith as he focused on the greater goal of pushing through a conservative revolution of the courts and of society at large.

Backed by a cabal of wealthy conservative patrons like industrialist David Koch, banker Richard Mellon Scaife, and the devout Catholic entrepreneur Frank Hanna, the Federalist Society under Leo became a breeding ground for conservative judges who were recruited at law school, groomed through the society's program of events and talks, and then bound together through their careers. "The key was to figure out how to develop what I call a 'pipeline'— basically, where you recruit students in law school, you get them through law school, they come out of law school, and then you find ways of continuing to involve them in legal policy," Leo later explained. In 2005, the Federalist Society began openly advocating for John Roberts—a former member—to be nominated to fill a vacant seat at the Supreme Court, the first time it had campaigned publicly for a particular candidate. A few months later, its sway had grown so much that it torpedoed President George W. Bush's own preferred candidate for another vacant seat on the Supreme Court—Harriet Miers, a judge and close friend of the president who wasn't a member of the

Federalist Society—and pressured him to nominate Samuel Alito, one of its members, in her place.

Leo worked closely with the Judicial Confirmation Network, a new nonprofit organization set up using funds from Robin Arkley, a California businessman known as the "foreclosure king," who had made billions buying up mortgages of people in financial difficulties. The idea for JCN had been hatched at a dinner in Washington attended by Leo, Ann Corkery, and Supreme Court Justice Antonin Scalia shortly after Bush's reelection in late 2004. JCN spent hundreds of thousands of dollars on radio and online advertisement to shape public opinion. It was run by Neil and Ann Corkery, a couple who had been supernumerary members of Opus Dei since at least the eighties. Neil had been a critical figure in getting a new numerary residence built in Reston, Virginia. "Opus Dei members preach their faith through their work as well as the friendships they develop," Ann explained. She and her husband would later preach their faith by becoming central figures in a series of nonprofits that would channel dark money for Leo's efforts.

Through his role in securing the nominations of Clarence Thomas, John Roberts, and Samuel Alito to the Supreme Court, Leo's political cachet began to grow. An avid networker, he cultivated friendships with other members of the court, spending a weekend in Colorado hunting with Judge Antonin Scalia—himself a devout Catholic and, like the Corkerys, close to Opus Dei. Surrounded by such religious zeal, it didn't take long for their example to reawaken his own Catholic faith, and Leo soon began tapping his network of dark-money backers to support religious causes. He twice bailed out the Becket Fund, a nonprofit named after a twelfth-century English martyr, that officially worked to protect religious freedoms, especially those that were important to conservative Catholics. He reveled in his reputation as the financial savior of this important community.

Soon afterwards, President Bush picked Leo as his representative to the United States Commission on International Religious Freedom, a federal agency set up to police religious freedom around the world. Despite its lofty aims, the commission had a tiny budget and its commissioners were unpaid. Within Washington circles, many saw it as nothing more than an office for amateurs who meddled in foreign policy. Undeterred by the skeptics, Leo made the most of his time at the commission to push his own Catholic agenda—traveling to places like Iraq, Nigeria, Saudi Arabia, South Sudan, and Vietnam to investigate allegations of religious persecution. His own faith seemed to grow during that time, with Leo occasionally reprimanding his staff for putting him in a hotel too far from a church, making it difficult for him to attend Mass. Some colleagues began to note a particular bias in the way he carried out a role that conflicted with the commission's stated aim of championing the freedom of *all* religions. He became embroiled in a lawsuit after one former colleague accused him of firing her because she was Muslim. Several staff members resigned because of the controversy, and Leo was fired not long after. Despite the scandal, his time at the commission deepened Leo's faith and helped him cultivate his image as a serious political figure.

By the time of the Federalist Society's twenty-fifth anniversary dinner in November 2007, his influence was clear. Leo shared the stage with the president and three sitting Supreme Court Justices—Antonin Scalia, Clarence Thomas, and Samuel Alito. Chief Justice John Roberts sent a video message. "Thanks in part to your efforts, a new generation of lawyers is rising," President Bush told the assembled members.

At the time of this dinner, Leo was still recovering from the sudden death of his daughter Margaret just a few weeks before her fifteenth birthday—an event that had a profound impact on him. Margaret had been born with spina bifida and used a wheelchair. Events around her death had reinforced Leo's faith. The previous summer, during a family vacation, Leo had promised Margaret that he would try to go to Mass more regularly. Over the years, Margaret had developed an obsession with anything religious, and would nag her parents to take her to Mass. She especially loved angels—and priests, insisting on a hug every time she saw one. The day after they returned from vacation, Leo got up early to go to Mass—as promised—and looked in on Margaret. As he was walking down the hall, she started gasping for breath and died shortly afterward. "I will always think that she did her job," he later said. "She did her job."

After her death, strange signs appeared. The real estate billionaire Robin Arkley—the man who had provided the money to lobby for Roberts and Alito's nomination to the Supreme Court—invited the Leos to spend some time at his ranch in California. On the way there, they spent a night in a hotel in San Francisco. After checking in, they went up to their room and Margaret's younger sister Elizabeth rushed over to a bowl of complimentary candy and dug her hand into it. In it, she discovered a Sacred Heart medal. On the last day at the ranch, Leo's wife Sally came across another medal. A few weeks later, someone visiting Leo at work told him they found another medal in their airplane seat. The Leos told friends that they were convinced these medals were signs from heaven that Margaret was both safe and still with them. The experience would deepen his faith, marking him out as a crusader—and a target for Opus Dei.

By 2008, with the economy in meltdown and a landslide victory by Democratic presidential candidate Barack Obama seeming increasingly likely, Washington's Catholic conservative circles were in deep despair. Just as the Culture of Life Foundation had done during the 2000 election campaign, Opus Dei–linked institutions pulled out all the stops to prevent an Obama victory. The attempt two years earlier to amend the Constitution and define marriage as being between a man and a woman had failed spectacularly, and momentum was building in various states to enshrine same-sex marriage into law. While Obama had come out in opposition to same-sex marriage, partly in a sop to the Christian vote, there were widespread concerns among the conservative Catholic movement about what a Democrat in the White House might mean for their pro-life, anti-gay agenda. The Witherspoon Institute published a speech by Archbishop Charles Chaput, a good friend of Opus Dei, a few weeks ahead of the election, seeking to drum the message into the faithful that the Democratic candidate was a danger to their Catholic belief system. "I believe that Senator Obama, whatever his other talents, is the most committed 'abortion-rights' presidential candidate of either major party since the Roe v. Wade abortion decision in 1973," the archbishop said. The publication of this speech struck a similar note to other pieces written by Robby George in the preceding weeks under inflammatory titles such as "Obama's Abortion Extremism" and "Obama and Infanticide."

Tellez wrote to his donors outlining an action plan for the coming battle against liberalism. "Let me remind you that we are not electing God but only the president of the United States," he wrote. "Presidents make mistakes and they will make mistakes. And presidential candidates are also humans, and they spin things to their advantage. Don't we all?" With just over three weeks to go until election day, Tellez was scathing about the Obama ticket, concluding that "the leadership of the Democratic party has been co-opted by forces that make it pro–gay marriage and pro-choice to the extreme."

He offered them a glimmer of hope via details of his latest project, called the National Organization for Marriage—another nonprofit run out of his office on Nassau Street, in Princeton. The idea for the initiative had come from Maggie Gallagher, an outspoken conservative columnist who had moved to D.C. predominantly so her son could attend the Opus Dei school there. Gallagher had shared her idea with Robby George—who in turn told her to speak with Luis Tellez. "I was basically trying to help provide the resources—basically raising money for the project," recalled Tellez. The longtime Opus Dei operative Neil Corkery was also brought in as treasurer. The Opus Dei money men were immediately successful: during 2008, its first full year in operation, the National Organization for Marriage brought in almost $3 million in donations. A large chunk of that money came from the Mormon Church, which Tellez had begun to cultivate for donations after the son of one of the organization's elders was admitted to Princeton on a Witherspoon Institute scholarship. That same year, the National Organization for Marriage spent $1.8 million in California, gathering signatures to put forward a proposition to outlaw marriage between same-sex couples in the state and mounting an aggressive campaign to get the conservative vote out. "NOM spearheaded the effort of collecting over one million signatures to qualify for a proposition to go on the ballot this November to let the people of California decide whether marriage should be reserved to one man and one woman," wrote Tellez. "No one at the time expected the effort to collect signatures and the requisite money . . . the general mood the fight for marriage was over (we had lost). It is important for you to know this."

Obama was elected president on November 4, 2008. But that same day, Tellez and his coalition of conservatives scored another, less-reported victory. In California, Proposition 8—defining marriage as between a man and a woman—was passed with 52 percent of the votes cast. "A pro-traditional marriage win in California is a very significant victory," Tellez explained. And it was. Just as he had done at Princeton with the James Madison Program and the Witherspoon Institute, on the back of its victory in California,

Tellez was able to position the National Organization for Marriage as a rallying point for conservative donors. The organization would assemble a $25 million war chest over the next three years. While styling itself as a grassroots organization and highlighting its thousands of small donors, in reality almost all its money came from a handful of religiously motivated individuals and organizations—such as the Knights of Columbus and the Mormon Church. But at its core would be a group of Opus Dei activists like Tellez and Corkery. They took their political advice from Jeff Bell, a Washington political operative and a supernumerary, and his business partner Frank Cannon, a donor to The Heights, an Opus Dei school in the city. Their public relations efforts were run by Creative Response Concepts, the self-styled "blue-collar" communications agency for the conservative movement. The group had brazenly run a litany of disinformation campaigns over the years, including the "Swift-Boat" campaign against John Kerry. It would later seek to discredit the testimony of a sexual abuse victim in its efforts to have a right-wing justice appointed to the Supreme Court. The firm's president, Greg Mueller, had been the spokesperson for Steve Forbes—one of Tellez's biggest backers—in his failed presidential bid in 2000. A staunch Catholic, Mueller had encouraged Forbes to campaign on the issue of abortion as "the way you get to the heart and soul of the Republican Party." He would later go into business with Leonard Leo to stack the Supreme Court with like-minded conservatives, and would become a major donor to—and a board member at—Opus Dei's Catholic Information Center in Washington.

At the center of the National Organization for Marriage's efforts was a $1.5 million television advertising campaign called "The Gathering Storm," which showed one concerned citizen after another standing against a backdrop of lightning and dark clouds, talking about how "gay marriage" activists were taking away their parental rights and religious freedom. The campaign was widely condemned. Tellez, wishing to maintain his "nice kind" of conservatism reputation at Princeton, sank back into the shadows while the organization's other board members spouted anti-LGBTQ+ vitriol. Gallagher described homosexuality as a "sexual disability" in one article, while John Eastman—who was appointed chairman of the National Organization for Marriage in 2011—equated abortion and homosexuality to barbarism. "Evil will be with us always, and it requires constant vigilance to defeat," he said.

"There will always be threats to institutions grounded in human nature by those who think human nature doesn't define limits." Eastman would later become an advisor to President Donald Trump and be indicted for his role in trying to overturn the result of the 2020 election.

Tellez's efforts to surreptitiously influence the political arena didn't end there, though. As the National Organization for Marriage was fueling hatred toward the LGBTQ+ community, he was quietly working with Jeff Bell and Frank Cannon on another initiative. The American Principles Project had political ambitions far beyond the gay marriage question that stretched deep into the fabric of American life. "Expose Obama as a social radical," read one confidential document setting out its aims. "Develop side issues to weaken pro-gay marriage political leaders and parties and develop an activist base of socially conservative voters. Raise such issues as pornography, protection of children, and the need to oppose all efforts to weaken religious liberty at the federal level. This is the mission of the American Principles Project." The organization would soon inject millions of dollars directly into election battles—and try to get the supernumerary Jeff Bell elected to the Senate. This new initiative would be funded by Sean Fieler, a wealthy hedge fund manager and devout Catholic who had met Tellez through the Witherspoon Institute and who described the numerary as a major influence. Across the country, forces were being rallied for the re-Christianization of America. And the general commanding them was a numerary of Opus Dei. Soon, they would gather more firepower than they could have ever imagined in their quest to realize Escrivá's distorted vision.

12

THERE BE DRAGONS

Buenos Aires, Argentina—August 2009

AMONG THE CAST AND CREW GATHERED BESIDE ROLAND JOFFÉ AT THE official press launch of the acclaimed director's new film sat three unlikely figures: an Opus Dei priest and two supernumerary lawyers. Their presence there that day attested to the organization's growing hubris—and the vast financial resources at its disposal. After two decades of failing to live up to the promise of *The Killing Fields* and *The Mission*, both of which earned him Oscar nominations as best director in the eighties, Joffé had been tempted out of semi-retirement with a $40 million budget to shoot a new picture about Escrivá. For Villa Tevere, the film was the culmination of a years-long dream to bring the founder to the silver screen. Del Portillo had sent one member to Hollywood to set up a film company in the early nineties, and his successor Echevarría had become obsessed with the idea of a biopic after watching a film about the life of Padre Pio. Urgency about the project ramped up after *The Da Vinci Code*: a production company called "The Work LLC" was established in California and a script commissioned for the project, tentatively called *The Founder*. It was poorly received. Hugh Hudson, who had directed *Chariots of Fire*, thought it "smelled pro-Franco," while Alejandro González Iñárritu—the Mexican who had shot to fame with *21 Grams* and *Babel*—rejected it outright. Joffé initially turned it down too, but found himself fascinated with the figure of Escrivá after watching some old footage. After the script was rewritten, the financing for the film magically came together, thanks to two Spanish supernumerary lawyers—and a mysterious foundation in Spain that people on the film referred to only as the "golden investor." At the launch, Joffé waxed lyrical about *There Be Dragons*—the new name for the film—which promised to be an epic drama filled with passion, betrayal, love, and religion.

During breaks from shooting, cast members and their Opus Dei minders would sometimes visit the main numerary residence in the Argentine capital. Such visits were a demonstration of the audacity that had seeped into the organization's presentation of itself to the outside world, following its successful handling of *The Da Vinci Code*. For years, the residence in Buenos Aires, where it now entertained the *There Be Dragons* cast and crew, had allegedly been home to one of Opus Dei's largest and most ruthless slave labor operations. This prime piece of real estate had effectively been gifted to the organization by the military junta in 1972, in a sign of its cozy relationship with a regime that, at the time, was "disappearing" tens of thousands of people across the country—first torturing them in illegal detention centers and then throwing them, drugged and beaten, out of military planes over the Atlantic Ocean. The residence was home to dozens of numeraries and students and soon established itself as extremely successful in attracting new recruits. Every morning and every evening, the men would gather in prayer in the large chapel on the ground floor, watched over by an image of Escrivá that had been fixed into one of the stained-glass windows. Next door, in an adjoining tower block connected to the residence through an underground tunnel, sixty women lived out their vocations as numerary assistants. Some say they had been recruited as young as twelve from poor communities in the north of Argentina, and from neighboring Paraguay and Bolivia, by numeraries who drove there looking for vocations, promising the girls a better life if they would come with them to Buenos Aires to study at a hospitality school there. Suitable girls were identified and pressured into joining. One victim says she was flown to Buenos Aires on a government plane. Others say their border crossings were facilitated by a numerary who worked for the Ministry of Foreign Affairs. They were told it was their calling to join

Opus Dei, that their families would be rewarded in heaven if they agreed—or condemned to hell if they refused. Ironically, it would be from this cohort of the most vulnerable in society that the biggest threat—perhaps an existential threat—would rise up against Opus Dei.

The women lived a life of servitude. They were woken up at 5:50 a.m. by a buzzer installed on each floor of the tower block. They were expected to get out of bed immediately, and to kneel on the floor and kiss the ground, while uttering *"Servium"*—Latin for "I serve." After a visit to the toilet, they put on their uniforms, then had a quick coffee, before prayers in the chapel. At 6:10 a.m., it was time to start work, either in the kitchen or cleaning the rooms of their own block, until 7:40 a.m., when the time came to change into more formal clothing to go back to the chapel at 8 a.m. After another set of prayers there came Mass and communion. Then at 9:30 a.m., it was time to have breakfast and change before returning to work at 10 a.m. With the men next door out at work, the double doors to the adjoining male residence were unlocked and the women were allowed to scurry through the tunnel to clean the men's rooms, the bathrooms, and the common areas—until lunch at midday. After a half-hour break, it was time to clean the vast auditorium, before returning to change in time for the rosary and the daily conversation with the other numeraries about their faith and potential recruits. At 3 p.m., they returned to the chapel to collectively chant the *Preces*, the special set of prayers pledging allegiance to the prelature. Then followed another ninety minutes of work in the laundry or ironing room—until a coffee break at 5 p.m., after which the women had "free time" to confess or study, or possibly go out to visit a potential recruit with another numerary assistant (they were hardly ever allowed to go out alone), if the directress permitted them to do so. At 8 p.m. came dinner, and then back to their rooms to change into their maids' uniforms to serve the men next door. Some were allowed to serve the men at mealtimes—but only if they followed strict rules, and only if they averted their gaze at all times. After serving dinner and cleaning up after the men, there was time for one fifteen-minute group chat before a return to the chapel—and then to bed at 10 p.m. It was an arduous, backbreaking existence—one that had been meticulously designed by the Opus Dei founder. The exploitation, the abuse of power, and the lack of basic rights were all explained as "sacrifices" delivered to God. None of their daily reality was represented in the sanitized biopic of the Opus Dei founder being filmed across town.

Under the pressure to meet the meticulous targets set for them—the number of men's shirts they had to iron per hour, or the number of bathrooms to clean—and with no days off and little time to themselves, some of the women became suicidal. For many, the only glimmer of Christian compassion came from one priest who came to give Mass and hear confession. Father Danilo Eterovic often turned a blind eye to minor infractions of Opus Dei rules that were vigorously enforced by the rest of the staff. One numerary assistant who asked the director to borrow a book she had seen in the male numerary residence library was told that she could not because the material was inappropriate for someone of her standing; she ended up taking the book without permission but panicked when the time came to return it. She confessed this to Father Danilo, who offered to return it on her behalf—a rare demonstration of compassion within the center. Opus Dei would eventually take away all the responsibilities that Father Danilo had toward its members. His body was later found on the train tracks a short distance away, with a note asking the police to inform the residence of his suicide. When the police went there, the numerary who answered told the officers that nobody by that name lived there and that nobody knew who Father Danilo was. As the actors and crew working on the Escrivá biopic came and went next door, the lives of the numerary assistants—the reality of life within Opus Dei—remained hidden from the world. It would be another decade before the oppression of their existence would eventually come to light.

After wrapping up the shoot in Argentina, the *There Be Dragons* production team traveled back to Europe. Following more than a year of postproduction, the film was at last ready for its international release. It was a complete flop. "Beyond the lugubrious pageantry, there is no sign of emotional or spiritual life in the film, only windy posturing," said the *New York Times* reviewer, who described the movie as "a calamitous film" and "a fawning biography." "*There Be Dragons* belongs to a realm devoid of flesh and blood, where vacuous oratory reigns and religiosity passes for faith." The *Village Voice* was no less critical. "Joffé's inexplicable penchant for tear-jerking Catholic mysticism make *Dragons* more punishing than a hundred Hail Marys," its reviewer said. Opus Dei did its best to salvage Escrivá's reputation—and project his supposed saintliness. Joaquín Navarro-Valls, the numerary and longtime spokesperson for Pope John Paul II, grandly announced that Villa Tevere was receiving messages of thanks almost daily—from divorcees inspired by the film to return to their wives, from parents and children who reconciled after years apart, and from others who rediscovered their lost faith. The financials told another story. Almost all of the $40 million budget was lost. Worldwide, it grossed just $4 million. At the Vatican, Opus Dei was the butt of many a joke. "There may be dragons, but there certainly won't be any Oscars," went one.

While its venture into Hollywood had been a disaster, Opus Dei had a much more successful debut in New York. In May 2010, the IESE Business School welcomed the city's corporate elite to its new campus in Midtown, across the street from Carnegie Hall. Elegant and stylish, with a façade of cream-colored brickwork rising to a grand colonnade, the building had been originally commissioned by a famous Russian ballet dancer to house his dance studio and had once been the global headquarters of Columbia Artists Management, an agency for classical musicians that represented the likes of Sergei Prokofiev and Igor Stravinsky. Following an $18 million renovation, this grand building at 165 West 57th Street was about to embark on its next adventure—as the New York campus of a Spanish business school with big ambitions to become the first European institution to break into the lucrative U.S. market for MBAs, which had long been dominated by Columbia, Harvard, and Stanford. Inside the glitzy new auditorium, executives from multinational corporations including Bain & Company, Cap Gemini, and Pfizer listened to talks from staff members who had been flown in from Barcelona; they spoke about how companies could foster a culture of innovation and creativity, and about the great hopes they had for the new campus. Having just been named the number one business school in the world by *The Economist*, the institution's plans were already underway to assemble a large research team in the city, which would be tasked with advising the country's largest companies on important topics such as globalization, innovation, regulation, and corporate governance.

Little was said about the Opus Dei chapel upstairs—or, indeed, of the business school's deep links with the movement. The ties between the two went back to 1958, when Escrivá approved the school's creation. Right from the start, he made it clear that IESE was an apostolic mission of Opus Dei with a specific goal—to groom a new generation of businessmen who prioritized their religious values over everything else. Luis Valls-Taberner became an early supporter, extending loans to finance IESE's expansion and hiring the dean—a fellow numerary—for lucrative consulting work at the bank. Within five years, it had established an alliance with Harvard Business School and launched the first two-year MBA program in Europe. Expansion continued at breakneck speed. By the time of the grand opening of its New York campus, IESE boasted a global network—with outposts in São Paulo, Lagos, and Shanghai. While spiritual formation had never officially been part of the curriculum, the ambitious young professionals its programs attracted were prime recruitment material for the many numerary and supernumerary academics who taught there. Those academics could direct any interested students to the priests—always from Opus Dei—on hand in the campus chapel. With almost five hundred of the brightest business minds enrolled in its regular courses, a further two thousand attending shorter programs, and contracts to provide training for executives at some of the world's largest companies, like Citibank, Nestlé, and PriceWaterhouseCooper, by 2010 IESE was in a strong position to deliver on Escrivá's plans for the school. Following Opus Dei's success in the political capital of America, the opening of this new outpost in New York was an opportunity to secure influence in the country's business hub as well.

In an indication of the continued ties between the two institutions, the seven-story building on West Fifty-seventh Street had been purchased, not by the IESE Business School but by the Opus Dei–linked Clover Foundation. Set up in the eighties as a charity dedicated to helping young people in poorer countries to get a decent education, Clover had by 2010 strayed a long way from its founding principles to become a major source of finance for Opus Dei vanity projects around the world. Under the oversight of Luis Tellez, it had provided millions of dollars that could only tangentially be linked to its original aims. One of its biggest projects was to pay for an expansion of Villa Tevere, financing new state-of-the-art living quarters for the numerary men who worked for the prelature's internal government. In 2007, the

Clover Foundation received a sudden injection of almost $50 million from an offshore entity called Anatol Financial Assets Limited, which had been incorporated a few years earlier in the British Virgin Islands. It had been set up through intermediaries in Panama by the notorious law firm Mossack Fonseca, a favorite among those keen to hide their money from the authorities. The transfer coincided with a decision at IESE to expand to New York. Clover bought the building on West Fifty-seventh Street for $25 million in cash and rented it out to the business school at far below market value. Shortly after, the foundation gifted $4.2 million to IESE for refurbishments. Another $6.5 million was transferred the year of the opening. For all the talk about transparency and best practices at IESE, the confused finances linking the business school and Opus Dei were unlikely to ever feature as a case study.

Such financial entanglements were a hallmark of the web of foundations used to finance Opus Dei activities all around the world. By 2010, there were about a hundred such foundations operating in the United States alone controlling more than $600 million of assets. While most of them were small, with only a single real estate asset on their books—usually a numerary residence—others were decidedly not. The largest, the Association for Cultural Interchange, Inc., had been established in the fifties by two numeraries and had been used to buy up several lavish properties across the Northeast in the years that followed. By 2010, the foundation had spun off most of that real estate to other Opus Dei foundations, but it still managed an $85 million portfolio of stocks, bonds, mutual funds, and other real estate. No mention was made of Opus Dei on its tax filings or on its website; instead, the foundation purported to "provide a program of support and assistance to other not-for-profit organizations . . . that promote international understanding, the exchange of ideas and cultural activities that promote the dignity of the human person." A closer look at its finances revealed an almost symbiotic relationship with Opus Dei. Its board was filled with the same cast of numerary men—such as Luis Tellez and Julien Nagore, who was in charge of overseeing the global finances of Opus Dei from Rome—who were also named as directors at Clover and dozens of other supposedly independent foundations. Images of smiling schoolchildren in Africa were used in promotional materials, but such projects accounted for only a tiny proportion of the budget. Its biggest project had been the purchase and refurbishment of a former school close to Villa Tevere, which had been transformed into a residence for numerary women, a project which had cost almost $30 million. By contrast, just $20,000 was donated to the smiling children in Africa during the previous year.

Such spending patterns were mirrored by the hundreds of other Opus Dei foundations around the world, which publicly touted the support they provided to underprivileged communities—but which secretly diverted most of their funds to finance a global infrastructure of residences and grassroot initiatives aimed at only one thing: recruitment. By 2010, Opus Dei boasted 88,000 members and a presence in sixty-six countries—following recent expansion into Russia, Indonesia, South Korea, and Romania. It operated almost three hundred schools, a hundred and sixty vocational schools, over a dozen universities, several hospitals, and a vast network of student residences. Opus Dei priests and numeraries had formally been tasked with providing the "spiritual formation" for anyone at those institutions, bringing hundreds of thousands of mainly children and young people into its orbit every day. Care was taken to distance the prelature from these initiatives— and not just to protect Opus Dei's reputation but also to guard against scaring off recruits by openly advertising their links to the prelature. But in reality, almost everything was coordinated from Rome, which sent out orders to the regional governments about how the numeraries that ran these individual projects should operate, about how they should spend their money and what types of recruits they should seek.

This fictitious construct of independence had another clear advantage. In France, where Catherine Tissier was seeking to sue Opus Dei for the exploitation she had suffered as a numerary assistant, the distancing strategy had protected Opus Dei from criminal proceedings. During deliberations with the judge, the organization successfully argued that it had only been responsible for the spiritual formation of the young numerary assistant— and not for any breaches of labor law or alleged enslavement. The strategy was a major victory, absolving Opus Dei of any responsibility to the people who had given their lives to and been controlled by the organization. The ruling left individual numeraries who ran the hospitality school where Tissier worked facing serious charges—and potential prison time. Two of them were forced to stand trial at the Palais de Justice in Paris and defend the life-style of numerary assistants—a lifestyle set not by them but by their Opus Dei superiors in Rome. The judge threw out the case because the retreat center successfully demonstrated it had paid Tissier a salary—a fact that she had never contested. Her accusations of exploitation were based on the fact that she never had access to her money and was expected to sign blank checks that were used to transfer her money to other Opus Dei foundations. At the same time, Opus Dei was engaged in a legal tussle with six numerary assistants in Spain who had made similar allegations: they asserted that it had failed to pay their social security contributions, that they'd been forced to work without contracts, and had no say over where they worked or what they did. While Opus Dei washed its hands of any responsibility, this network of residences and social initiatives continued to generate hundreds more recruits for the organization every year.

There were calls from within for Opus Dei to reform and halt this systematic abuse. The complaints weren't only from numerary assistants; they came from numeraries, too. Despite their higher status, freedom from manual labor, and the ability to work outside the residence—human rights denied to their "little sisters"—they, too, were subject to endless abuses of their physical and psychological freedoms. Those who worked in internal jobs were particularly vulnerable; many were asked to leave their paid careers to fill administrative roles or run recruitment activities, and they were moved around from place to place according to their superiors' whims, forced to abandon their friends and family, and expected to work long hours without pay or social security payments. Cut off from any outside support, with no recourse to savings, unemployment benefits, or pension, many of them were basically trapped in the institution, lacking any independent means to start a new life. Opus Dei usually washed its hands of any responsibility to them once they left. "You appear to be confusing the role of Opus Dei in your life with that of your legal employer," wrote one superior to a numerary in England who left. "Opus Dei never has and I believe never will actually employ people, and people who work in its residences or the catering departments of those residences are employed by the legal body that owns them. . . . I have investigated all these bodies for any reference to your name as an employee and have drawn a complete blank." While striving to draw a clear division between Opus Dei and these supposedly independent residences and "catering departments," the superior strangely had access to *all* their records.

Discontent among numeraries escalated from the late 2000s onwards, due in part to the proliferation of smart phones, which numeraries were allowed to have for their external jobs—and for more efficient recruiting. But the organization's abusive practices endured. Villa Tevere's practice of handpicking the elite "elector" members—the men who discussed and voted on any major changes to its practices and statutes—entrenched the sycophantic culture that had prevailed since the sixties. Time and again, the numeraries in positions of authority failed to tackle instances of abuse—and sometimes went to extraordinary lengths to cover them up. In 2010, one numerary in Spain reported that he had been sexually abused on at least seven occasions by an Opus Dei priest—abuse that had started when he was still a teenager. The priest, Manuel Cociña, had held several important positions within the organization, including rector of Saint Michael's, the flagship Opus Dei church in central Madrid, and several initiatives involving high school students—and at one stage, he seemed destined to be a potential future prelate. One senior figure within the Spanish hierarchy of Opus Dei informed the victim the organization was already aware of the priest's "recklessness" and asked him not to make a formal complaint. "He said: 'Look, I can't say anything more but this isn't news to me, it doesn't surprise me—we've taken this person out of circulation, we've sent him to Galicia . . . don't worry, because he isn't going to have any more dealings with young people,'" recalled the victim. It would take another ten years for Opus Dei to publicly recognize the allegations against the priest—and only after they were reported by the media. Years after the *Boston Globe* exposé had forced sweeping reforms in the Church, Opus Dei remained stuck in the old mentality. The priest was eventually found guilty.

In other instances, Villa Tevere went to extraordinary lengths to downplay the complaints that were being raised. One numerary in Asia who had begun to question the detailed rules that governed every aspect of his existence wrote to Echevarría to flag to the prelate how these "instructions" from Villa Tevere were affecting ordinary numeraries like him. When no response came, he wrote again. This time, he was summoned to Rome. His superiors refused to engage with him on any of the points he had raised.

Instead, he was told to see a doctor who specifically dealt with "this type of medical check-up"—not a practicing medical professional, but an Opus Dei priest who used to be a doctor. The priest prescribed for him a cocktail of drugs to address his "obsessive" behavior, telling him, "Don't pay much attention to what it says on the leaflet, just take one in the morning and one at night." The priest and one of the directors checked several times to make sure he was taking his pills.

Shortly after his return to Asia, the numerary decided to confess to a priest who wasn't from Opus Dei, who advised him to leave. Despite being against Church law, speaking to priests from outside the prelature was forbidden within Opus Dei: the risk of receiving spiritual advice that might conflict with the interests of Opus Dei, like that received by the numerary, was evidently too great. Pope Benedict XVI, who had always been uncomfortable about Opus Dei's canonical status within the Church, found out about the practice not long afterwards and ordered Opus Dei to drop the requirement. The pope also ordered the organization to cease the practice of numeraries passing on to their superiors information gleaned from others as part of spiritual direction—during the "chat." Echevarría was forced to send out a pastoral letter to "clarify" the "misunderstanding." That Opus Dei was willing to lie about this "misunderstanding" not just to the pope but also to its own membership illustrated how far the organization would go to protect its own interests. It also underlined the effectiveness of keeping its internal rulebook hidden from the Vatican and from most of its own members. Hiding its internal rules allowed Opus Dei to dodge what might have been a serious investigation of its practices had the "instructions" and "experiences" been openly published.

When some parents appeared at an Opus Dei school on the outskirts of Bilbao in June 2011, to accuse a numerary who taught there of sexually harassing their son, the teacher was flown to another school in Sydney, Australia, where he taught Spanish to boys of a similar age despite the accusations hanging over him. The numerary was later sentenced to eleven years in prison. Even under the most generous of interpretations, such behavior indicated serious failures in the safeguarding of children at schools run by Opus Dei. But it also indicated a willingness, as had the sudden disappearance of McCloskey in 2004, to use this vast network of institutions to shield potential criminals from justice and to put other people in harm's way in order to save the prelature from scandal. As well as creating a network to capture new recruits, the money at Opus Dei's disposal provided a network to hide its worst crimes.

The benefits of Opus Dei's network weren't restricted to the physical world—its residences, schools, universities, and hospitality schools—but also extended into the spiritual. By the 2010s, many in the Catholic Church were concerned about a serious shortage of priests. Between 1970 and 2010, while the global Catholic population had almost doubled to 1.2 billion people, the number of priests had fallen, leaving almost fifty thousand dioceses without a priest and countless others forced to merge to cover for the lack of sufficient vocations. The problem was perhaps most acute in the United States, where the number of priests had fallen by a third over that same period, with the sexual abuse scandal accelerating what had already been a growing trend. Opus Dei stepped into this void. As the money distributed from Spain funded the expansion of its network around the world, generating new members—and new vocations for the Opus Dei priesthood—its number of priests more than doubled over the same period. Banco Popular had played a critical role in this expansion, with money from the bank going directly to subsidize a seminary outside Pamplona and directly paying the living costs for hundreds of priests—many of whom had joined Opus Dei in Latin America and Africa and been offered the chance to study for free in Europe, with their costs covered by the bank. While still a small part of the Catholic Church, there was no doubt that Opus Dei—thanks to the endless stream of cash from the bank—was ascending as a force within the Vatican. As a reflection of its growing might, by 2010 the prelature boasted twenty-four bishops around the world—in Ecuador, Argentina, Peru, Chile, the United States, Austria, Kenya, Colombia, Spain, Venezuela, Paraguay, and Brazil—as well as two cardinals. In April 2010, an Opus Dei priest—José Horacio Gómez—took over as Archbishop of Los Angeles, giving the prelature influence over the largest Catholic diocese in North America.

During his second three-year term as chaplain of the Catholic Information Center, Father Arne Panula introduced a number of new initiatives designed to generate a steadier stream of donations—and to better integrate Opus Dei with wealthy Catholics. His first big initiative copied a popular strategy that had proved lucrative in almost every industry: the awards dinner. By bestowing an award on Washington's most respected conservative Catholics, and then hosting a lavish dinner in their honor—to which all the city's wealthy Catholics were invited—he generated hundreds of thousands of dollars in a single evening and established the Catholic Information Center at the heart of this influential community. And so the John Paul II Award was born in 2012. The inaugural award went to Cardinal Donald Wuerl, the Archbishop of Washington, who was popular with conservative members of his flock and who had recently stoked controversy by becoming one of the most senior members of the Church to sign the Manhattan Declaration. This was an ecumenical statement drafted by Robert George, and co-signed by Luis Tellez, Maggie Gallagher, and other members of the Catholic right, which called on Christians not to comply with laws permitting abortion, same-sex marriage, and other practices that went against their beliefs. The following year the award went to George Weigel, a biographer of Pope John Paul II and a big figure within the American Catholic right. The Supreme Knight of the Knights of Columbus, an influential and wealthy Catholic brotherhood; the founder of the Becket Fund, a lobby group championing religious rights; and Supreme Court Justice Antonin Scalia would all become recipients over the next few years.

Father Arne set up another initiative called the Leonine Forum, a program for top graduates designed to provide them with "intellectual and spiritual seriousness." It, too, brought in generous donations from wealthy Catholics keen to steep the leaders of tomorrow in Church teachings. As ever, the Opus Dei name was kept out of any promotional material—but, even so, such events deepened the prelature's presence among America's most influential Catholics. For Father Arne, the ultimate goal of this outreach was transforming the political sphere, almost every aspect of which had grown more and more secular over the years. He believed that policy simply couldn't be made by people who weren't versed in the universal truths of the Church. His mission was to reverse this creeping secularism—and put Opus Dei at the heart of a spiritual awakening.

Luis Tellez used his network to advance Father Arne's goal of transforming the political sphere. With the National Organization for Marriage increasingly under attack because of its vitriolic campaigns and increasing questions about its links with Opus Dei and the Mormon Church, Tellez shifted his energy to the American Principles Project. Thanks to huge contributions from Sean Fieler—who had become a close friend and squash partner to the Mexican numerary in Princeton—APP and its affiliated political action committee directed millions of dollars to political candidates and causes aligned with the think tank's conservative Catholic agenda.

It also sought to shape Republican policies. In September 2011, the American Principles Project sponsored a televised debate between the party's candidates for president. After Obama's reelection the following year, the Republican National Committee authored a long postmortem, concluding that it was time for the party to become more "welcoming and inclusive" on issues like gay marriage and immigration. APP pushed back, commissioning its own report—with the help of pollster Kellyanne Conway—arguing for the opposite. The group also pumped money into swinging electoral races in New Jersey, where it tried to get supernumerary Jeff Bell elected to the Senate, as well as in Oregon. In Wyoming, it sought to derail the Senate ambitions of Liz Cheney. "The aim was to advance legislation that would be consistent with principles—conservative principles," recalled Tellez.

During this period, Tellez also used his position at the Witherspoon Institute to fund other stealth missions to shape policy—and attract wealthy donors. He spent $700,000 on commissioning a "study" into the impact that gay parenting had on children. A series of emails from Tellez to Mark Regnerus, the academic commissioned for the report, made clear his motivations: "It would be great to have this before major decisions of the Supreme Court," he wrote. He reassured his financial backers he was "confident that the traditional understanding of marriage will be vindicated by this study as long as it is done honestly and well." The findings of the study would later be widely debunked. But its impact as a rallying force for Catholic conservatives was not to be underestimated. Tellez also spent $1.4 million of Witherspoon Institute money organizing a conference at the Vatican that was billed as "an interreligious colloquium on the complementarity of man and woman." While the initiative was officially the idea of the Princeton academic Robby George, Tellez and his Opus Dei colleagues in Rome oversaw the organization of the conference. Witherspoon made a large donation to the Opus Dei university in Rome around the same time. "Oftentimes, Robby will open the door, you know," Tellez explained. "I'm a nobody." The Humanum conference created some additional cachet for Opus Dei operatives in the United States, who used this important gathering of religious leaders as an enticement to woo big-name Catholic conservatives. Leonard Leo was one of those invited to participate.

The invitation dovetailed with a wider effort at the Catholic Information Center to entice Leo into the Opus Dei orbit. At around the same time as the Humanum conference, Leo was invited onto the CIC board. Their two worlds were already entwined. Leo's children went to the two Opus Dei schools—The Heights for the boys and Oakcrest for the girls—and he and his wife played an active part in school life, donating thousands of dollars a year in addition to the many thousands they were paying in tuition for their various children. The Leos were also regulars at a deeply conservative church in McLean, not far from their home, that was popular with many of the city's Opus Dei members. Both parties were also becoming ever more aggressive politically. In 2011, Leo teamed up with Clarence Thomas's wife Ginni to co-found another nonprofit that successfully opposed an Islamic center being built near the site of the 9/11 attacks in New York, denigrated as the "Ground Zero Mosque." A year later, he joined the board of the Catholic Association, another non-profit linked to the Corkerys, that funded campaigns to oppose same-sex marriage. For its part, the Catholic Information Center—despite in theory being apolitical—had also joined a suit against the Obama administration, challenging the requirement that employers provide and pay for contraception, sterilization, and abortion-causing drugs as part of employee health insurance plans.

The appointment of Leo came despite misgivings among the Opus Dei national leadership, and illustrated a transactional attitude toward this increasingly influential figure with deep connections to dark money. "He's a figure in Washington, and he may have had kids in the school down there," explained Father Tom Bohlin, who headed Opus Dei in the United States at the time—and who met Leo at the Humanum conference in Rome. "I'm not sure he even understands Opus Dei, but at a certain level, he likes what we do—certain things—and wants to support that." The appointment of Leo marked a shift in the CIC board. For years, it had been run by Father Arne, another priest, and a smattering of volunteers drawn from the congregation. The makeup of the board was decidedly unpolitical—a mix of academics, lawyers, and volunteers who helped run the bookshop. Pat Cipollone, a lawyer who had been an assistant to Attorney General Bill Barr in the early nineties but who had since returned to the private sector, was the only board member who was remotely connected to the Washington political scene. But in 2014, all that changed. Alongside Leo, Bill Barr, the former attorney general, was also appointed. Leo and his ilk would soon become a bridge connecting the prelature with important people on Capitol Hill—and the world of dark money populated by secretive billionaires with a deeply conservative agenda. Together, they would form a coalition—unified by their political connections, religious fervor, and money—that would reshape American society and destroy many hard-won civil rights.

In Father Arne's view, his successful renewal of the apostolic mission of the bookshop and chapel on K Street was all part of a "Great Awakening" that was about to wash over the United States—and the world. In the wake of the Occupy Wall Street movement and the general disgruntlement of young people following the financial crisis, he saw this "Great Awakening" starting on university campuses, where Opus Dei had again begun to plant its flag with what he called "counter-institutions" such as the Catholic Information Center's Leonine Forum and the Witherspoon Institute at Princeton. "It isn't only a spiritual awakening that's coming," Arne Panula explained. "Students leave these schools with no jobs, no intellectual sustenance of worth, and a huge financial debt . . . students are being duped. There will be a utilitarian reaction to that chasm between what they're promised and what they're actually taught—market correction, of sorts, in education. But the deeper reaction is more personal. It's about betrayal. Some of these students come to realize that there's a world out there that they never knew existed. They've been purposefully sealed off from it by their teachers and other authorities. That begs for reaction. They've been sold a bill of secular progressive goods!" Opus Dei would help guide them toward this new world.

Arne Panula was right—a new "Great Awakening" was coming. But it wouldn't rise up from the student population. Instead, it would emerge out of the dark-money networks. At the precise moment when Banco Popular's cash flow started to falter, the prelature found another seemingly bottomless source of income. The recruitment of Leonard Leo would cement ties between Opus Dei and the U.S. Supreme Court that had been developing for decades. Antonin Scalia had once been at the center of this relationship—the Justice had given talks at the Catholic Information Center and at the Reston Study Center, which was the male numerary residence in Washington's suburbs that hosted regular get-togethers for Opus Dei members. Only the year before, Scalia had also attended an Opus Dei retreat at the prelature's $10 million, 844-acre property near the Shenandoah Mountains. His children and grandchildren attended Opus Dei schools. He was best friends with Father Malcolm Kennedy, an Opus Dei priest who often came around for dinner at Scalia's house, after which the two would often belt out Broadway tunes. But with Leo and his network of dark money, Opus Dei's penetration of Washington's political and judicial worlds would now reach unprecedented levels. That Christmas, like many Christmases before it, the Supreme Court hosted its annual holiday party. As always, Father Malcolm was seated at the piano, playing carols for the assembled dignitaries, having been invited by Scalia. As he played, the Justices—the most powerful legal figures in America—sang along to the tune played by the Opus Dei priest. It was a dark portent for what was to come.

13

TRUMP CARD

Cibolo Creek Ranch, Texas—February 2016

THE MEN WERE PUZZLED WHEN THE SUPREME COURT JUSTICE FAILED TO show for breakfast ahead of that morning's hunt. Antonin Scalia had arrived a day earlier, and he'd seemed genuinely excited at the prospect of spending the long Presidents' Day weekend shooting pheasant, partridge, and blue quail on the remote 30,000-acre ranch, nestled in the Chinati Mountains, fifteen miles from the Mexican border. Cibolo Creek Ranch was a popular spot for celebrities—past guests included Mick Jagger, Bruce Willis, and Julia Roberts—and had served as a backdrop for Hollywood blockbusters like *No Country for Old Men* and *There Will Be Blood*. But this weekend, the glitz and glamor had been replaced by guns and God. Most of the other men gathered there were high-ranking members of the International Order of Saint Hubertus, a secret society of elite hunters with ties to the Catholic Church, whose followers wear dark-green robes emblazoned with a cross and the motto *Deum Diligite Animalia Diligentes*—"Honoring God by honoring His creatures." Scalia, an avid huntsman who had been on the rifle team in high school and whose chambers were a veritable taxidermy museum, had been invited along to join them for the weekend—all expenses paid—by John B. Poindexter, owner of the ranch and a former soldier who had made his fortune by manufacturing trucks.

After the Justice failed to appear for breakfast, Poindexter knocked on his door. Hearing no answer, he assumed that either Scalia hadn't heard him or didn't want to be bothered. But when he had still failed to surface some three hours later, Poindexter knocked again—this time loudly. When there was again no answer, he decided to go in. There, they found the seventy-nine-year-old lying in bed, still in his pajamas, perfectly reposed, his hands folded on top of the sheets. Scalia was dead. The conservative world had lost one of its greatest icons. And Opus Dei had lost one of its most powerful and influential allies in the United States.

Leonard Leo was one of the first people beyond the Justice's immediate family to learn the news, after receiving a call from one of the Scalias. It made sense for the family to reach out to the Federalist Society executive vice-president—the two men had been close over the years, bound by their dogmatic originalist reading of the Constitution, their profound Catholic faith, and their shared mission to overturn *Roe v. Wade*. Scalia had made public demonstrations of his support for Leo and the Federalist Society by regularly attending its annual dinner, which gave the society even more cachet among the conservative legal elite. Leo showed his gratitude to the Supreme Court Justice by tapping his network of wealthy donors to arrange hunting trips for him; two summers earlier, the two men spent five days fishing in Montana together, and had also previously been hunting in Colorado.

But there were other, more consequential reasons for reaching out to Leo. The sudden passing of Justice Scalia presented President Barack Obama with an opportunity to tilt the balance of the Court decisively to the left, by replacing him with a more progressive jurist. Such an appointment would be a milestone in the Court's history, handing Democratic-appointed judges a majority after more than forty years of being outnumbered by their Republican peers. Given the dangerously divisive fight being played out in the media among candidates desperate to win the Republican Party nomination for the presidential election nine months hence, and the growing discontent among the grassroots about the party's inability to capitalize on its control of both houses of Congress, the loss of the Supreme Court at this critical juncture— the last remaining line of defense against the march of progressivism— would be a bitter blow. Reaching out to Leo was the Scalias' way of seeking to preserve the legacy of the late Antonin.

Leo relayed the news to the office of Mitch McConnell, leader of the Senate, and spoke to his advisor for judicial nominations. A plan came together. Within hours, McConnell put out a bombshell statement that made clear the conservative elite would do everything it could to prevent the president from replacing Scalia. "The American people should have a voice in the selection of their next Supreme Court Justice," it said. "Therefore, this vacancy should not be filled until we have a new president." Talking points were emailed to the party, including the false statement that it had been eighty years since a Supreme Court nominee had been confirmed during an election year. That evening, in a televised debate involving the candidates for the Republican Party nomination, the issue dominated the agenda. Donald Trump, the real estate tycoon and frontrunner in the race, was unusually fatalistic when asked whether he thought Obama would seek to fill the vacancy. "I would certainly want to try and nominate a justice . . . I'm sure that—frankly, I'm absolutely sure that—President Obama will try and do it," he said, ignoring the talking points that had been so carefully put together by Leo and McConnell. "This is a tremendous blow to conservativism. It's a tremendous blow frankly to our country," he added.

Ted Cruz, the senator from Texas who had served as a clerk at the Supreme Court in the nineties, followed with a much stauncher defense of the Republican position. After repeating McConnell's false line about the eighty-year precedent, he launched into a tirade about the consequences of allowing Obama to nominate a replacement. "We are one justice away from a Supreme Court that will strike down every restriction on abortion adopted by the states," he said. "We are one justice away from a Supreme Court that will reverse the *Heller* decision—one of Justice Scalia's seminal decisions—that upheld the Second Amendment right to keep and bear arms. We are one justice away from a Supreme Court that would undermine the religious liberty of millions of Americans." Cruz, a devout Baptist, was Leonard Leo's own preferred candidate for the Republican ticket, and his words that evening were a salve to Leo's worries about what Scalia's death would mean for the Court. But the debate would mark a critical turning point—for Leo and for Opus Dei's own influence over the highest levels of government. Ironically, Trump's lackluster performance that evening would soon bring the two men together, uniting them in an unholy pact that would decisively change the country's direction for many years to come.

Four days after Scalia's unexpected passing, Father Bob Connor left the numerary residence in New York and made the four-hour drive south to Washington, where he planned to pay his respects to his great friend "Nino," whose body was lying in repose in the Great Hall of the Supreme Court. On his first evening in the capital, he posted a blog criticizing Scalia for adhering too strictly to the words of the Constitution—for being led by a "sand of lexicology"—and for placing too little emphasis on the Christian beliefs of the men who wrote it almost 250 years earlier. "The question concerning the legal mind of Justice Scalia is the question of the absence of truth and the prevailing nihilism globally," he surmised, adding that the late judge's willingness to defer to the democratic passing of laws—rather than to a universal concept of "truth"—risked a descent into "a dictatorship of the arbitrary will of individuals." Evidently, the legalistic originalism of the country's most archconservative jurist was too wishy-washy for this Opus Dei priest. He would later retract his critique—perhaps under pressure from his superiors for being too political. But his words offered a glimpse into the "spiritual direction" that this Opus Dei priest gave to Scalia—and his advice about how a Supreme Court Judge might "sanctify" his or her work.

At the funeral three days later, mourners assembled for what was supposed to be "a simple parish family Mass" at the Basilica of the National Shrine of the Immaculate Conception, the largest Catholic church in North America. Among the hundreds of guests was Vice President Joe Biden, former Vice President Dick Cheney, Republican presidential candidate Ted Cruz, and a small Opus Dei delegation that included Father Connor. After opening remarks from the archbishop, Scalia's son Paul—a Catholic priest and pastor at Saint John the Beloved, in McLean, a popular church among Washingtonian Opus Dei members, gave the liturgy for his father. Immediately after, Leonard Leo climbed the steps, took a deep bow before the altar, and made his way up to the pulpit to deliver that morning's first reading. From his position high above the assembled dignitaries, Leo read from the *Book of Wisdom*, his voice breaking occasionally.

After another reading from Scalia's fellow Justice Clarence Thomas, who had grown up steeped in Catholicism and even toyed with becoming a priest before turning his back on the faith (and later being converted again by Paul Scalia), the son of the late Supreme Court Jurist delivered his homily. "God blessed Dad, as is well known, with a love for his country," he began. "He knew well what a close-run thing the founding of our nation was. And he saw in that founding, as did the founders themselves, a blessing, a blessing quickly lost when faith is banned from the public square, or when we refuse to bring it there. So, he understood that there is no conflict between loving God and loving one's country, between one's faith and one's public service. Dad understood that the deeper he went in his Catholic faith, the better a citizen and public servant he became. God blessed him with the desire to be the country's good servant *because* he was God's first." After Scalia's body was carried out of the basilica, flanked by a hundred priests robed in white, Leo was among the last to leave. For half an hour he stayed behind, working the room at this critical juncture for the Supreme Court.

A few days later, he received a call from the Trump team asking whether he might be willing to put together a list of Supreme Court candidates for the real estate mogul. The hole left by Scalia was fast becoming a hot campaign topic, and Cruz had increasingly been gaining the upper hand, especially over Trump, who had previously proposed his own sister—a "radical pro-abortion extremist," in the words of the Texan senator—as a possible candidate for the Supreme Court. Trump needed to overturn this narrative, and Leo was the man to help him do it. Leo met with the Republican presidential candidate at a downtown law office and handed over his list, which was meant to be a private cheat sheet that Trump could use when asked his thoughts about possible nominees. Neither Leo nor the Federalist Society was keen to wade into the Republican contest; the society still liked to maintain a veneer of neutrality, and some of its members had begun to balk at the increasingly high profile of its deeply Catholic executive vice president, whose anti-abortion stance conflicted with many of its members' libertarian politics. But Trump's showmanship would soon change all that—and drive a wedge between Leo and some parts of the society, forcing him to choose between his loyalty to an organization he had devoted his career to and his own longing for power, money, and a Catholic reawakening of society. Keen to boost his ratings, Trump surprised Leo and his own campaign team by proposing to release the list, and he called a press conference announcing this intention. Following his meeting with Leo, Trump became much more aggressive in his outlook toward the Supreme Court. He spoke no longer about how Scalia's passing was a "tremendous blow for conservatism" but instead about how Scalia's death might presage a complete right-wing takeover of the Court. "You might have five Supreme Court justices to be picked over the next four years—because we already have one, and you'll probably have four more," said Trump. "So, you could change the balance of the court very quickly, very easily. And one of the things I am going to do—and this is perhaps breaking—I am going to give a list of either five or ten judges that I will pick—that I will 100 percent pick, that I will put in for nomination."

Leonard Leo's contribution to this reshaping of the Court would soon involve much more than providing a list of amenable conservative justices. Within weeks of Scalia's death, he began to mobilize hundreds of millions of dollars to make his dream of reshaping the Court—and wider society—a reality. While his appointment to the board of Opus Dei's Catholic Information Center on K Street was still relatively recent at the time of Scalia's death, in reality Leo had been juggling several side hustles during his more than twenty years at the Federalist Society—usually at nonprofit organizations linked to Catholic causes close to his heart. In 2008, he had become the chair of Students for Life of America, an organization conceived along the same lines as the Federalist Society, but dedicated to setting up local chapters at high schools and colleges across the country devoted to fighting abortion. In 2012, he joined the Catholic Association, a small nonprofit dedicated to promoting the Catholic voice in the public arena that had been set up by the Opus Dei activist Neil Corkery. Leo's entrance coincided with a sudden upswing in the finances of the Catholic Association, which hitherto had raised next to no money—but which suddenly saw almost $2 million flood in. The money was used to set up two advocacy groups. One was called the Catholic Association Foundation, which soon became a conduit for funding various media initiatives—including a radio station in Maine, where a referendum on same-sex marriage legislation was on the ballot. The other was called Catholic Voices, which had been started by Jack Valero, Opus Dei's spokesperson in London, as a way to shift media narratives concerning Catholic issues. Within months of being set up, "volunteers" from the group had given interviews or published comment pieces on a variety of issues, including abortion and same-sex marriage, in the *New York Times*, the *Washington Post*, and the *Los Angeles Times*. At one conference hosted by the organization, a priest from Opus Dei was on hand to offer the benediction.

Much to the consternation of his Federalist Society colleagues, Leo had also begun cannibalizing the organization's own deep-pocketed donors to help finance some of his more personal initiatives—and those of his friends. In 2010, he co-founded along with Ginni Thomas an organization called Liberty Central; Thomas was the wife of his good friend Justice Clarence Thomas and they used a $500,000 donation from Dallas real estate billionaire Harlan Crow, also a donor to the Federalist Society. The group billed itself as "America's Public Square," promising to preserve freedom and reaffirm the core principles of the Founding Fathers. The following year, he joined the board of Chicago Freedom Trust, which had been set up by manufacturing billionaire Barre Seid as a pass-through to anonymously channel funds to initiatives he wished to support and to take advantage of the recent *Citizens United* ruling shielding big donors from disclosure. Leo met Seid through Eugene Meyer, president of the Federalist Society, who envisioned the wealthy manufacturing tycoon as a potential donor to the law society. Instead, Leo cultivated him as a funder of his own dark-money network. The move brought Leo into contact with other central figures of the conservative dark-money world—like Whitney Ball and Adam Meyerson, the main actors behind DonorsTrust, who were responsible for anonymously funneling hundreds of millions of dollars to various conservative grassroot groups, including some linked to the far right. He also used his influence there to divert funds to Opus Dei, with the pass-through soon becoming a regular donor to the Oakcrest School.

As Leo's access to the world of dark money grew, his supernumerary friends the Corkerys became critical as a front for the tens of millions of dollars streaming through Leo's hidden network of nonprofits. Neil and Ann had provided crucial cover for him during the campaign to secure the confirmations of John Roberts and Samuel Alito in 2005, hiding the hundreds of thousands of dollars spent to influence public opinion. As more dark money poured in starting in 2010, they began to do the same again through various nonprofits such as the Wellspring Committee and the Judicial Crisis Network. Their importance only grew following Scalia's death, as Leo pumped his network for ever larger sums. In the weeks after Scalia's death, the Corkerys began opening the purse strings in what would eventually become a $17 million campaign to stop Obama from replacing Scalia and instead ensure a reliable conservative filled the vacancy. It was just the start. Over the next five years, Leo and the Corkerys would oversee the transfer of almost $600 million of dark money to right-wing causes. Their hidden ecosystem would eventually enable a conservative takeover of the Supreme Court that would disassemble hard-won civil rights and turn back the clock on issues close to their hearts—on abortion, on affirmative action, and on vast swathes of what they saw as a progressive agenda.

They also used the network to line their own pockets. Over the next few years, their personal wealth would skyrocket as they skimmed off tens of millions of dollars in advisory fees. These pools of dark money were also used to boost various initiatives directly or indirectly that were associated with Opus Dei: the Catholic Association, the Catholic Association Foundation, Catholic Voices USA, and the Catholic Information Center on K Street, where Leo now sat on the board, all became beneficiaries of this largesse.

As Opus Dei's fortunes rose in America, they seemed to be in decline in its birthplace. Ten years after the death of Luis Valls-Taberner, Banco Popular was a shadow of its former self. Soon after his passing, Ángel Ron—the man handpicked as Valls-Taberner's successor—had embarked on a huge push into the booming real estate sector, extending billions of dollars in loans to property developers and construction companies, and issuing mortgages. For a while it had gone well. Profits at the bank climbed to record levels, pushing the value of the stake indirectly controlled by Opus Dei to around $2 billion, which generated tens of millions of dollars in dividends for the various foundations linked to the prelature. But the global financial crisis of 2008 ended that bounty. The Spanish real estate market collapsed, leaving a glut of unsold properties and ghost towns across the country, which pushed many developers and construction companies into bankruptcy, unable to pay back the billions they had borrowed from banks such as Popular.

With dozens of Spanish banks facing collapse, the government was forced to seek a $125 billion bailout from the European Union. While Germany and France felt compelled to help out their neighbor—to save the euro and themselves from possible contagion—they insisted that the money have strings attached. They ordered a thorough audit of all Spanish banks, which they suspected weren't telling the whole truth about the size of their losses. Indeed, huge holes were found in their balance sheets and dozens of banks, including Popular, were ordered to halt their dividends and to urgently raise capital or face being taken over by the government. The order brought an abrupt halt to the vast flows of money to the Opus Dei foundations—and it raised the possibility that they might lose complete control if they were unable to inject enough new capital before the deadline.

The Opus Dei men tasked with safeguarding its stake in the bank scrambled to raise the cash they needed to participate in the capital raise. The European Union of Investments, one of the main vehicles managing the prelature's stakes, ended up having to pledge hundreds of millions of Popular shares that it owned in order to secure $200 million of loans from three banks—including almost $80 million from Popular itself, a highly unorthodox arrangement that meant the bank was effectively providing the money for its own bailout. Together with contributions from the bank's other shareholders, Opus Dei managed to inject sufficient capital to avoid a government bailout. But the rescue came at a huge cost, leaving the main vehicle managing the prelature's stake in the bank highly indebted—and potentially in big trouble if Popular remained unable to restart its dividend payments. Which is exactly what happened. For months after the capital was raised, regulators refused to lift the moratorium, arguing that the bank's vitals still weren't healthy enough to restart payments to its shareholders. With the clock on the loan repayments ticking, the Opus Dei guardians put pressure on Ángel Ron to find another solution. In May 2013, a contact put him in touch with Antonio del Valle, a Mexican billionaire who offered to inject $600 million into Banco Popular. A deal was announced in December 2013. A week later, Ron gleefully announced that Popular would once again start paying its dividend. Opus Dei was saved.

But the celebrations would not last long. In their haste to get the prelature and its foundations out of their predicament, Ron and the other members of the board had let in an outsider—Del Valle—who would soon shift the delicate balance of power within the bank. For two years, Del Valle bided his time—but he pounced when a routine spot check by regulators unearthed a $3 billion hole in the bank's accounts, alongside suspicious activity involving Luxembourg-based shell companies that seemed to have been set up to pretend that payments were still being made on some big loans the bank had extended. Del Valle flew to Madrid to put his cards on the table, offering to provide a large proportion of the cash needed to fill the hole—in exchange for greater control over the bank. When Ron refused, Del Valle decided to go over Ron's head. In an extraordinary move that confirmed how widely known the prelature's influence over the bank really was, the Mexican billionaire demanded to see the head of Opus Dei. No such meeting was ever granted. Instead, the Opus Dei foundations again borrowed heavily to save the bank. In the frantic scramble to find the cash, the separation that supposedly existed between these "independent" foundations began to fade away. One company was forced to mortgage the Beatriz Building that had been bequeathed to it by Luis in the early 1970s and used the $200 million raised to ensure that another supposedly separate entity could participate in raising the capital and maintain Opus Dei's decades-long hold over the bank. Much of Opus Dei's hidden empire in Spain—the shares it held in Popular, the office buildings it owned, and the bonds in its portfolio—had been pawned in one last, desperate move to retain control. Banco Popular lived to fight another day, but Opus Dei was leveraged to the hilt.

Ron had massively underestimated the storm he had unleashed in his confrontation with the Mexican. As the Popular chairman proceeded with his plan, backed by the Opus Dei–heavy board of directors, Antonio del Valle launched a campaign to oust him from the bank. The refusal of Opus Dei to talk to Del Valle relit his longstanding hatred toward the religious order. As a young man he had been a member in Mexico but left under mysterious circumstances. Years later, he had joined the Legionaries of Christ, a movement set up in the late 1950s by Marcial Maciel, a Mexican priest who was later revealed to have been a long-time drug addict who had sexually abused the boys and young men in his care. The organization was another religious movement Pope John Paul II had favored because of the large financial contributions it made to the Church. But it had been taken over by the Vatican in 2010, following serious allegations of sexual abuse and cult-like practices, and in the years since a multi-billion-dollar network of businesses and off-shore assets had been discovered. The parallels were unsettling. One Popular board member even learned that Del Valle had been overheard talking about his investment in the bank as part of a much larger plan to join the forces of Opus Dei and Legionaries of Christ, in a move that would restore the tarnished religious movement to prominence. But the slight he had received from the prelature made the Mexican vengeful, and he grew determined to take over the bank and rid it of Opus once and for all. He set about convincing other members of the board, first targeting the few non–Opus Dei members and then eventually picking off other members individually. It wasn't long before the struggle being fought within the board also caught the attention of the Bank of Spain, which—fearing a collapse in confidence at one of the country's largest banks—made clear that it was time to find a new chairman whom the board could rally around.

It fell to Reyes Calderón, head of the bank's internal appointments board, to find a replacement. A relative newcomer who had joined the bank only a few months earlier as one of the supposed independent members of the board, Calderón was nevertheless seen as a safe pair of hands by the faction within the bank that was allied with the prelature. As deacon of the economics department at Opus Dei's University of Navarre, and a devout supernumerary with nine children, Calderón was generally viewed as likely to protect the prelature's interests. She approached her task with complete professionalism and soon settled her sights on Emilio Saracho, who—despite not being affiliated with Opus Dei—had the right profile for the bank. Short and bald with a neatly trimmed white beard, Saracho was one of the most senior bankers in Europe—a hotshot at JP Morgan in London, paid tens of millions of dollars a year. She approached him and made it clear that the board wanted someone who would defend Popular's "independence"—code lingering from the Luis Valls-Taberner days that effectively meant guarding the interests of Opus Dei against attack. Unsure, Saracho asked for a meeting with Ron, who had begrudgingly accepted that his time was up. While the two weren't friends, they had known each other for more than twenty years, and they had a professional respect for each other. Saracho wanted to pick Ron's brain about the challenges. But what began as a courteous meeting rapidly became tense. Saracho snapped, revealing his misgivings about the job, confronting Ron about rumors concerning the bank. "If I accept, is there any chance I'll end up sending you to prison?" he asked. "If you've got a problem in the bank that could end up with you in prison, then this conversation ends right here, Ángel. I don't want to screw with your life." Despite the heated conversation—and his serious misgivings about Banco Popular—Saracho accepted the job. A dangerous new era now dawned for Banco Popular.

After formally joining the bank in February 2017, Saracho spent three months tirelessly working toward a solution: courting potential buyers, identifying bits of the bank that might be sold off to raise cash, and sounding out investment banks about the possibility of raising new funds to fill the holes left in its accounts by selling new shares to investors. Each path led to a dead end. The financial troubles were bad enough, but Saracho soon discovered he had another, even more unexpected problem to deal with. The board—the people he needed to support his efforts to turn around the bank—seemed oddly divided into two rival Catholic sects. After almost forty years of dealing with companies of all sizes, from every corner of the world, he had never before seen anything like it. He had walked into of the middle of a religious turf war—Opus Dei versus the Legionaries of Christ. He reported his concerns about Popular's unusual corporate governance methods to the central bank and, in a highly unusual step that reflected the unorthodox way in which the bank operated, he decided to hire his own lawyer—rather than rely on Popular's counsel—to cover his back. Saracho rapidly grew suspicious about what was being hidden from him. To make matters worse, there were constant leaks to the press that undermined his efforts—leaks he suspected were coming from his predecessor, Ron. Each day seemed to bring new reports of serious financial problems at the bank, of bitter infighting between board members, and of a secret web of shell companies.

Then, at the beginning of April 2017, under pressure from its auditors, Popular was forced to put out a statement admitting to irregularities in its accounts. Saracho's second in command resigned. Popular's customers reacted with panic. Just two years earlier, many had watched in horror as the government in Greece—which like Spain had joined the European Union in the 1980s—had suddenly closed the banks, cutting people off from their savings and restricting ATM withdrawals to just 60 euros a day. Determined not to suffer the same fate, Popular's customers reacted to rumors about the bank's health by withdrawing their money. Though only a handful of people knew the full extent of the unfolding disaster, a huge bank run was set in motion. In the coming weeks, customers pulled more than twenty billion euros out of their accounts. Then, in early June, Banco Popular collapsed. And Opus Dei had lost the institution that had powered its growth for sixty years.

As all of this drama was playing out in Madrid, over at Villa Tevere, the senior members of Opus Dei were preoccupied with another crisis. Javier Echevarría, the prelate, had been admitted to an Opus Dei hospital in December 2016 with a lung infection. His condition soon worsened. Within a week of being hospitalized, the prelate was dead. Just over a month later, 156 Opus Dei priests and male numeraries converged on Rome from around the world to elect a new leader, who would be Escrivá's third successor. Fernando Ocáriz, a seventy-two-year-old Spaniard who had joined Opus Dei in the sixties while studying for a science degree in Barcelona, and who served as deputy to Echevarría, was duly elected as prelate.

Ocáriz took up his new duties during an era of huge upheaval in the Church. Almost four years after the shock resignation of Pope Benedict XVI, the election of Jorge Mario Bergoglio from Argentina—the first ever pope belonging to the Jesuit order, and the first to take the name Francis after the beloved saint of the poor—was still sending shockwaves throughout the Catholic establishment. Benedict had resigned against a backdrop of scandal and outrage, following leaks of documents exposing widespread corruption and misuse of Church funds right across the Holy See, in what became known as the Vati-Leaks scandal. Francis was keen to put a distinctive stamp on his papacy and return the Church to what he considered the true mission of Jesus Christ, after more than thirty years of domination by conservative forces under John Paul II and Benedict XVI. "How I would love a Church that *is* poor and *for* the poor!" he told the press in one of his first public addresses after being elected to the papacy. In coming days, he shocked the Church establishment—first by breaking with centuries of convention by refusing to move into the sumptuous papal apartment, and then a couple of weeks later by skipping the traditional Holy Thursday ceremony at which the pope would emulate Christ by washing the feet of priests, instead opting to visit a juvenile detention center, where he washed the feet of inmates, including two Muslim women. These were not publicity stunts—during his time as auxiliary bishop in Buenos Aires in the nineties, he had eschewed a chauffeur-driven car, preferring to walk or take public transport. When he was made archbishop there, he chose not to live in the archbishop's palace and skipped the traditional Holy Thursday at the cathedral to go and wash the feet of AIDS patients instead.

While he projected an aura of humility, Bergoglio was also known as a shrewd politician. A pragmatist with clear ideas, Francis made it clear that he would no longer stand for the corruption and misuse of Church funds, which his predecessors had tolerated. He formed a new council tasked with breaking the old guard's stranglehold on how the Holy See was governed and launched a separate investigation into the Vatican's finances. To prevent wiretaps and potential sabotage of the inquiry by the old guard, investigators were given brand new cell phones with Maltese—rather than Italian—telephone numbers, and a private line was set up to send passwords for access to encrypted documents. Francis took particular aim at the Congregation for the Causes of Saints, which had ballooned under John Paul II to become a "saints factory," and where suspicious activity had been detected involving missing documents, money, and possible corruption.

While Bergoglio was known as an astute political operator back home, he knew little about the inner workings of Vatican politics. As a result, even as he ushered in a complete overhaul of the Holy See's governance and its finances, he leaned heavily on the recommendations of Vatican insiders during his first few years in charge. After thirty years of riding the coattails of John Paul II and Benedict XVI—and having carved out a niche for itself as the go-to organization on anything to do with canon law or communications, thanks to the prowess of the Pontifical University of the Holy Cross—Opus Dei and its allies were well positioned to obtain a number of important new roles as part of the inevitable reshuffle that accompanied Francis's election. Above all, the new pope wanted competent people—and Opus Dei was nothing if not competent.

During Bergoglios's first few years as Archbishop of Buenos Aires, Opus Dei had little to do with him. But all that changed when he emerged as a surprise runner-up to Ratzinger in the conclave to elect a successor to John

Paul II in 2005. Shortly afterwards, the prelature sought to curry favor with him, sending Mariano Fazio—a warm, friendly, fellow Argentinian—to the General Conference of Bishops of Latin America, where he had the opportunity to get to know this rising star. Soon after establishing contact, Fazio was posted to Argentina as head of the region, where he deepened contact with Bergoglio. Opus Dei took over a school in a poor neighborhood of Buenos Aires—something completely out of character for the organization, which until then had only really run academies for Argentina's upper classes. It also sought to showcase the work it did with underprivileged young girls by inviting Bergoglio to a hospitality school paid for by Banco Popular—although presumably it didn't mention the pressure it placed on students to become numerary assistants or its history of forcing young girls to work for free. While it bothered Bergoglio that he had no jurisdiction over Opus Dei, they seemed to be doing all the right things.

The prelature's efforts paid off. Within weeks of his election, Francis named an Opus Dei bishop to the five-member commission charged with reforming Vatican finances—and made him the group's coordinator. Another Opus Dei figure elevated to an important role was the priest Lucio Ángel Vallejo Balda, the only clergyman—alongside seven lay experts from the worlds of economics, business, and law—on a critically important commission charged with overhauling the economic and administrative structures underpinning the Holy See. Balda had been recommended for the job by Cardinal George Pell, the rumbunctious Archbishop of Sydney who was known disparagingly as "Pedopell" and "Pell Pot" among some at the Vatican because of a police investigation into allegations he had sexually abused children. A friend of the prelature, Pell had removed informal restrictions on Opus Dei expanding into Melbourne in the nineties and defended it against allegations of brainwashing. Over the years the relationship had blossomed. The prelature always provided a confessor for Pell whenever he was in Rome. Opus Dei members would later regularly visit the disgraced archbishop in prison.

But by the time of Ocáriz's investiture, Opus Dei's carefully cultivated relationship with Pope Francis was on the rocks. The trigger for the sudden shift had come from Argentina, where a numerary had donated all her earnings and three apartments she owned to the organization. But she later

decided to leave. Penniless, she asked the prelature to return some of her donations so she could start a new life. Opus Dei refused to honor her request.
Francis, upon hearing about her plight from the Vatican's representative in
Buenos Aires, was incensed. He intervened, ordering the prelature to compensate the woman. Villa Tevere obeyed, although it took care to destroy any
paper trail between it and the woman, with the agreed $40,000 settlement
handed over in cash in a McDonald's paper bag. The incident, coupled with
murmurings of further scandals involving other new movements that had—
like Opus Dei—mushroomed around the Church in the past century, seemed
to awaken a new zeal within Francis to reestablish control over these fringe
groups, which for far too long had been allowed to operate outside of Vatican
oversight.

The deterioration in relations between the pope and Opus Dei would
soon explode into the public sphere. In November 2015, the Swiss guard
made a startling arrest at the Vatican—none other than Lucio Ángel Vallejo
Balda, the Opus Dei priest who had cozied up to the pope and had been nominated to help lead the cleanup of the Curia. Balda had been exposed as a double
agent, after having been found leaking sensitive documents to the press and
undermining Francis's efforts to quietly root out corruption and malpractice
within the Vatican. He would eventually be sentenced to eighteen months in
prison. Opus Dei quickly moved to distance itself from events, adding that it
was "surprised and saddened" by the arrest. "The Prelature of Opus Dei has
no information about this case," it said. "If the accusations turn out to be
true, it will be particularly painful because of the harm done to the Church."
Francis's next move was more difficult for Opus Dei to dismiss. Following
the investiture of Ocáriz in January 2017, the pope made it known that he
would not be ordaining the new head of Opus Dei as a bishop—contrary to
the privileges afforded to the prelate's two predecessors under John Paul II.
The move was a massive blow for Ocáriz, who could no longer preside over
the ceremonies of new priests being ordained into the movement. The first
battle between the two men was a clear victory for Francis. But these were
just the opening salvos in a war whose outcome was far from certain.

Across the Atlantic, Opus Dei was forming new, powerful alliances that
might tilt the balance back in its favor. After two decades or more courting

the reactionary forces of American politics, its efforts were finally beginning to pay off. The shock election of Donald Trump—a man Francis had described as "not Christian" during the campaign—would soon open the doors of the White House to men closely allied to Opus Dei. At the center of it all was Leonard Leo. Soon after Trump's victory, Leo flew to New York to see the president-elect at Trump Tower. He left the meeting in a state of elation, convinced not only that Trump would pick a new Supreme Court Justice from the list prepared by him but also that that he would have direct access to the president—giving him another avenue, besides the courts, to influence the country's direction. As the earthquake of Trump's victory shook Washington, many of the conservative Catholic figures around Leo subtly positioned themselves to take advantage of this unexpected shift. Ann Corkery was one of them. During the Republican primaries, she—alongside a number of other prominent conservatives close to Opus Dei, including Robert George—had signed a letter titled "An Appeal to Our Fellow Catholics." The letter implored them not to vote for the real estate mogul, stating that his record and campaign "promise only the further degradation of our politics and our culture." She later switched sides, using her position at Catholic Voices USA to push a pro-Trump agenda.

In one of Trump's first acts as president, he kept his word to Leo, nominating the conservative judge Neil Gorsuch to the vacant seat on the Supreme Court. Once again, Leo's hidden machine of nonprofits—fronted by the supernumerary Corkerys—cranked into action to secure his nomination. Other prominent members of the Washington Opus Dei network were soon elevated to high-profile positions in the new administration. Mick Mulvaney, a supernumerary, was made director of the Office of Management and Budget. Later, he'd be promoted to White House Chief of Staff. In between his meetings with billionaires, Wall Street executives, lobbyists, and conservative backers, Mulvaney also invited Jeff Bell—another supernumerary that Tellez and Fieler had tried to get elected to the Senate—to the White House. The subject of their meeting was recorded simply as "Opus Dei." Bell later said that the meeting covered "religious and political matters." Two members of the Catholic Information Center board would later join the administration: Pat Cipollone as White House counsel and Bill Barr as attorney general. Larry Kudlow, who had been converted by Father McCloskey, became director of the National Economic Council. Not since the Franco regime had the movement had such direct access to political power.

In May 2017, a group of lawyers and their wealthy backers gathered at a luxury hotel in New York for a black-tie event to honor a man at the front in the emerging battle at the core of American society. A hushed silence fell across the room as a film was played in tribute to Leonard Leo, who was set to be awarded a medal that evening from the Becket Fund, a legal support network and one of the biggest challengers to contraception healthcare coverage. The award commemorated his commitment to upholding religious values against what had until recently seemed like the unstoppable march of progressivism. A family picture of the Leos filled the screen, before the film cut to a photograph of Margaret Mary, their eldest daughter who had passed away almost a decade earlier. "In the last several decades we've had a number of setbacks for the cause of religious freedom," the voiceover explained, as a figurine of Christ filled the screen, before cutting to a bronze cast of a golden eagle and then panning to an image of the Supreme Court. "In many court cases religious freedom has been restricted in one way or another. Some would say that courts too often have tried to remove God and faith from the public square." Over the next three minutes, a cast of characters including multi-millionaire activists, a Catholic archbishop, and a disgraced former U.S. attorney general extolled the heroic virtues of the recipient of that evening's award.

The unlikely cast represented a new alliance which had, barely four months into the Trump presidency, already notched a series of important wins. Less than a month earlier, the confirmation of Neil Gorsuch as Scalia's replacement had been the alliance's most recent—and most high-profile—victory. His confirmation had been masterminded by Leo and a web of nonprofits fronted by the Corkerys that had organized a media blitz to sway public opinion and push Congress into approving the nomination. That engine had published opinion pieces, contributed 5,000 quotes to news articles, scheduled pundit appearances on television, and posted online videos that were viewed some fifty million times. As further images of Clarence Thomas and Antonin Scalia flashed on, smiling alongside various Leo offspring, Sean Fieler added his adulation. "Leonard has created not just an organization but a movement," he said, "that has created a bench of Justices that will adhere to the principles of the American experiment, I think, with greater fidelity."

Applause rang out as the film ended, and Leo was welcomed up to the stage. "Many faiths and denominations are represented here," he told those present, while glancing out across the room, "although I can't help but notice a heavy turnout by what Saint Thomas Becket would call 'the troublesome priests.'" A chuckle went up. Among this group of "troublesome priests," Leo singled out Cardinal Timothy Dolan, the controversial Archbishop of New York, who was usually a regular at the Becket Fund dinner, but who was on a pilgrimage to Lourdes. Despite being archbishop of one of the country's most liberal and diverse cities, Dolan had cultivated a reputation as a champion of the conservative arm of the American Church since the election of Francis, pandering to a small but deep-pocketed and increasingly vocal fringe who were unhappy with the direction the new pope was pushing the Church. Following Francis's provocative ousting of Cardinal Raymond Burke, the former champion of the conservative wing of the American Church, and a series of speeches in which the pope seemed to question the morality of capitalism, one wealthy American donor had even threatened to withdraw support from the $180 million restoration of Saint Patrick's Cathedral in midtown Manhattan. Dolan had come out to "clarify" the pope's message shortly afterwards, explaining that Francis knew that the answer to problems with the free market wasn't government control, and dismissing the Pontiff's critique of capitalism as a result of his experience with the "exploitative racket" of Argentinian economics—an experience that had little to do with American capitalism. As well as reassuring wealthy critics of Francis, Dolan moved to deepen his relationship with Opus Dei, offering the prelature a parish of its own in the heart of Manhattan, a few blocks from its headquarters in Murray Hill, and a prime location to capture Catholics commuting to work via Grand Central Station. It later emerged that Larry Kudlow, the free-market cheerleader recruited to Opus Dei by McCloskey, had helped out Cardinal Dolan with his op-ed piece clarifying the pope's remarks.

Leo explained to the audience that Trump's victory presented them with an unexpected opportunity to claw back some ground on the moral issues that defined their Catholic faith. "Many are still trying to sort out all the lessons of 2016," he told the audience. "But maybe one lesson is this. Sometimes, in a good cause, your breaks take you by surprise as much as your setbacks." His acceptance speech became a rallying cry for those with money to join him and his Opus Dei allies. "Politics is like the rest of life—we don't always control events as much as we like to think," he continued. "The result is that, in ways we never expected, right now we have reasons to be hopeful. And as an officer of the Federalist Society and a director of the Becket Fund, my goal remains the same and is simple to state. It is to protect the instrument that protects us all, to preserve and extend the influence of one of the greatest works of man: the Constitution of the United States."

He gestured over to a group of nuns, the Little Sisters of the Poor, who had failed to convince the Supreme Court to exempt them from a federal mandate to provide contraceptive coverage to employees. But a few days before the dinner, Trump had issued an executive order giving them carte blanche to ignore the law. By framing the issue as part of the culture wars, Leo had won the president—an unlikely upholder of Catholic values—to the cause. "In all the comfortable corners of elite culture, who defended the Little Sisters?" asked Leo. "Where were the indignant editorials speaking up for them, and denouncing the previous administration for its needless and obvious overreach? We get earnest lectures all the time about respect and protection for minority views in our diverse country. The silence in this case conveyed a familiar message: You just have to hold the right minority views . . . otherwise, well, you're on your own."

The pitch would further entice some of the most powerful forces in the American Catholic world into the orbit of Opus Dei at a critical time for the movement. With the pope chipping away at the organization's coveted status within the Church hierarchy, its finances in disarray following the loss of Banco Popular, and recruitment beginning to trail off around the world because of an increasing incompatibility of its message to speak to the vast majority of Catholics, positioning itself as a champion for disgruntled American Catholic billionaires offered Opus Dei a new lease on life. Even before the Trump victory, the strategy had already begun to bear fruit. In 2014 and 2015, donations to the Woodlawn Foundation, the Rosemoor Foundation, and the Association for Cultural Interchange, its main nonprofits in the

United States, ballooned. That was thanks to Opus Dei's access to new donors, who helped offset a more general decline in membership among regular
folk. For years, the foundations had typically brought in around $20 million
a year—entire salaries donated by numerary members and tithes of around
10 percent of the income of supernumeraries. Thanks to a series of one-off
donations, the income at those three foundations rose to more than $50 mil-
lion a year. The sudden inflows had come at what was a difficult time for
Opus Dei, and they had helped the organization make up for the losses caused
by the halt in dividends at Banco Popular. Suddenly, the United States became a major financer of Opus Dei projects around the world—the Association for Cultural Interchange in particular became a critical source of funds,
bankrolling a new $50 million pilgrimage center called Saxum on the out-
skirts of Jerusalem.

While this newfound largesse was directed to various vanity projects,
Opus Dei showed little concern for those who had been scarred by their
membership and their years of toil in the organization. As part of a ruling in
March 2013, a French court had ordered one Opus Dei foundation and two
numeraries employed there to pay compensation to Catherine Tissier. But
three years later, they had failed to pay her a penny, forcing Tissier to return
to court to get justice.

Opus Dei soon counted among its ranks some of the most influential
conservative Catholic activists and donors in the United States. Tim Busch, a
wealthy California lawyer described by the *National Catholic Reporter* as "easily
among the most influential laymen in the U.S. and Rome," joined Opus Dei
as a "co-operator" after being introduced to the organization by one of his
colleagues—and he was soon introduced to Father Tom Bohlin, its American figurehead, whom he now describes as a close friend. "I think they're
very approachable—they're very practical," said Busch, who explained he
was struck by how numeraries had to work "in the real world" before they
became priests. "You know, it's kind of a unique thing—right? They're like a
cult, if you really think about it."

He began receiving regular spiritual direction from Father Patricio
Mata—a numerary priest from Spain who prefers to go by Father Luke—
and became close to José Horacio Gómez, the Archbishop of Los Angeles and
Opus Dei's most senior figure in the American Catholic Church, who he has

described as "one of my closest advisors." He was invited to the Humanum conference in Rome organized by Luis Tellez, and he also attended retreats run by the prelature. Busch's inculcation into Opus Dei dovetailed with the creation of the Napa Institute, which he set up in response to concerns about the United States becoming a secularized country hostile to religious rights and traditional morality, and which Busch has described as a Catholic fortress in an increasingly godless America where the faithful "hunker down and survive" until secular society self-destructs. Archbishop Gómez showed his support for Napa by agreeing to be its main speaker at its first conference in 2011—and participating in a private pilgrimage to Mexico organized by Busch two years later. Opus Dei provided financial support as a sponsor. "Probably about twenty percent of the people there are Opus Dei," said Busch, who over the years has reciprocated with donations to various Opus Dei initiatives.

Buoyed by this influx of money and by its growing influence, the Catholic Information Center began to enjoy a renaissance. Following the death of Father Arne Panula, the Opus Dei priest credited with turning around its fortunes, in 2017, the chaplaincy of Opus Dei was passed to a Spanish priest from Barcelona. Carlos Trullols, a rising star within the prelature, had been posted to the United States following a short stint in Spain, just two years after being ordained—serving in Pittsburgh, South Bend, and Chicago. Youthful and friendly, with a background in the nonprofit world, he seemed like the perfect choice to front the reenergized Catholic Information Center. Trullols would revel in the role and become an increasingly important friend and counselor to Leonard Leo. But his would also be a difficult reign. Within months of taking over, the scandal that had forced his predecessor to flee to England resurfaced. This was after the woman who had been abused by McCloskey—and who had been reassured by Opus Dei that the priest would no longer have direct ministry with women following the financial settlement—found out he had been allowed to continue effectively without any restrictions, first in Chicago and then in San Francisco. The victim had stumbled across a piece in the New York Times, depicting McCloskey as sipping cocktails at his new home in Palo Alto and once again reveling in his celebrity, thereby leaving his interviewer in thrall and describing him as "the man with the unusual gift." "Some priests are known for their work among the poor, others for their learning, still others for decades of service to a par-ish," the article continued. "The Rev. C. John McCloskey III, a priest of the traditionalist Opus Dei order, has a different calling. He makes converts, often of the rich and Republican." Horrified, the victim went public with her story, revealing that Opus Dei had paid her almost $1 million to settle the allegations. Once again, McCloskey's transgressions—and the complic-ity of Opus Dei in allowing its star priest to escape justice and responsibility for his actions—threatened to destroy the work of the Catholic Information Center—right at the moment when it was enjoying its most success. The Opus Dei press machine went into overdrive, with Brian Finnerty—its U.S. spokesperson—breaking down into tears during one newspaper interview to demonstrate just how sorry the prelature was for the mistakes it had made in handling the case. Within weeks of the scandal's resurfacing, Father Trullols would lead the nation in prayer in a special event, in the White House Rose Garden, to commemorate the annual National Day of Prayer. Trullols was the first of the religious leaders there that day to be introduced by President Trump, who asked the Opus Dei priest to stand and take a round of applause.

A few weeks later, Fernando Ocáriz traveled to New York as part of a coast-to-coast tour of the United States. It would be the first visit of a prel-ate of Opus Dei to the country for thirteen years, and it reflected the rising importance of the United States within the prelature. During his American visit, he participated in a colloquium with conservative academics from vari-ous universities—including Robert George—as part of a new push organized by Luis Tellez to extend the reach of Opus Dei and its message. It would do that by replicating the Witherspoon Institute's success at Princeton and on various other campuses across the United States.

Thanks to its successful infiltration of the conservative Catholic elite, Opus Dei had a valuable opportunity to capitalize on its position in the United States. But its alliance with people like Leonard Leo, Tim Busch, and Sean Fieler would be a dangerous one, placing it directly at odds with the message of Pope Francis. Busch in particular would become the center of controversy when he came out in defense of an ousted cardinal who had published an explosive letter alleging that Pope Francis knew about—and ignored—accusations of sexual abuse.

The release of that letter was timed for maximum damage, published by an outlet close to Busch in the middle of a papal trip to Ireland. "Archbishop Viganò has done us a great service," Busch crowed. "He decided to come forward because if he didn't, he realized he would be perpetuating the cover-up." "Viganò has given us an agenda," he told one gathering of like-minded conservatives. "We need to follow those leads and push that forward." As tensions between the Vatican and this right-wing Catholic fringe began to escalate, Opus Dei would find itself dangerously exposed. In its pursuit of power and money, the prelature had forgotten the roots of its true legitimacy. The conflict would soon threaten to destroy everything that Escrivá and his followers had built during the previous century.

14

UPRISING

Buenos Aires, Argentina—August 2020

IT TOOK LUCÍA GIMÉNEZ MORE THAN FIFTEEN YEARS BEFORE SHE FINALLY found a lawyer who would take her case seriously. By then she was in her fifties and married with a teenage daughter. Her time as a numerary assistant might have seemed like a distant memory, were it not for the pain in her knees from the years spent scrubbing the bathroom floors for the men—and the fury that still burned inside about the exploitation and abuse she had endured during her eighteen years in Opus Dei. Giménez had been recruited at the age of thirteen from her village in central Paraguay by two numeraries sent out to tour the impoverished plains in search of young girls. The teenager was lured to the school they ran in the capital Asunción, some three hundred miles south, on false promises of a decent education and a better life. Giménez was soon pressured by one of her tutors into joining Opus Dei as a numerary assistant. The tutor told her that it was what God wanted for her. She initially tried to resist—and was scolded for her insolence. "Jesus died on the cross for us," her tutor lectured. "Are you so selfish and so uncaring as to be unwilling to give your heart to God?" Young, defenseless, and hundreds of miles from her family, she eventually gave in to the pressure, writing to the Father in Rome to formally ask for admission, carefully transcribing the words dictated to her by her tutor. She was flown undocumented, in a private plane, to neighboring Argentina, where Opus Dei had a much larger presence and where the demand for numerary assistants was greater. For almost two decades, she led a life of servitude—of cleaning and cooking at various residences around Buenos Aires, of twelve-hour workdays for no pay, with breaks only for meals and prayer, her nights spent sleeping on a wooden board. She tried to leave several times, only to be admonished by her director, who told her that such thoughts were the temptations of the Devil. She was moved from center to center and prescribed drugs to relieve her malaise.

By the time she left Opus Dei at the age of thirty-two, Giménez was a broken woman. While she felt violated—physically and emotionally destroyed—seeking justice was the last thing on her mind. Slowly, she started to rebuild her life. She found a job, worked during the day, and went to school in the evening, finally getting the education she had been promised by the numeraries who recruited her. During one history class about slavery, Giménez began to draw parallels, in her mind, between the workers on the cotton and sugar plantations hundreds of years ago and her own existence within Opus Dei in the 1970s, 1980s, and 1990s. She came to realize that she too had been a slave—she had spent eighteen years within Opus Dei, toiling from morning until night, and had not a cent to show for it. She resolved to claim the money that was rightfully hers.

A friend in the United States put her in touch with a well-known lawyer in Buenos Aires. A meeting was arranged, and the lawyer asked what evidence she had. Giménez shrugged. She had been brought into the country undocumented, she had never received a pay stub or signed a work contract; she had no evidence other than the mental scars she suffered. The lawyer told her that such a case would never stand a chance—especially against as powerful an institution as the Church. Years passed, and Giménez contacted other lawyers. One was particularly supportive, voicing his disgust at what Opus Dei had done to her, but it was the same story—without any evidence, the case was doomed. Another said he was all too familiar with the behavior of Opus Dei but was powerless to do anything about it.

Then, one day, she received a friend request from another former numerary assistant on Facebook. After checking that she wasn't still in Opus Dei, for fear she might have been asked by her superiors to make contact with Giménez, she approved it. The friend put her in touch with a group of former numerary assistants, which she became involved in, helping build a network sharing her determination to bring the organization to justice. One of the main organizers of the group, a former numerary assistant called Claudia Carrero, who just like Giménez had been recruited to the hospitality school in Buenos Aires as a young girl, was particularly supportive, and together they began to gather a group of women who had shied away from confronting their tormentors individually, but who collectively felt able to contemplate some kind of action against Opus Dei.

Through this group, she first heard the name Sebastián Sal. Sal was a partner at a law firm in Buenos Aires where he specialized in cases involving white-collar crimes. He had built up a formidable reputation over his thirty-year career, earning him a number of reputable postings, including as an advisor to Argentina's parliament, an academic speaker, and a member of an international body set up to implement the United Nations Convention Against Corruption. Over the years, Sal had also established a sideline in representing numerary assistants seeking financial compensation for their years of unpaid labor. Unlike other lawyers in the city, Sal had an intricate understanding of how Opus Dei operated, thanks to his own experience as a numerary. He had come into contact with the organization while studying law in the 1980s, through a friend of a friend who had been to a talk at a local Opus Dei center. Sal decided to check it out for himself. There were things that made him uneasy about the organization from the start. The priest he talked to wouldn't let him leave without agreeing to borrow a book, a gesture made to look like a generous act of friendship, but which Sal soon realized was simply a ruse to get him to come back, and so that the priest could obtain his name, address, and telephone number—just so they knew where the book was, he was told. As the weeks went on and Sal began to frequent the center more and more, he also began to suspect that things he had shared in private with the priest had been shared with the other numeraries, who seemed suspiciously well-informed about his likes, dislikes, and the personal issues he had confided to the priest. Such information was passed around to help the numeraries form a bond with this potential new recruit, and to engineer a "vocational crisis" in him. It was a coordinated attack during which the question of becoming a numerary is first raised, with the priest and the other numeraries working in concert to pressure the victim into submission. The maneuver was successful; the unsuspecting victim "whistled." It was a tactic Sal would soon learn how to use himself after asking to be admitted as a numerary.

It didn't take long, though, for Sal to question what he had signed up for. The numeraries who had been so warm and welcoming to him in the buildup to his vocational crisis soon turned their backs on him. He came to understand that real friendship between numeraries—as opposed to the simulated friendship shown to potential recruits—was deeply frowned upon. The rousing talk about spreading the Work—Sal had heard stories about numeraries being sent to exotic countries, as missionaries embarking on a holy crusade—fell away. In addition to the classes on doctrine and apologetics, he was taught how to "fish" vocations, learning the same techniques as had been used to lure him in. By the end of his first year, Sal considered leaving, but decided to continue, buckling under the pressure of his priest and director, who warned him against turning his back on the vocation that God had laid out for him, telling him that following the path of a "traitor" would leave him unhappy for the rest of his life.

He carried on, unhappy—making himself as busy as possible with work and winning new recruits so he didn't have too much time to think. When that didn't work, he thought a change of scenery might help, and he asked his superiors for permission to go abroad and study. They tried to dissuade him; Sal had proved successful in recruiting a number of young men and was needed in Buenos Aires to host circles for the married supernumerary members. But his resolution was firm, and he applied without their knowing for a place at the University of Pennsylvania, where he was accepted. They eventually relented, allowing him to go. He was posted to the closest male numerary residence at Princeton, an hour's train ride away, where he shared a house with Father C. John McCloskey, and where he regularly saw Luis Tellez, the man behind the Witherspoon Institute. He took a strong dislike to McCloskey, who made racist remarks about some of the other numeraries, and he wrote letters to New York and Rome complaining about the priest's inappropriate behavior. He never received a reply. By the time he returned to Argentina in 1997, his doubts about Opus Dei had become overwhelming. He began to openly challenge his superiors about the control they exerted over every aspect of his life. Soon after returning, he left the organization.

Claudia Carrero wrote to Sebastián Sal in August 2020, telling him about the group that she and Giménez were involved in; detailing how many of them were missing social security payments, which had left them unable to claim their pensions and other benefits; and asking him whether there was anything they could do about it. By this stage, they had amassed a group of forty-three women in exactly the same situation, who wanted to claim the social security payments they were owed. They asked Sal whether he would be willing to take on their case. While the number of parties involved was much bigger—up until that point the lawyer had only represented individuals—the fundamentals of the complaint seemed similar to previous cases he had made against Opus Dei, which were usually straightforward and ended in settlements. He agreed to take on the case. His first step was to check the social security database for contributions made on behalf of the women in question. It corroborated their claims—of the forty-three, twenty had no social security contributions during their time as numerary assistants, and the rest had only sporadic contributions on their records. By September, he approached Opus Dei about a potential settlement, whereby the prelature would make good on the missing contributions so the women could claim the pensions and benefits they were entitled to.

Initially, the signs were good. A lawyer representing Opus Dei requested a meeting, and the two discussed the case over coffee outside a Starbucks in downtown Buenos Aires. The meeting was cordial, and Sal left optimistic that a settlement could easily be reached. It didn't take long for that optimism to crumble, however. After the initial meeting with the lawyer, there had been a flurry of WhatsApp activity—an exchange of information detailing the names of the women and the missing social security contributions. But by the beginning of 2021, progress had ground to a halt. Sal was told that the office of the regional vicar—the head of Opus Dei in Argentina—could no longer discuss the case, and that Sal should instead direct his complaint to the women's branch. He was given an email address and told to resend the complaint there, which he duly did—but only after sending a copy to the regional vicar. Sal received a response from someone who made it extremely clear she was not acting on behalf of the prelature but, instead, for a charitable foundation that owned various residences around the country. A calculated handwashing operation was underway.

Unbeknownst to Sal, around the same time as he'd received the complaint from the forty-three women, the regional vicar in Buenos Aires had received another complaint from someone alleging they had been sexually abused by a numerary during an Opus Dei summer camp in the 1980s. The victim was responding to new rules introduced by Pope Francis to prevent such cases from being covered up and making it obligatory to report any allegations of sexual abuse directly to the Vatican. The victim asked for Opus Dei to heed the new rules and report the abuse to the Holy See. His request was ignored. Instead, the prelature responded with similar diversion tactics to those in Sal's case, washing its hands of the affairs and telling the victim that it wasn't required to report the incident as it had taken place at a summer camp run not by Opus Dei but by a charitable foundation that just happened to be run by a group of numeraries.

Sal was told that, in order to proceed, the women would need to meet individually with the lawyers representing the charitable foundation, or possibly in groups of two—and without his being present. It was a clear attempt to break up the group. Sal refused and asked to speak with the mysterious figure representing the foundation. The woman responded by saying she didn't have a phone. Sal offered to buy one for her and have it sent to her office if she would provide him with an address. There was no response.

Sal realized the negotiations had hit a dead end, and his team began detailed interviews with the numerary assistants, with a view to putting together a formal case—only to discover that they were dealing with serious crimes like the human trafficking of children and enslavement, as well as physical and psychological abuse. Given what he had discovered, he felt obliged to inform the Vatican and so asked for a meeting with the papal nuncio—the pope's official representative in Argentina.

The nuncio told Sal to send a letter to the pope. The lawyer eventually sent three, via different routes, to maximize the chances of at least one getting to Francis, as well as to prevent the complaint from being intercepted by other interested parties within the Vatican. In the letters, he detailed how what had initially been a case to reclaim missing social security payments had morphed into something much more grave. He outlined a series of human rights violations and criminal acts suffered by the women during their time in Opus Dei, including enslavement, privacy infringements, human trafficking, the employment of minors, deception, captivity, denial of access to medical care, control over access to the media, and general exploitation. He made four specific requests to Francis: that Opus Dei recognize the abuses committed, that it apologize to the women for the suffering caused, that it compensate them, and that it take measures to ensure that such violations never happen again.

He also outlined how Opus Dei used a network of foundations to hide its wealth and absolve itself of any legal responsibility, providing a detailed list of fifteen nonprofits in Argentina linked to the prelature, as well as the assets held in their name. He heard nothing back. By May, two months after sending the letters and almost eight months after approaching Opus Dei, the case seemed deadlocked. The women were growing impatient. They had no option other than to go public.

Opus Dei was furious when the article, under the headline "Servants of God? A Cavalry of 43 Women Clashes with Opus Dei," appeared in *La Nación*, one of the country's leading newspapers, in May 2021. The article was filled with damaging details of how the women had been recruited as young girls, of how they had been promised an education they never received, and how they were expected to work for up to fifteen hours a day for no pay. By sheer chance, the story came out on the day that Opus Dei was due to hold a fundraiser at its university on the outskirts of Buenos Aires. It scrambled to control the fallout, accusing Sal of having provided insufficient information for them to investigate the situation properly—even though all the women had lived and worked in Opus Dei centers, which according to the internal rules were required to keep their own detailed records on every resident. It stressed that each of the cases might well be very different and said that it remained open to "listening to each person"—continuing its attempts to break up the group.

Given the outrage that the story had provoked in Buenos Aires, where the pope had lived and worked for almost his entire life, Sal was puzzled by the ongoing silence from the Vatican. One day in the middle of 2021, he got a call from another well-known lawyer in the city who asked for them to meet.

"I have a message from Jorge," the lawyer said when the two finally met in person. Sal had no idea who he was talking about.

"Jorge? Who is Jorge?" Sal asked.

"The pope!" the other lawyer replied. He explained that, from Rome, Francis was watching this story closely and wished to send a personal message to Sal to continue his good work. Though he had previously dismissed the Vatican as uninterested, the encounter made Sal realize there was, in fact, a willingness to tackle Opus Dei's abuses—although clearly the pope, playing a delicate political game, couldn't publicly call for an investigation. He concluded that the next logical step was to file an official complaint with the Vatican against Opus Dei.

In September 2021, a thirty-two-page document was sent to the Abuse Section of the Vatican's Tribunal of the Doctrine of the Faith, detailing the systematic abuse of former numerary assistants over a period of more than forty years—from 1974 until 2015—at various Opus Dei residences in Argentina, Paraguay, Bolivia, Uruguay, Italy, and Kazakhstan. The document named the prelate Fernando Ocáriz and his deputy Mariano Fazio as being complicit in the abuse, along with at least twenty-four Opus Dei priests who had direct knowledge of what was happening to the women. As well as his four previous demands, Sal made one more: that the accused be stripped of their ecclesiastical posts and be sanctioned for their role in the abuse. What Sal had initially envisioned as a fairly straightforward case, one that would be resolved quickly with Opus Dei making good on its missed social security payments and a cash settlement with the forty-three women, was now taking on unexpected implications that reached right to the very top of the organization.

In November 2021, the case in Argentina was thrust onto the international stage, when the Associated Press published a story about the plight of the former numerary assistants and the complaint that they had filed at the Vatican. The article detailed the alleged labor exploitation and the years of abuse, and included interviews with several of the women—including Lucía Giménez, who told her story to an international audience for the first time. "They don't give you time to think, to criticize and say that you don't like it," she explained. "You have to endure because you have to surrender totally to God."

None of the women were prepared for the impact the article would have. Within minutes of its hitting the wire, their fight was front-page news on the websites of dozens of prominent newspapers all around the globe—from London to Lagos and Taipei. The story got relatively little play in the United States, however, where it was overshadowed by the breaking news that Steve Bannon, the former White House advisor, was being charged with contempt of Congress. So little play did the story get in Washington that, down on K Street, Father Trullols and the rest of the board at the Catholic Information Center felt confident enough to go ahead with the planned launch of the biggest fundraiser yet—a multimillion-dollar renovation of the Saint Josemaría Escrivá Chapel and bookshop.

Billed as the Saint Joseph the Builder Campaign, the renovation project promised to transform the venue into "the premier space for Catholics and those interested in the faith to gather downtown." The push sought to capitalize on the Catholic Information Center's return to prominence under the Trump administration, during which three of its board members had occupied important positions and Father Trullols had led the nation in prayer from the White House Rose Garden. Joe Biden's victory in the 2020 presidential election had taken some wind out of the CIC's sails, despite the new president being a practicing Catholic. But in the months since the inauguration, the CIC had repositioned itself as a shelter for the retreating army of conservative Catholics who had worked at the center of the Trump administration, but whose ideas—and record in government—had been roundly rejected by the eighty-one million Americans who voted for Biden, in an election that boasted the highest turnout in more than a century.

The election loss created tension between Trump and some of the conservative Catholics who had been staunch allies of the president throughout his tumultuous time in office. That included Bill Barr, who was fired as attorney general seven weeks after the lost election, when he publicly admitted that the Department of Justice had found no evidence the vote had been tampered with—a line being pushed vigorously by Trump and his allies. The CIC moved to position itself as a home and a platform for Barr, who was a previous board member at the Opus Dei chapel and bookshop, creating a new position called the Saint Thomas More Chair and naming the former attorney general as its first awardee.

Not all the conservative Catholics at the heart of the Trump administration retreated quietly from government, however. Ginni Thomas, who had been an advisor to the president and a key ally and close friend of Leonard Leo, exchanged texts with the White House Chief of Staff, Mark Meadows, in which she shared conspiracy theories about the Sandy Hook school shooting being a false-flag operation—as well as theories circulating online about how the U.S. military had helped to alter paper ballots in swing states. She also shared another unfounded rumor circulating among far right conspiracists that Biden, the president elect, was about to be arrested for ballot fraud and transferred to a barge off Guantanamo Bay, where he would face a military tribunal for sedition. Her willingness to buy into the stolen-election narrative—despite zero evidence backing up Trump's claims—reflected a fear common among Washington's conservative Catholic elite that the change in power would unleash a liberal revolution similar to what priests like McCloskey had long warned them about. "Do not concede," she implored Meadows. "It takes time for the army who is gathering for his back." A few days later, the White House chief of staff responded with a text that framed the fight against Trump's election loss as part of a religious crusade. "This is a fight of good versus evil," he wrote. "Evil always looks like the victor until the King of Kings triumphs. Do not grow weary in well doing. The fight continues. I have staked my career on it. Well, at least my time in DC on it." Thomas replied, "Thank you!! Needed that! This plus a conversation with my best friend just now . . . I will try to keep holding on. America is worth it!"

The exchange offered a window into the minds of those at the very top of government, of how their religious views—and the vitriol pushed onto them by conservative voices in the Church—had distorted their reality. When riots broke out in Washington, D.C., two weeks ahead of Biden's inauguration, and protesters stormed Congress, it was revealed that one of the main groups behind the self-anointed "March to Save America" rally that led to the riots had received millions of dollars from one of the dark-money vehicles run by Leonard Leo and the Corkerys.

Following Biden's inauguration, the CIC moved to take advantage of the brewing culture wars, giving a platform—and the Opus Dei ecclesiastical stamp of approval—to a small but vociferous group of Catholic conservatives engaged in rousing believers to fight against what was framed as the militant secularism of the new Biden administration, inciting them to rise up in the coming ideological war. Ignoring an appeal from Pope Francis following the election for Catholics to "show care and compassion, to work for reconciliation and healing, and to advance mutual respect and acceptance," the Opus Dei center on K Street escalated the culture war by giving a platform to those voices more likely to call for battle than to seek reconciliation. Its previous calendar of talks by Catholic writers on inspiring figures within the faith were soon replaced with vitriolic lectures that tapped into the Zeitgeist— railing against the rise of "gender ideology," transgender politics, and other *liberal* causes.

Barr played a key role in this group, having caused controversy while actively serving as attorney general by alleging that an "organized destruction" of religion was underway in the United States. "Secularists, and their allies among the progressives, have marshaled all the force of mass communications, popular culture, the entertainment industry, and academia in an unremitting assault on religion and traditional values," he said in an October 2019 speech—in comments reminiscent of Escrivá and Del Portillo. As the Opus Dei center's new Saint Thomas More Chair, he made a rousing speech against the indoctrination of children in the public school system concerning subjects like gender and sexuality, and defending the rights of parents to educate their children according to their own belief system. "Today, the signal feature of our age is man's abandonment of God," he told the audience. "We see all around us the stunning collapse of the Christian world view and the culture that's been based on that world view. It is being supplanted by a wholly alien belief system, one that is secular, materialist, and solipsistic." The talk exalted parents—rather than the state—as being best placed to make decisions about how their children should be educated and what ideas they should hear. "Our public schools have inevitably become cockpits for a vicious winner-take-all culture war over the moral formation of our children," he warned.

The pose of victimhood being struck at the CIC ignored the fact that Catholic conservatives had, during the Trump years, taken control of the Supreme Court, thanks to one of the CIC's own—Leonard Leo. Following the appointment of Neil Gorsuch to replace Antonin Scalia, two more seats had become vacant during Trump's presidency, allowing him to create a solid conservative majority. One of those seats had become vacant just weeks before the election, following the unexpected death of Ruth Bader Ginsburg. Determined not to miss the opportunity to decisively shift the balance of the court, the conservative legal elite forgot about the supposed time-honored tradition of never filling a Supreme Court vacancy during an election year, an argument they had used to stop Obama from filling Scalia's seat. Leonard Leo was once again asked to help find a replacement. At one Federalist Society event, his good friend Supreme Court Justice Clarence Thomas jokingly referred to Leo as the third most powerful man in the world, presumably behind the pope and the president of the United States. "God help us!" Leo had responded. But following Ginsburg's death, not even God could rein in his ambition.

Rather than offer a concession candidate, given the proximity of the election, Leo put forward Amy Coney Barrett, a protégé of Antonin Scalia who was openly hostile to *Roe v. Wade*. It was no coincidence. A few months earlier, Thomas E. Dobbs, the Mississippi health officer, had lodged an appeal at the Supreme Court after the Jackson Women's Health Organization—Mississippi's only abortion clinic—had successfully challenged a state law that banned abortions after fifteen weeks. An injunction against the state's enforcing the law had already been upheld by two separate courts, but a Dobbs win at the Supreme Court directly challenged the premise of *Roe v. Wade* and created the opportunity the Catholic right had craved for so long to overturn almost fifty years of abortion rights. Coney Barrett was confirmed on the Supreme Court just eight days before the election, critically giving the court a strong anti-abortion bias as the case was being considered.

Leo's status as the world's third most powerful figure soon made him a rich man. During his time at the Federalist Society, he had hardly been a pauper, bringing in around $400,000 a year. But with six children attending The Heights and Oakcrest, the two Opus Dei schools that charged up to $30,000 tuition annually per student, and a burgeoning taste for good food and expensive wines, it didn't take long to burn through his salary. But his life had taken a lavish turn after Trump's victory and his appointment as an unpaid advisor to the president on judicial appointments. The dramatic uptick in his personal fortune dovetailed with his joining a for-profit entity called CRC Advisors, alongside another CIC board member Greg Mueller. Mueller had spearheaded the National Organization for Marriage's vitriolic public relations strategy, and CRC quickly established itself as the go-to advisory firm for the dark-money network of nonprofit entities that Leo had helped set up over the years. Once again, the Corkery name was all over the money flow. The majority of CRC's income came from The 85 Fund, a dark-money non-profit that Leo repurposed to fund conservative causes nationwide, and that fund paid $34 million in fees to his new advisory firm over a single two-year period. As the money rolled in, Leo began to enjoy some of the same luxuries as the billionaires he had spent years courting. For most of his three decades in Washington, Leo had led a modest home life, living for years in a small apartment in the Randolph Towers complex in downtown Arlington, before moving to a single-story five-bedroom family home in suburban McLean in 2010. But in the years since 2016, he had spent millions of dollars on two new mansions in Maine, bought four new cars, and hired a wine buyer and locker at Morton's, an upscale steakhouse three blocks from the Catholic Information Center. It was only a foretaste of what was to come.

In 2020, Leo stepped back from his duties at the Federalist Society to focus on the dark-money network he had fostered as a side hustle during his time there. With him, he took one of the Federalist Society's biggest donors: a manufacturing billionaire from Chicago called Barre Seid, who was Jewish by heritage but who shared many of Leo's conservative views. Over two decades, Seid had pumped at least $775 million into campaigns for libertarian and conservative causes, quietly transforming himself into one of the most important donors on the political right. Almost ninety, Seid had decided to leave his money continuing that work—and concluded that Leo was the man to oversee that largesse. Leo had betrayed his bosses, who had tasked him with wooing the billionaire as a potential donor for the Federalist Society. Instead, Leo had cultivated him for his own network. Seid signed his business over to Leo, giving him control over a $1.6 billion war chest and transforming him from a proxy for dark-money donors into a donor himself.

Opus Dei soon benefited from these dark-money streams. DonorsTrust, which had provided the lion's share of funding for The 85 Fund, the source of much of Leo's newfound wealth, soon began donating millions to a foundation linked to the Catholic Association. The organization, which had been set up by Neil Corkery, had for years funded various media initiatives to promote Catholicism in the public square—including Catholic Voices USA, the failed Opus Dei–linked media training programs. It soon directed money to other Opus Dei initiatives. One of the biggest beneficiaries of the foundation was the Catholic Information Center on K Street. Before long, Opus Dei had begun cultivating donations directly from many of the billionaires who had also given huge sums of money to Leo's dark network. Sean Fieler began to increase his donations to Opus Dei initiatives, sending money to help fund its university in Rome—as well as an expansion of Luis Tellez's Witherspoon Institute, which was being rolled out on other Ivy League campuses under his latest scheme—the Foundation for Excellence in Higher Education. Over the coming years, the budget of FEHE would swell to over $10 million a year, thanks to seven-figure donations from arch-conservative donors such as Charles B. Johnson, the Franklin Templeton billionaire—as well as the Sarah Scaife Foundation and the Diana Davis Spencer Foundation. The donations would allow Tellez to expand the program to fourteen elite universities, including Columbia, Duke, Harvard, Princeton, Stanford, and Yale, as well as Oxford, reaching and forming thousands of young people who would go on to hold positions of cultural influence. For Tellez, FEHE marked a decision to target the next generation—a strategy tried by Escrivá in the 1930s and 1940s—after voters failed to engage with the message of the National Organization for Marriage and the American Principles Project. "When we lost in the political process and in the legal process, I did some thinking about where is it that I can be most helpful," he explained, referring to the defeat regarding same-sex marriage. "We're going to devote even more fully to the education of young men and women so that they themselves can take positions in public policy."

Tim Busch, who had founded the Napa Institute for arch-conservative Catholics like himself to plot ways, over gourmet food and fine wine, of bringing the country back to its Christian moorings, appointed Leo to his board and made regular donations to the prelature's various initiatives. Bohlin personally approved Busch's appointment as a "co-operator," an official designation for the organization's closest supporters. Welcoming Busch into Opus Dei as a co-operator was a controversial move; Busch had previously been accused of taking part in a plot accusing Francis of hushing up sexual abuse, and more recently was tied to a controversial project to influence the next papal conclave. Run by a mysterious foundation called Better Church Governance, the "Red Hat Report" involved hiring former FBI officers to gather information on prominent cardinals. The initiative billed itself as a service to the wider Church, which—despite the advent of the internet and the information revolution—they believed was less qualified to make important decisions than it was in the seventies. Busch would later speak openly about the human failings of the Vatican leadership, and how wealthy lay members were best positioned to lead evangelization efforts going forward. "I think the Church that Jesus Christ founded is perfect because it has been around for 2,000 years and even the mortal leadership of the Church can't screw it up," he explained. "They can taint it, but they can't bring it down. But from an evangelization perspective, I think it's the laity. It's the lay apostolates that are going to make a difference because they have better funding, they have smarter money, and they can be much more mobile."

Philip Nielsen, the frontman for Better Church Governance, met with a prominent Opus Dei journalist and apologist during one fundraising trip to Madrid.

"So, no spying?" asked the man, a former numerary.

"It depends what you mean by spying," responded Nielsen. "The first stage in the process is the graduate students doing research. Then we will identify the gaps in the research and, where we don't know enough about a given cardinal, we will research him further. We do have former FBI investigators that are working for us. They are very professional."

"No CIA guys?"

"There are CIA guys. I don't want to lie. Yeah."

"So, how is Better Church Governance going to influence Church leaders, so they can elect more accurately and more efficacious a better pope?"

"There is a difficulty now in electing a pope," responded Nielsen. "It used to be that all the Italians knew each other—and the pope was Italian. Then the first non-Italian was pope—Saint—John Paul II and in many ways that was possible as he made many trips to Rome and knew many of the Italians. Also, because there were two conclaves . . . a month apart and the cardinals spent twice as much time together, they got to know each other even better and they got to make a bold choice. For the last two conclaves, clearly there was not as much information and, in some ways, the election of the last pope reflected that lack of information."

In a clear show of support from Tim Busch, Nielsen had been due to launch the "Red Hats Report" initiative at a Napa Institute conference advocating for "authentic reform" in the Church in October 2018 attended by Leonard Leo, Rick Santorum, and Scott Hahn, a prominent member of Opus Dei. But when a recording of a meeting of those who were behind the project was leaked to the press, the launch was abruptly canceled. "For me, it's an honor that Americans are attacking me," Francis later told reporters aboard the papal aircraft, when asked about the "Red Hat Report" and the involvement of Tim Busch. The Napa Institute founder continued to give a platform to the pope's critics. Despite this, Bohlin approved him as a cooperator, in an indication of Opus Dei's true loyalties.

The prelature's coziness with these rising, controversial figures of the Catholic right was clearly displayed—on a plaque honoring the biggest donors to the Saint Joseph the Builder Campaign, at the grand reopening of the Catholic Information Center, following its lavish refurbishment in September 2022. Among the highest, so-called Saint Josemaría Circle of donors were Leonard and Sally Leo, as well as Busch's Napa Institute and Leo's business partner, Greg Mueller. As regulars wandered around the new white interior, some couldn't help but gape in wonder at the portrait which hung in the foyer, even more prominent than the photographs of Saint Josemaría, which were tucked away in a passageway off the main communal area. It was a painting of a young girl in a blue dress and a white cardigan, who sat smiling, her eyes bright and content. Behind her was a figure of Christ, whose right hand was raised in blessing while his left hand caressed the head of the young girl. From that hand, a golden light emanated, surrounding the girl's head like a halo. It was Margaret Mary Leo, the eldest daughter of the conservative activist who had passed away fifteen years earlier. At the reception desk, prayer cards bearing her image were being handed out, with "Margaret Leo of McLean, pray for us!" written at the bottom. In the portrait and on the prayer cards, Margaret was wearing a sacred heart medal like the ones that had supposedly appeared unexplainedly shortly after her passing. The story of the medals had begun to circulate ever more widely following the publication of a book, written by the Opus Dei supernumerary writer Austin Ruse, who like Leo was one of the founders of the National Catholic Prayer Breakfast. His book was called *Littlest Suffering Souls: Children Whose Short Lives Point Us to Christ* and it detailed the miracles. Ruse's public demonstration of love toward the disabled daughter of his wealthy, powerful friend Leonard Leo contrasted starkly with the vitriol he doled out online to those who disagreed with him. And that vitriol included publicly taunting a thirteen-year-old for his stutter and declaring that "single women should not be allowed to vote." He had previously supported Russia's anti-gay propaganda laws as a means to "curb the homosexual advance," and he had stated that "the hard left, human-hating people that run modern universities" should "all be taken out and shot." The contrast in the supernumerary's rhetoric between his friends and his enemies was a clear demonstration of how his worldview was shaped by an ultra-conservative ideology—rather than any desire to spread Christian values of love, compassion, and respect.

The prayer cards on display at the Catholic Information Center were a logical first step toward potentially beatifying young Margaret. Opus Dei had offered the lobby of its most public-facing institution in America to further this cause. The portrait symbolized a growing symbiosis between Opus Dei and Leo. The bookshop and chapel would soon provide a platform for Leo as he detailed the philosophy and worldview that would inform his decisions about spending the $1.6 billion bequest from Seid. The Washington Opus Dei crowd brimmed with pride and admiration as they gathered at the Mayflower Hotel, just around the corner from the CIC, to confer the center's greatest honor—the John Paul II New Evangelization Award—at a black-tie dinner in October 2022. The award ceremony was especially pertinent, given the success of the *Dobbs* case at the Supreme Court, which had overturned *Roe v. Wade* and had ended a woman's constitutional right to legal abortion in the United States. "It's particularly fitting that the very year in which *Dobbs* was decided we are honoring Leonard Leo," Bill Barr said in a congratulatory video played before the award ceremony. "No one has done more to advance traditional values and especially the right to life than Leonard." Paul Scalia spoke, too, recounting his memories of Margaret Mary. Father Trullols, the Opus Dei priest in charge of the Catholic Information Center, was shown holidaying at the Leo's mansion in Maine.

"Thank you so much, Father Charles—for this privilege, for your leadership of the Catholic Information Center, for your friendship," began Leo in his acceptance speech. "It's been a real privilege to be a part of this great enterprise and have you as a friend. I do think the real honor this evening should go to the CIC—along with the Leonine Forum, which I think is a very important piece of our future." By 2022, the "spiritual enrichment" program that had been started by the Opus Dei priest Father Arne Panula a decade earlier had been expanded to other cities, including New York, Chicago, and Los Angeles, and counted more than 800 alumni. "They are the cutting edge of the New Evangelization," continued Leo. "Few organizations are doing more to raise up a new generation of courageous and faithful Catholic men and women."

Without irony, Leo suggested that the audience that night, some of whom had paid as much as $25,000 a table, were the oppressed minority. "Catholicism faces vile and amoral current-day barbarians, secularists, and bigots," Leo continued. "These barbarians can be known by their signs: they vandalized and burnt our churches after the Supreme Court overturned *Roe v. Wade*, they show up at events like this one trying to frighten and muzzle us. From coast to coast, they are conducting a coordinated and large-scale campaign to drive us from the communities they want to dominate." Only a few weeks earlier, after a group of protestors had scrawled "dirty money lives here" on the sidewalk outside his home, Leo used his awards speech to blame such attacks on "the progressive Ku Klux Klan." "They spread false and slanderous rhetoric about Catholic apostolates and institutions like the one represented here tonight," he said, referring to Opus Dei.

Within weeks of giving his speech, Leo had begun work on his next big project—offering a glimpse into how he and his network would spend the $1.6 billion donated by Seid. Having orchestrated a conservative, Catholic takeover of the Supreme Court, Leo now set his sights on things much broader—and outlined his ambitions for orchestrating a similar revolution in other sectors of society, such as education, the media, Wall Street, and Silicon Valley. "Wokeism in the corporate environment, in the educational environment, one-sided journalism, entertainment that's really corrupting our youth—why can't we build talent pipelines and networks that can positively affect those areas?" Leo asked in a promotional video for his latest initiative Teneo, which promised to "crush liberal dominance." In short, he was creating a Federalist Society for everything. Almost a century after Escrivá's vision for Opus Dei, the organization—through the Catholic Information Center, through the Leonine Forum, and through the initiatives of prominent sympathizers like Leonard Leo—had its biggest opportunity yet to definitively influence society, just as the founder had envisioned.

Their ambitions went well beyond Washington. The Hawthorn Foundation was established in 2019 as a vehicle to create more Opus Dei schools in the United States, starting with one in Bedford, a town in Westchester County, New York. "These schools are found in strategic cities in order to influence the formation of future leaders across culture, politics, and business," the foundation's site boasted. Leonard Leo lent his support to the initiative, which he professed would give the next generation "an education imbued with the right training, a healthy freedom, and inculcation of personal responsibility." By the end of its second full year in operation, the foundation had amassed $20 million—although the source of those funds was not revealed. The lofty words of Leo and the Hawthorn Foundation's website contrasted, though, with the actual experience of students at other Opus Dei institutions in the United States. While it was raising money from donors based on this promise of "healthy freedom," Opus Dei's Oakcrest School in Washington was disciplining students suspected of being in gay relationships, while the leadership of the school was drawing up plans to monitor the students' daily life to prevent such relationships from developing.

While this campaign was underway, Luis Tellez and his wealthy backers were working to influence teaching and debate on university campuses through a multi-million-dollar expansion of the Foundation for Excellence in Higher Education, which aimed to replicate the success of the Witherspoon Institute across the country—and around the world. Tellez, drawing on Escrivá's early vision for Opus Dei, sees these outposts as a kind of "finishing school" for the next generation of leaders. By 2024, FEHE was present on campus at fourteen elite universities across the United States—and at Oxford, England. In New York, Opus Dei has made further inroads in the university environment, having been rewarded with the appointment of Father Roger Landry, an Opus Dei priest and chaplain for the city's Leonine

Forum program, as chaplain at Columbia University. Tellez plans to build on the expansion of FEHE with the establishment of a number of "Catholic institutes" on campus for those students interested in exploring their faith—just as Escrivá did in 1930s and 1940s Spain. He helped set up the first of these—the Aquinas Institute—at Princeton in 2018, and plans are afoot for another at Columbia. Officially, Opus Dei will have nothing to do with such establishments, but Tellez has discussed his vision for attracting today's youth with the prelate. He also has admitted that there is often a good deal of gray area at such "Catholic institutes." "It is a lay organization: there is no connection to Opus Dei formally, but there are some members of Opus Dei involved in doing this," he explained. "Some members of Opus Dei are good because they are reliable thinkers in this regard—they know how to do the legwork." Almost a century from its founding, Opus Dei appears to have come full circle, by fanning the culture wars and fueling deep divisions that risk ripping our society apart while at the same time seeking to surreptitiously recruit tomorrow's leaders on university campuses—just as it did in in 1930s and 1940s Spain.

As the rest of the world shrunk in horror at the allegations made against Opus Dei by the women in Argentina, the lack of coverage of that story in the United States allowed the prelature to cozy up to the Catholic right and embark on bold new initiatives there. For all its talk of loyalty to the pope, Opus Dei was aligning itself with forces that contradicted Francis's message and mission. But it would soon find itself in an uncomfortable spotlight.

A small delegation of supernumeraries and their children were on hand to greet Fernando Ocáriz as he touched down in Sydney on the morning of August 8, 2023, bearing homemade placards reading "G'day Father!" welcoming the prelate back to Australian soil. Tired from his overnight flight from Jakarta, Ocáriz nonetheless posed for photographs before being ushered into a car and driven an hour north, into the hills surrounding the city, where he was due to spend the next five days at a private retreat. His stay at the Kenthurst Study Centre offered a chance for the seventy-eight-year-old prelate to relax and recharge after a grueling two weeks on the road in the oppressive heat of the Philippines and Indonesia. As his first pastoral visit outside Europe since the pandemic—and the first since the Argentinian complaint had been filed at the Vatican—the journey was seen as a vital opportunity to reset the narrative as Opus Dei approached its centenary. As a result, the past two weeks had been filled with meetings and photo opportunities designed to shift attention away from the abuse allegations. The stay at Kenthurst offered Ocáriz a much-needed rest. Set on twenty-five acres of native bush, with views of the Blue Mountains, and boasting a swimming pool, tennis courts, and extensive walking trails, the retreat center had been bankrolled by Luis Valls-Taberner in the early 1990s as part of a major expansion of Opus Dei in Australia, which had seen the prelature construct three new schools in Sydney's wealthy suburbs. Pope Benedict XVI had made his own three-day private retreat there, ahead of the World Youth Day celebrations in Sydney in 2008. Villa Tevere had planned a relaxing time for Ocáriz, styling his stay at Kenthurst as "The Father's Rest" before he took up the second half of his tour across Australia and New Zealand.

But events ten thousand miles away in Rome would soon dash any hopes Ocáriz and his team had for a restful stay. Within a few hours of the prelate's arrival, news reached Kenthurst of a decree signed by the pope that effectively rescinded the privileges Opus Dei had enjoyed for forty years—ever since John Paul II had elevated the organization to the status of personal prelature in 1983. On the face of it, the *motu proprio*—"of one's own initiative" in Latin, indicating the move was a personal initiative of the pope—appeared nothing more than a handful of small, technical tweaks to existing canon law. But it didn't take long for the team with the prelate to realize the significance of the brief document. With a few strokes of his pen, the pope removed Opus Dei's direct authority over the vast majority of its 90,000 members and stripped it of its ability to operate independently of local dioceses. The document set free thousands of numeraries and numerary assistants, who had for years been told that the vows they had taken to Opus Dei were binding for life. Only its priests would remain directly under Opus Dei control.

Ocáriz and his team didn't know how to respond. Had the *motu proprio* been timed to coincide with the pastoral trip? Had Francis signed the decree when Ocáriz was as far from Rome as possible, to isolate and neutralize him during the biggest crisis to face Opus Dei in its ninety-five-year history? For two days, there was silence as the prelate and his team scrambled to liaise with the General Council in Rome and struggled with the wording of a statement that would need to appear loyal to the pope, but also reassure the membership and prevent a potential mass desertion. On August 10, Ocáriz signed off on the agreed wording. "The modifications established in these canons refer to the general law regarding personal prelatures," it read, in a clear attempt to downplay this as an attack against the movement and ignoring the fact that Opus Dei was the *only* personal prelature in the Church. "In the addition that refers to the laity, the fact that they are faithful of their dioceses, like any other Catholic, is made explicit," it continued. "In the case of the Work, moreover, they are members of this supernatural family, thanks to a specific vocational call." Opus Dei was buying time by muddying the waters, asserting that numeraries and supernumeraries had *always* been members of their local dioceses, while reaffirming that they were also part of the wider Opus Dei family.

While the timing and content of the *motu proprio* had been unexpected, the papal decree should have come as no surprise to Ocáriz, given the various warning shots Pope Francis had fired in the two years since Sebastián Sal had lodged the complaint against Opus Dei, alleging the systematic abuse of numerary assistants. Rather than taking the complaint as an opportunity to reform, Opus Dei had moved to protect its own interests almost as soon as it had been filed, transferring its most senior representative in Argentina—who had been named in the complaint—to neighboring Paraguay. Sal saw the reassignment as a calculated move to make it more difficult for authorities in Buenos Aires to investigate the matter. The new head of the region initially signaled an openness to resolving the situation, and even issuing an apology to the women, but talks soon broke down. By March 2022, with no real progress, the pope made his first move against Opus Dei by including a single line in a document outlining his reform of the Holy See. That line proposed transferring the oversight of personal prelatures from the Dicastery for Bishops to the Dicastery for Clergy. In essence, as the only personal prelature in existence, Opus Dei was being demoted within the Church hierarchy. It was moving from a body that reported directly to the pope, to a largely administrative body looking after priests not belonging to religious orders. It was a politically cautious and carefully thought-out opening salvo from Francis, who had learned, from his years of dealing with the military dictatorships in Argentina, to play the long game. Yet Opus Dei failed to take the hint. In Argentina, it continued to pursue its attempts to break up the group of more than forty numerary assistants by setting up what it called a Commission for Listening and Enquiry, manned by Opus Dei members from other regions.

This commission backfired massively. Recognizing it as an attempt to break up the group, the women held firm and issued a response through Sebastián Sal that they would only communicate as a group—and through him. And to the chagrin of Opus Dei, which had envisioned the commission as a shrewd move to quell publicity concerning the scandal, new accusations from former members began to surface.

The pope signed the demotion of Opus Dei into canonical law in July 2022, issuing a *motu proprio* specifying how it would take effect. Francis required Opus Dei to submit a new set of statutes for approval by the Holy See, and henceforth also submit an annual report to the Dicastery for Clergy detailing its operations—and how it was fulfilling its apostolic work. This first *motu proprio* included an additional clause that was particularly galling for Ocáriz, confirming that the head of Opus Dei would henceforth no longer automatically become a bishop. The pope's decree made it clear that he supported Opus Dei's fundamental mission to spread holiness in the world through the sanctification of work—but also hinted that the movement had strayed from that mission. Francis wrote that the *motu proprio* stemmed from a desire "to protect the charism of Opus Dei and to promote the evangelizing action carried out by its members in the world," hinting that the current structure of the organization was not fulfilling its purported aims. "It is intended to strengthen the conviction that, for the protection of the particular gift of the Spirit, a form of governance based on charism more than on hierarchical authority is needed," he added.

The decree was a shot across Opus Dei's bow, a warning to get its house in order—or face the consequences. As Opus Dei prepared for an Extraordinary General Congress of its most senior members in Rome to discuss how to respond to the decree, Francis fired another warning shot. As the tenth anniversary of his papacy approached, in March 2023—just a few weeks before the Congress—Francis gave a rare interview in which he highlighted his point. "Opus Dei has some marvelous things in the work it does, and it also has defects like any anyone, but they are local, not universal," he said.

The pope also appeared in a documentary called *The Pope: Answers*, which was distributed around the world on Disney Plus and Hulu two weeks before the big meeting at Villa Tevere, in which Francis took questions from ten young people from around the world. Halfway through the film, in the middle of a debate about abortion that Francis was handling extremely well, a man in his mid-twenties wearing a pink flannel shirt joined the debate.

"I'd like to look at all of this from the standpoint of the Church as an institution," he interjected. "I think . . . and I don't want to generalize, of course . . . but there is a huge amount of hypocrisy on issues such as this. There is a lot of talk about the *right* to life, of the need to protect life—that it is a sin. But at the same time, on other matters—for example . . ."—here the young man took a deep breath—"the issue of pedophilia within the Church. . . ."

At this point, the pope let out a heavy sigh. "Buf!"

"Many people within the Church deny the victims—or they side with the perpetrator," continued the young man. He was getting emotional. "And there this question of protecting life takes the back seat."

Francis had a far from impeccable record when it came to handling claims of sexual abuse. During a trip to Chile in 2018, the pope accused the victims of one Catholic priest—Chile's most notorious pedophile—of slander, in an extraordinary blunder that undermined a visit intended to heal wounds rather than open new ones. He defended a prominent bishop against claims he was complicit in covering up the crimes, saying that such accusations were "calumny." But the conversation was about to take an unexpected twist.

"I am Juan Cuatrecasas," the young man continued, "and I went to an Opus Dei school—in Bilbao. There . . . when I was about eleven or twelve, I was sexually abused by a numerary."

At this point, Cuatrecasas began to break down.

"*Tranquilo, tranquilo . . .*" the pope soothed him in Spanish. "Don't worry."

Cuatrecasas recalled how his father had written to the pope for advice, and he produced a reply from Francis in which the pope encouraged them to file a complaint with the Congregation for the Doctrine of the Faith, which handled such allegations.

"Did you get a response?" asked the pope. "I sent it there for them to handle."

Cuatrecasas responded that the Congregation for the Doctrine of the

Faith had written not to him but to the Opus Dei school the following year, stating that the investigation was being closed and ordering that the good name of the numerary be reinstated. A Spanish court later found the numerary to be guilty, sentencing him to eleven years in prison.

"My question is obvious—why?" asked Cuatrecasas.

"Child abuse is a tragedy—not just in the Church, but wherever it takes place," answered the pope. "But in the Church it is even more scandalous because, in a place where you are supposed to be caring for people, instead you destroy them. . . . If they are people of the Church it is hypocritic, it's a horrific double life."

After agreeing to reopen the case, the pope had some choice words for the way abuse had been previously handled—words which would echo in Argentina, where Opus Dei was still seeking to wash its hands of another sexual abuse case brought against a numerary there.

"It may well be that there are people who conduct themselves badly," the pope said. "That's why the policy now is to clean up. If someone is conducting themselves badly, they should be denounced, and we will clean up. Zero tolerance, that is the policy of the Church."

In Buenos Aires, the pope's native city, the message seemed to get through—regarding one case at least. Opus Dei issued a public statement on the opening day of the Congress, revealing for the first time that in the River Plate region—encompassing Argentina, Bolivia, Paraguay, and Uruguay— eight members, three of them priests and the rest numeraries, had been accused of abuse. But when it came to apologizing for the systemic abuse of numerary assistants and revising the internal rules written by Escrivá, Opus Dei proved incapable of reacting to the pope's appeal. At the Congress in April 2023, only minor revisions to the statutes were put forward. They were presented to the Vatican a few weeks later. Frustrated with Opus Dei's refusal to embrace real reform, Francis twice summoned Ocáriz to the papal apartment to explain why the movement hadn't heeded his call.

Another blow came a few weeks later, when two former numeraries in Spain filed a separate complaint with the Vatican, backed up by seven hundred documents—including dozens of internal records secreted out of the organization over the years. Those documents detailed the systematic abuse of members dating back to its founding. Antonio Moya and Carmen Rosario Pérez delivered the complaint by hand to the office of the papal nuncio in Madrid. After spending decades inside Opus Dei as numeraries, both had abandoned the movement, and through the website OpusLibros.org, they had discovered countless others who had suffered systematic abuse under the prelature. The complaint, which was signed by former members from Mexico, Guatemala, El Salvador, Argentina, Italy, Spain, and the United Kingdom alleged widespread abuse, the cover-up of criminal acts—including child abuse—as well as an institutionalized fraud toward the Church itself, with Opus Dei intentionally concealing its internal rules and practices from the Vatican. Dozens of documents detailing these internal practices had previously been published online, only for Opus Dei to sue the website, forcing them to be taken down. But the case in Argentina had inspired this group to get organized; if numerary assistants, the weakest members of Opus Dei, could rise up and fight the movement that had abused them, then so could the numeraries. The complaint asked that the Vatican directly intervene in the Work, eradicate its institutionalized system of abuse, and punish those in charge—including Ocáriz, his deputies, and the two bodies that oversaw the men's and the women's sections. "Opus Dei is based on an asymmetric relationship, which encompasses some of the features of a destructive sect," Moya told reporters as he delivered the complaint, adding that there were many good people in the Work, but that they had been induced into doing what they did because they believed that Opus Dei was operating with the full authority of the Church.

Viewed in the context of these developments, Francis's second *motu proprio* in August 2023 had not been altogether unexpected. Despite the papal bombshell, the pastoral trip to Australia continued as planned, as Opus Dei sought to project a message of business as usual—although the question of what that meant for the future of the Work hung over every event. During an appearance at Warrane College, the Opus Dei university residence where abuse of student privacy and safety led to protests in the 1970s, Ocáriz met with a room full of men and began his speech by invoking the story of Jesus's calming the storm. "Do not be afraid!" Ocáriz told the gathering, echoing the words of Christ.

But Ocáriz would soon have further cause for concern. On his first full day back in Sydney, following brief trips to visit Opus Dei centers in Brisbane and Melbourne, a story broke in the *Sydney Morning Herald* about children from supernumerary families in the city being forced to attend gay conversion therapy sessions—and being pressured by Opus Dei priests and their teachers at an Opus Dei school to suppress their sexual orientation. The scandal coincided with an Opus Dei rally at a racecourse that had been planned to showcase the prelature's presence in the country. There, Ocáriz sought to dismiss this latest attack on the prelature by turning to the Gospel. He told the story of the Canaanite woman whose daughter had been tormented by the Devil, who persevered and persevered—even when it seemed that Jesus wasn't going to help her. Ocáriz told the crowd that it was a lesson of perseverance in prayer—even when it feels that God isn't listening, even when we don't see the results we want. He made no mention of the fact that the school in question—along with another Opus Dei school in Sydney—had recently been investigated by the state education authorities, following an exposé by the national broadcaster ABC that laid bare the systematic recruitment, indoctrination, and abuse of young children and teenagers. At Tangara School for Girls, pupils as young as twelve and their parents had been allegedly told that they didn't need to take a cancer-preventing vaccine because the virus which caused it was sexually transmitted, and they would only ever have one sexual partner, their future husband—ignoring the fact that they might contract the virus from him. Teachers passed a piece of sticky tape around the room to demonstrate how having multiple sexual partners made a person dirty and "unusable." Chastity was drummed into the girls, who were made to watch videos and were taught that masturbation was an "objective disorder"—just like homosexuality—and that psychologists who argued it wasn't had been duped. Their chastity was celebrated at graduation in a ceremony where the girls wore identical white dresses symbolizing their purity.

At Redfield College, the school for boys, ABC found students had been encouraged to attend a local numerary residence after class for study supervision, camps, and activities where many of the boys were subjected to aggressive recruitment attempts—even though some were barely teenagers. One boy found a black book at the center with a list of their names, with each boy's weaknesses and what strengths they might offer as potential Opus Dei recruits. The State Premier, who was himself brought up in a supernumerary family and was an alumnus of Redfield College, had been forced to launch the investigation amid the outcry—although he also made it clear that he had been "blessed with a great education" at the Opus Dei school. The education authority, which reported to him, later dropped the investigation.

Rather than distance himself from the schools and the scandal, Ocáriz embraced them, dedicating his final day in Australia to visiting both schools. During his visits, the old origin story was repeated: how a group of faithful parents had spontaneously set up a school and then asked Opus Dei to take over. Nobody mentioned how the construction of both schools had been paid for with more than a million dollars from Banco Popular and Luis Valls-Taberner—or how these two schools were part of a global network of hundreds of Opus Dei schools whose main purpose was generating new recruits.

This dual reality continued when Ocáriz returned to Villa Tevere, where frantic talks began about how best to handle the pressure coming from the Pontiff. Publicly, the prelate emphasized his loyalty to the pope, writing a letter to members stating that Opus Dei was now working closely with the Vatican on revising its statutes. The letter failed to acknowledge the elephant in the room: revising the statutes was yesterday's fight. Indeed, the situation had deteriorated markedly since the pope had first asked for the revision a year earlier. "I thank you and understand your concern for the Work, which belongs to everyone," Ocáriz wrote to the pope. "Let us take advantage of this news to joyfully spread the spirit that we have received from our Lord."

Not everyone close to the Work was so diplomatic. Some of its most vocal sympathizers in Spain and the United States were quick to voice their anger. Salvador Sostres, a controversial newspaper columnist from Barcelona, penned an angry diatribe against the pope. "The attack from Francis against Opus Dei is populist, akin to a guerrilla war," he wrote. "Opus Dei is the elite of the Church, and Francis is going after them because he can't compete with them intellectually—or spiritually. Francis doesn't believe in God, he uses Him for his quest." The article, from such a prominent sympathizer of Opus Dei in its home country, didn't go unnoticed at the Vatican. The head of Opus Dei in Spain published a response stating his disgust at the article and stressing that he had no personal relationship with the author—although he never clarified whether Sostres had any links to Opus Dei. Nor was his disgust sufficient to actually remove another article by Sostres that had been published on the Opus Dei official website.

In the United States, Austin Ruse—a prominent supernumerary in

Washington who had helped organize the National Catholic Prayer Breakfast, and who had dedicated an entire chapter of one of his books to the miracles of Margaret Mary Leo, waded into the debate. "No matter what happens with the Vatican, I'll keep doing Opus Dei," he wrote. When Pope Francis hosted a synod at the Vatican dedicated to modernizing the church, Tim Busch led an event in New York that many felt seemed a throwback to the church of the 1950s. Priests in ornate vestments marched in the center of the city, behind the Eucharist held aloft under a gilded canopy. "We can retake the culture of America," declared the Opus Dei co-operator. While Villa Tevere publicly adhered to its *nothing to see here* stance, it was clear that the papal decree had sent a shockwave through the movement's sympathizers around the world.

As Opus Dei approaches its centenary, its future is more uncertain than at any other time since the Spanish Civil War. The recent allegations heaped upon it are nothing new. But they come at a time when Pope Francis is trying to push through a root-and-branch reform of the Church—ending years of corruption, mismanagement, and systematic cover-up of abuse—in hopes of returning the Church to its original mission. It has become impossible to ignore the clear abuses carried out by Opus Dei in the name of the Church—and in the name of God. Francis has handled the situation with understandable caution: the Work still commands influence, and there are factions in the Church that see it as a reliable ally in the counterrevolution against Francis's reforms.

Given its public declarations of loyalty, the best hope for Opus Dei of reaching its centenary intact hinge on Francis's dying before he can follow through on his clear desire to clip the wings of the Work and end its abusive practices. Now eighty-seven, and in failing health, Opus Dei sees that outcome as possible. While Francis has shown himself willing to act decisively against Opus Dei, his strategy of slowly eroding the movement's power means the end result he envisions may yet be years away—and he may not survive long enough to see the project through. Opus Dei may profess loyalty to the pope, but at the same time it has chosen to cozy up to controversial and destabilizing forces—especially in the United States. Those forces are clearly looking past the current papacy, which they see as a lost cause. Opus Dei is seeking to play both sides; publicly, it declares its love for Francis because it knows that its ability to recruit and perpetuate its abusive institutionalized systems depends on the authority the Church has bestowed upon it.

Yet at the same time, Opus Dei is courting people like Tim Busch. He has been linked to the "Red Hat Report" project, which has contracted with former FBI officers to compile dossiers on all potential candidates for the next pope, with a clear ambition to influence the conclave when it next convenes. Busch and some other conservative figures are optimistic that Francis may well run out of time—that this reforming pope might die, in other words. "I think something important is happening, something not so good," Busch told me when asked about Francis's moves against Opus Dei. "I think he's tightening the noose, but I don't think he's going to have enough time. And then you got to have a question: Is the next pope going to succeed in doing the same thing? Or are they going to back off?" But even the passing of Francis might still leave Opus Dei in peril. In December 2023, Cardinal Juan Luis Cipriani—one of only two remaining Opus Dei cardinals—turned eighty, disqualifying him from voting at the next papal conclave. Cardinal Julian Herranz, the other, is now in his nineties, so he also will not be able to participate in the election of the next pope. And it's unclear what influence Opus Dei now wields among the other electors.

The Church is now at a crossroads. If Opus Dei fails to reform itself along the lines Francis has indicated, then the Vatican could stage an intervention. A throwaway line in the second *motu propio* of August 2023 lays the groundwork for precisely that course of action. The first article in that decree states that the pope can approve—or issue—new statutes for personal prelatures. That looks like the most likely next step. Given how entrenched the Opus Dei position is about maintaining authority over its membership, it's unlikely that the movement will be able to push through the changes the Vatican wants. An intervention, as has already happened with other parts of the Catholic Church, like the Legionaries of Christ, therefore seems inevitable. But an intervention is unlikely to be a panacea, in that its would possibly fail to completely cleanse Opus Dei of the forces that have allowed abuse and control to fester for decades.

There are signs that Opus Dei is already preparing itself for more direct intervention. In November 2023, a deal was signed with the French luxury group LVMH, the owner of dozens of prestigious hotels, as well as iconic trains like the Venice Simplon-Orient-Express, to sell the Castello di Urio, a sumptuous sixteenth-century castle on the banks of Lake Como, that had once been used as a summer retreat by Escrivá. While a sale price was not disclosed, newspapers reported that the purchase and subsequent renovation could cost LVMH more than $100 million. Other grand properties are being sold off in other parts of the world, including in Boston, where the Tiffany mansion bought by Opus Dei in the sixties and later turned into a residence for female numeraries, is currently on the market for $15 million. Liquidating such overt Opus Dei assets and shifting the money to arms-length nonprofits will help ensure that the Vatican—and the thousands of disgruntled numeraries and numerary assistants—will likely never get a penny of the prelature's riches. It is also a way of creating a hidden cache of financial power to continue fighting the guerrilla war to remake society in Escrivá's image. "The destination of the proceeds from the sale will be taken by the owner company, in accordance with its statutes," Opus Dei made clear in a statement after the deal.

So long as Escrivá and Del Portillo continue to be venerated by the Catholic Church, the risk remains that a hardline faction of Opus Dei supporters will steer the organization according to the discredited views and methods of the founder and his successor. A real clean-up of Opus Dei has to mean taking another look at the legacy left by these two important figures. An objective look at the role they played in creating the systemic methods of control over members' lives, which inflicted abuse and caused serious pain for thousands of victims, would almost certainly lead to their being excommunicated—additionally, with Escrivá stripped of his sainthood and Del Portillo stripped of his beatification. For the Catholic Church, such dramatic steps would likely be outside its comfort zone.

If Francis dies before real reform happens—and if his successor proves unwilling or unable to carry on his initiative—then Opus Dei will emerge from its near-death experience invigorated and defiant. Revitalized, backed by its army of donors, the movement will plow forward with its plans to re-Christianize the planet, whether that's what people want or not. Gay marriage, secular education, scientific research, and the arts will fast become its next targets. Given its supporters' unexpected victory over abortion, it's quite possible that Opus Dei and its sympathizers could mastermind equally devastating victories in those areas.

Acknowledgments

THIS BOOK STARTED OUT AS A SERIES OF ARTICLES ABOUT THE COLLAPSE OF Banco Popular at *IFR*, where the editor—my longstanding boss Matthew Davies—has been an unwavering bastion of support for me over the past fifteen years. An old-school hack with a nose for a good story and a stomach to defend his journalists in a fight, Matthew somehow saw my potential and generously carved out a reporter-at-large position for me at the magazine at a time when the travails of the media business were pushing almost every other publication in the opposite direction. He tasked me with a single objective—of writing interesting stories that nobody else was publishing—and sent me to Russia, Saudi Arabia, Japan, and all over Europe to dig into whatever crackpot story idea I came up with. I am eternally grateful for such freedom and support. Without his patronage and encouragement, I would never have made the temporary move back to Madrid in early 2019—and certainly wouldn't have discovered the secrets hidden deep in the carcass of the defunct Banco Popular.

The Valls-Taberner family has been a vital source of information and support throughout this endeavor. Javier, who so generously gave me days and days of his time both in Spain and in Switzerland, and who regaled me with memories of his long life alongside his older brother Luis, provided the vital spark that revitalized what was until then primarily a financial story with an entirely new angle. His wife Cristina and son Luis were equally generous with their time, hospitality, and backing. Various other members of the

Valls-Taberner family have offered their support, too. I was also fortunate enough to speak with dozens of people who worked directly with Luis Valls-Taberner—including his personal secretaries Miguel Ángel Prieto and Ángel Rivera, his bodyguard of many years Armando Guerra, and countless others. While I completely understand that this book might shine an unwelcome spotlight on certain elements of Don Luis's life for those that were close to and who revered him, I sincerely hope they do not read it as a condemnation of him personally. I believe that Luis Valls-Taberner was as much a victim of Opus Dei's machinations as the thousands of others who passed through its abusive system of coercion and control. I believe that Don Luis was, like so many others drawn into the organization, a kind-hearted and devout Catholic seeking to do good in this world—only to be manipulated and pressured into turning over his life, his family, and his bank account to the insatiable demands of the founder and the wider organization. I hope my writing reflects the great admiration that those around him had for Don Luis.

The team at the Archivo Histórico Banco Santander very patiently and professionally handled my unending requests related to the vast Banco Popular papers held in Solares, Spain. Throughout the ever-changing pandemic and travel restrictions, they did everything in their power to facilitate my research, guiding me wisely through the millions of documents held at the archives and offering suggestions for further lines of inquiry. In Pamplona, the team at the University of Navarre kindly assisted in my various visits to trawl through the vast personal archives left by Luis Valls-Taberner. In the United States, Thomas P. Lester kindly dug deep into the historical records of the Archdiocese of Boston for anything that might be of interest, while Jane Freiman did a fantastic job of going through the papers of Antonin Scalia. Countless other public servants right across the United States assisted me with queries and Freedom of Information Act requests—with Allison Kole and Zehava Robbins providing valuable counsel about my various attempts to pry open public records. There were many others who helped me in my work who have asked not to be named—for fear of potential reprisals, or because they thought it could negatively impact their professional lives. This, in itself, speaks volumes to the powerful—and dangerous—influence that Opus Dei and its network of foundations and supporters still exert.

The OpusLibros.org, Opus Dei Awareness Network, and OpusDei-

Exposed Reddit communities were vital sources of contacts, context, and stimulus throughout the project. Made up of hundreds of former members—many of which have been through harrowing experiences of abuse, drugging, and manipulation—the communities play a crucial role in educating the public about the realities of life within Opus Dei and offer critical support to those seeking to leave or trying to recover from their ordeal. Such vital resources only exist thanks to the selfless commitments of these former members—and in the case of OpusLibros.org, a tiny budget that is almost constantly running out. Readers wanting to help survivors and prevent more people from being drawn into the Opus Dei cult would do well to contribute to these communities. I will certainly be offering my support. Such communities operate on the basis of anonymity—former members quite understandably don't want their new, unshackled existences to be defined by the years they spent within the organization—and I wish to uphold that principle in these acknowledgments. During the course of my research, I spoke to literally hundreds of former members through these various communities, and I wish to say a sincere thank you to everyone who has helped me understand life within Opus Dei. This book is dedicated to you all. Particular thanks go out to Sebastián Sal and to the forty-three former numerary assistants in Argentina, many of whom I spoke to.

As a fair-minded journalist whose sole aim is to find out the truth, it would have been remiss of me not to speak with people from inside Opus Dei. Over the past five years, I have dedicated hundreds of hours to speaking with its current members—from supernumeraries who couldn't be further removed from the machinations of the organization, right up to several of Opus Dei's most high-ranking members in Rome. Marco Carroggio, Jack Valero, and Brian Finnerty—spokesmen for the organization in Rome, London, and New York, respectively—were critical in setting up many of those meetings. Mónica Herrero in Rome and Josefina Madariaga in Buenos Aires also arranged various interviews. While I am under no illusion that they—and the dozens of senior Opus Dei members I spoke with—will be unhappy about this book, I hope they recognize that my approach to it and to all our interactions have been at all times professional, driven by nothing other than a desire to understand the truth. I sincerely hope that one day they will be able to read the book with sufficient distance to acknowledge that the serious issues raised merit decisive action, and that they will use the influence they have within the organization to advocate for real change. Thanks also go out to the many bishops, cardinals, and Vaticanologists who helped me understand the politics of the Holy See.

The abuse, manipulation, and machinations of Opus Dei detailed in this book are nothing new, and countless journalists and writers have over the years published exposé after exposé of the way the organization operates. I am particularly indebted to María del Carmen Tapia, Alberto Moncada, Jesús Ynfante, Vladimir Felzmann, John Roche, Eileen Johnson, Robert Hutchison, and also Michael Walsh, who kindly loaned me a large number of books to aid me in my research. In more recent years, Paula Bistagnino in Buenos Aires, Jesús Bastante in Madrid, and Antonia Cundy in London have added to the wealth of evidence against Opus Dei with their diligent and thorough reporting of abuses. Johnny Daukes has written about the sexual and psychological abuse he endured during the years he was connected to Opus Dei. Countless others have shared their experiences through the OpusLibros.org, Opus Dei Awareness Network, and OpusDeiExposed Reddit communities. This book owes much to all of the above. It is my hope that more people will now have the confidence to come forward—so that real criminal cases can be built against the people who allowed this to happen, and so that this can never happen again.

On Leonard Leo and the world of dark money, Lisa Graves and Evan Vorpahl have been indispensable guides. The indefatigable Tom Carter has also been the source of a wealth of material and insights. I have drawn heavily on the peerless reporting of Andy Kroll, Andrew Perez, Heidi Przybyla, Jay Michaelson, and Jane Mayer and am deeply indebted to them. John Gehring and Tom Roberts have helped me better understand the U.S. Catholic Church, while John Allen, Gerard O'Connell, and Massimo Faggioli have been excellent guides to the wider Vatican.

At Simon & Schuster, I could not have hoped for a better editor than Eamon Dolan. Right from our very first conversations, Eamon understood the import and complexity of this story—and saw the potential in the proposal before him. He helped me see the forest through the trees, to refine my hundred-page proposal into a much clearer, concise, and focused plan of action. His guidance, advice, suggestions—and frequent interjections of "VAGUE" in the margins—have made this an immeasurably better book. Thank you for taking this chance on me as a first-time author, Eamon. I will be forever in your debt. I'd also like to thank Larry Hughes, Stephen Bedford, and Rebecca Rozenberg, who have spearheaded the marketing of the book. At Scribe, Molly Slight was one of the first publishers I spoke to and she immediately offered her support. Carmen Esteban Escalante at Planeta has also been an unwavering champion of the project. I am immensely grateful to you both.

At C&W, my agent Richard Pike saw the potential of this story right from the beginning and responded almost instantly to my four-paragraph email pitch with clear enthusiasm: "This seems an incredible story." Over coffee on a rainy October afternoon in London, he attentively listened to me recount the story, walked me through the process of putting together a formal proposal, and patiently sifted through umpteen iterations, offering wise words and encouragement throughout. He has been supported by an excellent team of colleagues, including Saida Azizova, Kate Burton, and César Castañeda Gámez. I am much indebted to Luke Speed, and to Anna Weguelin and Theo Roberts at Curtis Brown. Bradley Hope also gets a mention for being so generous with his time and walking me through how getting a book published actually works. At CAA in New York, I could not have wished for a better agent to represent me in the United States than Andrianna deLone. She somehow convinced all the big publishers there that they needed to take meetings with me. Thank you, Andrianna. Both you and Richard have been wise counsels throughout this whole process.

Countless friends and family members have put me up—and put up with me—during my various work trips to research the book. Miguel Ángel Usoz and Caridad de la Fuente have treated me as one of their own, kindly offering me a bed, a car—and plying me with copious amounts of tortilla and red wine—on my numerous and lengthy trips to the archives in northern Spain. I owe them so much. Mikel and Frantxa did the same in Madrid, while Gary and Kelly kindly welcomed me into their home and ferried me around various appointments in and around New York. Thank you also to the rest of my friends and family who have listened to me bang on about this story for the past five years. I'm going to have to find something else to talk about now. My mother Dorothy passed away right at the start of this project, and I write these words exactly five years since she left us. My father

Jimmy died many years earlier. Not a day goes by when I don't miss the two of you. You were the two most generous people I ever met—neither of you had much, but you would give everything for your children. This book is dedicated to both of you.

Hannah, Emmie, and Alice—what can I say? You are the most wonderful daughters in the whole world. You make me so proud. Thank you for all your smiles, cuddles, and support.

And Maite. The final words have to be dedicated to you. This book would not have been possible without you. You have encouraged, supported, and endured me rabbiting on endlessly about this project for the best part of five years. Without ever once complaining, you have read through every page of this book (often several times) and consistently offered up suggestions for how to improve it. You have endured my unceasing questions about translations and been a critical source of expertise on the political and cultural backdrop to this story. You have endured my mood swings, my self-doubt, and numerous bouts of writer's block with grace, understanding, and care. Thank you for your unwavering support. I am so lucky to have you.

Notes

INTRODUCTION

1 **When Banco Popular suddenly collapsed:** Gareth Gore, "Rushed Popular Resolution Casts Long Shadow over Europe's Banks," *International Financing Review*, June 7, 2019, https://www.ifre.com/story/1586009/rushed-popular-resolution-casts-long-shadow-over-europes-banks-53fvxp7lqv, accessed January 13, 2024.

1 **one of the strongest and most profitable in the world:** Banco Popular topped the league table for the world's top one hundred banks compiled by *Euromoney* three times in the early 1990s.

1 **who had lost hundreds of millions of dollars overnight:** Christopher Spink, "Santander Pressed by Pimco over Banco Popular Sale," *International Financing Review*, April 4, 2018, https://www.ifre.com/story/1494960/santander-pressed-by-pimco-over-banco-popular-sale-2gr14v6f3p, accessed January 13, 2024.

3 **spawning more than a hundred lawsuits:** Gore, "Rushed Popular Resolution."

3 **the 300,000 shareholders:** According to bank records, Popular had 303,251 individual investors at the end of 2016. See *Informe Anual 2016* (Madrid: Banco Popular Español, 2017), 138.

3 **a gentlemen's agreement in the 1940s:** Gabriel Tortella, José María Ortiz-Villajos, and José Luis García Ruiz, *Historia del Banco Popular: La lucha por la independencia* (Madrid: Marcial Pons, 2011), 131.

3 **controlled almost 10 percent of the bank when it collapsed:** According to bank records, Sindicatura de Accionistas del Banco Popular Español owned 9.55 percent of the bank's outstanding share capital at the end of the previous full year. See *Informe Anual 2016*, 139.

3 **a stake worth more than $2 billion at its peak:** Banco Popular's share price climbed above 16 euros in April 2007. At the time, Sindicatura de Accionistas del Banco Popular Español represented more than 100 million shares in the bank. See *Informe Anual 2006* (Madrid: Banco Popular Español, 2007), 65–69.

3 **that it was to be dissolved:** Union Europea de Inversiones stock market filing, July 27, 2017, https://www.cnmv.es/webservices/verdocumento/ver?e=W0hG9W7Lw

%2f0H%2fVpi8oFxjbojc5caDaczWitwUsYwRmRQSRh0dt1K2vXNhAR3mLSV, accessed February 16, 2024.

3 **As much as $100 million a year passed:** This includes money paid in dividends to Union Europea de Inversiones, charitable donations paid to affiliated foundations, and rent paid to another foundation that owned the Popular headquarters. See Chapter Ten, this volume, for details.

4 **who had spent more than forty years at the bank:** Javier Valls-Taberner joined the bank in 1966 and was promoted to the position of co-chairman alongside his brother Luis in 1989. He remained in that position until he was ousted from the bank in 2006.

4 **"They had nicknames for the two of us . . .":** Author interview with Javier Valls-Taberner, November 2019.

5 **Javier had been unceremoniously ousted from the bank:** Luis died on February 25, 2006. His brother Javier was ousted from the bank less than a month later. See Banco Popular stock market filing, March 22, 2006, https://www.cnmv.es/webservices/verdocumento/ver?e=%2bZFQUOBFTyaGJsR6EyGsv3oVWDfesgkpo6eZDnmbdpma3phc%2fKDdGHMm7I9fOOVE, accessed February 16, 2024.

7 **a group of forty-two women in Argentina:** Débora Rey, "Women in Argentina Claim Labor Exploitation by Opus Dei," Associated Press, November 12, 2021, https://apnews.com/article/business-paraguay-europe-argentina-uruguay-43b48ed43c2f7ddebf05ec6203b12d8d, accessed September 6, 2023.

7 **which had bought up Popular's assets following its collapse:** Gareth Gore, "Santander Considered Bidding €1.6bn for Popular Weeks Before Collapse," *International Financing Review*, May 17, 2019, https://www.ifre.com/story/1592384/santander-considered-bidding-16bn-for-popular-weeks-before-collapse-vqwz9ywt2c, accessed February 16, 2024.

7 **someone had been there before him to purge this mysterious cache:** Author interview with José Antonio Gutiérrez Sebares (archivist in Solares), June 2022.

7 **the words "Balance Sheet of International Cooperation" on the front:** See "Balance de Cooperación Internacional" report, with snapshot of spending as of March 1995, AHBPE.

7 **alleged enslavement of the forty-two women in Argentina:** Fundación del Plata, the foundation that ran hospitality schools and various Opus Dei residences implicated in the scandal, was the biggest single recipient of cash from the network linked to the bank during the early 1990s. Asociación para el Fomento de la Cultura, another foundation implicated in the scandal, also received money. Balance de Cooperación International report.

8 **subsidiaries in Switzerland to accounts in Panama, Liechtenstein, and Curacao:** See Chapter Six, this volume, for more details.

8 **an annual tradition of a eucharistic procession:** Kurt Jensen, "New Eucharistic Procession Aims to Bring Christ into the U.S. Capital's Public Square," *Our Sunday Visitor*, May 2, 2023, https://www.oursundayvisitor.com/new-eucharistic-procession-aims-to-bring-christ-into-the-u-s-capitals-public-square/, accessed February 16, 2024.

8 **the Spanish priest gazed intensely up at the golden monstrance:** "2023 CIC Eucharistic Procession," video, May 20, 2023, https://www.youtube.com/watch?v=hBXR4YMSdDw, accessed February 16, 2024.

8 **"I have absolute faith in the many graces God will bestow onto our country . . .":** "Eucharistic Procession in Downtown DC," *Arlington Catholic Herald*, May 11, 2023, https://www.catholicherald.com/article/local/eucharistic-procession-in-down town-dc/, accessed February 16, 2024.

8 **Almost five hundred people had taken time out:** William Murray, "CIC Hosts its First Eucharistic Procession in Downtown Washington," *Catholic Standard*, May 25, 2023, https://cathstan.org/news/local/cic-hosts-its-first-eucharistic-procession-in-down town-washington, accessed February 16, 2024.

9 **made up of eight hundred members and countless sympathizers:** Author interview with Daryl Glick (director of one of the Opus Dei residences in the city), February 2023.

10 **"The Work, as the faithful of Opus Dei call it, is part of the Church":** Fernanda Lopes, "I Like to Think of Opus Dei as a Family of Families," July 13, 2022, https://opusdei.org/en-uk/article/i-like-to-think-of-opus-dei-as-a-family-of-families/, accessed February 16, 2024.

11 **it is officially affiliated with nineteen universities, twelve business schools, 275 elementary and high schools:** Email correspondence with Marco Carroggio (chief spokesperson for Opus Dei globally), February 2024.

12 **which downgraded the institution within the hierarchy of the Church:** See "Apostolic Letter Issued 'Motu Proprio' of the Supreme Pontiff Francis 'Ad Charisma Tuendum,'" July 22, 2022, https://press.vatican.va/content/salastampa/en/bollettino/pubblico/2022/07/22/220722a.html, accessed September 21, 2023.

12 **laying the ground for direct intervention by the Vatican if it fails to reform:** See "Lettera Apostolica in Forma di 'Motu Proprio' del Sommo Pontefice Francesco con La Quale Vengono Modificati i Cann. 295–296 Relativi Alle Prelature Personali," August 8, 2023, https://www.vatican.va/content/francesco/it/motu_proprio/documents/20230808-motu-proprio-prelature-personali.html, accessed September 20, 2023.

1. THE SYNDICATE

15 **the tens of thousands of investors who owned shares in the bank:** *Informe Anual 2003* (Madrid: Banco Popular Español, 2004), 81.

15 **electing instead to hold the meeting effectively:** Author interviews with two people involved in setting up the meeting, July and September 2022.

16 **the last few had been ominous markers for the gradual decline in his health:** Author interviews with Miguel Ángel Prieto (personal assistant to Luis Valls-Taberner, 1998–2004), July and September 2022.

16 **had begun to suffer from dizzy spells and blurred vision:** Prieto interviews.

16 **Don Luis remained conspicuous by his absence:** Author interviews with several Banco Popular employees, July and September 2022.

16 **taking care to remember small details:** Prieto interview, July 2022.

16 **But those walks had all but ceased:** Banco Popular employee interviews.

16 **eleven members of the board were suddenly dismissed en masse:** Banco Popular stock market filing, December 18, 2003, https://www.cnmv.es/portal/HR/Resul tadoBusquedaHR.aspx?division=3&nif=A28000727&page=124, accessed September 15, 2022.

17 **it was selling its entire $400 million stake:** María Jesús Pérez, "La Mutua Madrileña sale del Popular y compra un 1,2% del Santander por 531 millones," *ABC*, April 27, 2004, https://www.abc.es/economia/abci-mutua-sale-popular-y-compra -2por-ciento-santander-millones-200404270300-9621186021002_noticia.html, accessed July 21, 2023.

17 **new alliance that promised an exciting future for both parties:** "Spain's Mutua Madrilena Buys 3 pct of Popular," Reuters, November 5, 2003, accessed July 21, 2023.

17 **more than a billion dollars off the value of Popular:** The share price fell from a high of 50.25 euros in January 2004 to a low of 44.81 euros in May of that year, a fall of 10.8 percent. During the same time period, the broader Spanish IBEX 35 index remained roughly flat. Extrapolating from the bank's 227 million outstanding shares, the fall in value would be equivalent to 1.2 billion euros—or about $1 billion at the time. See *Informe Anual 2004* (Madrid: Banco Popular Español, 2005), 61.

17 **solid support among the board members for Don Luis:** Author interviews with two people involved in setting up the meeting, July and September 2022.

18 **kept Don Luis's speech as short as possible:** Interviews with two people involved in meeting.

18 **Don Luis had delivered the speech without a hitch:** Interviews with two people involved in meeting.

18 **the smaller shareholders:** Interviews with two people involved in meeting.

18 **The room was less than a quarter full—just twenty:** The number of shareholders present is announced in a VHS recording of the 2004 AGM, AHPBE, box 800, item 3.

18 **the more than seventy thousand shareholders:** *Informe Anual 2003* (Madrid: Banco Popular Español, 2004), 81.

18 **Don Luis tripped and fell on the stairs:** Author interviews with several people present, July and September 2022.

18 **The first to break the silence was Ángel Ron:** VHS of 2004 annual shareholder meeting, AHBPE.

18 **"You need to start . . . look, we have it here in the script":** VHS of 2004 annual shareholder meeting, AHBPE.

19 **Aparicio had joined the bank's board at the end of the previous year:** Banco Popular stock market filing, December 18, 2003, https://www.cnmv.es/portal/HR/Resultado BusquedaHR.aspx?division=3&nif=A28000727&page=124, accessed September 15, 2022.

19 **Don Luis had asked people to treat Paco as one of their own:** Author interviews with several Banco Popular employees, July and September 2022.

19 **celibacy, poverty, and obedience:** *1950 Constitutions of Opus Dei*, Part Two, Chapter II, Articles 1–3, republished by The Opus Dei Guidebook, https://sites.google.com/a/

realcatholiconline.org/the-opus-dei-guidebook/statutes-1/1950-constitutions, accessed September 23, 2022. Although the 1950 constitutions were replaced by the 1982 statutes, the former contains a much more detailed list of rules and is to this day considered by most members as the guidance to follow.

19 **he had even banned the few Opus Dei members:** Author interview with anonymous board member, September 2022.

19 **stopped serving meat on Fridays during Lent:** Author interview with anonymous bank executive, September 2022.

20 **Not a great start—it was still morning:** Although the meeting began at 1 p.m., which would be considered afternoon in many countries, in Spain this would certainly still be considered morning, as it is before lunch, which is typically eaten after 2 p.m. Indeed, the board members were scheduled to eat together after the shareholder meeting.

21 **an elevator had been installed and, following some recent falls:** Author interviews and visual confirmation during a visit to the Opus Dei residence where Luis Valls-Taberner lived at the time, July 2022.

21 **they were also part of what Don Luis used to call his *núcleo duro*:** Author interview with a board member and close confidant of Luis Valls-Taberner for many years, July 2022.

21 **mysterious alliance of unidentified investors collectively known as The Syndicate:** *Informe Anual 2003* (Madrid: Banco Popular Español, 2004), 82.

23 **modern, red-brick, residential complex:** Author visit to Mirasierra residence and interviews with residents, July 2022.

23 **had taken vows of poverty, chastity, and obedience to the movement:** *1950 Constitutions of Opus Dei.*

23 **The director of the men's residence had a key to unlock one door:** *Reglamento Interno de la Administración,* 1985, Article 18, subsection 1.

23 **Mixing of genders was strictly prohibited:** *Reglamento Interno de la Administración,* Article 8.

23 **the entire floor of the house in order to avoid accidental encounters:** *Reglamento Interno de la Administración,* Article 46, subsection 2.

23 **Any conversations to coordinate mealtimes or cleaning:** *Reglamento Interno de la Administración,* Article 24.

23 **Even then they weren't allowed to use each other's name:** *Reglamento Interno de la Administración,* Article 25.

23 **it was permitted to pass a note under the door—although it had to be typed and unsigned:** *Reglamento Interno de la Administración,* Article 33.

24 **a mandatory decoration:** *1950 Constitutions of Opus Dei,* Part Two, Chapter IV, 236.

24 **began to change out of his work clothes into something more comfortable:** Author reconstruction of Luis Valls-Taberner's habitual evening routine, drawing on interviews with residents, July 2022.

24 **designed to keep the body in a state of servitude:** *1950 Constitutions of Opus Dei,* 260.

24 **as the irrefutable course of the path that God had laid down for them:** *Vademécum del Gobierno Local,* 2002, 5.

25 **he had a habit of buying books for the residence:** Author interview with residents, July 2022.

25 **newspapers each morning to censor any sensitive material:** *Vademécum del Gobierno Local*, 117.

25 **which were shared with the regional Opus Dei headquarters in Madrid:** *Vademécum del Gobierno Local*, 24.

25 **was required to turn off the gas supply at the mains every night:** *Vademécum del Gobierno Local*, 187.

25 **to keep internal rulebooks under lock and key in his office:** *Vademécum del Gobierno Local*, 24–25.

26 **detailing how much was spent on food:** *Vademécum del Gobierno Local*, 201.

26 **any communications with regional headquarters had to be delivered by hand:** *Vademécum del Gobierno Local*, 20.

26 **neither email nor telephone was to be used to communicate with the regional headquarters:** *Vademécum del Gobierno Local*, 21.

26 **A special department in Rome was in charge of issuing the ratings:** *Guia Bibliografica 2003*, republished by Opus Dei Awareness Network at https://www.opuslibros.org/Index_libros/guia_general.htm, accessed September 22, 2022.

26 **one movie a month—and even then, it had to be something approved by Rome:** *Vademécum del Gobierno Local*, 155–156.

26 **Luis regularly watched movies on the projector in his office:** Author interviews with various people who watched movies with Luis, even as far back as the 1970s.

26 **normally wouldn't have been tolerated among the other residents:** *Vademécum del Gobierno Local*, 7.

26 **a loving act of "fraternal correction":** *Vademécum del Gobierno Local*, 106.

26 **had been specifically told by their superiors to leave him be:** Author interview with one numerary who went on one of the annual courses with him around this time.

27 **his intercession in the financial needs of the movement:** See "Saint Nicholas, Intercessor of Opus Dei," December 5, 2021, https://opusdei.org/en-uk/article/saint-nicholas-intercessor-of-opus-dei/, accessed November 22, 2023.

27 **liberate the founder from any worries about money:** Recollections of Father Escrivá written by Luis Valls-Taberner shortly after the death of the founder, written at Pozoalbero, August 30, 1975, GAPOD (uncataloged).

27 **"my Saint Nicholas":** Author interview with Luis Sánchez Socías, July 2022.

27 **visiting various shrines:** Sánchez Socías interview.

28 **openly discussed among the numerary members themselves:** *Vademécum del Gobierno Local*, 16.

28 **specifically instructed to steer clear of anyone of a nervous disposition:** *Vademécum del Gobierno Local*, 28.

28 **might physically find it difficult to live as part of a "family":** *Vademécum del Gobierno Local*, 28.

28 **parents who had failed to keep their bodies "clean" before marriage:** "Il capo dell'Opus Dei contro gli abusi sessuali," *Giornale di Sicilia*, April 10, 1997, reproduced

at https://www.opuslibros.org/nuevaweb/modules.php?name=News&file=article& sid=7883, accessed February 19, 2024.

28 **Medical check-ups were preferable before anyone was formally admitted:** *Vademécum del Gobierno Local*, 28.

28 **also advised against targeting anyone with bad grades:** *Vademécum del Gobierno Local*, 30.

28 **or anyone who was illegitimate:** *Vademécum del Gobierno Local*, 34.

29 **children could become "aspirant" members:** *Vademécum del Gobierno Local*, 38.

29 **such matters were to be referred to the regional commission for advice:** *Vademécum del Gobierno Local*, 30.

29 **a lecture on etiquette while he peeled an orange using a spoon:** Author interview with various residents who saw similar performances at the residence.

30 **residence for numerary men in Kalorama Heights:** Author interview with Daryl Glick, February 2023.

30 **a four-story mansion built in the 1920s with twelve bedrooms and ten bathrooms:** According to property records held by the District of Columbia Office of Tax and Revenue, accessed November 22, 2023.

30 **boasted the Thai and Yemeni embassies as neighbors:** Author visit to Wyoming House, February 2023.

31 **a couple of days after the American's arrival:** Father C. John McCloskey, "A Eucharistic Recollection of Pope John Paul the Great," https://www.catholicity.com/mc closkey/johnpaulthegreat.html, accessed September 28, 2022.

31 **"I was not fleeing the evil world of Wall Street . . .":** Father C. John McCloskey, "Mother Merrill," https://www.catholicity.com/mccloskey/merrill.html, accessed September 28, 2022.

31 **"I suppose you could also say . . .":** Raymond de Souza, "From Wall Street to the Ivy League," *National Catholic Register*, August 16, 1998, https://www.ncregister.com/in terview/from-wall-street-to-the-ivy-league, accessed September 28, 2022.

31 **ordained at a ceremony at Torreciudad:** Mary Claire Kendall, "Opus Dei Bishop to Be Beatified Saturday," *Aleteia*, September 2014, https://www.catholicity.com/mc closkey/opus-dei-bishop.html, accessed September 28, 2022.

31 **"A liberal Catholic is oxymoronic":** Chris Suellentrop, "The Rev. John McCloskey: The Catholic Church's K Street Lobbyist," *Slate*, August 9, 2002, https://slate.com/ news-and-politics/2002/08/the-catholic-church-s-k-street-lobbyist.html, accessed September 28, 2022.

31 **"the most exotic pagan mission territory":** De Souza, "From Wall Street to the Ivy League."

32 **"small families marked by contraceptive selfishness":** De Souza, "From Wall Street to the Ivy League."

32 **"The values of the secular elite university . . .":** De Souza, "From Wall Street to the Ivy League."

32 **began to meet regularly:** De Souza, "From Wall Street to the Ivy League."

32 **McCloskey was finally kicked out:** James Hitchcock, "Condom, Coercion, and Christianity: A Princeton Tale," *Academic Questions*, 4, no. 1 (Winter 1990–91),

republished at https://www.catholicity.com/mccloskey/princeton.html, accessed September 28, 2022.

32 **found murdered in the basement:** Hitchcock, "Condom, Coercion, and Christianity."

32 **received a phone call:** Joe Feuerherd, "Selling Orthodoxy to Washington Power Brokers," *National Catholic Reporter*, September 5, 2003, https://natcath.org/NCR_Online/archives2/2003c/090503/090503c.htm, accessed September 28, 2022.

32 **personally responsible for the conversion:** Joe Heim, "'Quite a Shock': The Priest Was a D.C. Luminary. Then He Had a Disturbing Fall from Grace," *Washington Post*, January 14, 2019, https://www.washingtonpost.com/local/quite-a-shock-the-priest-was-a-dc-luminary-then-he-had-a-disturbing-fall-from-grace/2019/01/14/99b48700-1453-11e9-b6ad-9cfd62dbb0a8_story.html, accessed accessed September 28, 2022.

33 **several big business names:** Laurie P. Cohen, "Tyco Scandal, Money to Opus Dei?," *Wall Street Journal*, June 4, 2003, https://www.wsj.com/articles/SB105467469545317500, accessed September 28, 2022.

34 **"It's delightful, delicious, the irony":** Feuerherd, "Selling Orthodoxy to Washington Power Brokers."

34 **he had sexually assaulted her:** Michelle Boorstein, "Opus Dei Paid $977,000 to Settle Sexual Misconduct Claim Against Prominent Catholic Priest," *Washington Post*, January 7, 2019, https://www.washingtonpost.com/religion/2019/01/08/opus-dei-paid-settle-sexual-misconduct-claim-against-prominent-catholic-priest/, accessed September 29, 2022.

34 **"He absolutely radiated holiness . . .":** Heim, "'Quite a Shock.'"

35 **"so he could fix it":** Boorstein, "Opus Dei Paid $977,000."

35 **nothing much seemed to happen:** See "Statements Regarding Fr. C. John McCloskey," which confirm that Opus Dei was informed of the allegation in November 2002, and that no limitations were placed on his ministry during the entire period until he left the United States in December 2003, https://opusdei.org/en-us/article/message-from-msgr-thomas-bohlin-2/, accessed November 2, 2023.

35 **"I love Opus Dei . . .":** Boorstein, "Opus Dei Paid $977,000."

35 **encouraged by another priest to seek legal action:** Boorstein, "Opus Dei Paid $977,000."

35 **McCloskey had a cover story for anyone who asked:** Father John McCloskey, "American Lessons from Europe's Fall," *National Catholic Register*, May 2004, https://www.catholicity.com/mccloskey/americanlessons.html, accessed November 2, 2023.

35 **"It's increasingly seen as more mainstream and more normal . . .":** Frank Bruni, "New Saint Reflects Lay Group's New Influence," *New York Times*, October 3, 2002, https://www.nytimes.com/2002/10/03/world/new-saint-reflects-lay-group-s-new-influence.html, accessed November 2, 2023.

36 **at a cost of $70 million:** According to tax records, in addition to the $5,095,600 spent on purchasing the six properties, Murray Hill Place, Inc., subsequently spent $57,818,675 on building works and an additional $6,918,761 on furnishing and equipment between 1995 and 2001.

36 **a magistrate ordered a raid on the French headquarters of Opus Dei in Paris:** Vladimir de Gmeline, "Opus Dei: l'enquête interdite . . . ," *Marianne*, April 15, 2017, https://www.marianne.net/societe/opus-dei-l-enquete-interdite, accessed February 19, 2024.

2. THE FAMILY BUSINESS

37 **José María Escrivá:** José María is a common compound name in Spain. While Escrivá decided to amalgamate them into the unusual Josemaría form from the 1960s onward, possibly with a view to posterity, in his earlier years he nonetheless used the standard form, which appears on his birth certificate.

37 **with Holy Week fast approaching, he should report for duty as soon as possible:** Andrés Vázquez de Prada, *El Fundador del Opus Dei I* (Madrid: Ediciones Rialp, 2010), 206.

37 **"they sent me there to screw with me":** Vázquez de Prada, *El Fundador*, 209.

37 **lasted only six weeks:** Vázquez de Prada, *El Fundador*, 184.

38 **who mockingly called him "the little gentleman":** Vázquez de Prada, *El Fundador*, 117.

38 **who spent his Sundays promenading along the river:** Vázquez de Prada, *El Fundador*, 62.

38 **"reward them on earth, since he won't be able to reward them in eternity . . .":** Vázquez de Prada, *El Fundador*, 70.

38 **a pretext to secure the relevant permissions:** See Vázquez de Prada, *El Fundador*, 202–207.

39 **a pathway to a better life:** Jesús Ynfante, *La Prodigiosa Aventura del Opus Dei* (Paris: Ruedo Ibérico, 1970), 4.

39 **"I had never thought of becoming a priest . . .":** Vázquez de Prada, *El Fundador*, 92.

39 **their poverty was relative only to the good life they had once enjoyed:** A telling detail in the official biographies of Escrivá is that neither his mother nor his older sister Carmen, who trained as a schoolteacher in Logroño, seems to have held a job during these years—despite their supposed dire straits. It seems probable that they had another source of income, perhaps from the family property they would later sell. And, while the priestly stipend of around five pesetas per Mass was low by the standards of the day, it was sufficient to pay room and board at the lodgings where Escrivá stayed. Later, he supplemented this income with teaching. Some workers, such as waiters, earned as little as one peseta a day despite putting in eight hours of work. See "El salario y la jornada en Madrid, Año de 1929," from the *Anuario 1930*, published by the Instituto Nacional de Estadística at https://www.ine.es/inebaseweb/pdfDispacher.do?td=45719.

39 **schools and soup kitchens:** Vázquez de Prada, *El Fundador*, 240.

40 **a defender of the brutally unjust political order:** Paul Preston, *The Spanish Civil War* (London: Harper Perennial, 2006), 27.

40 **Escrivá threw himself wholeheartedly into these "apostolic missions":** Preston, *Spanish Civil War*, 242.

40 **completed two courses toward his doctorate:** Vázquez de Prada, *El Fundador*, 551.

40 **took on another job:** Vázquez de Prada, *El Fundador,* 235–239.

40 **able to afford an apartment:** Vázquez de Prada, *El Fundador*, 235.

40 **well-to-do neighborhood:** Vázquez de Prada, *El Fundador*, 250.

40 **he started to fall behind:** For a detailed breakdown of his academic record, see Vázquez de Prada, *El Fundador*, 540–543 and 550–551.

40 **"because you were more dead than alive":** Vázquez de Prada, *El Fundador*, 21.

41 **Escrivá saw the outlines of a new way to serve God:** Vázquez de Prada, *El Fundador*, 252.

41 **"never—no way—will there be women in Opus Dei":** Vázquez de Prada, *El Fundador*, 273.

41 **"The extraordinary for us is the ordinary . . .":** Vázquez de Prada, *El Fundador*, 257.

41 **The idea for a lay brotherhood was nothing new:** See Michael Walsh, *The Secret World of Opus Dei* (London: Grafton Books, 1990), 32–34.

41 **"It would take the imagination of a novelist who is a raving lunatic . . .":** Vázquez de Prada, *El Fundador*, 293.

42 **his idea for Opus Dei with those around him:** José Luis González Gullón and John F Coverdale, *Historia del Opus Dei* (Madrid: Ediciones Rialp, 2022), 38.

42 **his previous opposition to women joining Opus Dei:** González Gullón and Coverdale, *Historia del Opus Dei*, 38.

42 **"I received an illumination about the entire Work . . .":** Vázquez de Prada, *El Fundador*, 252.

42 **asked one dying woman to intercede for him:** Vázquez de Prada, *El Fundador*, 267.

42 **"Yesterday evening, while walking down the street . . .":** Vázquez de Prada, *El Fundador*, 263.

42 **apply for a job as a civil servant:** *Gaceta de Madrid* 267 (September 24, 1929): 1924, accessed at https://www.boe.es/datos/pdfs/BOE/1929/267/A01923-01924.pdf on October 17, 2022.

42 **generous salary of 2,500 pesetas a year:** *Gaceta de Madrid* 197 (July 16, 1929): 370, accessed at https://www.boe.es/datos/pdfs/BOE/1929/197/A00370-00372.pdf on October 17, 2022.

43 **"May the Immaculate Virgin defend this poor Spain . . .":** Vázquez de Prada, *El Fundador*, 312.

43 **a shadowy group of Jews, Masons, and Communists:** Preston, *Spanish Civil War*, 49.

43 **alleged killing of a taxi driver:** Hugh Thomas, *The Spanish Civil War* (London: Penguin Books, 1965), 58.

43 **"The persecution has begun":** Vázquez de Prada, *El Fundador*, 313.

43 **the position was temporary and offered no pay:** Thomas, *Spanish Civil War*, 324.

44 **a falling out with the women at the Apostolic Ladies:** Thomas, *Spanish Civil War*, 324.

44 **an example to others, an inspiration for how everyone:** José María Escrivá, *Singuli Dies*, March 24, 1930, Article 4.

44 **importance of prayer, of standing firm against temptation, of remaining faithful:** José María Escrivá, *Videns Eos*, March 24, 1931, Articles 21, 23, and 47.

44 **complete loyalty to the movement:** José María Escrivá, *Res Omnes*, January 9, 1932, Articles 4 and 71.

44 **this message had been misunderstood by Church scholars:** José María Escrivá, *Res Omnes*, Article 91.

44 **"You don't come to the Work in search of something . . .":** Escrivá, *Res Omnes*, Article 85.

44 **who had recently opened an academic academy:** Ynfante, *La Prodigiosa Aventura*, 15.

44 **he was outlining a battle plan for an "army" of the faithful:** Escrivá referred to the membership of Opus Dei as an "army" and a "militia" of "soldiers" several times in the foundational documents he wrote. See *Videns Eos*, March 24, 1931, Article 54; *Vos Autem*, July 16, 1933, Article 3; *Instrucción acerca del espíritu sobrenatural de la Obra de Dios*, March 19, 1934, Article 45; and *Instrucción sobre el modo de hacer proselitismo*, April 1, 1934, Article 9.

45 **"I need to give up everything . . .":** Vázquez de Prada, *El Fundador*, 443.

45 **he asked for the name to remain a secret:** González Gullón and Coverdale, *Historia del Opus Dei*, 56.

45 **around a hundred students passed through its doors:** González Gullón and Coverdale, *Historia del Opus Dei*, 57.

46 **asked them to begin calling him** *Padre***:** González Gullón and Coverdale, *Historia del Opus Dei*, 59.

46 **"instructions" for his small but growing membership:** The first, titled *Instrucción acerca del espíritu sobrenatural de la Obra de Dios* (Instruction Concerning the Supernatural Spirit of the Work of God) was dated March 19, 1934, almost two months to the day since the DYA academy officially opened its doors.

46 **the "tempestuous times" they were living through:** Escrivá, *Instrucción acerca del espíritu*, Article 8.

46 **an additional duty required of his followers—action:** Escrivá, *Instrucción acerca del espíritu*, Article 32.

46 **"a rising militia":** Escrivá, *Instrucción acerca del espíritu*, Article 45.

46 **"apostles carrying out the orders of Christ":** Escrivá, *Instrucción acerca del espíritu*, Article 27.

46 **"The disease is extraordinary—and the medicine is just as extraordinary . . .":** Escrivá, *Instrucción acerca del espíritu*, Article 42.

46 **Instruction Concerning How to Proselytize:** José María Escrivá, *Instrucción sobre el modo de hacer proselitismo*, April 1, 1934.

47 **to focus their efforts on young people:** Escrivá, *Instrucción acerca del espíritu*, Article 44.

47 **wary of people that asked too many questions:** Escrivá, *Instrucción acerca del espíritu*, Article 46.

47 **planting seeds in the mind of the person being targeted:** Escrivá, *Instrucción acerca del espíritu*, Article 15.

47 **as a pretext for getting people together:** Escrivá, *Instrucción acerca del espíritu*, Article 86.

47 **"Never—ever!—try to capture a group . . .":** Escrivá, *Instrucción acerca del espíritu*, Article 18.

47 **"Instruct the new ones to** *shut up* **. . .":** Escrivá, *Instrucción acerca del espíritu*, Article 41.

47 **distance themselves from their families:** Escrivá, *Instrucción acerca del espíritu*, Article 25.

47 **he encouraged his followers to invent a pretext for the meeting:** Escrivá, *Instrucción acerca del espíritu*, Article 81.

47 **They were to target men at the top of their field:** Escrivá, *Instrucción acerca del espíritu*, Article 66.

47 **fill internal roles within the organization:** Escrivá, *Instrucción acerca del espíritu*, Article 67.

48 **program of spiritual life:** Vázquez de Prada, *El Fundador*, 410.

48 **used the discipline three times a week:** For a detailed breakdown of his mortification practices, see Vázquez de Prada, *El Fundador*, 515.

48 **"It is precisely against gluttony . . .":** Vázquez de Prada, *El Fundador*, 521.

48 **had to ban him from fasting:** Vázquez de Prada, *El Fundador*.

48 **to muffle the cracks of the whip:** Vázquez de Prada, *El Fundador*, 462 and 472.

49 **"A student residence is essential . . .":** Vázquez de Prada, *El Fundador*, 459.

49 **"Classes have started at DYA . . .":** Vázquez de Prada, *El Fundador*, 464.

49 **not a single student signed up:** Vázquez de Prada, *El Fundador*, 468.

50 **name him as the patron saint:** Vázquez de Prada, *El Fundador*, 471.

50 **"The Enslavement":** *Esclavitud* in Spanish. The name of the ceremony was later changed to the less polemic *Fidelidad*, or Fidelity. For more on the ceremony, see Vázquez de Prada, *El Fundador*, 475.

50 **one hundred and fifty students:** González Gullón and Coverdale, *Historia del Opus Dei*, 62.

51 **One architecture student who had put down painting as a hobby:** *Interview with Miguel Fisac*, 13–14.

51 **any talk of politics was banned:** González Gullón and Coverdale, *Historia del Opus Dei*, 67.

51 **setting up a new company:** Vázquez de Prada, *El Fundador*, 506.

52 **the purchase of an entire building:** González Gullón and Coverdale, *Historia del Opus Dei*, 67.

52 **"Madrid? Valencia? Paris? The world!":** Vázquez de Prada, *El Fundador*, 510.

52 *Instruction for Directors:* José María Escrivá, *Instrucción para los directores*, May 31, 1936.

52 **local directors were required to write everything down:** Escrivá, *Instrucción para los directores*, Articles 69, 70, and 71.

52 **read the personal correspondence of anyone living at the residence:** Escrivá, *Instrucción para los directores*, Articles 75 and 76.

52 **remain silent about any "contradictions":** Escrivá, *Instrucción para los directores*, Article 58.

52 **"People who don't belong to the Work don't have the spirit of Opus Dei . . .":** Escrivá, *Instrucción para los directores*, Article 35.

53 **"an apostolate that will go unnoticed":** Escrivá, *Instrucción para los directores*, Article 66.

53 **"no one, absolutely no one . . .":** Thomas, *Spanish Civil War*, 185.

53 **began to notice unusual activity on the street below:** Andrés Vázquez de Prada, *El Fundador del Opus Dei II* (Madrid: Ediciones Rialp, 2003), 12.

53 **Five hours of fighting followed:** Thomas, *Spanish Civil War*, 207.

54 **stray bullets ricocheted off the walls:** Vázquez de Prada, *El Fundador II*, 12.

54 **dozens of churches were set on fire:** Thomas, *Spanish Civil War*, 207.

54 **He was the first to leave:** Vázquez de Prada, *El Fundador II*, 12–13.

54 **called the residence to check on his followers:** The fact that the Escrivás had a telephone in their apartment is future proof that their finances were far from dire. They also had a maid.

54 **asked his followers to run errands for him:** For a detailed diary of the first days of the war, see Vázquez de Prada, *El Fundador II*, 864–868.

54 **He also began to hear talk of priests being rounded up:** Vázquez de Prada, *El Fundador II*, 14.

55 **he went to the home of a young professor:** Vázquez de Prada, *El Fundador II*, 22.

55 **eight different homes:** González Gullón and Coverdale, *Historia del Opus Dei*, 71.

55 **good reason to be scared:** González Gullón and Coverdale, *Historia del Opus Dei*, 71.

55 **"I told the driver that the person in the back seat was mentally ill...":** Vázquez de Prada, *El Fundador II*, 36.

55 **Escrivá spent five months in the asylum:** For more detail on his stay, see Vázquez de Prada, *El Fundador II*, 37–55.

55 **more than ten thousand people:** González Gullón and Coverdale, *Historia del Opus Dei*, 73.

56 **assigned numbers 23 and 92, respectively:** González Gullón and Coverdale, *Historia del Opus Dei*, 66.

56 **He claimed one million pesetas in damages:** González Gullón and Coverdale, *Historia del Opus Dei*, 81.

56 **violent acts of mortification:** González Gullón and Coverdale, *Historia del Opus Dei*, 92.

57 **The founder would leave behind his mother, sister, brother, and six of his followers:** González Gullón and Coverdale, *Historia del Opus Dei*, 269.

57 **"I supposed they tried to find me...":** *Interview with Miguel Fisac*, 4.

57 **"Deo gratias! Deo gratias!":** *Interview with Miguel Fisac*, 236.

58 **but received only seven responses:** *Interview with Miguel Fisac*, 298.

58 **attending a women's sewing bee:** González Gullón and Coverdale, *Historia del Opus Dei*, 79.

58 **implored them to push the claim for compensation:** Vázquez de Prada, *El Fundador II*, 317.

58 **asked them to send him money:** Vázquez de Prada, *El Fundador II*, 341.

58 **"I need a wee million...":** Vázquez de Prada, *El Fundador II*, 302.

59 **defiantly wearing his cassock and holding out his crucifix:** Vázquez de Prada, *El Fundador II*, 426.

59 **no heating, hot water, medicine, or surgical dressings:** Thomas, *Spanish Civil War*, 737.

59 **what he called "the family business":** Vázquez de Prada, *El Fundador II*, 299.

59 **two had been killed and another seven had left the movement:** González Gullón and Coverdale, *Historia del Opus Dei*, 81.

3. AN AUTOGRAPH FROM THE POPE

60 **a priest who used lights to hypnotize the innocent young men:** Andrés Vázquez de Prada, *El Fundador del Opus Dei II* (Madrid: Ediciones Rialp, 2003), 515.

60 **Opus Dei members being nailed to a huge wooden cross:** Vázquez de Prada, *El Fundador II*, 666.

60 **to station priests on the other side of the street:** Joan Estruch, *Saints and Schemers: Opus Dei and Its Paradoxes* (New York: Oxford University Press, 1995), 115.

60 **they paid visits to the families:** Vázquez de Prada, *El Fundador II*, 579.

60 **a diet of conspiracy theories constantly fed to them by the Franco regime:** Paul Preston, *A People Betrayed: A History of Corruption, Political Incompetence and Social Division in Modern Spain 1874–2018* (London: William Collins, 2020), 341.

60 **women who had been raped and had their children stolen:** Preston, *People Betrayed*, 334.

61 **"If you want to take up orders . . .":** Author interviews with Javier Valls-Taberner (younger brother of Luis), April and November 2019.

61 **returning to the city dressed as peasants:** For more on the family's escape, see Gonzalo Fernández de la Mora, *Semblanza de Luis Valls-Taberner* (2000), republished at https://www.luisvallstaberner.com/wp-content/uploads/2014/02/Semblanza -LVT-FERNANDEZ-DE-LA-MORA-2000.pdf, accessed April 17, 2024.

61 **speaking tours of Nazi Germany and Latin America:** José María Mas Solench, *Fernando Valls-Taberner: Una vida entre la historia y la política* (Barcelona: Planeta, 2004), 94–99.

61 **still reeling from the sudden death of his beloved father:** Javier Valls-Taberner interviews.

62 **on his bike to play hockey or polo:** Fernández de la Mora, *Semblanza de Luis Valls-Taberner*, 4.

62 **El Palau's shabbiness:** For more on El Palau, see Josep Masabeu, *Escrivá de Balaguer a Catalunya, 1913–1974* (Barcelona: Publicacions de l'Abadia de Montserrat, 2015).

62 **export licenses and military promotions were doled out:** Preston, *Spanish Holocaust*, 333.

62 **they chose the judge, the prosecutor, and the defense lawyer:** Preston, *Spanish Holocaust*, 336.

62 **he had decided to join Opus Dei:** Letter from Luis Valls-Taberner to Father Escrivá on the anniversary of six months in Opus Dei, October 5, 1945, GAPOD (uncataloged).

63 **Franco made religious studies compulsory:** Michael Walsh, *The Secret World of Opus Dei* (London: Grafton Books, 1990), 42–43.

63 **rented an apartment in Madrid:** For more on Opus Dei's immediate postwar expansion, see Vázquez de Prada, *El Fundador II*, chapter 12.

63 **reviving his system of report cards:** José Luis González Gullón and John F Coverdale, *Historia del Opus Dei* (Madrid: Ediciones Rialp, 2022), 93.

63 **weekend trips to other Spanish cities to target students there:** In the first academic year after the war, Opus Dei members made sixty such weekend trips to eleven cities across Spain; see González Gullón and Coverdale, *Historia del Opus Dei*, 92–95.

63 **special study weeks:** González Gullón and Coverdale, *Historia del Opus Dei*, 94.

63   **"I think we will end up having to bless the war . . .":** Vázquez de Prada, *El Fundador II*, 431.

63   **Opus Dei had grown to almost two hundred and fifty members:** González Gullón and Coverdale, *Historia del Opus Dei*, 107.

64   **The architecture students among them would organize sketching trips to interesting sites:** Letter from Luis Valls-Taberner to Escrivá, April 14, 1947, GAPOD (uncataloged).

64   **supposed to live their lives:** José María Escrivá, *Instrucción para la obra de San Miguel*, December 8, 1941.

64   **Escrivá made clear to the directors:** José María Escrivá, *Instrucción para los directores*, Articles 69, 70, and 71.

64   **weekly "chat" they were supposed to have with their director:** Escrivá, *Instrucción para la obra de San Miguel*, Article 20.

64   **"During the chat, the Lord shines a light to show us . . .":** Escrivá, *Instrucción para la obra de San Miguel*, Article 20.

65   **"Don't leave your work for tomorrow":** José María Escrivá, *The Way*, 15, republished at https://escriva.org/en/camino/, accessed April 17, 2024.

65   **"Get used to saying no":** Escrivá, *The Way*, 5.

65   **a modern, innovative, and avant-garde offshoot of the Church:** Escrivá, *The Way*, 22.

65   **requests to give retreats and formation classes all around the country:** For a detailed record of Escrivá's visits across Spain during this period, see Vázquez de Prada, *El Fundador II*, Appendix XXII.

65   **"absolutely" aligned with those of the regime:** See AFNFF, roll 228, document 27198.

65   **"very loyal":** AFNFF.

65   **a private, six-day retreat for himself and his wife at the El Pardo palace:** Vázquez de Prada, *El Fundador II*, 895.

65   **he began traveling by air:** Vázquez de Prada, *El Fundador II*, 592.

65   **moved into a three-story mansion:** González Gullón and Coverdale, *Historia del Opus Dei*, 96.

65   **"That's their business":** Vázquez de Prada, *El Fundador II*, 705.

65   **applied to change his surname:** Walsh, *Secret World of Opus Dei*, 21.

65   **Escrivá began to draw up "instructions" for a new class of membership:** Escrivá, *Instrucción para la obra de San Gabriel*, May 1941.

66   **"mobilization of souls":** Escrivá, *Instrucción para la obra de San Gabriel*, Article 5.

66   **"paganized world":** Escrivá, *Instrucción para la obra de San Gabriel*, Article 17.

66   **"the spirit of Christianity, which will permeate absolutely everything in the world":** Escrivá, *Instrucción para la obra de San Gabriel*, Article 7.

66   **to anyone else without express permission:** Escrivá, *Instrucción para la obra de San Gabriel*, Article 27.

66   **tasked with infiltrating every element of society:** Escrivá, *Instrucción para la obra de San Gabriel*, Article 101.

66   **"the plans of the enemies of Christ":** Escrivá, *Instrucción para la obra de San Gabriel*, Article 30.

66   **cultural, social, and government institutions as part of their mission:** Escrivá, *Instrucción para la obra de San Gabriel*, Article 101.

66 **"foment the multiplication of numerary vocations":** Escrivá, *Instrucción para la obra de San Gabriel*, Article 10.

66 **"to America, to Africa, to Australia":** Escrivá, *Instrucción para la obra de San Gabriel*, Article 138.

66 **"we first target the intellectuals . . .":** Vázquez de Prada, *El Fundador II*, 506.

67 **reported to the Special Tribunal for the Repression of Masonry:** González Gullón and Coverdale, *Historia del Opus Dei*, 106.

67 **a designation that could be easily handed out at diocese level:** Walsh, *Secret World of Opus Dei*, 47.

67 **sent him documents outlining what Opus Dei was:** González Gullón and Coverdale, *Historia del Opus Dei*, 98.

67 **"I have never known a chaste Mason yet":** Walsh, *Secret World of Opus Dei*, 45.

67 **should sign up to fight for the Nazis:** Alberto Moncada, *Historia Oral del Opus Dei* (Barcelona: Plaza & Janes Editores, 1987), 18.

68 **since they were but a few:** Moncada, *Historia Oral del Opus Dei*, 18.

68 **Escrivá had allowed them to take confession with other priests:** *"Es menester —aprovecho este momento para deciros algo que no es un mandato: es un consejo imperativo—, es menester que tengáis completa libertad para confesaros con quien queráis. Pero que vuestro director espiritual sea siempre un sacerdote de la Obra,"* José María Escrivá, *Instrucción sobre el modo de hacer proselitismo*, April 1, 1934.

68 **a separate body called the Priestly Society of the Holy Cross:** For more on this, see Vázquez de Prada, *El Fundador II*, chapter 14.

69 **Del Portillo's plane was almost shot down:** Vázquez de Prada, *El Fundador II*, 748.

69 **they were not to use the title "Father":** María del Carmen Tapia, *Beyond the Threshold* (New York: Continuum, 1997), 80.

69 **compiled its own report on Opus Dei:** González Gullón and Coverdale, *Historia del Opus Dei*, 106.

69 **"You and I are effectively following the orders of a King . . .":** José María Escrivá, *Instrucción sobre el modo de hacer proselitismo*, April 1, 1934.

69 **persuaded his mother to make a large contribution:** Letter from Luis Valls-Taberner to Escrivá, May 15, 1947, GAPOD (uncataloged).

70 **The city appeared majestically on the horizon:** For more on the journey to Rome, see Andrés Vázquez de Prada, *El Fundador del Opus Dei III* (Madrid: Ediciones Rialp, 2003), 25–29.

70 **the lit window of the Pope's private library:** Vázquez de Prada, *El Fundador III*, 28.

70 **"I have a handwritten blessing from the Holy Father . . .":** Vázquez de Prada, *El Fundador III*, 33.

71 **three numeraries and five "numerary servants" be sent out:** Vázquez de Prada, *El Fundador III*, 33.

71 **Numerary servants were a new development in Opus Dei:** Clause 440.2 of the 1950 Opus Dei constitution specifically defines these "numerary servants" as women "dedicated to the manual work or the domestic duties of the houses of the institution." Republished at https://www.opus-info.org/index.php/Constituciones_del_Opus_Dei_1950#Cap%C3%ADtulo_I:_De_su_modalidad,_su_fin_y_sus_miembros, accessed June 30, 2023.

71   **through cheap or even semi-slave labor:** Tapia, *Beyond the Threshold*, 66.

71   **"The numerary servants—I really mean this . . .":** Vázquez de Prada, *The Founder of Opus Dei: The Life of St. Josemaría Escrivá* (New York: Scepter, 2003), 2:444. This quotation has been removed from the original Spanish version of this book.

71   **"Before she 'only' peeled potatoes, but now she attains holiness by peeling potatoes":** Escrivá, *Furrow*, 498, republished at https://escriva.org/en/surco/, accessed April 17, 2024.

71   **Hitler had been unjustly accused:** Vladimir Felzmann, *A Journey to Eternity: My Years in Opus Dei 1959–1982* (Hartpury, UK: All Squared, 2023), 33.

72   **for being controlling, inflexible, and derogatory:** Moncada, *Historia Oral del Opus Dei*, 24–25.

72   **a critical organ in the Vatican's own fight against Marxism:** Robert Hutchison, *Their Kingdom Come: Inside the Secret World of Opus Dei* (London: Transworld, 1997), 103.

72   **"In Rome, I lost my innocence":** Vázquez de Prada, *El Fundador III*, 148.

72   **a sanctification of the kind of scheming:** Estruch, *Saints and Schemers*, 140.

72   **no more than the personal project of an unknown priest:** Estruch, *Saints and Schemers*, 112.

73   **a pledge before God to obey three strict conditions:** González Gullón and Coverdale, *Historia del Opus Dei*, 161.

73   **trying to recruit his brothers and sisters:** Letter from Luis Valls to Escrivá, May 14, 1950, GAPOD (uncataloged).

73   **persuading one of his relatives to donate a house they owned:** Letter from Luis Valls to Escrivá, May 14, 1950, GAPOD (uncataloged).

73   **rumored to have a large inheritance:** A report compiled on Luis by the reputable analytics firm Dun & Bradstreet in the early 1960s estimated his wealth at seventy-five million pesetas. Much of this was derived from family businesses inherited on the death of his father, according to the reports. See AGUN, collection 299, box 2, folder 1.

73   **invited Luis to accompany him:** Luis is photographed with Escrivá at the abbey in a photograph dated May 1948. Their names are on the back. AGUN, collection 299, box 14, folder 3.

74   **in 1949 Luis moved to Madrid:** Letter from Luis Valls to Escrivá, May 2, 1949, GAPOD (uncataloged).

74   **a shopwindow for Opus Dei:** González Gullón and Coverdale, *Historia del Opus Dei*, 138.

74   **a new job as head of publications:** Letter from José María Albareda Herrera, secretary general of the Research Council, to Luis Valls-Taberner, July 1949. AGUN, collection 299, box 125, folder 4.

74   **"the essential ideas that have inspired our Glorious Movement . . .":** Constitutional Charter of the Research Council, November 24, 1939, reproduced at https://www.boe.es/datos/pdfs/BOE/1939/332/A06668-06671.pdf, accessed April 17, 2024.

74   **almost 260 million pesetas in funding:** Hutchison, *Their Kingdom Come*, 92.

75   **made friends with the future education minister:** Walsh, *Secret World of Opus Dei*, 44.

75   **one of every sixteen:** González Gullón and Coverdale, *Historia del Opus Dei*, 103.

75 **took advantage of their overseas stays to put down roots:** González Gullón and Coverdale, *Historia del Opus Dei*, 103.

75 **instructed by his Opus Dei superiors to mark up his contracts:** Moncada, *Historia Oral del Opus Dei*, 33–34.

75 **"It really ate at my conscience . . .":** Moncada, *Historia Oral del Opus Dei*, 34.

75 **overrun with members of Opus Dei:** María del Carmen Tapia joined the Research Council shortly after Luis and wrote extensively about the prevalence of Opus Dei members at the institute. "Almost everybody on the top levels here at the Council is a member," she was told by her colleagues there. See Tapia, *Beyond the Threshold*, 10–12.

75 **a generous salary of ten thousand pesetas a year:** The average industrial worker earned about twelve pesetas a day—equivalent to around 3,000 pesetas a year—around this time. See Pedro González, "La depresión de la autarquía," *Público*, April 3, 2009, https://www.publico.es/actualidad/depresion-autarquia-1.html, accessed November 17, 2022.

75 **Luis had begun to fall behind in his studies:** Letter from Luis Valls to Escrivá, May 14, 1950, GAPOD (uncataloged).

76 **Escrivá's demands:** Fisac visited Escrivá several times in Rome. "He became more and more convinced of his own importance," he said. "Throughout the years I lived with him, this conceit increased." See *An Interview with Miguel Fisac* (Pittsfield, MA: Opus Dei Awareness Network, 2000), 28.

76 **enormous gates that led into a garden:** Vázquez de Prada, *El Fundador III*, 90.

76 **come in more than ten times over budget, costing well over a billion lira:** The purchase of the palace cost fifty million lira in 1947. Some small modifications were done in the first few months. More extensive work began in June 1949, and was initially expected to cost around ten million lira, but soon took on a "new level of dimensions" and a second contract had to be signed for more than ten times that amount. According to a study by Alfredo Méndiz, by the time the works were completed in 1960, "it would be closer to reality to add another zero" to the ten-times overspending, bringing the cost of the works to well over a billion lira. See Alfredo Méndiz, "Orígenes y primera historia de Villa Tevere. Los edificios de la sede central del Opus Dei en Roma (1947–1960)," in *Studia et Documenta* (Rome: Istituto Storico San Josemaría Escrivá, 2017), 11:153–225.

76 **two new floors added, which placed such a stress on the structure that additional support had to be added:** Méndiz, "Orígenes y primera historia de Villa Tevere," 205.

76 **He decided he would also need:** Méndiz, "Orígenes y primera historia de Villa Tevere."

76 **he had already divided the world up into seven separate regions:** González Gullón and Coverdale, *Historia del Opus Dei*, 164.

76 **six million pesetas:** Hutchison, *Their Kingdom Come*, 94.

76 **a six-month tour of the Americas:** González Gullón and Coverdale, *Historia del Opus Dei*, 164.

76 **signing off on the admission of supernumeraries at the beginning of 1948:** Vázquez de Prada, *El Fundador III*, 126–132.

77 **almost seven hundred people:** González Gullón and Coverdale, *Historia del Opus Dei*, 168.

77 **demanded up to three million lira every couple of weeks:** Méndiz, "Origenes y primera historia de Villa Tevere," 205.

77 **the stress of finding enough money left him unable to sleep:** Méndiz, "Origenes y primera historia de Villa Tevere," 207.

77 **requesting eight million pesetas of public funds:** Letter from Álvaro del Portillo to the Minister of Foreign Affairs, July 5, 1949, AFNFF, roll 110, document 12063.

77 **eventually donated one and a half million pesetas:** Méndiz, "Origenes y primera historia de Villa Tevere," 205.

77 **stayed in Italy for two weeks:** Stamps in his passport show him entering Italy on June 9 and leaving on June 23. AGUN, collection 299, box 1, folder 6.

77 **sleeping at Villa Tevere:** Work correspondence sent to Luis during his stay in Italy is sent to Via Bruno Buozzi 73, the address of Villa Tevere. AGUN, collection 299, box 125, folder 4.

77 **Luis was clearly impacted by his trip to Rome:** Letter from Luis Valls to Escrivá, July 20, 1950, GAPOD (uncataloged).

77 **ever having to worry about the finances:** *"No tenía sentido que tanto el Padre como D. Álvaro emplearan su tiempo, y anduvieran preocupados por problemas económicos. Para afrontar esos problemas podíamos y debíamos estar los demás, y, de este modo, liberar al Padre y a D. Álvaro de esa preocupación. A partir de esa fecha, de este primer viaje, decidí emplearme a fondo en esta cuestión, para liberar en lo que pudiera el peso que a mí se me antojaba que era como muy grande para ellos."* Recollections of Father Escrivá written by Luis Valls-Taberner shortly after the death of the founder, written at Pozoalbero, August 30, 1975, GAPOD (uncataloged).

78 **sent on another Opus Dei course:** During July, work and personal correspondence was being addressed to Luis at Molinoviejo in Segovia. AGUN, collection 299, box 125, folder 4.

78 **granted a visa to enter Andorra:** Visa appears in his passport. AGUN, collection 299, box 1, folder 6.

78 **cross borders into Andorra, France, or Portugal:** Moncada, *Historia Oral del Opus Dei*, 38.

78 **having been handed packages:** Tapia, *Beyond the Threshold*, 104.

78 **during the first half of the 1950s:** See stamps in his passports. AGUN, collection 299, box 1, folder 6.

78 **moved into the Opus Dei headquarters in Madrid:** His passport issued in 1952 states his permanent address as Diego de León, 14—site of the Opus Dei headquarters. AGUN, collection 299, box 1, folder 6.

78 **an endless stream of letters demanding more money:** Moncada, *Historia Oral del Opus Dei*, 36.

78 **Miguel Fisac even confronted Escrivá directly about it:** *Interview with Miguel Fisac*, 27.

78 **defending Villa Tevere's twelve dining rooms and fourteen chapels:** Tapia, *Beyond the Threshold*, 1.

78 **"It shows that we pray more than we eat":** Tapia, *Beyond the Threshold*.

79   **was keenly felt:** *"La España de los cincuenta era bastante pobretona y nuestras casas lo refle-jaban. Las numerarias y las sirvientas hacían milagros para darnos de comer, muchas legum-bres, mucha patata y recosían nuestras escasas ropas. La ducha fría era obligatoria porque no había caliente."* Article by Alberto Moncada, April 2009, http://www.opuslibros.org/nuevaweb/modules.php?name=News&file=print&sid=14586, accessed November 18, 2022.

79   **suddenly, miraculously cured:** See Vázquez de Prada, *El Fundador III*, 192–205.

79   **"I don't know if you fully realize what it will mean . . .":** Vázquez de Prada, *El Fun-dador III*, 184.

79   **"if only they could find the right arrangement":** Letter from Álvaro del Portillo to Francisco Franco, July 14, 1952, AFNFF, roll 103, document 10868.

79   **a castle on the Valencian coast:** El Castillo de Peñíscola, letter from Álvaro del Porti-llo to Francisco Franco, July 14, 1952.

79   **"There is so much work that can be done . . .":** Letter from Álvaro del Portillo to Francisco Franco, July 14, 1952.

80   **was at pains to distance himself from the regime back home:** John Allen, *Opus Dei: An Objective Look Behind the Myths and Reality of the Most Controversial Force in the Catholic Church* (New York: Doubleday, 2005), 57.

80   **turned down their request:** Letter from Luis Valls to Escrivá, November 21, 1952, GAPOD (uncataloged).

80   **who had helped put together the loan request to the Spanish central bank:** Letter from Luis Valls to Escrivá, August 16, 1952, GAPOD (uncataloged).

80   **"a definitive solution":** Letter from Luis Valls to Escrivá, November 21, 1952, GAPOD (uncataloged).

80   **about three thousand members:** In the early 1950s, there were 692 supernumerar-ies, accounting for 23 percent of the total members of Opus Dei, implying member-ship of just over 3,000 people. González Gullón and Coverdale, *Historia del Opus Dei*, 168.

4. NOT A THING OF THIS WORLD

81   **two unfamiliar faces in the crowd that afternoon:** For a detailed account of the plot to take over Banco Popular, see Alberto Moncada, *Historia Oral del Opus Dei* (Barce-lona: Plaza & Janes Editores, 1987), 41–45.

81   **the other hundred or so shareholders in attendance:** While Moncada states that the notorious intervention took place in 1952, it seems likely that this account—being written more than thirty years after the events—got the date slightly wrong. The bank's own records show that Mariano Navarro Rubio's first appearance at a shareholder meeting was in April 1954, and they confirm that he did indeed make an intervention at that meeting. Juan Caldés, the second supernumerary named in Moncada's account, isn't recorded by name in the bank records of the meeting, but it is possible that he was there representing a corporate entity called Laryc, which was controlled by Opus Dei members and which became critical in their takeover of Banco Popular. See Acta de la Junta General Ordinaria de Accionistas del Banco Popular Español, April 10, 1954, AHBPE, box 802.

81   **Both men were supernumeraries:** Moncada, *Historia Oral del Opus Dei*, 42.

81   **a huge scandal involving the chairman of Popular:** The account given by Moncada is backed up by an interview that Luis Valls-Taberner gave in 2000, in which he spoke of the secret deal in Paris and confirmed that two men—including Mariano Navarro Rubio—had been sent to a shareholder meeting, one of which was to make a scene and the other to establish his reputation with those present. See interview conducted by Fernández de la Mora with Luis Valls-Taberner for his article *Semblanza de Luis Valls-Taberner* (2000), republished at https://www.luisvallstaberner.com/wp-con tent/uploads/2014/02/Semblanza-LVT-FERNANDEZ-DE-LA-MORA-2000.pdf, accessed April 17, 2024.

81   **received spiritual direction from Opus Dei:** Moncada, *Historia Oral del Opus Dei*, 42.

81   **a cunning plan to profit from the situation:** Moncada's account is particularly credible because the numerary in question here—Antonio Pérez-Tenessa, who became head of the Spanish region for Opus Dei—was one of the main sources for his book. Documents held at AHBPE also confirm that Moncada himself was involved in the operation, so had direct knowledge.

82   **how the bank might best position itself to take advantage of the current environment:** Moncada's account is confirmed by the bank's own records of the meeting.

82   **Navarro Rubio would be placed in charge of the bank's day-to-day operations:** Navarro Rubio was nominated by Millet to the position of chief executive at the end of December 1954, eight months after the shareholder meeting. See Gabriel Tortella, José María Ortiz-Villajos, and José Luis García Ruiz, *Historia del Banco Popular: La lucha por la independencia* (Madrid: Marcial Pons, 2011), 119.

82   **were pressured to syphon off money and donate it to the cause:** Moncada, *Historia Oral del Opus Dei*, 36.

82   **was pressed to use his or her position to benefit the movement in some way:** Moncada, *Historia Oral del Opus Dei*.

82   *support companies:* José María Escrivá, *Instrucción para la obra de San Gabriel*, May 1941, Article 41.

83   **although that company had eventually gone bankrupt:** José Luis González Gullón and John F. Coverdale, *Historia del Opus Dei* (Madrid: Ediciones Rialp, 2022), 271.

83   **newspapers and magazines:** González Gullón and Coverdale, *Historia del Opus Dei*, 271.

83   **even set up its own business department:** Moncada, *Historia Oral del Opus Dei*, 40.

83   **boards of the individual companies:** Moncada, *Historia Oral del Opus Dei*.

83   **even established its own rules:** See González Gullón and Coverdale, *Historia del Opus Dei*, 268–272; and Moncada, *Historia Oral del Opus Dei*, 34–38.

83   **Esfina, which was headed by two numeraries, both of whom were rising stars:** González Gullón and Coverdale, *Historia del Opus Dei*, 271.

83   **read like a Who's Who of the Opus Dei elite:** Among those listed as board members are Antonio Pérez, Andrés Rueda, Rafael Termes, and Fernando Valenciano, AHBPE.

83   **he was featured in *Life* magazine:** "Shots Complicate $200,000 Will Case," *Life*, March 17, 1952, 41, https://books.google.co.uk/books?id=x1QEAAAAMBAJ, accessed November 21, 2022.

84   **helping secure a mortgage for the movement:** John Coverdale, *Putting Down Roots: Joseph Muzquiz and the Growth of Opus Dei* (New York: Scepter, 2009), chapter 9.

84   **would be the ultimate beneficiary of any such deal:** Letter from Sol Rosenblatt to Jorge Brosa Palau, May 23, 1957, AHBPE, box 447, folder 2057.

84   **had come close to buying a small savings bank a year before:** See interview in Fernández de la Mora, *Semblanza de Luis Valls-Taberner*.

84   **Capturing the bank would mean betraying his own family:** While Luis Valls-Taberner always subsequently presented the takeover of the bank as an amicable deal, and one initiated by Félix Millet, who approached him about selling, this is contradicted by various other sources. Letters from Millet written years later indicate that he felt duped and betrayed by Luis; see letter from Millet to Valls, February 2, 1962, AGUN collection 299, box 153, folder 7. See also Moncada, *Historia Oral del Opus Dei* for an account of someone else involved that contradicts Luis's version.

84   **a way of bowing out of the bank with his reputation intact:** See interview in Fernández de la Mora, *Semblanza de Luis Valls-Taberner*.

84   **a pretext to fire his chief executive:** Tortella et al., *Historia del Banco Popular*, 119.

85   **promoting the twenty-eight-year-old to "elector":** Letter from Escrivá to Luis Valls, October 2, 1954, GAPOD (uncataloged).

85   **given a special dispensation to hold both jobs:** Mariano Navarro Rubio, *Mis memorias: Testimonio de una vida política truncada por el 'Caso Matesa'* (Madrid: Plaza & Janes, 1991), 65.

85   **Millet wrote to him about a deal:** For details of the offer, see letter from Julián Navarro García to Félix Millet Maristany, April 25, 1955, AHBPE, box 445, folder 2056.

85   **totaling five million pesetas:** See accounts of Eolo and Laryc, AHBPE, box 540.

85   **set up by some Opus Dei members a few years earlier:** Moncada, *Historia Oral del Opus Dei*, 34. Alberto Moncada was one of the founding shareholders of Eolo from 1955 on, so his account carries some weight.

85   **the same company paid ten million pesetas:** See accounts of Eolo and Laryc, AHBPE, box 540.

85   **Two Opus Dei members were appointed to new positions in the bank:** José Luis Moris became secretary general and Jorge Brosa technical secretary in January 1956. Tortella et al., *Historia del Banco Popular*, 131.

85   **friendly faces were also elected to the board:** Tortella et al., *Historia del Banco Popular*.

86   **a fifteen million peseta loan for Eolo:** See accounts of Eolo and Laryc, AHBPE, box 540.

86   **to give them complete control of the bank:** See records of the March 1957 shareholder meeting, AHBPE (uncataloged).

86   **Millet resigned from the board:** Tortella et al., *Historia del Banco Popular*, 133.

86   **One board member voiced his consternation:** Tortella et al., *Historia del Banco Popular*.

86   **Opus Dei's ascendancy now seemed complete:** See Paul Preston, *Franco: A Biography* (London: Harper Press, 1993), chapter 25.

86   **"It's good, your constant attention to the work of Saint Nicholas":** Letter from Escrivá to Luis Valls, June 17, 1959, GAPOD (uncataloged).

87   **Many had died during construction:** Paul Preston, *A People Betrayed: A History of Corruption, Political Incompetence and Social Division in Modern Spain 1874–2018* (London: William Collins, 2020), 335.

87   **two men had never been close:** See Preston, *Franco*.

87   **At the most poignant moment in the ceremony:** Carlos Hernández Quero, "Silbidos y gritos de traidor: así fueron las tres veces que abuchearon en vida a Franco en el Valle de los Caídos," *Vanity Fair*, https://www.revistavanityfair.es/poder/articulos/silbidos-abucheos-y-gritos-de-traidor-asi-fueron-las-tres-veces-que-franco-sufrio-en-el-valle-de-los-caidos/41349, accessed December 2, 2022.

87   **"Franco, you traitor!":** Benjamin Welles, "Talk of Madrid: The Grapevine Flourishes, to Censor's Chagrin," *New York Times*, December 17, 1960, 13, https://www.nytimes.com/1960/12/17/archives/talk-of-madrid-the-grapevine-flourishes-to-censors-chagrin-franco.html, accessed April 17, 2024.

88   **his favorite hobbies:** Preston, *A People Betrayed*, 403.

88   **"I ask the Lord Our God to bestow good fortune on Your Excellency . . .":** Letter from José María Escrivá to General Francisco Franco, May 23, 1958, AFNFF, published by *Razón Española*, January-February 2001, republished at https://www.lamarea.com/2013/02/05/escriva-de-balaguer-y-su-pasion-por-la-libertad/, accessed July 28, 2023.

88   **a requirement to kneel in his presence:** Moncada, *Historia Oral del Opus Dei*, 72.

88   **all Opus Dei ministers were to come personally to receive him:** Moncada, *Historia Oral del Opus Dei*.

88   **drive five hours north to the border at Irún:** Moncada, *Historia Oral del Opus Dei*.

88   **"The Lord brought me here with hints of our Work . . .":** González Gullón and Coverdale, *Historia del Opus Dei*, 280.

88   **pushed and jostled to get close:** Andrés Vázquez de Prada, *El Fundador del Opus Dei III* (Madrid: Ediciones Rialp, 2003), 320.

89   **Opus Dei members roamed the streets singing songs:** For a detailed account of the events in Pamplona, see *La Vanguardia*, October 22, 1960, 4, http://hemeroteca.lavanguardia.com/preview/1960/10/22/pagina-4/32728121/pdf.html, accessed January 6, 2023.

89   **Directly behind him sat Luis Valls-Taberner:** In a photograph from the occasion, Luis is seen seated in the row directly behind and two seats to the right of Escrivá, the only man in a business suit among the academic gowns and cassocks, AGUN, collection 299, box 14, folder 3.

89   **had begun to refer to him affectionately as *mi banquero*:** Moncada, *Historia Oral del Opus Dei*, 13.

89   **learned to stay quiet at the monthly board meetings:** In the minutes of board meetings during his first few years at the bank, Luis Valls-Taberner is barely mentioned as contributing anything to the discussion. See AHBPE, box 402, folders 1041 and 1037.

89   **"In our interactions, and in social, professional, and family life . . .":** Article from the bank's internal magazine *Panorama*, October 1959, republished in Javier Pérez-Sala Valls-Taberner, ed., *Luis Valls-Taberner: Un personaje en la penumbra* (Madrid: Fundación para Atenciones Sociales, 2007), 37.

90 **to invite important clients and other members on the board to special V.I.P. retreats:** Luis received notes suggesting the names of bank personnel and important industrial clients to invite to upcoming retreats being held at Molinoviejo. See AGUN, collection 299, box 325.

90 **onboarded as clients and given loans on extremely favorable terms:** The official Banco Popular archives are peppered with mentions of various Opus Dei auxiliary companies, including Esfina, Eolo, Rotopress, and many others from 1957 on. In late 1962 and early 1963, the bank lent Eolo more than thirty million pesetas to participate in a capital increase, after it was unable to raise the money from its own Opus Dei shareholders. Records show that it paid not a single peseta of interest on what was then a very large amount of money. See AHBPE, particularly boxes 539 and 540.

90 **created a much more ambitious overseas network:** Tortella et al., *Historia del Banco Popular*, 143–144.

90 **Numerary members were put in charge:** Tesifonte López and Rafael Termes were placed in charge of overseas expansion. Both were numerary members of Opus Dei. Tortella et al., *Historia del Banco Popular*.

90 **"Did you know that Opus Dei is . . .":** Falange pamphlet attacking Opus Dei. AFNFF, roll 35, document 2424.

90 **involved in transferring vast sums overseas:** Falange pamphlet attacking Opus Dei. AFNFF.

90 **two bombs exploded at the Popular headquarters:** Benjamin Welles, "Red 'Front' Accused," *New York Times*, June 9, 1962, 10, https://timesmachine.nytimes.com/timesmachine/1962/06/09/82044449.html?pageNumber=10, accessed December 6, 2022.

91 **the founder demanded to be kept regularly updated:** Moncada, *Historia Oral del Opus Dei*, 43.

91 **The founder flew into frequent fits of rage:** Escrivá's short temper has been noted by several sources who personally spent time with the founder, and are mentioned in María del Carmen Tapia, *Beyond the Threshold* (New York: Continuum, 1997) and in Moncada, *Historia Oral del Opus Dei*. The author has also confirmed these accounts in an interview with Vladimir Felzmann (Escrivá's personal assistant in the early sixties), August 2020.

91 **using a secret code of numbers and letters:** Moncada, *Historia Oral del Opus Dei*, 75.

91 **asked to come up with lists of people who could be swindled:** Moncada, *Historia Oral del Opus Dei*, 53.

91 **initially reluctant when asked to name a fellow numerary to his ministry:** Moncada, *Historia Oral del Opus Dei*, 49–50.

91 **flying out to see the founder whenever he was summoned:** Stamps in his passport show him visiting Italy once in 1957, twice in 1958, twice in 1959, three times in 1960, and twice in 1961. These trips were sometimes for eight days or more and almost always took place outside the standard vacation period, when employees—even senior ones—would be expected to be working. AGUN, collection 299, box 1, folder 6.

91 **he and Laureano López Rodó—the de facto deputy prime minister—held court:** Moncada, *Historia Oral del Opus Dei*, 73.

91 **encouraged to set aside his own dreams and aspirations:** For an excellent exploration of this dynamic, based on his own experiences and those of other young professional Opus Dei men around him, see Alberto Moncada, *Los Hijos del Padre* (Barcelona, Argos: 1977).

92 **Luis lapped up every article he could get his hands on:** Aristóbulo de Juan, *De Bancos, Banqueros y Supervisores: 50 años desde la trinchera* (Barcelona, Deusto: 2021), 42.

92 **jokingly began to refer to his assistant as his Mac Bundy:** De Juan, *De Bancos*, 65.

92 **saddling the bank with huge amounts of debt:** Total lending was 3.2 billion pesetas at the end of 1956, just before the takeover, rising to 9.2 billion pesetas at the end of 1961. During the same period, leverage at the bank rose from roughly thirty-four times to fifty-three times. For the evolution of the bank's balance sheet, see Tortella et al., *Historia del Banco Popular*, 418.

92 **warned against such a reckless expansion:** See comments made by Juan Manuel Fanjul during the May 1959 board meeting, AHBPE, box 402, folder 1041.

92 **asked its shareholders to inject seventy million pesetas:** See resolution agreed at the board meeting held in July 1962, AHBPE, box 402, folder 1041.

92 **he borrowed money from the bank:** An account named "Cuenta Ampliación B.P.E en Eolo" shows that in January 1963, following the capital increase, there was a balance of thirty-one million pesetas overdrawn. The transaction lines above this show various share purchases corresponding to the rights issue. AHBPE, boxes 539 and 540.

92 **bailing out Opus Dei with a huge cash injection:** A letter from the bank to Abelardo Alonso dated February 18, 1963, asked how the deposits made by the Valls-Taberners—three million pesetas from Luis's mother, three million pesetas from his brother Javier, and another one million pesetas from Luis—should be credited. Ironically, the letterhead of the bank boasts that it now has 300 million pesetas of capital and reserves following the recent rights issue. AHBPE, boxes 539 and 540. AHBPE, boxes 539 and 540.

92 **bundled off to Pamplona:** Escrivá asks Luis to let him know what the doctors in Pamplona have said; letter from Escrivá to Luis Valls, June 17, 1963, GAPOD (uncataloged).

93 **"You and I, who have both been endowed with huge hearts . . .":** Letter from Escrivá to Luis Valls, July 16, 1963, AGUN, collection 299, box 153, folder 7.

93 **had reached as far as Kenya, Japan, and Australia:** See https://opusdei.org/en-uk/article/historical-overview/, accessed December 9, 2022.

93 **had climbed to about six thousand people:** González Gullón and Coverdale, *Historia del Opus Dei*, 280.

93 **he did it as a sign of his devotion to both Joseph and Mary:** González Gullón and Coverdale, *Historia del Opus Dei*, 16.

93 **demand an account of their time with him:** Vázquez de Prada, *El Fundador III*, 349.

93 **"Don't use the term *we*, use only the term *I* . . .":** Recollections of Father Escrivá written by Luis Valls-Taberner shortly after the death of the founder, written at Pozoalbero, August 30, 1975, drawing on contemporaneous notes taken by Luis during the meeting, GAPOD (uncataloged).

93   **138 "support companies" had been set up:** González Gullón and Coverdale, *Historia del Opus Dei*, 366.

94   **a complex system of bank accounts:** Moncada, *Historia Oral del Opus Dei*, 52.

94   **sometimes suddenly presented with a money belt to wear:** Tapia, *Beyond the Threshold*, 104.

94   **Opus Dei's money smuggler in chief:** Moncada, *Historia Oral del Opus Dei*, 38.

94   **made several trips:** He made trips to Portugal in September 1953, January 1954, September 1955, March 1956, and in January 1964. See stamps in his passports, AGUN, collection 299, box 1, folder 6.

94   **he announced he was the Archduke of Austria:** "Ortega Pardo Habría Desfalcado Casi Dos Millones de Dólares," *La República*, December 13, 1965; kept in the archives at AFNFF, roll 49, document 3631. His claim to be related to the Archduke of Austria is also repeated in a report prepared by the Spanish Ambassador to Portugal, José Ibañez-Martín for Francisco Franco, dated November 19, 1965, found at AFNFF, roll 48, document 3628.

94   **the lifestyles of some of the elite numerary businessmen:** see Moncada, *Los Hijos del Padre*, 12–13, for an exploration of the privileges enjoyed by Luis Valls-Taberner, Laureano López Rodó, and numerous other senior figures at their residence in Madrid around this time.

95   **Ortega was linked to a long list of companies:** For a detailed biography of Ortega Pardo prior to the incident in Venezuela, see Ibañez-Martín report, AFNFF.

95   **subsisted on a diet of whisky and coffee:** See Ibañez-Martín report, AFNFF.

95   **he needed to take some time away and returned to Spain:** See letter from José Ibañez-Martín to Pedro Salvador de Vicente at the Ministry of Foreign Affairs, November 10, 1965, AFNFF, roll 40, document 2879.

95   **seemed recovered and completely normal:** See Ibañez-Martín letter, AFNFF.

95   **he presented a suitcase full of banknotes to the manager:** See Ibañez-Martín report, AFNFF.

95   **might be part of a communist cell linked to a clandestine arms factory:** "Español detenido por la Policía venezolana," *Ya*, November 7, 1965, AFNFF, roll 25, document 1723.

95   **instead to follow him around the city:** See Ibañez-Martín report, AFNFF.

95   **almost a quarter of a million dollars:** See telegram from the Spanish Ambassador to Venezuela back to the Ministry of Foreign Affairs in Madrid, November 6, 1965, AFNFF, roll 25, document 1723.

95   **he told the police he was a university professor:** Telegram from the Spanish delegation to the United Nations back to the Office for Diplomatic Information in Madrid, November 8, 1965, AFNFF, roll 25, document 1723.

95   **brought the money into the country to buy some property:** "Español detenido," *Ya*, AFNFF.

95   **plans to open a new school for boys in Caracas:** Liceo Los Arcos finally opened its doors in September 1967.

95   **had been withdrawn legally:** See Ibañez-Martín report, AFNFF.

96 **shut himself in his office for several days:** De Juan, *De Bancos*, 77. Details in the bank archive also appear to confirm De Juan's observations. See Notas de Presidencia, November 17, 1965, AHBPE, box 771, folder 1.

96 **had known Ortega for many years:** The AHBPE contains numerous letters between the two men dating back to the 1950s.

96 **"How do we know you're not a sleeping communist ...":** De Juan, *De Bancos*, 77.

96 **relocating to a tiny room barely big enough to fit a desk:** De Juan, *De Bancos*, 78.

96 **selectively leaking information to the friendly Spanish ambassador:** *"Me consta, de fuente fidedigna, es decir, de las mismas personas que con él convivían, que no dijo la finalidad de su viaje a sus compañeros de vida y también, que en esa misma fecha, escribió cartas—que él mismo colocó en Correos—dimitiendo de sus cargos directivos en los organismos que actuaba,"* Ibañez-Martín report, AFNFF.

97 **extricating Ortega from the web of companies he still headed:** In November and December 1965, and through the first few months of 1966, the bank asked Ortega Pardo to sign several documents linked to such companies, implying that he still had some authority. AHBPE, box 771, folders 1 and 2.

97 **sign several blank sheets of paper before leaving on any trip:** Tapia, *Beyond the Threshold*, 204.

97 **found nothing wrong with the patient:** See Ibañez-Martín report, AFNFF.

97 **"with good sense and authentic love for their neighbor":** See Ibañez-Martín report, AFNFF.

97 **being held at a ranch in the countryside:** *"Ortega Pardo internado en una finca,"* *El Mundo*, December 29, 1965, AFNFF, roll 49, document 3631.

97 **conspired with the Opus Dei men in government:** The Notas de Presidencia record several meetings with senior regime members to discuss the Ortega affair— including the Minister of Commerce Alberto Ullastres, an Opus Dei numerary, and the Governor of the Bank of Spain Mariano Navarro Rubio, a supernumerary member of the religious group. AHBPE, box 771, folders 1 and 2.

97 **helped to smuggle as much as two million dollars abroad:** *"Ortega Pardo Habría Desfalcado Casi Dos Millones de Dólares,"* *La República*, December 13, 1965, AFNFF, roll 49, document 3631.

97 **"medical treatment proportionate to the danger he poses":** Notas de Presidencia, March 14, 1966, AHBPE, box 771, folder 2.

97 **encouraged to medicate fellow numeraries:** Examples of numerary members being drugged to alleviate perceived mental disorders are numerous. See Moncada, *Los Hijos del Padre*, 214–216; and the testimony of Eileen Johnson, a former numerary in the UK during the 1960s, at a conference held on cults in Bilbao in 2020 and republished at https://www.opus-info.org/index.php/Opus_Dei_Tactics_-_Testimony_of_Eileen_Johnson, accessed January 17, 2023.

97 **"He can't cope with staying in the asylum any longer ...":** Notas de Presidencia, March 27, 1966, AHBPE, box 771, folder 2.

97 **After signing various documents:** *"Visita de Termes y Butragueño. Se le recogió la firma de los documentos básicos sobre los hechos importantes de su actuación y se trato de la posible*

recuperación de algunas cantidades adeudadas por terceros a Ortega, conviniéndose que este facilitaría cartas de presentación para sus deudores, las cuales serán recogidas por Butragueño," Notas de Presidencia, March 26, 1966, AHBPE, box 771, folder 2.

98   **a new life that had been arranged for him in Argentina:** Notas de Presidencia, April 12, 1966, AHBPE, box 771, folder 2.

98   **"Don't get upset about any of it . . .":** This meeting took place on October 3, 1966, in the doorway of the chapel at Molinoviejo. Luis Valls stated clearly in his recollection that he believed the founder was referring to the incident in Portugal almost a year earlier. See Recollections of Father Escrivá written by Luis Valls-Taberner shortly after the death of the founder, written at Pozoalbero, August 30, 1975, GAPOD (uncataloged).

98   **"Never judge things by appearances . . .":** Father Escrivá recollections, August 30, 1975, GAPOD.

98   **"Opus Dei is not a thing of this world":** Father Escrivá recollections, August 30, 1975, GAPOD.

5. BECAUSE I SAY SO

99   **nobody waiting for her at Fiumicino Airport:** For a detailed account of her stay in Rome, see María del Carmen Tapia, *Beyond the Threshold* (New York: Continuum, 1997), 239–278.

99   **not long after being recruited as a numerary by her boss:** Tapia, *Beyond the Threshold*, 8–29.

100   **that female numeraries usually slept on:** Tapia, *Beyond the Threshold*, 240.

100   **including rheumatism, bad backs, and gynecological problems:** Tapia, *Beyond the Threshold*, 47.

100   **report immediately to the dining room in Villa Vecchia:** Tapia, *Beyond the Threshold*, 240.

100   **retained much of its former elegance and charm:** Author visit to the Villa Tevere complex, including a tour of the inside, November 2023.

100   **his suite of rooms included an office:** Tapia, *Beyond the Threshold*, 127.

100   **she approached Escrivá, knelt before him, and kissed his hand:** Tapia, *Beyond the Threshold*, 240.

100   **"How was the journey?":** The dialogue presented here is translated from the original Spanish version of Tapia's account of her time in Opus Dei, *Tras el Umbral: Una Vida en el Opus Dei* (Madrid: Ediciones B, 1992).

101   **there was a certain annoyance in his voice:** Tapia, *Beyond the Threshold*, 241.

101   **various commissions that had been set up to work on documents for the general congregations:** José Luis González Gullón and John F. Coverdale, *Historia del Opus Dei* (Madrid: Ediciones Rialp, 2022), 378.

101   **Escrivá turned down the offer:** González Gullón and Coverdale, *Historia del Opus Dei*, 378.

102   **diminished the status of Opus Dei within the Church:** Alberto Moncada, *Historia Oral del Opus Dei* (Barcelona: Plaza & Janes Editores, 1987), 25.

102   **the meaning of that label had become distorted over the years:** José María Escrivá, *Non ignoratis*, October 2, 1958, Article 9.

102   **accusing the new pope of being a Mason:** Michael Walsh, *The Secret World of Opus Dei* (London: Grafton Books, 1990), 27.

102   **"God in his infinite wisdom should take this man away":** Walsh, *Secret World of Opus Dei*, 72.

102   **"handbook for senior scouts":** Hans Urs von Balthasar, "Integralismus," *Wort und Wahrheit* 18 (1963): 737–744.

102   **criticized Opus Dei for "purchasing" spirituality:** Von Balthasar, "Integralismus."

102   **"Purchased spirit is a contradiction in itself":** Von Balthasar, "Integralismus."

103   **focus his time on recruiting schoolboys:** Vladimir Felzmann, *A Journey to Eternity: My Years in Opus Dei 1959–1982* (Hartpury, UK: All Squared, 2023), 18–19.

103   **even though he had no interest in doing so:** Felzmann, *Journey to Eternity*, 25.

103   **"Whatever the director told me to do was God's will . . .":** Felzmann, *Journey to Eternity*, 13.

103   **given the task of cleaning the central-heating boiler:** Felzmann, *Journey to Eternity*, 25.

103   **"I was told that in bullfights the bull had to be weakened . . .":** Felzmann, *Journey to Eternity*, 31.

103   **"all for the benefit of the institution":** Felzmann, *Journey to Eternity*, 23.

103   **she was summoned before the founder again to receive a formal admonition:** Tapia, *Beyond the Threshold*, 248.

104   **she had dared to question Escrivá's rules and regulations:** Tapia, *Beyond the Threshold*, 249.

104   **She also learned of the punishment for her transgressions:** Tapia, *Beyond the Threshold*, 250.

104   **she was a prisoner inside Villa Tevere:** Tapia, *Beyond the Threshold*, 251.

104   **microphones the founder had installed in many parts of the complex:** Tapia, *Beyond the Threshold*, 256.

105   **"Surrounded by a bubble of affection, I was utterly uncritical . . .":** Felzmann, *Journey to Eternity*, 32.

105   **agreed to set up a post office box for her:** Tapia, *Beyond the Threshold*, 257.

105   **accompanied by another numerary whenever she left the complex:** Tapia, *Beyond the Threshold*, 267.

106   **interrogated her about the details of the post office box:** Tapia, *Beyond the Threshold*, 271.

106   **in search of any incriminating evidence:** Tapia, *Beyond the Threshold*, 272.

106   **told what to write in her letter of resignation:** Tapia, *Beyond the Threshold*, 275.

106   **almost three million dollars on expansion overseas:** González Gullón and Coverdale, *Historia del Opus Dei*, 368.

106   **knowing the way to his parishioners' hearts—and to their wallets:** For a detailed profile of Cardinal Cushing, see "The Unlikely Cardinal," *Time*, August 21, 1964, https://content.time.com/time/subscriber/article/0,33009,876036,00.html, accessed January 11, 2023.

107   **responsible for at least $250 million worth of construction:** "Unlikely Cardinal," *Time*.

107   **deliver a prayer at the 1961 presidential inauguration:** William J. Jorden, "Smoke Signals Stir Inaugural," *New York Times*, January 21, 1961, 8, https://timesmachine.nytimes.com/timesmachine/1961/01/21/97650363.html?pageNumber=8, accessed January 11, 2023.

107   **a one-acre lot four blocks from Harvard Yard for $200,000 in cash:** Work of God, Inc., bought 44,503 square feet of land at the corner of Ellery Street and Broadway in October 1963. The newspaper report cited the price as $200,000. There was no mortgage taken out on the property. See Southern Middlesex County property records, book 10371, page 84.

107   **given permission to build a residence for two hundred students:** Herbert A. Kenny, "Cardinal to Erect Cultural Site," *Boston Globe*, June 26, 1963, 22.

107   **"I don't know anything about your work in Boston . . .":** Letter from Cardinal Richard Cushing to Father Joseph Múzquiz, April 16, 1964, Archive of the Archdiocese of Boston, Cardinal Cushing Papers, boxes 7 and 8.

107   **two six-story redbrick houses in the wealthy Back Bay area:** Work of God, Inc., bought two properties at 22 and 24 Marlborough Street in November 1953 for around $50,000. The residence was known as Trimount House. See Suffolk County property records, book 6912, page 46.

107   **a large clapboard house on Follen Street in Cambridge:** Work of God, Inc., bought the property at 25 Follen Street in September 1959 for around $50,000. There was no mortgage taken out on the property. See Southern Middlesex County property records, book 9456, page 7.

107   **where it hosted weekend retreats for young men and boys:** John Arthur Gueguen describes the residence, known as Wynnview, as a country place that would soon become the first conference and retreat center of Opus Dei in the United States, and host future ski trips as well as summer camps and courses. See John Arthur Gueguen, "The Early Days of Opus Dei in Boston as Recalled by the First Generation (1946–1956)," in *Studia et Documenta* (Rome: Istituto Storico San Josemaría Escrivá, 2007), 1:97.

107   **"mighty upset":** Letter from Cardinal Richard Cushing to Father Joseph Múzquiz, April 16, 1964, Archive of the Archdiocese of Boston.

107   **demanded the group immediately halt any plans:** Letter from Father Joseph Collins to Father Francis Sexton dated April 24, 1964, following a meeting with Cushing, during which Collins heard him give these orders to Father Robert Bucciarelli, an Opus Dei priest affiliated with Trimount House. Archive of the Archdiocese of Boston, SI-195.

108   **a series of companies in places like Maryland:** Work of God, Inc., was the first of these companies to be set up, established in Chicago in the late 1940s. It was followed by the establishment of the Maryland Institute of General Studies, Inc., in 1957 and the Association for Cultural Change, Inc., in 1958. The articles of association filed by the directors of the Maryland Institute of General Studies, Inc., clearly state that they are "acting on behalf of the Roman Catholic Institution commonly known as Opus Dei."

108   **often crossed the Atlantic by air:** Passenger lists accessed via ancestry.com show that

Barturen made no fewer than nineteen flights from New York to Europe between May 1956 and December 1962. These were mainly to Madrid, but he also made trips to Rome, Paris, and Lisbon.

108   **a former New Jersey butcher:** Dan Davies, *Lying for Money: How Legendary Frauds Reveal the Workings of Our World* (London: Profile Books, 2018), 50.

108   **Tino blamed the whole thing on Opus Dei:** Norman C. Miller, *The Great Salad Oil Swindle* (New York: Coward McCann, 1965), 107–110.

108   **he had purchased a fifteen-room house:** See Cook County property records, PIN 20-14-106-020-0000.

109   **the Opus Dei pioneers had their first American recruit:** González Gullón and Coverdale, *Historia del Opus Dei*, 227.

109   **another five men asked to be admitted:** John F. Coverdale, *Putting Down Roots: Father Joseph Múzquiz and the Growth of Opus Dei* (New York: Scepter, 2009), chapter 6.

109   **"We are making progress on furniture and decorations . . .":** Coverdale, *Putting Down Roots.*

109   **the Work of God, Inc., closed on another property:** See Suffolk County property records, book 6412, pages 46 and 48.

109   **who was working on a translation of *The Way* into English:** John Arthur Gueguen, "The Early Days of Opus Dei in Boston as Recalled by the First Generation (1946–1956)," in *Studia et Documenta* (Rome: Istituto Storico San Josemaría Escrivá, 2007), 1:80.

109   **excommunicated from the Church after making a speech:** Federico M. Requena, "Fr. William Porras, un capellán católico en la Universidad de Harvard," in *Studia et Documenta* (Rome: Istituto Storico San Josemaría Escrivá, 2018), 12:325.

109   **invited to Spain by Opus Dei some years earlier:** Requena, "Fr. William Porras," 12:334.

109   **had seen first-hand its great work there:** Cardinal Cushing told those attending the ceremony at Trimount House, "I met Opus Dei in Spain some years ago, in the residence in Santiago de Compostela. I was so impressed that I began to foster a hope that Opus Dei would come to Boston." Gueguen, "Early Days," 1:82.

110   **recruited about four hundred Americans:** González Gullón and Coverdale, *Historia del Opus Dei*, 229.

110   **"It is my experience that in a mixed group . . .":** Letter from Father Bill Porras to Father Lawrence Riley, December 12, 1957, Archive of the Archdiocese of Boston, M-2178.

110   **had to ask another two Opus Dei priests:** Elizabeth W. Green, "Opening the Doors of Opus Dei," *The Crimson*, April 10, 2003, https://www.thecrimson.com/article/2003/4/10/opening-the-doors-of-opus-dei/, accessed January 12, 2023.

110   **"I possess several documents and have many facts . . .":** Father Joseph Collins letter to Father Francis Sexton, Archive of the Archdiocese of Boston.

110   **bought a private school sitting on more than eighty acres of land:** Maryland Institute of General Studies, Inc., purchased the property in Pembroke in June 1964 for approximately $120,000. It took out a mortgage on the property for $35,000. See Plymouth County property records, book 3116, pages 284 and 287.

110 **a boarding school for rich girls:** An advertisement in 1968 for "Arnold Hall Academy" in East Pembroke describes it as a "two-year boarding school" for girls aged between 14 and 17. The plan seems to have ended in failure, as the property became a center for Opus Dei retreats shortly after. See *Boston Globe*, September 29, 1968, 16-A.

110 **a five-story Tiffany mansion on Commonwealth Avenue:** The property was put back on the market for $14,995,000, almost fifty years later. For the realtor's listing and details of the property, see https://tiffanyayermansion.com/, accessed January 12, 2023.

110 **set Opus Dei back $400,000:** Association for Cultural Interchange, Inc., bought three adjoining properties at 395, 397, and 399 Commonwealth Avenue in December 1964 for roughly $400,000. A mortgage of $300,000 was taken out against the three properties, implying a cash payment of the $100,000 balance. See Suffolk County property records, book 7916, pages 285 and 286.

111 **a string of lavish property purchases around the world that year:** González Gullón and Coverdale, *Historia del Opus Dei*, 297.

111 **Escrivá had an audience with Pope Paul VI:** González Gullón and Coverdale, *Historia del Opus Dei*, 381.

111 **ten times for an audience with the Pope—but was turned down every time:** González Gullón and Coverdale, *Historia del Opus Dei*, 384.

111 **he sent Del Portillo to Greece:** Kenneth L. Woodward, "A Questionable Saint," *Newsweek*, January 12, 1992, https://www.newsweek.com/questionable-saint-197568, accessed December 4, 2023.

111 **soon led to a number of senior departures:** Antonio Pérez-Tenessa, Raimundo Panikkar, and María del Carmen Tapia—along with Miguel Fisac, who left a few years before them—are the primary sources in Alberto Moncada's book *Historia Oral del Opus Dei*. Moncada himself left shortly afterwards.

112 **He had wanted to leave for years:** Antonio Pérez-Tenessa, "No hablaré mal de la Obra," *El País*, April 12, 1992, https://elpais.com/diario/1992/04/13/sociedad/703116007_850215.html, accessed July 28, 2023.

112 **to launch a manhunt to track him down:** Joaquín Prieto, "Una crisis en el Opus Dei," *El País*, April 12, 1992, 4, http://opuslibros.org/nuevaweb/modules.php?name=News&file=article&sid=12847, accessed July 28, 2023.

112 **that he keep quiet about his time in the movement:** Pérez-Tenessa, "No hablaré mal de la Obra."

112 **he was visited by two Opus Dei priests:** Eileen Johnson, who was told of the incident by Fisac himself, recounted it to the *Scottish Catholic Observer* in 1994, prompting Opus Dei to write to the newspaper refuting the story. This then provoked Fisac to write to the newspaper insisting that the account was in fact true. See https://www.opus-info.org/index.php/Opus_Dei_Tactics_-_Testimony_of_Eileen_Johnson, accessed January 17, 2023.

112 **where members actively competed for resources and fought against each other:** Moncada cites Antonio Pérez-Tenessa: "*Y lo mismo que en el caso de la política, se vio en seguida que en el mundo de los negocios, las tensiones internas, las peleas entre hermanos, eran*

un perjuicio mucho mayor que los beneficios, que tampoco eran tan claros," Moncada, *Historia Oral del Opus Dei*, 50.

112   **a frustrated Escrivá decided the time had come to reset the narrative:** "*Los mensajes sobre tensiones y conflictos iban y venían a Roma donde Escrivá, muy zarandeado ya por la crítica internacional a la politización franquista de la Obra, empezó a tener también disgustos graves por esta causa,*" in Moncada, *Historia Oral del Opus Dei*, 50.

112   **The "interviews" were in fact entirely stage-managed:** Author interview with one of the people tasked with preparing answers for Escrivá, February 2023.

113   **the founder was once again being treated for his diabetes:** One person who lived with him in Rome during the period coinciding with the interviews said that Escrivá had a dietician and a masseur brought in regularly because of a flare-up in his diabetes. Author interview with person tasked with preparing answers.

113   **openly talked about a growing crisis:** González Gullón and Coverdale, *Historia del Opus Dei*, 293.

113   **pointed to a new school called The Heights:** *Conversations with Monsignor Escrivá de Balaguer* (Manila: Sinag-Tala Publishers, 1977), 81.

113   **a huge school-building program in Spain and Latin America:** González Gullón and Coverdale, *Historia del Opus Dei*, 306–370.

113   **Popular had held back:** A twenty million peseta loan request from Matesa was discussed at the bank's credit committee on December 7, 1966. It was rejected. See Notas de Presidencia, December 9, 1966, AHBPE, box 771, folder 1.

113   **was found abandoned at the docks in Barcelona:** Robert Hutchison, *Their Kingdom Come: Inside the Secret World of Opus Dei* (London: Transworld, 1997), 132.

113   **made its way to various Opus Dei initiatives:** Jesús Ynfante, who spent many years investigating and publishing books on Opus Dei, alleged that 270 million pesetas were sent to Villa Tevere, 120 million split among Opus Dei centers in Rome, Barcelona, and Pamplona, as well as the University of Navarre, while a further 900 million were sent to two new schools in the United States and 1.2 billion pesetas were sent to a new Opus Dei university being built at the time in Peru. See Jesús Ynfante, *Opus Dei: Así en la Tierra Como en el Cielo* (Barcelona: Grijalbo Mondadori, 1996), 416. See also Hutchison, *Their Kingdom Come*, 134; and Paul Preston, *A People Betrayed: A History of Corruption, Political Incompetence and Social Division in Modern Spain 1874–2018* (London: William Collins, 2020), 435.

114   **countless other projects:** A subsequent Andorran investigation found that large sums of cash, in bundles of 1,000 peseta notes, were taken by car from Madrid or Barcelona to the principality, where the Spanish peseta was legal tender alongside the French franc, and where it was deposited with the Credit Andorra bank, affiliated with Opus Dei since the 1950s. The court concluded that the money then went from Andorra to Switzerland. A separate route of money out of Spain, via a Luxembourg company called Sodetex, was never investigated by Spanish authorities. Hutchison, *Their Kingdom Come*, 134.

114   **"What have you got against the Opus Dei?":** Paul Preston, *Franco: A Biography* (London: Harper Press, 1993), 1087.

114   **his worsening Parkinson's disease:** Preston, *People Betrayed*, 436.

114 **dismissing the Falangists from their posts immediately:** Preston, *Franco: A Biography*, 1041–1045.

114 **would later admit that he had been taken advantage of:** Preston, *Franco: A Biography*, 1046.

114 **took out his gun, and shot himself in the head:** Richard Eders, "Falangist Commits Suicide in Apparent Protest," *New York Times*, November 24, 1969, 7, https://timesma chine.nytimes.com/timesmachine/1969/11/24/79438149.html?pageNumber=7, accessed January 19, 2023.

114 **a special commission was being set up to investigate a raft of criticism against Opus Dei:** González Gullón and Coverdale, *Historia del Opus Dei*, 383.

115 **had begun to openly challenge the Pope's authority:** González Gullón and Coverdale, *Historia del Opus Dei*.

115 **oversee the commission were openly hostile to the movement:** González Gullón and Coverdale, *Historia del Opus Dei*.

115 **a significant riposte to pontifical authority:** Walsh, *Secret World of Opus Dei*, 73.

115 **to win its approval as a secular institute:** "As a logical consequence of these fundamental demands of the spirit of Opus Dei, we will proceed to the revision of our particular law, in those places in which there was no other alternative but to accept provisionally certain concepts or terms proper to the law of the so-called state of perfection or the religious state," cited in Amadeo de Fuenmayor, Valentín Gómez-Iglesias, José Luis Illanes Maestre, *The Canonical Path of Opus Dei: The History and Defense of a Charism* (Princeton: Scepter, 1994), 355.

115 **the internal process of reform that was now underway:** González Gullón and Coverdale, *Historia del Opus Dei*, 383.

116 **accusations that one senior member had been using his position at the Vatican to spy on the Holy See:** Andrés Vázquez de Prada, *El Fundador del Opus Dei III* (Madrid: Ediciones Rialp, 2003), 552.

116 **Escrivá was asked to give "explicit assurance":** Vázquez de Prada, *El Fundador III*, 555.

116 **Escrivá was granted his first audience with the pope in almost six years:** Vázquez de Prada, *El Fundador III*, 556.

116 **Villa Tevere arranged for the founder across Latin America:** Vázquez de Prada, *El Fundador III*, 610–637.

116 **current member would openly challenge him:** María Eugenia Ossandón Widow, "Josemaría Escrivá de Balaguer en Santiago de Chile (1974)," in *Studia et Documenta* (Rome: Istituto Storico San Josemaría Escrivá, 2017), 11:130.

117 **"seem to do nothing but have sex . . .":** *Catequesis en América*, II:43.

117 **missives to the membership bemoaning the state of the Church:** See, for example, the three "Campanadas" missives that he sent out between 1973 and 1974.

117 **by helicopter:** Vázquez de Prada, *El Fundador III*, 658.

117 **"It is marvelous . . .":** Vázquez de Prada, *El Fundador III*, 659.

117 **his followers tried for ninety minutes to resuscitate him:** For an account of his death and the frenzy of activity trying to resuscitate him, see Álvaro del Portillo, *Nuestro Padre en el Cielo*, June 29, 1975.

117 **the Caudillo appeared before a huge crowd at the Palacio de Oriente:** For a detailed account of the Caudillo's gradual deterioration and death, see Preston, *Franco: A Biography*, 1084–1087.

6. HABEMUS PAPAM

119 **had been in Rome for a couple of days:** George Weigel, *Witness to Hope: The Biography of Pope John Paul II* (New York: Harper Perennial, 2009), 242.

119 **invited to a quiet dinner with an old friend:** For an account of the dinner between Karol Józef Wojtyła and Álvaro del Portillo in August 1978, and an account of their friendship and the future pope's relations with Opus Dei, see https://opusdei.org/en-uk/article/stories-about-john-paul-ii/, accessed January 30, 2023.

119 **books and circulating them among the Vatican hierarchy:** Martin A. Lee, "Their Will Be Done," *Mother Jones*, July/August 1983, https://www.motherjones.com/politics/1983/07/their-will-be-done/, accessed July 31, 2023.

119 **Escrivá had actually asked for a different inscription:** José Luis González Gullón and John F. Coverdale, *Historia del Opus Dei* (Madrid: Ediciones Rialp, 2022), 437.

120 **knelt in silence before his tomb:** Opus Dei doesn't say specifically that the two men visited the tomb of Escrivá. However, it does say the two men visited, knelt, and prayed in the Chapel of the Blessed Sacrament. This chapel is in the same crypt where Escrivá was initially laid to rest after his death in June 1975. See https://romanchurches.fandom.com/wiki/Santa_Maria_della_Pace_dell%27Opus_Dei, accessed January 30, 2023.

120 **known for his simple tastes and dislike of the Venetian elite:** Weigel, *Witness to Hope*, 246.

120 **Four different signals, each of indeterminate color:** Weigel, *Witness to Hope*, 245.

120 **understand what God was trying to tell them:** Weigel, *Witness to Hope*, 251.

120 **thirty-six possible successors put out to the press:** Betty Clermont, *The Neo-Catholics: Implementing Christian nationalism in America* (Atlanta: Clarity Press, 2009), 58.

120 **hailed by progressives and conservatives in equal measure:** Penny Lernoux, *People of God: The Struggle for World Catholicism* (New York: Viking, 1989), 28.

121 **"CRIS, one of Opus Dei's most successful projects—ever . . .":** Vladimir Felzmann, *A Journey to Eternity: My Years in Opus Dei 1959–1982* (Hartpury, UK: All Squared, 2023), 68.

121 **in Chile to overthrow the country's democratically elected government:** Michael Walsh, *The Secret World of Opus Dei* (London: Grafton Books, 1990), 130–131.

121 **former numerary who had written an embarrassing exposé about his time in the movement:** Maurice Roche, "The Secrets of Opus Dei," *Magill*, April 30, 1983, https://magill.ie/archive/secrets-opus-dei, accessed January 31, 2023.

121 **listening devices that had been installed around Villa Tevere:** According to the account of one person involved in the removal of these listening devices, the edict was issued in early 1977. See http://www.opuslibros.org/nuevaweb/modules.php?name=News&file=article&sid=27985, accessed December 6, 2023.

122 **who had specifically named Del Portillo as his successor:** González Gullón and Coverdale, *Historia del Opus Dei*, 440.

122 **"We have been bequeathed a gift . . .":** González Gullón and Coverdale, *Historia del Opus Dei*, 439.

122 **"the matter continues to be open":** Amadeo de Fuenmayor, Valentín Gómez-Iglesias, and José Luis Illanes Maestre, *The Canonical Path of Opus Dei: The History and Defense of a Charism* (Princeton, NJ: Scepter, 1994), 396.

122 **told to prepare the proper documentation:** Fuenmayor et al., *Canonical Path of Opus Dei*, 396.

123 **who agreed to consider the matter:** Fuenmayor et al., *Canonical Path of Opus Dei*.

123 **"This isn't an audience, it's a family meeting":** González Gullón and Coverdale, *Historia del Opus Dei*, 454.

123 **a letter of congratulations to Opus Dei on its fiftieth anniversary:** Walsh, *Secret World of Opus Dei*, 77.

123 **He spent most of his week at a country house owned by Banco Popular:** Luis began using the property the bank owned in San Rafael, about an hour outside of Madrid, following its closure to staff in the late 1970s. His routine was to work in Madrid on Mondays and Tuesday mornings, leave for the mountains during the afternoon, and stay there until Saturday morning, when he would return to the Opus Dei residence. He loved the countryside, the solitary lifestyle that the location afforded him, and the freedom from oppressive rituals back at the numerary residence. Author interviews conducted with former colleagues—including numerary members of Opus Dei—July and September 2022.

123 **his newfound freedom was like a breath of fresh air:** Author interviews with various people at San Rafael and at the bank who worked closely with Luis Valls-Taberner, September 2023.

123 **a modernist concrete hulk that occupied an entire block:** For more on the Beatriz Building, see Eduardo Delgado Orusco, *The Hard Skin: Beatriz Building, Madrid* (Madrid: Lampreave, 2013).

123 **Luis had named it after Beatriz Galindo:** Gabriel Tortella, José María Ortiz-Villajos, and José Luis García Ruiz, *Historia del Banco Popular: La lucha por la independencia* (Madrid: Marcial Pons, 2011), 177–178.

124 **a former television executive and supernumerary member of Opus Dei:** Paul Preston, "Adolfo Suárez Obituary," *The Guardian*, March 23, 2014, https://www.theguardian.com/world/2014/mar/23/adolfo-suarez, accessed February 10, 2023.

124 **"The press has always been very kind to me . . .":** Luis Valls-Taberner interview with *El Pais*, published on December 5, 1976, and cited in Tortella et al., *Historia del Banco Popular*, 245.

124 **began to write articles for various national newspapers:** Tortella et al., *Historia del Banco Popular*, 244–254.

124 **"I've never had the power to *name* ministers":** Interview with Luis Valls-Taberner, *Televisión Española*, 1977.

124 **a grand Council of Europe summit at the bank's headquarters:** See Actas de Presidencia, November 18, 1978, AHBPE, box 37, folder 170.

124 **received 5 percent of the bank's profits every year:** Tortella et al., *Historia del Opus Dei*, 224.

124 **boasted more than two billion pesetas:** The foundation had 2.1 billion pesetas in assets at the end of 1981, of which 710.6 million had been extended in soft loans to various social projects and a further 129.2 million had been donated to good causes. The biggest recipients of money were the Fundación Aliatar (an Opus Dei–run cultural and social center in Andalusia), Asociación de la Juventud de La Pedriza (a holiday camp for boys in the mountains around Madrid that was run by an Opus Dei network of schools), and Colegio Mayor Bonaigua (an Opus Dei university residence in Barcelona for women only). See Fundación Hispánica Annual Report 1982, AHBPE, box 422, folder 2020.

124 **these sums were going to "good causes":** Tortella et al., *Historia del Banco Popular*, 224.

124 **a holiday camp for children run by Opus Dei priests and numeraries:** Since opening in 1978, Las Cabañas—the holiday camp run by Asociación de la Juventud de La Pedriza and funded by the Hispanic Foundation—has hosted around 40,000 children of school age. See https://www.tajamar.es/las-cabanas-otro-plan-de-mejora/, accessed February 10, 2023.

125 **eventually stretch to three hundred schools around the globe:** González Gullón and Coverdale, *Historia del Opus Dei*, 628.

125 **there were eight hundred numeraries teaching children in Opus Dei schools:** González Gullón and Coverdale, *Historia del Opus Dei*, 517.

125 **because classes were taught by "experts" rather than normal teachers:** Maxine Shaw, "Opus Dei School Is Unique, Experimental," *Catholic News Service*, October 1, 1970, https://thecatholicnewsarchive.org/?a=d&d=cns19701001-01.1.8&srpos=1&e=------197-en-20--1--txt-txIN-%22the+heights%22-------Washington%2c+DC, accessed February 3, 2023.

125 **Chicago:** Northridge Prep in Chicago opened its doors with thirty-three boys and eight faculty members, renting space from the Park View School in Mount Prospect, in 1976.

125 **Boston:** Opus Dei opened Oakcrest School for girls in the Virginia countryside around Washington, D.C., in 1976. It opened the Montrose School for girls on the outskirts of Boston in 1979.

125 **drawing up plans to almost double the size:** See Montgomery County, "History of The Heights School and the Existing Special Exception Operations," 7–9, https://www.montgomerycountymd.gov/OZAH/Resources/Files/pdf/2015/CBA-2197-C%2C%20Heights%20School%20ModificationReport%20(Grossman)-signed.pdf, accessed February 3, 2023.

125 **its largest student residence yet:** González Gullón and Coverdale describe the size of the 200-bed residence as unusual for Opus Dei. González Gullón and Coverdale, *Historia del Opus Dei*, 420.

125 **only three-quarters of rooms rented out:** Letter from Graeme Robertson to editor, *Tharunka*, April 27, 1971, 5, https://digitalcollections.library.unsw.edu.au/nodes/view/1943#idx4247, accessed February 13, 2023.

125 **burst into the rooms of students who were forbidden from locking their doors:** Stanley Joseph, "Octopus Dei," *Tharunka*, April 6, 1971, 5, https://

digitalcollections.library.unsw.edu.au/nodes/view/1941#idx4273, accessed February 13, 2023.

126   **adult men and women might dance together:** Joseph, "Octopus Dei."

126   **methodically recorded by the college and then later used:** Joseph, "Octopus Dei."

126   **"Opus Dei is a very deadly form of cancer . . .":** Letter from Stan Correy to editor, *Tharunka*, April 27, 1971, 4, https://digitalcollections.library.unsw.edu.au/nodes/view/1943#idx4245, accessed February 13, 2023.

126   **cover story was a piece about sexual freedom:** Liz Fell, "Family Issue," *Tharunka*, July 28, 1971, https://digitalcollections.library.unsw.edu.au/nodes/view/1950, accessed February 13, 2023.

126   **attention naturally turned to Opus Dei:** José Manuel Cerda, "Like a Bridge over Troubled Water in Sydney: Warrane College and the Student Protests of the 1970s," in *Studia et Documenta*, edited by Maria Carla Giammarco (Rome: Istituto Storico San Josemaría Escrivá, 2010), 4:171–172.

126   **pelted with objects, rubbish, and water bombs:** Cerda, "Like a Bridge," 173.

126   **a mock Passion Play:** Cerda, "Like a Bridge," 176.

126   **locking all the fire escapes of the eight-story, two-hundred-bed building:** Account of Dennis Dubro, an Opus Dei numerary who was assigned to work at Warrane College from 1974, reproduced at https://www.opus-info.org/index.php/Seventeen_Years_in_Opus_Dei, accessed February 13, 2023.

126   **better for all the residents to burn in this life:** Dubro account.

126   **the fire escapes were locked once again:** Dubro account.

126   **to falsify the college's accounts:** "The first thing I discovered was that there was money missing. The dormitory had been submitting false audits for many years." Dubro account and author interview with Dennis Dubro, February 2022.

127   **to take sedatives prescribed by an Opus Dei doctor:** "This was an extremely stressful time for me in which I found it difficult to sleep. At one point, my directors wanted me to take sedatives which they would get from one of our doctors. This was a complete abomination! It was a lack of everything spiritual! Here were directors who claimed to have special spiritual gifts to carry out their God-given responsibilities, and rather than taking away the silencing, the false accusations of disobedience, and the inexperienced and bad-tempered directors, they suggested covering up the effects with drugs!" Dubro account.

127   **had to be closed down not long after opening:** John F. Coverdale, *Putting Down Roots: Father Joseph Múzquiz and the Growth of Opus Dei* (New York: Scepter, 2009), chapter 9.

127   **wood-paneled rooms hung with Spanish paintings and two grand pianos:** "Old Ways Reign in Columbia Hall," *New York Times*, January 10, 1971, 53, https://timesmachine.nytimes.com/timesmachine/1971/01/10/91262231.html?pageNumber=53, accessed February 3, 2023.

127   **"a private residence hall for men who want something special":** *Columbia Daily Spectator* 114, no. 97 (April 24, 1970): 4, https://spectatorarchive.library.columbia.edu/cgi-bin/columbia?a=d&d=cs19700424-01.1.4&e=-------en-20--1-byDA-txt-txIN-%22schuyler+hall%22------, accessed February 3, 2023.

127   **residents being pressured to follow Opus Dei practices:** Fred Schneider, "Schuyler

Hall Administration Accused of Biased Practices," *Columbia Daily Spectator* 116, no. 113 (June 5, 1972): 5, https://spectatorarchive.library.columbia.edu/cgi-bin/columbia?a=d&d=cs19720605-01.2.18&srpos=35&e=-------en-20--21-byDA-txt-txIN-%22schuyler+hall%22------, accessed February 3, 2023.

127 **a ban on residents seeing their families:** David Raab, "Opus Dei: Spirit Behind Schuyler," *Columbia Daily Spectator* 97, no. 105 (April 13, 1973): 1 and 3, https://spectatorarchive.library.columbia.edu/cgi-bin/columbia?a=d&d=cs19730413-01.2.7&srpos=4&e=-------en-20--1-byDA-txt-txIN-%22schuyler+hall%22+%22families%22------, accessed February 3, 2023.

127 **who had been beaten up for speaking to the press:** See https://www.columbiaspectator.com/the-eye/2017/11/17/blinks-in-the-archives/, accessed February 3, 2023.

127 **even going so far as to set up their own alternative governing body:** Interview with Daryl Glick (regional administrator for Opus Dei in the United States during the 1970s), February 2023.

127 **a private bank in Switzerland:** Banque d'Investissements Mobiliers et de Financement, also known as Imefbank.

128 **supposedly as a "guarantee" to the seller:** Letter from Banco Popular to Mariano Navarro Rubio, August 10, 1965, AHBPE, boxes 283–286. There is no evidence that the bank actually paid the deferred second payment to the former owners of Imefbank mentioned in the letter to Navarro Rubio.

128 **on behalf of a Panamanian company:** The Panamanian company Argesco, which had been set up well ahead of the deal in 1953, bought a 35 percent stake in the bank at the same time as Banco Popular. Documents from the Banco Popular archive show that this stake was funded using a loan from another Panamanian entity called Credito Suizo Latinoamericano, a subsidiary of Imefbank. See AHBPE, boxes 283–286.

128 **Opus Dei's top men in Switzerland:** Edwin Zobel was named director of Argesco, the company that bought the secret stake. For a biography of Zobel, and his role within Opus Dei, see https://opusdei.org/fr-ch/article/deux-intrepides-et-un-appartement/, accessed February 7, 2023.

128 **conduit that covertly moved money out of Spain:** Credito Suizo Latinoamericano, a subsidiary of Imefbank that funded the Argesco stake in the bank, made a number of large loans equivalent to millions of dollars from 1972 onward, including to Opus Dei–linked entities such as Sexim, Valfinsa, and Bartyzelinvest. AHBPE, boxes 283–286.

128 **run by senior members of Opus Dei in the United States and Mexico:** Bartyzelinvest, a Liechtenstein company that received almost $6 million in loans, was run by Carl Schmitt and Paul Deck. Both were numerary members of Opus Dei in New York. Paul Deck said that he was asked to take on the role because "they needed an American," but said he did not recall the purpose of the company or its activities. The company was later taken over by Alberto Pacheco Escobedo, one of the first Opus Dei members in Mexico who later became a priest, and Carlos Llano Cifuentes, a founder of the Opus Dei university in Mexico City. Author interview with Paul Deck, February 2023. Also AHBPE, boxes 283–286.

128 **struggled to pay back the $6 million that had been lent to them:** As mentioned, Bartyzelinvest, the company run by Carl Schmitt and Paul Deck, received almost $6 million in loans.

128 **difficult questions about the Swiss bank's finances:** See report "Perspectiva de resultados a corto plazo y sugerencia de una política a seguir para incidir sobre los mismos," March 15, 1975, AHBPE, boxes 283–286.

128 **millions of dollars to save the Swiss bank from collapse:** Jesus Cacho, "Ruiz-Mateos implica al Banco Popular y al Opus Dei en una operación financiera realizada en Suiza en 1978," *El País*, July 10, 1986, https://elpais.com/diario/1986/07/10/econo mia/521330402_850215.html, accessed February 7, 2023.

129 **in negotiations to buy the Sears chain of department stores:** Ernesto Erkaizer, *José María Ruiz-Mateos: El Último Magnate* (Barcelona: Plaza & Janes, 1985), 354.

129 **which he credited with helping him get started in business:** For an account of these years, see Erkaizer, *José María Ruiz-Mateos*, 50–76.

129 **showed his gratitude with large regular donations:** Between 1963 and 1982, Rumasa made more than 3.3 billion pesetas in donations to charity—often to foundations linked to Opus Dei. See Erkaizer, *José María Ruiz-Mateos*, 509.

129 **always felt looked down on by the Opus Dei elite:** Author interviews with several close associates of José María Ruiz-Mateos, conducted between March 2021 and February 2023.

129 **breaking into what he saw as the inner sanctum of the movement:** Author interviews with Ruiz-Mateos associates.

129 **inviting the billionaire to his mountain retreat:** According to records found in the Banco Popular archives, the two men met three times in 1979, eight times in 1980, four times in 1981, and seven times in 1982. Seven of these meetings took place in the bank's mansion in San Rafael. See AHBPE (uncataloged).

129 **to prevent anyone from listening in:** Erkaizer, *José María Ruiz-Mateos*, 522.

129 **business deal involving a German brewery:** Erkaizer, *José María Ruiz-Mateos*, 74.

129 **"I see too many bees . . .":** Robert Hutchison, *Their Kingdom Come: Inside the Secret World of Opus Dei* (London: Transworld, 1997), 305.

129 **various Opus Dei educational initiatives around the world:** Erkaizer, *José María Ruiz-Mateos*, 509–511.

129 **make a contribution to this new initiative:** Erkaizer, *José María Ruiz-Mateos*, 261.

129 **failing to pay billions of pesetas in tax:** Enrique Díaz González, *Rumasa: La verdadera historia del holding desde su inicio en los años sesenta hasta el momento de su expropiación* (Barcelona: Planeta, 1983), 12–13.

129 **indicated to Ruiz-Mateos that he might be able to help:** Exactly what help Luis Valls-Taberner offered to José María Ruiz-Mateos would later become a public court battle. The Andalusian businessman alleged until his death that the Banco Popular chairman had offered to facilitate bribes to the right people in the government to make Ruiz-Mateo's tax problems go away. Valls-Taberner always denied this.

130 **formally submitted its application to change its status:** De Fuenmayor et al., *Canonical Path of Opus Dei*, 398.

130 **primarily as means for ordaining priests outside of the local diocese structure:**

"To carry on special pastoral or missionary work for various regions or social groups which are in need of special assistance, prelatures composed of priests from the secular clergy equipped with special training can be usefully established by the Apostolic See," *Motu Propio Ecclesiae Sanctae* issued by Pope Paul VI, August 6, 1966, Article 4, https://www.vatican.va/content/paul-vi/en/motu_proprio/documents/hf_p-vi_motu-proprio_19660806_ecclesiae-sanctae.html, accessed December 6, 2023.

130 **the authority to ordain priests into the movement:** *Motu Propio Ecclesiae Sanctae.*

130 **projects linked to the personal prelature:** *Motu Propio Ecclesiae Sanctae.*

130 **he expected them to study the application closely:** González Gullón and Coverdale, *Historia del Opus Dei*, 461.

131 **present almost unanimously threw out the application:** González Gullón and Coverdale, *Historia del Opus Dei*, 462.

131 **create a new mobile battalion of priests and laymen:** Juan Arias, "El Opus Dei intenta cambiar su 'status' jurídico dentro de la Iglesia," *El País*, November 8, 1979, 1 and 27, https://elpais.com/diario/1979/11/08/sociedad/310863602_850215.html, accessed January 31, 2023.

131 **boasted about its infiltration of higher education and the media:** Arias, "El Opus Dei intenta cambiar."

131 **more than seventy-two thousand members in eighty-seven different countries:** Arias, "El Opus Dei intenta cambiar."

131 **probably fewer than sixty thousand:** González Gullón and Coverdale cite official Opus Dei statistics which show that membership was only 32,800 in 1975, climbing to 61,700 in 1984, five years after this report was prepared for the Vatican. Membership appears to have crossed the seventy thousand threshold only in the early 1990s. See González Gullón and Coverdale, *Historia del Opus Dei*, 485.

131 **the backing of the Pope:** González Gullón and Coverdale, *Historia del Opus Dei*, 463.

131 **sending ambassadors around the world:** González Gullón and Coverdale, *Historia del Opus Dei*, 463.

131 **a separate branch of the Church with complete autonomy:** "The New Face of the 'Opus Dei': A Personal Prelacy?," anonymous pamphlet distributed in Vatican circles, cited in González Gullón and Coverdale, *Historia del Opus Dei*, 465.

132 **with some parts of the clergy openly questioning his pronouncements:** Lee, "Their Will Be Done."

132 **one which the Pope clung to dearly:** David Remnick, "The Pope in Crisis," *The New Yorker*, October 9, 1994, 52, https://www.newyorker.com/magazine/1994/10/17/the-pope-in-crisis, accessed July 31, 2023.

132 **exposé on the darker side of Opus Dei:** Clifford Longley, "A Profile of Opus Dei," *The Times* [London], January 12, 1981.

132 **measures designed to prevent potential abuse:** See "Guidelines for Opus Dei within the Diocese of Westminster," issued by the Archbishop of Westminster on December 2, 1981, and republished at https://www.opus-info.org/index.php?title=Guidelines_for_Opus_Dei_within_the_Diocese_of_Westminster, accessed March 2, 2023.

132 **would effectively create a church within a church:** *"Hic habemus criterium voluntarium, et ad Eccle- siam particularem aliquis non secundum suam voluntatem intrat; si haberetur*

criterium subiectivum, non fuisset Ecclesia particularis sed specialis, in qua omnes seipsos eligunt: Ecclesia quaedam electorum, et hoc non!," minutes of the Pontifical Commission for the Interpretation of Canon Law, October 20–29, 1981, http://www.opuslibros.org/libros/raztinger/CONGREGATIO_PLENARIA.pdf, accessed July 31, 2023.

132   **"It would be a Church of the elect and we cannot have that!":** Pontifical Commission.

133   **approved the movement's new status from his hospital bed:** González Gullón and Coverdale, *Historia del Opus Dei*, 467.

133   **more than sixty cardinals voicing opposition:** González Gullón and Coverdale, *Historia del Opus Dei*, 468.

133   **was particularly opposed:** González Gullón and Coverdale, *Historia del Opus Dei*, 468.

133   **the body of an Italian banker was found hanging:** Charles Raw, *The Money Changers: How the Vatican Bank Enabled Roberto Calvi to Steal $250 Million for the Heads of the P2 Masonic Lodge* (London: Harvill, 1992), 447.

133   **founded in 1896 by a priest in Milan with a vision:** Rupert Cornwell, *God's Banker: The Life and Death of Roberto Calvi* (London: Counterpoint, 1984), 27–28.

133   **these companies were owned by the Vatican itself:** Cornwell, *God's Banker*, 20.

133   **$1.4 billion in assets secreted out the country:** Cornwell, *God's Banker*, 180.

134   **threw herself to her death:** Cornwell, *God's Banker*, 191.

134   **"religious warfare is not easy":** Giuseppe Zaccaria, "Parla Calvi: il 'complotto' le banche, i giornali, la P2," *La Stampa*, June 15, 1982, 1–2, http://www.archiviolastampa.it/component/option,com_lastampa/task,search/mod,libera/action,viewer/Itemid,3/page,1/articleid,1040_01_1982_0123_0001_17374437/, accessed February 8, 2023.

134   **new information emerged about a meeting in which John Paul II:** Cornwell, *God's Banker*, 177.

134   **startling revelations in the *Wall Street Journal*:** [no title], *Wall Street Journal*, August 19, 1982.

134   **"The answer lies in the final act of Roberto…":** Ennio Caretto, "Le accuse della vedova di Calvi 'Perché uccisero mie marito,'" *La Stampa*, October 7, 1982, 1–2, http://www.archiviolastampa.it/component/option,com_lastampa/task,search/mod,libera/action,viewer/Itemid,3/page,2/articleid,1043_01_1982_0216_0002_14928817/, accessed February 8, 2023.

134   **A jury later ruled the cause of his death to be inconclusive:** "Inquest Jury Undecided on Calvi," *New York Times*, June 28, 1983, D1 and D6, https://timesmachine.nytimes.com/timesmachine/1983/06/28/260111.html?pageNumber=60, accessed February 8, 2023.

134   **parliamentary investigation into the influence of secret societies there:** John L. Allen Jr., *Opus Dei: An Objective Look Behind the Myths and Reality of the Most Controversial Force in the Catholic Church* (New York: Doubleday, 2005), 136.

135   **emergency decree expropriating the entire conglomerate:** Enrique Díaz González, *Rumasa* (Barcelona: Planeta, 1983), 67.

136   **halt all outstanding operations with any of Ruiz-Mateos's businesses:** Memo on Grupo Rumasa circulated by the regional directorate of Banco Popular in Barcelona, sent January 5, 1983 and republished in Díaz González, *Rumasa*, 324.

136 **who else knew about his financial connections with the movement:** Hutchison, *Their Kingdom Come*, 310.

136 **Luis advised him to flee the country:** Erkaizer, *José María Ruiz-Mateos*, 21 and 29; Luis Valls-Taberner later confirmed this in a newspaper interview, a television interview, and in court. See court records of his testimony given on April 7, 1986, AHBPE, folder "Rumasa."

136 **the disgraced businessman staged a dramatic escape:** Mariano Guindal, "Ruiz Mateos escapó a Londres, desapareció en Jamaica y finalmente fue detenido en Francfor," *La Vanguardia*, December 1, 1985, 59.

136 **ordered to conceal his membership in Opus Dei:** Hutchison, *Their Kingdom Come*, 311.

136 **secreted out of the country to companies in Panama:** Erkaizer, *José María Ruiz-Mateos*, 477.

136 **billion pesetas that had been withdrawn in cash:** Erkaizer, *José María Ruiz-Mateos*, 462.

136 **Jews wishing to escape the Nazis:** Testimony of Michael D. Bulmash, published by institutional repository of Kenyon College, https://digital.kenyon.edu/bulmash/1615/, accessed March 3, 2023; see also Erkaizer, *José María Ruiz-Mateos*, 561–567.

136 **helped set up the first Opus Dei foundation in Switzerland:** Harald Schützeichel, *Opus Dei: Goals, Claims and Influence* (Düsseldorf: Patmos Verlag, 1992), 124.

136 **Opus Dei foundation in The Netherlands:** Erkaizer, *José María Ruiz-Mateos*, 482.

136 **earmarked for bribing government officials:** "*El destino de tal dinero se manifestó a mi representado era única y exclusivamente el de resolver sus problemas, no indicándole los medios ni destinos concretos del mismo. . . . Lejos de solucionar la situación, los querellados se han adueñado del dinero, presumiblemente en provecho propio, negando incluso su recepción.*" Court documents, copies of which can be found in the Banco Popular archives, AHEPE (uncataloged).

136 **"look straight into his eyes . . .":** Erkaizer, *José María Ruiz-Mateos*, 519.

136 **apologizing for what had happened and feigning innocence:** Author interview with Benedicto Alguacil de la Blanca (also known as Ben Whyte), a close associate of Ruiz-Mateos, who had the letter read out to him by the disgraced businessman during a walk in Hyde Park in 1983. Interview conducted February 2023.

137 **"I never met Calvi, but some people say I will end up like Calvi":** "This Is Only the Start of a Very Long Film," *Financial Times*, April 30, 1983.

137 **Luis flew to London to calm the situation:** For an account of this meeting, see Erkaizer, *José María Ruiz-Mateos*, 521. Stamps in the passport of Luis Valls-Taberner also confirm this visit to London. See AGUN, collection 299, box 1, folder 6.

137 **invited the banker over for lunch at his house in Chelsea:** The scene is reproduced in Erkaizer, *José María Ruiz-Mateos*, 520–522.

137 **Ruiz-Mateos concluded that there were two sides to Opus Dei:** Hutchison, *Their Kingdom Come*, 312–313.

137 **"Everything has been taken from me . . .":** Hutchison, *Their Kingdom Come*, 318–319.

138 **"How is your soul? Have you been following the norms?":** Hutchison, *Their Kingdom Come*, 319–320.

138 **official creation of the Prelature of the Holy Cross and Opus Dei:** González Gullón and Coverdale, *Historia del Opus Dei*, 475.

7. BLESSED DAY

139 **had come to California with that same spirit of evangelization:** For an account of his trip, see Javier Medina Bayo, *Álvaro del Portillo: Un hombre fiel* (Madrid: Ediciones Rialp, 2012), chapter 20.

139 **Opus Dei's building a shrine in North America:** For more on the Shrine of Mary, Mother of Fairest Love, see https://www.fairestloveshrine.org/about, accessed December 11, 2024.

139 **"We want Christ's reign here on Earth to become a reality . . .":** Medina Bayo, *Álvaro del Portillo*, chapter 20.

140 **openly criticizing the administration:** See Penny Lernoux, *People of God: The Struggle for World Catholicism* (New York: Viking, 1989).

140 **responded with disciplinary measures against the bishops:** Lernoux, *People of God*, 168.

140 **to withhold their contributions to Rome in protest:** Lernoux, *People of God*, 227.

140 **almost derailed a papal visit to the United States in 1987:** Lernoux, *People of God*, 207.

140 **new publications and foundations that exposed liberal bishops:** Lernoux, *People of God*, 175.

140 **"Love your children—do not block the sources of life . . .":** Medina Bayo, *Álvaro del Portillo*.

141 **to fund the growth of Opus Dei in other parts of the world:** Monsignor James Kelly, "Priestly Life in the Writings and Example of Venerable Álvaro del Portillo," written for the Arnold Hall Seminar for Priests, April 21, 2014, https://www.catholicpreaching.com/wp/wp-content/uploads/2014/03/Msgr.-Jim-Kelly-on-Venerable-Alvaro-del-Portillo.pdf, accessed December 11, 2023.

141 **from one wealthy supernumerary family to pay its bills there:** Author interview with John Haley (regional administrator for Opus Dei at the time), September 2023.

141 **was the brains behind that transformation:** Haley interview.

141 **had already investigated dozens of numeraries because of suspicious activity:** Haley interview.

142 **meetings that had never taken place:** See the account of one person asked to do that, at https://opuslibros.org/nuevaweb/modules.php?name=News&file=article&sid=28316, accessed February 23, 2024.

142 **to compile a list of potential wealthy donors:** Haley interview.

142 **indications for $3 million came in:** Haley interview.

142 **barely enough to cover the fundraiser's wages:** Haley interview.

142 **"Everybody needs a new kitchen":** Haley interview.

142 **donate as much as $1 million for the right project:** Haley interview.

143 **rebranded as the "Second Generation Campaign":** Haley interview.

143 **the first $1 million donation for Opus Dei in the United States:** Haley interview.

143 **Dorothy Bunting Duffy was one of them:** See obituary of Dorothy Bunting Duffy, archived at https://webcache.googleusercontent.com/search?q=cache:SIgakRU-lHIJ:

https://www.ncadvertiser.com/past_obituaries/article/Obituary-Dorothy-Duffy-79
-Montessori-founder-14037834.php&hl=en&gl=uk, accessed December 12, 2023.

143 **they fell in with Opus Dei and became supernumeraries:** Author interview with
Mary Ellen Kranzlin (daughter of Dorothy and Joe Duffy), November 2023.

143 **they gave generously to the movement:** Haley interview.

143 **sold to consumer products giant Procter & Gamble for $1.3 billion:** Mark Potts, "Noxell
Accepts Takeover by Procter & Gamble," *Washington Post*, September 23, 1989, https://www
.washingtonpost.com/archive/business/1989/09/23/noxell-accepts-takeover-by-procter
-gamble/2d5aa411-e38a-49f6-9010-d95f420b00b8/, accessed December 12, 2023.

144 **joined Opus Dei as a numerary while studying at Harvard:** Author interview with
Monsignor James Kelly, October 2023.

144 **Kelly was told to get better at asking for money:** Monsignor Kelly interview.

144 **to target its recruitment efforts at teenagers:** Monsignor Kelly interview.

144 **Church's policies and initiatives at national level:** *Vademécum del apostolado de la opin-
ión pública*, 1987, 11.

144 **letters that might be published and read by the general public:** *Vademécum del apostolado*, 12.

144 **whenever the opportunity arose:** *Vademécum del apostolado*, 17.

145 **first be run by the regional commission:** *Vademécum del apostolado*, 32.

145 **were fulfilling the movement's expectations:** *Vademécum del apostolado*, 21.

145 **reading over articles before publication to check for "inaccuracies":** *Vademécum del
apostolado*, 35.

145 **personal dispensation from the prelate himself:** See *Catecismo de la Prelatura de la
Santa Cruz y Opus Dei*, 5th ed., April 1983, Articles 210, 226, and 236.

146 **never removed from Opus Dei premises:** *Vademécum de los Consejos Locales*, 1987, 142.

146 **prohibited the recruitment of anyone younger than eighteen:** According to Article
97 of the *Code of Canon Law*, "A person who has completed the eighteenth year of age
has reached majority; below this age, a person is a minor." Article 98 further states
that "A minor, in the exercise of his or her rights, remains subject to the authority
of parents or guardians except in those matters in which minors are exempted from
their authority by divine law or canon law. In what pertains to the appointment of
guardians and their authority, the prescripts of civil law are to be observed unless
canon law provides otherwise or unless in certain cases the diocesan bishop, for a
just cause, has decided to provide for the matter through the appointment of another
guardian." Furthermore, Article 20 of the *Statutes of Opus Dei*, approved by the Vatican, states clearly that "for someone to be admitted to the Prelature, it is required
. . . that they be at least seventeen years of age." Opus Dei habitually targeted and
groomed minors to become members, and oftentimes instructed the numeraries carrying out such recruitment to hide said recruitment from the parents of the minors.

146 **a new category invented to get around Church restrictions:** *Catecismo de la Prelatura*,
Article 60. Further details are given in the *Vademécum de los Consejos Locales*, 19–21.

146 **some of whom were only thirteen—to masturbate:** Author interview with one
member of that family who was repeatedly sexually abused by an Opus Dei numerary, October 2023.

146 **while also subjecting them to horrific sexual abuse:** Interview with sexually abused boy.

146 **between the ages of twelve and sixteen:** This was according to court documents seen by the author.

146 **"These clubs had much to recommend them . . .":** Johnny Daukes, *Shadowman: Records of a Life Corrupted* (Des Moines, IA: Red Door Press, 2022), 34.

147 **groom Dauke into submission:** Daukes, *Shadowman*, 44.

147 **retreat center out in the English countryside:** Author interview with Johnny Daukes, February 2024.

147 **"frequently took place on Opus Dei premises . . .":** Daukes interview.

147 **running Opus Dei schools:** Daukes interview.

147 **at least one other boy during that time:** Daukes interview.

147 **The abuse was never reported:** Daukes interview; and Daukes, *Shadowman*, 362.

147 **published a book called *Parent's Guide to Opus Dei:*** J. J. M. Garvey, *Parent's Guide to Opus Dei* (New York: Sicut Dixit Press, 1988).

147 **purportedly set up to teach them English and about the American way of life:** See account of Tammy DiNicola, "I Was Shocked by Hidden Agendas Behind Opus Dei 'Service Projects,'" published by the Opus Dei Awareness Network, June 10, 1993, http://www.opus-info.org/index.php?title=I_Was_Shocked_by_Hidden_Agendas_Behind_Opus_Dei_%22Service_Projects%22, accessed December 13, 2023.

148 **"underwater fishing":** See Tammy DiNicola, "Fishing for Vocations in Opus Dei," Opus Dei Awareness Network website, March 19, 1994, https://www.opus-info.org/index.php?title=Fishing_for_Vocations_in_Opus_Dei, accessed December 13, 2023.

148 **"They were vulnerable, unsuspecting youth . . .":** DiNicola, "I Was Shocked."

148 **being tempted by the devil when she asked to leave:** Tammy DiNicola, "Deception and Drugs in Opus Dei," https://odan.org/tw_deception_and_drugs, accessed February 23, 2024.

148 **even gave her Rohypnol, explaining that it would help her get some rest:** DiNicola, "Deception and Drugs."

148 **discussions he had with such patients with the numeraries' superiors:** Author interview with one person treated by this doctor who knew of many others who had received the same treatment, February 2024.

149 **"Opus Dei aimed to spread the Kingdom of God using deceit . . .":** Vladimir Felzmann, *A Journey to Eternity: My Years in Opus Dei 1959-1982* (Hartpury, UK: All Squared, 2023), 68.

149 **offering a cigarette was a great way to break the ice:** Felzmann, *Journey to Eternity*, 33.

149 **more successful in recruiting more members to the cause:** Felzmann, *Journey to Eternity*, 45.

149 **spun off a large portfolio of businesses in the late 1960s:** About sixty companies were spun off into three entities—Sociedad de Gestion de Industrias SA, Sociedad de Gestion de Servicios SA, and Sociedad General Fiducaria SA. See AHBPE (uncataloged).

149 **including one that owned the Banco Popular headquarters:** That was Viviendas y Oficinas SA.

149 **to buy up these assets:** By 1979, the original portfolio of companies owned by

Sogefi—BEN, Financiera Alcalá, Heller Factoring, Iberleasing, Sociedad Anónima de Financiación, Fiventas, Sogeval—had been expanded to include Banco de Andalucia, Vividendas y Oficinas, Union Europea de Inversiones, Arte y Regalos, and others. AHBPE, box 481, folder 6.

149   **One of the subsidiaries was run by Santiago Escrivá:** A 1978 report showed that just seven people were employed by Sociedad General Fiducaria SA, and the highest paid member was Santiago Escrivá with a salary of 1.9 million pesetas, which would be well over $250,000 today. The report bemoans the fact that the salaries are unaffordable owing to the lack of business, and a proposal is put forward to bring the people onto the bank's books. AHBPE, box 481, folder 6.

149   **Luis had transferred ownership of these assets:** Fundación para Atenciones Sociales would be founded the following year. From 1982 onward, it would take over Fundación Hispánica's 5 percent share of Banco Popular's annual profits. Eventually it would become the owner of many of the assets grouped under Sociedad General Fiducaria SA. See Gabriel Tortella, José María Ortiz-Villajos, and José Luis García Ruiz, *Historia del Banco Popular: La lucha por la independencia* (Madrid: Marcial Pons, 2011), 224; and AHBPE, boxes "Sogefi" 1, 2, 4, 5, 8, and 12.

150   **almost six billion pesetas:** By the end of March 1995, some 5.8 billion pesetas had been spent on international projects linked to Opus Dei. See Balance de Cooperación Internacional report with snapshot of spending as of March 1995, AHBPE (uncataloged).

150   **pumped millions of dollars into the expansion of Opus Dei in thirty-seven different countries:** A total of 2.7 billion pesetas were spent on projects in Europe—in order of magnitude—in France, Sweden, Belgium, the UK, the Netherlands, and Italy. A further 870 million pesetas were spent in Argentina, 314 million in Canada, and 290 million in Australia. AHBPE (uncataloged).

150   **hundreds of thousands of dollars generated by Banco Popular:** Between July 1991 and March 1995, the Spanish foundations linked to Banco Popular made payments of 2.9 million French francs—equivalent to around $600,000 at the time—to the École Hôtelière Dosnon and the adjoining retreat center. See "Balance de Cooperación Internacional" report with snapshot of spending as of March 1995, AHBPE (uncataloged).

150   **a rush of property acquisitions by Opus Dei:** José Luis González Gullón and John F. Coverdale, *Historia del Opus Dei* (Madrid: Ediciones Rialp, 2022), 297.

151   **connected by an underground tunnel:** See summary of facts in the ruling made by the Appeals Court of Amiens, case of *Catherine Tissier v. Association de Culture Universitaire et Technique, Claire de Bardon de Segonzac, and Agnés Duhail* on July 27, 2016, https://www .opus-info.org/images/1/1d/Arr%C3%AAt_de_la_Cour_d%27Appel_d%27Amiens_ confirmant_le_jugement_de_la_Cour_d%27Appel_de_Paris.pdf, accessed March 22, 2023.

151   **pressure to join Opus Dei as numerary assistants:** Testimony of Catherine Tissier and several other girls who attended the École Hôtelière Dosnon during the 1980s and 1990s; summary of facts, Appeals Court of Amiens.

151   **to provide cheap labor for the retreats being held next door:** Testimonies of various girls, including Alexandra Thibaut, Aline Deswarte, and Anne Cécile Renard; summary of facts, Appeals Court of Amiens.

151 **worked through until ten at night, seven days a week:** Testimony of Anne Cécile Renard; summary of facts, Appeals Court of Amiens.

151 **impressed by the staff's friendliness and professionalism:** Perrine Cherchève, "La boniche de l'Opus Dei," *Marianne*, April 14, 2017, 40–44, https://www.marianne .net/societe/la-boniche-de-l-opus-dei, accessed March 22, 2023.

151 **None of the staff mentioned the school's affiliation with Opus Dei:** Cherchève, "La boniche de l'opus Dei."

151 **follow the strict timetable of prayers and meditation:** Testimony of Catherine Tissier; summary of facts, Appeals Court of Amiens.

151 **write to Álvaro del Portillo asking for admission:** Tissier testimony, summary of facts, Appeals Court of Amiens.

151 **asked to write a will ceding all her earthly possessions to Opus Dei:** Summary of facts, Appeals Court of Amiens.

151 **rewarded with the gift of a Bible and a crucifix:** Cherchève, "La boniche de l'Opus Dei."

151 **"Your daughter is now an adult . . .":** Cherchève, "La boniche de l'Opus Dei."

152 **moved from one residence to another on short notice:** Summary of facts, Appeals Court of Amiens.

152 **only allowed out if accompanied by another member:** Cherchève, "La boniche de l'Opus Dei."

152 **regularly asked to sign blank checks:** Tissier testimony, summary of facts, Appeals Court of Amiens.

152 **who prescribed for her antipsychotics and tranquilizers:** Cherchève, "La boniche de l'Opus Dei."

152 **be taken off the cocktail of drugs:** Medical opinion of Dr. Caumont following examination on January 12, 2001, cited in summary of facts, Appeals Court of Amiens.

152 **other parents had made similar allegations against the school:** The parents of Nelly Peugnet made similar accusations against the school; cited in summary of facts, Appeals Court of Amiens.

152 **in Argentina:** More than 120 million pesetas were sent to the ICIED foundation, which ran a center for women that was later linked to abuse cases. See "Balance de Cooperación Internacional" report, AHBPE (uncataloged).

152 **including Belgium:** More than three hundred million pesetas were sent to the Cooperative Centres Culturels foundation, which ran a hospitality school at the Château de Dongelberg; "Balance de Cooperación Internacional" report, AHBPE.

152 **Sweden:** More than 450 million pesetas were sent to the Stiftelsen Pro Cultural Foundation, which ran a hospitality school called Trädlärkan; "Balance de Cooperación Internacional" report, AHBPE.

152 **the Philippines:** Almost 130 million pesetas were sent to the Foundation for Professional Training, which ran a hospitality school in the country; "Balance de Cooperación Internacional" report, AHBPE.

153 **not for any breaches of labor law or alleged enslavement:** See "Confusion About a Court Case in France," press release from Béatrice de la Coste, from the Opus Dei

information office in France, https://opusdei.org/en-uk/article/confusion-about-a-court-case-in-france/, accessed June 20, 2023.

153 **keeping Del Portillo updated on the global push to recruit more numerary assistants:** Author interview with the numerary in question, November 2023.

153 **charged with coordinating this global operation:** Numerary interview.

153 **accreditation for the schools' training programs:** Numerary interview.

153 **went straight to work in a numerary residence:** Numerary interview.

153 **The United Nations definition of human trafficking:** Article 3 of the United Nations Protocol to Prevent, Suppress, and Punish Trafficking in Persons, Especially Women and Children, states that:

> For the purposes of this Protocol: (a) "Trafficking in persons" shall mean the recruitment, transportation, transfer, harbouring or receipt of persons, by means of the threat or use of force or other forms of coercion, of abduction, of fraud, of deception, of the abuse of power or of a position of vulnerability or of the giving or receiving of payments or benefits to achieve the consent of a person having control over another person, for the purpose of exploitation. Exploitation shall include, at a minimum, the exploitation of the prostitution of others or other forms of sexual exploitation, forced labour or services, slavery or practices similar to slavery, servitude or the removal of organs;
>
> (b) The consent of a victim of trafficking in persons to the intended exploitation set forth in subparagraph (a) of this article shall be irrelevant where any of the means set forth in subparagraph (a) have been used;
>
> (c) The recruitment, transportation, transfer, harbouring or receipt of a child for the purpose of exploitation shall be considered "trafficking in persons" even if this does not involve any of the means set forth in subparagraph (a) of this article;
>
> (d) "Child" shall mean any person under eighteen years of age.

See UN General Assembly, Resolution 55/25, Protocol to Prevent, Suppress and Punish Trafficking in Persons, Especially Women and Children, Supplementing the United Nations Convention against Transnational Organized Crime, Article 3 (November 15, 2000), https://www.unodc.org/res/human-trafficking/2021the-protocol-tip_html/TIP.pdf, accessed April 22, 2024.

154 **many of the young women were coerced:** Author interviews with dozens of former numerary assistants who worked in Opus Dei residences around the world. Some of these women were part of the group of forty-two women who filed an official complaint with Cardinal Luis Francisco Ladaria Ferrer, who was at the time prefect of the Dicastery for the Doctrine of the Faith, the Vatican authority charged with investigating accusations of abuse within the Catholic Church. The complaint, which was filed with the Vatican in September 2021, alleges that the women were all recruited into Opus Dei between the ages of twelve and sixteen by existing members

who "took advantage of their precarious situations . . . and specifically abus[ed] their vulnerability on account of their young age, offering them the possibility of coming to Buenos Aires under the false promise—made to them and their families—of completing their secondary education and improving their life chances." It alleges that, once in Buenos Aires, girls and women were exploited, forced to work without pay, and moved to other centers when they complained. Similar accounts, including ones from women who were recruited in Europe and elsewhere, have also been published by the Associated Press, the *Financial Times*, and other outlets. See Débora Rey, "Women in Argentina Claim Labor Exploitation by Opus Dei," Associated Press, November 12, 2021, https://apnews.com/article/business-paraguay-europe-argentina-uruguay-43b48ed43c2f7ddebf05ec6203b12d8d; Antonia Cundy, "The Opus Dei Diaries," *Financial Times*, March 16, 2024, https://www.ft.com/content/53bbc8a8-1c5b-4c6e-8d50-8b7c00ffa5f8; Nicolás Cassese and Paula Bistagnino, "¿Servidoras de Diós? El calvario de 43 mujeres que enfrentan al Opus Dei," *La Nación*, May 18, 2021, https://www.lanacion.com.ar/sociedad/servidoras-de-dios-el-calvario-de-las-43-mujeres-que-enfrentan-al-opus-dei-nid17052021/; and Paula Bistagnino, "La Escuela de Mucamas del Opus Dei," *Anfibia*, June 26, 2023, https://www.revistaanfibia.com/la-escuela-de-mucamas-del-opus-dei/.

154 **Opus Dei members from around the globe converged on Rome:** Albert Escala, "La beatificación del fundador del Opus Dei congregó a doscientas mil personas," *La Vanguardia*, May 18, 1992, 25, https://hemeroteca.lavanguardia.com/preview/1992/05/18/pagina-25/33512643/pdf.html, accessed March 8, 2023.

155 **more than a hundred flights that the prelature had chartered:** See https://opusdei.org/es/article/17-de-mayo-del-92-una-experiencia-que-vale-la-pena-repetir/.

155 **transferred half a mile down the road to the Basilica of Saint Eugene:** Bulletin on the Life of Msgr. Escriva, Special Edition, 21, https://cedejbiblioteca.unav.edu/web/centro-de-estudios-josemaria-escriva/biblioteca-virtual/en/viewer/13708/blessed-josemaria-escriva-founder-of-opus-dei-bulletin-10-special, accessed March 8, 2023.

155 **were planning to kidnap his remains:** Robert Hutchison, *Their Kingdom Come: Inside the Secret World of Opus Dei* (London: Transworld, 1997), 5–6.

155 **two hundred thousand people flocked to Saint Peter's Square:** Escala, "La beatificación del fundador."

155 **beatification to Rome by offering to heavily subsidise their trips:** Author interviews with University of Navarre students at the time, who were offered cut-rate trips to Rome coinciding with the beatification, despite having no desire to be involved in Opus Dei.

155 **watched the ceremony from his seat on the steps of Saint Peter's:** Photos of Luis Valls-Taberner at the beatification in 1992 show that he had a front-row seat, up on the stage next to the papal dais. AGUN, collection 299, box 14, folder 2.

155 **to attend the ceremony:** "Numerosos vip en la ceremonia," *La Vanguardia*, May 18, 1992, 25, https://hemeroteca.lavanguardia.com/preview/1992/05/18/pagina-25/33512643/pdf.html, accessed March 8, 2023.

155 **"Why does the press speak so favorably of Mother Teresa . . .":** González Gullón and Coverdale, *Historia del Opus Dei*, 457.

156 **had begun the process well before the statutory five-year waiting period:** Hutchison, *Their Kingdom Come*, 10.

156 **a third of the time it normally took:** Kenneth L. Woodward, "A Questionable Saint," *Newsweek*, January 12, 1992, https://www.newsweek.com/questionable-saint-197568, accessed March 9, 2023.

156 **the cousin of Mariano Navarro Rubio:** Hutchison, *Their Kingdom Come*, 14.

156 **was also a member:** Raffaello Cortesini, who was president of the medical commission at the Vatican's Congregation for the Causes of Saints during the time that the beatification of Escrivá was being assessed, was around the same time also named as chairman of the international scientific committee at the Università Campus Bio-Medico di Roma, an Opus Dei-affiliated medical institute. See Martina Ballmaier, "Opus Dei Works for the Future of Italian Biomedical Science," *Nature Medicine* 2, no. 9 (September 1996): 957. https://www.nature.com/articles/nm0996-957a.pdf, accessed March 8, 2023. Also see Hutchison, *Their Kingdom Come*, 14.

156 **speak out against the beatification—including Antonio Pérez-Tenessa:** Antonio Pérez-Tenessa, "No hablaré mal de la Obra," *El País*, April 12, 1992, https://elpais.com/diario/1992/04/13/sociedad/703116007_850215.html, accessed July 28, 2023.

156 **soon came forward to reveal that they had been refused a hearing:** Woodward, "A Questionable Saint."

156 **gave an interview to *Newsweek*:** Kenneth L. Woodward, "A Questionable Saint," *Newsweek*, January 12, 1992, https://www.newsweek.com/questionable-saint-197568, accessed December 4, 2023.

156 **requesting more time to investigate Escrivá's alleged failings:** González Gullón and Coverdale, *Historia del Opus Dei*, 544.

157 **"We cannot portray as a model of Christian living . . .":** Interview with Juan de Dios Martín Velasco, who had held senior positions within the Archdiocese of Madrid, in *Il Regnio*, reproduced in Hutchison, *Their Kingdom Come*, 14.

157 **his counterreformation against the Church's leftward drift:** See Lernoux, *People of God*, for an exploration of this topic.

157 **summoned to Rome to account for his views on sexual conduct:** David Remnick, "The Pope in Crisis," *The New Yorker*, October 9, 1994, 52, https://www.newyorker.com/magazine/1994/10/17/the-pope-in-crisis, accessed July 31, 2023.

157 **"The Hitler trials were certainly more dangerous . . .":** Remnick, "Pope in Crisis."

157 **the Pope refused to let one cardinal kiss his ring:** Lernoux, *People of God*, 60.

157 **an outraged Pope had shouted *"Silencio!"* during an open-air Mass:** Lernoux, *People of God*, 61.

157 **apprentice bullfighter who left the ring to train as a doctor:** Remnick, "Pope in Crisis," 56.

158 **John Paul II's image as the virile, athletic picture of health:** Remnick, "Pope in Crisis."

158 **recruitment video for Opus Dei:** Remnick, "Pope in Crisis."

158 **start to unduly influence decision-making:** Remnick, "Pope in Crisis."

158   **Del Portillo had been named a bishop:** González Gullón and Coverdale, *Historia del Opus Dei*, 479.

158   **compared with three under Paul VI:** See https://www.catholic-hierarchy.org/diocese /dqod0.html, accessed December 13, 2023.

8. A NEW DEMOGRAPHIC

159   **as a staff member on an obscure Catholic magazine called *Crisis*:** Joe Feuerherd, "The Real Deal: How a Philosophy Professor with a Checkered Past Became the Most Influential Catholic Layman in George W. Bush's Washington," *National Catholic Reporter*, August 19, 2004, https://www.nationalcatholicreporter.org/update/bn HOLD081904.htm, accessed December 15, 2023.

159   **Hudson seemed to thrive on academia:** Feuerherd, "Real Deal."

159   **"Something seemed wrong . . .":** Feuerherd, "Real Deal."

159   **"handbook for senior scouts":** Hans Urs von Balthasar, "Integralismus," *Wort und Wahrheit* 18 (1963): 737–744.

160   **Daryl Glick, a numerary from the Midwest:** Author interview with someone with direct knowledge of the incident, November 2023.

160   **an after-school club for bright children in the sixties:** Robert A. Best, *The Lord and the Links* (Phoenix: Leonine Publishers, 2012), 149–151.

160   **path to liberation was through the traditions of the Church:** Colman McCarthy, "Celebrating Good Men," *Washington Post*, April 14, 1995, https://www.washington post.com/archive/lifestyle/1995/04/14/celebrating-good-men/3fbe6855-8694 -426b-a3b5-f9fd3880b02a/, accessed December 15, 2023.

160   **decline in purity and innocence in American culture:** David Ruppe, "Opus Dei: A Return to Tradition," ABC, June 18, 2001, https://culteducation.com/group/1086-opus -dei/15629-opus-dei-a-return-to-tradition.html, accessed December 19, 2023.

160   **"But it's immoral for them to wear their hair that long . . .":** Lisa Socarra, "Vocation Thursdays: Father Ron Gillis," *Catholic Herald*, December 29, 2011, https://apriest life.blogspot.com/2011/12/vocation-thursdays-father-ron-gillis.html, accessed December 15, 2023.

161   **S.A.T. program that some of the male numeraries ran:** Evan Thomas, "Washington's Quiet Club," *Newsweek*, March 8, 2001, https://www.newsweek.com/washing tons-quiet-club-149005, accessed June 6, 2023.

161   **"to respond with generosity should the Lord call them":** *Experiencias de las labores apostólicas*, 2003, 115. While this is comes from an internal document published later, this was an update of a similar text that had been in use since 1987.

161   **sessions to extract more money from the supernumerary base:** *Experiencias de las labores apostólicas*, 128.

161   **"apostolic tasks" deemed helpful to Opus Dei:** *Experiencias de las labores apostólicas* 142.

161   **considered "immoral or contrary to the common good":** *Experiencias de las labores apostólicas*, 153.

161   **"they are simply not aware of their capabilities . . .":** *Experiencias de las labores apostólicas*, 158.

161 **deemed useful allies in the "doctrinal and moral battles" ahead:** *Experiencias de las labores apostólicas.*

162 **"The importance of engaging with leading intellectuals . . .":** *Experiencias de las labores apostólicas,* 159.

162 **had been run by the Redemptorists since the 1950s:** According to a background document provided by the Opus Dei press office in New York.

162 **a relative of the Nazi general who tried to assassinate Adolf Hitler:** Guy Lamolinara, "Against Hitler: Exhibition Commemorating German Resistance Opens," *Library of Congress Information Bulletin* 53, no. 16 (September 5, 1994), https://www.loc.gov/loc/lcib/94/9416/open.html, accessed April 24, 2024.

162 **Opus Dei should take over the chapel and bookstore:** Author interview with Damian von Stauffenberg, November 2023.

162 **"The vision was to lure people in through books . . .":** Von Stauffenbrg interview.

163 **without really knowing what it was:** Best, *Lord and the Links,* 3.

163 **A teammate called him a "killer" in the locker room:** Best, *Lord and the Links,* 5.

163 **Best assumed they meant the pope:** Best, *Lord and the Links,* 4.

163 **"having jumped into something I knew little about . . .":** Best, *Lord and the Links,* 4.

163 **The three men greeted each other with the traditional *"Pax"*:** Best, *Lord and the Links,* 33.

163 **"No, my son, America has a great soul . . .":** Best, *Lord and the Links,* 138.

163 **"Nixon's finest hour, but he never knew it":** Best, *Lord and the Links,* 139–140.

163 **Hawaiian hotel and a grower of Christmas trees:** Best, *Lord and the Links,* 35–40.

164 **His superiors rejected the idea:** Von Stauffenberg interview.

164 **much of the money went to Opus Dei projects:** Von Stauffenberg interview; and Best, *Lord and the Links,* 41.

164 **The cardinal asked Del Portillo whether he could help:** Von Stauffenberg interview.

164 **while studying to be an engineer at Harvard:** See obituary at https://www.washingtonpost.com/archive/local/1999/02/07/obituaries/b890d4cd-2665-4287-95e5-192b5ece5c15/, accessed December 15, 2023.

165 **before settling on its shorter, more forthright name:** Feuerherd, "Real Deal."

165 **"emergency dinners" to stave off bankruptcy were common:** Feuerherd, "Real Deal."

165 **quadrupling its readership and its budget:** Feuerherd, "Real Deal."

165 **retreats that the movement held for select members:** Author interview with one person who was present, November 2023.

165 **Supreme Court Justice Antonin Scalia was one of those in attendance:** Interview with person present.

165 **live with the founder in Rome:** James Rosen, *Scalia: Rise to Greatness* (Washington, DC: Regnery, 2023), 1:31.

165 **getting drawn in by his friend's enthusiasm:** Rosen, *Scalia,* 1:71.

165 **old schoolfriend, who had since been ordained as an Opus Dei priest:** Rosen, *Scalia,* 1:31.

166 **the Supreme Court Justice was a regular at the V.I.P. retreats hosted by Opus Dei:** Scalia's attendance dates back to at least 1988; see Antonin Scalia papers, Harvard Law School Library, box 79, folder 7.

166 **A numerary sent him a list of thirty-six colleges:** Scalia papers, Harvard Law School Library.

166 **regularly had him over to the family home for dinner:** See account by Hadley Arkes, in NR Symposium, "Antonin Scalia—A Justice in Full," *National Review*, February 29, 2016, https://www.nationalreview.com/2016/02/antonin-scalia-supreme-court -justice-remembrances/, accessed June 12, 2023.

166 **other attendees to the V.I.P. Opus Dei:** Author interview with one person who was present, November 2023.

166 **almost a fifth of its entire readership at that stage:** Feuerherd, "Real Deal."

166 **Bradley and Scaife foundations, which made six-figure contributions:** Feuerherd, "Real Deal."

166 **redevelop six properties:** The properties were 239, 241, and 243 Lexington Avenue and 137, 139, and 141 East 34th Street. The purchases were completed on September 8, 1993. See https://a836-acris.nyc.gov/DS/DocumentSearch/DocumentDetail?doc _id=FT_1740000445174, accessed March 10, 2023.

166 **Most of the money for the purchase had actually been transferred from another nonprofit:** According to tax filings, Association for Cultural Interchange, Inc., made a loan of $4 million to National Center Foundation, Inc., in September 1993. The loan had a tenure of ten years and had a 4 percent interest rate, with no principal payable in the first two years.

167 **would include a hundred bedrooms:** "A Catholic Organization Builds a New Head-quarters," *New York Times*, February 21, 1999, sec. 11, 1, https://timesmachine.ny times.com/timesmachine/1999/02/21/403083.html?pageNumber=385, accessed March 10, 2023.

167 **the $70 million cost of making them a reality:** According to tax records, in addition to the $5,095,600 spent on purchasing the six properties, Murray Hill Place, Inc., subsequently spent $57,818,675 on building works and an additional $6,918,761 on furnishing and equipment between 1995 and 2001.

167 **just three thousand members across the entire United States:** "Catholic Organiza-tion Builds New Headquarters."

167 **a staunch defender of the modernization of the Church:** Steven P. Millies, "If We'd Listened to Cardinal Bernardin, the Catholic Church Would Not Be Where It Is Today," *National Catholic Reporter*, November 4, 2021, https://www.ncronline.org/ news/if-wed-listened-cardinal-bernardin-catholic-church-would-not-be-where-it -today, accessed December 14, 2023.

167 **The move provoked an outcry:** "Opus Dei Appointment Questioned by Clergy," *Na-tional Catholic Reporter*, January 18, 1991.

167 **to buy a former seminary for $9 million:** Robert McClory, "Diocese May Sell Semi-nary to School Tied to Opus Dei," *National Catholic Reporter*, February 24, 1995.

168 **concern about the organization's aggressive, dogmatic approach:** Robert McClory, "Chicago Rejects Bid from Opus Dei for Seminary," *National Catholic Reporter*, May 26, 1995.

168 **the two initiatives would eventually raise more than $70 million:** According to a document provided by the Opus Dei press office in New York.

168 **returning from a trip to the Holy Land:** The trip took place from March 14, 1994, until March 22, 1994. See José Luis González Gullón and John F. Coverdale, *Historia del Opus Dei* (Madrid: Ediciones Rialp, 2022), 442.

168 **would be a retreat center of its own in the Holy Land:** González Gullón and Coverdale, *Historia del Opus Dei*, 576.

168 **the pope never attended funeral Masses, even when a cardinal died in Rome:** According to Pope John Paul II's spokesman, as told to Jordi Picazo, https://www .roterdamus.com/blog---roterdamus/joaquin-navarro-valls-el-ser-humano-no-esta -fabricado-tiene-que-hacerse-con-su-libertad, accessed December 14, 2023.

168 **138 "electors":** González Gullón and Coverdale, *Historia del Opus Dei*, 558.

169 **"These people are the moderators of civic society . . .":** González Gullón and Coverdale, *Historia del Opus Dei*, 561.

169 **donations collected by the Red Cross:** "R. Templeton Smith Services Tomorrow," *Pittsburgh Post-Gazette*, August 11, 1967, 15, https://www.newspapers.com/article/ pittsburgh-post-gazette-obituary-for-r/42538441/, accessed December 14, 2023.

169 **ventured into insulin production after the war:** John L. Allen Jr., *Opus Dei: An Objective Look Behind the Myths and Reality of the Most Controversial Force in the Catholic Church* (New York: Doubleday, 2005), 223–225.

169 **who were Presbyterians:** Allen, *Opus Dei: Objective Look.*

169 **advocating for women's rights:** For an overview of the life of Eliza Kennedy Smith, see "Mrs R. Templeton Smith: Pittsburgh Civic Leader," *Congressional Record* (Washington, DC: U.S. Government Printing Office, 1965), 111:Part 29, A3040– A3041, https://play.google.com/books/reader?id=lmdOrBDimukC&pg=GBS.SL1 -PA2870&hl=en_GB, accessed March 13, 2023.

169 **who would run the company for the next twenty years:** See In Brief news feature in industry publication *The Pink Sheet*, January 29, 1996, https://pink.pharmaintel ligence.informa.com/PS027549/In-Brief-Ben-Venue, accessed March 13, 2023.

169 **when he was converted to Catholicism by a Byzantine priest:** Author email exchange with Mary Elizabeth Podles (daughter of Kennedy Smith), March 2023.

169 **The two youngest sons—Frederick and Mark—even became numeraries:** Author interview with Luis Tellez (who has known the Smith family for many years), October 2023.

170 **takeover bid by a German company the year after their father's passing:** Raquel Santiago, "German Drug Giant to Acquire Ben Venue," *Crain's Cleveland Business*, November 3, 1997, https://www.crainscleveland.com/article/19971103/SUB/7110 30734/german-drug-giant-to-acquire-ben-venue, accessed December 14, 2023.

170 **Sandy and Mark would receive $80 million from the deal:** Allen cites the value of the stock donated to Opus Dei after the bid as $80 million; see Allen, *Opus Dei: Objective Look*, 223. This figure is backed up by IRS tax filings by the Sauganash Foundation and the Rockside Foundation, which valued their stakes at $35 million each on transfer.

170 **Sauganash Foundation:** See IRS tax filings at https://projects.propublica.org/non profits/organizations/311538838, accessed December 14, 2023.

170 **Rockside Foundation:** See IRS tax filings at https://projects.propublica.org/non profits/organizations/311538837, accessed December 14, 2023.

170   **"number of Donor Trustees by at least one":** Both entities had this written into their statutes; see IRS tax filings.

170   **Opus Dei would whittle their inheritance down to almost nothing:** IRS tax filings show the Sauganash Foundation had assets of less than $1 million in 2014, while the Rockside Foundation had assets of $3.4 million.

170   **$100 million from one of the country's wealthiest businessmen:** Author interview with Lucas Niklison (numerary who works closely with Austral), June 2023.

171   **false invoices revealing that money had gone missing:** Author interviews with two Argentinian numeraries who were active in the country at the time, June 2023.

171   **side projects he hadn't approved originally:** Author interview with the person in question, June 2023.

171   **half-built campus:** Author visit to the campus, which had a model of the original plans, June 2023.

171   **couple from Pittsburgh had made this generous donation:** Author interview with Brian Finnerty (spokesperson for Opus Dei in the United States), February 2023.

171   **encouraged to call these two benefactors "Mamoo" and "Papoo":** Finnerty interview.

172   **aggressively conservative preaching style:** Patrick Allitt, "The Bitter Victory: Catholic Conservative Intellectuals in America, 1988–1993," in *Catholic Lives, Contemporary America*, ed. Thomas J. Ferraro (Durham, NC: Duke University Press, 1997), 156.

172   **after being banned from campus by university authorities:** Author interview with Sebastián Sal (numerary who shared the Mercer Street residence with McCloskey during these years), June 2023.

172   **"I was looking out from where I was standing . . .":** Barbara Matuswo, "The Conversion of Bob Novak," *Washingtonian*, June 1, 2003, https://www.washingtonian.com/2003/06/01/the-conversion-of-bob-novak/, accessed December 19, 2023.

173   **becoming known as the "convert maker":** The blurb and marketing material for McClosky's 2005 book *Good News, Bad News: Evangelization, Conversion and the Crisis of Faith* even described him this way. See https://www.catholicity.com/mccloskey/goodnews.html, accessed June 8, 2023.

173   **the refined splendor of The University Club around a block away, on Sixteenth Street:** Thomas, "Washington's Quiet Club."

173   **grand surroundings for social gatherings:** See the overview of the club's storied history at https://www.universityclubdc.com/history, accessed June 8, 2023.

173   **played squash with the powerful and the influential:** Thomas, "Washington's Quiet Club."

173   **prominent conservatives to the Catholic Church:** "An Opus Dei Priest with an Unusual Gift," *Crux*, June 12, 2015, https://cruxnow.com/church/2015/06/an-opus-dei-priest-with-an-unusual-gift, accessed June 8, 2023.

173   **matters of "natural law" or of "divine revelation":** Charles P. Pierce, "The Crusaders," *Boston Globe*, November 2, 2003, http://archive.boston.com/news/globe/magazine/articles/2003/11/02/the_crusaders/, accessed June 8, 2023.

173 **theologically inspired politics in the United States:** Betty Clermont, *The Neo-Catholics: Implementing Christian Nationalism in America* (Atlanta: Clarity Press, 2009), 132.

173 **priests were warriors for Jesus Christ:** Michael S. Rose, "The Conversion Specialist," in *Priest: Profiles of Ten Good Men Serving the Church Today* (Bedford, New Hampshire: Sophia Institute Press, 2013), available at https://www.catholicity.com/mccloskey/conversionspecialist.html, accessed June 8, 2023.

173 **"someone who believes in the sanctity of marriage . . .":** Pierce, "The Crusaders."

174 **a condition he called Friendship Deficit Syndrome:** Father John McCloskey, "The Key to the Evangelization of Men," https://www.catholicity.com/mccloskey/friendship.html, accessed June 8, 2023.

174 **"Once Father John gets his claws into you, he never lets go":** "An Opus Dei Priest."

174 **while struggling with an addiction to alcohol and cocaine:** "An Opus Dei Priest."

174 **feared might even push him to suicide:** Steve Fishman, "The Convert," *New York Magazine*, July 30, 2004, https://nymag.com/nymetro/news/people/features/9572/, accessed June 8, 2023.

174 **the two became good friends:** Laurie P. Cohen, "Tyco Scandal, Money to Opus Dei?," *Wall Street Journal*, June 4, 2003, https://www.wsj.com/articles/SB105467469545317500, accessed June 9, 2023.

174 **"I thank God every day for the gift of mistaken e-mail addresses:** Cohen, "Tyco Scandal."

174 **Bowie Kuhn, Lew Lehrman, and Bob Best:** Fishman, "The Convert." 4

174 **"I'm on fire with the faith":** Fishman, "The Convert."

174 **"human guardian angel":** Fishman, "The Convert."

174 **"everything (but I still miss you . . .)":** Fishman, "The Convert."

175 **following a drunken sexual encounter between them:** Feuerherd, "Real Deal."

175 **"idealism from offices that bind our culture together . . .":** Feuerherd, "Real Deal."

175 **political attitudes of American Catholics:** Feuerherd, "Real Deal."

175 **"swing voters are *active* Catholics":** "The Catholic Vote—A Special Report: The Mind of the Catholic Voter," *Crisis*, November 1, 1998, https://crisismagazine.com/vault/the-catholic-vote-a-special-report-the-mind-of-the-catholic-voter, accessed December 18, 2023.

175 **opportunity to tap into a new demographic:** Peter J. Boyer, "Party Faithful," *The New Yorker*, September 1, 2008, https://www.newyorker.com/magazine/2008/09/08/party-faithful, accessed December 18, 2023.

176 **$3.4 million from the sale of restricted shares:** Cohen, "Tyco Scandal."

176 **"$2M toward my pledge to the new Sanctuary/Altar":** Cohen, "Tyco Scandal."

176 **receive more than $50 million from his employer:** Cohen, "Tyco Scandal."

176 **had recently been set up by Bob Best:** Cohen, "Tyco Scandal."

176 **"especially the poor, the elderly and those who have no voice":** See Culture of Life Foundation & Institute website, archived at https://web.archive.org/web/20030627092233/http://christianity.com/CC_Content_Page/0,,PTID4211%7cCHID116414%7cCIID,00.html, accessed December 20, 2023.

176 **counted a number of high-profile supporters:** Culture of Life Foundation website.

176 **basically a one-man band:** According to IRS filings made by the Culture of Life Foundation, Best was the only paid member of the board and the only one of the board members who regularly spent hours working for the foundation and who lived in the Washington area; see https://projects.propublica.org/nonprofits/display_990/522055185/2002_05_EO%2F52-2055185_990_200012, accessed December 20, 2023.

176 **address from his old Private Sector Initiatives Foundation offices to 815 15th Street:** Culture of Life Foundation IRS filings.

177 **she hadn't taken the news well:** Cohen, "Tyco Scandal."

177 **most of those present were members of the prelature:** Cohen, "Tyco Scandal."

177 **even misleading government investigators:** Cohen, "Tyco Scandal."

177 **"Justice triumphs—and the Founder comes through again!":** Cohen, "Tyco Scandal."

177 **six-figure donation to the Culture of Life Foundation:** Cohen, "Tyco Scandal."

177 **a commemorative mass was held at the Catholic Information Center:** Christine Creech, "Cardinal Hickey Dedicates Chapel Honoring Josemaria Escriva," *Catholic Way*, September 15, 2000, http://sites.silaspartners.com/partner/Article_Display_Page/0,,PTID5339_CHID28_CIID155862,00.html, accessed March 27, 2023.

177 **had flown in from Rome for this symbolically important event:** Creech, "Cardinal Hickey Dedicates."

177 **deep fissure running through the U.S. congregation:** Robert D. McFadden, "Cardinal James A. Hickey of Washington Dies at 84," *New York Times*, October 25, 2004, sec. B, page 7, https://www.nytimes.com/2004/10/25/obituaries/cardinal-james-a-hickey-of-washington-dies-at-84.html, accessed March 27, 2023.

178 **"another effort in the new evangelization":** McFadden, "Cardinal James A. Hickey."

178 **the Fairfax County Planning Commission across the river in Virginia had approved:** Record CP-86-C-121-13: Tyson Study Center, Inc., retrieved from https://plus.fairfaxcounty.gov/CitizenAccess/cap/CapDetail.aspx?type=1000&Module=Zoning&capID1=09HS5&capID2=00000&capID3=000BK&agencyCode=FFX&FromACA=Y, accessed December 20, 2023.

178 **a $9 million development that was to be called the Reston Study Center:** See IRS tax filing for Reston Study Center, filed for tax year ending June 2006, https://projects.propublica.org/nonprofits/display_990/541826300/2006_12_EO%2F54-1826300_990_200606, accessed December 20, 2023.

178 **financial consultant and supernumerary called Neil Corkery:** Neil Corkery is named as treasurer for the project; see IRS tax filing for early 2000s, https://projects.propublica.org/nonprofits/organizations/541826300, accessed December 20, 2023.

9. CLOAK AND DAGGER

179 **he'd be back in time for Sunday dinner with the family:** Major Garrett, host, *Agent of Betrayal: The Double Life of Robert Hanssen*, episode 8, "Dosvedanya," CBS News podcast, https://podcasts.apple.com/us/podcast/dosvedanya/id1505853304?i=1000635011298, accessed December 20, 2023.

179 **a part-time theology teacher at nearby Oakcrest School:** Author interview with former students, February 2023.

179   **a childhood friend of Robert Bucciarelli:** Craig Unger, *American Kompromat: How the KGB Cultivated Donald Trump, and Related Tales of Sex, Greed, Power, and Treachery* (London: Scribe, 2021), 105.

179   **first school in the city, back in the seventies:** Author interview with Father John Wauck (younger brother of Bonnie and an Opus Dei priest), November 2023.

180   **had grown to embrace his membership in Opus Dei:** Garrett, *Agent of Betrayal*, episode 2, "The Spy Next Door," https://podcasts.apple.com/us/podcast/the-spy-next -door/id1505853304?i=1000629481398.

180   **aggressively foist his Catholic faith onto his colleagues:** Garrett, *Agent of Betrayal*, episode 2.

180   **big donor to the movement, to attend the regular "circle":** Author interview with Mary Ellen Kranzlin (daughter), November 2023.

180   **widely rumored to be a member, too:** Kenneth L. Woodward, "Opus Dei in the Open," *Newsweek*, October 6, 2002, https://www.newsweek.com/opus-dei -open-146563, accessed December 20, 2023.

180   **drive out to Dulles Airport herself:** Garrett, *Agent of Betrayal*, episode 8.

180   **the agents had a warrant to search their house:** Garrett, *Agent of Betrayal*, episode 8.

180   **conducted by F.B.I. agents and their colleagues at the Central Intelligence Agency:** Garrett, *Agent of Betrayal*, episode 7, "Room 9930," https://podcasts.apple.com/us/ podcast/room-9930/id1505853304?i=1000634235035.

180   **information about a dead-drop planned for that Sunday:** Garrett, *Agent of Betrayal*, episode 7.

180   **suspicious activity which might mean he was being monitored:** Garrett, *Agent of Betrayal*, episode 7.

181   **Bonnie took him to Father Robert Bucciarelli:** Unger, *American Kompromat*, 105; for further reading about the incident, see David Wise, *Spy: The Inside Story of How the FBI's Robert Hanssen Betrayed America* (New York: Random House, 2003); and David A. Vise, *The Bureau and the Mole: The Unmasking of Robert Philip Hanssen, the Most Dangerous Double Agent in FBI History* (New York: Atlantic, 2002).

181   **Bucciarelli called to say that he had changed his mind:** Unger, *American Kompromat*, 106.

181   **movement's most prominent families would reflect badly on the Work:** Unger, *American Kompromat*, 106.

181   **gave up valuable military and counterintelligence secrets:** See "A Review of the FBI's Performance in Deterring, Detecting, and Investigating the Espionage Activities of Robert Philip Hanssen," Office of the Inspector General, August 14, 2003, https://oig.justice.gov/sites/default/files/archive/special/0308/index.htm, accessed February 20, 2023.

181   **to the Holy See at the American Embassy:** Rachel Donadio, "Leaked Cables Show Vatican Tensions and Diplomacy with U.S.," *New York Times*, December 11, 2010, A9, https://www.nytimes.com/2010/12/11/world/europe/11vatican.html, accessed August 1, 2023.

181   **not a single penny after 1992:** Donadio, "Leaked Cables."

181   **close to the top of the F.B.I. pay scale:** "Review of the FBI's Performance."

182 **the thousands of dollars that Hanssen spent on tuition:** "Review of FBI's Performance."

182 **Hanssen reaped more than $600,000 from the Russians:** "Review of FBI's Performance."

182 **"Request for urgent meeting struck post as unusual . . .":** Donadio, "Leaked Cables."

182 **boasted more than eighty thousand members:** According to data published in the *Annuario Pontificio*, which is the official annual directory of the Holy See of the Catholic Church, published by the Vatican. A historical series of the data is available at https://www.catholic-hierarchy.org/diocese/dqod0.html, accessed June 15, 2023.

182 **had a physical presence in sixty countries across six continents:** See https://opus dei.org/en-uk/article/historical-overview/, accessed December 21, 2023.

183 **as auxiliary bishop to the Archdiocese of Denver:** Vatican press release, January 23, 2001, https://press.vatican.va/content/salastampa/it/bollettino/pubblico/2001/01/23/0048/00132.html, accessed March 27, 2023.

183 **"We are not a sect . . .":** Charles W. Bell, "Catholics' Strict Offshoot," *Daily News*, May 13, 2001, available at https://culteducation.com/group/1086-opus-dei/15624-cath olics-strict-offshoot-.html, accessed March 27, 2023.

183 **the founder of the power company AES Corporation, Dennis Bakke:** Author interview with Daryl Glick (who identified the donor as one of the founders of AES), February 2023.

183 **844-acre property near the Shenandoah Mountains:** According to the "Woodlawn Foundation Campaign for the Twenty First Century" document, provided by Opus Dei press office in the United States.

183 **had begun moving into Murray Hill Place the previous fall:** Bell, "Catholics' Strict Offshoot."

183 **it said was unfinished construction:** Bell, "Catholics' Strict Offshoot."

183 **indictment of Hanssen on twenty-one counts of espionage:** The indictment was published the day before the planned ceremony and would have been front-page news in all the papers that day. See https://irp.fas.org/ops/ci/hanssen_indict.html, accessed December 21, 2023.

183 **exclusive as the lead story on its front page:** James Risen and David Johnston, "Wife Says Suspect Told a Priest 20 Years Ago of Aiding Soviets," *New York Times*, June 16, 2001, A1, https://www.nytimes.com/2001/06/16/us/wife-says-suspect-told-a -priest-20-years-ago-of-aiding-soviets.html, accessed December 21, 2023.

183 **met with the double-agent in the context of spiritual guidance:** Risen and Johnston, "Wife Says Suspect Met."

183 **kicked off frenzied speculation:** Noam Friedlander, *What Is Opus Dei?: Tales of God, Blood, Money and Faith* (London: Collins & Brown, 2005), 125.

184 **establishment might also be involved with the group:** Friedlander, *What Is Opus Dei?*

184 **both named as possible sympathizers:** Evan Thomas, "Washington's Quiet Club," *Newsweek*, March 8, 2001, https://www.newsweek.com/washingtons-quiet -club-149005, accessed June 6, 2023.

184 **"especially the poor, the elderly and those who have no voice"**: See Culture of Life Foundation & Institute website, https://web.archive.org/web/20030627092233/http://christianity.com/CC_Content_Page/0,,PTID4211%7cCHID116414%7cCIID,00.html, accessed December 20, 2023.

184 **"Once people have made a decision to discard the leftover embryo . . ."**: "Stem Cell Research," *Washington Journal*, C-SPAN, video, July 6, 2001, https://www.c-span.org/video/?165054-4/stem-cell-research&desktop=#!, accessed December 21, 2023.

185 **pro-life figures to the foundation as advisors**: See Culture of Life Foundation & Institute website, https://web.archive.org/web/20020601121852/http://www.christianity.com:80/CC_Content_Page/0,,PTID4211%7cCHID116414%7cCIID,00.html, accessed December 21, 2023.

185 **director of an Opus Dei numerary residence there**: Author interview with Luis Tellez (one of the Opus Dei numeraries who became close to him), October 2023. He was also close to Father McCloskey.

185 **after being aggressively hounded by Father Bob Connor**: "Pro-Life Doctor Recalls Life in the Trenches," *Defend Life*, January-February 2005, https://www.defendlife.org/newsletters/Feb2005/hogan.shtml, accessed December 21, 2023.

185 **sudden rise in interest in the stem cell with a stream of press releases**: See Culture of Life Foundation & Institute, https://web.archive.org/web/20011120134550/http://www.christianity.com:80/CC_Content_Page/0,,PTID4211%7cCHID120680%7cCIID,00.html, accessed December 21, 2023.

186 **had helped double the foundation's budget from two years earlier**: See IRS tax filing for the Culture of Life Foundation, Inc., for year ending December 31, 2000, https://projects.propublica.org/nonprofits/display_990/522055185/2002_05_EO%2F52-2055185_990_200012, accessed December 21, 2023.

187 **pumped out reams of disinformation and pseudo-science on its website**: See Culture of Life Foundation & Institute, https://web.archive.org/web/20010204013000/http:/culture-of-life.org/news_lrci.html, accessed June 9, 2023.

187 **"then going on to dance the night away . . ."**: Robert A. Best, "Our Nobility," https://web.archive.org/web/20000816033602/http://www.culture-of-life.org/cull_best_ournobility.htm, accessed June 9, 2023.

187 **Democratic candidate's "tolerance" of homosexuals**: "Gore Cites His 'Tolerance' of Homosexuals," https://web.archive.org/web/20000816034734/http://www.culture-of-life.org/gores_tolerance_of_gays.htm, accessed December 21, 2023.

187 **complain about plans for two openly gay superheroes**: "DC Comics to Include Homosexual Couple!," https://web.archive.org/web/20000816034754/http://www.culture-of-life.org/dc_comics_homo.htm, accessed December 21, 2023.

188 **pledging to restrict funding to research on tissues extracted from adults**: See Letter from President Bush to the Culture of Life Foundation, https://web.archive.org/web/20020807201432/http://www.christianity.com/partner/Article_Display_Page/0,,PTID4211%7cCHID102753%7cCIID442205,00.html, accessed December 21, 2023.

188 **announced in a televised address to the nation the following month**: See "Address to the Nation on Stem Cell Research," August 9, 2001, https://www.presidency

.ucsb.edu/documents/address-the-nation-stem-cell-research, accessed December 21, 2023.

188 **had racked up huge losses every year since:** According to author interview with Álvaro Sánchez-Carpintero (university's director of promotion and development), the running costs have never been covered by the fees paid by students; interview November 2023.

188 **a conduit for money diverted from other Opus Dei foundations:** According to Jack Valero (spokesperson for Opus Dei in the United Kingdom), independently run foundations all around the world habitually receive requests from Rome to contribute toward the university's running costs; author interview with Jack Valero, July 2023.

188 **more than $2 million to the university:** See IRS tax filing for Pontifical University of the Holy Cross Foundation for tax year ending December 31, 2002, https://projects.propublica.org/nonprofits/display_990/133458562/2003_12_EO%2F13-3458562_990_200212, accessed December 22, 2023.

188 **Other foundations in Chile, Germany, Italy, and Spain performed similar roles:** José Luis González Gullón and John F. Coverdale, *Historia del Opus Dei* (Madrid: Ediciones Rialp, 2022), 507.

188 **"at the service of the whole Church":** See the official profile and mission statement of the university, https://en.pusc.it/chi-siamo, accessed December 22, 2023.

188 **hard-up dioceses in Europe, Latin America, and Africa:** Sánchez-Carpintero interview.

188 **secretary of the Pontifical Council for Legislative Texts:** Juan Ignacio Arrieta, who headed up the school of canon law for much of the eighties and nineties, was promoted in February 2007.

189 **"cornering the market":** Author interview with Jack Valero (spokesperson for Opus Dei in the United Kingdom), September 2023.

189 **"The Grandeur of Ordinary Life":** See https://web.archive.org/web/20020927025252/http://www.escriva2002.org/, accessed December 22, 2023.

189 **important conservative allies:** "Congress at the Pontifical University of the Holy Cross, Rome," *Romana: Bulletin of the Prelature of the Holy Cross and Opus Dei*, 34, https://romana.org/en/34/the-centennial-of-his-birth/congress-at-the-pontifical-university-of-the-holy/, accessed December 22, 2023.

189 **which would include conferences:** See "Centennial of Saint Josemaría Escrivá's Birth," https://opusdei.org/en-us/article/centennial-of-saint-josemaria-escrivas-birth/, accessed December 22, 2023.

189 **his wife's devout Catholic parents:** Author interview with Father Tom Bohlin (former Opus Dei regional vicar for the United States), September 2023.

189 **regularly attended its V.I.P. retreats out in rural Virginia:** According to another person present; author interview, November 2023.

189 **by paying him a speaking fee:** Stephanie McCrummen and Jerry Markon, "Rick Santorum's Journey to Devout Catholicism, View of Religion in Governance," *Washington Post*, March 19, 2012, https://www.washingtonpost.com/national/rick-santorums-journey-to-devout-catholicism-view-of-religion-in-governance/2012/03/16/gIQAj4NzNS_story.html, accessed December 22, 2023.

189 **covered by the foundation in Princeton:** Jennifer Rubin, "Exclusive: Santorum the homebody?," *Washington Post*, blog, March 20, 2012, https://www.washington post.com/blogs/right-turn/post/exclusive-santorum-the-homebody/2012/03/20/ gIQAn0pBPS_blog.html, accessed December 22, 2023.

190 **famous phrase attributed to the founder:** John L. Allen Jr., "Opus Dei Prestige on Display at Centenary Event," *National Catholic Reporter*, January 18, 2002, https://natcath.org /NCR_Online/archives2/2002a/011802/011802f.htm, accessed December 22, 2023.

190 **"to leave one's Catholicism aside . . .":** Allen, "Opus Dei Prestige."

190 **to uphold absolute truths—"blessed Josemaría guides my way":** McCrummen and Markon, "Rick Santorum's Journey."

190 **such views had caused "much harm in America":** Allen, "Opus Dei Prestige."

190 **"All of us have heard people say . . .":** Allen, "Opus Dei Prestige."

190 **Wojtyła presented McCloskey with a rosary:** Allen, "Opus Dei Prestige."

190 **Pope John Paul the Great, as McCloskey called him:** Allen, "Opus Dei Prestige."

190 **devastating exposés by a group of journalists at the** *Boston Globe***:** See https://www .bostonglobe.com/news/special-reports/2002/01/06/church-allowed-abuse-priest -for-years/cSHfGkTIrAT25qKGvBuDNM/story.html for a list of articles published over the course of 2002 by the Spotlight team at the paper, accessed April 27, 2023.

191 **"not a problem of pedophilia . . .":** "La Iglesia de E.U. Sacudida por los Casos de Pederastia de Sacerdotes," *Aceprensa*, April 3, 2002, an interview with Father John McCloskey, available at https://www.catholicity.com/mccloskey/pederastia.html, accessed December 22, 2023.

191 **stepping down risked creating a "domino effect" that could rip through the Church:** Betty Clermont, *The Neo-Catholics: Implementing Christian nationalism in America* (Atlanta: Clarity Press, 2009), 170.

191 **"People with these inclinations just cannot be ordained":** Melinda Henneberger, "Vatican Weighs Reaction to Accusations of Molesting by Clergy," *New York Times*, March 3, 2002, https://www.nytimes.com/2002/03/03/us/vatican-weighs-reac tion-to-accusations-of-molesting-by-clergy.html, accessed December 22, 2023.

191 **played his recent appearance on** *Meet the Press* **on a continual loop:** Author interview with several attendees around that time, February and November 2023.

191 **"The church is not run by opinion polls . . .":** As stated on *Meet the Press*, NBC, March 31, 2002.

192 **had a very public falling out with McCloskey:** Charles P. Pierce, "The Crusaders," *Boston Globe*, November 2, 2003, http://archive.boston.com/news/globe/magazine/ articles/2003/11/02/the_crusaders/, accessed June 8, 2023.

192 **had broken the seal of confession by sharing very personal information with someone else:** Author interview with someone familiar with the situation, November 2023.

192 **the venue would host five hundred people to its weekend retreats:** See 2002 IRS tax filing for Wyoming House, Inc., which owns both the Wyoming Avenue property and the Longlea Conference Center that hosted retreats, https://projects.propublica.org/ nonprofits/display_990/521760051/2003_08_EO%2F52-1760051_990_200212, accessed June 6, 2023.

192 **were attending its monthly evenings of recollection:** Wyoming House, Inc., IRS tax filing.

193 **Catholics to choose if, when, and how often they took part:** See Canon 630 under the 1983 code, https://www.vatican.va/archive/cod-iuris-canonici/eng/documents/cic_lib2-cann607-709_en.html#CHAPTER_IV, accessed April 17, 2024.

193 **"The confidence—that sincere chat, full of supernatural meaning . . .":** Javier Echevarría, *Experiencias sobre el modo de llevar charlas fraternas*, March 2001, 4.

193 **"who are gifted with the necessary graces to help you . . .":** Echevarría, *Experiencias sobre el modo de llevar charlas fraternas*, 5.

193 **"Advice will normally take the form of guidance or suggestions . . .":** Echevarría, *Experiencias sobre el modo de llevar charlas fraternas*, 12.

193 **a weak, trembling voice that betrayed the extent of his Parkinson's:** See video at https://opusdei.org/es-co/article/canonizacion-de-san-josemaria/, accessed March 27, 2023.

193 **the Vatican was struggling to keep secret:** Nick Pisa, "Vatican Hid Pope's Parkinson's Disease Diagnosis for 12 Years," *Daily Telegraph*, March 19, 2006, https://www.telegraph.co.uk/news/worldnews/europe/italy/1513421/Vatican-hid-Popes-Parkinsons-disease-diagnosis-for-12-years.html, accessed March 27, 2023.

194 **a Spanish doctor supposedly cured of his cancer:** See Vatican announcement, https://www.vatican.va/latest/documents/escriva_miracolo-canoniz_en.html, accessed March 27, 2023.

194 **the pope invited Echevarría into his vehicle to tour the crowd:** Vatican announcement.

194 **the Vatican would at long last admit what had been obvious for many years:** Pisa, "Vatican Hid Pope's Parkinson's Disease."

10. THE ALBINO ASSASSIN

195 **still riding high from the positive coverage:** Author interview with Brian Finnerty, February 2023.

195 **had set the publishing world ablaze with excitement:** Charlotte Abbott, "Code Word: Breakout," *Publishers Weekly*, January 27, 2003, https://www.publishersweekly.com/pw/print/20030127/32725-code-word-breakout.html, accessed April 24, 2023.

196 **"What keeps this baroque conceit from collapsing . . .":** Abbott, "Code Word."

196 **a clear priority for his bosses at Villa Tevere:** See https://opusdei.org/en/article/chronology-of-the-cause-of-canonization-of-bishop-alvaro-del-portillo/, accessed May 17, 2023.

196 **corner in its relationship with the press:** Finnerty interview.

196 **the foresight to secure the opusdei.org domain:** Finnerty interview.

196 **stumbled across a set of bound galleys of the book:** Finnerty interview.

196 **the words "A Novel" were emblazoned on the cover:** "The Da Vinci Code," *Publishers Weekly*, February 3, 2003, https://www.publishersweekly.com/9780385504201, accessed April 25, 2023.

196 **"The Vatican prelature known as Opus Dei is a deeply devout Catholic sect . . .":** Dan Brown, *The Da Vinci Code* (London: Bantam Press, 2003), 2.

197 **rules controlling the information they consumed:** Accounts of numeraries and numerary assistants from various countries, speaking on the condition of anonymity.

197 **by putting together his own list:** E.B.E., *Opus Dei as Divine Revelation: Analysis of Its Theology and the Consequences in Its History and People* (self-published, 2019), 170.

197 **approved by an Opus Dei priest in Rome:** E.B.E., *Opus Dei as Divine Revelation.*

197 **framed these false accusations as acts of religious persecution:** Escrivá described the attacks against Opus Dei in the early days of the movement as "like the one that Jesus suffered at the hands of the priests and the local princes: calumnies, lies, trickery, insults," and modern-day attacks on the prelature were often viewed through that same lens. See *Meditations*, 29-III-1959.

197 **new assignment as Opus Dei's most senior man in the States:** See announcement "Rev. Thomas G. Bohlin Appointed Regional Vicar of the Prelature of Opus Dei in the United States," December 11, 2002, https://opusdei.org/en-uk/article/rev -thomas-g-bohlin-appointed-regional-vicar-of-the-prelature-of-opus-dei-in-the -united-states/, accessed May 17, 2023.

197 **living out their faith in the world as lawyers or doctors or politicians:** Author interview with Father Thomas Bohlin, September 2023.

198 **he began to like the job—but was soon transferred to another role:** Bohlin interview.

198 **Bohlin had never been keen on becoming a priest:** Bohlin interview.

198 **informed of their new posting only when the needs of the Work required it:** Author interview with dozens of numeraries who were informed of their new postings without any real consultation, July 2022 to November 2023.

198 **being groomed for another, more important role:** "I think you know, what they do with young people . . . you work with them and you get trained. You're getting trained. I didn't realize." Bohlin interview.

199 **Bohlin went back to accept:** Bohlin interview.

199 **expanding to seven new countries:** The countries were Estonia, Slovakia, Lebanon, Panama, Uganda, Kazakhstan, and South Africa. Bohlin interview.

199 **just five thousand new members had joined:** According to data published in the *Annuario Pontificio*, the official annual directory of the Holy See of the Catholic Church published by the Vatican each year. A historical series of the data is republished at https://www.catholic-hierarchy.org/diocese/dqod0.html, accessed June 15, 2023.

199 **barely recognized the events they had supposedly experienced:** See the video posted on YouTube by former numerary member David Gilbert, "The Key to Understanding Opus Dei," https://www.youtube.com/watch?v=Ip6FFDQvEtY, accessed June 6, 2023.

199 **fiction that was unlikely to have much impact:** Finnerty interview.

199 **"Brian, don't worry, the novel sounds so silly that nobody will ever buy it":** Marc Carroggio, Brian Finnerty, and Juan Manuel Mora, "Three Years with The Da Vinci Code," a paper prepared for a conference, titled Strategic Management of Church Communications: New Challenges, New Directions, organized by the Pontifical

University of the Holy Cross, April 2006, http://bib26.pusc.it/jjgn/seminar06/com_pdf/carroggio_finnerti_en.pdf, accessed April 25, 2023.

200 **decked out with promotional material for the book:** Finnerty interview.

200 **Doubleday, had put into the promotional campaign:** Abbott, "Code Word."

200 **"In this gleefully erudite suspense novel . . .":** Janet Maslin, "Spinning a Thriller From a Gallery at the Louvre," *New York Times*, March 17, 2003, E8, https://www.nytimes.com/2003/03/17/books/books-of-the-times-spinning-a-thriller-from-a-gallery-at-the-louvre.html, accessed April 25, 2023.

200 **top of the bestseller list during its first week on sale:** Bill Goldstein, "As a Novel Rises Quickly, Book Industry Takes Note," *New York Times*, April 21, 2003, C11, https://www.nytimes.com/2003/04/21/business/media-as-a-novel-rises-quickly-book-industry-takes-note.html, accessed April 25, 2023.

200 **the book had a disclaimer saying it was fiction:** Account of a numerary member based in the United States at the time, May 2023.

200 **"marketing promotion and its pretension to authentic scholarship . . .":** "The Da Vinci Code, the Catholic Church, and Opus Dei: A Statement from the Prelature of Opus Dei in the United States on The Da Vinci Code," press release, September 30, 2003, https://web.archive.org/web/20040101040351/http://www.opusdei.org/art.php?w=32&p=6437, accessed April 25, 2023.

201 **the prelature also included links to several reviews critical of the book:** "Da Vinci Code, Catholic Church, and Opus Dei," statement.

201 **pieces in the *Chicago Tribune* and *Newsday*, and on National Public Radio giving voice:** For a list of media coverage of the publication of *The Da Vinci Code*, including links to the original pieces, see https://odan.org/opus_dei_in_the_media, accessed April 25, 2023.

201 **part of a series it was doing on secret societies:** "Secret Societies: Opus Dei," *Anderson Cooper 360°*, CNN, December 9, 2003, http://edition.cnn.com/TRANSCRIPTS/0312/09/acd.00.html, accessed April 25, 2023.

201 **requesting that the name of Opus Dei not be used:** Carroggio et al., "Three Years with The Da Vinci Code."

201 **a call to the press office from the producers of *The Sopranos*:** Finnerty interview.

201 **"You think I don't know what that is? It's for Opus Dei . . .":** "Rat Pack," *The Sopranos*, Series 5, episode 2. HBO, March 14, 2004.

202 **the prelature's star priest in Washington, in November 2002:** See statements regarding Fr. C. John McCloskey by Msgr. Thomas Bohlin, Vicar of Opus Dei in the U.S., posted online, January 7, 2019, https://opusdei.org/en-us/article/message-from-msgr-thomas-bohlin-2/, accessed April 26, 2023.

202 **pressed himself against her, kissed her hair, and caressed her:** Joe Heim, "'Quite a Shock': The Priest Was a D.C. Luminary. Then He Had a Disturbing Fall from Grace," *Washington Post*, January 14, 2019, https://www.washingtonpost.com/local/quite-a-shock-the-priest-was-a-dc-luminary-then-he-had-a-disturbing-fall-from-grace/2019/01/14/99b48700-1453-11e9-b6ad-9cfd62dbb0a8_story.html.

202 **only for him to absolve her of her sins:** Michelle Boorstein, "Opus Dei Paid $977,000 to Settle Sexual Misconduct Claim Against Prominent Catholic Priest,"

Washington Post, January 7, 2019, https://www.washingtonpost.com/religion/2019/01/08/opus-dei-paid-settle-sexual-misconduct-claim-against-prominent-catholic-priest/.

202 **failing to even ascertain the charges against McCloskey:** "The real accusation didn't come until a few years later because the woman didn't tell us everything." Bohlin interview.

202 **given assurances that Father McCloskey would be dealt with:** Author interview with one person with knowledge of the investigation and its aftermath, February 2023.

202 **"I'm a salesman for the church . . .":** Joe Feuerherd, "Selling Orthodoxy to Washington Power Brokers," *National Catholic Reporter*, September 5, 2003, https://natcath.org/NCR_Online/archives2/2003c/090503/090503c.htm, accessed April 26, 2023.

202 **she resolved to seek justice through the courts:** Author interview with one person with knowledge of the investigation and its aftermath, February 2023.

203 **fundraiser event for the new numerary residence:** Scalia attended an event for the Reston Study Center in May 2003; see Antonin Scalia papers, Harvard Law School Library, box 99, folder 45.

203 **who might also be involved with the group:** Noam Friedlander, *What Is Opus Dei? Tales of God, Blood, Money and Faith* (London: Collins & Brown, 2005), 125.

203 **federal funding for research on previously discarded human embryos:** Best had been particularly incensed by the president's willingness to green-light federal funding for research on previously discarded human embryos; Robert A. Best, *The Lord and the Links* (Phoenix: Leonine Publishers, 2012), 47.

203 **Best fell on some marble steps and broke both kneecaps:** Best, *Lord and Links*, 47.

204 **provided seed funding:** See tax filing from National Catholic Prayer Breakfast in 2004, where it declares a loan made to it from the Culture of Life Foundation, https://projects.propublica.org/nonprofits/display_990/200408543/2006_02_EO%2F20-0408543_990R_200412, accessed June 12, 2023.

204 **office space:** According to their respective 2004 IRS tax filings, both organizations were registered to 1413 K Street NW, Suite 1000.

204 **Bohlin had quietly ordered:** Bohlin interview.

204 **had spotted some cognitive issues that made it difficult for the priest to write:** Bohlin interview.

204 **he played an active role in the Catholic community:** Christopher White, "Case of Opus Dei Priest Raises Fresh Questions About Clerical Abuse Crisis," *Crux*, January 15, 2019, https://cruxnow.com/church-in-the-usa/2019/01/case-of-opus-dei-priest-raises-fresh-questions-about-clerical-abuse-crisis, accessed April 27, 2023.

204 **a thousand in attendance for the breakfast:** See archived web page at https://web.archive.org/web/20050407192956/http:/www.catholicprayerbreakfast.com/inaugural.html, accessed June 12, 2023.

204 **"unexpectedly I was able to take several months of sabbatical":** Father John McCloskey, "American Lessons from Europe's Fall," *National Catholic Register*, May 2004,

https://www.catholicity.com/mccloskey/americanlessons.html, accessed April 27, 2023.

205 **U.S. presidential candidate John Kerry:** *Evening News*, CNN, April 12, 2004, https://tvnews.vanderbilt.edu/broadcasts/752820, accessed April 27, 2023.

205 **Opus Dei lobbied the local archbishop in London:** White, "Case of Opus Dei Priest."

205 **"without adding to it—precisely as it is!":** José Luis González Gullón and John F. Coverdale, *Historia del Opus Dei* (Madrid: Ediciones Rialp, 2022), 439.

205 **An approach endorsed by his own successor, Echevarría:** González Gullón and Coverdale, *Historia del Opus Dei*, 560–561.

206 **Opus Dei had no legal or financial connection:** John L. Allen Jr., *Opus Dei: An Objective Look Behind the Myths and Reality of the Most Controversial Force in the Catholic Church* (New York: Doubleday, 2005), 207–208.

207 **stake in the bank was worth more than a billion dollars:** The shares were officially owned by a web of companies and foundations which officially operated independently, but which in practice were often run by the same numerary members, who coordinated activity and who funneled any income from the holdings back to Opus Dei projects around the world—often in consultation with Rome. At the end of 2003, four entities closely linked to Opus Dei—Sindicatura de Accionistas del Banco Popular Español SA, Instituto de Educación e Investigación SA, Popularinsa SA, and Naarden International SA—owned more than twenty-five million shares in the bank, either directly or indirectly through affiliated companies and subsidiaries. Those shares were worth almost 1.2 billion euros at the time. See *Informe Anual 2003* (Madrid: Banco Popular Español, 2004), 82.

207 **"Don't use 'we,' conjugate using only 'I'":** Recollections of Father Escrivá written by Luis Valls-Taberner shortly after the death of the founder, written at Pozoalbero, August 30, 1975, GAPOD (uncataloged).

207 **which were generating close to $50 million a year in dividends:** The twenty-five million shares that were controlled either directly and indirectly by the four Opus Dei–linked entities were paid more than forty million euros in dividend payments in 2003. See *Informe Anual 2003*, 84.

207 **An additional $50 million was generated along this route:** "El Banco Popular destina 40 millones de euros a acción social," *La Gaceta*, available at https://www.ccoo-servicios.info/noticias/imprimir/8060.html, accessed May 2, 2023.

207 **had made it his personal mission to "liberate" the founder and the Opus Dei elite from any financial worries:** "*No tenía sentido que tanto el Padre como D. Álvaro emplearan su tiempo, y anduvieran preocupados por problemas económicos. Para afrontar esos problemas podíamos y debíamos estar los demás, y, de este modo, liberar al Padre y a D. Álvaro de esa preocupación. A partir de esa fecha, de este primer viaje, decidí emplearme a fondo en esta cuestión, para liberar en lo que pudiera el peso que a mí se me antojaba que era como muy grande para ellos.*" Recollection of Father Escrivá, GAPOD (uncataloged).

208 **nicknamed "The Terminator":** Author interviews with various Banco Popular colleagues, July and September 2022.

208 **a coup with one of the bank's largest shareholders:** Interviews with Banco Popular colleagues.

208 **Ángel Ron, a young protégé of Luis:** Interviews with Banco Popular colleagues.

208 **installed Ron to replace him:** Bank announcement to the Spanish stock market regulator, March 5, 2002, https://www.cnmv.es/Portal/hr/verDoc.axd?t={b05dd1ea-4ada-46bb-bcc8-063d47072a8d}, accessed May 4, 2023.

208 **"We would have expected that a measure of such magnitude . . .":** Letter from Diethart Breipohl, the board member representing Allianz, to Javier Valls-Taberner, March 12, 2002, AHBPE, box 297, folder 745.

209 **was appointed to the board:** Bank announcement to the Spanish stock market regulator, October 21, 2002, https://www.cnmv.es/Portal/hr/verDoc.axd?t={a5fbf4c8-df74-4290-ba76-a7f8126730c7}, accessed May 4, 2023.

209 **A deal was soon struck for Banco Popular to buy his bank:** The deal to buy Banco Nacional de Crédito Inmobiliario was announced on January 23, 2003. After the deal, its owner, Américo Amorim, ended up with a stake greater than 5 percent in Banco Popular, making him the third largest shareholder behind the Opus Dei–aligned Sindicatura de Accionistas del Banco Popular Español SA and the German insurer Allianz. See *Informe Anual 2005* (Madrid: Banco Popular Español, 2005), 61.

209 **so that he might marry:** Author interviews with José Ramón Rodríguez García (board member and fellow supernumerary), July and September 2022.

209 **Luis rushed to his house with a pile of sensitive documents for supposed "safe keeping":** Rodríguez García interview.

209 **Spanish insurance company that began buying up shares in Popular:** Platero also held a senior position on the board of Mutua Madrileña and helped broker an agreement to buy a 1 percent stake in Popular. When the insurance company increased its stake to above 3 percent, Luis feared another coup and dismissed Platero from the board. See bank announcement to the Spanish stock market regulator, November 7, 2003, https://www.cnmv.es/Portal/hr/verDoc.axd?t={7fbab4a2-e94c-44b9-baec-9f30b89cc276}, accessed May 4, 2023.

209 **he sent Ron to do his dirty work:** Author interview with one of those present, September 2022.

209 **Platero was so overcome that he needed to be taken to the hospital:** Author interview with one of those present.

210 **his fellow numerary Paco as general secretary of the bank:** Bank announcement to the Spanish stock market regulator, December 18, 2003, https://www.cnmv.es/Portal/hr/verDoc.axd?t={84d274fc-3cf5-45d2-8616-2ce364896e50}, accessed May 4, 2023.

210 **Sold an entire $400 million stake in the bank:** María Jesús Pérez, "La Mutua Madrileña sale del Popular y compra un 1,2% del Santander por 531 millones," *ABC*, April 27, 2004, https://www.abc.es/economia/abci-mutua-sale-popular-y-compra-2por-ciento-santander-millones-200404270300-9621186021002_noticia.html.

210 **after boasting about it as a "safe" and "very profitable" investment:** "Spain's Mutua Madrilena buys 3 pct of Popular," Reuters, November 5, 2003.

210 **increasingly unable to venture outside his room unaided:** Rodríguez García interview.

211 **was subject to the watchful eye of the local director:** This practice is well

documented. See opuslibros.org for various accounts by numeraries, and the control over the correspondence.

211 **he was being prevented from seeing his brother:** Author interviews with Javier Valls-Taberner, April and November 2019.

211 **a man he had trusted with Banco Popular's most intimate secrets:** Javier was one of only three directors named on the Panamanian company Crédito Suizo Latinoamericano, the vehicle used to channel money to various Opus Dei–linked companies in Europe and the Americas. AHBPE, boxes 283–286.

211 **instructions from Rome to safeguard the assets still in his brother's name:** Crédito Suizo Latinoamericano, AHBPE.

211 **"a request, which won't come as a surprise to you . . .":** Note sent to Javier Valls-Taberner, purportedly at the request of his brother Luis, dated January 17, 2006, and found in the personal archives of the recipient.

212 **who sat on the board were summoned to see Luis:** Rodríguez García interview.

212 **"Because you are loyal":** Rodríguez García interview.

212 **plans were put together to merge their various holdings under a single umbrella:** See filing made by Union Europea de Inversiones to the Spanish stock market regulator, March 1, 2006.

213 **buying additional Banco Popular shares:** See prospectus for capital increase filed by Union Europea de Inversiones to the Spanish stock market regulator, November 23, 2006, https://www.cnmv.es/Portal/verDoc.axd?t={a2788e70-fab4-43e4-a317 -9048e1c303f7}, accessed May 26, 2023.

213 **lion's share of the money would come from the foundations:** The majority of the funds came from three sources—Fundación IEISA, Fundación Para el Desarollo y la Cooperación, and Viviendas y Oficinas—which were affiliated with Opus Dei. See changes in the shareholder base between December 2005 and December 2006 for details on this, filed with Spanish stock market regulator.

213 **a solid bloc of Opus Dei–allied shareholders holding 20 percent:** The group included the collective holdings of Francisco Aparicio, Americo Ferreira de Amorim, Luis Herrando, Casimiro Molins, Luis Montuenga, José Ramón Rodríguez, and Sindicatura de Accionistas de BPE and was equivalent to more than 250 million shares, or 20 percent of the bank's outstanding share capital at the end of 2005. See *Informe Anual 2005*, 58.

213 **students were encouraged to file past the corpse:** Author interview with Armando Guerra (personal bodyguard and driver for Luis Valls-Taberner for many years), September 2022.

214 **failed despite numerous attempts to elicit any kind of reassurance from Sony Pictures:** Carroggio et al., "Three Years with The Da Vinci Code."

214 **Opus Dei had flown its communications teams:** Carroggio et al., "Three Years with The Da Vinci Code."

214 **screen adaptation would be faithful to the novel:** Devin Gordon, "The 'Code' Breakers," *Newsweek*, December 26, 2005, https://www.newsweek.com/code-break ers-114221, accessed May 26, 2023.

214 **"That's news to me—I'll have to get back to you":** Gordon, "The 'Code' Breakers."

214 **make something more palatable out of the lemons they had been dealt:** Carroggio et al., "Three Years with The Da Vinci Code."

214 **an affront—not just to Opus Dei but also to all Christians:** Carroggio et al., "Three Years with The Da Vinci Code."

215 **The "real-life Silas":** Carroggio et al., "Three Years with The Da Vinci Code."

215 **small box outside the entrance, containing literature about the prelature:** Carroggio et al., "Three Years with The Da Vinci Code."

215 **"Ignorance is always a great evil and information a good . . .":** Véronique Groussett, "Statut, Argent et Prosélytisme: Les Réponses du «Pape» de l'Opus Dei," *Le Figaro*, April 21, 2006, https://www.lefigaro.fr/lefigaromagazine/2006/04/21/01006-20060421ARTMAG90513-statut_argent_et_proselytisme_les_reponses_du_pape_de_l_opus_dei.php, accessed May 26, 2023.

215 **"To millions and millions of readers . . .":** *Hardball with Chris Matthews*, NBC, May 18, 2006, https://www.nbcnews.com/id/wbna12870827, accessed February 23, 2024.

216 **victim of McCloskey's sexual misconduct:** Boorstein, "Opus Dei paid $977,000."

216 **silence her from ever revealing anything about its star priest:** See Bohlin statement regarding Fr. C. John McCloskey.

217 **"God's mercy is much greater than our sexual sins . . .":** See YouTube posting of interview, https://www.youtube.com/watch?v=uYZRkID96X4, accessed June 12, 2023.

217 **a documentary aimed at helping Catholics become "marriage material":** See archived webpage for *Road to Cana* at https://web.archive.org/web/20051125130328/http://roadtocana.com/, accessed June 12, 2023.

11. A MARRIAGE OF CONVENIENCE

218 **a political stunt by party grandees that had no real chance of passing:** Maria Newman, "Bush Backs Gay Marriage Ban as Senate Debates," *New York Times*, June 5, 2006, https://www.nytimes.com/2006/06/05/washington/05cnd-bush.html, accessed January 7, 2024.

218 **Its real aim was re-energizing the conservative base:** Jim Rutenberg, "Conservatives Watching Senate Debate on Gay Marriage," *New York Times*, June 6, 2006, https://www.nytimes.com/2006/06/06/washington/06bush.html, accessed January 7, 2024.

219 **"How many constituents do you have?":** Jeff Sharlet, "God's Senator," *Rolling Stone*, February 9, 2006, https://www.rollingstone.com/politics/politics-features/sam-brownback-gods-senator-883564/, accessed January 7, 2024.

219 **the Opus Dei chapel on K Street presided over by McCloskey, he converted:** Chris Suellentrop, "The Rev. John McCloskey: The Catholic Church's K Street lobbyist," *Slate*, August 9, 2002, https://slate.com/news-and-politics/2002/08/the-catholic-church-s-k-street-lobbyist.html, accessed January 7, 2024.

219 **his time in the Senate to serving that one constituent—God:** Sharlet, "God's Senator."

219 **"how societies have been built for thousands of years . . .":** See *Congressional Record*

152, no. 69 (June 5, 2006), https://www.congress.gov/congressional-record/vol ume-152/issue-69/senate-section/article/S5401-11, accessed January 7, 2024.

220 **academics and activists such as Robert George, Hadley Arkes, and Maggie Galla-gher:** See the speaker list at https://web.archive.org/web/20041204180904/http:// www.winst.org/index2.html, accessed January 7, 2024.

220 **a beachhead for Opus Dei at American universities across the United States:** Author interview with Luis Tellez, November 2023.

221 **one of three brothers in a family of eight who joined Opus Dei as numeraries:** Tellez interview.

221 **who wanted to leave their fortune to good causes:** Francisco Gómez Franco and Begoña Laresgoiti Foix set up the charity, initially called the Mass Foundation, in 1985. Their idea was to create a foundation that would support projects in Mexico and other parts of the world. These projects would be for charitable, educational, and cultural purposes. See https://www.cloverfdn.org/our-history/, accessed June 16, 2023.

221 **they agreed to put him in charge of the endowment:** Tellez interview.

221 **It would eventually swell in size to almost $130 million:** See IRS tax filings at https://projects.propublica.org/nonprofits/organizations/742390003, accessed December 30, 2023.

221 **the Mexican numerary immediately became enamored with the town:** Tellez interview.

222 **It was at Princeton that Luis Tellez met Robert George:** Tellez interview.

222 **on the books in order to assert these moral standards:** James Merritt, "Heretic in the Temple: Robby George Once Worked for George McGovern; Now He's the Hero of the Intellectual Right," *Princeton Alumni Weekly*, October 8, 2003, https://www .princeton.edu/~paw/archive_new/PAW03-04/02-1008/features1.html, accessed February 26, 2024.

222 **funding a postdoctorate chair using money from the Clover Foundation:** Tellez interview.

223 **"I wanted to make friends. And I did both . . .":** Tellez interview.

223 **given permission to relocate full time to Princeton:** Tellez interview.

223 **including the Clover Foundation and some Opus Dei donors:** "Spotted History Aside, Opus Dei Forges Close Campus Links," *Daily Princetonian*, March 21, 2005, https://www.dailyprincetonian.com/article/2005/03/spotted-history-aside-opus -dei-forges-close-campus-links, accessed June 12, 2023.

223 **activists and fellowships for conservative professors and students:** Max Blumenthal, "Princeton Tilts Right," *The Nation*, March 13, 2006, https://www.thenation .com/article/archive/princeton-tilts-right/, accessed December 30, 2023.

223 **"solving the political-correctness problem in the academy as a whole:** Blumenthal, "Princeton Tilts Right."

224 **outraged Forbes and conservative moralists like Robby George:** Blumenthal, "Princeton Tilts Right."

224 **The Smith family, heirs to the Ben Venue pharmaceutical fortune, also contributed:** Tellez interview.

224 **other Ivy League universities and later across the world:** Tellez interview.

224 **the study of constitutional law and political thought:** Blumenthal, "Princeton Tilts Right."

224 **revolve solely around the question of religion's role in society:** Deborah Yaffe, "A Conservative Think Tank with Many Princeton Ties," *Princeton Alumni Weekly*, July 16, 2008, http://www.princeton.edu/~paw/web_exclusives/plus/plus_071608witherspoon.html, accessed June 12, 2023.

224 **called the Higher Education Initiatives Foundation:** Tellez interview.

224 **that the prelature was setting up in New York City:** See IRS tax filings, reproduced at https://www.guidestar.org/profile/22-3576915, accessed January 7, 2024.

225 **donations from the Opus Dei foundation during its first three years:** IRS tax filings.

225 **James Madison Program received an additional $187,000:** IRS tax filings.

225 **"to fund several projects to experiment . . .":** Tellez interview.

225 **"I can tell you categorically we have never taken a dime from Opus Dei":** Yaffe, "A Conservative Think Tank."

225 **how compatible that would be with her role as a future mother:** See interview with Ana Samuel, posted on YouTube, https://www.youtube.com/watch?v=oLxxL7eI98g, accessed January 7, 2024.

225 **"Unless you're an active leaven, you're not going to raise the dough . . .":** Author interview with Father Tom Bohlin, September 2023.

225 **new office for the Witherspoon Institute on Stockton Street:** Author interview with Luis Tellez, January 2024.

226 **"Nothing I do is a recruiting tool . . .":** "Spotted History Aside," *Daily Princetonian*.

226 **employing dialogue rather than invective:** Yaffe, "A Conservative Think Tank."

226 **Mercer House, the Opus Dei residence in town, were once again teeming with college students:** "Spotted History Aside," *Daily Princetonian*.

226 **"having the right people in the right places—and seeing what they can do":** Bohlin interview.

226 **struggling to revive its former status in the capital:** Author interviews with two board members, February 2023.

226 **moved to Rome shortly afterwards to study under the founder:** For a biography of Father Bill Stetson, see his obituary, https://angelusnews.com/obituaries/monsignor-william-h-stetson/, accessed July 7, 2023.

226 **Attendance at the daily Mass began to suffer:** Author interview with one board member, February 2023.

227 **Donations dramatically tailed off, too:** Author interview with one board member, February 2023.

227 **it was unable to pay its rent:** Author interview with one board member, February 2023.

227 **had to be bailed out by the Opus Dei headquarters in New York:** This account is borne out by tax filing of the Woodlawn Foundation, the main conduit for tithes from the men's section in the United States, which details loans made in its 2007 and 2008 filings to the Catholic Information Center; see https://projects.propublica.org/nonprofits/organizations/133055729, accessed July 7, 2023.

227 **carefully selected cardinals at an Opus Dei villa on the outskirts of Rome:** Sandro Magister, "Ruling in the Shadow of John Paul II: The Vatican Four," *Chiesa*, https://web.archive.org/web/20061015221317/http:/www.chiesa.espressonline.it/print Dettaglio.jsp?id=19630&eng=y, accessed January 7, 2024.

227 **Herranz began an active campaign to lobby the cardinals:** Betty Clermont, *The Neo-Catholics: Implementing Christian Nationalism in America* (Atlanta: Clarity Press, 2009), 226.

227 **"working within the power structure of the Roman Curia that can make a difference":** Clermont, *The Neo-Catholics.*

227 **what he called the "pre-conclave" about what the priorities of his papacy ought to be:** Julián Herranz, *Dos papas: Mis recuerdos con Benedicto XVI y Francisco* (Madrid: Ediciones Rialp, 2023), 55.

228 **Father Arne had grown up in a small town on the shores of Lake Superior:** For a biography of Father Arne Panula, see his obituary, https://www.colefuneral.com/obituary/FrArne-Panula, accessed July 7, 2023.

228 **and had become a close friend of Peter Thiel:** Mary Eberstadt, *The Last Homily: Conversations with Father Arne Panula* (Steubenville, OH: Emmaus Road, 2018), 148–149.

228 **the two men bonded over their shared disdain for government:** Thiel's libertarian views are well known. Panula also saw government intervention disapprovingly. On government action to save the environment, he said: "The trouble with environmentalism as some now construe it is that if you say the problem is 'carbon emission' or 'the ozone layer' or related abstractions, individuals find that overwhelming. That's why people become resigned to having government discharge the moral obligation, or try to, because it looks like only a big organization can solve such a big problem. . . . And that's precisely what sets the stage for potential malfeasance: the fact that individuals have effectively outsourced their concern to a faceless entity over which they exercise little oversight." See Eberstadt, *Last Homily*, 61–62.

228 **liberalize Mass by the Vatican in the sixties, which had led to "confusion" for men of the cloth:** "Any priest who says Mass every day, or the Liturgy of the Hours, or any of the rest of the discipline embraced within Opus Dei, isn't fertile territory for the evil seeds that led to the scandals. Those seeds were planted during the 1960s and 1970s under quite the opposite circumstances, at a time when many within religious orders, especially, ceased living as religious. . . . It was a time of great confusion, and people swept up in that confusion, and drawn to that confusion, ended up creating the scandals." Eberstadt, *Last Homily*, 77.

228 **"that's inimical to society's flourishing . . .":** Eberstadt, *Last Homily*, 112.

229 **reinvigorate the pipeline of donations that Father C. John had been so successful at:** Author interview with board member at the time, February 2023.

229 **he became spiritual director to Arthur C. Brooks:** Eberstadt, *Last Homily*, 138.

229 **"the most powerful direction I have ever received":** Eberstadt, *Last Homily*, 138.

229 **"friend and confidant to billionaires and Supreme Court Justices":** Eberstadt, *Last Homily*, 137.

229 **while only a toddler, lost his father—a pastry chef—to cancer:** Jeffrey Toobin, "The Conservative Pipeline to the Supreme Court," *The New Yorker*, April 10, 2017, https://

www.newyorker.com/magazine/2017/04/17/the-conservative-pipeline-to-the
-supreme-court, accessed July 11, 2023.

229 **was chosen as the "Most Likely to Succeed" in the yearbook:** Andy Kroll, Andrea
Bernstein, and Ilya Marritz, "We Don't Talk About Leonard: The Man Behind the
Right's Supreme Court Supermajority," *ProPublica*, October 11, 2023, https://www
.propublica.org/article/we-dont-talk-about-leonard-leo-supreme-court-superma
jority, accessed January 7, 2024.

229 **with dollar signs painted on their glasses:** Kroll et al., "We Don't Talk About Leonard."

229 **his classmates nicknamed him the "Moneybags Kid":** Kroll et al., "We Don't Talk
About Leonard."

229 **encouraged the young Leonard to follow their lead:** Toobin, "Conservative Pipeline."

229 **building the case for a novel legal doctrine known as originalism:** Kroll et al., "We
Don't Talk About Leonard."

229 **student organization called the Federalist Society:** Robert O'Harrow Jr. and Shawn
Boburg, "A Conservative Activist's Behind-the-Scenes Campaign to Remake the Nation's Courts," *Washington Post*, May 21, 2019, https://www.washingtonpost.com
/graphics/2019/investigations/leonard-leo-federalists-society-courts/, accessed April
19, 2024.

230 **She decided to convert not long before her marriage:** See Austin Ruse, *Littlest Suffering Souls: Children Whose Short Lives Point Us to Christ* (Charlotte, NC: TAN Books,
2017), chapter 7.

230 **who had recently been appointed to the D.C. circuit:** O'Harrow and Boburg, "Conservative Activist's Behind-the-Scenes."

230 **through his contentious confirmation process for the Supreme Court:** O'Harrow
and Boburg, "Conservative Activist's Behind-the-Scenes."

230 **Backed by a cabal of wealthy conservative patrons:** The Federalist Society Annual Report 2007, 29, https://fedsoc-cms-public.s3.amazonaws.com/update/pdf/
Mm5ulxBoFDTe0z0bjuG5uaxCIuloUjHFBmE2u5Dy.pdf, accessed July 11, 2023.

230 **"The key was to figure out how to develop what I call a 'pipeline' . . .":** Toobin,
"Conservative Pipeline."

230 **a former member:** Charles Lane, "Roberts Listed in Federalist Society 97-98 Directory," *Washington Post*, July 25, 2005, https://www.washingtonpost.com/wp-dyn/
content/article/2005/07/24/AR2005072401201.html, accessed July 11, 2023.

230 **the first time it had campaigned publicly for a particular candidate:** Jackie Calmes,
Dissent: The Radicalization of the Republican Party and Its Capture of the Court (New York:
Twelve, 2021), 31.

231 **Samuel Alito, one of its members, in her place:** Calmes, *Dissent*, 31.

231 **set up using funds from Robin Arkley:** Viveca Novak and Peter Stone, "The JCN
Story: How to Build a Secretive, Right-Wing Judicial Machine," *Daily Beast*, April 14,
2017, https://www.thedailybeast.com/the-jcn-story-how-to-build-a-secretive-right
-wing-judicial-machine?utm_content=buffer271c0&utm_medium=social&utm_
source=twitter.com&utm_campaign=buffer, accessed July 12, 2023.

231 **known as the "foreclosure king":** Stephanie Mencimer, "These Right-Wing Groups

Are Gearing Up for an Onslaught on Obama's Supreme Court Nominee," *Mother Jones*, March 19, 2016, https://www.motherjones.com/politics/2016/03/right-wing -groups-gearing-up-onslaught-merrick-garland-supreme-court/, accessed July 14, 2023.

231 **buying up mortgages of people in financial difficulties:** See description of Ark-ley's businesses at https://web.archive.org/web/20080208124445/http://www.snsc .com/AboutUs.aspx, accessed July 12, 2023.

231 **after Bush's reelection in late 2004:** Novak and Stone, "JCN Story."

231 **to shape public opinion:** Novak and Stone, "JCN Story."

231 **a couple who had been supernumerary members of Opus Dei since at least the eighties:** Carol Brzozowski, "Love of God Is Shrouded in Secrecy Opus Dei Wants Others to Understand Devotion," *Sun Sentinel*, May 25, 1990, https://web.archive .org/web/20181202104027/https://www.sun-sentinel.com/news/fl-xpm-1990 -05-25-9001100227-story.html, accessed July 12, 2023.

231 **"through their work as well as the friendships they develop":** Brzozowski, "Love of God."

231 **spending a weekend in Colorado hunting with Judge Antonin Scalia:** Leo and Scalia went hunting in Colorado in October 2006, according to the former Justice's papers, Harvard Law School Library, https://hollisarchives.lib.harvard.edu/reposito ries/5/archival_objects/2953039, accessed July 11, 2023.

231 **He twice bailed out the Becket Fund:** Jay Michaelson, "The Secrets of Leonard Leo, the Man Behind Trump's Supreme Court Pick," *Daily Beast*, July 24, 2018, https:// www.thedailybeast.com/the-secrets-of-leonard-leo-the-man-behind-trumps-su preme-court-pick, accessed July 12, 2023.

231 **He reveled in his reputation as the financial savior of this important community:** Author interview with someone who worked closely with Leo during this period, July 2023.

231 **representative to the United States Commission on International Religious Free-dom:** See presidential announcement, https://georgewbush-whitehouse.archives. gov/news/releases/2007/05/text/20070510-10.html, accessed July 14, 2023.

232 **to investigate allegations of religious persecution:** For a complete list of the visits that Leo made, see annual reports published by the commission, https://www.uscirf .gov/annual-reports, accessed July 14, 2023.

232 **making it difficult for him to attend Mass:** Author interview with someone who worked closely with Leo during this period.

232 **and Leo was fired not long after:** Michaelson, "Secrets of Leonard Leo."

232 **Chief Justice John Roberts sent a video message:** Toobin, "Conservative Pipeline."

232 **"a new generation of lawyers is rising . . .":** "President Bush Delivers Remarks at Federalist Society's 25th Annual Gala," November 15, 2007, https://georgewbush -whitehouse.archives.gov/news/releases/2007/11/20071115-14.html, accessed July 11, 2023.

232 **he would try to go to Mass more regularly:** Toobin, "Conservative Pipeline."

232 **Margaret had developed an obsession with anything religious:** See Ruse, *Littlest Suffering Souls*, chapter 7.

232 **and would nag her parents to take her to Mass:** See Ruse, *Little Suffering Souls.*

232 **Leo got up early to go to Mass—as promised—and looked in on Margaret:** Toobin, "Conservative Pipeline."

232 **"I will always think that she did her job . . .":** Toobin, "Conservative Pipeline."

232 **Robin Arkley . . . invited the Leos to spend some time at his ranch in California:** See Ruse, *Littlest Suffering Souls.*

233 **were signs from heaven that Margaret was both safe and still with them:** Ruse, *Littlest Summering Souls.*

233 **partly in a sop to the Christian vote:** Tom McCarthy, "Obama's Gay Marriage Controversy: 'I Am Just Not Very Good at Bullshitting,'" *The Guardian,* February 10, 2015, https://www.theguardian.com/us-news/2015/feb/10/obama-frustrated -same-sex-marriage-david-axelrod-book, accessed January 7, 2024.

233 **"I believe that Senator Obama, whatever his other talents . . .":** Archbishop Charles Chaput, "Little Murders," *Public Discourse,* October 18, 2008, https://www.thepub licdiscourse.com/2008/10/127/, accessed January 7, 2024.

233 **such as "Obama's Abortion Extremism" and "Obama and Infanticide":** Chaput, "Little Murders."

233 **"but only the president of the United States . . .":** Email from Luis Tellez, October 10, 2008, http://robertaconnor.blogspot.com/2008/10/email-on-election-abortion -and-gay.html, accessed January 7, 2024.

234 **so her son could attend the Opus Dei school there:** Mark Oppenheimer, "The Making of Gay Marriage's Top Foe," *Salon,* February 8, 2012, https://www.salon.com/ 2012/02/08/the_making_of_gay_marriages_top_foe/, accessed February 28, 2024.

234 **Robby George—who in turn told her to speak with Luis Tellez:** Tellez interview, January 2024, corroborated in email correspondence with Maggie Gallagher, February 2024.

234 **"provide the resources—basically raising money for the project":** Tellez interview.

234 **The long-time Opus Dei operative Neil Corkery was also brought in as treasurer:** See IRS tax filing for the year ending December 31, 2008, https://proj ects.propublica.org/nonprofits/display_990/260240498/2010_08_EO%2F26 -0240498_990O_200812, accessed January 7, 2024.

234 **organization's elders was admitted to Princeton on a Witherspoon Institute scholarship:** Tellez interview.

234 **"A pro-traditional marriage win in California is a very significant victory":** Email from Luis Tellez, October 10, 2008.

235 **would assemble a $25 million war chest over the next three years:** See IRS tax filings, https://projects.propublica.org/nonprofits/organizations/260240498, accessed January 7, 2024.

235 **came from a handful of religiously motivated individuals and organizations:** Sofia Resnick, "National Organization for Marriage's 2010 Financial Records Raise Questions," *Washington Independent,* December 12, 2011, https://web.ar chive.org/web/20120107203322/http://washingtonindependent.com/116452/ nom%E2%80%99s-2010-financial-records-raise-questions, accessed January 7, 2024.

235 **took their political advice:** See court documents in case of *National Organization for Marriage and American Principles in Action v. Walter F. Mckee et al.*

235 **a Washington political operative and a supernumerary:** Gustav Niebuhr, "Catholic Organization Opus Dei Struggles to Shed Image of Secrecy," *Washington Post*, December 29, 1993, https://www.washingtonpost.com/archive/politics/1993/12/29/catholic-organization-opus-dei-struggles-to-shed-image-of-secrecy/42cfeda2-dfa6-4d3a-ab62-88f9c91ea272/, accessed January 7, 2023.

235 **a donor to The Heights, an Opus Dei school in the city:** See https://onlyattheheights.files.wordpress.com/2012/10/ar_final_updated.pdf, accessed January 7, 2024.

235 **public relations efforts were run by Creative Response Concepts:** See court documents in case of *National Organization for Marriage and American Principles in Action v. Walter F. Mckee et al.*

235 **the self-styled "blue-collar" communications agency for the conservative movement:** Kevin Merida, "The GOP's Town Criers," *Washington Post*, July 9, 1997, https://www.washingtonpost.com/archive/lifestyle/1997/07/10/the-gops-town-criers/5cd071ce-fff3-441a-9c5f-60ade6f61ed3/, accessed February 28, 2024.

235 **including the "Swift-Boat" campaign against John Kerry:** Eliana Johnson, "PR Firm Helped Whelan Stoke Half-Baked Kavanaugh Alibi," *Politico*, September 21, 2018, https://www.politico.com/story/2018/09/21/ed-whelan-kavanaugh-tweets-pr-firm-836405, accessed February 28, 2024.

235 **later seek to discredit the testimony of a sexual abuse victim:** Johnson, "PR Firm Helped Whelan."

235 **in his failed presidential bid in 2000:** Howard Kurtz, "Forbes Ads Target Abortion Opposition," *Washington Post*, January 12, 2000, https://www.washingtonpost.com/wp-srv/WPcap/2000-01/12/004r-011200-idx.html, accessed February 28, 2024.

235 **A staunch Catholic:** Greg Mueller self-defines as a "Catholic, Husband, Father, conservative who likes to shoot, golf and ski" on his X profile, https://twitter.com/gregmcrc?lang=en, accessed February 28, 2024.

235 **a major donor to:** According to a plaque inside the Catholic Information Center, Greg Mueller and his wife were among the biggest donors to its 2022 renovation; author visit in February 2023.

235 **a board member at:** See https://cicdc.org/faqs/, accessed February 28, 2024.

235 **a $1.5 million television advertising campaign called "The Gathering Storm":** Michael Foust, "A Winning Strategy to Stop 'Gay Marriage'?," *Baptist Press*, April 17, 2009, https://web.archive.org/web/20120320070909/http://www.sbcbaptistpress.org/BPnews.asp?ID=30303, accessed February 25, 2024.

235 **"sexual disability":** Reproduced at https://www.goodasyou.org/maggie2000.png, accessed February 25, 2024.

235 **equated abortion and homosexuality to barbarism:** See "Anti-Gay Animus," published by NOM Exposed, https://web.archive.org/web/20120314175745/http://hrc.org/nomexposed/section/anti-gay-animus, accessed January 7, 2024.

235 **"Evil will be with us always, and it requires constant vigilance to defeat . . .":** Tim Drake, "National Organization for Marriage Names John Eastman Chairman of the Board," *National Catholic Register*, September 28, 2011, https://www.ncregister.com/

news/national-organization-for-marriage-names-john-eastman-chairman-of-the
-board, accessed February 25, 2024.

236 **"Expose Obama as a social radical . . .":** See court documents in case of *National Organization for Marriage and American Principles in Action v. Walter F. Mckee et al.*

236 **who had met Tellez through the Witherspoon Institute:** Tellez interview.

236 **who described the numerary as a major influence:** "Interview with Sean Fieler," *Philanthropy* Winter 2019, https://www.philanthropyroundtable.org/magazine/interview-with-sean-fieler/, accessed August 23, 2023.

12. THERE BE DRAGONS

237 **an Opus Dei priest and two supernumerary lawyers:** Oscar Ranzani, "¿La respuesta a 'El código Da Vinci'?," *Página* 12, August 25, 2009, https://www.pagina12.com.ar/diario/suplementos/espectaculos/5-15057-2009-08-25.html, accessed February 29, 2024.

237 **to Hollywood to set up a film company:** Author interview with Heriberto Schoeffer, June 2023.

237 **become obsessed with the idea of a biopic:** Schoeffer interview.

237 **"The Work LLC" was established in California:** See initial filing for "The Work, LLC" made with the State of California on July 7, 2005, https://bizfileonline.sos.ca.gov/api/report/GetImageByNum/161079078173232217223238190134240219075137167012, accessed June 29, 2023.

237 **tentatively called *The Founder*:** Schoeffer interview; author interview with Barbara Harrington (neé Nicolosi), June 2023.

237 **thought it "smelled pro-Franco":** Laurie Goodstein, "Bringing a Saint's Life to the Screen," *New York Times*, August 21, 2009, https://www.nytimes.com/2009/08/22/movies/22opus.html, accessed June 14, 2023.

238 **rejected it outright:** Goodstein, "Bringing a Saint's Life to the Screen."

238 **figure of Escrivá after watching some old footage:** Elizabeth Nash, "Opus Dei Lets Film Director in on Some of Its Secrets," *The Independent*, June 8, 2009, https://www.independent.co.uk/news/world/europe/opus-dei-lets-film-director-in-on-some-of-its-secrets-1699227.html, accessed June 15, 2023.

238 **on the film referred to only as the "golden investor":** Author interview with Dámaso Ezpeleta, June 2023.

238 **an epic drama filled with passion, betrayal, love, and religion:** Nash, "Opus Dei Lets Film Director."

238 **main numerary residence in the Argentine capital:** Author interview with Father John Wauck (Opus Dei priest on set), June 2023.

238 **the military junta in 1972:** Paula Bistagnino, "La sede principal del Opus Dei en la Argentina, un regalo de dos dictaduras militares," *El Diario AR*, August 8, 2021, https://www.eldiarioar.com/politica/sede-principal-opus-dei-argentina-regalo-dictaduras-militares_1_8202696.html, accessed June 30, 2023.

238 **established itself as extremely successful in attracting new recruits:** Author interviews with former residents, June 2023.

238 **as twelve from poor communities:** Paula Bistagnino, "La Escuela de Mucamas del

Opus Dei," *Anfibia*, June 26, 2023, https://www.revistaanfibia.com/la-escuela-de-mucamas-del-opus-dei/, accessed June 30, 2023.

238 **who drove there looking for vocations, promising the girls a better life:** Bistagnino, "La Escuela de Mucamas."

238 **worked for the Ministry of Foreign Affairs:** Author interviews with some of the women—then girls—who came to Argentina via this route, June 2023.

239 **if they agreed—or condemned to hell if they refused:** Author interview with various numerary assistants who passed through the hospitality school and later worked at the Recoleta residence, June 2023.

239 **buzzer installed on each floor of the tower block:** This account is based on a published account of a numerary assistant who lived in the center, which had been corroborated through author interviews with other numerary assistants there, conducted in person in Buenos Aires in June 2023. See http://www.opuslibros.org/nuevaweb/modules.php?name=News&file=article&sid=26627, accessed June 30, 2023.

240 **some of the women became suicidal:** Author interview with one numerary assistant who lived at the center in the 2000s, who said that others felt similar, June 2023.

240 **material was inappropriate for someone of her standing:** Author interview with one numerary assistant who lived at the center in the 2000s, July 2023.

240 **responsibilities that Father Danilo had toward its members:** The events of Father Danilo's life are discussed at length in an online article on OpusLibros.org, which includes images of the note left on his body and the police report following a visit to the Opus Dei residence indicated. See http://www.opuslibros.org/nuevaweb/modules.php?name=News&file=article&sid=23037, accessed July 3, 2023.

240 **nobody knew who Father Danilo was:** OpusLibros.org article.

240 **"emotional or spiritual life in the film, only windy posturing…":** Stephen Holden, "A Guess-the-Flavoring Game, and Then Along Comes a War," *New York Times*, May 5, 2011, https://www.nytimes.com/2011/05/06/movies/there-be-dragons-roland-joffes-film-review.html?ref=movies, accessed February 28, 2024.

240 **"*Dragons* more punishing than a hundred Hail Marys":** Mark Holcomb, "There Be Historical Inaccuracies and Lame Storytelling in *There Be Dragons*," *Village Voice*, May 4, 2011, https://www.villagevoice.com/there-be-historical-inaccuracies-and-lame-storytelling-in-there-be-dragons/, accessed February 28, 2024.

241 **Villa Tevere was receiving messages of thanks almost daily:** Jesús Colina, "Movie Inspires a Forgiveness Movement," *Zenit*, May 4, 2011, https://web.archive.org/web/20111112103926/https://zenit.org/article-32479?l=English, accessed February 28, 2024.

241 **Worldwide, it grossed just $4 million:** The figure is taken from IMDbPro, a respected industry database; see https://www.boxofficemojo.com/title/tt1316616/, accessed July 14, 2023.

241 **"There may be dragons, but there certainly won't be any Oscars":** Author interview with several people in Rome at the time, November 2023.

241 **welcomed the city's corporate elite to its new campus in Midtown:** "IESE's New York Center Hosts First Programs," https://web.archive.org/web/20100909214826/http://www.iese.edu/en/ad/NY/1011/iese_ny_center.html, accessed June 15, 2023.

241 **famous Russian ballet dancer to house his dance studio:** "IESE'S New York Center: Past & Future of a Landmark," https://web.archive.org/web/20100602094458/http://www.iese.edu/en/ad/NY/0910/past-and-future-of-a-landmark.html, accessed June 15, 2023.

241 **Following an $18 million renovation:** See Consolidated Financial Statements for year ending December 31, 2018, issued by Clover Foundation and Subsidiary, https://www.cloverfdn.org/financial-information/, accessed June 15, 2023.

241 **first European institution to break into the lucrative U.S. market:** "New Frontier: European Schools in America," *The Economist*, November 11, 2009, https://www.economist.com/business/2009/11/11/new-frontier, accessed June 15, 2023.

241 **including Bain & Company, Cap Gemini, and Pfizer listened to talks:** "IESE's New York Center Hosts First Programs."

241 **named the number one business school in the world by *The Economist*:** "New Frontier."

241 **tasked with advising the country's largest companies:** "New Frontier."

242 **when Escrivá approved the school's creation:** Beatriz Torres, *Los Orígenes del IESE* (Madrid: LID Editorial, 2015), chapter 2.

242 **who prioritized their religious values over everything else:** José Luis González Gullón and John F. Coverdale, *Historia del Opus Dei* (Madrid: Ediciones Rialp, 2022), 258.

242 **extending loans to finance IESE's expansion:** See *Notas de Presidencia*, April 23, 1969, AHBPE, box 461, folder 1, for one example among various in the archives confirming the financial support offered to IESE.

242 **a fellow numerary—for lucrative consulting work at the bank:** Gabriel Tortella, José María Ortiz-Villajos, and José Luis García Ruiz, *Historia del Banco Popular: La lucha por la independencia* (Madrid: Marcial Pons, 2011), 151.

242 **always from Opus Dei:** "The IESE Chaplaincy provides a context for the spiritual growth of all members of the IESE community based on Christian principles. . . . The priests who serve in the IESE Chaplaincy are members of Opus Dei." See https://www.iese.edu/chaplaincy/, accessed June 16, 2023.

242 **enrolled in its regular courses:** See IESE Annual Report, 2009–2010, https://www.iese.edu/wp-content/uploads/2018/10/IESE-Annual-Report-2009-2010.pdf, accessed June 16, 2023.

242 **a further two thousand attending shorter programs:** IESE Annual Report, 2009–2010.

242 **some of the world's largest companies, like Citibank, Nestlé, and PriceWaterhouseCooper:** IESE Annual Report, 2009–2010.

242 **poorer countries to get a decent education:** Francisco Gómez Franco and Begoña Laresgoiti Foix set up the charity, initially called the Mass Foundation, in 1985. Their idea was to create a foundation that would support projects in Mexico and other parts of the world. These projects would be for charitable, educational, and cultural purposes. See https://www.cloverfdn.org/our-history/, accessed June 16, 2023.

242 **Under the oversight of Luis Tellez:** He is named as treasurer and is identified as the person to whom any applications for financial aid should be addressed, as per various

tax returns from the early 2000s. See https://projects.propublica.org/nonprofits/organizations/742390003, accessed June 16, 2023.

242 **who worked for the prelature's internal government:** The Villa Fontana initiative is listed on its website as one of the projects of the Clover Foundation. See https://www.cloverfdn.org/portfolio/villa-fontana/, accessed June 16, 2023.

243 **almost $50 million from an offshore entity:** See Clover Foundation tax return for 2007, at https://projects.propublica.org/nonprofits/display_990/742390003/2008_05_PF%2F74-2390003_990PF_200712, accessed June 16, 2023.

243 **by the notorious law firm Mossack Fonseca:** Documents found in the "Panama Papers," access to which was facilitated by the International Consortium of Investigative Journalists, confirmed this.

243 **Clover bought the building on West Fifty-seventh Street for $25 million in cash:** See Consolidated Financial Statement for year ending December 31, 2018, produced by Clover Foundation and Subsidiary, https://www.cloverfdn.org/financial-information/, accessed June 15, 2023.

243 **rented it out to the business school at far below market value:** "The Foundation charges rent to the tenant in an amount equal to the Foundation's depreciation expense on the building. Depreciation of the property recorded using the straight-line method over 30 years." See Consolidated Financial Statement, 2018, 7.

243 **the foundation gifted $4.2 million to IESE for refurbishments:** Consolidated Financial Statement, 2018.

243 **Another $6.5 million was transferred the year of the opening:** Consolidated Financial Statement, 2018.

243 **controlling more than $600 million of assets:** Various organizations, including the Opus Dei Awareness Network, a registered 501(c)3 nonprofit set up by former members, have compiled lists of foundations and nonprofits linked to the prelature. The author has taken these and updated them. Figures are based on the total assets declared by those nonprofits in annual IRS tax filings. See https://odan.org/foundations, accessed June 19, 2023.

243 **lavish properties across the Northeast in the years that followed:** See Chapter Four, this volume, for more details of the real estate purchases made by Association for Cultural Interchange, Inc.

243 **portfolio of stocks, bonds, mutual funds, and other real estate:** See Association for Cultural Interchange, Inc., tax filing for 2010, https://projects.propublica.org/nonprofits/display_990/526054124/2011_12_EO%2F52-6054124_990_201012, accessed June 19, 2023.

243 **or on its website:** See https://web.archive.org/web/20140111043516/http://culturalinterchange.org/, accessed June 19, 2023.

243 **"to other not-for-profit organizations . . .":** See Association for Cultural Interchange, Inc., tax filing for years 2010 through 2022, https://projects.propublica.org/nonprofits/organizations/526054124, accessed April 19, 2024.

243 **Images of smiling schoolchildren in Africa were used in promotional materials:** For example, see https://www.culturalinterchange.org/projects/, accessed June 19, 2023.

244 **a project which had cost almost $30 million:** See Fixed Asset & Depreciation Schedule, part of the 2006 tax filing, https://projects.propublica.org/nonprofits/display_990/526054124/2007_08_EO%2F52-6054124_990_200612, accessed June 19, 2023.

244 **just $20,000 was donated to the smiling children in Africa during the previous year:** See Association for Cultural Interchange, Inc., tax filing for 2010.

244 **Opus Dei boasted 88,000 members:** This is according to data in the *Annuario Pontificio*, the official annual directory of the Holy See of the Catholic Church, published by the Vatican each year. A historical series of the data is available at https://www.catholic-hierarchy.org/diocese/dqod0.html, accessed June 15, 2023.

244 **a presence in sixty-six countries:** See https://opusdei.org/en-uk/article/historical-overview/, accessed June 19, 2023.

244 **what types of recruits they should seek:** Author interviews with various numeraries and directors who were directly involved in many of these initiatives, various times in 2022, 2023, and 2024.

244 **not for any breaches of labor law or alleged enslavement:** See "Confusion About a Court Case in France," press release from Béatrice de la Coste, Opus Dei information office in France, https://opusdei.org/en-uk/article/confusion-about-a-court-case-in-france/, accessed June 20, 2023.

245 **forced to stand trial at the Palais de Justice in Paris:** Estelle Maussion, "Un procès pour travail dissimulé vise les pratiques de l'Opus Dei," *La Croix*, September 23, 2011, https://www.la-croix.com/Actualite/France/Un-proces-pour-travail-dissimule-vise-les-pratiques-de-l-Opus-Dei-_NG_-2011-09-23-714929, accessed June 20, 2023.

245 **had paid Tissier a salary:** Maussion, "Un procès pour travail dissimulé."

245 **never had access to her money and was expected to sign blank checks:** See summary of facts in the ruling made by the Appeals Court of Amiens, in the case of *Catherine Tissier v. Association de Culture Universitaire et Technique, Claire de Bardon de Segonzac, and Agnés Duhail*, July 27, 2016, https://www.opus-info.org/images/1/1d/Arr%C3%AAt_de_la_Cour_d%27Appel_d%27Amiens_confirmant_le_jugement_de_la_Cour_d%27Appel_de_Paris.pdf, accessed March 22, 2023.

245 **no say over where they worked or what they did:** Antonio Rubio and Santiago Saiz, "Seis mujeres denuncian al Opus Dei por presunto fraude a la Seguridad Social," *El Mundo*, January 29, 2012, https://www.elmundo.es/elmundo/2012/01/29/espana/1327838306.html, accessed July 14, 2023.

245 **work long hours without pay or social security payments:** Jack Valero, the UK spokesperson of Opus Dei, confirmed several times to the author that Opus Dei directors and priests received no salary or social security contributions until relatively recently. Other numeraries confirmed they also received no salary or social security contributions after being asked to leave their jobs and transferred to internal positions within the organization.

245 **"You appear to be confusing the role of Opus Dei in your life with that of your legal employer . . .":** According to correspondence seen by the author, dated 2002.

246   **due in part to the proliferation of smart phones:** Author interviews with several numeraries, various times in 2022, 2023, and 2024.

246   **sexually abused on at least seven occasions by an Opus Dei priest:** Jesús Bastante, "Un sacerdote del Opus Dei, investigado por Doctrina de la Fe por abusar de varios estudiantes después de la confesión," *Religión Digital*, April 10, 2019, https://www.religiondigital.org/espana/Manuel-Cocina-Karadima-Opus-Dei-religion-abusos-sevilla-granada_0_2111188883.html, accessed March 1, 2024.

246   **seemed destined to be a potential future prelate:** Bastante, "Un sacerdote del Opus Dei."

246   **"He said: 'Look, I can't say anything more but this isn't news to me …'":** Bastante, "Un sacerdote del Opus Dei."

246   **for Opus Dei to publicly recognize the allegations against the priest:** See "Conclusión del proceso canónico contra un sacerdote de la Prelatura," July 16, 2020, https://opusdei.org/es-es/article/comunicado-16-julio-2020/, accessed March 1, 2024.

246   **"instructions" from Villa Tevere were affecting ordinary numeraries like him:** The account of this numerary is at http://www.opuslibros.org/libros/MI_VIDA.htm, accessed July 5, 2023.

247   **"this type of medical check-up":** Account of numerary.

247   **"just take one in the morning and one at night":** Account of numerary.

247   **Echevarría was forced to send out a pastoral letter to "clarify" the "misunderstanding":** González Gullón and Coverdale, *Historia del Opus Dei*, 572–573.

247   **where he taught Spanish to boys of a similar age:** Koldo Domínguez, "Un viaje previo a Australia, clave para determinar el riesgo de fuga del exprofesor de Gaztelueta," *El Correo*, November 20, 2018, https://www.elcorreo.com/bizkaia/viaje-previo-australia-20181120224610-nt.html, accessed July 4, 2023.

247   **later sentenced to eleven years in prison:** Julio Núñez, "Condenado a 11 años de prisión un profesor de un colegio del Opus de Bizkaia por abusos sexuales," *El País*, November 15, 2018, https://elpais.com/sociedad/2018/11/15/actualidad/1542273994_044195.html, accessed July 4, 2023.

248   **the number of priests had fallen:** See "Frequently Requested Church Statistics," collated by the Center for Applied Research in the Apostolate, a nonprofit affiliated with Georgetown University, https://cara.georgetown.edu/faqs, accessed July 4, 2023.

248   **leaving almost fifty thousand dioceses without a priest:** "Frequently Requested Church Statistics."

248   **the number of priests had fallen by a third over that same period:** "Frequently Requested Church Statistics."

248   **its number of priests more than doubled over the same period:** Around 2,100 diocesan priests were members of Opus Dei in 2010, according to the *Annuario Pontificio* published by the Vatican. According to González Gullón and Coverdale, the number of diocesan priests belonging to the prelature expanded by around 600 during the Álvaro del Portillo years. Working back using the Vatican figures, this indicates that there were fewer than 1,000 when the founder died in 1975. See González Gullón and Coverdale, *Historia del Opus Dei*, 485–486; and https://www.catholic-hierarchy.org/diocese/dqod0.html, accessed July 4, 2023.

248 **by 2010 the prelature boasted twenty-four bishops around the world:** According to the *Annuario Pontificio.*

248 **as well as two cardinals:** See *Annuario Pontificio.*

248 **better integrate Opus Dei with wealthy Catholics:** Author interview with a Catholic Information Center board member who was serving at the time, February 2023.

249 **The inaugural award went to Cardinal Donald Wuerl:** For a list of past winners, see https://cicdc.org/john-paul-ii-new-evangelization-awardees/, accessed July 11, 2023.

249 **an ecumenical statement drafted by Robert George, and co-signed by Luis Tellez, Maggie Gallagher, and other members of the Catholic right:** See "Manhattan Declaration: A Call of Christian Conscience," drafted on October 20, 2009, and released on November 20, 2009, https://web.archive.org/web/20130901171332/http://de mossnews.com/manhattandeclaration/press_kit/manhattan_declaration_signers, accessed July 11, 2023.

249 **provide them with "intellectual and spiritual seriousness":** See outline of the Leonine Forum, ahead of its planned launch in the fall of 2013, https://web.archive .org/web/20131027085506/http://cicdc.org/sites/cicdc/leonine/, accessed July 11, 2023.

249 **people who weren't versed in the universal truths of the Church:** Author interview with a Catholic Information Center board member who was serving at the time, who knew Father Arne well, February 2023.

250 **televised debate between the party's candidates for president:** Paul Steinhauser, "Next Two Months Could Shake Up GOP Race," *CNN*, September 9, 2011, https:// edition.cnn.com/2011/POLITICS/09/05/gop.two.months/index.html, accessed March 1, 2024

250 **Kellyanne Conway—arguing for the opposite:** Jack McCordick, "The Shadowy Right-Wing Think Tank Pushing Transphobia," *New Republic*, October 25, 2023, https://newrepublic.com/article/176012/american-principles-project-think-tank -pushing-transphobia, accessed March 1, 2024.

250 **also pumped money into swinging electoral races:** See https://www.opensecrets .org/outside-spending/detail/2014?cmte=C00544387&tab=targeted_candidates, accessed March 1, 2024.

250 **"legislation that would be consistent with principles—conservative principles":** Author interview with Luis Tellez, January 2024.

250 **impact that gay parenting had on children:** Ari Rabin-Havt, "This Is How to Invent a Lie: An Essay from the Author of Lies, Incorporated," https://knopfdoubleday .com/2016/05/18/this-is-how-to-invent-a-lie/, accessed January 7, 2024.

250 **"It would be great to have this before major decisions of the Supreme Court":** Rabin-Havt, "This Is How to Invent a Lie."

250 **"this study as long as it is done honestly and well":** Rabin-Havt, "This Is How to Invent a Lie."

250 **Tellez also spent $1.4 million of Witherspoon Institute money:** See the Witherspoon Institute, Inc., IRS tax filings for year ending December 31, 2014, https:// projects.propublica.org/nonprofits/display_990/550835528/2015_06_EO%2F55 -0835528_990_201412, accessed March 4, 2024.

250 **"an interreligious colloquium on the complementarity of man and woman":** Edward Pentin, "Humanum Conference Highlights Sanctity and Beauty of Marriage," *National Catholic Register*, November 20, 2014, https://www.ncregister.com/news/humanum-conference-highlights-sanctity-and-beauty-of-marriage-i809vcr3, accessed March 4, 2024.

250 **colleagues in Rome oversaw the organization of the conference:** Tellez said that he asked Villa Tevere to recommend someone to organize the conference. He hired the person they recommended. He also asked for advice about how to handle relations with the Vatican. Tellez interview.

250 **to the Opus Dei university in Rome around the same time:** See the Witherspoon Institute, Inc., IRS tax filings for 2014.

251 **"Oftentimes, Robby will open the door, you know . . .":** Tellez interview.

251 **Leonard Leo was one of those invited to participate:** John Gehring, "Leonard Leo Has Reshaped the Supreme Court. Is He Reshaping Catholic University Too?," *National Catholic Reporter*, December 15, 2022, https://www.ncronline.org/news/leonard-leo-has-reshaped-supreme-court-he-reshaping-catholic-university-too, accessed March 4, 2024.

251 **The Heights for the boys:** Anthony Leo is listed as a student at The Heights in a document published by the school, https://issuu.com/heightsschool/docs/upper school_faculty_v5, accessed July 12, 2023.

251 **Oakcrest for the girls:** Elizabeth Leo is listed as a student at Oakcrest in a document published by the school, https://anyflip.com/gyntu/vujz/basic, accessed July 12, 2023.

251 **donating thousands of dollars a year:** Sally and Leonard Leo are classified as "Cavalier Circle" donors in the 2011–2012 annual report published by The Heights school. See https://issuu.com/robwright31/docs/ar_final_updated, accessed July 12, 2023.

251 **The Leos were also regulars at a deeply conservative church in McLean:** Sally and Leonard Leo have been named numerous times in the Mass intentions of the church around this time; see https://www.stjohncatholicmclean.org/bulletins/bulletin-archive/february-9-2014/, accessed July 12, 2023.

251 **Islamic center being built near the site of the 9/11 attacks in New York:** Jay Michaelson, "The Secrets of Leonard Leo, the Man Behind Trump's Supreme Court Pick," *Daily Beast*, July 24, 2018, https://www.thedailybeast.com/the-secrets-of-leonard-leo-the-man-behind-trumps-supreme-court-pick, accessed April 19, 2024.

251 **that funded campaigns to oppose same-sex marriage:** See Catholic Association, Inc., IRS tax filing for 2012, https://projects.propublica.org/nonprofits/display_990/208476893/2013_12_EO%2F20-8476893_990O_201212, accessed July 14, 2023.

251 **pay for contraception, sterilization, and abortion-causing drugs as part of employee health insurance plans:** See "Catholic Groups File Suit in DC Court Against HHS Mandate," press release, Catholic News Agency, October 23, 2013, https://www.catholicnewsagency.com/news/28302/catholic-groups-file-suit-in-dc-court-against-hhs-mandate, accessed July 12, 2023.

251 **"He's a figure in Washington, and he may have had kids in the school down there . . .":** Author interview with Father Tom Bohlin, September 2023.

252 **a mix of academics, lawyers, and volunteers who helped run the bookshop:** See list of board members, https://web.archive.org/web/20140216205948/http://www.cicdc .org:80/about/staff-and-board-of-directors/, accessed July 11, 2023.

252 **Bill Barr, the former attorney general, was also appointed:** See list of board members.

252 **all part of a "Great Awakening" that was about to wash over the United States:** Mary Eberstadt, *The Last Homily: Conversations with Father Arne Panula* (Steubenville, OH: Emmaus Road, 2018), 33.

252 **"counter-institutions":** Eberstadt, *Last Homily*, 34.

252 **"It isn't only a spiritual awakening that's coming . . .":** Eberstadt, *Last Homily*.

253 **given talks at the Catholic Information Center:** Scalia gave a talk in October 2012, according to the former Justice's papers, Harvard Law School Library, https://hol lisarchives.lib.harvard.edu/repositories/5/archival_objects/2954305, accessed July 12, 2023.

253 **and at the Reston Study Center:** Scalia gave a talk in May 2003, according to the former Justice's papers at the Harvard Law School Library.

253 **Scalia had also attended an Opus Dei retreat:** Scalia attended the four-day retreat at Longlea at the end of 2013, according to the former Justice's papers, Harvard Law School Library.

253 **after which the two would often belt out Broadway tunes:** "Antonin Scalia—A Justice in Full," *National Review*, February 29, 2016, https://www.nationalreview.com/ 2016/02/antonin-scalia-supreme-court-justice-remembrances/, accessed July 12, 2023.

253 **Father Malcolm was seated at the piano:** Author interview with John Coverdale, February 2023.

13. TRUMP CARD

254 **failed to show for breakfast ahead of that morning's hunt:** Alan Blinder and Manny Fernandez, "Ranch Owner Recalls Finding Justice Antonin Scalia's Body," *New York Times*, February 14, 2016, https://www.nytimes.com/2016/02/15/us/ ranch-owner-recalls-finding-justice-antonin-scalias-body.html, accessed August 14, 2023.

254 **shooting pheasant, partridge, and blue quail:** Molly Hennessy-Fiske, "Scalia's Last Moments on a Texas Ranch—Quail Hunting to Being Found in 'Perfect Repose,'" *Los Angeles Times*, February 14, 2016, https://www.latimes.com/local/lanow/la-na -scalia-ranch-20160214-story.html, accessed August 14, 2023.

254 **backdrop for Hollywood blockbusters:** Valerie Edwards, "Inside the Luxury West Texas Ranch Where Scalia Died, Which Is Beloved by A-list Celebrities (and Randy Quaid Who Ran up a $25,000 Unpaid Bill)," *Daily Mail*, February 14, 2023, https:// www.dailymail.co.uk/news/article-3446321/Inside-30-000-acre-West-Texas-re sort-Scalia-died-counts-Mick-Jagger-Bruce-Willis-Jerry-Hall-Julia-Roberts-previ ous-guests.html, accessed August 15, 2023.

254 **members of the International Order of Saint Hubertus:** Amy Brittain and Sari Horwitz, "Justice Scalia Spent His Last Hours with Members of This

Secretive Society of Elite Hunters," *Washington Post*, February 24, 2016, https://www.washingtonpost.com/world/national-security/justice-scalia-spent-his-last-hours-with-members-of-this-secretive-society-of-elite-hunters/2016/02/24/1d77af38-db20-11e5-891a-4ed04f4213e8_story.html, accessed August 14, 2023.

254 **whose chambers were a veritable taxidermy museum:** Jeffrey Toobin, *The Nine: Inside the Secret World of the Supreme Court* (New York: Doubleday, 2007), 200.

254 **a former soldier who had made his fortune by manufacturing trucks:** Christopher Helman, "Fighting a Two-Front War," *Forbes*, September 30, 2009, https://www.forbes.com/2009/09/30/poindexter-trucks-vietnam-entrepreneurs-medal.html?sh=73400e281ba1, accessed August 14, 2023.

255 **hadn't heard him or didn't want to be bothered:** Hennessy-Fiske, "Scalia's Last Moments."

255 **perfectly reposed, his hands folded on top of the sheets:** Blinder and Fernandez, "Ranch Owner Recalls Finding Justice."

255 **after receiving a call from one of the Scalias:** Jackie Calmes, *Dissent: The Radicalization of the Republican Party and Its Capture of the Court* (New York: Twelve, 2021), 150.

255 **Federalist Society by regularly attending its annual dinner:** Scalia attended the event in 2007, 2008, and 2009, according to the former Justice's papers, Harvard Law School Library, https://hollisarchives.lib.harvard.edu/repositories/5/archival_objects/2953305, https://hollisarchives.lib.harvard.edu/repositories/5/archival_objects/2953554; and https://hollisarchives.lib.harvard.edu/repositories/5/archival_objects/2953758, accessed August 14, 2023.

255 **the two men spent five days fishing in Montana together:** Leo and Scalia went fishing in Montana in August 2014, according to the former Justice's papers, Harvard Law School Library, https://hollisarchives.lib.harvard.edu/repositories/5/archival_objects/2953039, accessed August 14, 2023.

255 **had also previously been hunting in Colorado:** Leo and Scalia went hunting in Colorado in October 2006, according to the former Justice's papers, Harvard Law School Library.

255 **way of seeking to preserve the legacy of the late Antonin:** Calmes, *Dissent*, 150.

256 **and spoke to his advisor for judicial nominations:** Calmes, *Dissent*.

256 **"voice in the selection of their next Supreme Court Justice . . .":** Calmes, *Dissent*, 151.

256 **Supreme Court nominee had been confirmed during an election year:** Calmes, *Dissent*.

256 **"I would certainly want to try and nominate a justice . . .":** Republican Presidential Debate, *CBS News*, February 13, 2016, https://www.youtube.com/watch?v=w5FAskZH7n8, accessed August 14, 2023.

256 **"Supreme Court that will strike down every restriction on abortion adopted by the states . . .":** Republican Presidential Debate.

256 **was Leonard Leo's own preferred candidate for the Republican ticket:** Author interview with a political operative who knew Leo and his thinking well during this period, February 2023.

257 **pay his respects to his great friend "Nino":** Mark Pattison, "Thousands Pay Respects

to Scalia at Supreme Court," *Catholic Herald*, February 22, 2016, https://catholich erald.org/news/nation-and-world/thousands-pay-respects-to-scalia-at-supreme -court/, accessed August 14, 2023.

257 **he posted a blog:** Robert A. Connor, "A Critique of Justice Scalia's Legal Philosophy," blog, February 17, 2016, https://robertaconnor.blogspot.com/2016/02/a-critique -of-justice-scalias-legal.html, accessed August 14, 2023.

257 **"sand of lexicology":** Connor, "A Critique."

257 **"question of the absence of truth and the prevailing nihilism globally":** Connor, "A Critique."

257 **"a dictatorship of the arbitrary will of individuals":** Connor, "A Critique."

257 **He would later retract his critique:** Robert A. Connor, "I Now Consider My Piece on Scalia's 'Originalism' [Repeated Here] To Be Mistaken," blog, March 16, 2016, https://robertaconnor.blogspot.com/2016/03/i-now-consider-this-piece-on-scal ias.html, accessed August 15, 2023.

257 **"a simple parish family Mass":** Roxanne Roberts, "Who Showed up at Scalia's Funeral—and Who Didn't," *Washington Post*, February 20, 2016, https://www.washing tonpost.com/lifestyle/style/who-showed-up-at-scalias-funeral--and-who-didn't, accessed August 15, 2023.

257 **to the pulpit to deliver that morning's first reading:** Justice Antonin Scalia funeral mass, video, C-SPAN, February 20, 2016, https://www.c-span.org/video/?404962 -1/justice-antonin-scalia-funeral-mass, accessed August 15, 2023.

258 **later being converted again by Paul Scalia:** Evan Thomas, "Washington's Quiet Club," *Newsweek*, March 8, 2001, https://www.newsweek.com/washingtons-quiet -club-149005, accessed August 15, 2023.

258 **list of Supreme Court candidates for the real estate mogul:** Carl Hulse, *Confirmation Bias: Inside Washington's War over the Supreme Court, from Scalia's Death to Justice Kavanaugh* (New York: HarperCollins, 2019), 50–55.

258 **in the words of the Texan senator—as a possible candidate for the Supreme Court:** Katie Zezima, "Cruz Calls Trump's Sister a 'Radical Pro-abortion Extremist' Judge," *Washington Post*, February 15, 2016, https://www.washingtonpost.com/news/post -politics/wp/2016/02/15/cruz-calls-trumps-sister-a-radical-pro-abortion-ex tremist-judge/, accessed August 15, 2023.

258 **Trump could use when asked his thoughts about possible nominees:** Calmes, *Dissent*, 158–159.

258 **anti-abortion stance conflicted with many of its members' libertarian politics:** Calmes, *Dissent*, 160.

258 **campaign team by proposing to release the list:** Calmes, *Dissent*.

259 **called a press conference announcing this intention:** Jenna Johnson, "Donald Trump to Release List of His Top Picks for the Supreme Court," *Washington Post*, March 21, 2016, https://www.washingtonpost.com/news/post-politics/wp/2016 /03/21/donald-trump-to-release-list-of-his-top-picks-for-the-supreme-court/, accessed August 15, 2023.

259 **"we already have one, and you'll probably have four more . . .":** Johnson, "Donald Trump to Release List."

259 **In 2008, he had become the chair of Students for Life of America:** See IRS tax filing for year ending December 31, 2008, https://projects.propublica.org/nonprofits/display_990/521576352/2009_12_EO%2F52-1576352_990_200812, accessed August 15, 2023.

259 **In 2012, he joined the Catholic Association:** See IRS tax filing for Catholic Association, Inc., for year ending December 31, 2012, https://projects.propublica.org/nonprofits/display_990/208476893/2013_12_EO%2F20-8476893_990O_201212, accessed August 15, 2023.

259 **but which suddenly saw almost $2 million flood in:** Catholic Association IRS 2012 tax filing.

259 **which soon became a conduit for funding various media initiatives:** See IRS tax filing for Catholic Association Foundation, Inc., for year ending December 31, 2012, https://projects.propublica.org/nonprofits/display_990/202387967/2013_12_EO%2F20-2387967_990_201212, accessed August 15, 2023.

260 **"volunteers" from the group had given interviews or published comment pieces on a variety of issues:** See IRS tax filing for Catholic Voices, Inc., for year ending December 31, 2012, https://projects.propublica.org/nonprofits/display_990/454626789/2013_12_EO%2F45-4626789_990_201212, accessed August 15, 2023.

260 **a priest from Opus Dei was on hand to offer the benediction:** The priest was Father Roger Landry; see IRS filing.

260 **he co-founded along with Ginni Thomas an organization called Liberty Central:** Jay Michaelson, "The Secrets of Leonard Leo, the Man Behind Trump's Supreme Court Pick," *Daily Beast*, July 9, 2018, https://www.thedailybeast.com/the-secrets-of-leonard-leo-the-man-behind-trumps-supreme-court-pick, accessed August 15, 2023.

260 **used a $500,000 donation from Dallas real estate billionaire Harlan Crow:** Kenneth P. Vogel, John Bresnahan, and Marin Cogan, "Justice Thomas's Wife Now Lobbyist," *Politico*, February 4, 2011, https://www.politico.com/story/2011/02/justice-thomass-wife-now-lobbyist-048812, accessed August 15, 2023.

260 **also a donor to the Federalist Society:** Joshua Kaplan, Justin Elliott, and Alex Mierjeski, "Clarence Thomas and the Billionaire," *ProPublica*, April 6, 2023, https://www.propublica.org/article/clarence-thomas-scotus-undisclosed-luxury-travel-gifts-crow, accessed August 15, 2023.

260 **he joined the board of Chicago Freedom Trust:** See IRS tax filing for Chicago Freedom Trust, Inc., for year ending December 31, 2011, https://projects.propublica.org/nonprofits/display_990/264123223/2012_12_PF%2F26-4123223_990PF_201112, accessed August 15, 2023.

260 **wealthy manufacturing tycoon as a potential donor to the law society:** Heidi Przybyla, "Leonard Leo Used Federalist Society Contact to Obtain $1.6B donation," *Politico*, May 2, 2023, https://www.politico.com/news/2023/05/02/leonard-leo-federalist-society-00094761, accessed August 15, 2023.

260 **a funder of his own dark-money network:** Przybyla, "Leonard Leo Used Federalist Society."

260 **with the pass-through soon becoming a regular donor to the Oakcrest School:** The

donations to the Oakcrest School started in 2013. See IRS tax filing for Chicago Freedom Trust, Inc., for year ending December 31, 2013, https://projects.propublica.org/
nonprofits/organizations/264123223/201430699349100408/full, accessed August 15, 2023.

261 **$17 million campaign to stop Obama from replacing Scalia:** Michaelson, "Secrets
of Leonard Leo."

261 **almost $600 million of dark money to right-wing causes:** Evan Vorpahl, "Leon-
ard Leo's Court Capture Web Raised Nearly $600 Million Before Biden Won; Now
It's Spending Untold Millions from Secret Sources to Attack Judge Ketanji Brown
Jackson," *True North Research*, March 22, 2022, https://truenorthresearch.org/2022/
03/leonard-leos-court-capture-web-raised-nearly-600-million-before-biden-won
-now-its-spending-untold-millions-from-secret-sources-to-attack-judge-ketanji
-brown-jackson/, accessed August 16, 2023.

261 **skimmed off tens of millions of dollars in advisory fees:** Heidi Przybyla, "Dark
Money and Special Deals: How Leonard Leo and His Friends Benefited from His Judicial Activism," *Politico*, March 1, 2023, https://www.politico.com/news/2023/03/
01/dark-money-leonard-leo-judicial-activism-00084864, accessed August 16, 2023.

261 **all became beneficiaries of this largesse:** Vorpahl, "Leonard Leo's Court Capture."

261 **pushing the value of the stake indirectly controlled by Opus Dei to around $2 bil-
lion:** The Banco Popular share price hit a high of 13.83 euros in December 2006.
At the time, Sindicatura de Accionistas del Banco Popular Español, which was
wholly owned by foundations linked to Opus Dei, owned 83 million shares in the
bank. Unión Europea de Inversiones, which was about 43 percent owned by foundations linked to Opus Dei at the time, owned almost 66 million shares. Therefore
approximately 111 million shares could be said to be linked to Opus Dei at the time,
a stake valued at just over 1.5 billion euros. See Banco Popular Español annual report for the year ending December 31, 2006, 65–69, available at https://www.cnmv.
es/portal/consultas/datosentidad.aspx?nif=A28000727; see also UEI annual reports
for that year. Available at https://www.cnmv.es/Portal/Consultas/DatosEntidad
.aspx?nif=A-08149957.

261 **generated tens of millions of dollars in dividends:** A stake of 111 million Banco
Popular shares would have generated just over 40 million euros in dividends during
2006. See Banco Popular Español 2006 annual report.

261 **the government was forced to seek a $125 billion bailout from the European
Union:** Gareth Gore, "Spain Eyes Support from Banks," *International Financing Review*, June 15, 2012, https://www.ifre.com/story/1227010/spain-eyes-support
-from-banks-tmhyh6mfxf, accessed August 16, 2023.

262 **huge holes were found in their balance sheets:** "Spanish Bank Audit Buys More
Time for Rajoy," *International Financing Review*, September 28, 2012, https://www
.ifre.com/story/1242375/spanish-bank-audit-buys-more-time-for-rajoy-wmrxvw
zyhw, accessed August 16, 2023.

262 **including Popular:** "Popular to Avoid Bailout with Rights," *International Financing
Review*, October 5, 2012, https://www.ifre.com/story/1245205/spain-popular-to
-avoid-bailout-with-rights-pl0dvlv9vw, accessed August 16, 2023.

262   **it owned in order to secure $200 million of loans from three banks:** See Unión Europea de Inversiones (EUI) annual report for the year ending December 31, 2012, 27–29. Available at https://www.cnmv.es/Portal/Consultas/DatosEntidad .aspx?nif=A-08149957.

262   **With the clock on the loan repayments ticking:** EUI was due to make repayments of more than 11 million euros in 2014 and almost 131 million euros the following year. See EUI 2012 annual report, 31.

262   **a contact put him in touch with Antonio del Valle:** See José García Abad, *Cómo se Hundió El Banco Popular* (Madrid: El Punto Prensa, 2017), chapter 3.

262   **offered to inject $600 million into Banco Popular:** See García Abad, *Cómo se Hundió.*

262   **A deal was announced in December 2013:** See regulatory filing made by Banco Popular on December 11, 2013, https://www.cnmv.es/WebServices/VerDocumento/ Ver?e=mkE9N1SD3%2bAY%2fByocdggE7ojc5caDaczWitwUsYwRmRQSRh0dt1K 2vXNhAR3mLSV, accessed August 16, 2023.

262   **A week later, Ron gleefully announced that Popular would once again start paying its dividend:** See regulatory filing made by Banco Popular on December 19, 2013, https://www.cnmv.es/WebServices/VerDocumento/Ver?e=BqyUGk7K3EBAdbuM cuYGgbojc5caDaczWitwUsYwRmRQSRh0dt1K2vXNhAR3mLSV.

263   **when a routine spot check by regulators unearthed a $3 billion hole in the bank's accounts:** Gareth Gore, "ECB Knew of Financial Irregularities Ahead of Banco Popular Rights Issue," *International Financing Review*, April 5, 2019, https://www.ifre .com/story/1590298/ecb-knew-of-financial-irregularities-ahead-of-banco-popu lar-rights-issue-kq2kltd8nm, accessed August 16, 2023.

263   **suspicious activity involving Luxembourg-based shell companies:** Gore, "ECB Knew of Financial Irregularities."

263   **cash needed to fill the hole—in exchange for greater control over the bank:** See García Abad, *Cómo se Hundió*, chapter 5.

263   **the Mexican billionaire demanded to see the head of Opus Dei:** "Del Valle recurrió 'al jefe del Opus Dei' para tomar el control de Banco Popular," *Vozpópuli*, March 17, 2018, https://www.vozpopuli.com/economia_y_finanzas/empresas/del -valle-recurrio-jefe-opus-dei-tomar-control-banco-popular_0_1117989054.html, accessed August 16, 2023.

263   **participate in raising the capital and maintain Opus Dei's decades-long hold over the bank:** See Viviendas y Oficinas annual report for the year ending December 31, 2016.

263   **As a young man he had been a member in Mexico but left under mysterious circumstances:** José Luis Panero, "Popular y Opus Dei. La obsesión de Antonio Del Valle por 'desopusizar' el banco," *Hispanidad*, May 11, 2017, https://www.hispani dad.com/hemeroteca/confidencial/popular-y-opus-dei-la-obsesion-de-antonio-del -valle-por-desopusizar-el-banco_282072_102.html, accessed August 17, 2023.

263   **sexually abused the boys and young men in his care:** Philip Pullella, "Legionaries Founder Sexually Abused 60 boys, Religious Order's Report Says," Reuters, December 22, 2019, https://www.reuters.com/article/mexico-abuse-idINKBN1YQ02W, accessed August 17, 2023.

263 **large financial contributions it made to the Church:** Pullella, "Legionaires Founder Sexually Abused 60 Boys."

264 **network of businesses and offshore assets had been discovered:** Jason Berry, "Legion of Christ's Deception, Unearthed in New Documents, Indicates Wider Cover-up," *National Catholic Reporter*, February 18, 2013, https://www.ncronline.org/news/accountability/legion-christs-deception-unearthed-new-documents-indicates-wider-cover, accessed August 17, 2023.

264 **part of a much larger plan to join the forces of Opus Dei and Legionaries of Christ:** Author interview with said board member (who asked to remain anonymous), July 2023.

264 **made clear that it was time to find a new chairman whom the board could rally around:** Author interview with senior board member involved in the discussions (who spoke on the condition of anonymity), July 2023.

264 **It fell to Reyes Calderón, head of the bank's internal appointments board, to find a replacement:** Emilio Saracho testimony to Spanish parliament, July 12, 2018, https://www.congreso.es/public_oficiales/L12/CONG/DS/CI/DSCD-12-CI-70.PDF, accessed August 17, 2023.

264 **the board wanted someone who would defend Popular's "independence":** Saracho testimony.

265 **"If I accept, is there any chance I'll end up sending you to prison . . .":** Saracho testimony.

265 **seemed oddly divided into two rival Catholic sects:** Author interview with one person familiar with his thinking (who spoke on condition of anonymity), October 2019.

265 **he decided to hire his own lawyer:** Interview with person familiar with his thinking.

265 **statement admitting to irregularities in its accounts:** Regulatory filing made by Banco Popular on April 3, 2017, https://www.cnmv.es/WebServices/VerDocumento/Ver?e=Y%2fZ8Oxrgypo6IaMBTqb21afqoTZheLsWaW8eg8EG1exQSRh0dt1K2vXNhAR3mLSV, accessed August 17, 2023.

265 **Saracho's second in command resigned:** Regulatory filing made by Banco Popular on April 3, 2017, https://www.cnmv.es/WebServices/VerDocumento/Ver?e=kmEwHjxa6YYMy6ZuJwbb%2fafqoTZheLsWaW8eg8EG1exQSRh0dt1K2vXNhAR3mLSV, accessed August 17, 2023.

265 **cutting people off from their savings and restricting ATM withdrawals to just 60 euros a day:** "Greek Council Recommends 60 Euro Limit on ATM Withdrawals from Tuesday," Reuters, June 28, 2015, https://www.reuters.com/article/us-eurozone-greece-limits-idINKCN0P811A20150628, accessed August 17, 2023.

266 **In the coming weeks, customers pulled more than twenty billion euros out of their accounts:** Bank of Spain report into the collapse of Banco Popular, April 8, 2019, 242.

266 **in December 2016 with a lung infection:** "Bishop Javier Echevarría Passes Away," *Romana*, 63, https://romana.org/en/63/bishop-javier-echevarria-passes-away/december-12-bishop-javier-echevarria-passes-away/, accessed August 18, 2023.

266   **156 Opus Dei priests and male numeraries converged:** According to Opus Dei, 194 "faithful of Opus Dei"—some 94 priests and 100 lay persons—took part in the entire process. However, this figure includes 38 women who met separately from the men a day before, and who were not allowed to cast a vote in the actual election. They merely put forward possible names for the men to consider, although the men were not bound to any of these recommendations. For more details of the election, see *Romana*, 64, https://romana.org/en/64/msgr-fernando-ocariz-prelate-of-opus-dei/, accessed August 18, 2023.

266   **the first to take the name Francis after the beloved saint of the poor:** See John Gehring, *The Francis Effect: A Radical Pope's Challenge to the American Catholic Church* (Lanham: Rowman & Littlefield, 2015), chapter 1.

266   **corruption and misuse of Church funds right across the Holy See:** See Gianluigi Nuzzi, *Merchants in the Temple: Inside Pope Francis's Secret Battle Against Corruption in the Vatican* (New York: Henry Holt, 2015).

266   **"How I would love a Church that *is* poor and *for* the poor!":** See "Address of the Holy Father Pope Francis," Paul VI Audience Hall, March 16, 2013, https://www.vatican.va/content/francesco/en/speeches/2013/march/documents/papa-francesco_20130316_rappresentanti-media.html, accessed August 19, 2023.

266   **refusing to move into the sumptuous papal apartment:** See Gehring, *Francis Effect.*

267   **washed the feet of inmates, including two Muslim women:** See Gehring, *Francis Effect.*

267   **eschewed a chauffeur-driven car, preferring to walk or take public transport:** Colm Tóibín, "The Bergoglio Smile," *London Review of Books*, January 21, 2021, https://www.lrb.co.uk/the-paper/v43/n02/colm-toibin/the-bergoglio-smile, accessed January 6, 2024.

267   **go and wash the feet of AIDSs patients instead:** Tóibín, "Bergoglio Smile."

267   **stranglehold on how the Holy See was governed:** Nuzzi, *Merchants in the Temple*, 8.

267   **launched a separate investigation into the Vatican's finances:** Nuzzi, *Merchants in the Temple*, 24.

267   **set up to send passwords for access to encrypted documents:** Nuzzi, *Merchants in the Temple*, 28.

267   **missing documents, money, and possible corruption:** Nuzzi, *Merchants in the Temple*, 24–44.

268   **where he had the opportunity to get to know this rising star:** For a biographical outline of Mariano Fazio, see https://opusdei.org/en-uk/article/mons-mariano-fazio/, accessed September 8, 2023.

268   **run academies for Argentina's upper classes:** Interview with a senior member of the Opus Dei government at the time, June 2023.

268   **inviting Bergoglio to a hospitality school paid for by Banco Popular:** Author interview with a person familiar, November 2023.

268   **it bothered Bergoglio that he had no jurisdiction over Opus Dei:** Author interview with one person familiar with the Pope's thinking, November 2023.

268   **made him the group's coordinator:** Junno Arocho Esteves, "Pope Francis Establishes Commission to Gather Information on IOR," *Zenit*, June 27, 2013, https://zenit

.org/2013/06/27/pope-francis-establishes-commission-to-gather-information -on-ior/, accessed January 5, 2024.

268 **overhauling the economic and administrative structures underpinning the Holy See:** John L. Allen Jr., "A Revolution Underway with Pope Francis," *National Catholic Reporter*, August 5, 2013, https://www.ncronline.org/news/vatican/revolution-un derway-pope-francis, accessed January 5, 2024.

268 **"Pedopell" and "Pell Pot," among some at the Vatican:** See Francesca Immacolata Chaouqui, *Nel nome di Pietro* (Milan: Sperling & Kupfer, 2017), prologue.

268 **expanding into Melbourne in the nineties:** Chris McGillion, "Pell, Opus Dei and Signs of a New Elitism," *Sydney Morning Herald*, January 22, 2002, https://culteduca tion.com/group/1086-opus-dei/15672-pell-opus-dei-and-signs-of-a-new-elitism .html, accessed January 5, 2024.

268 **defended it against allegations of brainwashing:** Alan Gill, "A Long-Serving Force in Opus Dei," *Sydney Morning Herald*, December 31, 2003, https://www.smh.com.au/ national/a-long-serving-force-in-opus-dei-20031231-gdi2ot.html, accessed January 5, 2024.

268 **a confessor for Pell whenever he was in Rome:** See Cardinal George Pell, *Prison Journal: The Cardinal Makes His Appeal* (San Francisco: Ignatius Press, 2020), Week 7: Perfection through Suffering.

268 **the disgraced archbishop in prison:** See Pell, *Prison Journal*, Week 9: Easter Week.

269 **Vatican's representative in Buenos Aires, was incensed:** Author interview with one person directly involved, November 2024.

269 **with the agreed $40,000 settlement handed over in cash in a McDonald's paper bag:** Author interview with one person directly involved, November 2024.

269 **root out corruption and malpractice within the Vatican:** Elisabetta Povoledo, "Two Convicted of Conspiring to Leak Vatican Secrets in 'Vatileaks 2,'" *New York Times*, July 7, 2016, https://www.nytimes.com/2016/07/08/world/europe/two-convicted-of -conspiring-to-leak-vatican-secrets-in-vatileaks-2.html, accessed August 19, 2023.

269 **"surprised and saddened":** Statement from the Rome Communications Office of the Prelature of Opus Dei, November 2, 2015, https://opusdei.org/en-uk/article/ press-release-2-november-2015-surprise-and-sadness/, accessed August 19, 2023.

269 **"The Prelature of Opus Dei has no information about this case . . .":** Statement from Rome Communications Office.

269 **new priests being ordained into the movement:** Author interview with a senior Opus Dei figure close to Ocáriz, November 2023.

270 **a man Francis had described as "not Christian" during the campaign:** Philip Pul-lella, "Pope Says Trump 'Not Christian' in Views, Plans over Immigration," Reuters, February 18, 2016, https://www.reuters.com/article/us-usa-election-trump-pope -idUSKCN0VR277, accessed August 23, 2023.

270 **he would have direct access to the president:** Calmes, *Dissent*, 163.

270 **"An Appeal to Our Fellow Catholics":** Robert P. George, George Weigel, et al., "An Appeal to Our Fellow Catholics," *National Review*, March 7, 2016, https://web.ar chive.org/web/20160323235004/http:/www.nationalreview.com/article/432437/ donald-trump-catholic-opposition-statementk, accessed September 25, 2023.

270 **using her position at Catholic Voices to push a pro-Trump agenda:** Author interview with Jack Valero (Opus Dei spokesperson and co-founder of Catholic Voices), September 2023.

270 **a supernumerary:** Kurt Jensen, "Bishop Olmsted Says 'Love of Christ' Compels Him to Proclaim Gospel of Life at National Catholic Prayer Breakfast," *Catholic Sun*, April 23, 2019, https://www.catholicsun.org/2019/04/23/national-catholic -prayer-breakfast/, accessed March 1, 2024.

270 **The subject of their meeting was recorded simply as "Opus Dei":** Justin Elliott, "Koch Lobbyists and Opus Dei—Who's Dropping in on Trump Budget Czar Mick Mulvaney?," *ProPublica*, November 21, 2017, https://www.propublica.org/article/ whos-dropping-in-on-trump-budget-czar-mick-mulvaney, accessed March 1, 2024.

270 **Bell later said that the meeting covered "religious and political matters":** Elliott, "Koch Lobbyists and Opus Dei."

271 **film was played in tribute to Leonard Leo:** *Leonard Leo: Becket's 2017 Canterbury Medalist*, video, https://www.youtube.com/watch?v=5XhJNEQKthY, accessed August 22, 2023.

272 **"Many faiths and denominations are represented here . . .":** Leonard Leo, Acceptance Speech, 2017 Canterbury Medal Gala, https://www.becketlaw.org/leonard -leo-speech-2017-canterbury-medal-gala/, accessed August 22, 2023.

272 **Francis's provocative ousting of Cardinal Raymond Burke:** See Gehring, *Francis Direct*.

272 **Saint Patrick's Cathedral in midtown Manhattan:** Michelle Caruso-Cabrera, "Pope's Sharp Words Make a Wealthy Donor Hesitate," CNBC report, December 30, 2013, https://www.cnbc.com/2013/12/30/pope-francis-wealthy-catholic-donors -upset-at-popes-rhetoric-about-rich.html, accessed August 22, 2023.

272 **experience with the "exploitative racket" of Argentinian economics:** Cardinal Timothy Dolan, "The Pope's Case for Virtuous Capitalism," *Wall Street Journal*, May 22, 2014, https://www.wsj.com/articles/SB100014240527023041985045795725 71508689630, accessed August 22, 2023.

272 **offering the prelature a parish of its own in the heart of Manhattan:** Angelo Stagnaro, "Faith and the City: Opus Dei Assumes Responsibility for St. Agnes Church," *National Catholic Register*, June 15, 2016, https://www.ncregister.com/news/faith- and-the-city-opus-dei-assumes-responsibility-for-st-agnes-church, accessed August 22, 2023.

272 **had helped out Cardinal Dolan with his op-ed piece clarifying the pope's remarks:** See Gehring, *Francis Effect*.

273 **its main nonprofits in the United States, ballooned:** According to IRS tax filings for the Woodlawn Foundation, the Rosemoor Foundation, and the Association for Cultural Interchange for those years.

274 **bankrolling a new $50 million pilgrimage center called Saxum on the outskirts of Jerusalem:** The IRS tax filing for the year ending December 31, 2017, details more than $59 million spent by ACI on the Saxum project in Jerusalem, https://projects .propublica.org/nonprofits/organizations/526054124/201833189349302328/ full, accessed March 1, 2024.

274 **forcing Tissier to return to court to get justice:** See ruling by the Appeals Court of Amiens, July 27, 2016, https://www.opus-info.org/images/8/82/SENTENCIA_CATHERINE_TISSIER_2016.pdf, accessed March 1, 2024.

274 **"easily among the most influential laymen in the U.S. and Rome":** Dan Morris-Young, "Tim Busch, Conservative Activist-Philanthropist, Rejects Anti-Francis label," *National Catholic Reporter*, June 12, 2019, https://www.ncronline.org/news/tim-busch-conservative-activist-philanthropist-rejects-anti-francis-label, accessed March 1, 2024.

274 **whom he now describes as a close friend:** Author interview with Tim Busch, October 2023.

274 **"I think they're very approachable—they're very practical ...":** Busch interview.

274 **began receiving regular spiritual direction from Father Patricio Mata:** Busch interview.

274 **who he has described as "one of my closest advisors":** Harriet Ryan, "The Fight to Move the Catholic Church in America to the Right—and the Little-Known O.C. Lawyer Behind It," *Los Angeles Times*, December 18, 2023, https://www.latimes.com/california/story/2023-12-18/this-o-c-lawyer-is-the-most-important-catholic-youve-never-heard-of, accessed March 1, 2024.

275 **hostile to religious rights and traditional morality:** John Gehring, "Napa Institute Expands to Fight the Culture War." *National Catholic Reporter*, August 4, 2021, https://www.ncronline.org/news/people/napa-institute-expands-fight-culture-war, accessed January 6, 2024.

275 **"hunker down and survive" until secular society self-destructs:** "Tim Busch: Is Catholicism Anti-Capitalist?," *Patrick Coffin Show*, podcast, https://www.patrickcoffin.media/tim-busch-is-catholicism-anti-capitalist/, accessed March 1, 2024.

275 **pilgrimage to Mexico organized by Busch two years later:** See "Pilgrimage to Mexico City," https://web.archive.org/web/20130311174318/http:/napa-institute.org/other-events/pilgrimage-to-mexico-city/, accessed January 6, 2024.

275 **Opus Dei provided financial support as a sponsor:** See "Pontifical University of the Holy Cross Foundation Sponsors the 2012 Napa Institute," https://web.archive.org/web/20120520041657/http:/www.napa-institute.org/latest-news/, accessed January 6, 2024.

275 **just two years after being ordained:** See biography at https://cicdc.org/speakers/fr-charles-trullols/, accessed August 23, 2023.

275 **"the man with the unusual gift":** Mark Oppenheimer, "An Opus Dei Priest with a Magnetic Touch," *New York Times*, June 12, 2015, https://www.nytimes.com/2015/06/13/us/rev-c-john-mccloskey-iii-an-opus-dei-priest-with-a-magnetic-touch.html, accessed June 23, 2023.

275 **"still others for decades of service to a parish ...":** Oppenheimer, "An Opus Dei Priest."

276 **paid her almost $1 million to settle the allegations:** Michelle Boorstein, "Opus Dei Paid $977,000 to Settle Sexual Misconduct Claim Against Prominent Catholic Priest," *Washington Post*, January 7, 2019, https://www.washingtonpost.com/religion/2019/01/08/opus-dei-paid-settle-sexual-misconduct-claim-against-prominent-catholic-priest/, accessed August 23, 2023.

276 **for the mistakes it had made in handling the case:** Michelle Boorstein, "In Emotional Interview, Opus Dei Spokesman Said He 'Hated' How Prominent Priest's Sexual Misconduct Case Was Handled," *Washington Post*, January 8, 2019, https://www.washingtonpost.com/local/social-issues/an-emotional-interview-opus-dei-spokesman-said-he-hated-how-prominent-priests-sexual-misconduct-case-was-handled/2019/01/08/4993575e-1397-11e9-90a8-136fa44b80ba_story.html, accessed August 23, 2023.

276 **to be introduced by President Trump:** "President Trump Observes National Day of Prayer," video, C-SPAN, May 2, 2019, https://www.c-span.org/video/?460357-1/president-trump-observes-national-day-prayer, accessed August 23, 2023.

276 **colloquium with conservative academics from various universities:** "In New York," press release, July 12, 2019, https://opusdei.org/en/article/the-prelate-arrives-in-new-york/, accessed August 23, 2023.

277 **"Archbishop Viganò has done us a great service . . .":** Elizabeth Dias and Laurie Goodstein, "Letter Accusing Pope Leaves U.S. Catholics in Conflict," *New York Times*, August 27, 2018, https://www.nytimes.com/2018/08/27/us/catholic-church-pope-francis-letter.html, accessed March 1, 2024.

277 **"Viganò has given us an agenda . . .":** Heidi Schlumpf, "At 'Authentic Reform,' Conservative Catholics Rally to 'Fix' Church Failures," *National Catholic Reporter*, October 5, 2018, https://www.ncronline.org/news/authentic-reform-conservative-catholics-rally-fix-church-failures, accessed March 10, 2024.

14. UPRISING

278 **finally found a lawyer who would take her case seriously:** Author interview with Lucía Giménez, June 2023.

278 **years spent scrubbing the bathroom floors for the men:** Débora Rey, "Women in Argentina Claim Labor Exploitation by Opus Dei," Associated Press, November 12, 2021, https://apnews.com/article/business-paraguay-europe-argentina-uruguay-43b48ed43c2f7ddebf05ec6203b12d8d, accessed September 6, 2023.

278 **tour the impoverished plains in search of young girls:** Author interviews with Lucía Giménez, June 2023 and September 2023.

278 **"Jesus died on the cross for us . . .":** Giménez interviews.

278 **carefully transcribing the words dictated to her by her tutor:** Giménez interviews.

279 **in a private plane, to neighboring Argentina:** Giménez interviews.

279 **of twelve-hour workdays for no pay, with breaks only for meals and prayer:** Rey, "Women in Argentina Claim."

279 **prescribed drugs to relieve her malaise:** Giménez interviews.

279 **toiling from morning until night, and had not a cent to show for it:** Giménez interviews.

280 **recruited to the hospitality school in Buenos Aires as a young girl:** See http://www.opuslibros.org/nuevaweb/modules.php?name=News&file=article&sid=28032, accessed September 23, 2023.

280 **a partner at a law firm in Buenos Aires where he specialized in cases involving white-collar crime:** For biographical details of Sebastián Sal, see https://www

.sal-morchio.com.ar/staff/?lang=en and https://www.linkedin.com/in/sebas
tiansal/?originalSubdomain=ar, accessed September 7, 2023.

280 **financial compensation for their years of unpaid labor:** Author interviews with
Sebastián Sal, January 2023, June 2023, and September 2023.

280 **had been shared with the other numeraries:** Sal interviews.

281 **learning the same techniques as had been used to lure him in:** Sal interviews.

281 **would leave him unhappy for the rest of his life:** Sal interviews.

282 **Carrero wrote to Sebastián Sal in August 2020:** Email from Claudia Carrero to Sebastián Sal, August 12, 2020.

282 **had only sporadic contributions on their records:** Nicolás Cassese and Paula Bistagnino, "¿Servidoras de Diós? El calvario de 43 mujeres que enfrentan al Opus
Dei," *La Nación*, May 18, 2021, https://www.lanacion.com.ar/sociedad/servidoras
-de-dios-el-calvario-de-las-43-mujeres-que-enfrentan-al-opus-dei-nid17052021/,
accessed September 8, 2023.

283 **by a numerary during an Opus Dei summer camp in the 1980s:** See "Comunicado
sobre un caso de 1989 denunciado al Coordinador de protección de menores en el
año 2020," April 4, 2023, https://opusdei.org/es-ar/article/comunicado-sobre-un
-caso-de-1989-denunciado-al-coordinador-de-proteccion-de-menores-en-el-2020/,
accessed September 8, 2023.

283 **just happened to be run by a group of numeraries:** Paula Bistagnino, "Francisco
Ferro, víctima de pederastia del Opus Dei: 'Desde hace 34 años encubren mi abuso
sexual,'" *El Diario*, April 9, 2023, https://www.eldiario.es/sociedad/francisco-ferro
-victima-pederastia-opus-dei-34-anos-encubren-abuso-sexual_1_10096420.html,
accessed September 8, 2023.

284 **suffered by the women during their time in Opus Dei:** Letter from Sebastián Sal to
Pope Francis, March 5, 2021.

284 **He made four specific requests to Francis:** Letter from Sebastián Sal to Pope Francis.

284 **"Servants of God? A Cavalry of 43 Women Clashes with Opus Dei":** Cassese and
Bistagnino, "¿Servidoras de Diós?"

284 **fundraiser at its university on the outskirts of Buenos Aires:** Sal interviews.

284 **to investigate the situation properly:** See "Comunicado de la Oficina de Comuni-
cación del Opus Dei en Argentina," May 18, 2021, https://opusdei.org/es-ar/article/
comunicado-de-la-oficina-de-comunicacion-del-opus-dei-en-argentina/, accessed
September 8, 2023.

285 **"I have a message from Jorge":** Author interview with one person familiar with the
meeting, January 2023.

285 **former numerary assistants over a period of more than forty years:** Detailed in
"Denuncia de Abusos de Poder y de Conciencia con ulterior sometimiento de las víc-
timas a situaciones de explotación personal," sent to Cardenal Luis Francisco Ladaria
Ferrer, Prefect of the Congregation for the Doctrine of the Faith–Abuse Section,
dated September 7, 2021.

285 **direct knowledge of what was happening to the women:** "Denuncia de Abuosos de
Poder."

285   **and be sanctioned for their role in the abuse:** "Denuncia de Abusos de Poder."

285   **and the complaint that they had filed at the Vatican:** Rey, "Women in Argentina Claim."

286   **was being charged with contempt of Congress:** Devlin Barrett, "Steve Bannon Indicted After Refusal to Comply with Jan. 6 Committee Subpoena," *Washington Post*, November 12, 2021; this breaking news story appeared around the time that the Argentina story disappeared, https://web.archive.org/web/20211112211632/https://www.washingtonpost.com/national-security/steve-bannon-indicted/2021/11/12/eebd4726-43fa-11ec-a3aa-0255edc02eb7_story.html, accessed September 13, 2023.

286   **and naming the former attorney general as its first awardee:** See https://cicdc.org/speakers/william-p-barr/, accessed September 25, 2023.

287   **U.S. military had helped to alter paper ballots in swing states:** Bob Woodward and Robert Costa, "Virginia Thomas Urged White House Chief to Pursue Unrelenting Efforts to Overturn the 2020 Election, Texts Show," *Washington Post*, March 24, 2022, https://www.washingtonpost.com/politics/2022/03/24/virginia-thomas-mark-meadows-texts/, accessed September 14, 2023.

287   **where he would face a military tribunal for sedition:** Woodward and Costa, "Virginia Thomas Urged."

287   **"Do not concede . . .":** Woodward and Costa, "Virginia Thomas Urged."

287   **"This is a fight of good versus evil . . .":** Woodward and Costa, "Virginia Thomas Urged."

287   **"Thank you!! Needed that! . . .":** Woodward and Costa, "Virginia Thomas Urged."

287   **dark-money vehicles run by Leonard Leo and the Corkerys:** Between 2014 and September 2020, the Judicial Crisis Network—previously called the Judicial Confirmation Network, and later renamed to the Concord Fund, which since the mid-2000s has been run by Leonard Leo and his friends the Corkerys—gave almost $1.6 million to the Rule of Law Defense Fund and almost $11 million to its sister organization, the Republican Attorney Generals Association. The Rule of Law Defense Fund was one of the main organizers of the protest. See https://www.accountable.us/wp-content/uploads/2021/01/formatted_2021-01-14-Research-on-Capitol-Riot-Rally-Backers-FINAL-1.pdf, accessed September 14, 2023.

288   **"work for reconciliation and healing, and to advance mutual respect and acceptance":** Courtney Mares, "Pope Francis Calls for 'Culture of Care' in 2021 World Peace Day message," *Catholic News Agency*, December 17, 2020, https://www.catholicnewsagency.com/news/46944/pope-francis-calls-for-culture-of-care-in-2021-world-peace-day-message, accessed September 14, 2023.

288   **vitriolic lectures that tapped into the Zeitgeist:** For a list of events following the January 2021 presidential inauguration, see https://cicdc.org/events/list/?tribe_paged=3&tribe_event_display=list&tribe-bar-date=2021-01-01, accessed September 14, 2023.

288   **"organized destruction" of religion was underway in the United States:** David Rohde, "William Barr, Trump's Sword and Shield," *The New Yorker*, January 13, 2020, https://www.newyorker.com/magazine/2020/01/20/william-barr-trumps-sword-and-shield, accessed September 14, 2023.

288 **"Secularists, and their allies among the progressives . . .":** Rohde, "William Barr, Trump's."

288 **made a rousing speech:** See "An Evening with William P. Barr, CIC 2021–2022 St. Thomas More Chair," news release, April 27, 2022, https://cicdc.org/event/saint -thomas-more-chair-barr/, accessed September 14, 2023.

288 **"Today, the signal feature of our age is man's abandonment of God . . .":** "Evening with William P. Barr."

288 **"cockpits for a vicious winner-take-all culture war over the moral formation of our children":** "Evening with William P. Barr."

288 **two more seats had become vacant during Trump's presidency:** Anthony Kennedy retired from the court in July 2018 and was replaced with Brett Kavanaugh. Ruth Bader Ginsburg died while in office in September 2020 and was replaced with Amy Coney Barret.

289 **Leonard Leo was once again asked to help find a replacement:** Andrew Chung and Steve Holland, "Trump to Name Supreme Court Pick by Saturday as Democratic Hopes of Blocking Nomination Dim," Reuters, September 21, 2020, https://www.re uters.com/article/uk-usa-court-ginsburg-idUKKCN26C2NA, accessed September 15, 2023.

289 **jokingly referred to Leo as the third most powerful man in the world:** See "Justice Clarence Thomas at the Federalist Society," video, C-SPAN, September 8, 2018, https://www.c-span.org/video/?450905-1/justice-clarence-thomas-federalist-soci ety, accessed September 15, 2023.

289 **"God help us!":** "Justice Clarence Thomas at Federalist."

289 **a protégé of Antonin Scalia:** Joan Biskupic, "Antonin Scalia's Legacy Looms over the Amy Coney Barrett Hearings," CNN, October 13, 2020, accessed September 15, 2023, https://edition.cnn.com/2020/10/12/politics/scalia-barrett-supreme-court -hearing/index.html.

289 **who was openly hostile to *Roe v. Wade*:** Jackie Calmes, *Dissent: The Radicalization of the Republican Party and Its Capture of the Court* (New York: Twelve, 2021), 394–395.

289 **lodged an appeal at the Supreme Court:** See "Petition for a Writ of Certiorari," filed at the Supreme Court, June 15, 2020, https://www.supremecourt.gov/DocketPDF/ 19/19-1392/145658/20200615170733513_FINAL%20Petition.pdf, accessed September 15, 2023.

289 **Coney Barrett was confirmed on the Supreme Court just eight days before the election:** Calmes, *Dissent*, 395.

289 **bringing in around $400,000 a year:** See various IRS tax filings by the Federalist Society, https://projects.propublica.org/nonprofits/organizations/363235550, accessed September 15, 2023.

289 **that charged up to $30,000 tuition annually per student:** See https://heights.edu/ admissions/tuition-grants-and-scholarships/ and https://www.oakcrest.org/admis sions/affording-oakcrest for tuition fees, accessed September 15, 2023.

289 **a burgeoning taste for good food and expensive wines:** Jeffrey Toobin, "The Conservative Pipeline to the Supreme Court," *The New Yorker*, April 10, 2017, https://

www.newyorker.com/magazine/2017/04/17/the-conservative-pipeline-to-the
-supreme-court, accessed September 15, 2023.

289 **unpaid advisor to the president on judicial appointments:** Heidi Przybyla, "Dark
Money and Special Deals: How Leonard Leo and His friends Benefited from His
Judicial Activism," *Politico*, March 1, 2023, https://www.politico.com/news/2023/
03/01/dark-money-leonard-leo-judicial-activism-00084864, accessed September
15, 2023.

289 **dovetailed with his joining a for-profit entity called CRC Advisors:** Przybyla,
"Dark Money and Special Deals."

290 **Once again, the Corkery name was all over the money flow:** Przybyla, "Dark Money
and Special Deals."

290 **repurposed to fund conservative causes nationwide:** Jonathan Swan and Alayna
Treene, "Leonard Leo to Shape New Conservative Network," *Axios*, January 7, 2020,
https://www.axios.com/2020/01/07/leonard-leo-crc-advisors-federalist-society,
accessed September 15, 2023.

290 **paid $34 million in fees to his new advisory firm over a single two-year period:**
The 85 Fund paid $12.1 million in fees to CRC Advisors in 2020 and $21.7 million to the same firm in 2021, according to IRS tax filings. See https://projects
.propublica.org/nonprofits/organizations/202466871/202223199349301462/
full, accessed September 15, 2023.

290 **family home in suburban McLean in 2010:** This is according to Fairfax County
property records, which are not repeated here to respect the family's privacy.

290 **hired a wine buyer and locker at Morton's:** Przybyla, "Dark Money and Special
Deals."

290 **campaigns for libertarian and conservative causes:** Andy Kroll, Justin Elliott, and
Andrew Perez, "How a Billionaire's 'Attack Philanthropy' Secretly Funded Climate
Denialism and Right-Wing Causes," *ProPublica*, September 6, 2022, https://www
.propublica.org/article/barre-seid-heartland-institute-hillsdale-college-gmu, accessed September 15, 2023.

290 **Leo had cultivated him for his own network:** Heidi Przybyla, "Leonard Leo Used
Federalist Society Contact to Obtain $1.6B Donation," *Politico*, May 2, 2023, https://
www.politico.com/news/2023/05/02/leonard-leo-federalist-society-00094761,
accessed September 15, 2023.

290 **giving him control over a $1.6 billion war chest:** Kenneth P. Vogel and Shane Gold-
macher, "An Unusual $1.6 Billion Donation Bolsters Conservatives," *New York Times*,
August 22, 2022, https://www.nytimes.com/2022/08/22/us/politics/republican
-dark-money.html, accessed September 15, 2023.

290 **millions to a foundation linked to the Catholic Association:** Evan Vorpahl, "Leonard Leo's Court Capture Web Raised Nearly $600 Million Before Biden Won; Now
It's Spending Untold Millions from Secret Sources to Attack Judge Ketanji Brown
Jackson," *True North Research*, March 22, 2022, https://truenorthresearch.org/2022/
03/leonard-leos-court-capture-web-raised-nearly-600-million-before-biden-won
-now-its-spending-untold-millions-from-secret-sources-to-attack-judge-ketanji
-brown-jackson/, accessed August 16, 2023.

291 **was the Catholic Information Center on K Street:** According to IRS filings, the Catholic Association Foundation donated more than $1 million to the Catholic Information Center and a further $100,000 to its Leonine Forum program between 2019 and 2021, https://projects.propublica.org/nonprofits/organizations/208476893, accessed September 15, 2023. The CIC also received donations directly from DonorsTrust.

291 **expansion of Luis Tellez's Witherspoon Institute:** According to IRS tax filings for Fieler's Chiaroscuro Foundation, see https://projects.propublica.org/nonprofits/organizations/205858767, accessed September 15, 2023.

291 **the budget of FEHE would swell to over $10 million a year:** See IRS tax filings, https://projects.propublica.org/nonprofits/organizations/461439784, accessed January 6, 2023.

291 **such as Charles B. Johnson, the Franklin Templeton billionaire:** Author interview with Luis Tellez, January 2024.

291 **Sarah Scaife Foundation:** See IRS tax filing for year ending December 31, 2021, https://projects.propublica.org/nonprofits/organizations/251113452/202223189349101212/IRS990PF, accessed January 6, 2024.

291 **Diana Davis Spencer Foundation:** See IRS tax filing for year ending December 31, 2021, https://projects.propublica.org/nonprofits/organizations/203672969/202243199349104294/IRS990PF, accessed January 6, 2024.

291 **to expand the program to fourteen elite universities:** See "2023–24 Key Developments," report by Foundation for Excellence in Higher Education.

291 **"I did some thinking about where is it that I can be most helpful:"** Tellez interview.

291 **made regular donations to the prelature's various initiatives:** While Tim Busch was already making donations to Opus Dei initatives as far back as 2016, mainly to its local operations in California, they increased substantially soon after Leo joined the board, with donations to Murray Hill Place, the Leonine Forum, and eventually the Catholic Information Center. See IRS tax filings for Napa Institute Support Foundation, https://projects.propublica.org/nonprofits/organizations/811190021, accessed September 15, 2023.

291 **Bohlin personally approved Busch's appointment as a "co-operator":** According to the internal Opus Dei document entitled "Experiencias de las labores apostólicas," published in 2003, the regional vicar has to personally approve any new co-operators.

292 **plot accusing Francis of hushing up sexual abuse:** Leigh Baldwin et al., "How Pope Francis Became a Hate Figure for the Far Right," *openDemocracy*, April 13, 2019, https://www.opendemocracy.net/en/5050/how-pope-francis-became-hate-figure-far-right/, accessed September 25, 2023.

292 **controversial project to influence the next papal conclave:** Baldwin et al., "How Pope Francis."

292 **"perfect because it has been around for 2,000 years . . .":** Michael E. Hartmann, "A Conversation with Catholic Philanthropist Timothy R. Busch," May 17, 2023, https://capitalresearch.org/article/a-conversation-with-catholic-philanthropist-timothy-r-busch/, accessed March 4, 2024.

292 **"So, no spying?":** "My Interview to Philip Nielsen, Founder of Red Hat Report: FBI

and CIA Will Help in a Better Election of Pope, an Interview by Jordi Picazo," web posting, https://www.academia.edu/38458546/My_interview_to_Philip_Nielsen_Founder_of_Red_Hat_Report_FBI_AND_CIA_WILL_HELP_IN_A_BETTER_ELEC TION_OF_POPE_-_an_interview_by_Jordi_Picazo, accessed January 6, 2024.

293 **attended by Leonard Leo, Rick Santorum, and Scott Hahn, a prominent member of Opus Dei:** Heidi Schlumpf, "At 'Authentic Reform,' Conservative Catholics Rally to 'Fix' Church Failures," *National Catholic Reporter*, October 5, 2018, https://www .ncronline.org/news/authentic-reform-conservative-catholics-rally-fix-church-failures, accessed January 6, 2024.

293 **the launch was abruptly cancelled:** Judy Roberts, "The 'Red Hat Report': Should Laypeople Investigate Cardinals?," *National Catholic Reporter*, October 16, 2018, https://www.ncregister.com/news/the-red-hat-report-should-laypeople-investi gate-cardinals, accessed January 6, 2024.

293 **continued to give a platform to the Pope's critics:** Morris-Young, "Tim Busch, Conservative Activist-Philanthropist."

293 **approved him as a co-operator:** Author interview with Thomas Bohlin, September 2023.

293 **Leonard and Sally Leo, as well as Busch's Napa Institute:** Author confirmed this during a visit to the CIC, February 2023.

293 **tucked away in a passageway off the main communal area:** Bohlin interview.

294 **the Opus Dei supernumerary writer Austin Ruse:** Author interview with Austin Ruse, June 2023, during which he confirmed he was a supernumerary member of Opus Dei.

294 **detailed the miracles:** See Austin Ruse, *Littlest Suffering Souls: Children Whose Short Lives Point Us to Christ* (Charlotte: TAN Books, 2017), chapter 7.

294 **publicly taunting a thirteen-year-old for his stutter:** Tweet by Austin Ruse @aus-tinruse, August 21, 2020, screenshot at https://twitter.com/DaveHolmes/status/ 1296832000188284928, accessed March 4, 2024.

294 **"single women should not be allowed to vote":** Tweet by Austin Ruse @aus-tinruse, April 17, 2020, screenshot at https://twitter.com/jennycohn1/status/ 1763435533437657360, accessed March 4, 2024.

294 **"curb the homosexual advance":** Austin Ruse, "Letter From Moscow," *Catholic Thing*, July 26, 2013, https://www.thecatholicthing.org/2013/07/26/letter-from -moscow/, accessed March 4, 2024.

294 **"the hard left, human-hating people that run modern universities" should "all be taken out and shot":** Brian Tashman, "Austin Ruse Says Left-Wing University Professors 'Should All Be Taken Out And Shot,'" *Right Wing Watch*, March 12, 2014, https://www.rightwingwatch.org/post/austin-ruse-says-left-wing-university-pro fessors-should-all-be-taken-out-and-shot/, accessed March 4, 2024.

294 **"was decided we are honoring Leonard Leo . . .":** CIC video celebrating the award being given to Leonard Leo, October 28, 2022, YouTube video, https://www.youtube .com/watch?v=7M8sPOrbVJU, accessed September 19, 2023.

295 **"leadership of the Catholic Information Center, for your friendship . . .":** CIC video of remarks given by Leonard Leo at the dinner, November 30, 2022, YouTube

video, https://www.youtube.com/watch?v=DtsXLstn77M, accessed September 19, 2023.

295 **counted more than 800 alumni:** Author interview with Father Roger Landry (chaplain to the Leonine Forum's program in New York), February 2022.

295 **some of whom had paid as much as $25,000 a table:** See sponsorship details of the John Paul II New Evangelization Award Dinner, October 2022, https://web.archive .org/web/20220930094708/https://cicdc.org/jp2award/, accessed September 19, 2023.

295 **scrawled "dirty money lives here" on the sidewalk outside:** Kenneth P. Vogel, "Leonard Leo Pushed the Courts Right. Now He's Aiming at American Society," *New York Times*, October 12, 2022, https://www.nytimes.com/2022/10/12/us/politics/ leonard-leo-courts-dark-money.html, accessed September 25, 2023.

295 **"build talent pipelines and networks that can positively affect those areas":** Andy Kroll, Andrea Bernstein, and Nick Surgey, "Inside the 'Private and Confidential' Conservative Group That Promises to "Crush Liberal Dominance," *ProPublica*, March 9, 2023, https://www.propublica.org/article/leonard-leo-teneo-videos-doc uments, accessed September 19, 2023.

296 **which promised to "crush liberal dominance":** Kroll et al., "Inside the 'Private and Confidential.'"

296 **"future leaders across culture, politics, and business":** See Hawthorn Foundation website, https://www.hawthornfoundation.com/, accessed March 4, 2024.

296 **"and inculcation of personal responsibility":** Hawthorn Foundation.

296 **the foundation had amassed $20 million:** See IRS tax filings at https://projects .propublica.org/nonprofits/organizations/843042040/202323199349310807 /full, accessed March 4, 2024.

296 **monitor the students' daily life to prevent such relationships from developing:** See the now-defunct "Oak for Change" website, archived at https://web .archive.org/web/20211218131145/http:/oakforchange.com/, accessed March 4, 2024.

296 **a kind of "finishing school" for the next generation of leaders:** Tellez interview.

296 **and at Oxford, England:** See https://excellenceinhighered.org/network/, accessed March 10, 2024.

297 **plans are afoot for another at Columbia:** Tellez interview.

297 **Tellez has discussed his vision for attracting today's youth with the prelate:** Tellez interview.

297 **"there is no connection to Opus Dei formally, but there are some members of Opus Dei involved in doing this . . .":** Tellez interview.

297 **"G'day Father!," welcoming the prelate back to Australian soil:** See "The Prelate lands in Australia," August 8, 2023, news release, https://opusdei.org/en-au/article/ the-prelate-lands-in-australia/, accessed September 20, 2023.

297 **where he was due to spend the next five days at a private retreat:** See "Program of the Prelate of Opus Dei in Australia and New Zealand," news release, https://opus dei.org/en/article/program-of-the-prelate-of-opus-dei-in-australia-and-new-zea land/, accessed September 20, 2023.

298 **Set on twenty-five acres of native bush, with views of the Blue Mountains:** "Pope to Holiday at Semi-Rural Australian Retreat: Report," *Sydney Morning Herald*, July 6, 2008, https://www.smh.com.au/world/pope-to-holiday-at-semirural-australian-retreat-report-20080706-32k8.html, accessed September 20, 2023.

298 **bankrolled by Luis Valls-Taberner in the early 1990s:** The Education Development Association, the arms-length Opus Dei foundation that owns the retreat center, as well as several numerary and university residences, received 1.5 million in Australian dollars from Fomento de Fundaciones in 1993 for the construction of Kenthurst. The Pared Foundation, a separate arms-length organization that runs Opus Dei schools in the country, received 1.6 million Australian dollars to finance construction at two Sydney schools about the same time. See Balance de Cooperación Internacional report, with snapshot of spending, as of March 1995, AHBPE (uncataloged).

298 **Pope Benedict XVI had made his own three-day private retreat there:** Balance de Cooperación International report.

298 **before he took up the second half of his tour:** See "Program of the Prelate of Opus Dei in Australia and New Zealand," news article, https://opusdei.org/en/article/program-of-the-prelate-of-opus-dei-in-australia-and-new-zealand/, accessed September 20, 2023.

298 **rescinded the privileges Opus Dei had enjoyed for forty years:** See "Lettera Apostolica in Forma Di 'Motu Proprio' Del Sommo Pontefice Francesco con La Quale Vengono Modificati i Cann, 295–296 Relativi Alle Prelature Personali," August 8, 2023, https://www.vatican.va/content/francesco/it/motu_proprio/documents/20230808-motu-proprio-prelature-personali.html, accessed September 20, 2023.

298 **stripped it of its ability to operate independently of local dioceses:** "What the pope changed about prelatures," *The Pillar*, August 9, 2023, https://www.pillarcatholic.com/p/what-the-pope-changed-about-prelatures, accessed September 20, 2023.

299 **"canons refer to the general law regarding personal prelatures . . .":** See "Letter from the Prelate on the Motu Proprio Regarding Personal Prelatures," August 10, 2023, https://opusdei.org/en/article/letter-from-the-prelate-on-the-motu-proprio-regarding-personal-prelatures/, accessed September 20, 2023.

299 **"like any other Catholic, is made explicit . . .":** "Letter from the Prelate on the Motu Proprio."

299 **timing and content of the *motu proprio* had been unexpected:** Opus Dei was given a three-week heads-up on the first *motu propio* in July 2022, but was given no advance notice at all on the second. Author interview with one person with direct knowledge of the situation, November 2023.

299 **transferring its most senior representative in Argentina:** Decree from Fernando Ocáriz, dated September 29, 2021, published in *Romana*, 73, https://romana.org/en/73/establishment-of-new-circumscriptions/establishment-of-the-circumscription-of-la-plata-u/, accessed September 20, 2023.

299 **make it more difficult for authorities in Buenos Aires to investigate the matter:** Sal interview, September 2023.

299 **including a single line in a document outlining his reform of the Holy See:** See

Article 117 of the *Praedicate Evangelium*, March 19, 2022, https://www.vatican.va/content/francesco/en/apost_constitutions/documents/20220319-costituzione-ap-praedicate-evangelium.html, accessed September 20, 2023.

300 **manned by Opus Dei members from other regions:** See "Comisión de escucha y estudio (2022)," June 23, 2022, https://opusdei.org/es-ar/article/comunicado-de-la-oficina-de-comunicacion-del-opus-dei-en-argentina-23-de-junio-2022/, accessed September 20, 2023.

300 **would only communicate as a group—and through him:** Sal interview.

300 **new accusations from former members began to surface:** Author interview with Juan Pablo Cannata (former spokesman for Opus Dei in Argentina), June 2023.

300 **issuing a *motu proprio* specifying how it would take effect:** See "Apostolic Letter Issued 'Motu Proprio' of the Supreme Pontiff Francis 'Ad Charisma Tuendum,'" July 22, 2022, https://press.vatican.va/content/salastampa/en/bollettino/pubblico/2022/07/22/220722a.html, accessed September 21, 2023.

300 **to submit a new set of statutes for approval by the Holy See:** "Apostolic Letter Issued 'Motu Proprio,'" Article 3.

300 **and how it was fulfilling its apostolic work:** "Apostolic Letter Issued 'Motu Proprio,'" Article 2.

300 **would henceforth no longer automatically become a bishop:** "Apostolic Letter Issued 'Motu Proprio,'" Article 4.

300 **"promote the evangelizing action carried out by its members in the world":** "Apostolic Letter Issued 'Motu Proprio,'" Article 4.

300 **"It is intended to strengthen the conviction . . .":** "Apostolic Letter Issued 'Motu Proprio.'"

300 **"Opus Dei has some marvelous things in the work it does . . .":** Jorge Fontevecchia, "Papa Francisco: 'Se puede dialogar muy bien con la economía, no se puede dialogar con las finanzas,'" *Perfil*, March 11, 2023, https://web.archive.org/web/20230314003941/https://www.perfil.com/noticias/periodismopuro/papa-francisco-se-puede-dialogar-muy-bien-con-la-economia-no-se-puede-dialogar-con-las-finanzas-por-jorge-fontevecchia.phtml, accessed September 21, 2023.

301 **a documentary called *The Pope: Answers*:** Video titled *Amén. Francisco responde*, directed by Marius Sánchez and Jordi Évole, Disney+, 2023, https://www.disneyplus.com/en-gb/video/cd6b11aa-85a8-4790-b879-5c7e5b6091a2, accessed September 21, 2023.

301 **Chile's most notorious pedophile—of slander:** Nicole Winfield, "Pope Shocks Chile by Accusing Sex Abuse Victims of Slander," Associated Press, January 19, 2018, https://apnews.com/article/77f4a7e9779940a48e2347c852516d3c, accessed January 6, 2024.

301 **"Did you get a response? . . .":** Winfield, "Pope Shocks Chile."

302 **"Child abuse is a tragedy—not just in the Church, but wherever it takes place . . .":** Winfield, "Pope Shocks Chile."

302 **"It may well be that there are people who conduct themselves badly . . .":** Winfield, "Pope Shocks Chile."

302 **Opus Dei issued a public statement:** See "Información sobre denuncias de abusos en

la Región del Plata," April 12, 2023, https://opusdei.org/es-ar/article/informacion -sobre-denuncias-de-abusos-en-la-region-del-plata/, accessed September 21, 2023.

302 **explain why the movement hadn't heeded his call:** Author interview with a person familiar with the two meetings, June 2023.

302 **systematic abuse of members dating back to its founding:** See "Institutional Complaint Against Opus Dei," signed by Antonio Moya Somolinos and others, June 26, 2023.

303 **to the office of the papal nuncio in Madrid:** José Manuel Vidal, "Ex miembros presentan una denuncia canónica por 'fraude normativo institucional' contra el Opus Dei," *Religión Digital*, July 3, 2023, https://www.religiondigital.org/espana/Opus -Dei-Denuncia-Escriva-Obra-espana-nunciatura-fraude_0_2574942485.html, accessed September 22, 2023.

303 **complaint:** "Institutional Complaint Against Opus Dei."

303 **concealing its internal rules and practices from the Vatican:** "Institutional Complaint Against Opus Dei."

303 **"which encompasses some of the features of a destructive sect":** Vidal, "Ex miembros presentan una denuncia canónica."

303 **was operating with the full authority of the Church:** Vidal, "Ex miembros presentan una denuncia canónica."

304 **to suppress their sexual orientation:** Caitlin Fitzsimmons, "Jeremy Was 16 and Depressed. A Psychiatrist Offered Therapy to Suppress His Attraction to Boys," *Sydney Morning Herald*, August 19, 2023, https://www.smh.com.au/politics/nsw/jeremy -was-16-and-depressed-a-psychiatrist-offered-therapy-to-suppress-his-attraction -to-boys-20230817-p5dxd9.html, accessed September 22, 2023.

304 **Canaanite woman whose daughter had been tormented by the Devil:** Matthew 15:21–28.

304 **even when we don't see the results we want:** See "2,000 Gather in Sydney to See the Father," news release, August 21, 2023, https://opusdei.org/en-au/article/ 2-000-gather-in-sydney-to-see-the-father/, accessed September 22, 2023.

304 **had recently been investigated by the state education authorities:** Maureen Dettre, "Opus Dei Schools to Be Investigated," *Canberra Times*, January 30, 2023, https:// www.canberratimes.com.au/story/8066101/opus-dei-schools-to-be-investigated/, accessed September 22, 2023.

304 **systematic recruitment, indoctrination, and abuse of young children and teenagers:** Louise Milligan, Mary Fallon, and Stephanie Zillman, "Power and Purity," ABC, January 29, 2023, https://www.abc.net.au/news/2023-01-30/inside-sydney -opus-dei-affiliated-private-schools/101777060, accessed September 22, 2023.

305 **"blessed with a great education":** Luke Costin, "Perrottet 'Blessed with Great Opus Dei Education,'" *Canberra Times*, February 1, 2023, https://www.canberratimes.com .au/story/8069937/perrottet-blessed-with-great-opus-dei-education/, accessed September 22, 2023.

305 **Ocáriz embraced them:** See "Monsignor Fernando Ocariz, Prelate of Opus Dei, Visits the school," news release, August 24, 2023, https://news.redfield.nsw.edu.

au/newscentre/monsignor-fernando-ocariz-prelate-of-opus-dei-visits-the-school
-jtpmnkqrao/, accessed September 22, 2023.

305 **set up a school and then asked Opus Dei to take over:** See https://www.pared.edu
.au/our-people/, accessed September 22, 2023.

305 **was now working closely with the Vatican on revising its statutes:** See "Letter from
the Prelate," September 13, 2023, https://opusdei.org/en-uk/article/letter-from
-the-prelate-13-september-2023/, accessed September 22, 2023.

305 **"The attack from Francis against Opus Dei is populist, akin to a guerrilla war . . .":**
Salvador Sostres, "Esto se ha llenado de patanes," *ABC*, August 12, 2023, https://
www.abc.es/opinion/salvador-sostres-llenado-patanes-20230812161739-nt
.html, accessed September 23, 2023.

305 **he had no personal relationship with the author:** See https://twitter.com/opusdei_
es/status/1691332268764119040, accessed September 23, 2023.

305 **had been published on the Opus Dei official website:** See "Busquem l'ascensor social a través de l'èxit escolar i de la inserció laboral," https://opusdei.org/ca/article/
josep-masabeu-braval-barcelona-exit-escolar-insercio-laboral/, accessed September
23, 2023.

306 **"No matter what happens with the Vatican, I'll keep doing Opus Dei":** Austin
Ruse, "I'll Be Doing Opus Dei No Matter What," *Crisis*, September 15, 2023, https://
crisismagazine.com/opinion/ill-be-doing-opus-dei-no-matter-what, accessed September 23, 2023.

306 **many felt seemed a throwback to the church of the 1950s:** Harriet Ryan, "The
Fight to Move the Catholic Church in America to the Right—and the Little-Known
O.C. Lawyer Behind It," *Los Angeles Times*, December 18, 2023, https://www.latimes
.com/california/story/2023-12-18/this-o-c-lawyer-is-the-most-important-catho
lic-youve-never-heard-of, accessed March 1, 2024.

307 **"I think something important is happening, something not so good . . .":** Author
interview with Tim Busch, October 2024.

308 **to sell the Castello di Urio:** See "Comunicato stampa sul Castello di Urio," November
14, 2023, https://opusdei.org/it-it/article/comunicato-stampa-sul-castello-di-urio/,
accessed March 10, 2024.

308 **the purchase and subsequent renovation could cost LVMH more than $100 mil-
lion:** Eva Morletto, "LVMH and Its Belmond Hotel Group Acquire Castello di Urio
on Lake Como, Italy," *Luxury Tribune*, November 20, 2023, https://www.luxury
tribune.com/en/lvmh-and-its-belmond-hotel-group-acquire-castello-di-urio-on
-lake-como-italy, March 10, 2024.

308 **is currently on the market for $15 million:** See https://www.christiesrealestate
.com/sales/detail/170-l-775-2203180921381964/the-tiffany-ayer-mansion-louis
-comfort-tiffanys-masterpiece-back-bay-boston-ma-02215, accessed March 10,
2024.

308 **"in accordance with its statutes":** See "Comunicato stampa sul Castello di Urio,"
November 14, 2023, https://opusdei.org/it-it/article/comunicato-stampa-sul-cas
tello-di-urio/, accessed March 10, 2024.

Index